W9-AAE-307

Fifth Edition

Motivation
Theories and Principles

Robert C. Beck
Wake Forest University

PEARSON
Prentice
Hall

Upper Saddle River, New Jersey 07458

Library of Congress Cataloging-in-Publication Data

Beck, Robert C. (Robert Clarence)
  Motivation: theories and principles / Robert C. Beck.—5th ed.
    p. cm.
Includes bibliographical references and index.
  ISBN 0-13-111445-X
  1. Motivation (Psychology) I. Title.
  BF503 .B38 2004
  153.8—dc21   2003009370

*I dedicate this book to my wife, Bettianne,
and our children and grandchildren,
all of whom have made life interesting.*

Editor-in-chief: Leah Jewell
Senior Acquisitions Editor: Jayme Heffler
Editorial Assistant: Jennifer Conklin
Production Liaison: Fran Russello
Project Manager: Patty Donovan/Pine Tree Composition
Prepass and Manufacturing Buyer: Tricia Kenny
Art Director: Jane Conte
Cover Designer: Kiwi Design
Cover Art: Spike Mafford/Getty Images, Inc.
Executive Marketing Manager: Sheryl Adams

This book was set in 10/12 Baskerville by Pine Tree Composition, Inc., and was printed and bound by Courier Companies, Inc. The cover was printed by Phoenix Color Corp.

© 2004, 2000 by Pearson Education, Inc.
Pearson Education, Inc.
Upper Saddle River, New Jersey 07458

All rights reserved. No part of this book may be reproduced, in any form or by any means, without permission in writing from the publisher.

Printed in the United States of America
10 9 8 7 6 5 4 3 2

ISBN 0-13-111445-X

Pearson Education LTD.
Pearson Education Singapore, Pte. Ltd
Pearson Education, Canada, Ltd
Pearson Education—Japan
Pearson Education Australia PTY, Limited
Pearson Education North Asia Ltd
Pearson Educación de Mexico, S.A. de C.V.
Pearson Education Malaysia, Pte. Ltd
Pearson Education, Upper Saddle River, New Jersey

Contents

Preface

When I wrote the first edition of *Motivation* (1978), my goal was to provide an empirically based introduction to a broad range of motivational theories and principles. The phenomena described ranged from homeostatic motives in animals to motives for human social interactions. Many theoretical viewpoints were covered, as they should be in a text, but my own predilection was for hedonic theory with a liberal sprinkling of learning theory. This was explicitly stated and the concepts of desire and aversion were considered the most fundamental concepts in the book. About that same time, research on emotion rapidly began to expand, and in the second (1983) and subsequent editions a chapter on emotion was added. This fifth edition of *Motivation: Theories and Principles* expresses the same orientation as that found in earlier editions. It is an experimentally oriented survey of research and theory on animal and human motivation, emphasizing hedonic principles.

In the first edition I noted that it is difficult to maintain a completely logical and consistent conceptualization of motivation without sacrificing a large amount of material that many people consider important to the topic. This is still true. Motivation theorists and researchers are still fragmented in their efforts to understand motivation. Much of the reason for this, it still seems to me, is that *evolution* has not been a logical and consistent process. Consequently, theoretical principles developed in the context of one species or motivational problem, say eating behavior in omnivores (like humans and rats), may not be applicable to a different set of motivational problems or to the same problems in different species (such as eating in herbivores or carnivores). The end result is a great diversity of approaches to motivation, none of which is *the* correct approach but all of which have their own strengths. For reasons such as this, the first chapter is still devoted to discussion of the nature of scientific *theory*, just so the student can gain greater insight as to what theories and theorizing are all about, and why they are essential.

Given the same ambitions as before, there are similarities with the previous editions as well as differences. One of these similarities is the attempt to weave an historical perspective into as many topics as reasonable in a limited space. Some older concepts and theories may not be as important as they once seemed (such as drive theory) but such concepts have a way of reappearing, sometimes under new names. The strengths and weaknesses of the earlier concepts may apply to the new concepts, and it seems to me there is much to be gained by at least familiarizing students with some of the older concepts. Reflecting recent scholarship, however, there are numerous changes in content and references for this edition.

ACKNOWLEDGMENT

I would like to acknowledge Stephen W. Brown, Rockhurst University; August Hoffman, California State University–Northridge; and Kraig Schell, Angelo State University. Michelle Ayers and Caleb Masling were also a great help in checking various details for the revised manuscript.

I would like to recognize my intellectual debt to five great teachers and psychologists who inspired my efforts: G. Robert Grice, J. McV. Hunt, O. H. Mower, Lawrence I. O'Kelly, and Paul Thomas Young. They hardly ever seemed to agree on much theoretically, but all were creative, energetic, and devoted to the process of teasing out nature's psychological secrets as best they could. They were all inspirations and the diversity they provided was a stern warning not to take any single idea as *the* truth. Finally, over my years as a teacher many students and colleagues have pushed or pulled me in new directions and further enriched my scholarship.

R.C.B.

CHAPTER ONE

The Nature of Motivation Theory

What is motivational psychology about?

Are we free to behave as we wish or do outside forces control us?

How closely related are our minds and bodies?

What is scientific theory and why must we have it?

How is the language of science different from our everyday language?

How can we put together a good theory?

How can we define motivation in exact terms?

What Is Motivational Psychology About?

On August 1, 1966, Charles Whitman, twenty-five years of age, climbed to the observation deck of the Tower Building at the University of Texas. In two hours he killed fourteen people and wounded twenty-four others before he was slain by the police. The question raised for all psychology, and especially for motivation theory, is Why? By any common meaning of the term, Whitman was not rational, even though his actions seemed carefully planned. There were numerous interesting little twists in the accounts that followed. Many people thought him a fine young man. He liked children, worked hard, and had been an Eagle Scout at the age of twelve. He had a good sense of humor, and most of his friends and acquaintances seemed to regard him highly. And the night before, he had also killed his mother and father.

There are many possible explanations for Whitman's spree. He had a need for achievement, particularly to surpass his father, but was frustrated by not doing as well in school as he had hoped. He was continually stressed by overwork; he carried heavy academic loads and part-time jobs. His family had an abiding interest in guns, which reporters saw in every room of his parents' house after the incident. And there was possibly a specific biological disorder: He was reported (upon autopsy) to have a brain tumor in an area known to be related to aggressive behaviors. Any of these factors, as well as others not considered here, might have led to the final tragic outcome. We cannot really know the answer to this particular drama, because the central character is gone. This much we do know: the answer is not simple. But it is the kind of mystery that psychologists are supposed to help unravel.

We also see in this example the possibility that many motives might be present at the same time. Sometimes a single motive seems to provide adequate explanation, such as "I ate because I was hungry." But to explain a situation as complex as Charles Whitman's, we might find ourselves discussing many different motivational concepts, such as drives, goals, incentives, frustration, conflict, aggression, and needs for achievement or power. We might also wish to consider brain damage or drug use as possible factors.

Motivation is one of the explanations we use when we try to account for the variability of behavior. Under virtually identical external circumstances, there are variations in individual behavior that may be due to differences in motivation. For example, why do some kids do well in school when equally talented ones fail? This dilemma suggests that there may be differences in motivation for achievement. Why do some children steal, when others of equal social status or income are scrupulously honest? Why do some people take drugs, when others under similar living circumstances ignore them? Why do some people work harder than others at the same job? Why do we have wars and killings? Why do people create? Why would anybody repeatedly eat until they vomit or starve themselves when food is easily available? The individual variations in these activities suggest the need for motivational explanations, as well as the possibility of producing change for the better.

A Preliminary Definition of Motivation

Let us start with a very general definition of what we mean by motivation. The word *motivation* is derived from the Latin verb *movere*, which means "to move." Motivation is then concerned with our movements, or actions, and what determines them. These factors may be internal (such as being hungry, thirsty, in pain) or external (such as the presence of tasty food, an attractive person, or cues indicating imminent danger). Motivation is a broad *theoretical concept* that we often use to explain why people (or animals) engage in particular actions at particular times. Why do we eat rather than drink, play rather than work, read rather than exercise? We do not assume that organisms are inert unless prodded into action by some motive. The nervous system is continually active, sometimes violently, even as we sleep. The motivational problem is how to account for fluctuations in the choices made among the possible things an organism might do.

Our basic motivational premise is that organisms *approach goals*, or engage in activities that are expected to have *desirable outcomes*, and *avoid events* that are expected to have unpleasant or *aversive outcomes*. This premise is called *psychological hedonism*. We must use this premise with a certain amount of care for detail, however. First and foremost, we are taking a scientific approach and must define desire and aversion objectively. A common criticism of hedonistic approaches is that what is considered pleasant or unpleasant depends on subjective experience, and since subjective experiences are not objective scientific data, desire and aversion are not useful scientific concepts. As we shall see, this line of argument is simply not correct. Later in this chapter we shall see in detail how to define desire and aversion objectively. First, however, there are a number of basic issues that we need to explore, because the way these issues are resolved determines how we shall approach the topic of motivation, or any other scientific concept related to behavior. These issues are (1) How free are we to act as we choose? (2) How are our minds and bodies related? and (3) What really is a scientific theory?

HOW FREE ARE WE TO ACT AS WE WISH?

The Problem of Freedom

One of the most fundamental ideas implied by the very existence of psychological theory and research is that *human behavior can be understood and predicted*. This must mean that behavior has causes, and therefore we are not free to choose our behaviors so that we can do anything we want. To the contrary, if we knew the causes of a behavior, then we could make that behavior occur by producing those causes.

The conclusion that behavior is caused may jar the sensibilities of some readers because it has powerful implications for life in general, as well as for psychological science, and runs contrary to much popular belief. We all like to feel free to act as we choose and the idea of determinism challenges that feeling. From a scientific point of view, though, total freedom to choose poses a problem: If we can do anything we wish at any time, then we could not predict behavior. Science aside, if we could not predict the behavior of other people, how would we ever know how to interact with them? Would not utter social chaos arise? Obviously, we do a pretty good job at predicting the behavior of others in everyday life, and our interactions are not always chaotic.

However, society as a whole deals inconsistently with the question of freedom. A person may be imprisoned because that person "chose" to commit a crime. On the other hand, if we assume complete freedom of choice, then such punishment would be useless because it should not deter future choices to commit crimes. Punishment would be nothing more than retribution for crime, an "eye for an eye." Punishment makes sense only if we expect it to alter (determine) future behavior. Even the argument that punishment sets an example for others assumes that the threat of punishment will partly determine their behavior. Because of such inconsistencies in the freewill argument, as well as because of the impossibility of having a science of behavior without assuming determinism, determinism is considered to be as necessary for the behavioral sciences as it is for the physical sciences, where it is taken for granted.

Determinism

Stated simply, determinism means that if Cause A occurs, then Effect B will follow. If I suddenly make a loud sound behind you, you will jump. If I am hungry, I will eat. In mathematical terminology we would say that the Effect is a function of the Cause, or Effect = f (Cause). In psychological terminology we say that Response = f (Stimulus, Organism) or Behavior = f (Person, Environment). Both of these statements mean that behavior results from a combination of external events (stimulus, environment) and internal events (organism, person). Motivation is just one of the "internal events," along with knowledge gained from experience, for example. In the psychology laboratory, we can repeatedly do experiments with human subjects and obtain the same results under the same conditions. Indeed, most undergraduate experimental psychology laboratories use at least some "tried and true" demonstration experiments that almost always work, such as simple experiments in human learning or perception. We depend on the predictability of behavior to make such demonstrations reliable.

Behavior is affected by many different conditions, however, and to the extent that we do not know what conditions are prevailing at a given time, our predictions are less reliable. A psychologist is unwilling to predict the behavior of a person at a party for the same reason that a physicist balks at predicting the behavior of a handful of confetti thrown at that party: We just do not know all the conditions bearing on these behaviors. Prediction in psychology is also made more difficult because the internal "organism" or "person" variables influencing behavior are usually not open to direct observation by outsiders. For example, the "impressions" of past experiences obviously affect the way we act, but we cannot recall all our own past experiences nor know all those of other people.

"Freedom," then, often comes down to lack of predictability. Freedom of behavior is perceived differently according to where the cause(s) of a particular behavior are located. If a particular behavior is mainly controlled by external, observable events, we tend to say that it is determined. If the behavior is primarily controlled by internal, unobservable events, we might say that it is free. The more choices we have, the "freer" we seem (Tomkins, 1981). Failure to predict behavior with perfect accuracy is not the same thing as freedom, though. It is just failure to predict perfectly.

The question of social freedom or control is not the issue here. Belief in freedom does not change the laws of behavior, and belief in determinism does not imply any particular kind of social control. It is possible, of course, that different beliefs may partly determine how people behave. A person who believes in freedom *might* (or might *not*) behave differently than one who believes in determinism. Political leaders who believe in freedom may try to exert different social controls than the leaders who believe in determinism, just as leaders who hold a particular set of religious beliefs might try to exert different controls than someone with a different set of beliefs. By the same token, however, anyone asking for improved teaching methods, cures for mental illness, or less violence in society is asking, "What can we do to produce those ends?" These very questions *assume determinism* since they imply that if we had the answers, we could make things happen the way we want.

A closer look at causation. We do research to find the causes of events and our explanations of events involve statements of causation. "Why did George's knee jerk?" "Because the doctor struck him below the knee with a rubber hammer." The blow caused the knee jerk. Or if a child started crying when a dog approached, we might say that the dog caused the child to cry. But what is a cause? All we can know about in the world is the impression it makes on our sense organs, either directly or indirectly by means of instruments. We say that one thing causes another when we perceive that the events occur closely in time and space. Thus, because the dog appeared and the child cried, we say that the dog caused the child to cry. But perhaps the child's parent said something that made the child cry, and the innocent dog just happened on the scene at a bad time. Causes are what we perceive or think them to be, and nothing more. Scientists do not find ultimate truths or ultimate causes. Rather, on the basis of observations, they write statements, called laws, about observed events. The causality is in the statements, the language of science, rather than directly in the physical world. That is one of the reasons why we want to be as precise as we can with language.

THE MIND-BODY PUZZLE

If we accept the principle of determinism, as we must if we believe that psychological science and theory is possible, then we have another problem. We often see psychology defined as the science that uniquely studies both mind and body. This may imply that mind and body are different, and going by our own experience we might be inclined to say that our mind causes our body to engage in certain actions. But this point of view raises problems that have puzzled critical thinkers for literally thousands of years. What do we mean by mind? What do we mean by body? And how are the two related?

For the average person, the relationship of mind to body probably is clear. The "official doctrine" (Ryle, 1949) is that "body" is physical and material; that it is limited in space, time, and size; and that it is objectively observable. "Mind," on the other hand, bears the opposite of all these qualities. It is subjective, directly known only to the individual possessing it, unlimited in physical dimensions, and, perhaps, everlasting. This distinction is essentially the same doctrine generally accepted in western theology to maintain the separation of "body" and "soul." It goes back to the Greek philosopher Plato around 400 B.C., came into Christianity with St. Augustine about seven hundred years later, and reemerged in the seventeenth century with the French philosopher René Descartes. As a "person on the street" might view the situation, we are aware of our circumstances, feelings, and ideas. Faced consciously with several possible courses of action, we consciously and freely *will* ourselves to take this or that action. Even scientists may hold this view without ever having thought much about it; it is just part of western cultural history (Searle, 2000). We have already seen that "free will" is not the direction we want to take. But what are the alternatives to the mind-body relation? It is important to analyze these because the alternative we settle on determines how we approach psychology in general, especially motivation.

There are two general classes of opinion regarding mind and body. The proponents of *dualism* assume that mind and body are qualitatively different. The proponents of *monism* assume that the mind and body really are qualitatively the same. Within each of these camps there are subdivisions.

Dualisms

Interactionistic dualism.   This is the view developed by Descartes, commonly called Cartesian dualism. Mind and body are considered qualitatively different categories, immaterial and material, and what the body does depends on the mind. That is, there is a causal relation between mind and body, which is illustrated in Figure 1–1. However, where and how do these qualitatively different substances interact? Descartes ([1650] 1892) suggested the pineal gland in the brain as the point of interaction and developed a physical model based on reflected light rays. He proposed that light energy comes into the eyes and activates "spirits" that are reflected one way or another by the **pineal gland**, which he saw as something like a pivoting mirror. Depending on where the spirits are reflected, different movements of the body occur. The term reflex, referring to an automatic movement following a particular stimulus (such as a knee jerk when the patellar tendon is struck), comes from Descartes's description of the "reflection of spirits." According to Descartes, animal behavior consists entirely of reflexes, but humans have the capacity to mentally will behavior to occur in addition to reflexes.

The logical problems with such a theory are painfully difficult. If our minds and bodies really are so unlike each other, how could they interact? How can an immaterial mind cause any behavior to occur? We know that it takes physical energy to make the body move, so if the mind has no energy it cannot make the body move. We also know that the pineal gland serves no function like the one that Descartes imagined and that he hit upon the pineal gland only because, unlike other parts of the brain, it was not duplicated in the two hemispheres. Most scientists, as well as philosophers, have rejected Descartes's system for these reasons.

Parallelistic dualism.   This approach retains a mind-body dualism but without the mind causing the body to do anything. Suppose we set two atomic clocks to exactly the same time and then leave them to run out their separate existences. Whenever we look at the first clock, we will be able to tell what the second says. The German philosopher Gottfried Wilhelm Leibniz proposed such a view of mind and body (Duncan, 1890). Just as the first clock does not cause the second to tell a particular time, so the mind does not cause the body to do a particular thing. There is only a correlation between experience and behavior. This view recognizes some kind of dual existence of mental life and body activity, but it does not raise the problem of how they could interact in any causal way. For many scientists, parallelism may simply make a practical distinction between mind and body: The methods for studying mental activity are sufficiently different from the methods of studying other phenomena that the mind-body distinction is worth maintaining for this reason alone. This principle is called a *methodological dualism.*

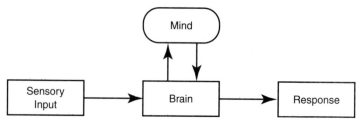

A. Cartesian dualism. Arrows indicate causal
relationship between mind and brain.

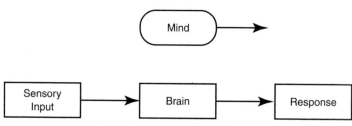

B. Parallelism. No causal relation between mind
and brain. They just run in parallel.

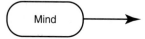

C. Idealistic monism (idealism). There is nothing but mind.

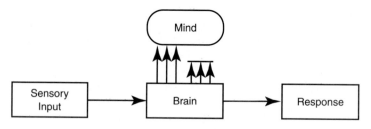

D. Materialistic monism (identity theory). Mind is a
function of brain processes and has no causal
properties. All mind states have corresponding
brain states, but not all brain states have
corresponding mind states.

FIGURE 1–1.   Possible causal relations between mind and body. The brain is the most important aspect
of body here.

Monisms

Monism is the idea that there is only a single "substance," encompassing both mind and body. This view completely does away with any problems of interaction because there are not two different substances to interact. As one might expect, however, this view has its own problems, depending on what view of monism one proposes: mentalistic or materialistic.

Mentalistic monism.   How do we know about the existence of a world outside our own minds? It seems obvious that we know about this world through our consciousness of it, through our minds. But what proof could we offer that things exist outside our minds? Our dreams in all their terror or sensuousness seem real when they occur, but we know they are not "real." Neither are hallucinations. Mentalistic monism is the view that if we know the world only from experiences, then experience (mind) may be all there is. This view was proposed by the British philosopher Bishop George Berkeley ([1710] 1939). The great German physiologist Johannes Mueller proposed a similar view in the early nineteenth century, but in biological terms. Mueller said we are not directly aware of the external world, we are aware only of the activity of our own nervous systems.

Another British philosopher, David Hume ([1748] 1939), proposed an even more extreme view, called *solipsism*. Hume's logical extension of Berkeley is the possibility that there is but a *single mind* and that any other apparent minds are only the experience of this one mind, just as apparent objects are also the experience of this one mind. There are no physical objects, no bodies, no other minds. Someone may ask, however, "Why do thorns pain me unless thorns exist?" The direct answer to this question is that the existence of thorns has to be *assumed* before the question can even be asked. The assumption that thorns exist is built into the question. The assumption of the solipsistic point of view is just the opposite, that such things as thorns do not exist outside the mind, nor does anything else. If the experience of pain accompanies the experience of thorns, that is just the way experiences are. No experience can be proof of a separate existence of things outside experience. "But," may come another objection, "surely a mind would not produce pain for itself." This is irrelevant. The mind does not pick and choose its experiences, they just happen. Indeed, even the objections to my argument do not exist outside my own mind because there is no separate "you" outside my own mind. The mind-body problem disappears since there is only the mind. As the philosopher John Searle says, "We need to overcome the philosophical tradition that treats the mental and the physical as two distinct metaphysical systems" (Searle, 2000, p. 557).

Materialistic monism.   This view holds that the single underlying reality is material and that "the mind is what the brain does." That is to say, the mind is the brain in operation. Consider an analogy with a dump truck. The truck moves about, picks up and drops things, generally acting (functioning) as a dump truck should. We do not, however, believe that these functions of the truck actually cause the truck to behave as it does or that they exist separately from the truck. From this point of view, the body, especially the nervous system, is so constructed that one of its functions is consciousness. This function does not cause behaviors to occur, however; the nervous system causes them to occur. This process is illustrated in Figure 1–10.

One variation of materialistic monism, called *neural identity theory*, says that the material nervous system can be viewed in two different ways, just as we view two sides of a coin differently. The physiologist's description of the brain and a person's description of his own experience are both descriptions of the same thing (Pepper, 1959). Both describe the activity of the brain, but from different points of view and with different languages. For example, the person talks about seeing the color red, whereas the physiologist talks about certain neurons firing when the eye is stimulated with a certain wavelength of light. This theory is also sometimes called *double aspect theory* in reference to looking at two aspects of the brain (from the "inside" and from the "outside").

According to neural identity theory, for every conscious mental event, there is a corresponding brain event, but the converse is not true. That is, we are not aware of everything that goes on in our nervous systems, for example, the neural activities that control breathing. Nor at a given moment are we aware of all of the things we can possibly remember. Neural processes involved in motivation, emotion, and memory may influence our behavior without our being aware of them at the moment. Neural activities of which we are aware may be especially important for such activities as learning, but this is speculation, and its validity must be determined by research. (Considerable research does show, for example, that we can learn little or nothing while sound asleep.)

The neurobiological problem is how brain processes produce conscious states. We do not yet have an answer to this question, but the close identity of conscious experience and brain function is shown by many examples, such as the following:

- Some individual neurons in the visual part of the brain respond only to lines with vertical orientations, others to horizontal lines, and some to both orientations. Other neurons respond only to moving stimuli, not to stationary ones, or to some colors but not others. Amazingly, it seems that the form, color, and movement that we perceive in an object occur in activity in different parts of the brain and are combined in some way to produce our experience of a single moving, colorful shape. Such relationships have been found in frogs, cats, and monkeys, and it is reasonable to assume that they also exist in humans.
- If the two hemispheres of the brain are surgically separated, there are two independent "minds," whereas before there was only one mind. Each half of the

brain is now an independent unit, and things learned in one half are unknown to the other half (e.g., Gazzaniga, 1967). Experience deceives us because the split-brain patient is unaware that his two half-brains are disconnected and to a large extent functioning independently of each other. To the patient, the experience is still that of a single brain. Reason or logic based solely on our conscious experience would therefore never have predicted that splitting the brain into two hemispheres would produce two minds, but this is dramatically shown with laboratory tests.

- Many drugs have mind-altering effects, such as producing hallucinations, making us more sleepy or alert, reducing our anxiety, or making us feel more happy.

Here is one final point on the mind-body problem. By nature and definition, science deals with observable events. For psychology these observable events are behaviors, body activities ranging from filling out attitude-survey questionnaires to throwing baseballs to describing drug experiences. Do we need to infer something behind those behaviors that is uniquely different from what the nervous system can reasonably be expected to do? The answer is no. This is not to say that all experience is expressed in behavior or that behavior tells us everything about a person. From a scientific point of view, however, the minds of other people are inferred from their words or other behavior. We are not questioning the existence of consciousness but do argue that the immediate experience of consciousness is not usable scientific data because it is not open to observers other than oneself.

In summary, the popular view that mind and body are different and that mind controls body is but one of several logical possibilities. The particular belief anyone has in this matter may have important practical consequences—deciding how to go about studying and treating "mental" disorders, for example. Indeed, what could be the possible reason for using drug therapy for mental disorders if the mind did not involve activity of the nervous system?

SECTION SUMMARY

1. Every science starts with the assumption that there is a predictable relationship between causes and effects. Psychology assumes that human behavior can be understood and predicted.

2. **Determinism** means that if Cause A occurs, then Effect B will follow. We may say that Response = f (Stimulus, Organism) or Behavior = f (Person, Environment). In either case, we assume that behavior can be predicted.

3. **Causes** are inferred from observations we make and the goodness of our causal statements depends on the goodness of our observations. Causal statements are necessarily tentative because new knowledge may contradict old statements of causation.

4. Psychological science uniquely faces the issue of the relationship between mind and body. The "official doctrine" commonly held by the public is that mind and body are separate and that an immaterial mind freely wills a person to act in a certain way. This view, commonly referred to as **Cartesian dualism**, is untenable for a science of psychology.

5. Of the several possible views of the relationship between mind and body, the one most widely accepted by psychological theorists is **materialistic monism**. This holds that the single underlying reality is material and that the mind is the brain in operation. For every conscious mental event there is a specific underlying brain event. The converse is not true; we are not aware of all of our brain activity.

SCIENTIFIC THEORY

Why We Must Have Theory

Consider the following scenario. A friend says to you, "You're studying psychology, tell me why my daughter Susy is so aggressive toward her little brother." What kind of answer would you give? Would you give some very specific reasons? Probably not, because you don't know enough about Susy. You might say something about her upbringing (a psychological answer in terms of learning and environment), you might talk about a cultural effect (a sociological answer), you might mention some physical reason (a biological answer), or you might mention something about morality (a theological answer). You might even answer in terms of motivation, for example, she is angry about something and taking it out on her brother. All these possible answers deal with some kinds of *general principles* that might apply to the question at hand. In other words, they are answers in terms of some *theory* that you want to apply to the question. To repeat an old saying, there's nothing so practical as a good theory.

The daily lives of most of us are not fraught with the murder and mayhem of Charles Whitman's final hours, but we do have motivational questions about things that are important to us. You might ask, "How could I have done better on my last exam?" or, "Why does Ellen have so many friends when Mary has so few?" "How can I get the job I want?" "How can I reduce the stress in my life?" The answers to such specific questions call for general psychological principles to apply to specific situations. To *explain* an event means to apply a general principle to a specific situation. Discovering general principles and weaving them into theory is what psychological research is all about. When theory has been sufficiently developed, we can apply it to such specific problems as aiding clients with weight disorders, helping a manufacturer sell his or her product, helping an athlete perform better, or helping an unhappy marriage. Our purpose in this section is to see what a theory actually is and how to distinguish a good theory from a bad theory. We should learn how to keep from being misled by bad theories.

Nature of Scientific Theory

A scientific theory is like a map. We commonly refer to theories as being like models. We use the word model in a broad sense, referring to an actual physical model, to a set of blueprints, to a set of mathematical equations, or to a map (Toulmin, 1953). Let us think of a theory as a map of some part of the world of interest to us. A theory is a *representation* of real things and places in the world, and it relates those things to each other by a set of rules. It organizes some part of the world and guides us just as a road map does.

A map has *objectively definable* names for places (e.g., North America is such and such; Mount Rushmore is such and such; Kernersville is such and such). Figure 1–2 shows a map with different places linked together so that we can relate them to each other (e.g., Kernersville is seventeen miles east of Winston-Salem on I-40). If we follow the map and actually get to Kernersville from Winston-Salem as the map says we should, we have evidence that the map is good. If we follow the map and arrive in Statesville (which is actually about twenty miles west of Winston-Salem), we know that the map has some serious flaws. It is pretty easy to tell when we have a good or a bad road map.

Even a very accurate map, however, is an incomplete representation of the world, but useful for some purposes. A map of the United States will not tell us how to get to the psychology building on our campus, and a highway map doesn't help a lot if we want to go someplace by boat. There may be many different maps of the same area, corresponding to different aspects of the environment: road maps, geodetic maps, temperature maps, ocean-floor maps, and so on. None of these maps is completely right or wrong; they are merely different because they organize different things in different ways and have different uses. Similarly, there are many theories of motivation (or, of learning or perception), none of which explains everything but each of which is useful for explaining some things. For example, theories of feeding,

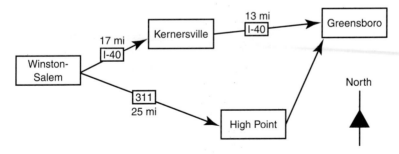

FIGURE 1–2. A theory of how to get from Winston-Salem to Greensboro in North Carolina. This rough mapping of distances and directions from Winston-Salem to Kernersville and on to Greensboro should be accurate enough to get us there in a predicted amount of time, if we know what the names refer to and have established the distances accurately. If the map is to scale, we should even be able to estimate traveling time by the alternate High Point route. Note that the map leaves out a lot. Are the omitted things important?

achievement motivation, and fear all have to do with motivation but deal with different domains of behavior. We develop and use the theories that are appropriate to the situation at hand.

Making measurements.   The classic method of mapping is to send out an explorer, compass in hand, who measures distances and directions, recording what that explorer finds. Different ways of measuring the "same thing" may give different results, however. Suppose that there are two rivers separated by a mountain and that we ask what the distance is between the rivers? Is the distance the walking distance going straight up and down over the mountain? Is it the distance walking around the mountain? Is it the distance as the crow flies in a straight line? (And if this, how was this distance measured before we had aircraft and could not actually travel in a straight line? Think about it.) If we are measuring people's attitudes, do we record what they say about things if asked directly? Do we use attitude scales? Do we use physiological measures? Clearly, we have options about how to measure the things that interest us, and depending on the method of measurement, we may end up with quite different descriptions of events. New and improved methods produce new and improved maps. Satellite mapping systems and PET scans give us dramatically improved methods for looking at the earth and at the brain, respectively. Digital computers allow us to look at and organize psychological data in ways never before possible.

Objectivity in observation.   Several times we have used the word objective to refer to observations. Most people probably think of objective observation as being "perfect," free from any subjective bias on the part of the observer. But a little reflection tells us that this definition cannot be entirely true. Counters and clocks all have to be read by someone, and such readings can be biased, even by such small factors as the angle at which the instrument is observed. Since all observations are subject to some kind of error, the terms objective and subjective are just relative. Objective means that several observers are in high agreement about what they observe, and subjective means that they agree very little. It is easier to agree on what an automatic counter says than to agree on a number that we have had to count in our heads so we may consider data from the counter as objective. We may be satisfied that a single person reading a counter is adequate because we have previously established that people usually agree on such readings. In psychology, however, we often must make observations in situations where it is necessary to demonstrate that there is high agreement among observers. Suppose that we are watching an infant's face and are recording the frequency and duration of smiles over a period of time. To be objective, we would want to have more than one observer doing the recording and to verify that their recordings are similar. Or we might videotape the infant for later counting of smiles by several observers.

Drawing a map. Given that we have obtained the data from which to make a map (or theory), how are we to draw the map? Again, there are choices. If we draw a rectangular map, we run into problems when we try to represent the whole earth, because areas near the poles will be disproportionately large on the map. If we try to represent the globe on a flat surface, in the way it would look if we made cuts in a ball and flattened it out, we get a map that is very difficult to follow, and so on. Instead of a drawing, our representation of the world may be linguistic. The title to a particular piece of property is both pictorial (a diagram of land shape with locations indicated) and a purely verbal description in terms of latitude and longitude and particular landmarks. We can also map behavior over time and space just as we map the orbits of planets over time and space (see Figure 1–3a). For example, we may measure "general activity" of animals over days as we study circadian rhythms. Or we can describe behavior over both time and space, as with the dances of honey bees that show the distance and direction of food from the hive, as illustrated in Figure 1–3b. These dynamic maps might be described mathematically rather than verbally or graphically. Once we have drawn a map or developed a theory, however, how do we know it is a "good" map or theory?

Criteria for Goodness of a Theory

Four qualities distinguish a good theory from a bad theory: testability, fruitfulness, simplicity, and comprehensiveness.

- **Testability.** Most people might say that a good theory is one that cannot be proven false. In fact, however, the single most important characteristic of a good theory is that it can be shown wrong by being tested (Popper, 1959). A

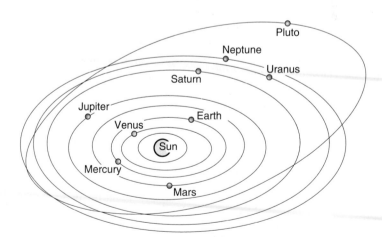

FIGURE 1–3A. Dynamic mapping of the solar system, showing the orbits of the planets around the sun. The orbits can be described mathematically as well.

Round Dance

Tail-wagging Dance

FIGURE 1–3B.   Dances of bees to show location of food. The round dance shows only that food is nearby. A worker bee returns to the hive and just goes around in circles, exciting the others to go get food. The tail-wagging dance shows the direction of the food (by the direction of the wavy line in the middle), and the speed of the dance indicates distance. The faster the dance, the closer the food is. A classic book on the dances of bees is Von Frisch (1967).

good theory makes predictions specific enough to be "risky," so that some outcome other than the predicted outcome can possibly occur and disconfirm (falsify) the theory. A theory that cannot be falsified is not a good theory, because it cannot be tested. Suppose I propose the theory that I am being followed by little green men who are known only to me and who disappear when I turn around to look at them. This "theory" is a very bad theory, because there is no way to find out whether it is right or wrong, no way to test it. Compare this with the theory that gravity on the moon is only one-sixth of the gravity on Earth. We've had a theory of gravitational pull for about three hundred years, and it has worked very well in accounting for planetary motion, but we could not test it with human beings on the moon until thirty years ago. Unlike the little-green-men theory, however, the moon's gravity was testable in principle as soon as it was proposed by Isaac Newton in the seventeenth century. We just had to wait for technology that would get us to the moon. In the meanwhile, of course, there was much other evidence to support the theory, and what a surprise it would have been had we been wrong when we got to the moon!

- **Fruitfulness.** A fruitful theory generates research so that more knowledge is gained. Hull's (1943) theory of behavior (which we look at in more detail later) generated a great deal of research, much of which showed the theory to be wrong in many ways. The theory was thus also good because it was falsifiable. Built-in obsolescence as a result of being fruitful and testable is a mark of good theory. Sometimes a theory is proposed that sounds good at the time but that generates virtually no further research and does not aid in development of the field. Such an unfruitful theory is inevitably assigned to the dustbin of history.

- **Simplicity.** If there are two explanations for an event, the simpler of the two is preferable. This principle of *parsimony* is also called *Occam's razor*. Simplicity may refer to the number of concepts in a theory (the fewer the better if they are adequate to the job) or to the complexity of the relationships among the concepts. A variation of this, called *Lloyd Morgan's Canon*, is applied especially to psychology. Morgan was a comparative psychologist studying many different kinds of animals who argued that we should not apply more complex mental activities to explain animal behavior than are necessary to account for the behavior. For example, we all know that moths tend to fly into flame (a phototropism). How would we explain this? We might say that, like Icarus of Greek mythology, the moth was trying to reach the sun and burned its wings. Or we might say that the moth had a death wish. But we might also say that a moth has photo receptors in its wings that automatically make it fly toward light and that it is quite accidental that the moth flies into the flame. Which theory is simplest and still does the job?

- **Comprehensiveness.** The better a theory is, the greater number of observations it explains. Einstein's theory of relativity was more complicated than Newton's theory of gravity, but it was also more comprehensive. Newton's theory is still quite adequate for many practical purposes, such as working out the trajectories of shells fired from cannons. Einstein's theory would be of no practical use in improving gunnery on earth, but is certainly better for understanding many mysteries of the universe. In motivation there is a theory called expectancy-value theory, which says that we make decisions on the basis of the value to us of possible outcomes of our choices. This theory has been applied to animals foraging for food, economic decisions, choice of a mate, and satisfaction with one's job. It is one of psychology's most durable and comprehensive theories.

Explanation

We want theories to *explain* past observations and *predict* future ones. But what does it mean to explain something? One kind of scientific explanation is to identify a specific event as an instance of a more general principle or law. One principle in psychology is the serial position effect in verbal learning. Words in the middle of a learned list are harder to remember than words at the beginning or end of the list. If someone were having trouble learning the middle of a list, we could explain this difficulty as an instance of the serial position effect. Identifying something as an "instance" of a particular phenomenon is a "low-level" explanation. A higher-level explanation would explain the serial position effect itself, as well as other facts of memory. Such an explanation was achieved by Postman and Phillips (1965) who accounted for it in terms of the difference between long-term and short-term memories. They found that if subjects were tested on word lists immediately after study that the serial position effect was present. If subjects were delayed before testing, however, only the primacy effect was found. They concluded that the primacy effect was due to long-term memory and the recency effect was due to short-term memory. Following a delay, the recent material was lost from short-term memory. The concepts of long-term and short-term memory, of course, account for many other facts of learning and memory than just the serial position effect.

THE LANGUAGE OF SCIENCE

Science is as precise as it can be at any given time. One of the great scientific steps leading to precision was the introduction of *measurement* of times, speeds, distances, weights, and temperatures. There is a big difference, for

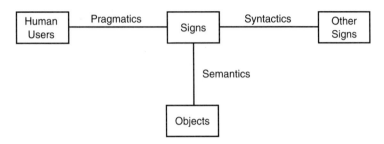

FIGURE 1–4. Three areas of semiotic: syntactics, semantics, and pragmatics.

example, between saying that water freezes when it gets cold and that water freezes at 32 degrees Fahrenheit. We try to carry this precision of measurement over to the language of science. The philosopher Charles Morris (1938) established a system for understanding scientific language, called *semiotic.* The three subareas, illustrated in Figure 1–4, are *syntactics* (the relations of different signs to each other), *semantics* (the relations of signs to the objects to which they refer), and *pragmatics* (the relations of signs to their users). Signs are any linguistic conventions, words, or numbers. We are interested here in syntactics and semantics.

Syntactics: Rules for Using Signs

Syntactics is concerned with the establishment and use of agreed-on rules by which we can relate signs (symbols or words) to each other. Every language, including logic and mathematics, has such formal rules. In English, for example, the rule is generally that nouns come before verbs in a sentence, but in German the rules are different and verbs come at the very end of the sentence, and so on. In mathematics we apply the basic rules of arithmetic and algebra to manipulate signs. For example, the formula $M = \Sigma X/N$ can be changed to read $NM = \Sigma X$ or $N = \Sigma X/M$. As any psychology student would recognize, this is the formula for the arithmetic mean, in which M equals the mean, ΣX is the sum of the individual scores, and N is the number of scores. Using the formal rules we can move the signs around into different combinations even if the signs *do not actually refer to anything* in the real world. No matter what the symbols refer to, all we need to manipulate them is knowledge of the rules. In science, of course, we do want the symbols to be more than a word game; we want them to refer to actual things.

Semantics: Rules for Using Words

Semantics refers to the rules by which we assign symbols to objects or events; these are the rules for *defining* terms. The simplest definition is the *ostensive,* or pointing, definition. For example, we may say "That is what I mean by dog," while pointing to a dog. All definitions eventually have to appeal to some kind of sense observation in this way. We might read that a dog is "a four-legged animal that barks and is commonly used as a house pet," but we then have the problem of knowing what is meant by the words "four," "legged," "animal," and "barks," and we are back to observation. We usually assume that everybody knows color names, simple numbers, and so on, from previous experience, and we progress from there to build more complex definitions via language. If we say that "a group is two or more people," we assume that our reader knows already what the words "two," "more," and "people" mean.

Operational definitions.   The physicist P. W. Bridgman proposed that we should define a concept in terms of how we measure it. The procedures for *measuring* length are what we *mean* by the term length, just as the procedures for measuring temperature are what we mean by temperature. *The meaning of any concept is synonymous with the corresponding set of measurement operations* (Bridgman, 1927, p. 5). Without measurement procedures, such words as length, weight, and time are meaningless and are not related to the "real world." We can measure length, of course, by laying down a standard rod repeatedly and counting the number of times it takes to go from one end of an object to the other. A soccer field is a hundred and twenty meters long, and for many years a meter was defined the length of a rod kept in the International Bureau of Standards. But what about situations in which we cannot perform this particular measurement operation or one derived from it. The diameter of the sun, the diameter of an atom, or the distance of the stars cannot be measured by "laying down a rod." Neither can the length of an object moving at high speed (such as a photon) be measured in this manner. We have to have new kinds of measurement procedures for these situations. And when any new measurement procedure is introduced, we may be led to changes in fundamental concepts, whether in physics or in psychology. The development of modern statistical methods (such as factor analysis) has had a profound impact on the way psychological measurements, such as personality tests, are constructed and used. These new tests, in turn, strongly impact our understanding of human personality and intellect.

Operational Definitions of Psychological Concepts

There is an old saying that "intelligence is what intelligence tests measure." In a trivial sense, this remark seems to deny that we have any understanding of intelligence. Operationally, however, it means that our understanding of intelligence depends on the procedures (operations) by which intelligence is measured. If intelligence is defined in terms of some vague hypothetical property like "problem-solving ability," we do little to understand it and nothing to measure it. But if we set up a series of problems and measure the ability to solve them (such as how fast they are solved), we have taken a step in the right direction. Alfred Binet did just this when he defined mental age in terms of successful completion of tasks of increasing difficulty. Now, someone might want to argue that a particular intelligence test is a poor way to measure intelligence or to say, "That's not what I mean by intelligence." It is then incumbent on the critic to say what her or his alternative way of measuring intelligence would be. The critic's way of measuring intelligence would give us his or her operational definition of intelligence.

Circular Definitions

Suppose that two rats run down an alleyway to a goal box where there is water. One rat runs very quickly, the other runs slowly. We might be inclined to say that one rat runs to water fast because it is thirsty and that the other runs slowly because it is not thirsty. But what is the evidence for their being thirsty or not? The evidence is that they run fast or slow! This is a **circular definition**, in which something is defined in terms of itself. We would be saying that the fast animal runs fast because it runs fast. This is no definition at all. It is simply giving a name (thirst) to something observed. As another example, we might see a flock of sheep gathered together and ask why they are doing so. An answer might be that "they have a herding instinct." How do we know that they have a herding instinct? The answer is because they are gathering together. Again, the definition is circular and does nothing more than put a name (herd instinct) to the observed behavior (gathering together). Circular definitions are dangerous to theory because they deceptively appear to be saying something when they are not. This dilemma is avoided by defining concepts as intervening variables.

Intervening Variables

Let us go back to our rats running down the alleyway to water. Suppose we found that the fast-running rat had been without water for a day and the slow-running rat had actually drunk its fill just before being tested. If we asked why one rat ran faster, we could say because it was thirsty. And how do we know it was thirsty? Our answer is that it had been without water for a day. The concept (thirst) is defined by observable *antecedent* and *consequent* conditions, that is, deprivation on the one hand and running on the other, as shown in Figure 1–5. The concept is "anchored" by objectively observable events on the antecedent and consequent sides, which in an experiment cor-

Antecedent Condition	Intervening Variable	Consequent Condition
24-Hour Water Deprivation·····················Thirst··Running Fast
No Water Deprivation·····························No Thirst·· Running Slow

FIGURE 1–5. Defining an intervening variable (thirst) in terms of antecedent and consequent conditions.

respond to the familiar independent variable that the experimenter manipulates and the dependent variable that the experimenter measures.

The two disciplines of scientific psychology. Lee Cronbach (1957) argued that there are "two disciplines of scientific psychology," *experimental* and *psychometric* (measurement and comparisons of individual differences). Spence (1944) and Kimble (1994a, b) made the same distinction in terms of intervening variables. Experimental psychologists *manipulate* variables to study their effects on behavior, whereas psychometric psychologists *correlate* different measures of behavior to find which are related.

Experimentally defined intervening variables. Suppose we wanted to study the effect of fear on speed of response to a signal. We might manipulate level of fear experimentally by telling subjects that they will get zapped with an electric shock if they do not respond quickly enough. We would compare the performance of these fearful subjects with the performance of nonfearful control subjects to determine the effect of the threat. This situation is illustrated in Figure 1–6.

Psychometrically defined intervening variables. Instead of using stimulus manipulation of fear as an antecedent condition, we might use scores on a test of anxiety as an antecedent condition. Suppose we think that anxiety will hurt test scores in a classroom test but we cannot manipulate the anxiety level for experimental purposes. Since our hypothesis is about students who bring their anxiety with them into the testing situation, we could set up our study to distinguish among subjects who normally differ in level of anxiety and compare their test performances. We could administer an anxiety scale to all the students and then correlate these scores with the subsequent classroom test scores. We must, of course, be careful to control for such extraneous factors as intelligence, year in school, and the like. The research design would then look like Figure 1–7. A significant negative correlation between anxiety scores and test performance (i.e., subjects with higher scores on the anxiety scale performing more poorly on the test) would support our hypothesis. We should be cautious about interpreting the results to mean that anxiety *caused* poorer performance, however, because we did not manipulate anx-

Antecedent Condition (Stimulus)	Intervening Variable	Consequent Condition (Response)
Threat of Shock	Fear	Fast Response to Signal
No Threat of Shock	No Fear	Slower Response to Signal

FIGURE 1–6. Experimentally defined (manipulated) intervening variable. The intervening variable is defined in terms of experimentally manipulated antecedent condition (threat of shock) and is therefore under experimental control.

Antecedent Condition (Response 1)	Intervening Variable	Consequent Condition (Response 2)
Scores on Anxiety Scale ·············· Anxiety Level ······························· Test Performance		

FIGURE 1–7. Psychometrically defined intervening variable. The antecedent condition is defined by one set of responses (scores on anxiety scale), and consequent condition is defined by a different set of responses (test performance). The antecedent condition is not manipulated; it is measured and is not under experimental control.

iety as an experimental variable (as we did with threat). It is always possible that some other unmeasured factor accounts for the correlation.

A variation of this psychometric approach is to select and compare the *extremes* of subjects who are high and low on some personality characteristic of interest, such as anxiety. We might do this because of the time and expense of dealing with all the available subjects. We might administer our anxiety test to a large number of potential subjects and then collect further data only from subjects in the top and bottom 25 percent of the scores. We then compare subsequent experimental task performance by the two groups, but using only half as many subjects as we would otherwise. This method is shown diagrammatically in Figure 1–8. This method gives the appearance of using an experimental intervening variable in an experimental study because we are comparing two independent groups. But, of course, it is still just a correlational procedure because we did not experimentally manipulate the level of anxiety. Therefore, we still have the same reservations about interpreting anxiety as the cause of differences between the groups as we have when we are correlating scores.

Putting Together a Theory

We have examined the elements of a theory, so let us see what they look like when put together. Consider first the formal structure of a theory in abstract terms, as illustrated in Figure 1–9. The concepts of the theory are defined in terms of observable events, and the theory states how these concepts

Antecedent Condition (Test Scores)	Intervening Variable	Consequent Condition (Task Scores)
High Anxiety Scale Scores ·············· High Anxiety ······························· Test Performance		
Low Anxiety Scale Scores ·············· Low Anxiety ······························· Test Performance		

FIGURE 1–8. Psychometrically defined intervening variable with subject selection. Scores are gathered from a large group of subjects, but only those subjects who score high or low on this antecedent measure (an anxiety scale in this example) are actually used for measurement of the consequent condition (task scores). This may be a more efficient use of subjects, but even though it may look like an experiment, it is not. The antecedent condition is not manipulated.

Level of Theoretical Concepts	$\mid (A)$	$\times$	$(B) \mid$	$+$	C	$=$	D
Definition	$\uparrow$		$\uparrow$		$\uparrow$		$\downarrow$
Level of Observations	(a) Control		(b) Control		(c) Control		(d) Measure

FIGURE 1–9. Formal structure of a theory. Theoretical concepts (A, B, and C) are defined in terms of observations. They are intervening variables. Concept D is defined according to the syntax of the theory ([A × B] + C = D). D is measured in terms of some appropriate response. If any two of A, B, and C were held constant, then D would reflect the change in the variable not held constant. For example, if A and B were held constant and C were varied, then D would reflect the variation in C.

are related to each other. Predictions about other observable events in the world are made on the basis of the syntax of the theory, which is determined by both observation and logic. The example in Figure 1–9 uses a completely arbitrary syntax just for the purpose of showing what syntax is. *A, B,* and *C* are theoretical concepts defined by specific experimental control procedures (operations) *a, b,* and *c.* Concept D, however, is defined by the syntax of the theory $D = (A \times B) + C$. If we know the values for *A, B,* and *C* (the independent variables in the experimental situation), then we can predict the value for *D,* which is measured as the dependent variable in the situation. We can study any one of the independent variables individually by holding the others constant. If the theory does not predict accurately, we will change its syntax, add new concepts, or eliminate old ones. We may have to scrap the theory if it never works right.

As a specific example, Hull (1943) proposed that learning multiplies with motivation to determine performance. He symbolized learning as *H* (for habit), motivation as *D* (for drive), and performance potential as *E* (for excitatory potential). The syntax for these was

Excitatory Potential = Habit × Drive, or $E = H \times D$

He operationally defined the magnitude of *H* in terms of number of previous learning trials (the more trials, the greater is *H*), magnitude of *D* in terms of hours of food deprivation (more hours of deprivation produces greater *D*), and *E* as $H \times D$. Putting this into the preceding format provides the theoretical concepts defined as shown in Figure 1–10.

Given the concepts and the syntax, we can make many specific predictions about experimental outcomes. For example, the theory says that running speed depends on the multiplication of habit and drive. If a particular

Level of Theoretical Concepts	H	$\times$	D	$=$	E
Definition	$\uparrow$		$\uparrow$		$\downarrow$
Level of Observations	Number of Learning Trials		Hours of Deprivation		Speed of Running

FIGURE 1–10. Hull's theory. Habit and drive (H and D) are defined as intervening variables, and excitatory potential (E) is defined by the syntax of the theory (E = H × D). The strength of E is measured by some appropriate response, in this example the speed of running.

response has not been learned ($H = O$) or if there is no drive ($D = O$), then $E = O$. If $E = O$, there would be no performance; the subject would not run. To make exact predictions, we would need exact numerical values for the concepts, such as numerical values for habit and drive. In psychological research there is seldom such high precision, and we are more likely to predict something like twenty-two hours of food deprivation produces more "drive" than two hours, and performance should be better (running faster to food) at twenty-two hours. Still and all, however, the theory is testable. In fact, the theory was widely tested and found to be flawed in many details. The virtue of this theory was what did it in; it was very testable.

SECTION SUMMARY

1. **Theory** is necessary to weave together the myriad of facts that would be meaningless in isolation from each other. We use theories and general principles to account for specific events that occur. A theory is like a map. It is a representation of real things and the relationships among those things. It helps organize the world for us.

2. Two crucial aspects of science are **observation** and **measurement**, where we try to be as objective as possible. In practice, objectivity means that many observers can agree upon what they have observed. Such agreement is greatly facilitated by such instruments as clocks, thermometers, and balances.

3. Four criteria for the goodness of a theory are **testability, fruitfulness, simplicity**, and **comprehensiveness**. With such multiple criteria there may be disagreement over whether one theory is clearly superior to another.

4. The language of science needs to be as precise as we can make it. We define word as precisely as we can (**semantics**) and relate terms to each other by rules (**syntactics**). We use **operational definitions** for our concepts, especially in research. This means that we define concepts (such as learning or motivation) in terms of how we measure them. For example, aggression may be defined as the number of times one child pushes another on the playground.

5. Many concepts are defined as **intervening variables**, which have **antecedent** and **consequent conditions. Experimentally-defined** (S-R) intervening variables have some experimental manipulation as the antecedent condition, such as a fear-arousing procedure. **Psychometrically-defined** (R-R) intervening variables have one response measurement as the antecedent condition, such as a score on an anxiety scale, and a different response measurement as the consequent condition.

6. A theory is put together by combining carefully defined concepts according to some set of rules from which we can make testable predictions and can explain observed events.

DEFINING MOTIVATION

One of the most important tasks for a motivation theorist is to define motivation. This is complicated by the fact that different theorists approach motivation differently and disagree on their definitions because they may have fundamentally different views of what motivation is about. Two major differences in emphasis are represented by the *regulatory* and *purposive* approaches to motivation.

The Regulatory Approach

The regulatory approach emphasizes the body's responses to such disruptive internal forces as hunger and pain and the way that the body tries to *restore* internal equilibrium. This process is called *homeostasis*. The emphasis is on what happens in the body when an organism needs food or water, for example. What does an organism do to counteract the disruptions?

The regulatory approach has a biological tradition, traceable to Darwin's theory of evolution and to experimental medicine. At the turn of the twentieth century, psychologists asked how does mental activity help organisms adapt to their environment? About the same time, however, the study of reflexes became popular. Such reflex responses as salivating were behaviors simple enough to be analyzed in detail. Complex behaviors were interpreted as "strings" of reflexes, and so, it was theorized, understanding reflexes could also lead to understanding complex social behaviors. The most extreme position was John B. Watson's behaviorism. Watson (1924) denied any role for "mental" events in the determination of behavior, and had no use for the notion of purpose.

These early approaches relied solely on stimuli as causes of behavior, without a separate motivational concept. Some stimuli were motivating stimuli, however. In 1918, Robert S. Woodworth argued that like an automobile, behavior had a *drive* mechanism and a *steering* mechanism. The driving mechanism provided the power or energy (drive) to make an otherwise motionless organism active and environmental stimuli steered the organism's activity in one direction or another. A biologically adaptive act, then, consisted of the following sequence:

Internal Need → Drive → Activity → Goal → Quiescence

Need for food drives an organism to be active until it finds and consumes food, after which it is quiet until some new need increases drive again. In this approach, goals come into play in the restoration of homeostatic equilibrium.

The Purposive Approach

The purposive approach emphasizes the *goal-directed* nature of behavior. This approach is more future-oriented and relatively less concerned with the physiology of regulation. Many goals, such as to get a college education or to have the best collection of baseball cards in the world, do not have any easily defined physiological basis. The origins of the purposive approach are found in ancient philosophical views about choices of goals and behaviors, often couched in terms of choices between good and evil. Scientifically, the question is phrased in terms of what makes a person choose *any* kind of goal over its alternatives. Why choose steak rather than fish for supper? Why select this person for a spouse, and not that person? According to the purposive approach, we look to the future, at the potential outcomes of choosing different possible courses of action. Then we strive toward goals that we anticipate will be of the greatest value to us. Given the choice between two potential spouses, we choose the one who we anticipate will provide the greater satisfaction. Concepts of internal need or drive are not necessary from the purposive point of view.

The regulatory and purposive approaches both have important things to say about motivation, and a major problem for the modern motivation theorist is to bring them together. In effect, doing this means that any definition has to be rather "loose," including a large number of specific concepts under the umbrella of motivation.

Motivational Intervening Variables

At the beginning of the chapter, we said that our basic motivational premise is that organisms engage in activities that are expected to have desirable outcomes, and avoid activities expected to have unpleasant or aversive outcomes. This is *psychological hedonism* and our intervening variables are desire and aversion. Let us now define these objectively, using principles we have been discussing. Using this approach we can study both internal states and goals. We shall say that an intervening variable is a motivational variable rather than, for example, learning or fatigue or illness, *If a difference in the level of an intervening variable, X, is related to a difference in preference, persistence, or vigor of behavior, the intervening variable is motivational.* We simply call the intervening variable "X" because we can define many different intervening variables, with different names, using this definition. Using this approach we can manipulate both internal states (e.g., food or water deprivation) and goals (e.g., food versus water) to see how these affect performance. In this way, we bring the regulatory and purposive approaches together. The motivational variables of most importance to us are desire and aversion.

Desire and Aversion as Intervening Variables

The hedonic axiom.   Our first assumption is that, at any given moment, there is an ordering of events along a continuum ranging from very aversive, through neutral, through very desirable. This is called the *hedonic continuum.* The details of the hedonic continuum may vary from one organism to another, or for the same organism at different times. At any given time, however, it is assumed to be fixed for a given organism. Our second assumption is the *hedonic axiom* (Irwin, 1971), which states that organisms direct their behaviors to maximize pleasure and minimize distress. This axiom has been held by all hedonic theorists, from ancient times to the present (e.g., Kahneman, Diener, & Schwarz, 1999). According to the hedonic axiom, organisms always make choices in favor of the direction of the arrow, as shown in Figure 1–11.

The concepts of desire and aversion both hinge on the idea of *neutrality*, or affective zero. Obviously, the fact that something is preferred does not necessarily mean that it is desirable. Suppose we have made preference tests for six different foods and found the order of preference from *A* to *F*, with *A* the most preferred and *F* the least preferred. Which of the outcomes are desirable, and which are aversive? This question can be answered only with reference to a neutral point. If a behavioral outcome, *A*, is preferred to a neutral outcome, then *A* is desirable. If a neutral outcome is preferred to *A*, then *A* is aversive. In Figure 1–12 a neutral point has been inserted, and we can see that although all the foods except *F* are preferred to some other food, only *A*, *B*, and *C* are desirable.

To take an everyday example, close to the hearts of both students and instructors, consider how we might be misled if we uncritically equate preference with desire. An instructor teaches a course that always has a high enrollment. The instructor concludes that he is a superb teacher of a fascinating course. He "knows" it is desirable because students flock to it in preference to all the other courses they might take. The students may have a different perspective. They know it is a course required for graduation, and they prefer taking the course to not graduating. If the requirement were removed, the enrollment would plummet. The instructor might be quite surprised at this result, however. With reference to the Figure 1–12, his course might have been *E*, taken in preference to *F*. With the new requirements, even a mildly aversive course is preferable to the previously required course.

In very concrete and specific terms, how do we find a neutral point or zone of neutrality in a real situation? In many situations, including the example just given, perhaps we cannot. We cannot change a curriculum structure just to answer such a question (although we might find some other ways to answer it). Technical difficulty in determining a neutral point is not a fatal flaw in the definitions of desire and aversion, however, and in laboratory re-

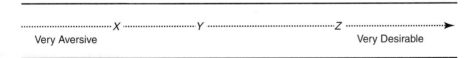

FIGURE 1–11. Hedonic Continuum and Hedonic Axiom. Objects or events can be placed on the hedonic continuum from very aversive to very desirable (e.g., at positions *X*, *Y*, and *Z*). According to the hedonic axiom, organisms prefer less aversive or more positive conditions. Therefore, *Z* would be preferred to *X* and *Y*, and *Y* would be preferred to *X*.

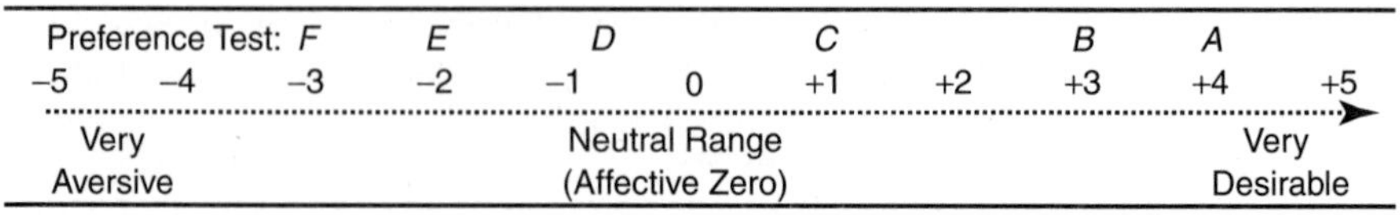

Preference Test:	*F*	*E*		*D*		*C*		*B*	*A*	
−5	−4	−3	−2	−1	0	+1	+2	+3	+4	+5
Very Aversive				Neutral Range (Affective Zero)					Very Desirable	

FIGURE 1–12. Preference alone does not tell us whether something is desirable or aversive. We can determine this only in relation to some neutral point. A desirable object is preferred to neutral, but an aversive object is less preferred than neutral. *D* is preferred to *E*, but *D* is still aversive.

search we can overcome most of the practical difficulties encountered in field research. Figure 1–13 illustrates a classic problem in choice, a rat turning right or left in a T-maze. We can operationally define desire and aversion in terms of this situation.

Operationally defining desire and aversion.   There are two possible outcomes in this situation, 01 and 02, which occur when the rat turns either left or right. The rat has chosen 02, which follows the right turn. There are three possible explanations: 02 is less aversive than 01, 01 is aversive and 02 desirable, or 01 is desirable and 02 more desirable. Only if we can establish a neutral point can we decide among these alternatives. Establishing a neutral point is done as follows:

• **Neutrality.** First, we determine that the rat is indifferent between outcomes 01 and 02 at the beginning of the experiment. For example, we could put it into

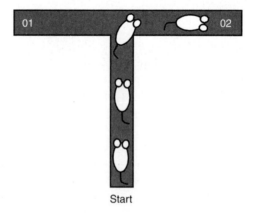

Start

FIGURE 1–13. Why does the rat turn right? All we know at the moment is that 02 is preferred to 01. The motivational problem is to determine the difference between 02 and 01, which will tell us why.

the empty maze several times and record its choices. No matter which choice the animal makes, the outcomes are essentially neutral, or at least equal. Let us assume that the rat is indifferent between the outcomes of the two choices: $O1 = O2 = $ Neutral. We can now define desire and aversion with reference to neutral.

- **Desire.** An outcome is desirable if it is preferred to a neutral outcome or some other already known desirable outcome. If without changing the neutral left side (O1) we added food to the right side (O2) and the animal preferred O2 over a number of test trials, we conclude that the food is desirable. Food (O2) is preferred to the neutral outcome (O1).

- **Aversion.** An outcome is aversive if a neutral or less aversive outcome is preferred to it. If we put electric shock in the floor of the left side, without changing the neutral right side, and if the animal prefers to go to right side, we can conclude that the left side (O1) is aversive because a neutral outcome (O2) is preferred to it.

Other measures of motivation.   We consider preference to be the best behavioral measure for defining desire and aversion, but for practical purposes other correlated measures are sometimes more useful, such as speed, vigor, or persistence in responding. The different measures do not always produce the same results, however, because the measures themselves can be influenced by different variables. For example, if an animal were already showing a 100 percent preference for one outcome over another, making the better alternative more attractive could not possibly show an effect on preference. A measure of vigor or persistence of responding might show a difference, however. Vigor of response (such as speed or force) may also be difficult to interpret because vigor can be part of what is learned. Even the rat will run or lever-press fast or slow if it is selectively rewarded for responding fast or slow (Logan, 1960). Capaldi and Davidson (1979) even got rats to run more rapidly with a short period of food deprivation than with a long period simply by not rewarding the rats if they ran too fast when very hungry. Finally, we must be cautious about interpreting the results obtained with any particular behavior without reference to other possible behaviors in the situation (Atkinson & Birch, 1978). For example, a child washing dishes is more easily tempted away by ice cream than a child playing a favorite game. Much motivational research, especially with animals, has not been approached with such multiple responses in mind.

Desire and aversion as classes of variables.   Many different operationally defined concepts can be put under the broad headings of desire or aversion even though they are different concepts and affected by different variables. For example, sweet food, sex objects, and good music may all be desirable and approached, but all they have in common behaviorally is that they are approached. Similarly, pain, foul odors, and screechy noises are aversive, but not otherwise identical. At some underlying physiological level, there may be common processes for all desirable and all aversive events, but this is not necessarily the case. The following list illustrates some motivational concepts that fit under the umbrellas of desire and aversion:

DESIRE	AVERSION
need for achievement	fear of failure
positive incentives	negative incentives
rewards	punishers
cognitive consistency	cognitive dissonance
love	fear
hope for power	fear of power
relaxation	stress

Motives are hierarchical.   Each of us strives more persistently toward some goals than others. If such goals are ranked in order of importance, there is a *hierarchy* of motives (Karniol & Ross, 1996), with more important goals nearer the top. The establishment of goal hierarchies can be considered as a process in *setting priorities* for goals. Abraham Maslow (1970) argued that motives are ordered from lower to higher in the same manner for all people, as follows: (1) physiological (hunger, etc.), (2) safety, (3) belongingness and love, (4) esteem (e.g., achievement), and (5) self-actualization (fulfilling one's unique potential, whatever it may be). Maslow also stipulated that higher level needs do not come into play until lower needs are satisfied and that the same hierarchy applies to all individuals. Although widely quoted, there is little supporting evidence for Maslow's hierarchy. Clearly, however, each individual has her or his own hierarchy of motives, and an important question is, On what grounds do people establish hierarchies of motives (goals)?

A hierarchy of goals is precisely what the hedonic continuum and hedonic axiom refer to (Figure 1–12.) The ordering of outcomes from left to right is a hierarchy of *desirability of goals.* The top of the hierarchy (i.e., the goal furthest to the right on the continuum) is the most preferred goal at the moment. As noted earlier, goals are influenced by both internal and external states and can fluctuate in importance with these. For example, a steak may be highly desirable when you are hungry but very undesirable if you have already eaten more than your fill. As another example, a student wishing strongly to graduate from college would choose activities that lead to this goal or at least are not in conflict with it. The hierarchy might change, however, if other opportunities goals presented themselves. For example, a student might have the opportunity to become a professional athlete. Or, another student might see the possibility that computer programs are the wave of the future and drop out of school to start a company to develop computer software.

SECTION SUMMARY

1. Two major approaches to motivation are **regulatory** and **purposive**. Regulatory approaches tend to emphasize **internal states** and such biological motives as hunger or fear. Organisms work to reduce such states. Purposive approaches emphasize the **goals** that organisms anticipate and pursue.

2. Two major classes of motivational variables are **desire** and **aversion**. Desire is defined as a preference for a behavior whose outcome is preferred to a neutral outcome. Aversion is defined as a preference for a behavior whose outcome is less preferred than a neutral outcome. Many different specifically defined motivational intervening variables may fall within these two classes, such as "hope of success" and "fear of failure."

3. The **hedonic axiom** states that organisms work to minimize aversive outcomes and to maximize desirable outcomes. It is an objective and empirical question whether an outcome is desirable or aversive, however, and not a subjective decision on the part of an observer.

4. **Preference** is considered the most basic motivational index, but **persistence** and **vigor** of behavior are often correlated with preference and, under particular conditions, may be better measures.

5. Motives are **hierarchical**, which means that some particular motives (goals) are stronger and more persistent than others. The specific motives in a hierarchy varies from one person to another.

CHAPTER TWO

Emotional Foundations of Motivation

What do we mean by emotion?

Why do we have emotions? What purpose do they serve?

How does emotion differ from temperament or mood?

How can we define emotion?

How do we measure emotion?

What are the biological bases of emotion?

How many emotions are there?

Do emotions vary from one person or culture to another?

How is emotion related to cognitive (thought) processes?

How is emotion related to motivation?

INTRODUCTION

Throughout the history of Western thought, philosophers have asked why people choose to act the way they do. The answers have always involved some interplay between passion and reason. Socrates in the fourth century B.C. taught that people do what they perceive to be the "right thing" to do, that is, a logical, rational analysis of a situation automatically leads a person to do the right thing. It may be difficult to determine what the right thing is, because such passions as love and hate may cloud our reason, but reason ultimately prevails. Other Greek philosophers, such as Epicurus and Aristotle, argued that passion plays a central role in our choices of action and that we act to maximize our pleasure and minimize our discomfort. Reason helps us to determine which actions will be to our benefit (pleasure) or harm (discomfort). This hedonistic viewpoint carried forward to Thomas Hobbes and Alexander Bain in the seventeenth and nineteenth centuries and into contemporary psychology. The role of emotion in psychological theory declined over the first sixty years of the twentieth century, but is now regaining its previously central role (Cacioppo & Gardner, 1999; Ekman & Davidson, 1994; Kahneman, Diener, & Schwarz, 1999; Lewis & Haviland-Jones, 2000; Oatley & Jenkins, 1996).

What Purpose Do Emotions Serve?

Let us begin with the idea that, at the very least, emotion involves our feeling of pleasantness and unpleasantness. Why do we have such feelings? If emotions simply confound and confuse us, they would not serve us at all. But if this were the case, why would they have evolved and been passed from generation to generation over thousands of years? Should they not have hindered survival and dropped out of the gene pool? Since we do have emotions we may presume that even the negative ones somehow benefit us. We may say that positive emotions are rewards for doing things that are good for us and negative emotions are punishment for doing things that are bad for us. For example, we are rewarded with pleasant taste and smell for eating foods that are good for us (tasty foods tend to be good for us) and are punished by bad taste, smell, and perhaps nausea for eating foods that are bad for us (putrid or bitter tasting substances tend to be bad for our health). Cues associated with these good or bad characteristics arouse the same emotional responses as do the taste substances themselves, so that we can judge in advance the likely benefit or harm from approaching or avoiding such stimuli.

Psychologists frequently distinguish the following four types of rewards and punishers that encourage or discourage preceding behaviors (Rescorla & Solomon, 1967; Rolls, 1999). The common emotion terms for the anticipation of each of these are in parentheses.

Reward 1 (Hope): Presentation of a stimulus (e.g., food, praise) produces positive affect. The reward encourages repetition of the behavior that preceded it.

Punisher 1 (Disappointment): Removal of source of positive affect (e.g., taking away privileges or social contact) leads to negative affect and discourages the behavior that preceded the loss.

Punisher 2 (Fear): Presentation of a stimulus producing negative affect (e.g., pain, verbal abuse) discourages preceding behavior.

Reward 2 (Relief): Removing source of negative affect (e.g., pain, threat of danger) encourages preceding behaviors.

For example, if a person experiences pain in a particular situation, that person may learn to anticipate a bad event (fear) and to behave so as to prevent the bad event from occurring. The subsequent reward is relief. We go into such situations in more detail in later chapters.

THE BEGINNINGS OF MODERN RESEARCH AND THEORY

The James-Lange Theory

William James (1884, 1890) provided the impetus to modern research on emotion. Prior to this time, said James, the common view was that emotion is aroused by some event and we act in accordance with the emotion. He also said that this view was wrong. We do not run (respond) because we are afraid (emotion). Instead, our *response* to an emotion-arousing situation (such as running away) comes *before* the emotional experience (James, 1884). *The emotional experience is the perception of the response to the situation.* To use his famous example, we do not see a bear, become afraid, and then run. Rather, we see the bear, run, and then are afraid. We must observe, however, that James emphasized responses of all kinds, not just muscular activity. A response to a bear might only be a pounding heart, without any running, such as with a person who is frozen with fear. James especially emphasized the sympathetic nervous system and the bodily responses it controls, such as heart rate, blood pressure, perspiration, and gastrointestinal functions. Figure 2–1 shows the brain, sympathetic nervous system, and the viscera controlled by the system. It also followed from James's theory that different emotional experiences have their unique physiological counterparts; otherwise, emotions would be indistinguishable. This has been called the *identity theory of emotion*, meaning there is a one-to-one relation (identity) between experienced emotion and physiology. A Danish physiologist, Carl Lange (1885), proposed a similar theory that is restricted to vascular system changes; the theory is known as the James-Lange theory. One of the greatest contributions of the theory was to shift the emphasis of emotion research to the study of physiology.

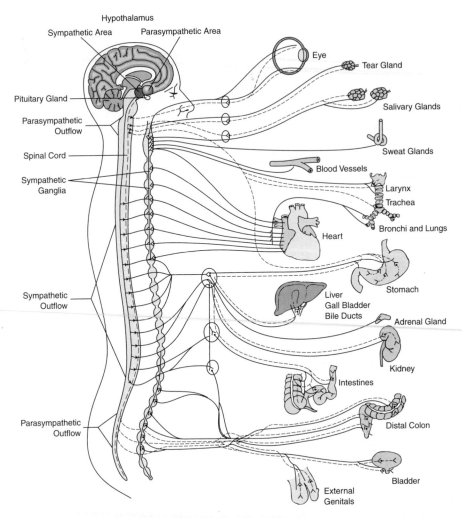

FIGURE 2–1. The autonomic nervous system and the body organs it controls. The limbic system is a set of brain structures surrounding the hypothalamus. (Reprinted from Krech, Crutchfield, & Livson, 1970. Copyright 1970 by Alfred A. Knopf. Used by permission.)

The Cannon-Bard Theory

The inevitable attack on James's theory came from Walter Cannon (1927), who argued that (1) separating the viscera from the nervous system does not change emotional behavior; (2) the same visceral changes occur in different emotional states, as well as in such nonemotional states as violent activity; (3) the viscera are relatively insensitive structures; (4) visceral changes occur too slowly (a matter of seconds) to be the source of sudden emotional changes, and (5) artificial induction of the visceral changes typical of strong emotions does not produce these same strong emotions. Cannon therefore proposed that neural impulses from the sense organs flow into the **thalamic area** in the middle of the brain, are directly experienced as emotion, and only later produce visceral changes. Studies of patients with spinal cord damage have recently provided tests of the opposing views of these theories. Hohmann (1966) reported that amount of spinal cord damage was correlated with amount of loss of emotional experience, apparently supporting James. Subsequently, however, research with better methodology and more subjects has contradicted Hohmann's results. In two studies, patients with severe spinal cord damage and very limited body feeling commonly reported experiencing emotions as more intense than they had experienced prior to their injuries (Bermond, Nieuwenhuyse, Fasotti, & Schuerman, 1991; Chwalisz, Diener, & Gallagher, 1988). Therefore, the visceral responses typically occurring during emotion-arousing situations are not themselves necessary for emotional experience.

Discovery of Important Subcortical Brain Structures

The brain is more complicated than conceived by either James or Cannon, and many areas below the cortex are involved in emotion. James Papez (1937) theorized that a set of pathways in the core of the brain constitute the neural circuitry underlying emotional experience and behavior. This **Papez circuit** (now generally referred to as the **limbic system**, Figure 2–2) is buried deep inside all mammalian brains, and accounts for most of the brain mass of reptiles. Such recently evolved brain structures as the neocortex exert some control over the limbic system, but this primitive emotional circuitry may still not be fully adapted to life in modern civilization (Malmo, 1975). The brain mechanisms that evolved for such strong actions as fight or flight still produce intense physiological arousal in situations where strong action is inappropriate. Emotional arousal maintained for a long time is stressful and potentially harmful to our health.

CONTEMPORARY STUDY OF EMOTION

The study of emotion has been complicated by the fact that there are many different approaches and seemingly contradictory data. At the heart of all this, however, we have the basic phenomenon of interest to most people— our feelings. The common term for these feelings is **affect** and developing an organization or *structure* for different types of affect helps bring order to the study of emotion.

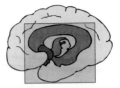

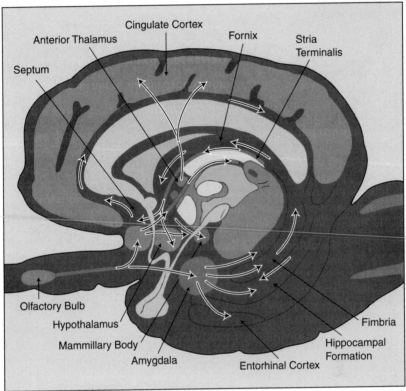

FIGURE 2–2. Schematic and simplified representation of the limbic system. (From Carlson, 1987. Copyright © 1987 by Allyn and Bacon, Inc. Used by permission.)

Structure of Affect

feelings = affect

Affect refers to experiences that have the quality of being either pleasant or unpleasant. Three different aspects of affective experience are **temperament**, **mood**, and **emotion**.

Temperament. Temperament refers to very stable tendencies toward having positive or negative affect. These tendencies appear early in life and endure over years, suggesting a genetic basis (Goldsmith, 1993; Oatley & Jenkins, 1996). The most notable genetic tendency is along the dimension of introversion-extraversion, or shy versus outgoing, which is related to negative versus positive affect. Children identified at an early age as withdrawn tend to remain so throughout life (Kagan, Reznick, & Snidman, 1988). Genetic studies suggest that 25 to 50 percent of the variability in extraversion across people is genetically determined.

Moods.   Moods are typically characterized as (1) being relatively weak but pervasive affective experiences, (2) not having a specific object that a person recognizes as having produced the mood, and (3) being relatively enduring (e.g., minutes to hours) but not as long lasting as temperament. For example, we may "get out of bed on the wrong side" and be irritable for half the day or have a "blue Monday." Moods are a low-level background of affect that "color" our thoughts and behaviors. Things look better or worse according to our mood, but we may not even be aware of our mood until it is pointed out to us. The effects of different moods on perception, learning, memory, and social interactions have been studied.

Emotions.   Emotions are relatively more brief and intense than moods and have some specific object toward which there is a tendency to act (approach or avoid). We are happy *with* someone, sad *about* something, angry *at* someone, or afraid *of* something. Emotions call for actions most broadly described as being approach or avoidance, and for some theorists such action tendencies are part of the definition of emotion (Frijda, 1986, 1988). The action aspect of emotion also highlights the intimate relationship between motivation and emotion. Motivation is said to "move" us, to initiate and maintain behavior (action). For example, fear is clearly an emotion with the power to move us to strong action.

Defining Emotions as Intervening Variables

In order to study emotion, we need to define the term more specifically. Consider a common question, How many emotions are there? The answer depends on who you ask and how they define emotion. Scientific definitions of emotion go beyond reports of emotional experience to include the details of the situations in which emotional experiences, behaviors, and physiological changes occur. This leads us to define emotions as intervening variables. In William James's illustration, if a person sees a bear and his heart rate accelerates and he runs away, we may conclude that he is afraid. Seeing the bear is the antecedent condition; heart rate acceleration, running away, and self-report of experience are consequent conditions; and the emotion of fear is the intervening variable (Figure 2–3). The meaning of emotion is embedded in the conditions under which emotion occurs and the way(s) that we measure emotion.

If a person sees a bear and *approaches* it, we would infer that either that person is not afraid or that she has some more powerful reason to approach the bear than to run from it. (In June 1998 a mother hiking in Big Bend Na-

Antecedent Condition	Intervening Variable	Consequent Conditions
Seeing Bear	FEAR	Verbal Behavior ("I'm afraid") Running Away Heart Pounding

FIGURE 2–3. Fear defined in terms of antecedent and consequent conditions.

tional Park, Texas, with her three children held off an attacking cougar with a knife as they slowly worked their way back to their car. The mother's concern for her children made her behave very differently than she probably would have behaved had she been alone. We can safely assume that she was afraid even though she did not run.) We distinguish among different emotions by analyzing antecedent and consequent conditions, as illustrated in Table 2–1. This table is not meant to be an exhaustive listing of emotions, but it does show how we can organize our thinking about emotion. One important lesson to be learned is that no specific consequent condition is a completely unambiguous index of any emotion.

The Measurement of Emotion

Verbal behavior.   We cannot directly observe other people's emotional experiences, but we can record what they say about them. Psychotherapists listen attentively to what patients say about their emotional problems, but also use psychological tests and scales as somewhat less ambiguous and more quantifiable indicators of emotion than open-ended discussion. Verbal behavior is subject to many biases, however, and has to be assessed cautiously. People often say what they think is expected rather than just what they are feeling. Furthermore, language is often inadequate to convey emotional experience, or a person may intentionally want to disguise his feelings, or a past emotional experience may not be remembered well enough to be described accurately.

Nonverbal Behavior.   This is any behavior besides talking that a person or animal might engage in and that can readily be seen by the naked eye, such as facial expression or body movements. If I clench my fist, an observer might conclude that I am angry. There is the possibility of error, though; I might have clenched my fist for emphasis while speaking, or as a sign of victory. This shows why we need antecedent as well as consequent conditions to define emotion. A clenched fist in a threatening situation signifies one thing but a clenched fist after making a great golf putt indicates something very different.

The study of escape and avoidance behavior in animals (where verbal description by the subjects is not possible anyway) is particularly useful

TABLE 2–1. Potential antecedent and consequent conditions used to define emotions as intervening variables. We may commonly think of these as causes and effects of emotion. The table is intended to show how we go about distinguishing emotions, not to indicate that the list of emotional names is the list that all theorists would use.

ANTECEDENT CONDITIONS	INTERVENING VARIABLES	CONSEQUENT CONDITIONS
WHAT CAUSES A PARTICULAR EMOTION?	WHAT EMOTIONS ARE DEFINED BY ANTECEDENT AND CONSEQUENT CONDITIONS?	WHAT ARE THE EFFECTS OF EMOTIONS?
Environmental Events	**Positive Emotions**	**Feelings**
Home team's winning ball game	Happiness	Verbal self-report scales
Sight of loved one	Interest	**Behaviors**
Snarling dog	Surprise	**Expressive Behaviors**
Loss of fortune	Sexual arousal	Facial expressions
Sight of someone throwing up	Love	Body language
Cognitive Events	**Negative Emotions**	**Approach/Avoidance**
Memories	Fear	**Task Performance**
Evaluations of events	Sadness	Work
	Anger	Sport
Body Changes	Disgust	**Cognitive Processes**
Biochemical changes (e.g., drugs)		Attention
Fatigue		Thinking
Disease		Learning
Physical activity (e.g., running)		Memory
		Physiologic Events
		Central nervous system
		Autonomic nervous system
		Neurohormones (e.g., endorphins)
		Neurotransmitters (e.g., dopamine, adrenaline, noradrenaline, etc.)

because these are analogous to many anxiety-based human behaviors. Animals can, for example, learn to avoid electric shock in an experimental apparatus and may successfully do so for hundreds of trials. We would surely be astounded at seeing an animal compulsively moving back and forth in an apparatus for no apparent reason if we didn't know its history. If we know how a problem behavior came to be learned, however, the behavior makes sense, and we can form better ideas about how to change it. Psychologists have long been concerned with giving accounts of anxiety disorders, for example, so that some of the "strange" behaviors of humans could be as understandable as the behavior of persistently avoiding rats.

Physiology.   A large number of physiological activities and anatomical locations have been described in relation to emotion, as suggested in Table 2–1. Many of the body changes related to emotion cannot be observed with the naked eye, but can be measured with appropriate instruments. The most common measures with humans are (1) heart rate; (2) blood pressure; (3) galvanic skin response, an increase in the electrical conductivity of the skin during emotional arousal; (4) respiration (breathing) rate; (5) blood volume change, easily recorded at the tips of the fingers; (6) perspiration; (7) muscle tension; and (8) skin temperature, an indirect measure of blood flow. All these measures also have to be interpreted with caution, however, because these body changes also occur in situations unrelated to emotion, such as exercise. Other measures, such as of hormone levels, can be obtained from blood and urine samples. With animals, experimental surgery is also possible. The body damage from nature's experiments with humans (accidents or disease) also occur with such frequency that we can learn a great deal about emotion from clinical cases, as exemplified in the earlier discussion of spinal cord damage.

SECTION SUMMARY

1. **Emotion** involves feelings of **pleasantness** and **unpleasantness**. From an evolutionary perspective, an important purpose of emotions is to **reward** us when we do things that are biologically beneficial to us and to **punish** us when we do things that are biologically bad for us.

2. We are rewarded by the presentation of positive stimuli or the removal of negative stimuli. We are punished by the presentation of negative stimuli or the removal of positive stimuli.

3. According to the **James-Lange theory**, emotion is the perception of body changes that occur in response to stimulus events. The theory provided major impetus to the physiological study of emotion. The **Cannon-Bard theory** proposed that emotional experience need only involve activity of the brain in response to environmental events. Emphasis subsequently shifted more to the emotional roles of biologically primitive subcortical brain areas, especially in the limbic system.

4. The study of **affect** (feelings of pleasant and unpleasant) is organized into the topics of (a) long-term **temperament**, as seen in such stable personality characteristics as extraversion; (b) **moods** that are more temporary, but vague, affective experiences; and (c) **emotions** that are relatively brief, intense, and focused on some source.

5. We may define emotions as intervening variables, with environmental events as antecedent conditions and verbal reports of experience, behaviors, and physiological changes as consequent conditions. Differences in antecedent and/or consequent conditions help us to define different emotions.

THE BIOLOGY OF EMOTION

Because biology is so basic to emotion, we begin with some biological facts. Our most reliable knowledge is related to positive and negative affect, but more specific emotions can also be categorized as either positive or negative.

Divisions of the Nervous System

Table 2–2 outlines the major divisions of the nervous system. The nervous system is divided into the **central nervous system** (**CNS**, brain and spinal cord) and the **peripheral nervous system** (everything else). It is also divided into somatic and autonomic portions. The **somatic nervous system** regulates interactions with the environment: sensory inputs and muscle movements. The **autonomic nervous system** (**ANS**) regulates internal body activities involved in maintaining and replenishing the body.

The ANS controls heart muscle, the smooth muscle of the body cavity, such as stomach and intestines, and the release of hormones from glands, such as the pituitary and adrenals. The **parasympathetic** portion of the ANS is concerned with digestive activity. The **sympathetic** portion of the ANS is concerned with such emergency functions as preparation of the body for fight or flight (Cannon, 1939a), which are considered reactions to strong emotions. The intense activity we feel in our bodies when we are very active, angry, or frightened reflects the activity of the sympathetic nervous system and the arousal of the internal organs.

The parasympathetic and sympathetic systems (see Figure 2–1) each affect every visceral organ and are generally antagonistic to each other. When the sympathetic system is strongly aroused, the parasympathetic system is relatively suppressed, and vice versa.

We commonly speak of "adrenaline flowing" during excitement. This and related hormones are circulated through the body via the bloodstream and are also released from nerve endings in the sympathetic system. This double-barreled action produces both quick and widespread preparation of the body for emergency activity. This preparation includes the release of

TABLE 2–2.   Divisions of the nervous system. The somatic nervous system is involved in interactions with the external environment. The autonomic system is more involved with the regulation of the internal activity and chemistry of the body.

	SOMATIC	AUTONOMIC
Central	Brain and spinal cord	Limbic system, hypothalamus, and brain stem
Peripheral	Nerves to skeletal muscles and from sense organs	Sympathetic, parasympathetic

blood sugar into the body, more rapid breathing, quicker circulation of oxygen, and perspiration for cooling.

Hemispheric Differences in Emotion

The brain is divided into two halves, the right and the left **cerebral hemispheres,** which function somewhat differently in humans. For example, the left hemisphere is relatively more involved in such sequential, analytic activities as language, which is almost always localized in the left hemisphere. The right hemisphere is relatively more concerned with "holistic impressions," a more immediate grasp of a spatial situation. The right hemisphere also relates to emotion recognition and expression better than the left (Rinn, 1984; Toates, 2001).

Both hemispheres, of course, contribute to emotion, but in somewhat different ways. If a humorous visual stimulus is presented in such a way that it goes only to the right hemisphere, a research subject may smile but cannot say why she is smiling. The emotional quality of the stimulus has been detected by the right hemisphere but cannot be put into language because the left hemisphere has not gotten the information. Lesions in the right hemisphere, but not the left, impair the ability of the affected person to detect emotion in other people (but see Leventhal & Tomarken, 1986, for controversies).

There is also a right hemisphere dominance for negative emotions and left hemisphere dominance for positive emotions. Left hemisphere damage or sedation by a drug injected into the hemisphere is associated with excessive worry, pessimism, and crying whereas right hemisphere damage or suppression is associated with euphoria or laughing (Tucker, 1981). There are also right and left hemisphere differences ("asymmetries") in brain wave activity in emotion, with more left brain activity when a person experiences positive affect and more right brain activity during negative affect (Davidson, 1994; Jacobs & Snyder, 1996; Spence, Shapiro, & Zaidel, 1996; Tomarken, Davidson, Wheeler, & Doss, 1992; but also see Collet & Duclaux, 1986). These differences are also shown by people with different personality characteristics; extraverts show more left brain activity than introverts, and introverts show more right brain activity. Similarly, experimental manipulations of positive versus negative affect produce greater activity in left and right hemispheres, respectively.

Subcortical Structures for Positive Affect

Pleasure centers.   In 1954, James Olds and Peter Milner reported one of the monumental neurological discoveries of the twentieth century: A tiny amount of electric current, put into the brain of a rat by means of a permanently implanted electrode, was a powerful reward. The data indicated that such a reward is effective because it is pleasurable and the authors proposed that "pleasure centers" in the brain are excited by *any stimulus* that we would find rewarding. More and more data indicate that Olds and Milner were correct in their analysis.

Figure 2–3a illustrates an animal pressing a lever for brain stimulation reward. Figure2–3b illustrates the power of such reward, showing the results for a single animal pressing a lever for brain stimulation over thirteen hours. The animal pressed steadily when stimulated but stopped pressing when the current was turned off and the lever press had no effect. Such results were typical and Olds (1958) subsequently reported an animal that responded about two thousand times an hour for twenty-four consecutive hours before collapsing from fatigue.

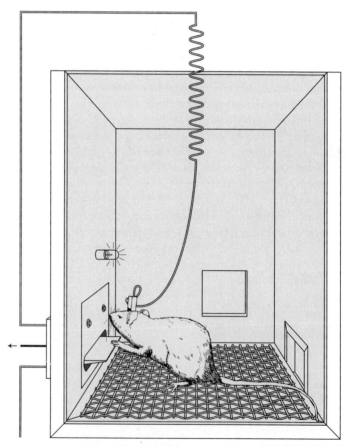

FIGURE 2–3A.   A self-stimulation circuit is diagrammed here. When the rat presses on the treadle, it triggers an electric stimulus to its brain and simultaneously records action via wire at left. (From Olds, 1956, p. 108. Copyright © 1956 by *Scientific American, Inc.* Reprinted by permission.)

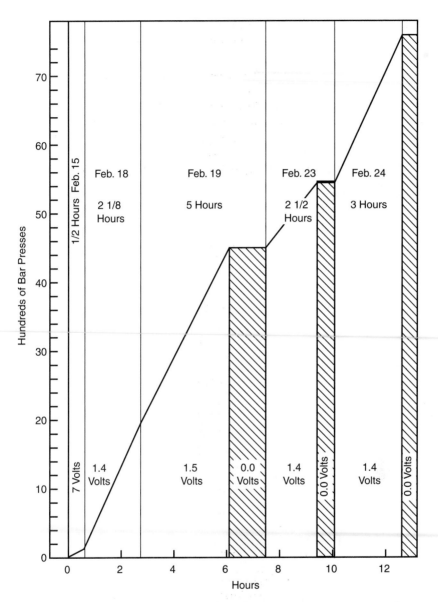

FIGURE 2–3B. Smoothed cumulative response curve for a rat. (From Olds & Milner, 1954, p. 424. Copyright © 1954 by the American Psychological Association. Reprinted by permission.)

Locations of pleasurable stimulation effects. Anatomical and biochemical studies reveal that locations ranging from the neocortex and frontal lobes all the way down to the brain stem can be rewarding with electrical self-stimulation. These locations are in the areas of the **medial forebrain bundle, lateral hypothalamus**, and **ventral tegmental area** (**VTA**), shown in

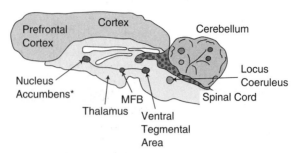

*Stimulation is reinforcing along pathway between n.a. and VTA.

FIGURE 2–4.   The dopamine "pleasure system" in the rat brain, running from the ventral tegmental area (VTA) through the hypothalamus and medial forebrain bundle (MFB), and on to the nucleus accumbens. When electrically stimulated, this area produces a highly pleasurable effect. It is involved in feeding and drug addiction.

Figure 2–4. These are areas of the brain that utilize **dopamine** as a neurotransmitter (Stellar & Stellar, 1985). The dopamine system is also where such addictive drugs as cocaine and the amphetamines produce their pleasurable effects. Whether activated by such substances as pleasant food or addictive drugs, or by direct electrical activation, the common effect of arousing this system is pleasurable.

Other areas of the brain are also involved, however (Kalat, 1988). The brain stimulation electrode must be placed in a dopamine-rich area, but the dopamine system connects to the **endorphin** system in the **nucleus accumbens** (Figure 2–4). The endorphins, the brain's natural opiates, may be the key neurotransmitters for reward (Wise, 1989) and involved in all forms of addiction. Furthermore, if other "motivating" stimuli are added to brain stimulation, animals work more for the stimulation (Hoebel, 1969). For example, if animals have sucrose put into their mouths passively when they are pressing a lever for electrical self-stimulation, they respond more rapidly.

Brain differences in liking and wanting.   We typically think that animals, including ourselves (Gilbert & Wilson, 2000), like what they want and want what they like. The rat that likes sucrose also wants it, as shown by the fact that it works for it. Liking and wanting are separable in the brain, however, and have different characteristics (Berridge, 1996). To demonstrate this, we need a measure of liking separate from working for the food (wanting). Liking is seen in the way animals or humans consume tasty fluids. The rat licks steadily at the drinking tube, is careful to swallow all it can get, and so on. Animals show similar movements if the fluid is injected directly into the mouth so that they can taste and swallow it without having to do any work at all. Conversely, if they do not like the fluid, they try to spit it out, withdraw from it, let it dribble from their mouths, or wipe it away with their paws. These highly

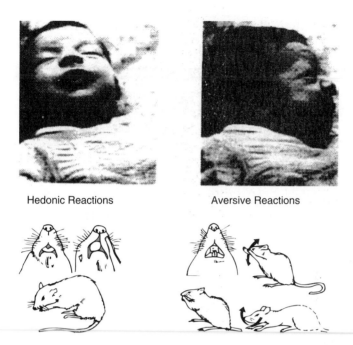

Hedonic Reactions   Aversive Reactions

FIGURE 2–5.   Affective reactions to taste. Hedonic reaction of a three-week-old infant to a sweet solution (left; 1 M sucrose) versus aversive reaction to an unpleasantly salty solution (right; 0.15 M NaCl) are shown in videotape frames at top. Various hedonic and aversive reactions of rats, which would be elicited by the same tastes, are drawn below. Hedonic reactions include tongue protrusions, lateral tongue protrusions, and paw licks. Aversive reactions include gapes, headshakes, face/paw wipes, and forelimb flails. Infant video from unpublished observations collected by G. Harris, D. Booth, and K. Berridge at the University of Birmingham, England [following Steiner (130, 131)]. Rat drawings of taste reactivity components follow Grill and Norgren (63). (From Berridge, 1996, Figure 2.)

stereotyped acceptance and rejection behaviors (illustrated in Figure 2–5) are recorded on videotape for later analysis and are readily distinguished by observers. These reactions do not require conscious recognition and occur in human infants born without parts of the brain necessary for consciousness. Various experimental manipulations that alter human perception of palatability, such as food deprivation, increase the number of positive reactions (Berridge, 2000).

If dopamine in the tegmental system is temporarily "wiped out" by injection of **6-hydroxydopamine**, animals will not work for sweet foods. If, however, a sweet solution is injected directly into the mouths of these same animals, they show the head movements that indicate liking. Administration of **naloxone**, a drug that counteracts opiate activity in the brain, eliminates these liking responses. Liking thus appears to be related to the endorphins, and wanting is related to the dopamine system.

Subcortical Structures for Negative Affect

The amygdala. More is known about the role of the amygdala in emotions than any other specific brain area (Aggleton & Young 2000; LeDoux, 2000). In primates, probably including humans, the amygdala is important for *expressing* emotion, for *recognizing* emotional expression in others, and for *learning* emotional associations. The evidence for all these effects is particularly strong with regard to fear. For example, animals with lesions of the amygdala do not respond in an appropriately fearful manner to threat gestures by other animals and do not readily learn to be fearful in the presence of stimuli that signal dangerous events. The amygdala also has many connections to the frontal lobes of the brain, which are important in planning future activities. Our specific choice of plans to initiate and carry out actions depends in part on our anticipation of whether the outcomes will be good or bad, requiring connections between the frontal lobes and such subcortical brain areas as the amygdala and ventral tegmental dopamine system. There is also evidence for the role of the amygdala in positive emotion, but this evidence is fairly scanty (Hamann, Ely, Hoffman, & Kilts, 2002).

SECTION SUMMARY

1. Many parts of the body are involved the expression of emotion. The **brain** controls the **autonomic nervous system** which controls the general level of **arousal** of the body. Activity in the **sympathetic nervous system** prepares an animal for energetic action.

2. **Cerebral cortex** in the right half of the brain is more active in negative emotion and in the left half is more active in positive emotion. Overall, the right cerebral hemisphere is more active in emotion.

3. At the **subcortical** level, the **ventral tegmental dopamine** system and the **nucleus accumbens** are generally active for positive emotion involving what are called the pleasure centers in the brain. These areas are activated by all kinds of rewards and give rewards their pleasurable characteristics. Different parts of the brain are involved in **wanting** and seeking things as compared with **liking** and disliking things.

4. The **amygdala** is active during negative emotion and has been extensively studied for its role in negative emotion, especially fear. There is limited evidence that the amygdala is also involved in positive emotion.

THEORIES OF EMOTION

Discrete Emotion Theories

The number of emotion-related words in the English language runs into the thousands, but not all of these words represent different emotions. Many of the words are synonyms (e.g., joy, ecstacy), and others represent different intensities of the same emotions (e.g., irritation, anger, rage, fury). Discrete emotion theories assume that there is some small number of core emotions and that the many emotion words apply only to these core emotions and their combinations. The core emotions are thought to be specific, biologically determined emotional responses whose expression and recognition is fundamentally the same for all individuals and peoples. This is a Darwinian evolutionary viewpoint running counter to many previously accepted notions of cultural anthropologists who argued for culture-specific emotions (Ekman, 1998). The number of core emotions is typically in the range of seven to ten, depending on the particular theory (e.g., Ekman & Oster, 1979; Izard, 1977; Plutchik, 1980; Tomkins, 1981). Table 2–3 shows the discrete emotions identified by various theorists. These are not much different than those proposed by René Descartes in the seventeenth century or Charles Darwin in the nineteenth.

Evidence for Discrete Emotions

Facial expression in humans.   Figure 2–6 shows six different posed emotional expressions. Can you identify them? Darwin himself (1872/1998) observed that many species show similar expressions of emotion. Dogs, cats, and monkeys draw back their lips and bare their teeth when angry, and these emotional displays may replace actual fighting. In humans such displays are often pale reflections of those shown by lower animals, but the evolutionary relationship to our animal ancestors is clear. Evidence from such diverse cultures as preliterate mountain natives of New Guinea and the modern United States suggests universal recognition of expressions of happiness, anger, sadness, disgust, surprise, fear, and contempt. People who have neither seen Caucasians nor been exposed to photographs or television can correctly identify specific facial expressions as indicative of the emotions that a person in a

TABLE 2–3.   Discrete emotions according to several theorists.

IZARD	TOMPKINS	EKMAN	PLUTCHIK
1. Interest-excitement	Interest	—	Expectancy
2. Joy	Joy	Happiness	Joy
3. Surprise	Startle	Surprise	Surprise
4. Distress-Anguish	Distress	Sadness	Sadness
5. Anger-Rage	—	Anger	Anger
6. Disgust	—	Disgust	Disgust
7. Contempt-Scorn	—	Contempt	—
8. Fear-Terror	Fear	Fear	Fear
9. Shame-Shyness	—	—	—
10. Guilt	—	—	—
11. —	Laughter	—	—
12. —	—	—	Acceptance

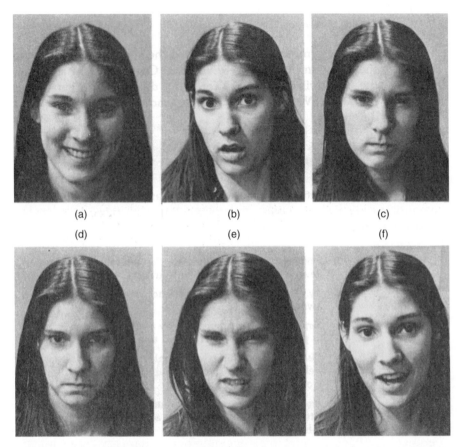

(a)   (b)   (c)

(d)   (e)   (f)

FIGURE 2–6.   Facial expressions of emotion like those used in research on emotion. These six are common around the world. Can you identify them?

(a) Happy, (b) fear/surprise, (c) anger, (d) sorrow, (e) disgust, (f) surprise/happy.

story would express (Ekman, 1994, Ekman & Friesen, 1971, Ekman & Friesen, 1975; Ekman & Friesen, 1986). Deaf and blind children also show the typical facial expressions for these emotions (Ekman & Oster, 1979). Such emotional expressions might be universal because they are biologically valuable forms of communication for infants, arousing caretaking by adults.

Anatomy of facial expression.   Facial expressions are determined by contractions of muscles in the face that contort the skin to form the visible expression. The specific muscles that contract during different facial expressions have been cataloged by Ekman & Friesen (1978), in what they call the *Facial Action Coding System* (FACS). Figure 2–7 shows a simplified diagram of some of the muscles that are important for the facial expression of emotion. The **frontalis** muscles produce wrinkles in the forehead; the **corrugator** mus-

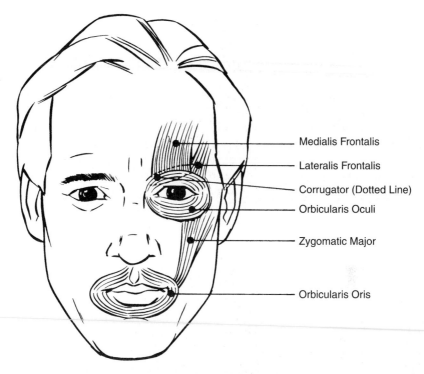

Medialis Frontalis

Lateralis Frontalis

Corrugator (Dotted Line)

Orbicularis Oculi

Zygomatic Major

Orbicularis Oris

FIGURE 2–7.   Important muscles involved in pleasant and unpleasant facial expressions.

cles produce frowning eyebrows; the **orbicularis oculi** muscles produce the crows' feet that characterize smiling; and the **zygomatic major** and **orbicularis orbis** muscles around the cheeks and mouth produce smiling. When we change moods from negative to positive, activity of the corrugators decreases, and activity of the zygomatic and orbicularis orbis increases (Cacioppo, Petty, Losch, & Kim, 1986). Not surprisingly, zygomatic activity is also greater during the presentation of sexual stimuli (Sullivan & Bender, 1986).

The facial feedback hypothesis.   An interesting question, raised by William James, is whether facial muscle activity actually produces emotion. Can we make ourselves feel better by "putting on a happy face"? James's theory stated that the experience of emotion is the perception of one's responses to the environment, leading him to consider whether actors, for example, actually felt the emotions that they were mimicking with their faces (James, 1890). He concluded that the evidence was ambiguous, probably because the actors could not easily produce the appropriate visceral changes to go along with the facial expressions. Tomkins (1962) and Izard (1971) argued, however, that the facial musculature is complex enough that the feedback produced is adequate to produce the experience of different emotions.

If this is true, then artificial manipulation of facial expressions should modify emotional experience.

Manipulation of facial reactions has been studied by directly manipulating facial muscles, by instructing subjects to express or hide a particular emotion (Leventhal & Tomarkan, 1986), and by using such cues as "canned laughter" to facilitate such humorous responses as smiling and laughing. Laird (1974) reported that subjects instructed to frown also reported feeling aggressive in response to photographs but that smiles induced positive feelings toward these same photos. It appears that expressive changes can alter subjective states but that such effects are small (Leventhal & Tomarken, 1986). Matsumoto (1987) analyzed the data from sixteen experiments on manipulation of facial expression and found that facial feedback accounts for only about 12 percent of the variation of reported emotional change. This 12 percent is equivalent to a correlation of .35, however, which is typically what researchers consider to be a meaningful correlation in personality research. By this criterion, the effect is far from trivial.

Carroll and Russell (1997) challenged the notion that activity of the specific facial muscles described by the Facial Action Coding System automatically indicate specific emotions. Film clips of Academy Award–winning performances were shown to subjects who were asked to identify the emotions being portrayed without reference to any particular muscles. There was a high agreement about the portrayed emotions, but except for upturned corners of the mouth for happiness, the facial musculature did not correspond to the FACS. Carroll and Russell (1996) also revived the old idea that facial expressions of emotion are judged by the context in which they appear. They found that "most observers judged the expresser [the person expressing the emotion to be judged] to be feeling the emotion anticipated from the situation rather than the one allegedly signaled by the face" (p. 215). They believe that the only distinctive facial features are related to pleasure-displeasure and level of arousal.

Emotional expression as social communication: display rules. Even if facial expressions of emotion were genetically programmed, there are variations in expression. Ekman (1972) proposed that cultural "display rules" tell us when and how we ought to express grief, joy, and other emotions. Such rules may interfere with "basic" emotional expressions. Thus, if I win a lottery, I will feel happy and communicate that happiness. If I were to feel happy at someone else's misfortune, however, I would probably try to mask my joy. Ekman and Oster (1979) reported that Japanese people watching a movie controlled their facial expressions if they knew they were being observed more than Americans did. The stereotypes of the "stoic" Britisher, the "inscrutable" Oriental, or the "excitable" Latin may have arisen because of such specific cultural influences on the expression of emotion. Overt expressions of emotion may be aroused more readily by social cues than by other events. For example, bowlers, hockey fans, and people strolling down the street were more likely to smile in response to other people than to cues regarding sports results that should have made them happy, such as good bowling scores (Kraut & Johnston, 1979). The concept of display rules has been criticized, however, as an attempt to "save" discrete emotions theory. That is, if a person shows some theoretically "appropriate" discrete facial expression, it is considered support for the theory. If the person does not show this, display rules are blamed for the failure to observe the "appropriate" response. The theory then becomes nearly untestable until we are given the rules that tell us when and how display rules will come into play.

Voluntary versus spontaneous emotional expression.   Spontaneous reactions to stimuli are stronger in terms of both facial expression and reported feelings than are artificial reactions. In fact, voluntary and involuntary (spontaneous) emotional responses appear to "originate" in different motor systems in the brain (Rinn, 1984). Involuntary emotional responses operate through the **extrapyramidal motor system** in the brain, and voluntary responses through the **pyramidal motor system**. A person with damage to the extrapyramidal system may laugh or cry uncontrollably, expressing emotion inappropriate to the situation. Voluntary expression of emotion, however, is not affected. Conversely, a person with pyramidal damage has difficulty making voluntary expressions of emotion but shows appropriate involuntary responses. This dual control system would account for the fact that there is sometimes emotional leakage. When people try to disguise their emotions (pyramidal control), their "true" emotion may still "leak" through in facial expression (extrapyramidal control). An angry person may try to hide his anger, but some component of the involuntary emotional response cannot be inhibited and can be detected by others.

Development of facial expression.   The facial muscles of newborn humans are fully operative, and adultlike expressions occur early. In the first few hours of life, infants show expressions of distress, disgust, and startle. Imitation of adult facial expressions may occur as early as two or three weeks of age. At about three months, smiling begins to occur reliably, and infants begin to distinguish adult facial expressions and respond differently to them (Ekman & Oster, 1979). Preschool children know most of the common facial expressions and what elicits them, although this knowledge continues to grow until at least age ten.

Cultural variations in emotion.   Although cross-cultural research has been presented by some researchers as evidence for the universality of discrete emotions (e.g., Ekman, 1998), other researchers argue that emotions are culture-specific and that cross-cultural research provides evidence against the existence of biologically determined discrete emotions (e.g., Kitayama &

Markus, 1994; Mesquita & Frijda, 1992). Mesquita and Frijda (1992, p. 52) say that "[e]motions occur when an event is appraised by the individual as relevant to his or her concerns (goals, motives, values)." Therefore, two individuals in the same situation may experience very different emotions because they have different concerns. Such individual differences in appraisals and concerns may also be characteristics of cultures. For example, in individualist cultures, like the United States, members are concerned with individual goals and achievements, and signs of individual failure produce distress. In collectivist cultures, commonly found in Far East countries (e.g., Japan), there is greater concern with one's place in the group, and signs of individual failure are less likely to produce distress than signs of failure to live up to group standards. A major question here is whether the emotions differ or whether the (antecedent) conditions that lead to the emotions differ.

Dimensional Theories of Emotion

Dimensions of emotion are usually researched by studying reported similarities and differences in facial expressions or emotion words. Starting with many words or pictures representing emotions, the problem is to find a smaller number of threads (dimensions) running through these. If a word or picture is judged similarly to other words or pictures, there is overlap in their meanings. For example, if the words joy, happiness, and euphoria are judged similarly they do not represent entirely different emotions but do share a common element, such as positive affect. Similarly, if such words as angry, unhappy, and distraught are judged to be similar, the common element would be negative affect. When appropriate statistical analyses (such as factor analysis or multidimensional scaling) are applied to such data, we obtain sets of words that vary along such dimensions as pleasant-unpleasant and high arousal–low arousal.

Far and away the most important such dimension, which we have discussed as the hedonic continuum, is the pleasant-unpleasant dimension. Stimuli are aligned on this dimension according to their capacity to arouse positive or negative affect. The pleasant-unpleasant is *bipolar,* which means that the one dimension has opposites at the two ends and is neutral in the middle. An advantage of such a dimension to an organism is that it allows comparison of stimuli according to a single criterion, their *value.* Such varied stimuli as a person, an animal, an insect, a food, or a loud noise can all be compared in terms of how good or bad they are to the individual judging them (Cacioppo & Gardner, 1999). Affect is the common currency in a psychological monetary system with emotion rather than gold as the standard. We can more quickly decide to approach or avoid events on the basis of our emotional evaluation than we can on the basis of more thoughtful evaluation. This should confer considerable survival advantage by allowing organisms to respond more quickly in changing situations, especially those involving danger. Indeed, as we shall see later, a person need not even be fully aware of such stimuli to make rather accurate judgments of their being good or bad—potentially beneficial or harmful.

Pleasant-unpleasant is the most important dimension but level of arousal is consistently the second most important, as summarized in Table 2–4. Different emotions are described as lying at different specific points along each dimension and can be located in a geometric space defined by those dimensions, as illustrated in Figure 2–8 (Russell, 1980). We see, for example, that alarmed, afraid, and angry are unpleasant and have high levels of arousal, whereas calm and relaxed are pleasant and have low arousal, and so on. Because such emotion plots often form a circle, with different emotions blending into each other, this type of geometric representation is called a *circumplex model* of emotion.

Whether there are important emotional dimensions beyond pleasant-unpleasant and level of arousal is still unanswered. Thayer (1978) distinguishes two dimensions of arousal, which he calls tense-relaxed and energetic-sleepy. The former is characterized by the tension that builds up during a day full of hassles, following which a person may just want to relax. The latter is characteristic of hard work or play, following which a person is sleepy. He has more recently likened these to dimensions of positive and negative affect, however. A possible third dimension, which may be called control–lack of control, has appeared under such names as *competence* (Davitz, 1970), *dominance-submission* (Russell & Mehrabian, 1977), and *potency* (Osgood, Suci, & Tannenbaum, 1957). In recent years, the perception of control has been extensively studied and lack of control is considered an important element in the experience of anxiety and stress. This is discussed in Chapter Ten.

TABLE 2–4.   Dimensions of emotion found by a number of different researchers.

| NAME | DIMENSIONS | | |
	FIRST	SECOND	THIRD
Wundt (1902)	Pleasant-Unpleasant	Tense-Relaxed	Excitement-Depression
Titchener (1910)	Pleasant-Unpleasant	—	—
Schlosberg (1954)	Pleasant-Unpleasant	Tense-Relaxed	Acceptance-Rejection
Osgood, Suci, & Tannenbaum (1957)	Evaluative (Good-Bad)	Activity (Fast-Slow)	Potency (Strong-Weak)
Davitz (1970)*	Hedonic Tone (Comfort-Discomfort)	Activation	Competence
Russell and Mehrebian (1977)	Pleasure-Displeasure	Degree of arousal	Dominance-Submission

* Davitz also identified a fourth dimension that he termed "relatedness."

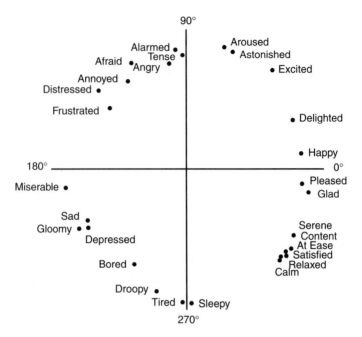

FIGURE 2–8. Russell's circumplex model of emotion. A representation of twenty-eight emotion-related words on the two dimensions of pleasant-unpleasant and level of arousal. (From Russell, 1980, Figure 2. Copyright 1980 by the American Psychological Association. Reprinted by permission.)

Bipolar versus unipolar representations of affect. Historically, researchers have described affect as a *single bipolar dimension* with pleasant at one end and unpleasant at the other, but this has a very important implication that may not be immediately obvious. It says that pleasant and unpleasant emotions are *not independent* because you cannot feel both good and bad simultaneously. At a particular point in time your feeling falls at one point along the dimension, and you cannot simultaneously be at two points.

We can also describe positive and negative affect as *separate (unipolar) dimensions* that can each take on any value from low to high. That is, positive and negative affect *can be aroused simultaneously* at any level of intensity independently of each other. Being high or low on one dimension is unrelated to how high or low you are on the other dimension as shown in Figure 2–9 (see also Cacioppo & Berntson, 1994; Cacioppo, Gardner, & Berntson, 1997; Watson, Weise, Vaidya, & Tellegen, 1999). The emotion that is *experienced* may be the algebraic sum of the underlying positive and negative affective arousals (e.g., Lang, Bradley, & Cuthbert, 1989) or the two systems may set up conflicting responses (e.g., to approach or avoid a particular situation Cacioppo & Berntson, 1994, and see Chapter Nine), but in either case we have two sys-

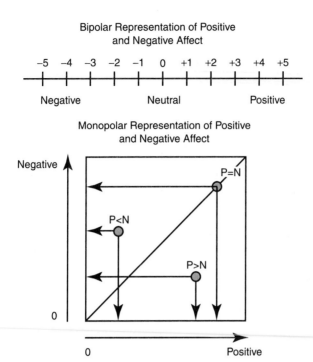

Bipolar Representation of Positive
and Negative Affect

Monopolar Representation of Positive
and Negative Affect

FIGURE 2–9.   Bipolar and monopolar representations of positive and negative affect. With the bipolar, a person's affect is located at a point along the line from negative to positive, and it cannot simultaneously be positive and negative. With the monopolar, the underlying biological systems for positive and negative affect could be aroused simultaneously and independently in any degree. The affect experienced depends on the relative strengths of the positive and negative affect. If positive is greater than negative (P>N), there would be a positive experience. If positive is less than negative (P<N), there could be negative experience. (See text for discussion.)

tems combining. Two kinds of evidence bear on the issue, behavioral and physiological.

Behavioral evidence.   According to the bipolar model, if a person reports feeling very good, then that person should also report *not* feeling very bad, and vice versa. Such reports should be highly negatively correlated. This cannot be tested, however, with a bipolar scale because the scale guarantees a negative correlation (being high on the positive end automatically makes one low on the negative end). If, however, subjects are asked to report on separate unipolar scales how good and how bad they feel (neutral to very positive and neutral to very negative), a zero correlation is possible and near-zero correlations are often found. Green, Goldman, and Salovey (1993), in support of the bipolar approach, suggested that the usual lack of correlation results from using scales with low reliability, which would automatically produce less-than-perfect correlations. Larsen, McGraw, and Cacioppo (2001), however, found that people coming out of a movie theater reported feeling both happy and sad after the seeing the film *Life Is Beautiful* and that students leaving their dormitories or graduating from college also had such conflicting emotions. Most of the participants reported feeling happy or sad (a bipolar model prediction) rather than both, but the fact that any of them felt both shows that it is possible to do so.

Physiological evidence.   Biological evidence strongly favors separate underlying systems for positive and negative affect even though we may experience only one affect which is a combination of these systems. First, we have already seen that the left hemisphere is more specialized for positive affect and the right hemisphere for negative affect (Cacioppo & Gardner, 1999; Davidson, 1994). Second, there are different subcortical brain systems corresponding to positive and negative emotion. In particular, the positive system is the ventral tegmental system which uses dopamine as its major neurotransmitter (Berridge, 1996; Wise, 1989), and the negative system is related to the amygdala (LeDoux, 1994) and perhaps the neurotransmitter **serotonin**. Measures of affect in animals show that these systems can function independently (Berridge, 1996).

Temporal dynamics of emotion: opponent process theory.   A theory that assumes that there are separate underlying positive and negative emotional systems is the Solomon and Corbit opponent-process theory. Previous theories generally assumed that a particular stimulus could arouse either a pleasant or an unpleasant emotion, but not both. Opponent process theory says that a situation that arouses positive affect also leads automatically to negative affect and negative affect automatically leads to positive (Solomon, 1980; Solomon & Corbit, 1974).

Consider this illustration from Solomon and Corbit. A woman discovers a lump in her breast and is immediately fearful of cancer. She makes an appointment with her doctor but frets about it until he reports that the tumor is benign. Her strong anxiety is then replaced by great elation. An opposite example would be the sudden loss of something or someone that has brought us great pleasure; we are depressed. The crux of the opponent process theory is that every affective state, whether pleasurable or aversive, tends to arouse the opponent state. Extreme fear arouses the opponent process of pleasure, and when the source of the fear is removed, the pleasure process becomes dominant and lingers for a while. At any given time, the affective experience of the individual is the algebraic sum of both of these processes.

The initial affective process aroused is called an A-state, whether positive or negative. The opponent process that is automatically aroused by the A-state is called the B-state. It is said that the B-state is a slave to the A-state because its occurrence depends on the prior A-state. The person who does something very frightening, such as jumping out of an airplane, initially has a fearful A-state aroused, and the joyful B-state automatically follows. The A-state is initially dominant until the person lands safely on the ground and the danger is over. The joyful B-state is then very strong for a while. The A-state and B-state are the underlying affective processes. They combine to produce a single positive or negative affective state, the *manifest affect,* which is what we experience. If the A-state and B-state were exactly equal, there would be a neutral manifest affect. The strength of the B-state increases with the number of times that the A-state has occurred. This means that the B-state has a greater neutralizing effect on the manifest affect the more times the A-state is aroused. Stronger arousal of the A-state is then necessary just to get the same degree of pleasure from the positive A-state that was initially obtained. If the stimuli arousing the A-state are removed, the B-state remains. Figures 2–10a and 2–10b illustrate the temporal course of events with the A-state and B-state as a function of the number of times the A-state has occurred.

Cognitive Theories of Emotion

According to strong versions of cognitive theories, the occurrence of emotion *depends* on how we appraise or evaluate situations. In particular, emotion is related to our readiness to act in a certain way, depending on how

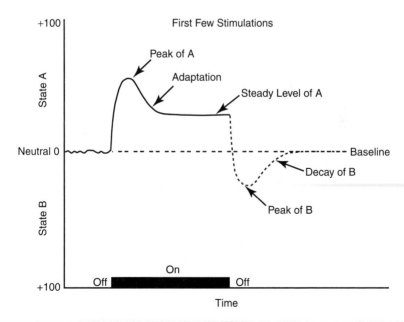

FIGURE 2–10A. The manifest temporal dynamics generated by the opponent process system during the first few stimulations. (The five features of the affective response are labeled.) The curves are the algebraic summation of the opponent processes. Note the high level of A relative to B. (Solomon & Corbit, 1974, p. 128. Copyright © 1974 by the American Psychological Association. Reprinted by permission:)

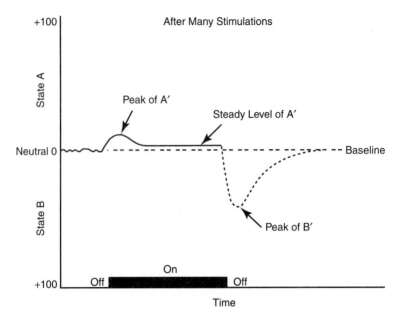

FIGURE 2–10B. The manifest temporal dynamics generated by the opponent process system after many repeated stimulations. (The major features of the modified patterns are labeled.) Compared with the curves in Figure 8-8, note the low level of A and the relatively high level of B.

the situation might affect us (Frijda, 1994). If a person hears footsteps in the dark, he may appraise them as bad (a burglar) and be anxious, or may appraise them as good (a friend or loved one) and be relieved or happy. In the former case, he is prepared to defend himself against the intruder, whereas in the latter, he is prepared to approach the intruder in a friendly manner. The "objective situation" may be the same in either case, but the responses are entirely different. Psychologists do not question that cognition has a role in emotion but have disagreed among themselves over just what that role is.

Is cognition necessary for emotion?   One dispute is whether cognitive appraisal is *necessary* for emotion to occur at all. Robert Zajonc (1984, 2000) takes the position that cognition is *not* necessary for emotion, that emotional responses to stimuli can be immediate and do not require cognitive appraisal. For example, people report liking stimuli more if they have previously been exposed to those stimuli, even though they do not remember the earlier exposure. This is called the *mere exposure effect* (Zajonc, 1968, 2001). Since the change in liking occurs without awareness, Zajonc concludes that cognitive appraisal is not a necessary condition for all emotional responses. Furthermore, after the mere exposure effect has been induced in laboratory subjects, it appears that they are also generally in a better mood and find other stimuli more likeable as well (Monahan, Murphy, & Zajonc, 2000).

Murphy and Zajonc (1993) also reported that emotional responses could be *primed* with stimuli presented too briefly to be recognized. They flashed pictures of male and female faces expressing either happiness or anger for either 4/1000 of a second (4 msec) or for 1000 msec (1 second). These pictures were followed immediately by Chinese ideographs, which are affectively neutral stimuli. The question was whether the happy and angry faces (primes) would induce positive and negative affect into the ideographs. The subjects rated their degree of liking/disliking on a five-point scale with the results shown in Figure 2–11. When the faces were exposed for only 4 msec, the ratings for the ideographs changed appropriately in comparison with a control condition with no primes. When the faces were exposed for a full second, however, there was no effect. The authors interpreted their data to mean that affective responses were aroused by stimuli presented too quickly to be consciously recognized, hence supporting Zajonc's argument. But why was there no change in liking for the ideographs with the 1-second primes? One possibility is that the longer presentations gave subjects enough time to attach the emotion expressed in the faces to the faces themselves.

MURPHY AND ZAJONC PRIMING EXPERIMENT

4-msec Exposure of faces – too fast to identify

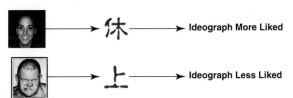

1-sec Exposure of faces— plenty of time to identify

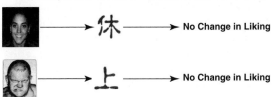

FIGURE 2–11. Summary of Murphy and Zajonc's (1993) results. When positive and negative faces were presented so briefly (4 msec) preceding the Chinese ideographs that the subjects could not identify them, the faces affected subsequent reports of liking for the ideographs. If the faces were presented long enough so that they were easily identified (1 sec), they had no effect on subsequent reports of liking for the ideographs.

Therefore, they did not transfer to the ideographs. With the brief presentations, however, emotional responses were aroused but not associated with any discernible stimuli. Therefore, these responses became attached to the first discernible stimuli to occur, the ideographs. In another experiment, subjects were quickly flashed pictures of happy or angry faces, immediately followed by neutral faces so that only the neutral faces were actually seen. Nevertheless, recordings from electrodes placed on the face showed that subjects mimicked the happy and angry expressions even though not aware of the differences in the faces they were viewing, nor of their own responses to those faces. In face-to-face communication, people may be able to pick up very subtle emotional cues from facial expression, even though not aware of them (Dimberg, Thunberg, & Elmehed, 2000).

Many other problems await the theorist who argues that appraisal is absolutely necessary for emotion. For example, we do not appraise our stereo loudspeakers as beneficial or threatening before being emotionally aroused by the sounds they emit. There is something in the music itself that produces an emotional effect (Ellsworth, 1994). Some theorists argue that all emotional responses to music are learned, but this seems unlikely since we find some selections either pleasant or unpleasant upon first hearing. Also, there are emotional rebounds, such as the emotional letdown following a prolonged positive experience. According to opponent process, this occurs automatically, without appraisal. Frijda says (1994, p. 198), "I believe that nobody contests the essentially noncognitive determination of the likes and dislikes for particular smells, tastes, and bodily sensations, at least for certain ones. Nothing other than direct prewired determination appears to be involved in the practically universal liking for moderately sweet substances, caresses, and sexual climaxing." In brief, the evidence for emotional arousal without appraisal seems convincing.

Richard Lazarus (1984) argues in favor of cognition's being necessary for emotion by pointing to extensive research from his own lab and others. For example, subjects viewing rather grisly accident scenes in a movie can have a galvanic skin response exaggerated or attenuated according to the narrative that accompanies the film. Lazarus argues that the appraisal necessary for emotion need not necessarily be conscious. The debate, then, seems to hinge on the question of how we are to define appraisal. If appraisal, by definition, is a conscious process, then appraisal may not be necessary. But if appraisal, by definition, can sometimes be unconscious, then appraisal may be necessary. One way this might work is illustrated in Figure 2–12. Sensory inputs come into the brain and follow two pathways (LeDoux, 1993). A very short path goes to the amygdala where emotional appraisal occurs. A longer path goes to the sensory cortex and on to other parts of the brain where the stimulus is consciously identified, for example, as a face. With brief presentations of stimuli, the longer pathway may never be completed. Hence, there may be an emotional response without any awareness of a recognizable stimu-

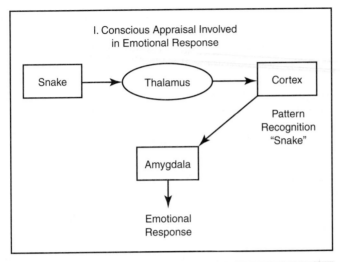

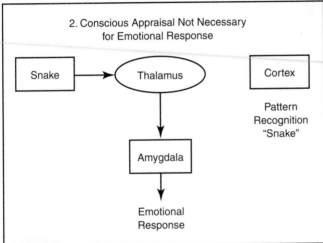

FIGURE 2–12. The upper part of the figure shows a "long" pathway by which an emotional stimulus goes through the visual cortex and is consciously recognized when the emotional response occurs. The lower part of the figure indicates that a shorter pathway from the thalamus to the amygdala can activate an emotional response when a stimulus is presented too briefly to follow the thalamus-cortex-amygdala path. This allows for an emotional response to a stimulus before it is consciously recognized.

lus. Appraisal occurs just for the positive or negative emotional character of the stimulus, not for its other distinguishing features.

Attribution theory and emotion.   In the early 1960s a new approach to emotion grew out of attribution theory in social psychology. Attribution theory is concerned with how people seek and find causes for behavior. It was a short step to propose that people also seek causes to account for how they feel and to interpret their feelings in terms of the situation in which they find themselves. If a person feels herself becoming aroused, she might interpret this arousal in any of several ways. If a large, unfriendly dog is approaching, she might interpret the arousal as fear. If someone has just insulted her, she might interpret the arousal as anger. If a friend is approaching, she might interpret the arousal as joy. Mandler (1962) and Schachter and Singer (1962) simultaneously proposed that such interpretations are necessary for emotional experience. The latter also presented an experiment purporting to show that the same state of nonspecific arousal could be interpreted as either happiness or anger, depending on environmental circumstances and proposed cognitive arousal theory to explain such results.

Cognitive-arousal theory.   Schachter and Singer's theory stated that perceived emotion is a joint function of *nonspecific arousal* and a *cognition* with which to label the arousal. The labeling, such as referring to the arousal as fear, is a cognitive activity based on an active search for the cause of the arousal. If either the cognition or the arousal is missing, there is no emotional experience. Schachter and Singer tested this hypothesis by giving subjects injections of adrenaline (to produce arousal) and then putting them into different situations calculated to produce different cognitive labeling of the arousal. Some subjects were subjected to conditions calculated to make them happy, others to make them angry. They reported positive results, and a happy reading public eagerly embraced the theory and many textbooks still report the results uncritically (but see Beck, 1990, for detailed analysis of the shortcomings of their data). The most glaring deficiency was that subjects in the anger-inducing conditions never reported themselves to be angry, varying only in their degree of reported happiness.

Subsequent research rarely gave support to the theory. Reisenzein (1983) and Leventhal and Tomarken (1986) concluded that the *only* adequate support came from research involving *misattributed arousal* from an irrelevant source, such as attributing exercise-induced arousal to sexual arousal in the presence of sexual cues. There was no evidence that unexplained arousal instigates a search for the cause of such arousal. In addition, Maslach (1979) and Marshall and Zimbardo (1979) found that subjects uniformly described the arousal produced by adrenaline injections as unpleasant regardless of their experimental condition. They did not describe themselves as happy when placed in the happy experimental condition previously used by Schachter and Singer.

Excitation-transfer theory.   The one area of support for cognitive-arousal theory, noted before, involves what is called *excitation transfer* (Zillman, 1978). According to this theory, when arousal occurs, it takes some period of time for the arousal to decay. While arousal is still decaying, a person may incorrectly identify the source of arousal. Thus, for example, already-existing feelings of anger, aggression, or sexual arousal might be intensified by irrelevant arousal produced by exercise.

Excitation-transfer theory differs from cognitive-arousal theory in important ways (Leventhal & Tomarken, 1986). First, excitation-transfer theory does not assume any causal search for the source of unexplained arousal. Misattributions (mistaken attributions) occur by accident, not as a result of a search for the cause of unexplained arousal. Second, excitation-transfer theory assumes that misattribution is most likely to occur when people are actually becoming *less aware* of their arousal. For example, Cantor, Zillman, and Bryant (1975) studied the effect of prior physical exercise on self-reports of sexual arousal from erotic films. They had separate groups of subjects view a film entitled *Naked under Leather* at either zero, five, or nine minutes after exercising, when the exercise-induced arousal is high, imperceptible, or back to preexercise baseline. Actual arousal level was measured by heart rate change from baseline. Only subjects in the five-minute group, who had imperceptible residual arousal, rated their level of sexual arousal higher. Presumably, the zero-delay group recognized that much of their arousal was attributable to exercise, and the nine-minute group was no longer aroused by the exercise and so had no excitation to transfer. Results from this line of research seem robust.

Valins's attribution theory. Valins (1966, 1970) extended the Schachter-Singer approach by suggesting that the perception of physiological change is a sufficient condition for experienced emotion, whether or not the perception is accurate. If we only think we have been aroused, we can interpret this apparent arousal as emotion. Valins (1966) tested his hypothesis by giving male subjects false information about their heart rates as they viewed slides of *Playboy* centerfolds. Slides associated with either an increase or a decrease in heart rate were rated more attractive than those not associated with change. Overall, the results supported Valins's hypothesis that when subjects heard the fake heart rate changes, they searched the slides for characteristics of the models (such as parts of the anatomy) that might have caused the cardiac changes and then attributed the changes to these "attractive" features. In short, subjects reached the attribution that they had made emotional responses to slides that were more attractive. Unfortunately for the hypothesis, the effect can readily be obtained under conditions that do not correspond to the attribution search hypothesis (Beck, Gibson, Elliott, Simmons, Matteson, & McDaniel, 1988). For example, tourist slides of Rome, Italy, were rated more attractive simply by bringing subjects' attention to them. There is little emotion in this activity. Beck et al. interpreted the results as due to *experimenter demand.* Given the experimental situation in which some slides are selected for more attention than others, a subject looking at nude slides might say to himself: "What am I expected to do here? I am in an experiment on emotional arousal, looking at pictures of naked women; they tell me my heart rate is higher for some pictures than for others, and I am supposed to rate the pictures. Perhaps I should give higher ratings to pictures where my heart rate changes." Quite apart from emotional arousal, the situation may set up a demand to rate repeated slides as more attractive.

We conclude that cognitive factors, including attributions, can affect emotional responses. However, the evidence does not support cognitive-arousal theory as a general theory of emotion, nor does it support the attribution-search hypothesis very well. The false-feedback experiments seem to indicate more about conditions under which a person will make particular ratings about any stimulus than about what might be true emotional responses.

SECTION SUMMARY

1. **Discrete emotion theories** assume that there is some fixed number of genetically programmed emotional reactions to specific kinds of situations. Six have been reliably identified across many cultures: happiness, anger, sadness, disgust, surprise, and fear. Others have been reported less consistently.

2. **Facial expressions** are among the most reliable indicators of emotion, but physiological recording from facial muscles most consistently shows distinctions only between positive and negative emotions. There is evidence that manipulation of facial muscles may produce changes in affect. The recognition of emotional expression depends on the context of the situation, as well as the actual expression. There are also cultural variations in emotional expression.

3. **Dimensional theories** of emotion emphasize the fact that emotional expressions can be organized along a limited number of dimensions, most notably those of **pleasant-unpleasant** and **level of arousal**. If more specific emotions are plotted on the two axes formed by these dimensions, they tend to fall in a circle that is called a **circumplex model** of emotion.

4. There is some dispute whether positive and negative affect can be experienced simultaneously. Since there are different underlying brain systems, it appears that different levels of arousal in the separate systems may combine to produce a particular type of consciously experienced affect.

5. The **opponent process theory** of emotion says that if either positive or negative affect is aroused, the opposite affect automatically follows. Following repeated experiences with a particular emotion-arousing situation, the opponent process is more strongly aroused, and when the initial process terminates, the opponent process continues for some time. This can account for the depression that often follows pleasurable experience or the relief that follows unpleasant experience.

6. **Cognitive theories** of emotion emphasize that emotional responses are largely determined by how we evaluate or **appraise** situations. A controversial issue is whether such evaluations are necessary in order to have any emotional experience at all and, if so, whether such evaluations are necessarily conscious.

7. Research with the **mere exposure** effect and **stimulus priming** indicate that emotions can be aroused without our being conscious of this happening. Emotional changes in facial expression also occur without conscious awareness. These studies indicate that cognition is not indispensable for emotional arousal.

8.   **Cognitive-arousal** theory proposes that both **visceral arousal** and an **attribution** of the cause of the arousal are necessary for emotional experience. Different interpretations of the same arousal are said to produce different emotional experiences. Research has not supported this theory very well. A limited variation called **excitation transfer theory** says that irrelevant physiological arousal, such as from exercise, may be interpreted as emotional arousal.

OVERVIEW OF MOTIVATION AND EMOTION

Many theorists agree on two important points. First, emotion is concerned with reactions to rewards and punishments, learned or unlearned. Motivation involves the control of behavior through the anticipation of such rewards or punishers. Second, there is only a small number of specific emotion systems, perhaps three or four. There are widely differing points of view on many fundamental issues, however. Without any "standard" theory of emotion, there is no complete integration of motivation and emotion to satisfy everyone. We can, however, point out how each of the three main approaches to emotion that we covered (discrete, dimensional, and cognitive theories) can relate to motivation.

Discrete Theories

Throughout the text we make reference to particular emotions, for example, love, happiness, anger, anxiety, depression, and fear, thereby implying that there are such discrete emotions. The number of such emotions is small and the degree to which they are biologically fixed is debatable. Some concepts, such as fear, are equally central to both emotion and motivation theory. Fear activates behaviors to escape or avoid, for example.

Dimensional Theories

Dimensional theories divide emotions into pleasant and unpleasant, which is a particularly good fit to the hedonic approach to motivation outlined in Chapter One. The motivational concept of desire corresponds to the anticipation of a pleasant emotional outcome, and the motivational concept of aversion corresponds to the anticipation of an unpleasant emotional outcome. These anticipations are based on prior pleasant or unpleasant experiences, and we try to re-create the pleasant experiences and avoid the unpleasant. Such anticipations are motives, and approach and avoidance are motivated behaviors.

Cognitive Theories

Cognitive theories are concerned with the effect that appraisal or evaluation of a situation has on what emotion is aroused, pleasant or unpleasant. Such appraisals determine whether a situation is approached or avoided. We may relate appraisal to other theoretical approaches. For example, if I appraise a situation as dangerous (cognitive theory), I may be afraid (discrete theory) and try to reduce this unpleasant state (dimensional theory) by running away. Or, if I interpret some personal slight to me as intentional, I may become angry and perhaps aggressive, whereas if I perceive the slight as accidental, I do not become angry and behave entirely differently.

In summary, emotion and motivation are intimately related regardless of what theoretical approach to emotion we may favor. At a particular time, one approach may be more appropriate, whereas at a different time another approach may serve better.

CHAPTER THREE

Species Specific Behaviors

Is there such a thing as instinctive behavior?

Where did the concept of instinct come from?

What is the ethological approach to behavior?

How do we distinguish between genetic and environmental contributions to behavior?

What is the theory of evolution?

What is evolutionary psychology about?

How do stimuli control behavior?

How do external stimuli interact with internal body conditions?

INTRODUCTORY EXAMPLES

The Curious Case of the Cowbird

Cowbirds are a curiosity because they never raise their own young. They lay eggs in other birds' nests and then depart forever. The unwitting foster mother hatches the egg and cares for the cowbird baby until it can go out on its own. There are a number of such brood parasites, but cowbirds stand out among this group because they parasitize the nests of over two hundred other species. This behavior raises numerous questions (West, King, & Eastzer, 1981). How do the females go about exchanging eggs? How can the baby cowbirds get so many different kinds of mothers to care for them? And most important of all: How do cowbirds recognize other cowbirds and know with whom to mate? It has generally been assumed that birds learn appropriate species-recognition songs from their parents, but this is clearly not so with the cowbird.

Songs by cowbirds reared in isolation. Shortly after cowbirds leave the foster parent's nest, they manage to seek out other cowbirds and travel in flocks. They obviously recognize each other, but not necessarily by song. In the case of mating, however, song plays a demonstrably important role. When a male sings his song of love, the female adopts a specific and identifiable posture that can be used to judge the effectiveness of a male's song. And the result is striking. Male cowbirds reared in isolation from all other birds from two days after hatching until adulthood are more successful at evoking the female copulatory posture than are males who have lived with other cowbirds. We thus have a specific behavior that appears to be unlearned but is more effective than the same behavior with opportunity for learning. Isolate-reared cowbird songs, played to females on a tape recorder, evoke copulatory responses about 60 percent of the time, whereas normally reared males are only about 25 percent effective. However, if the isolates are now placed with other males, the isolates' songs are degraded to the lower effectiveness of normally reared birds. Or if normally reared birds are isolated in adulthood, their songs become more effective. In short, socialization has the perverse effect of making male cowbird songs less appealing to female cowbirds. Finally, the cowbirds with the most effective songs actually do mate more than those with less effective songs. Why, then, does socialization lead to less lovable cowbird males?

Isolation, dominance, and aggression. The elegant studies of West, King, and Eastzer (1981) show that isolate cowbirds have a particular frequency component in part of their song that is especially attractive to females. Socialized birds do not have this component because it evokes attack on them by other males. Only those birds that are at the top of the dominance hierarchy in a group can sing the most effective song with impunity and can mate most often. In terms of natural selection, this ability does tend to guarantee that the most fit males breed. Isolate birds have not learned to suppress the critical song component and are attacked and even killed if they sing it when introduced to a group. Conversely, birds put into isolation learn that they will not be attacked and start to sing the most happy song. If a dominant bird from one group is put into another group, he is no longer dominant, but he does not know this. He therefore sings his best song, is attacked, and either changes his ways or is killed.

The conclusion, then, is that the male cowbird comes out of its shell equipped to sing a highly enticing mating song but learns not to sing it unless he becomes a dominant bird. The female comes into the world prepared to respond to this song during the mating season. There is, therefore, a complex set of genetic, hormonal, and social learning experiences that operate on natural selection. It is the genetic component, the apparently prewired ability to sing on the one hand and to respond appropriately to the song on the other, which keeps the notion of "instinct-as-specific-response" alive. Biologists, of course, are less interested in calling this instinct than in finding out the exact sensory-neural-muscular mechanisms that can account for such behaviors. For this kind of study, we turn to a simpler organism, the cricket, whose song is less lyrical than that of the birds but effective for its purpose.

Cricket Song

Research on cricket song by Bentley and Hoy (e.g., Bentley, 1977; Bentley & Hoy, 1972; Hoy & Casaday, 1979) has identified a very specific neural location for controlling the mating song of the cricket. The cricket's song is produced by opening and closing the wings. The rough end of the wing (the scraper) rubs against a row of ridges (the file) under the cover of the opposite wing. This rubbing produces the familiar summertime chirping sound. The cricket song is limited to different temporal patterns and intensities, and the males of different species identify themselves solely by their own species-specific variation in these. What humans normally hear is the calling song, which loudly proclaims the singer as an adult male of a particular species, with a territory of his own and ready for action. Sexually receptive females respond to the unique male song of their species. In order to mate, the cricket must precisely control its wing movements. The question is, How?

The cricket wings are controlled by muscles in the thorax, which in turn are connected to a nerve bundle called the thoracic ganglion. The delicate wing timing is controlled by a single neuron in the brain, the command interneuron. Direct electrical stimulation of this neuron produces neural impulses, which have the appropriate species-specific rhythm. These neural impulses stimulate the thoracic ganglion, thus stimulating the thoracic muscles and wing movement and subsequent chirping. The correct calling song can be produced by such artificial stimulation even in otherwise brainless crickets. Under normal conditions, brain cells probably put together such information as time of day and weather, and if everything is "right," the command in-terneuron fires, and so on. Crickets reared in isolation through the ten moult-ings preceding adulthood still sing the right song. By isolating males and fe-males of different species together, it is possible to produce hybrid offspring that have a greater variety of calls. These are apparently the result of having more than one command interneuron, each with its unique timing control (Al-cott, 1979). Again, both genetics and experience are involved in species-specific behaviors, but the relative contributions of these sources of behavior variation differ according to the species and the behavior in question.

The cowbirds and the crickets illustrate why the instinct concept sur-vives: Every so often someone researches a behavior that just does not seem accountable in terms of standard learning theory principles. Besides different physical characteristics, each species has unique behaviors that set it apart. Spiders construct webs that are even specific to subspecies of spiders, and dif-ferent species of birds build their own peculiar nests. Such behaviors are often called instinctive, usually to imply they are not learned. William James (1890, p. 393) said that instinct was the "faculty of acting in such a way as to produce a certain end without foresight of that end, and without the individ-ual's having previous education in that performance." More recently, the bi-ologist Nikolaas Tinbergen (1951) defined instinct by four criteria: (1) the behavior is stereotyped and constant in form; (2) the behavior is characteris-tic of the species; (3) the behavior appears in animals reared in isolation from each other; and (4) the behavior develops fully formed in animals pre-vented from practicing it. The main questions here are whether the concept of instinct is actually useful in explaining such behavior and whether other explanations might fit better.

THE PROBLEMS OF INSTINCT THEORY

Meanings of Instinct

Whether we should consider "instinct" a motivational concept depends on how we use the term. Unfortunately, the term instinct is so loosely used, sometimes in contradictory ways, that there is no clear-cut meaning to the term, either motivational or nonmotivational.

Instinct as universal behavior. We may apply the term instinct when a particular behavior occurs very commonly in a species, including humans. Maternal behavior may be said to be instinctive, since most mothers engage in something called maternal activities. William James (1884) thought no hen could resist the charm of an egg-to-be-sat-upon and that no woman could resist the charm of a small, naked baby. John B. Watson (1924), however, noted that in hospitals where they could be closely observed, new mothers were very awkward with their first child and did not do all those tender, loving things that supposedly characterize the "maternal instinct." Watson pointed out the pitfalls of attributing any behavior to a universal instinct.

Instinct as unlearned behavior. A second way in which the term is applied is to activities that seem to occur without much forethought. The prize-fighter who is quick to dodge his opponent's jabs may be said to "duck instinctively," but very little imagination is necessary to see that one either learns to duck or gets out of the business. In this kind of example, the term instinct is used as if some people have it (the capacity to respond quickly) and some do not. Thus, it seems to be used as an account of differences within a species rather than as an explanation for the universality of a species behavior. This is just the opposite of the use described in the preceding paragraph or in Tinbergen's definition.

Instinct as urge versus instinct as behavior. Another kind of confusion arises in treating instinct as an urge toward some activity (thus being like a motive or an emotion) as compared with referring to such specific behaviors as web building. James and Freud both talked more in terms of urges than of behaviors. In fact, what are usually referred to as instincts in Freudian theory (sex and aggression) come from the German word *Trieb*, which can be translated as either "instinct" or "drive." As it happened, the term instinct was originally used and hence picked up connotations that Freud did not necessarily intend. Freud (1915) talked about instincts as having **source, impetus, aim**, and **object**, implying that either internal or external stimulation (source) produces "instinct"; that the instinct carries some degree of force (impetus) that is related to the intensity of behavior; that the person tries to reduce the tension (aim); and, finally, that this process is all ended by some object. Freud saw neither fixed behaviors nor invariant objects related to instincts; both, in his view, are subject to change because of particular individual experiences. For Freud these built-in urges might find their outlets in very disguised forms because of social pressures. He saw many behaviors as being apparently irrational because they are stimulated by instincts that the individual cannot identify but that such behaviors can be studied and their "hidden" causes determined.

William McDougall (1923) argued that instincts were innate tendencies to engage in certain actions under certain conditions but that the goals of actions should be taken into account. Thus one animal might follow another with the goal of either mating, fighting, or eating (prey). In order to identify the instinct, one must know the behavioral outcome. McDougall also believed that each separate instinct had its own unique emotional experience accompanying it.

Most serious theorists have argued that as far as specific responses are concerned, the term instinct should be limited to some very small segments of behavior, almost at the level of reflexes. All major instinct theorists have stated that there were some inborn tendencies or urges but that these are overshadowed by learning. James, for example, described instinct as being without the foresight of its end, but he also said that once an instinctive activity occurred, there would be foresight of its end on future occasions. This foresight of consequences of an activity would either facilitate or block the expression of the instinct. James (1890, p. 395) even referred to the idea of invariable instincts as "mystical" and observed that "the minuter study of recent years has found continuity, transition, variation and mistake wherever it has looked for them"; he decided that what is called an instinct is usually only a tendency to act in a way of which the average is pretty constant, but which need not be mathematically "true." McDougall believed that instincts were often more permanent than James believed, but that they still could be modified.

History of the Instinct Concept

Origins.   Given the considerable agreement that so-called instinctive behavior is never as invariant as supposed, how did the concept gain such a foothold and still maintain such a grip on popular opinion? One reason is that it keeps getting revived by people like Lorenz (1965b) and Ardrey (1966), who argued, respectively, that aggression and territorial behaviors in humans are instinctive. Although most biologists have been skeptical of these views, they have had great popular appeal.

A deeper running current, however, is that the instinct concept derived from theology rather than biology (Beach, 1955). The line of reasoning, still applicable today in some circles, is as follows: People get to heaven or hell according to their earthly choices. If they make the correct moral decisions, their reward is paradise; if not, their "reward" is perdition. But the whole problem is meaningless unless we assume that people are free to choose. This capacity to make moral choices was considered to be a unique property of the rational soul of humans, just as an afterlife was said to be reserved to them. But without a capacity to make rational decisions, how could animals carry on the complex activities that they obviously do? It was simply postulated that animals are not rational and do not have to make decisions because their behavior consists of predetermined responses to particular situations. This view of theology is still widely held, as we saw in Chapter One, and still lends credence to the concept of instinct in animals.

The anti-instinct revolt.   Darwinian biology partly bridged the gap between animals and humans by proposing that humans also have instincts. Both William James and William McDougall believed that humans actually have more instincts than other animals. And though they saw these more as urges than specific behaviors, less sophisticated writers proposed human instincts running into the hundreds. By about 1920 a number of psychologists became alarmed by this proliferation, which in effect was nothing more than putting names to behaviors without further explanation. Knight Dunlap

(1919) and Zing Yang Kuo (1922) were particularly strident in their attacks on the practice, arguing for the greater importance of environmental determinants on behavior.

Kuo went further in undertaking a productive program of research on what were commonly thought to be instinctive behaviors. He showed that not all cats do "naturally" kill rats and that such factors as familiarity are involved (1930). Figure 3–1 illustrates this: a cat and laboratory rat (both pets of the author) sleeping together, clearly not enemies. From his extensive investigation of the development of the embryonic chick, Kuo also made a convincing argument (1932) that the "instinctive" pecking and swallowing of the newborn chick has its origins in embryonic movements that are "forced" in the course of morphological development. For example, after the embryonic heart starts to beat, the chick's head is moved back and forth in the egg, the mouth opens and closes, and there is some swallowing. As a result of many such attacks on the instinct concept, it fell into ill repute in American psychology in the 1920s.

Resurgence of interest at mid-twentieth century. In 1938, Karl Lashley spoke out in favor of instinct. He gave fifteen examples of what he believed were "confirmed" instinctive behaviors, most of which involved mating or maternal activities. But as Beach (1955) pointed out, few American psychologists had ever seen any of the behaviors listed (e.g., responses of the sooty tern to her nest and young). And Beach once more emphasized the point that the

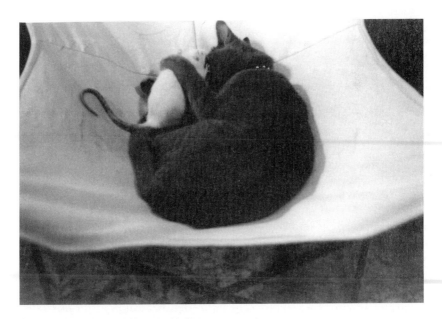

FIGURE 3–1. Pet cat and rat sleeping together.

more closely any behavior is studied, the less likely it is to be considered automatic. Gradually, however, increasing numbers of examples of species-specific behaviors, such as the mating of the stickleback fish, caught the attention of both psychologists and biologists, particularly after World War II.

An article by Breland and Breland (1961) was particularly interesting to learning-oriented psychologists. Entitled "The Misbehavior of Organisms," a switch on the title of B. F. Skinner's classic work, *Behavior of Organisms* (1938), it attracted attention in part because it was an insider's account of the difficulties of doing operant conditioning (training animals by giving them rewards for behaviors) with many different species. Originally students of Skinner's, Keller and Marian Breland were so impressed by the power of operant conditioning that they started a business training animals for shows. They reported that certain behaviors simply could not be trained with some species. In one act, for example, a pig was supposed to carry a large, simulated gold coin to a piggy bank. This behavior was learned, but then, in spite of continued reward for success, the pigs began dropping the coin on the ground, rooting around at it, and never got it to the bank anymore. It seemed as if the pigs were trying to "root" the coin, much as they would root for food in the ground. Similarly, racoons had great difficulty in letting go of objects that they were supposed to deposit someplace else, tending to hold them in their hands and to "wash" them. The Brelands referred to such problems as a drift from learned to instinctive behavior. To avoid the difficulties of this **instinctive drift**, they eventually built all their acts around what the animals would do reliably rather than trying to train responses arbitrarily selected.

Present status of the instinct concept.   Psychologists and biologists agree that behavior is in part genetically determined, but the actual term instinct rarely appears in the biological literature on behavior, except perhaps to put it into historical perspective (e.g., Eibl-Eibesfeldt, 1975). Instead, it is argued that genes establish the potential for species-specific behaviors and that this potential is fulfilled to greater or lesser degree under different environmental conditions. The problem, then, is to determine what specific mechanisms are inherited and what environmental conditions bring them into play. This kind of analysis proceeds nicely without any concept of instinct, except as it may refer generally to such motivational systems as hunger or reproduction.

A sophisticated differentiation of the concepts of instinct and motivation was proposed by Alan Epstein (1982), who argued that a large amount of animal behavior is unlearned. If we look at a wide spectrum of animal life, we find that most of the earth's animal population is far less complicated than primates, or even vertebrates, and that it is among the masses of insects, mollusks, and arachnids that instinctive behaviors are most likely to occur. Epstein distinguishes instinctive and motivated behaviors in terms of behavioral characteristics as summarized in Table 3–1. Briefly stated, motivated be-

TABLE 3–1. A comparison of instinct and motivation (adapted from Epstein, 1982).

I. COMMON CHARACTERISTICS

1. Both employ innate mechanisms for behavior.
2. Both employ acquired (learned) components.
3. Both are organized sequentially into highly variable goal-seeking behavior, followed by more specific consummatory responses[1]
4. Both are drive induced (i.e., induced by some physiological imbalance).
5. Both contribute to homeostasis.

II. DIFFERENCES

A. INSTINCT

1. Species-specific in terms of the kinds of stimuli that *release* the behavior and the specific organizations of behaviors.
2. Goal-seeking (appetitive) behavior not changed by expectancy (i.e., is not changed by learning).
3. Nonemotional.
4. Biologically common, occurring across many different phyla and orders.

B. MOTIVATION

1. Goal-seeking behavior that can be modified by learning.
2. Anticipating goals.
3. Accompanied by expression of emotion.
4. Biologically rare (very few animals show it).

Source: A. N. Epstein, 1982. Copyright © 1982 Springer-Verlag. Used by permission.
[1]These are commonly referred to as *appetitive* and *consummatory* phases.

haviors are characterized by *variability, foresight,* and *emotion,* but instinctive behaviors lack these features.

SECTION SUMMARY

1. **Species-specific behaviors** are those activities unique to a particular species that have at least partial genetic determination.
2. Species-specific behaviors have often been called **instinctive,** but early in this century, the indiscriminate use of the term instinct brought it into disfavor among both biologists and psychologists. Historically, American psychologists have placed greater emphasis on learning than on genetic factors, but there is a rising increase in interest in genetics and it is found that even personality characteristics have a significant genetic component.
3. The term instinct has been rather indiscriminately applied both to **universal** behaviors, to **unique** behaviors, and to motivational **urges.** The usage most closely approximating a motivational concept is that of the urge to do something.
4. Epstein distinguished "instinctive" behaviors from "motivated" behaviors by saying that motivated behaviors show variability, foresight, and emotion but that instinctive behaviors do not. Instinctive behaviors (e.g., web weaving of spiders) occur more commonly with simpler organisms than primates.

THE ETHOLOGICAL APPROACH TO BEHAVIOR

Ethology is a part of biological science concerned with animal behavior, initiated largely in Europe under the leadership of Konrad Lorenz, Nikolaas Tinbergen, and Karl von Frisch. Tinbergen (1951) considered the main question of ethology to be, Why does the animal behave as it does? His answer was that behavior is the joint product of environmental events and internal conditions, which is also the psychologist's standard answer to the same question. The difference is that the ethologists have placed more emphasis on (1) detailed study of animal behavior in natural settings, (2) closer attention to the development of behavior, (3) genetics and the phylogenetic development of a species, and (4) studies of birds, fish, and insects, as well as mammals. Psychologists have also incorporated these approaches into their research.

The Ethogram

The first step in the ethological analysis of behavior is to map out the typical behavior of a species in its normal environment. Activities are observed, recorded, and counted, as are the circumstances under which they occur. This behavioral map is the ethogram. The description of the cowbird's behavior is an ethogram, valuable because it gives a baseline of normal behavior against which the effects of changing the organism or its surroundings can be evaluated.

Erbkoordination

The general name given to an "instinctive" pattern of behavior is **Erbkoordination**. It is a core of more or less complex and fixed "inborn" movement forms. This fixed core was originally referred to as a *fixed action pattern* (FAP), but is now called a *modal action pattern* (MAP; Toates, 2001), to make the point that no behavior is "fixed." The MAP does not involve all the behavior in any such sequence as feeding or mating; instead, it generally refers to the terminal behavior in the sequence, or **consummatory behavior** that is the final phase of a "motivated act." An animal may engage in widely variable movements, or *appetitive behaviors*, which bring it into contact with food or a sexual partner. As the animal gets closer to the end of the sequence, the behavior is relatively more stereotyped. As an example of such stereotypy, the drinking rate of a rat licking from a water tube is relatively constant, at about six licks per second. This number may vary with circumstances, but under any normal conditions, it is never reported as low as three nor as high as ten per second; the range is small. The distinction between appetitive and consummatory behaviors is essentially the same as the distinction that psychologists usually make between instrumental (or operant) and consummatory behaviors. The MAP constitutes only a small fragment of an overall sequence of motivated behavior.

The early Lorenz-Tinbergen analysis emphasized that **reaction-specific energy** (RSE) builds up in the organism much as water fills a tank. The RSE was so called because it was considered specific to particular kinds of behavior such as feeding, mating, or aggressive activities. The concept of RSE is a motivational concept, separate from specific behaviors but attempting to serve as an explanation for their occurrence. A particular behavior was said not to be stimulated by external events, but to be *released* by them. Until a specific stimulus called a **releaser**, or **sign stimulus**, is presented to the organism, the RSE is internally blocked and is not expressed overtly. The releaser is a "key" that fits the "lock" of an **innate releasing mechanism** (IRM). When a releaser (such as the gaping mouth of a baby bird) is presented, the appropriate behavior is released (the parent putting food into the mouth).

Hierarchical Ordering of Action

A crucial concept is that the neural centers storing the RSE are ordered in a hierarchy according to complexity. At the highest level, there are "moods," which correspond to such broad kinds of behavior as are involved in feeding, mating, sleeping, or aggression. Within each mood, there are successively "lower" levels of hierarchy corresponding to more and more specific kinds of behaviors involved in the total activity, down to the movements of specific muscle groups. Figure 3–2 (Tinbergen, 1951) shows the nature of this hierarchical structure in the specific example of stickleback mating behavior. The hierarchical concept has been given support in research described by von Holst and von St. Paul (1962), using electrodes permanently implanted in chicken brains so that behavior could be artificially stimulated. Depending on exact electrode placement, either an overall "mood" or very specific behaviors could be produced. The sleepy chicken, for example, goes through a standard ritual in preparation for sleep, including standing on one leg and putting its head under a wing. Von Holst reported that, at one electrode site, the entire "sleepy" mood could be stimulated, with all the behaviors in sequence and the chicken actually going to sleep. Presumably, the electrode had tapped into a fairly high position in the hierarchy. With other locations, only very specific parts of the overall behavior pattern were evoked, such as putting the head under the wing, but the other behaviors did not occur, and the chicken did not sleep.

Vacuum Reactions and Displacement

If a releasing stimulus is not presented to "unblock" the IRM, the buildup of a particular RSE may be so great that the reaction occurs anyway. The reaction is called a **vacuum reaction** because it presumably occurs in the absence of external stimulation. Continuing the previous hydraulic analogy, the "water tank" overflows so that a MAP occurs, such as "spontaneous" aggressive behavior or inappropriate sexual activity, perhaps with an animal try-

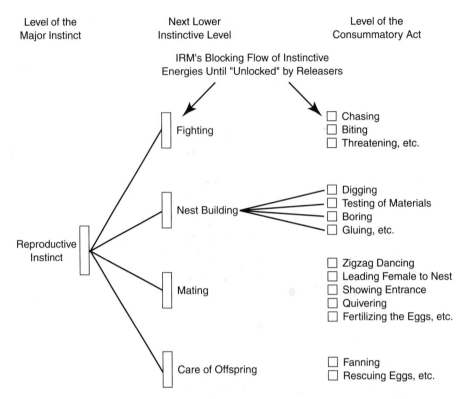

| Level of the Major Instinct | Next Lower Instinctive Level | Level of the Consummatory Act |

IRM's Blocking Flow of Instinctive Energies Until "Unlocked" by Releasers

FIGURE 3–2. The reproductive instinct of the male three-spined stickleback, showing the hierarchical ordering of action, with different levels of instinct indicating innate releasing mechanisms. (Modified from Tinbergen, 1951, p. 104.)

ing to mate with an inanimate object or a member of another species. Or, if two incompatible reactions are simultaneously released, as with courtship and aggressive activities, the animal cannot really complete either. In such a case, there may be an alternation between attack and enticement, and some unexpected response may suddenly appear. A chicken may suddenly start pecking at the ground, for example. This is called **displacement activity** and is thought to be caused by released energy from the conflicting (and blocked) RSE's "spilling over" to release other behaviors. Both vacuum and displacement reactions, including reactions to unusual stimuli, are based on the "full water-tank" model. Although it is an interesting analogy, biologists do not take the hydraulic model seriously as an explanation of behavior. There is no known neurological mechanism that has the properties of such a model. In the case of displacement, moreover, Zeigler (1964) showed how specific kinds of stimulation could determine what behaviors would occur when conflicting activities block each other. In the courtship-fighting conflict, a bird might start to preen because of the engorgement of blood close to the skin. Similarly, "vacuum" reactions do not occur completely in isolation from the environment; they are also responses to some kind of stimulation.

SECTION SUMMARY

1. The primary motivational concept in ethology for a long time was that of **reaction-specific energy** (RSE). A system of "energy reservoirs" was conceived to underlay each specific behavior, or fixed action pattern (FAP). The term **modal action pattern** (MAP) has replaced the FAP.

2. Behavior is ordered **hierarchically** in pyramid fashion. Very specific muscle movements are organized at a higher level so that they are part of coordinated activity.

3. The various RSEs were said to "build up" spontaneously, and if not released by a **sign stimulus** (also called **releaser**) in the environment, the reservoir for a particular FAP would "overflow" into the behavior appropriate to that energy but not necessarily appropriate to the situation. Such spontaneous activities are called **vacuum reactions** or **displacement behaviors**. Evidence does not generally support the notion of RSEs.

THE EVOLUTION OF BEHAVIOR

Darwin's Theory

Charles Darwin's *The Origin of the Species* ([1859] 1936) was not the first attempt to describe continuously evolving life, but it was certainly the most influential. Based on a myriad of observations during his worldwide travels on the *Beagle*, Darwin's thesis was that there is a **natural selection** of organisms based on their fitness to reach maturity and reproduce themselves. Or as Wilson (1975) put it, natural selection is the process whereby certain genetic material gains increased representation in the following generation. Such "survival of the fittest" does sometimes depend on savagery and cunning, but not always. The opossum, which exhibits neither of these characteristics in great amount, has survived for over 60 million years. So has the cockroach.

Specific survival rules are not laid down in advance, however. Evolution is opportunistic, and whatever assists survival at a given time and place is the physical or behavioral character selected in a species. Just in consideration of appearance, for example, some animals survive by being inconspicuous, their form and coloring providing camouflage that allows them to blend almost invisibly into their environment. Insects are particularly adept at this, but the spotted coat of the fawn, the stripes of the zebra, and the white fur of the polar bear are also protective. The polar bear's fur presumably hides it from prey, however, rather than predators. Other animals show mimicry, looking like different species that are more dangerous than they are. For example, one species of butterfly (*Limenitis archippus*) survives in part because it looks like the Monarch butterfly, which feeds on poisonous plants and is rejected by such predators as the bluejay because it tastes bad. Many animals have such rituals as spreading feathers or puffing up the cheeks that make them appear more dangerous and threatening than they really are.

Selection itself, however, depends on two other factors: **genetic variation** (which Darwin simply referred to as "natural variation") and **environmental pressure**. Darwin recognized that there could be no selection unless there were alternatives to be selected from and reasons for them to be selected. Unless organisms differed from their parents, and hence from each other, all the members of a species would be equally likely to perish or survive. As an example of such pressure, in England the industrial revolution led to cities that became black with coal dust and smoke. Moths that were darker could survive and multiply in the cities, where they literally blended into the walls (camouflage) and were protected, but the lighter colored moths of the same species could not. In more rural areas, however, lighter colored moths were less conspicuous and continued to survive better than the darker ones. If there had been no variation among the moths, with complete adaptation to the country living, city survival would not have been possible. This would have been an instance of overspecialization in natural selection.

Abrupt environmental changes may provide pressures that a species cannot withstand because it does not possess sufficient variability among its members. It then becomes extinct. Shifting land masses and bodies of water possibly had such effects on the dinosaur. Sometimes the introduction of a new species plays havoc because the new species is better adapted to survival in the environment than the established inhabitants. Thus the placental jackrabbit was better adapted to life in Australia than the indigenous marsupials and rapidly multiplied when introduced there. The incessant movement of humans into wilderness areas has caused extinction of numerous species and endangered many others. Sometimes, however, environmental changes in the form of such geographic upheavals may give new life to a species. Some of Darwin's observations most important to his theory were made of the variations of finches among the different Galapagos Islands of volcanic origin. The finches experienced different environmental pressures on these different, suddenly appearing islands and therefore developed along different lines.

Mendel's Theory of Genes

Gregor Mendel did his work on inheritance in the middle 1880s, but it was about 1900 before it became evident that his discoveries provided the mechanism of Darwin's natural variation. An organism passes some of its characteristics to its offspring. The mechanism of transmission is the genes (Mendel himself just referred to "factors"). A particular organism has a **genotype**, the actual genes it receives from its parents, and a **phenotype**, that part of its genetic inheritance that is actually expressed in observable characteristics under appropriate environmental conditions.

Each adult individual has pairs of genes for a particular character, such as eye color. The genes may be of the same kind, or they may be different. Such different forms of the same gene are called **alleles**. When reproductive cells, or **gametes**, are formed in the adult individual, only one member of each gene pair goes into the gamete. In the combination of gametes from each parent, the offspring gets a full complement of genes; the exact combinations depend on which genes from a particular parent went into the gamete and on which adults happen to mate with each other. If one allele, which we may call A, is **dominant** over another allele, A', which is **recessive**, then an individual receiving A from one parent and A' from the other will have the phenotype of A. Suppose that A represents the allele for brown eyes and A' for blue, and that A is dominant (which it is). We may then ask what the eye color of the offspring will be on the basis of the parental phenotypes and genotypes.

Figure 3–3 shows some of the possibilities for genetic combinations. We show here the combinations of the two phenotypes, but with different underlying genotypes. If one parent is AA, then the offspring will be brown-eyed, because no matter what allele the other parent brings to the situation, A will always be dominant in the combination. If both parents are AA', they will have brown eyes, but it is expected that one out of four offspring will be blue-eyed (an A'A' combination).

If both parents are blue-eyed, then we know immediately what the genotype of the offspring will be. Both parents have to be A'A', so there is no way for the offspring to be anything but A'A' and hence blue-eyed. Such genetic crosses as we have described produce these particular phenotypes in the specific cases in which dichotomous characters (such as eye color) are controlled by a particular gene and are unrelated to other genes. If the genes in question interact with other genes, the outcomes may be quite different. As it happened, the garden peas that Mendel studied did show such simple dominant and recessive characters. Other genetic crosses may show "blends," or combinations of the phenotypic characters of the parents. For example, in flowers a red male and a white female may produce a pink offspring. Two pinks may produce either red, white, or pink.

Somewhere along the way, however, there may be a genetic error. Perhaps a gene is not reproduced correctly or is not passed on to the offspring. An offspring that does not get the normal genetic complement from each parent is a **mutant** (there is a mutation, or genetic change). Usually this is lethal, sometimes harmless, and only rarely advantageous. Advantageous mutations have had time in their favor, however—millions of years to occur, to be selected, and to become part of the gene pool of a species. It is through gene mutations that the variability in species is maintained, which is necessary for the operation of natural selection.

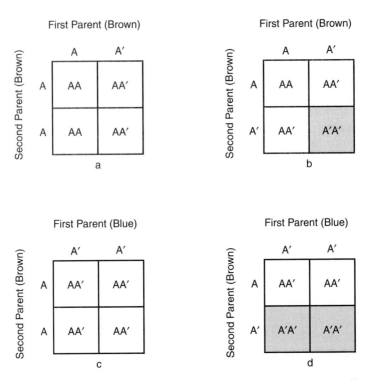

FIGURE 3–3. Illustrative genetic tables for brown-eyed and blue-eyed parents and their offspring. The margins of each table show the genotypes of the parents (A = Brown, dominant; A′ = Blue, recessive). Blue occurs only when two recessive blue genes are paired. The phenotypes of the parents are indicated in the marginal parentheses, and the blue phenotype for offspring is in the stippled cells in (b) and (d). Note that the parental phenotypes are the same in (a) and (b) (both brown), but the genotypes are different, and one out of four off-spring in (b) is expected to be blue-eyed. In (c) and (d) there is one blue-eyed and one brown-eyed parent, but only in (d) are there blue-eyed offspring.

Genetic versus Environmental Contributions to Behavior

The problem of "nature versus nurture" or "heredity versus environment" generates heated discussions on topics such as personality, intelligence, and criminal tendencies. At various times, the pendulum has swung in favor of the one or the other view. The inevitable conclusion, however, is that both factors are involved and that the problem is to determine the conditions under which one or the other is relatively more influential. We cannot judge by simple observation the extent to which a particular behavior is more or less dominated by nature or nurture. By using appropriate analytic and/or experimental procedures, however, we can estimate the relative amounts of variation in behavioral or other characteristics caused by genetic and environmental factors in groups of animals. These techniques may involve experiments with selective breeding of particular individuals, comparisons of monozygotic twins (from a single egg and hence with identical genes) with dizygotic twins or other relatives, or statistical studies of behaviors in populations of individuals.

Selective breeding.   If we take an unselected sample of subjects from some population and measure a specific behavior, we find that there is a distribution of scores for that behavior around some average (mean) value. The amount of variation among the scores, how widely they spread, can be determined by calculation of a statistic called the **variance** (which is the square of the standard deviation). This population variance, **Vpop**, consists of two components: (1) the individual differences caused by genetics, or the genetic variance, **Vgen**, and (2) differences caused by environmental factors, or the environmental variance, **Venv**. Now, we take a group of subjects that are, say, very close to the group mean and selectively inbreed them. (We could inbreed subjects at the extremes of the distribution.) With each succeeding generation, we continue to inbreed those subjects closest to the group average. Over successive generations, we will find that the variance of the inbred groups gets progressively smaller until, after about twenty generations, it reaches a stable value and is no longer reduced by further inbreeding. At this point, we have a **homozygous group** (all the members have virtually identical genotypes with regard to the character being bred for). There is still some variability, however, that must be caused by environmental factors. Now, we have already said that **Vpop = Vgen + Venv**. In our experimental breeding procedure, since we reduced Vgen to zero, any remaining variability is attributable to environmental factors and thus constitutes Venv. We then can determine Vgen by this simple formula: **Vgen = Vpop − Venv**.

This process is illustrated in Figure 3–4. Suppose that the initial unselected population variance was 10 and that the twentieth generation variance was 3. Then Vgen = 10 − 3 = 7. The final step would be to obtain a **heritability coefficient**, which is calculated as **Vgen/Vpop** = 7/10 = .70. This ratio is the proportion of the unselected population variance that is caused by genetic factors. It does not say that 70 percent of the behavior of any *particular* animal is caused by genetics and 30 percent by environmental factors, but it does say that for the group as a whole, 70 percent of the variance among animals is genetic and 30 percent is environmental.

Many such selective breeding experiments have been done, both in laboratories and in agricultural situations. The latter are often less quantitative, but from them we know that animals can be bred for specific features. Horses, cattle, chickens, turkeys, hogs, and others can be bred for commercially desirable characteristics. Dogs can be bred as gentle pets for children, as hunters, or for sheep herding. In laboratories, fruit flies have been bred for such characteristics as phototaxis (tendency to approach a light), and mice have been bred for aggressiveness or for either high or low emotionality

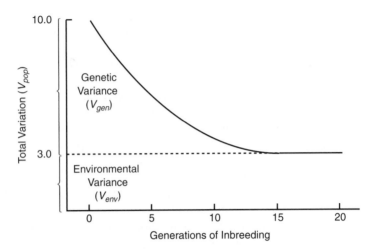

FIGURE 3–4. Stylized representation of change in population variance over successive generations of inbreeding. When further inbreeding produces no further reduction in variance of the breeding characteristic, it is assumed that only environmental variance remains. The proportion of variance that is genetic in this examine is the 10.0−3.0 = 70 percent. See text for details.

(fearfulness). The common laboratory rat, intentionally or not, has been bred for tameness. In one of the early studies of behavior genetics, Tryon (1940) inbred rats that quickly learned a standard maze and rats that were slow to learn the maze. Within twenty generations, he had bred virtually non-overlapping populations of animals for the maze task.

Twin studies.   Identical twins are homozygous because they come from a union of the same sperm and egg. Nonidentical twins or siblings do not have the same genes because the eggs and sperm from which they come are not genetically identical. The closer the familial relationship, the more similar are the genetics of two individuals, however. Using a **coefficient of concordance**, one can compare the likelihood of one identical twin having a certain characteristic if the other has it and so on through the rest of the familial relations. For example, if one member of every pair of one hundred twins has a particular characteristic and if eighty of the second members have it, the coefficient of concordance is .80. If a particular characteristic is genetically determined, then identical twins should have the highest coefficients, siblings next, and randomly paired members of the population as a whole should have the lowest. Using this approach, Kallmann (1946) found that schizophrenia seemed to have a large genetic component. One might argue that this might be due to more closely related members of a family also having more similar environments. The answer to this challenge is that identical twins reared in very different environments have higher concordance ratios than nonidentical twins reared in the same general environment. We could also calculate a heritability coefficient from twin data. If we assume that any variation between identical twins is environmental, then we could compare this variance to the total population variance. Thus, **Vgen = Vpop − Vtwin**. We could go from there to calculate the heritability coefficient: Vgen/Vpop.

Population genetics. Selective breeding is not feasible with humans, and the occurrence of particular phenotypic characteristics with twins may not be frequent enough to be enlightening about the genetic basis of a particular human characteristic of interest to us. Data on the frequency of particular phenotypic characters in families or other genetically close groups can give us much information, however. A variety of characteristics are thus found to be hereditary, including blood type, extra fingers, the Rh factor in blood, some forms of mental retardation, color blindness, and hemophilia (excessive bleeding). Some genes may be carried by both sexes but be sex-linked in their expression. Thus, color blindness occurs almost exclusively in males.

A particular group, because of its geographic or social isolation, may contain a gene virtually unknown in other groups. For example, in the United States, sickle cells in the blood are found only among African Americans and are pathological (sickle-cell anemia). In Africa, however, sickle cells were apparently naturally selected because they are resistant to malaria and hence had a positive value in prolonging life. Similarly, the Jewish population shows a much higher incidence than other populations of a recessive gene for Tay-Sachs disease (a lethal central nervous system disorder). At the same time, however, a genetic defect called **phenylketonuria** (PKU), which produces mental retardation, is virtually unknown among Jews. Other religious groups (such as the Amish and the Muslems) also have particular recessive pathological genes that are uncommon in other populations. Hemophilia is caused by a recessive gene and although occurring rarely in any broad population, is found with considerable frequency in European royal families. These families have intermarried so frequently over the years that the probability that two individuals with the recessive gene will mate is much higher than the chance pairing in the general population.

Cognitive abilities also have a genetic component that appears only after adolescence (Plomin, Fulker, Corley, & DeFries, 1997). This finding was made in a twenty-year longitudinal adoption study that compared 245 adoptive children, their adoptive and biological parents, and 25 matched non-adoptive parents and children. On several measures of cognitive ability, adoptive children are never like their adoptive parents but become more like their natural parents as they pass through adolescence. Eventually they have the same degree of similarity to their biological parents as do children raised with their own biological parents. In general, it appears that somewhere between 20 percent and 50 percent (depending on the study and the characteristics measured) of the variation in human personality is genetically determined (Hamer, 1997).

EVOLUTIONARY PSYCHOLOGY

Edmund Wilson (1975) popularized the term **sociobiology** in his widely cited book of the same name, but his application of biological principles to sociological events was not a new idea. Indeed, for higher-life forms, social interaction is the sine qua non of evolution and obviously dates back to Darwin and earlier. The evolutionary process of natural selection is based on genetic variation and transmission from one generation to another, which among animals usually requires some degree of social interaction, that is, mating. The question of who mates with whom and how this affects survival requires examination of aggressive male behavior, development of mating rituals, attractiveness, coloration, seasonal estrus, and on and on. All these problems have been studied for many years by biologists and psychologists under the general rubric of **adaptation**.

Adaptations.   Adaptation to conditions of life is the key to evolution. An adaption is an inherited characteristic that appears through natural selection because it enhances survival and facilitates reproduction. Although an adaptation is inherited, the expression of an adaptation depends on many events in the life of the individual organism. Intrauterine conditions affect development of intelligence (e.g., measles during pregnancy may lead to mental retardation), as can extreme social isolation after birth. Along with adaptations there may be incidental by-products that are not part of the adaptive solution. For example, bones are white because of the calcium they contain (which adds strength), not because whiteness solves any evolutionary problem (Buss, Haselton, Shackelford, Bleske, & Wakefield, 1998). Whiteness of external coloration (e.g., on polar bears) obviously does have adaptive value in camouflaging the bear as it hunts prey. Sometimes there are just random effects in reproduction, neutral with regard to adaptation and not linked (as with whiteness of bones) to some adaptive effect (calcium in bones). Although adaptation is the key to evolution, some newer concepts have been added.

Expanded adaptation theory.   Gould (1991) has argued that many present functions of organisms were not initially selected because they were adapted for these present functions. For example, feathers are important for bird flight but seem initially to have evolved because of their thermal properties. Evolved first for one function (keeping warm), they began to be used ("co-opted") for a different function (flying). Gould calls this **exaptation**. A feature that now enhances fitness for one function (feathers for flying) was originally adapted because it enhanced fitness for a different function (keeping warm). In both cases the feathers are functional. Another example is handgrip, which evolved for one function but is now used for holding hammers, tennis rackets, ski poles, and for friendly encounters.

Another concept of Gould's is **spandrels**. A spandrel is an incidental by-product that subsequently became a functional adaptation. Gould suggests that the human brain was adapted for just one use (survival) but that reading, writing, fine arts, commerce, and war are incidental by-products of brain evolution. Adaptation is still the key to evolution, but the twisting and turning evolutionary road is more like a back-country trail than a carefully engineered superhighway.

Buss and colleagues (1998) cited examples of empirical discoveries about humans generated by the concepts of adaptation and selection, but were unable to find examples of discoveries about humans based on the concepts of exaptations or spandrels. In any case, the point is that a broader view of evolution may reap a richer harvest of applications to psychology, for which new concepts are needed. In the evolution of science, not all new concepts survive, but new concepts are necessary for the evolution of science to occur at all.

Inclusive fitness theory. One concept that seems to bear fruit is **inclusive fitness**. We generally think of fitness in terms of individual genetic characteristics that are passed on directly by that individual to his or her offspring. Other characteristics may indirectly serve this function, however. For example, one man may be able to protect his small family so that his children live longer than those of a man with a large family who cannot protect them. The former may have his genes passed on with greater frequency because he helps his offspring to survive longer and hence to mate more. Similarly, a person who protects his extended family (brothers, sisters, nieces, nephews), which shares his genes, also helps more of these shared genes to be passed on. Inclusive fitness, then, refers to a person's own reproductive success plus the effects of his or her behavior on the reproductive success of genetic relatives (Hamilton, 1964).

SECTION SUMMARY

1. **Charles Darwin's** theory of **evolution** states that organisms best adapted for survival will reproduce more often and gain increased representation over successive generations. The three operating characteristics are **natural selection**, **natural variation**, and **environmental pressure**. Survival involves selection of individuals who can respond behaviorally with the most efficiency in their particular historical time and place and who therefore breed more frequently and have more offspring.

2. **Gregor Mendel's** postulation of specific **genetic inheritance** and of **gene mutation** provided the variation in organisms upon which natural selection could work.

3. Any behavior is the joint product of **genetic** and **environmental** effects (including the intrauterine environment before birth). Heredity versus environment arguments always reduce to the question of "How much variability in any species characteristic (including behavior) is due to genetic differences, and how much to environmental differences?" Such questions are studied in animals by **selective breeding**, and in humans by studies of **twins**, families, and other genetically related groups.

4. **Expanded evolutionary theory** has developed other concepts besides natural selection. The concept of **inclusive fitness** is that an organism can help pass on its own genes by protecting its own family members, who also carry its genes. Other concepts that have been proposed to expand beyond the idea of adaptation to the environment are **exaptation** and **spandrel**.

5. **Evolutionary psychology**, also referred to as **sociobiology**, is the application of evolutionary concepts to social behaviors. One such application is **mate selection** and the principles by which one individual selects a member of the opposite sex for breeding purposes.

STIMULUS CONTROL OF SPECIES-SPECIFIC BEHAVIOR

Examples

Of the many energy forms in the environment, living organisms are sensitive to only a few. An animal's sensory system operates as a filter that lets some energy forms "pass" into the animal's nervous system but excludes others. If an animal has a receptor mechanism for transducing a particular environmental energy into neural activity, it is sensitive to that energy. The kinds of receptors that an animal has, and the kind and complexity of neural machinery for processing the sensory inputs, determine that animal's perceptual world. We may all occupy the earth, but we do not all live in the same perceptual world and do not respond the same ways to the same stimuli. For example:

1. Humans can hear from about 20 hertz (Hz) to 20 kilohertz (kHz; hertz is the term for cycles per second) sound waves, but dogs and rats hear up to about 40 kHz, and bats and porpoises into the range of 80–100 kHz.

2. Migrating birds are sensitive to the earth's magnetic fields, which they use for navigation, but humans are apparently not.

3. Bees and some birds are sensitive to polarized light, to which humans are blind.

4. Humans are sensitive to light wavelengths in the range of 400 to 700 millionths of a millimeter but are blind to infrared and ultraviolet wavelengths just on either side of the visible spectrum, as well as to radio frequencies. Many mammals seem to be color-blind, but birds typically have excellent color vision.

5. Sea animals, such as sharks, do not have particularly good vision, but have highly developed smell which is essential to them for the location of food. A

variety of land animals also have excellent smell and utilize body secretions called **pheromones** to communicate with other members of the species, particularly for sexual attraction. Male butterflies can detect and locate female odors at distances of up to several miles. According to Wilson (1975), such chemical communication is virtually universal among living organisms.

Such a list could go on and on, but the point is made: there are large differences in perceptual sensitivity, and on the basis of our own perceptions, we cannot make any assumptions about what nonhumans are perceiving.

Given that a particular species is sensitive to a particular range of stimuli, the species then has to respond appropriately to stimulus configurations within that range. Such responding may be based on inherited neural mechanisms for responding in relatively specific ways to specific configurations and/or may depend on prior experience. We may refer to these respectively as **releasing stimulus control** and **acquired stimulus control**.

Releasing Stimulus Content

Releasing stimuli.   Many species may be sensitive to a particular stimulus pattern, but only some are uniquely responsive to them. Thus, releasing stimuli depend on species-specific sensorimotor organizations for their effectiveness, in addition to stimulus sensitivity per se. For example, many species are sensitive to other organisms looking at them, but primates are especially aggressive in response to being stared in the eye. Rhesus monkeys bare their teeth, scream, and may attack. Male squirrel monkeys, on the other hand, make penile displays as a ritualistic response that has apparently replaced fighting.

Both mother love and love for mother suffer at the hands of the ethologists, however, because it turns out that the effective stimuli for releasing many social behaviors are only a small fraction of the total stimulus input from another organism. We find out what the effective stimuli are by making models with varying degrees of similarity to living organisms, or parts thereof, until it is determined what minimal aspect of the natural stimulus will release a particular behavior. The following examples illustrate such minimal stimuli:

1. For the stickleback, a wooden model on a stick lowered into the water tank will release male sexual behavior, but all that is required of the model is that it look vaguely like the swollen belly of a female with eggs.
2. The gaping behavior of hungry baby birds can be released by a stick with a spot on it (in some cases, a ring around it), similar to the bill of the parent.
3. Male turkeys get excited by a model of a female turkey head, although a real head is better (whether or not attached to a body).
4. The squirrel monkey's penile display is released by a mirror reflection of nothing more than its own eyeball.
5. A cardboard model of a "hawk" produced fearful behavior in chickens when the model was "flown" over the flock, but the same model "flown" in reverse (now

having a long neck on the leading edge and looking more like a goose) did not. The exact interpretation of this phenomenon is controversial, but it seems well established that such a phenomenon occurs.

6. Frogs strike out at any small, buglike objects in motion, but not if the stimuli are stationary. Frogs respond to large, dark stimuli by escaping.

7. There are also **supernormal stimuli**, which are artificial stimuli that are better releasers than natural ones. Thus, gulls will take care of oversize artificial eggs in preference to their own.

Desmond Morris (1967) tried to make the argument that human female breasts and lips are sexual releasers because of their similarity to the female buttocks and genitalia. The argument was that in the course of the evolution of walking erect, women minimized the display of those sexual releasers that are obvious in the more typical bent-over primate position; therefore, new releasers were evolved. As Eibl-Eibesfeldt (1975, p. 495) notes, however, "the artificially up-lifted breast of a movie star may evoke such an association, but a normal breast is as dissimilar from a buttock as lips are from the labia." Besides which, men also have lips.

Interaction of Internal States and Releasers

A stimulus that will release a behavior such as sexual activity at one time may not do so at another time. Responsiveness depends on internal hormonal conditions that may be present only at a particular time of the month in cyclic fashion (estrus, for example) or at certain seasons of the year (as with ungulates). In the case of seasonal mating, sex hormone changes are initiated by the pituitary gland, which, in turn, is under the control of dark-light cycles. Sexual arousability by members of the opposite sex is therefore under the control of complex organismic and environmental interactions. Only in the human species do females seem prepared to mate at any time, and even here the common restrictions against intercourse during menstruation are based on social taboos rather than on biological factors. Human females are also more sensitive to musk odors (as in perfumes) during their childbearing years; men are sensitive to them only if injected with estrogen prior to the odor test. We have much more to say about the interaction of internal states and external stimuli in subsequent chapters.

Acquired Stimulus Control

Besides the innate releasing mechanisms, organisms learn to use stimuli as cues. They learn that a particular food is good or bad, that a particular event is painful, or that a stimulus signals a pleasant or an unpleasant situation to come. Depending on the individual circumstances of learning, the range of stimuli to which an animal responds in a particular way may be widened or narrowed. A child may learn to be afraid either of all dogs or of only one special dog.

Depending on the particular structural characteristics of a species, some things are learned more readily than others. Presumably in the course of evolution, animals have developed mechanisms for responding to stimuli that are biologically important to them. In the case of releasers, there was phylogenetic selection for such responsiveness. Even in the case of learning, there appears to be some preprogramming so that there is a bias in ontogenetic selection as well; that is, there is greater ease of learning some things than others. Seligman (1970) has referred to this as **preparedness**. In humans, for example, Valentine (1930) reported that it was easy for a child to learn to be afraid of caterpillars but that children did not readily become conditioned to fear opera glasses or a bottle. As Hebb (1955) suggests, there may be a latent fear of certain things that makes it easy to condition them. Such a "latent fear" is a genetic predisposition.

Imprinting.   William James (1890) described the phenomenon we now call **imprinting** and cited the experimental work of his contemporaries. Imprinting is a particular kind of learning occurring most reliably with precocial birds, such as chickens and ducks, which are born with down and are active immediately after hatching. The behavior usually studied is the following response of newborn precocial birds. These birds follow any object that moves in front of them on the first day or so of life, but there is a critical period of time after hatching during which a permanent attachment to the moving object can develop. Mallard ducklings follow a duck-mother model or a ball or a box that moves, and they are imprinted most strongly at about sixteen hours after hatching (Hess, 1962). In the normal course of duckling events, fortunately, the most likely moving stimulus that the baby encounters is its real mother.

For different species there are different critical periods for imprinting, but in all cases there is considerable variability. Hinde, Thorpe, and Vince (1956) found imprinting in coots as late as six days after hatching and were able to correlate the end of the imprinting period with the onset of a flight period. That is, the birds would imprint until they reached an age at which they became afraid of strange objects and would not follow them, hence they did not become "attached." There apparently is no unique physiological process involved in imprinting; it is just that after awhile, birds (or other animals) become afraid of novel stimuli and do not become attached to them. This same view of attachment behavior in mammals has been expressed by Scott (1962) and may be seen in humans. For about the first three months of life, human infants show little response to parental billing and cooing; then they begin to smile and make answering noises. At about six months of age, many infants suddenly become frightened by unfamiliar stimuli, including new faces. This response is often to the chagrin of grandparents or friends who may arouse screaming and crying when they expect laughing and smiling. Eventually, of course, most children lose such extreme fear of unfamiliar stimuli.

Lorenz (1965a) had argued that imprinting is very nearly irreversible, citing the case of an adult shell parakeet that made sexual advances toward a human to whom it had been imprinted in early life. He believed that this aberrant sexual behavior had been caused by imprinting when the parakeet was young. He did not believe it represented instrumental conditioning because the response had not occurred at the time of imprinting. What does more systematic research indicate, however?

Permanence, or irreversibility, of imprinting can refer either to (1) lack of generalization of the imprinted behavior to other stimuli, so that the response is only to a very specific stimulus, or (2) a failure of the strength of the imprinted response to decline. The evidence seems to be largely negative in either case. Hinde, Thorpe, and Vince (1956) found that coots would follow objects very dissimilar to the one on which they were imprinted, and Fabricius (1951) found that, although he could establish a strong following response in tufted ducks, shovellers, and eiders, the following response gradually diminished beginning at about three weeks of age. The most likely explanation for the attractiveness of humans to parakeets is that they were in each other's company over a long period of time, during which a strong attachment developed. Furthermore, as Moltz (1960) suggested, what is "imprinted" may be primarily an emotional response that leads to generalized approach behavior toward a given stimulus rather than a specific response toward that stimulus. Gallagher and Ash (1978), however, report that imprinting of Japanese quail to an albino hen during the first ten days of life is strong, being demonstrated by adult sexual preferences of the imprinted males for albino hens. Postimprinting experience with hens different from the imprinted hen can change this preference. But lacking later experience, the early establishment of a social bond does last into adulthood. Perhaps the learning is persistent because of lack of interference by other stimuli. At any rate, the general conclusion from research on imprinting is that it is not a unique process but is a fairly typical kind of emotional learning that happens to occur at a particular stage in life.

SECTION SUMMARY

1. **Releasing stimulus control** of behavior refers to responsiveness to particular stimulus configurations due to genetically programmed stimulus-response connections, such as the gaping mouth of a baby bird eliciting feeding from a parent. The effective releasing stimulus is often only a small fragment of the total stimulus. Responsiveness to such stimuli often depends on internal states, such as the level of circulating sex hormones.

2. **Acquired stimulus control** refers to any kind of learning that involves responding to stimuli. Considerable evidence indicates that **genetic predispositions** make it easier for a given species to learn some things rather than others.

3. A form of learning called **imprinting** is exemplified by the following behavior of ducklings. It is said to occur only during a **critical period** after birth and to be very enduring. Evidence indicates that critical periods vary a great deal, that imprinting is reliably found mainly with precocial birds, and that it is not as permanent as has often been stated. It is questionable whether imprinting is a unique kind of learning at all.

CHAPTER FOUR

Eating and Taste

Why do we eat more when hungry?

Do we eat for pleasure or because we must have food?

What internal cues tell us when we should start or stop eating?

Do our bodies only respond to need for food or can we anticipate our food needs?

What role does the brain play in our eating?

What does the pleasure of eating have in common with other pleasures?

How does learning affect our likes and dislikes for different foods?

What roles do society and culture play in when, where, and what we eat?

Why do people overeat to the point of producing health problems?

What can be done to help people with eating disorders?

Over the last thirty years, there has been a revolution in the study of consummatory behavior which is still gaining momentum in both research and theory. The new view emphasizes the roles of pleasure, learning, and environmental and social factors in the control of feeding and drinking. This chapter reflects the new outlook and the way that it reorganizes our thinking about how we survive.

CLASSIC HOMEOSTATIC THEORY

Constancy of the Internal Environment

Biological approaches to motivation have largely grown out of Darwin's theory of evolution. If complex organisms are to reproduce, they must survive. To do this, they must monitor the status of their **internal environments** and make the behavioral adjustments necessary to keep healthy, such as eating and drinking. The internal environment consists of the fluids that bathe our body cells, protecting them from dehydration, bringing them nutrients, and removing metabolic waste. Claude Bernard ([1865] 1957), often called the father of experimental medicine, developed the dictum that the *necessary condition for a free life is constancy of the internal environment.* An animal is "free" when it can carry its internal environment from place to place in the external environment without undue threat of cell destruction. When all the controls necessary for life become portable and are protected from the environment by the skin, an animal is free.

Homeostasis

Walter Cannon (1939b) built on Bernard's ideas by developing the concept of **homeostasis,** which he called "the wisdom of the body." Cannon described homeostasis as the automatic adjustments the body makes to restore stability when there is a departure from the narrow tolerance ranges the body has for temperature, acidity, glucose concentration, salt and water balance, and so on. These automatic adjustments are under the control of the brain and autonomic nervous system, but can do only so much until behavior becomes necessary to replenish depleted stores of food and water or to aid other systems. For example, when the body becomes overheated, perspiration promotes evaporative cooling, but at the cost of losing body water. Automatic mechanisms come into play to conserve water, but eventually the organism must take action to replace lost water and/or to cool itself without evaporation, such as moving into a cooler environment. The study of such **regulation** of internal states is a major part of the study of motivated behavior. A deficiency in the body sends **start signals** to trigger appropriate regulatory behaviors such as eating and **stop signals** to terminate the behavior when the deficiency has been offset. The question for homeostatic theorists is, What are these start and stop signals and how and where they are they generated?

Homeostatic Signals

Peripheral theories.   Walter Cannon (e.g., 1934) argued for a peripheral theory of motivation, which says that start and stop signals are generated outside the central nervous system. Cannon proposed that the signal to start eating was contractions of the stomach and the signal to stop was stomach expansion. Experiments by Anton Carlson, using balloons in the stomach to sense stomach contractions indicated that the stomach did contract at the same time human subjects were reporting "hunger pangs." Other research showed, however, that animals or people without stomachs still ate normal amounts of food. Furthermore, stomach contractions recorded from electrodes on the abdomen did not correlate with reported hunger pangs. Therefore, stomach contractions and expansion cannot be the *necessary* start and stop signals. Similarly, Cannon thought that a dry mouth signaled thirst, but a man without salivary glands drank normal amounts of water (Steggerda, 1941). Peripheral start and stop signals may exist, as discussed later in this chapter, but they cannot be the whole story.

Central theories.   Other researchers emphasized start signals generated within the brain, such as for instinctive behaviors (including eating; Lashley, 1938) and sexual behavior (Beach, 1942). Clifford Morgan (1943, 1959) extended this line of thinking with his concept of **central motive states** (CMS), a hypothetical system of brain centers and pathways concerned with particular kinds of motives. A specific CMS was defined in terms of the kinds of environmental stimuli to which an animal responds. Responsiveness to food indicates a hunger CMS, responsiveness to water indicates a thirst CMS, and so on. Morgan said that once it is triggered, the CMS persists for some time without further stimulation; it predisposes an organism to act in a certain way to particular stimuli (e.g., to approach food) but not to other stimuli (e.g., a sex object); and it emits certain behaviors. For example, the sexual movements of a female rat in heat might occur as a direct response to a CMS and its hormones. Morgan held that hormones were probably more important than external stimuli in arousing and maintaining CMSs because circulating hormones could maintain a state of excitability over a long period of time. Elliot Stellar (1954) proposed more specifically that motivated behavior results from arousal of excitatory centers in the **hypothalamus** of the brain. The activity of these excitatory centers is determined by (1) *inhibitory centers* that depress the excitatory centers, (2) *sensory stimuli*, (3) *humoral factors*, and (4) *cortical and thalamic* centers that can produce either excitatory or inhibitory effects on the hypothalamus. Stellar's ideas were the driving force for much research during the last half of the century, but newly discovered peripheral factors (such as release of chemicals into the stomach during eating) have also stimulated research. Whether an animal eats depends on the relative strength of the start and stop signals. It is not clear where or how these signals are measured or compared by the brain, but it is likely that such "computations" would occur, if at all, in the general region of the hypothalamus.

HUNGER AS A HOMEOSTATIC NEED

Feedback and Feed Forward Signals

Feed backward (negative feedback) signals. Negative feedback signals tell us when to stop an activity. In the case of hunger, these signals are also often anticipatory and tell the animal to stop eating before food can be absorbed and homeostasis restored. Negative feedback signals are generated as food passes through the mouth, stomach, and small intestine. Having a full stomach (feedback from stomach distention) may be one such signal, but is not the only signal. Even if the vagus nerve from the stomach is severed so that stomach stretch receptors can no longer send signals to the brain, animals still stop eating after normal-size meals.

A major negative feedback signal appears to be the release of the hormones **cholecystokinin (CCK)** and **bombesin** from the stomach and intestinal walls. One effect of CCK is to reduce the pleasure from the ingested food so that the animal stops eating. There are also more specific chemical satiety signals released by eating particular kinds of foods so that we may become satiated ("full") for one food but immediately start consuming another (Hetherington & Rolls, 1996). In modern American culture where there is plenty of food available, this may be one reason for obesity. There are so many different foods that when we get satiated with one food we just eat another—leading to overeating (Raynor, 2001).)

Energy monitoring. Different *specific hungers* also initiate searches for specific kinds of food, such as sugar, salt, fats, and amino acids. However, the only specific physiological start signal known is a decline of blood sucrose of about 12 percent in the case of the rat, and no particular cue is specifically known for humans (Smith & Gibbs, 1995). What then is the brain "watching" that tells it when we should eat? The brain may monitor the *overall energy status* of the body, regardless of the particular food being utilized (Bernardis & Bellinger, 1996; Ramsay, Seeley, Bolles, & Woods, 1996). For example, oxidation rate in the liver is correlated with the uptake of free fatty acids in the lateral hypothalamus (LH). Sugars, proteins, and fats all contribute to this, and specific receptors for each food type are not needed. When energy production in the body declines (as shown by decreased liver activity), there is a change in the activity of hypothalamic neurons, and this change triggers feeding. As the organism eats, metabolic activity in the liver increases, fatty acids in the hypothalamus increase, and feeding declines. This is a nice homeostatic account, which says that the constancy of the internal environment is maintained by monitoring energy level rather than by monitoring particular food deficits. By and large, though, it appears that organisms use such energy signals as a last resort, in emergencies that arise when body needs have not been anticipated in some other way.

Feedforward signals.   For the complex organisms (e.g., mammals), the capacity to *anticipate* events, not just respond to them, is important to survival. For example, the regulation of body temperature keeps the core of the body within a narrow temperature range. As the body starts to cool, our hands get cold before core temperature drops. This is an anticipatory signal that we should do something to get warm before there is a truly dangerous drop in core temperature. In a similar manner, food-seeking activity may be triggered by distant cues for food (e.g., seeing food at a distance) even before food stimuli reach the mouth or nose. Once an animal can smell or taste food, approach to food and eating are intensified. Anticipations are partly unlearned (e.g., animals approach some odors that are inherently "good" and avoid others that are "bad"), but are in large part learned. We learn times of day to eat, cues to what foods are available, and so on. These cues are part of the "start" mechanism for feeding.

Woods (1991) has argued that the act of eating must in itself be highly disruptive to homeostasis, because it produces large internal changes suddenly. We usually think of the parasympathetic division of the autonomic nervous system as having a calming influence as food is digested and of the sympathetic system as being dominant during exciting fight-flight episodes of activity. Actually, the sympathetic system is active, and epinephrine, norepinephrine, and other stress hormones are released into the blood as we eat. It would therefore seem that at least some aspects of feeding should be aimed at protecting the organism from this stress. And, indeed, a separate set of feedforward signals may warn the animal to act before feeding disruption becomes overly severe. Most feedforward signals appear to be learned.

Cephalic insulin.   An excellent example of a physiological feedforward signal in feeding is called **cephalic insulin** (Woods, 1991). Insulin is released from the **pancreas** into the blood in response to increases of glucose, fat, or amino acids. Insulin release is a homeostatic mechanism that helps the body return to its normal blood glucose level by removing the newly consumed foods from the bloodstream and into body cells. If the insulin supply is inadequate, as in the case of **diabetes mellitus,** there is a surplus of unabsorbed glucose in the blood. Insulin release is triggered by food in the mouth, but also by the sight, taste, and smell of food. It can also be conditioned to occur in response to such arbitrary external stimuli as lights, sounds, or odors. All these can lead to the arrival of insulin in the blood before the animal/person actually starts to eat, preparing the body to move the homeostatic-disruptive food from the blood so that homeostasis is restored more quickly (Woods, 1991).

Inherent Limitations of the Homeostatic Model

Herman (1996) points out that the homeostatic model is often kept in its dominant theoretical position by simply ignoring "other" factors that affect eating or by considering them "exceptions" to the homeostatic rule. In fact, however, animals or people seldom eat because they are food-depleted. Rather, they eat to *prevent* depletion (e.g., Collier, Hirsch, & Hamlin, 1972; Collier, Kanarek, Hirsch, & Marwine, 1976). The homeostatic model predicts that amount of eating should increase steadily with the amount of time since the last meal (or until the next one), but such correlations are rarely found in free-feeding animals. Each kind of animal in its own particular ecological niche knows how to keep from getting overly hungry. In the case of humans, the types of food or beverage that people consume within a meal or over a day is more influenced by such factors as time of day, other people eating, taste, and so on, than by any responses to homeostatic imbalance (De Castro, 1993).

Does nature know best?   All animals must meet certain minimal dietary requirements to maintain health. For humans, there are three major food components. **Fats** are found in meats, milk products, and oils, each of which breaks down into fatty acids and glycerol. **Carbohydrates** are found in breads, pasta, and fruits which break down into the sugars glucose and fructose. **Proteins** are found in vegetables, meats, and beans which break down into the twenty or so different amino acids. In addition, we need vitamins and minerals which we typically get from the above food groups rather than having separate sources. A nutritionally balanced diet contains about 15 percent protein, 65 percent carbohydrates, and 15 to 20 percent fats. But how do animals, including humans, know how to select a balanced diet from all the possible choices available? Has nature "hardwired" us with this ability so that we just automatically select proper foods, or do we learn what to eat? Both these explanations are correct, but of varying importance depending on the species involved.

Some animals are **feeding specialists,** and others are **feeding generalists.** Such feeding specialists as koala bears, which feed exclusively on eucalyptus leaves, are genetically wired to select the proper food. This diet is adequate, and their only problem is getting enough to eat. Feeding generalists, like omnivores, can find an adequate diet among many combinations of foods and must make wise choices about what to eat, not just how much to eat. Evolution provided the generalists with a particularly important genetic decision-making aid: taste. Good-tasting things tend to be healthy, and bad-tasting substances tend to be deadly. There is a correlation of about +.80 between how bad something tastes and how toxic it is (Scott, 1990). Taste allows us to estimate whether something is good or bad for us before it goes to the stomach. We can therefore usually decide whether to continue eating before irreparable harm is done. Many animals, but not all, can regurgitate bad substances if they get too far into the digestive tract. But does this, or any other automatic mechanism, guarantee good nutrition?

There have been two schools of thought on this issue: those who believe that "nature knows best" and those who believe that "nature is fickle" when it comes to self-selected diets. In early **cafeteria studies,** animals (or children; Davis, 1939) were given all the foods necessary for a well-rounded diet and allowed to eat freely whatever they wanted. The animals tended to eat appropriately over a period of time, apparently supporting the "nature knows best" argument. Cafeteria diets are successful, however, only if the necessary foods are available and if there is not some high-preference food in the mix, such as a delicious desert. When high-preference foods are available, animals do not eat any more wisely than humans; they eat what tastes good. For example, Young and Chaplin (1945) found that rats deprived of protein preferred a high-protein food in comparison with a regular laboratory chow diet, but not in preference to a sugar-laced diet. Galef (1991) also points out that half the cafeteria studies have *not* shown that animals "naturally" select a nutritionally adequate diet and, many wild animals do not survive to adulthood because they do not eat properly. Nature can be a very fickle mistress.

P. T. Young (1966) therefore argued that food acceptance is determined by at least four groups of determinants:

- **Organic conditions.** These include metabolic needs such as those that are induced by deprivation, but also include other organic states. Illness, for example, overrides deprivation and often abolishes any desire for food.
- **Peripheral stimulations.** These involve not only the immediate impact of food on the head receptors (taste, smell, touch, vision, audition) but also complex social and cultural factors.
- **Previous experience.** This includes dietary history, as well as feeding habits, attitudes, and expectancies.
- **Bodily constitution.** This includes not only types of taste receptors, which vary from species to species, but also more complex body differences. Thus, if a feeding specialist like the koala bear is limited to eating eucalyptus leaves, then its body must be able to derive all its nutritional requirements from these leaves. Other animals cannot do this.

SECTION SUMMARY

1. **Homeostasis** refers to the automatic adjustments the body makes to maintain a constant internal environment of the body fluids surrounding individual cells. The body can store limited amounts of fat or sugar, for example, to be released as they are needed. Eventually, however, animals must seek out foods in order to maintain homeostasis.

2. **Homeostatic behaviors** are triggered by cues that signal departures from homeostatic balance. According to **peripheral theories,** signals outside the central

nervous system signal homeostatic imbalances. According to **central theories,** the brain (especially the **hypothalamus**) detects homeostatic imbalances and their restoration, such as changes in blood sugar level. Both kinds of processes are involved in the regulation of food intake.

3. **Positive feedback signals** to initiate and maintain eating involve taste and smell. **Negative feedback signals** are generated as food passes through the mouth, stomach, and small intestine. Negative feedback signals are **anticipatory** and tell the animal to stop before food is actually absorbed and can restore homeostasis. **Cholecystokinin** and **bombesin** are **hormones** released within the gastrointestinal tract that operate as negative feedback signals.

4. A drop in **blood glucose** level is the only specific physiological signal known to reliably precede eating in the laboratory rat. Another possible signal is the uptake of **fatty acids** in the brain, which is correlated with the amount of work the **liver** is doing in breaking down foods. The brain's activity may thus reflect **energy production,** indicated by liver activity, as the basis for stopping and starting eating.

5. **Feedforward signals** anticipate body needs and initiate compensatory activity before strong needs arise. For example, **insulin** release is triggered by the taste and smell of food (as well as by other learned signals for food) so that it is in the blood prior to the delivery of glucose to the blood by digestion.

6. Limitations to the homeostatic model revolve around the fact that food intake is controlled by many **nonhomeostatic factors,** including sensory pleasure, previous individual experiences, family history, cultural background, emotions, and social factors. These seem to control feeding more than does hemostatic imbalance, but they contribute to homeostasis by regulating feeding.

7. The multitude of external factors in control of feeding may lead to bad feeding and work against homeostasis. For example, the pleasurable tastes of nonhealthy foods may override the nutrition provided by other foods. Neither humans nor other animals always eat wisely if left to their own choices.

BRAIN MECHANISMS FOR FEEDING

Many parts of the brain are involved in feeding. Sensory systems must help locate and discriminate among possible foods, memory systems are needed to remember where foods are found, muscle systems must be activated to collect and eat food, and so on. Following the arguments of Stellar (1954), the hypothalamus has been at the center of much research.

The Dual Hypothalamic Theory of Hunger

According to the **dual hypothalamic theory** of hunger, the **lateral hypothalamus** (LH) is an **excitatory area** (start mechanism) for feeding, and the **ventromedial hypothalamus** (VMH) is an **inhibitory area** for feeding (stop mechanism; see Figure 4–1). The great bulk of laboratory research on hunger is done with laboratory rats which are highly similar to humans in their preferences for foods and their physiology of hunger.

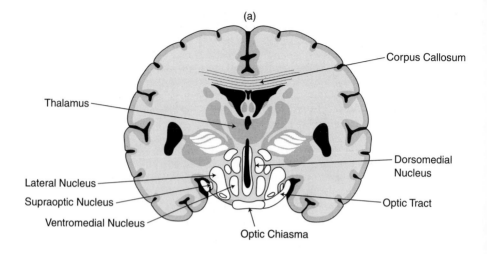

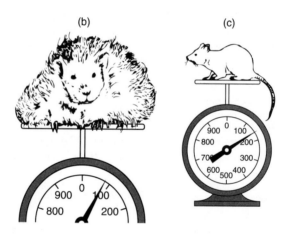

FIGURE 4–1. Hypothalamic nuclei. The cross-section of the brain (a) shows several of the hypothalamic nuclei. The obese rat (b) has lesions in the ventromedial nuclei. A normal rat (c) is shown for comparison. A rat with lesions in the lateral nuclei starves itself. (From Schneider & Tarshis, *An Introduction to Physiological Psychology*, 1975, p. 278. Reprinted with permission of Random House, Inc.)

Lateral hypothalamic syndrome. Direct electrical stimulation of the LH by permanently implanted electrodes leads to **stimulus bound eating,** which lasts only as long as the stimulation is on. Conversely, when the lateral hypothalamus is destroyed by passing an electrical current through it with carefully placed electrodes, animals stop eating and drinking for times ranging from days to weeks, depending on the size and locations of the lesions. As the animals recover, they go through a sequence of feeding changes called the **lateral hypothalamic syndrome.** Initially, they have to be tube fed because they will not eat or drink anything. Then the animals begin to accept such highly palatable foods as chocolate chip cookies ground up in milk but will not eat regular lab chow (which is similar to dry dog food). Finally, they will voluntarily eat enough lab chow and drink enough water to maintain their body weight, apparently regulating their food and water intake according to their need (Teitelbaum & Epstein, 1962). As it turns out, however, the animals get enough water only accidentally, as a side effect of drinking while eating. Their thirst system is permanently impaired and unlike normal animals they do not respond to water deprivation by increasing their water intake.

The LH contains its own nerve cells but is also part of the ventral tegmental dopamine pathway previously discussed in Chapter Two. Some of the pathways running through the lateral hypothalamus go to a motor area of the forebrain (the **globus pallidus**). Since LH animals are very sloppy eaters, as if they could not eat and swallow food normally, it was suggested in the early days of this line of research that the lesions may have produced a deficit in muscle coordination rather than in motivation. It was demonstrated, however, that if the animals were required to press a lever to get food, they showed the same sequence of deficit and recovery as animals who had only to eat the food available. Even if the acts of grasping, eating, and swallowing food had been impaired, there was also a motivational deficit, because a behavior not disturbed by the lesions (bar pressing) was also affected. The motivational hypothesis was favored also by the fact that during recovery, animals could and would eat highly palatable foods even when they would not eat lab chow, suggesting that the palatability of the regular diet was altered by the lesions.

Ventromedial hypothalamic effects.   Electrical stimulation of the VMH puts a stop to eating, and destruction of the VMH produces animals that eat voraciously, to the point of doubling or tripling their body weight. Figure 4–2 shows how animals gain weight. Stimulation of the VMH also inhibits just about anything an animal might be doing, however, so that the VMH is not involved only in the control of eating. In addition, VMH-lesioned animals have shown other food-related changes. They overeat to the point of gross obesity and are overreactive to good and bad tastes. Compared with normal animals, they eat more of sweet-tasting food but less of bitter-adulterated food. Furthermore, in spite of their ravenous appetites and responsiveness to good tastes, they often will not work as much as normal animals to get food. The LH and VMH effects converge on the idea that something about the taste of food is critical to feeding and that particular parts of the brain are important for liking foods.

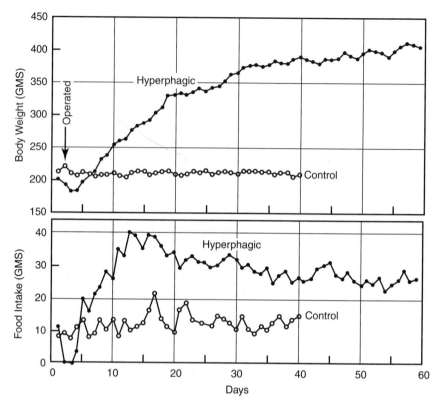

FIGURE 4–2. Effects of ventromedial hypothalamic lesions on intake and weight changes in the rat. (From Teitelbaum, 1961. Reprinted from 1961 *Nebraska Symposium on Motivation,* by permission of University of Nebraska Press. Copyright © 1961 by University of Nebraska Press.)

Pleasure Centers and Feeding

As we saw in Chapter Two, a tiny amount of electric current put into the brain of a rat by means of a permanently implanted electrode is a powerful reward. This research immediately seemed to be in conflict with the homeostatic idea that rewards are effective because they reduce body needs and restore homeostasis. The data pointed toward the classic hedonic concept that rewards are effective because they are pleasurable. We now know that whether this dopamine system is activated by such substances as pleasant food or addictive drugs, or direct electrical stimulation, the effect is pleasurable. The endorphins, the brain's natural opiates, may be the key neurotransmitters for reward (Wise, 1989). Lateral hypothalamic lesions may damage this system so that the pleasurable effects of eating regular lab chow are diminished and the animals eat only highly palatable foods for a while before they begin to eat lab cow again.

Brain differences in liking and wanting. We also saw in Chapter Two that the functions of liking and wanting are separable in the brain and have different characteristics (Berridge, 1996). Liking and disliking are shown by the way laboratory rats or other animals consume fluids. Rats drink tasty fluids eagerly. They lick steadily at the drinking tube, are careful to swallow all they can get, and so on. They show similar movements if the fluid is injected directly into the mouth so that they can taste and swallow it without having to do any work at all. Conversely, if they do not like the fluid, they try to spit it out, withdraw from it, let it dribble from their mouths, or wipe it away with their paws. Various experimental manipulations that alter human perception of palatability, such as food deprivation, increase the number of positive reactions (Berridge, 2000). Berridge (1991) also showed that positive affective reactions to food were reduced when the animals became satiated but that aversive reactions did not increase. Thus, the usual decline in palatability that occurs with satiation is a reduction in liking (endorphin related) rather than actual aversion to food. Just the **brainstem,** disconnected from the thalamus, hypothalamus, and the cerebral hemispheres, is sufficient neural tissue for the rat to demonstrate its liking or disliking. The animal cannot survive this operation without being tube fed, but if food is squirted into its mouth through a tube, it responds to different taste stimuli the same way a normal animal does. By all tests thus far devised, once an animal has food in its mouth, it hardly seems to miss the parts of its brain above the brainstem (Grill & Kaplan, 1990). Organization of activities for approaching and learning about foods do involve a higher level of brain organization than found in the brainstem.

SECTION SUMMARY

1. According to the **dual hypothalamic theory** of hunger, the **lateral hypothalamus** is an **excitatory** area of feeding, and the **ventromedial hypothalamus** is an **inhibitory** area for feeding. When the lateral hypothalamus is damaged, animals stop eating and only gradually recover in a progression called the lateral **hypothalamic syndrome.** When the ventromedial area is damaged, animals overeat and gain a great amount of weight.

2. So-called **pleasure centers** in the brain are involved in feeding. This system involves neurons that have **dopamine** as a neurotransmitter and are related to the release of **endorphins** in the brain. The system is activated by feeding.

3. Two aspects of eating and other motivations have been distinguished, called liking and wanting, that are related to the pleasure system. Liking is shown by preference for foods, and wanting is indicated by the amount of effort put forth to obtain food. Liking is related to the endorphin system, and wanting to the

dopamine system. Preferential responses to tastes can be shown by animals with only the brainstem intact.

TASTE AND FEEDING

Palatability

Palatability refers to any features that make food more or less appetizing, including taste, odor, texture, temperature, color, and even shape. Some of these are genetically determined, others are learned. Food manufacturers have fine-tuned palatability to provide us with such culinary delights as fruit- and sweet-flavored cereals that have bright colors, fun shapes, and that don't get soggy in milk. They have also given us hamburgers, french fries, and chocolate milk shakes.

Taste Qualities and Their Stimuli

The single most important palatability factor is probably taste. Humans have bout three-hundred thousand taste receptor cells collected into about six thousand taste buds (Scott, 2001). In humans, there are four commonly recognized taste qualities: **sweet, bitter, salty,** and **sour.** The prototype stimuli for these are sucrose (table sugar), quinine, sodium chloride (table salt), and citric acid (as found in citrus fruits). Other taste qualities seem to be either a combination of these four or a mixture of taste and smell. Other species may have more or fewer tastes than humans. Rats are equally responsive to the same stimuli as humans but also appear to have a receptor for **polyglucose,** a more complex sugar than sucrose (Sclafani, 1991). Some of the food specialists have taste receptors for very particular substances and are taste-blind to all else, for example, the koala bear's responding only to eucalyptus leaves and the tomato worm's responding only to tomato leaves. Dogs love sweets, but cats are indifferent to them.

Sweet taste is produced by a variety of organic compounds, including sugars, glycols, and alcohols, with no specific chemical similarities among them yet known. Salty taste is produced by water-soluble salts, with both positive and negative ions contributing to the taste. Sour taste is correlated with the concentration of hydrogen ($H+$) ions, with a number of different acids having the same taste. Alkaline substances are bitter, but there is no known specific chemical structure for all stimuli that have a bitter taste.

Primary Taste Qualities and Hunger

It is no accident that the primary taste qualities are so important to feeding. The different taste receptors are tuned to respond to different stimuli that play crucial roles in survival.

Sweet. Sugar is one of our most motivationally potent stimuli. Sucrose breaks down into fructose and glucose, the body's most important source of energy. Glucose provides energy to the muscles, but the body's most gluttonous user of glucose is the brain. Consider, then, the following:

- Food deprivation increases animals' liking for sugars, so that they consume more (e.g., Collier & Myers, 1961), a phenomenon known as **allesthesis** (Cabanac, 1979, 1990).
- If glucose is injected directly into the blood of a hungry animal before it eats, it eats less sugar.
- Glucose in the mouth stimulates firing of sweet-taste receptors on the tongue, which leads to firing of "sweet" neurons in the brain, thereby signaling that something in the mouth is good. But if glucose is injected directly into the blood, these brain responses are inhibited; the brain detects that the body has enough glucose.
- Diabetic humans tend to overeat because they have a strong liking for sweets, which are not being absorbed because of lack of insulin. Their bodies then continue to signal that they are hungry. Injection of insulin also inhibits neural responses to a glucose taste stimulus.

Salt. Salt is needed for regulating the amount of water in the body and for normal nerve and muscle activity. Severe salt deficiency is rare, but is a health-threatening problem. Most people like food a little salty, and wild animals will travel miles to get to a salt lick. Laboratory rats normally prefer about a 1 percent solution of salt water to plain water. However, if their adrenal glands are removed so that the salt-regulating hormone **aldosterone** is lost, they drink more salt solution and prefer a higher concentration (3 percent), which is normally very aversive. People with **diabetes insipidus,** a disease of the adrenal gland, lose massive amounts of salt in their urine and subsequently consume large amounts of salt. But what triggers increased salt intake during salt deprivation?

Curt Richter (1936), a pioneer in the study of behavior and homeostasis, suggested that animals whose adrenal glands are removed become more *sensitive* to the taste of salt. Research showed, however, that the minimal salt concentration sufficient to activate the taste system is the same for normal animals and those with their adrenal glands removed (Pfaffman & Bare, 1950). Furthermore, even a normal rat can discriminate between water and very low concentration saline if it is motivated to do so by being punished for failing to discriminate. Therefore, salt deprivation increases the *preference* for salt, not sensitivity to salt, and there is strong evidence that this change in preference occurs without prior learning. For example, after a single salt depletion, animals show greater preference for salt. No prior experience is necessary (A. N. Epstein, 1967; Falk, 1961; Krieckhaus & Wolf, 1968). Further supporting the hedonic interpretation for increasing salt preference, Scott (1990) measured the activity of individual taste neurons in the brain and found that salt-responsive neurons had different patterns of firing than sugar-responsive neurons. When animals were salt deprived, however, salt-responsive neurons began to behave more like sugar-responsive neurons. Increased preference for salt may thus be explained by the fact that the brain begins to respond to salt more like it was sugar.

Bitter. The prototype bitter taste is quinine, once the standard treatment for malaria. There is no concentration of quinine that animals prefer to purified water, the standard "neutral stimulus" in taste research. Quinine is always avoided by animals that can taste it. Could such a strong aversion be reversed by early experience with quinine? Both rats and guinea pigs have been exposed to quinine immediately after birth and throughout infancy. It becomes tolerated at low concentrations, but as soon as animals are given the choice of water, they avoid the quinine in the same way as animals that have never tasted it. This aversive reaction to quinine is genetically determined, just as the approach reaction to sugar and salt is genetic. The only way yet discovered to make a bitter taste more attractive is by introducing the taste in a social context with another person or animal (Galef, 1996).

Sour. Sour tastes are generally aversive but can become attractive under some conditions, especially in combination with sweet, such as in sour candy or lemonade. The sour taste of pickles is enjoyed by some, but as with bitter, this characteristic seems to develop in a social context.

Fat. Although fat is not a basic taste, it is such an important determinant of food preference that we put it with the others. Fat is important because it and sugar are two of the most highly preferred human tastes and because excess fat produces health problems. Fat combined with sugar makes a potent taste package, no secret among cookie manufacturers.

SECTION SUMMARY

1. **Palatability** refers to features of foods that make them more or less appetizing. Innate taste preferences and aversions are related to the four primary taste qualities: **sweet, salty, bitter,** and **sour.** Fat is not considered a basic taste, but is highly palatable.
2. The basic tastes are related to such critical biological functions as regulating the level of salt in the body. Purified sugar and salt are used to exaggerate the palatability of many foods.
3. Under deprivation conditions, the acceptability of particular tastes is increased, a phenomenon called **alliesthesis.** This increases the likelihood that a needed substance will be consumed.

LEARNING AND CONSUMMATORY BEHAVIOR

In order to understand how our experience is related to feeding behavior, we must first understand a few of the basic principles of **classical (Pavlovian) conditioning.** Classical conditioning is not the only form of learning that affects our eating, but it has been studied in the laboratory for well over a hundred years and accounts for phenomena ranging from learning what foods are good or bad to promoting or devaluing political candidates by publicly associating them with good or bad events. Conditioning is also an important component of the feedforward mechanisms discussed earlier.

The Classical Conditioning Paradigm

While doing research on salivary reflexes, Ivan Pavlov normally put food on the tongue of a dog and recorded the amount of salivation stimulated by the food. He observed that the dogs sometimes began to salivate before food was placed on the tongue (which he called "psychic secretions"), even as they were being put into the experimental apparatus. The salivary reflex had been conditioned to cues in the environment (Pavlov, 1927). Classical conditioning is generally considered a form of **associative learning,** which means that a relationship, or association, between two events is learned. Pavlov's dogs learned the association between the laboratory environment and getting food, so that they came to anticipate food in that situation.

We begin by defining four terms that are at the heart of the process. These terms and their relationships are illustrated in Figure 4–3. The terms are defined as follows:

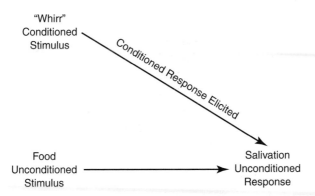

FIGURE 4–3. The basic arrangement and terminology to describe classical conditioning of salivation. The "whirr" of the can opener is associated with food and comes to elicit salivation as the food does. See text for more details.

Unconditioned stimulus (UCS): Any stimulus, such as food, which will reliably elicit a response before conditioning occurs. The stimulus could be positive (food) or negative (painful or unpleasant).

Unconditioned response (UCR): The response elicited by an unconditioned stimulus, such as a salivary reflex elicited by putting food in the mouth. The response might also be a reaction to a painful stimulus, such as change in heart rate.

Conditioned stimulus (CS): Any a stimulus that gains the power to evoke the response produced by the UCS by preceding the UCS in time. For example, the sound of a buzzer (CS) could come to evoke salivation (CR) if paired with food presentation (UCS).

Conditioned response (CR): The response, such as salivation, evoked by the CS. The CR may not be exactly like the UCR, but has some of the characteristics of the UCR.

The following *processes* are basic to classical conditioning.

Acquisition.   Acquisition is the process of learning to associate the CS with a meaningful stimulus (the UCS). This is diagrammed in Figure 4–4. If you use an electric can opener to open food for your dog, he will eventually associate the whirring sound with food. You may not see the salivation (which

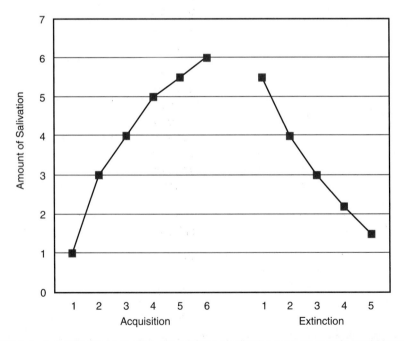

FIGURE 4–4. Acquisition and extinction of a conditioned salivation response over six acquisition trials and extinction over six trials. Curves are illustrative, and amount of salivation is in arbitrary numbers.

in the laboratory is measured by special instruments), but you can see the dog "perk up" and get excited when it hears the sound, just as it does when it sees or smells the food. The conditioned response becomes "stronger" with more pairings of the CS and UCS . Each CS-UCS pairing is called a **trial.** The *magnitude* of the response (amount of saliva) to the CS is measured, and learning is demonstrated when the response increases over trials. Other possible response measures of conditioning are faster responding to the CS over trials or an increase in the likelihood (probability) of responding. In research on classical conditioning, it is necessary to have proper control conditions to rule out other possible causes of a change in responsiveness to the CS besides learning the CS-UCS relationship. One such cause might be a increase in excitement which might facilitate any response, not just salivation.

Extinction.   Extinction is the decline of the conditioned response when the CS is presented without the UCS. If you stopped feeding the dog after using the can opener, he would lose interest and stop salivating when the can opener whirred. Extinction is not the same as forgetting, however. If one day you suddenly started feeding your dog again after using the can opener, the dog would almost immediately start salivating again.

Stimulus generalization.   When we are conditioned to one CS, we are also conditioned (less strongly) to similar stimuli. This is stimulus generalization. Generalization protects us from having to learn everything anew. If we are hit by a Buick, we may associate our pain with Cadillacs, Chevrolets or even Hondas.

Discrimination.   If we always generalized to other stimuli, generalization would be as maladaptive as if we never generalized at all. A second process then comes into play, called discrimination. We continue to respond to the CS, but responses to other stimuli extinguish because they are not followed by the UCS. If a large brown dog growled and bit us, we might become afraid of this dog and generalize our fear to other dogs. As we discover that other dogs do not growl and bite, however, our fear of other dogs would probably decline.

What Is Learned in Classical Conditioning?

Psychologists once believed that classical conditioning involved nothing but specific responses being conditioned to specific stimuli, such as the salivary reflex becoming conditioned to a new sound. This is referred to as a **stimulus substitution model,** meaning that one stimulus (the CS) comes to substitute for another stimulus (the UCS) in evoking the same response (e.g., salivation). It was believed that *contiguity* (presenting CS and UCS close to each other in time) was sufficient for this conditioning. Figure 4–5 illustrates the stimulus substitution model. In this illustration we see that the food stim-

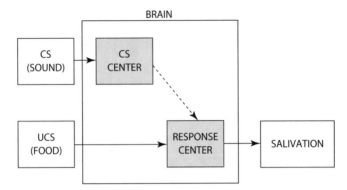

FIGURE 4–5. Simple stimulus substitution model of classical conditioning. The UCS (food) activates the salivation response center in the brain which produces salivation. After conditioning, the CS center in the brain activates the response center and evokes salivation. The conditioned response of salivation should therefore be identical to the unconditioned response of salivation.

ulus goes to some area(s) of the brain, which we call the *UCS center,* which automatically activates the salivary response. By pairing the CS and UCS, the CS now activates the UCS center (stimulus substitution) and automatically activates the response of salivation.

We now know that stimulus substitution is *not* how classical conditioning works for the following reasons.

1. *The conditioned response is frequently not the same as the unconditioned response.* Salivation is rather misleading because the unconditioned and conditioned responses appear to be the same, and therefore the stimulus substitution model seems adequate. With many other responses, the stimulus substitution model clearly has problems. For example, the unconditioned heart response to a painful stimulus is an *increase* in heart rate. However, the conditioned response to a CS is a *decrease* in rate, just the opposite of the unconditioned response. There are many such examples, but suffice it here to say that a simple stimulus substitution model fails to account for observed differences between responses to the UCS and to the CS.

2. *UCS Devaluation.* Suppose that during conditioning we had been feeding the dog a particularly tasty food out of the can following our noisy can opening. For a period of time thereafter, however, we feed the dog a much less tasty food out of already-opened cans, not exposing him to the can opener as we did before. Now, we go back to opening cans as we did before. What should be the dog's reaction? According to the stimulus substitution model, the dog should respond just as it had previously because we have done nothing to change the relationship between the CS and the UCS center. In fact, however, animals (including humans) respond *less* than previously. This is called UCS devaluation. Devaluation is explained by a **stimulus representation model,** which says that the CS is associated with a representation (or image) of the UCS in the brain. The relation between this image and the response can be readily changed without the CS being present, unlike the fixed relationship between the UCS center and the re-

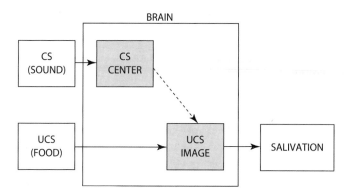

FIGURE 4–6. Stimulus representation model of classical conditioning. The UCS (food) activates a UCS image (or, representation) which triggers the salivation response. After conditioning, the CS Center activates the UCS image rather than directly activating a response center. If the UCS value is reduced (e.g., by satiating the animal), this makes a less desirable UCS image, and there is less salivation. The response is changed without directly changing pairings of CS and UCS.

sponse. This is illustrated in Figure 4–6. Thus, in our example of making food less tasty, the CS activated a less attractive UCS representation and hence a weaker salivation response. In general, any procedure that might change the UCS representation (including a bigger or better UCS representation as well as a devalued UCS) will lead to a modified CR. This is important for our understanding of how classical conditioning works in relation to eating behavior, as well as to our later discussions of fear, anxiety, and stress.

3. *Contiguity alone is not always sufficient to establish conditioning.* In many situations a stimulus is more likely to become an effective CS if it reliably *predicts* that another stimulus (the UCS) will follow (Gordon, 1989; Rescorla, 1987). This is called the **contingency theory** of conditioning, which means that the occurrence of the UCS is contingent on (depends on) the occurrence of the CS. Another way of saying this is that the CS provides **information** about the coming of the UCS. The whir of the can opener is an effective CS because it reliably informs the dog that dinner is on the way. If the can opener sounded randomly in relation to feeding, the sound would not become as reliable a CS because it would not reliably tell the dog anything about coming food. If the food just appeared at random times the dog (or any other animal) would have no way of anticipating and preparing itself for the food. If the CS reliably comes before the food, and only before the food, the dog is informed that the food is on its way and can make whatever the appropriate preparations are.

A phenomenon that forcibly brings home this point is called **blocking.** Suppose we condition a light with food so that we get a good conditioned response to the light. Now, with the same subject we present the light and a sound together before presenting the food. Finally, we test for conditioning to the sound by presenting it alone. If contiguity were sufficient for conditioning, we should get a conditioned response to the sound because it was paired with food. In fact, however, there is virtually no conditioned response to the sound, because the sound does not tell the subject anything that was not already signaled by the light. The sound is a redundant and uninformative stimulus; nothing is contingent on the sound alone.

Conditioning and Feeding Behavior

As earlier noted, feeding generalists eat a variety of foods, but have the problem of selecting the right foods for a nutritious diet. A great number of specific taste preferences have been uncovered among the generalists (omnivores, especially), leading us to ask whether every apparent dietary deficiency has a mechanism to make some specific foods more preferred. Classical conditioning is a general process that accounts for the development of many preferences and aversions.

Odor-taste conditioning in early experience.   When newborn rats are stimulated around the mouth (e.g., with a Q-tip) they grasp the mother's nipple and suck, which is rewarded by getting milk. The sucking response can be classically conditioned to other stimuli, such as odors. Cheslock, Varlinskaya, Petrov, and Spear (2000) studied infant rats that had never had actual contact with the mother's nipple. The rats first were presented with a lemon odor, followed by direct infusion of milk into the mouth. Then, the lemon odor was presented to them and they were allowed contact with an artificial nipple that provided no fluid. Compared with appropriate control conditions, the pups that had previous odor-milk pairings grasped the nipple more consistently and for longer periods of time. This same procedure was also effective using sucrose or saccharin as the UCS (not just milk), supporting the hypothesis that the common element was engagement of the endorphin system.

Taste aversion conditioning.   If you ask almost anyone, they are likely to tell you that they have an aversion to some food that made them sick. In several survey studies, over half the respondents had developed such an aversion to some food (Schafe & Bernstein, 1996). Such aversions are typically learned in a single experience, with delays of minutes or hours between eating and getting sick, and are most likely to occur with new foods.

In the first laboratory report of taste aversion conditioning (Garcia & Koelling, 1966), there were four experimental conditions, indicated in Table 4–1. In two conditions the CS was water accompanied by lights and noise; in two others the CS was saccharine-flavored water. For each CS, there were two aversive UCSs: drug-induced illness and foot shock. The test was the amount of solution consumed after conditioning. Drinking less indicates aversion to the CSs. Aversion to the saccharin taste CS occurred with illness as the UCS, but not shock, and aversion to the bright-noisy CS occurred with shock but not illness. The experiment demonstrated taste aversion learning, but also showed that some stimulus combinations are more readily associated than others. In a similar experiment, Garcia and Ervin (1968) found that animals

TABLE 4–1. Taste aversion conditioning experiment. Saccharin-flavored water was a good CS when illness was the UCS, but not when shock was the UCS. Bright, noisy water was a good CS when shock was the UCS, but not when flavor was the UCS. See text for more details. (From Garcia & Koelling, 1966.)

CONDITIONED STIMULI	UNCONDITIONED STIMULI	CONDITIONING OCCURS
Saccharin flavor	Illness	Yes
Saccharin flavor	Shock	No
Bright, noisy water	Illness	No
Bright, noisy water	Shock	Yes

learned to discriminate between two sizes of food pellet with shock as the UCS, but not illness. Garcia and Ervin hypothesized that it is easy to develop external (size)–external (shock) associations or internal (taste)–internal (illness) associations, but not external-internal associations. The ease of association of different stimuli varies across species, however. For example, quail, which are more visually oriented animals than rats, show aversion to colors that precede illness but not to tastes (Wilcoxin, Dragoin, & Kral, 1971).

Taste aversion conditioning experiments challenged two pieces of conventional wisdom about classical conditioning and forced rethinking about classical conditioning principles. The first was that short intervals between CS and UCS are necessary for conditioning. When the initial laboratory reports of taste aversion learning appeared in the 1960s, one prominent learning theorist publicly remarked that conditioning with such long delays between CS and UCS was about as likely as finding bird dung in a cuckoo clock. The second principle challenged was that all CSs and UCSs can be associated with equal ease. We now know that the ease with which different kinds of stimuli can be associated differs from species to species (see reviews by Revusky & Garcia, 1970; Rozin & Kalat, 1971). In the course of evolution, different species apparently developed somewhat different mechanisms of learning, specific to their own needs.

Learned safety.   All rats approach new stimuli timidly, and wild rats are especially **neophobic**. A new food associated with illness is dangerous and avoided, but if nothing dangerous happens, the new stimulus is considered safe and the animal returns to it. The rat learns to eat new foods as it discovers they are safe. According to learned safety theory, then, animals avoid foods that are associated with illness and tentatively try out new foods until they find one that is safe. The new food becomes associated with well-being and is attractive (Rozin & Kalat, 1971). This mechanism allows for development of a "specific hunger" for practically any food that turns out to be safe. The theory requires only that the animal be able to recognize differences between foods so it can associate them with danger or well-being. In probably the first of such studies showing this, it was found that vitamin B deficiency was corrected by dietary choice only if the vitamin were tagged with a distinctive licorice flavor (Harris, Clay, Hargreaves, & Ward, 1933).

Social Factors in Eating

The manager of a college cafeteria told me that he could never satisfy his student customers because they all wanted food like their mothers made. Even rats learn to prefer foods that they were first exposed to as infants, which would also typically be foods associated with the mother (Galef, 1971; Galef & Henderson, 1972). Infant rats actually prefer foods that their mothers ate while they were still in the womb. Food tastes are transferred to the fetuses through the placenta, familiarizing the offspring with tastes that they will later encounter. Young rats become familiar with "safe" tastes and subsequently prefer them.

Among humans, whole cultures have "eating habits" that seem so natural to them that they reject the equally popular eating habits of other whole cultures. Many foods that we prize or abhor (chili peppers, eyeballs, raw octopus, lizards, monkey brains, corn on the cob) have become pleasurable or aversive because of the way they are treated within our own culture (Rozin, 1996). This is not just a matter of exposure to foods, because animals do not always share the food preferences of the human cultures in which they live. In one instance, an expressive cat I owned kept begging for food as I ate at the table. I put some of the food in a bowl for her and set it on the floor. She took one smell, turned around, and tried to cover it with her back paw. She was not acculturated enough to eat chili. Additional social influences are necessary.

Direct social influences require that another person or persons be present during eating. For example, the more people there are at a meal, the more each individual tends to eat (De Castro & Brewer, 1991). Children prefer foods eaten by admired others (Birch & Fisher, 1996), as well as those eaten by members of their peer group. In a social context, humans will develop a liking for otherwise unpalatable foods. Bitter substances such as coffee, quinine water, and burnt food become popular as do such irritants as alcohol, chili pepper, ginger, and raw garlic or onion (Rozin, 1996). In the case of chili peppers, young children are exposed to the burning sensation in the atmosphere of family and friends, and these positive situations encourage a liking for the burning sensation. Dogs in the same family context do not develop such a liking, indicating that it is socialization, not just familiarity, that produces the liking.

Even with the rat, social factors are powerful influences in food preferences. For example, young rats prefer foods found in the presence of an adult rat that is anesthetized and just lays near a food source. Preferences for foods associated with adults have been found with rats, cats, sheep, and chickens. Galef (1996) argues that the physical presence of one individual at a location attracts others and makes it more likely they will eat the food found there. An animal learns to eat (or not to eat) foods by observing other members of its species eating the foods and not becoming (or becoming) ill.

Indirect social influences on eating and nutritional adequacy occur without the intervention of another person. For example, the cuisine that is characteristic of a particular culture is used whether other individuals are present or not. "Cuisines are defined by the basic ingredients they employ (e.g., rice, potatoes, fish), the characteristic flavors (flavor principles) employed (e.g., a combination of chili pepper with either tomato or lime for Mexico, a varied mixture of spices called "curry" for India), and particular modes of food preparation (e.g., stir-frying for China)" (Rozin, 1996, p. 236). Each culture has its rules about how foods are prepared, what foods are served in combination, what is appropriate for special occasions, what is appropriate at each time of day, and so on.

As an example, corn is a staple in Mexican cuisine but is inadequate as a nutrient because it is low in niacin (a B vitamin) and calcium, and does not have an adequate pattern of essential amino acids. Making corn into tortillas solves a number of these problems because the corn is soaked in a solution of lime that increases the level of niacin, adds calcium, and improves the amino acid pattern. Since the tortilla is usually eaten along with beans and chili peppers, there is an adequate protein source. If you ask Mexican women why they soak the corn, however, they say that it makes the tortillas easier to roll out. The cultural tradition promotes a healthy diet, but the participants aren't aware of the problem that the tortilla-making technology solved (Rozin, 1996).

Beliefs and attitudes also play a major role. In Hindu culture the sacredness of cows prohibits eating them and Hebrews shun pork. Such beliefs affect the way food is perceived, commercialized, and eaten.

SECTION SUMMARY

1. **Classical (Pavlovian) conditioning** is a form of **associative learning** by which a **conditioned stimulus** can come to elicit a response previously elicited by an **unconditioned stimulus.** For example, a tone can come to elicit salivation after having been paired with food. Basic conditioning processes include **acquisition, extinction, stimulus generalization,** and **extinction.**

2. Conditioning does not just involve the substitution of one stimulus for another to evoke a specific response. Instead, the conditioned stimulus evokes a **mental representation** of an unconditioned stimulus (such as food). This representation can be modified in may ways and can have a different response than the original unconditioned response to the unconditioned stimulus.

3. Conditioning is related to feeding in several ways. New **taste preferences** or **aversions** can be learned by associating tastes with "good" consequences (e.g., sugars or fats) or bad consequences (illness following consumption of a particu-

lar taste substance). In early infancy odors are associated with taste and facilitate nursing.

4. According to the **learned safety** principle, animals come to prefer food tastes that they associate with **well-being.** If an animal becomes ill because of dietary deficiency, it can associate a particular taste with the well-being that follows eating the needed substance (e.g., vitamins).

5. **Social factors,** including both **familial** and **cultural** eating habits, have a strong influence on food likes and dislikes. Foods considered delicacies in one culture may be considered disgusting in another. **Social reinforcement** seems to be the only way to get people to like bitter/sour tastes.

EATING DISORDERS AND THEIR TREATMENT

Definition of Eating Disorders

An eating disorder is any change in eating behavior that leads to impaired physical or psychological health. "Typical" eating disorders are **obesity, anorexia nervosa,** and **bulimia nervosa.** "Atypical" eating disorders may have some of the characteristics of anorexia and bulimia but also include overeating or vomiting associated with other disturbances and eating unusual substances (such as feces or chalk; Fairburn & Walsh, 1995).

Obesity

What is obesity?   Obesity is usually defined as a body weight 20 percent greater than the ideal weight for a given height, as established by life insurance norms (L. Epstein, 1990). This excess weight is associated with the storage of fat. Somewhere between a third and a quarter of the United States population over age thirty is obese by this criterion, but the social acceptability of obesity varies with cultures. In some places obesity is a sign of success, that is, eating more food than the minimum required for survival. In other places obesity is a negative characteristic with regard to appearance, especially for women. The prevalence of obesity in this country may reflect dietary habits and the availability of high-fat foods.

What causes obesity?   According to Drewnowski (1996, p. 304), "The question of who becomes obese and why remains unsolved." Increases in average national weight found in large-scale studies reflect obese people becoming fatter, not everyone becoming fatter. A large part of the population is resistant to getting fat. A number of hypotheses about the causes of obesity, or differences between normal weight and obese people, have been proposed, tested, and rejected over the last twenty-five years. Two of these hypotheses are **taste preferences** with obesity, and **set point theory.**

- **Taste preferences in obesity.** Obese individuals have a substantial preference for foods that are high sweet and/or high fat, but there are some sex differences. Men prefer meats more than do women (97 percent versus 86 percent); both prefer carbohydrates/fats equally (93 percent versus 92 percent); and women prefer high-fat sweets more than men (81 percent versus 68 percent) (Drewnowski, 1996). However, taste preferences between normal or overweight groups are overshadowed by the great variation within each group. Hence, taste preferences do not predict who will be obese.

- **Set point theory.** According to set point theory (Keesey & Powley, 1986), different people have different biologically determined "set points" for body weight, and some people are just "naturally" heavier than others. The main line of support for this theory is that although there are fluctuations in body weights, most people have a relatively stable body weight after they reach maturity. A set point operates like the thermostat on a furnace. When our body detects that we are below the set point, it "turns on" the eating system just as the thermostat turns on the furnace. A fat person is said to have a very high set point and therefore has to eat more than a skinny person just to keep his or her weight at the set point. Being "fat" may actually be "normal" for some people, if they are maintaining their weight at their own set point. The set point idea is appealing because it is like the control systems concept often used with reference to homeostatic mechanisms. Also, it may make some people more comfortable if they believe that "biology is destiny" and that it is not their fault they are overweight. Actual evidence for a body weight set point is scanty, however.

Other factors gaining support include the following:

- **Genetics and obesity.** There are genetic differences in susceptibility to obesity among humans, as well as among rodents. An example is that the Pima Indians of the southwest United States have an unusually high prevalence of obesity. Another is that identical twins reared apart are more similar in obesity than are nonidentical twins reared together (Van Itallie & Kissileff, 1990). Given free access to food, some strains of mice become obese, and other strains do not. Even this tendency interacts with the specifics of diet, however. Genetically obese animals gain weight on a diet of standard lab chow, whereas other strains become obese only with intensely sweet, high-fat diets (Drewnowski, 1996). This strongly suggests that there is no single genetic factor accounting for obesity.
- **Food cravings involve endorphin release.** Beta-endorphins are associated with overeating in genetically obese mice and rats. In humans, administration of naloxone, an opiate antagonist, suppressed consumption of sweet, fat foods for binge eaters but not in nonbingers. Overall food intake was not reduced (Drewnowski, Krahn, Demitrack, Nairn, & Gosnell, 1992). Since not all obese individuals overeat on highly palatable foods, the endorphin hypothesis does not account for all obesity.

How can weight be controlled?   The best way to control weight is to back away from the dining table sooner. In addition, regular exercise helps reduce the craving for food, making dieting easier. The problem is that some people cannot stay on diets, and will not exercise nor do anything else long enough to reduce weight significantly. Some kind of psychological intervention is called for when the simpler, more obvious solutions do not work. **Behavior therapy** appears to be the most successful psychological treatment and is now part of most obesity programs (Epstein, 1990). The behavioral approach assumes that, unless there is a true medical disorder, obesity is mainly a problem of bad eating habits and that the solution is to change these habits (Ferster, Nurnberger, & Levitt, 1962). Behavior therapy has been one of the major success stories of an area of laboratory animal research (operant conditioning) being applied to a significant human clinical problem. By 1983 behavioral programs had progressed to the point where the average weight loss was in the range of fifteen to twenty-five pounds.

Behavioral treatment is done in a graduated series of steps with the individual, may involve family members, and extends to general lifestyle problems in addition to eating. The first step is for the patient to keep track of when and how much she or he eats. This step alone is very useful, because many obese people simply do not realize how often they snack or "finish off a plate" before washing it. Can you remember everything you have eaten in the last twelve hours? The patient also keeps a careful record of her or his weight so that she or he will be reinforced for eating less by the satisfaction of seeing body weight go down. This process is not unlike standing in front of a mirror so that you can see your muscles bulge as you exercise. Eating is done only at specific times and places, such as in the dining room at mealtime, using a clean tablecloth and silverware. Doing this cuts down on snacking and eating right out of the refrigerator or cupboard. The patient may have a contract with the therapist, having to donate a specified amount of money to charity any week that the weight loss contract is not met. The behavior therapy approach is both effective and less dangerous than some of the faddish diets that have been promoted in best-selling books and touted on television. Medical treatment of some form may be required for any kind of weight disorder if the individual has reached a life-threatening weight level.

Anorexia Nervosa

Anorexia nervosa (self-starvation) is characterized by refusal to maintain an appropriate minimum body weight, intense fear of becoming fat (even though underweight), disturbance in the perception of one's own body size or shape (as being heavier than one actually is), and amenorrhea (absence of menstrual cycles). This self-starvation is seen mostly in intelligent young women who may take on the appearance of starved prisoners of war. The cause is not clear, but it is thought that they may be responding to social pressure to look thin and that in their own eyes, they may appear to look heavier than they actually are. Professional models and beauty pageant contestants weigh less than average for their height, and so if a women judges herself against such standards, she is likely to perceive herself as overweight.

The most effective treatment for anorexia again appears to be behavior therapy. The therapist rewards the client with whatever is effective only when the client eats. The reward may simply be to talk to the client when the client takes a bite of food. Opportunity for exercise is often an effective reward, which is rather surprising in light of the client's poor state of health.

Anorexia Bulimia

Anorexia bulimia is characterized by repeated episodes of binge eating (an inordinate amount of eating in a short period of time). Often called the **binge-purge syndrome,** bulimia is characterized by excessive eating followed by such inappropriate compensatory behaviors as self-induced vomiting, misuse of medications (e.g., laxatives), fasting, or excessive exercise (Garfinkel, 1995). During an average binge, a bulimic eats two to three thousand calories, usually of junk food. Persons of any weight, from anorectic to obese, may behave in this manner. The typical bulimic individual, however, is a slender female who is college educated and working, who may take care of a house and children, and who is highly achievement oriented. Bulimics may suffer from a number of serious health problems resulting from the repeated binge-purge cycle, such as ulcers and other intestinal difficulties. There may be dental problems, and the sudden chemical imbalances in the body caused by bingeing and purging may lead to heart attacks (Mitchell, 1986). Bulimics typically fear the shame and embarrassment of being caught binging or purging.

Although social factors seem obviously important in the etiology of both anorexia and bulimia, more basic physiological factors may also be involved. We know that taste plays a role because binging involves good-tasting foods. Therefore, taste abnormalities might be implicated in the development and/or maintenance of the disorder or might be produced by the disorder. With normal-weight subjects, hedonic ratings of sucrose typically decline following a high calorie lunch or drinking glucose, but do not decline for bulimics (Garfinkel, Molodofsky, and Garner, 1979; Rodin, Bartoshuk, Peterson, & Schank, 1990). This suggests that bulimics do not have the normal experience of satiation after eating. Whether this taste modification causes bingeing or results from purging is not known. The acid reflux from purging does damage taste receptors, which may facilitate purging by making it less obnoxious to taste. The binge-purge cycle is therefore made easier and more frequent and may affect satiety mechanisms.

The causes of bulimia are not clearly different from those of anorexia, and the most promising treatments are still behavioral. Close medical supervision may be required because of the bulimic's poor state of health.

SECTION SUMMARY

1. Obesity is a common eating problem whose causes are not well understood, but that may involve genetic and taste factors. Obese individuals may not be sensitive to the "stop cues" for feeding in the same way that "normal weight" individuals are. The most successful weight loss programs involve **behavior therapy.**

2. Several hypotheses proposed to account for obesity are **different taste preferences** for obese individuals, **set-point theory** (people have different biologically determined weight levels), a **genetic susceptibility** to obesity, and greater release of **endorphins** in obese individuals. Behavior therapy is the most successful treatment for obesity.

3. **Anorexia nervosa** and **bulimia nervosa** are eating disorders most commonly found in young, well-educated women. In the former, eating is so reduced that the individual may become emaciated. In the latter, there are periodic eating **binges** followed by **vomiting** and **dieting.** Again, the most successful treatments have been behavior therapies.

CHAPTER FIVE

Thirst, Temperature Regulation, Addiction, and Reproduction

What happens to us if we don't get enough water?

How do we keep a constant amount of water in our bodies?

How do we know when to start and stop drinking?

How does the brain control drinking?

How do our bodies respond to excesses of heat and cold?

How does body temperature affect hunger and thirst?

Is fever good for us?

What is drug addiction?

What kinds of drugs are most commonly addicting?

What brain systems are involved in addiction?

What is the difference between sexual arousal and arousability?

What produces sexual arousal?

What role do hormones play?

How is emotion related to sex?

What are the characteristics of the human sexual response?

Do we know what causes homosexuality?

The combination of motives presented in this chapter may seem unusual to the reader. However, they have the following in common: (1) they are powerful determinants of behavior; (2) all but addiction are necessary for survival, of the species as well as the individual; and (3) they all have a powerful hedonic component. From the hedonic point of view of that we have taken overall, each of the motives discussed here affects approach and avoidance behaviors and the common underlying neurological systems for these, as discussed in Chapters One and Two.

THIRST AND DRINKING

Our bodies are 60 to 70 percent water, and we begin to get thirsty with as little as a 1 to 2 percent loss of body fluid. People may survive for weeks without food, but in a hot, dry environment a person without water may die most unpleasantly within hours. Our bodies do not store surplus water nor can we completely halt its loss as it evaporates when we breathe and perspire, or when we urinate. Without sufficient water, our bodies become a hostile and deadly environment for the cells within. How then do we maintain the right amount of body fluid?

Different species have solved the problem of regulating the amount of body water in different ways. Some desert animals, such as the kangaroo rat, can metabolize water from dry seeds and survive without ever drinking, but most land animals do rely on drinking to replenish body fluids. Water consumption, whether by drinking water or other fluids, or by obtaining water in food, is the way humans control the body's water supply. The factors influencing how we get fluid are, however, as variable as those for getting food. Drinking is not controlled just by some homeostatically determined need for a certain amount of water (Rowland, 2002; Toates, 1979). We divide drinking into two types. First, there is **regulatory drinking**, which is in direct response to need for water. Second, there is **nonregulatory drinking**, which is in response to other factors rather than immediate water need.

Regulatory Drinking

What cues tell us to start drinking? Animals can be induced to drink or to work for water, by water deprivation, eating dry food, working in a hot environment, consuming excess salt, or losing blood. It would seem, however, that there must be some smaller number of internal start cues activated by these various conditions. Contemporary theory is dominated by the **double depletion hypothesis**, which says that there are two independent mechanisms for stimulating us to drink. The first depends on what happens to the fluid within cells, an **intracellular mechanism**. The second depends on changes in the volume of body fluid, an **extracellular mechanism**.

The osmotic gradient: an intracellular mechanism. Body fluids are normally about 0.9 percent salt, and if a more concentrated solution is injected into an animal, it drinks. This occurs without any change in the amount of water in the body. In Figure 5–1 we see a body cell and its **intracellular fluid** surrounded by **extracellular fluid**, which is all body fluids not found inside cells. When salt is put into the extracellular fluid, water is pulled by osmosis from the less concentrated fluid inside the cell to the more concentrated extracellular fluid. Water easily passes through the cell membrane, but salt does not. Gilman (1937) demonstrated that the *difference* in concentration inside and outside the cell was critical for drinking. He injected dogs with urea, a substance that readily passes into the cell so that there is an equal increase in concentration both inside and outside the cells. Urea produced very little drinking, whereas injections of saline produced a lot. Specialized brain cells, called **osmoreceptors**, are thought to detect the concentration difference and signal the brain to initiate appropriate action.

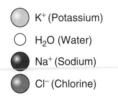

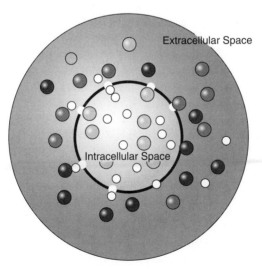

FIGURE 5–1. Intracellular and extracellular water spaces. Small water molecules easily move across the cell membrane to and from the intracellular space. Potassium ions are trapped inside the cell, and sodium and chlorine ions are kept outside. If water is lost from the extracellular space, there is a higher concentration of sodium and chloride, so that water moves from inside the cell to outside the cell by the process of osmosis. The cell therefore shrinks and provides a stimulus to drinking.

Any mechanical distortion of the osmoreceptors may trigger drinking, however. If salts are removed from the extracellular space, water moves into the cell and makes it swell and triggers drinking. This process can lead to a condition called **water intoxication**, characterized by excessive drinking and urination, and mental aberration. The treatment, paradoxically, is to give the patient more salt. The water then leaves the cells, which return to normal size, and excessive drinking is no longer stimulated.

Where are the osmoreceptors?   The hypothalamus and surrounding areas are crucial to water regulation, which involves conservation of water as well as increased intake. In the normal animal, the **supraoptic nucleus** of the hypothalamus manufactures **antidiuretic hormone** (**ADH**), which is released when the animal is water deprived. This hormone increases the rate of reabsorption of water from the kidneys, so that less is lost by excretion. Without ADH, the animal urinates excessively and has to drink excessively to make up the loss, a clinical condition known as **diabetes insipidus** (Ranson, Fischer, & Ingram, 1938). Direct injections of very small quantities of saline into the hypothalamus induce voracious drinking (Andersson, 1952). A one-milliliter (1/1000 of a liter) injection of 15 percent saline may induce a goat to drink a gallon of water. Drinking can be elicited also by electrical stimulation of the hypothalamus and limbic system, as well as by various drugs placed in small quantity into the limbic system (e.g., Fisher, 1964). There are also osmoreceptors in the gut as well as the brain. Since such solutes as sodium enter the body through the gut, receptors for osmotic change are stimulated very quickly and do not have to wait on changes in circulating blood as the central osmoreceptors do (Rowland, 2002). This means that osmotic changes in the gut can produce very rapid changes in the regulation of body water, including drinking.

Fluid volume: the extracellular mechanism.   Thirst often accompanies blood loss, vomiting, or diarrhea, even though these do not change osmotic pressure (Wolf, 1958). Fitzsimmons (1972) and others have shown that if the blood supply to the kidneys is reduced, drinking increases. This condition occurs if the aorta is tied off above the renal arteries (which carry blood to the kidneys) or if the vena cava (going directly to the heart) is blocked. There appear to be independent sets of pressure receptors in the heart and in the renal blood supplies (Carlson, 1980). These receptors may send direct signals to the brain, but they also initiate a major chemical mechanism. When the venous pressure drops, the kidneys release **renin** into the bloodstream, which is in effect a "thirst hormone." The renin reacts with another substance to form **angiotensin**, which acts on brain receptors to incite drinking. Injected directly into the brain, angiotensin is the most powerful stimulus to drinking yet found. The location of the brain receptors for angiotensin has provided a lively dispute among those interested in the problem, but the two prime candidates (the **subfornical organ** and the **organum vascularis of the lamina terminalis**) both lie near the ventricles of the brain, in the vicinity of the hypothalamus.

What cues tell us when to stop drinking?   According to the homeostatic model, an animal should stop drinking when it has drunk enough water to offset its deficit. In support of this, after injections of saline that increase salt concentration in the body, rats accurately drink enough to dilute the injected saline to normal body-fluid concentration (Corbit, 1969; Rowland, 2002). There must be some kind of "meter" running to tell the animal when it has had enough and to stop drinking. There is no specific brain area yet known to be a satiety area for drinking, but there are several possible cues for the animal.

Mouth metering.   If a normal dog is deprived of water, it offsets its water deficit with nearly 100 percent accuracy by drinking. If a fistula (tube) is inserted into the esophagus of the dog so that ingested water runs out of the tube and does not reach the stomach, the dog may drink twice as much as it needs to offset its deficit. Its intake is still proportional to the number of hours it has been without water, however (Bellows, 1939). This tells us that the process of lapping and swallowing water are one stop mechanism, but cannot be the only one. There is evidence for water receptors in the mouth (Nicholaidis, 1968),

Stomach distention.   To determine if a "full" (distended) stomach might be a cutoff cue for drinking, Towbin (1949) put balloons into the stomachs of thirsty dogs. He found that as more air was pumped into the balloon, the dog drank less. On the other hand, if a thirsty dog had enough water tubed directly into its stomach to offset its deficit, it would immediately drink the same amount of water all over again. It is as if the dog did not know that water had been put into its stomach. If drinking were delayed for just a few minutes after tubing water into the stomach, however, the animal did not drink. This whole sequence is just the opposite of how stomach distention should work as a cutoff mechanism. If distention were the cue, the animal should not drink just after tubing when distention is greatest but should drink after a delay. Stomach distention does not then seem to be a major cue for cutting off drinking, in the dog at least. Water by itself is not actually very good for producing distention because water drains through the stomach very quickly as the animal drinks.

Reversal of the initiating stimulus.   Water ingestion has often been thought to cease before there is time to reverse the stimulus that triggered drinking. In fact, however, about 25 percent of water tubed into the stomach of the rat is absorbed within fifteen minutes (e.g., O'Kelly & Beck, 1960). Novin (1962) recorded changes in electrical resistance of fluids in the region of the hypothalamus and found them to change within ten minutes of the onset of drinking by the rat. In other words, water was getting from the intestine to the brain within ten minutes, several minutes before the rats voluntarily stopped drinking. Reversal of the initiating stimulus, then, may be another cutoff cue.

Nonregulatory Drinking

Why do we get thirsty when we eat?   Eating and drinking usually occur together. In the normal animal, insulin is released upon eating, and the insulin, in turn, stimulates the release of **histamine** from endocrine-like cells in the gastric lining. Histamine receptors in the intestines are activated, and drinking occurs (Kraly, 1984). **Serotonin**, another neurotransmitter, may also be released when the rat eats, and it also stimulates drinking in its own right. Histamine and serotonin effects on drinking are due to two independent mechanisms that together produce greater drinking than either by itself (Kraly, Simansky, Coogan, & Trattner, 1985). The histamine and serotonin effects are eliminated if the **vagus** nerve from the stomach is cut, so that there is no signal from the stomach to the brain via the autonomic nervous system.

The importance of taste.   The rat can regulate its water balance without smelling or tasting water, by pressing a lever that produces a squirt of water directly into its stomach (Teitelbaum & Epstein, 1962). A normal animal, however, does have taste and smell to guide it, and behavioral studies show that these are important in water-regulatory behavior. Humans can reduce their need to drink water by consuming soft drinks, for example, which are ingested primarily for taste. Thus, taste indirectly serves to maintain homeostasis.

For an animal not water deprived or not eating, water does not seem to be very palatable, and animals do not drink much of it. If nonthirsty rats are forced to lap water from a tube to avoid shock, they let the water dribble out of their mouths without really swallowing it (Williams & Teitelbaum, 1956). Neal Miller (1959) developed what he called the "quinine test" for thirst. If thirsty animals have their drinking water adulterated with a small amount of quinine, they drink less. The more water deprived they are, the more quinine they will tolerate. We might conjecture, then, that when an animal is thirsty, water tastes better, and the "good" taste overcomes the "bad" taste of quinine. Water-deprived animals consume water avidly and show less of a preference for sugar water over plain water (Beck & Bidwell, 1974; Beck, Nash, Viernstein, & Gordon, 1972; Sclafani & Nissenbaum, 1987). Under some conditions water may even be preferred to sugar solution (Cohen & Tokieda, 1972). Recall, also, that LH-lesioned animals early in their recovery drink only sweet solutions, as if a mechanism for making water taste good to the normal animal had been impaired. We begin to piece together the picture of an animal that generally finds water not very palatable until it becomes thirsty. Desire for water then overrides the bitterness of quinine and competes with the sweetness of sugar.

Mouth cooling.   Both rat and human data suggest that mouth cooling is a major factor in drinking. Mendelson and Chillag (1970) found that thirsty rats would lick at a drinking spout that delivered a stream of cool air instead of water. Boulze, Montatruc, and Cabanac (1983) studied the effect of water temperature on both the pleasantness ratings of water and the amount consumed by dehydrated humans. Subjects either were sweating profusely or had been mountain climbing. As water temperature increased from 32°F to 56°F, the subjects drank more, but above 56° intake went down as temperature increased. Water never became more pleasant with temperatures above 56° and was considered unpleasant at higher temperatures.

Ecology, effort, and satiation.   A simple regulatory theory would say that animals should drink until they restore water balance, but a more ecologically oriented argument takes other factors into account. Thus even when there is an unlimited supply of water available, rats consistently drink less when more effort is required to obtain the water (Toates, 1979, 2001). For example, if animals have to press a lever to obtain water, they take less water when more presses are required. Similarly, if thirsty rats are required to run six feet to obtain each sip of water, they give up on running after obtaining far less water than animals required to run only two feet (O'Kelly & Beck, 1960). The amount of water required to "satiate" an animal therefore depends on such factors as effort and taste, not just the amount of water needed to offset a deficit.

Do Animals Learn to Avoid Getting Thirsty?

Fitzsimmons and LeMagnen (1969) reported data suggesting that rats learn to anticipate the osmotic water deficit that results from eating thirst-arousing food. Specifically, they shifted rats from a high-carbohydrate (low thirst-arousal) diet to a high-protein (high thirst-arousal) diet. In the first few days, the animals drank more after the meal but gradually began to drink more during the meal, as if anticipating thirst. This finding suggests that animals learn behaviors that prevent a departure from homeostasis so that homeostatic mechanisms do not come into play as strongly, much as Woods (1991) proposed for eating.

SECTION SUMMARY

1. We must maintain our bodies at about 70 percent water in the face of the fact that we continually lose water through evaporation or urination. In most mammals, body water is restored or maintained by drinking and by eating foods with water in them.

2. According to the **double-depletion theory** of thirst, drinking is initiated by **intracellular** and **extracellular** changes. The intracellular cues to drinking result from increased salt concentration of body fluids outside the cells. This is detected by **osmoreceptors** in the hypothalamus, which trigger water conservation as well as drinking. The extracellular mechanism involves activation of **pressure receptors** in the vascular system. Reduced pressure triggers a chemical reaction, which leads to stimulation of hypothalamic cells by a chemical called **angiotensin**, which elicits drinking behavior. Drinking is also stimulated by **histamine** and **serotonin**, which are released when food is ingested.

3. Drinking is terminated by stop cues from the mouth and stomach, and by absorption of water, which turns off the cues that initiated drinking. Termination of drinking is also determined by such behavioral factors as the amount of effort required to get water, not just amount of water consumed.

4. An important **nonregulatory** factor in drinking is the palatability of fluid which seems to involve cooling as well as taste. People or animals may drink enough tasty fluids to forestall serious thirst. Animals may learn to drink to prevent dehydration, as well.

REGULATION OF BODY TEMPERATURE

Temperature regulation is important because temperature plays a major role in the chemical reactions necessary for life. Physiologically, the proper utilization and transfer of substances within the body, including nerve transmission, involve chemical reactions that can only occur within an appropriate temperature range. Psychologically, extremes of temperature in either direction are unpleasant, and we spend a great deal of effort and money to reduce such unpleasantness. The largest electrical energy use of the year comes during summer heat waves when air conditioning is at its peak. Indeed, a major factor in the improved economy of the south after World War II was the availability of air conditioning, as it also is in desert towns such as Las Vegas or Phoenix. The second largest electricity use is in winter cold spells. In hedonic terms, when we are cold, warmth is pleasant, and when we are hot, coolness is pleasant. This was clearly demonstrated in an experiment where human subjects had their body temperatures raised or lowered by immersion in a temperature-controlled bath. Once their temperatures had stabilized above, below, or at normal temperature (98.6°F) they immersed their hands into water of varying temperature and rated the pleasantness of the hand bath. Figure 5–2 summarizes the results (Mower, 1976). In the neutral condition, hand-bath temperatures either above or below body temperature were unpleasant. However, when the subjects were cold, higher temperatures were more pleasant, but when they were warm, the same temperatures became unpleasant.

In the face of extreme temperatures, we all know of the failures of temperature regulation, death by freezing or death by heatstroke. In fact, how-

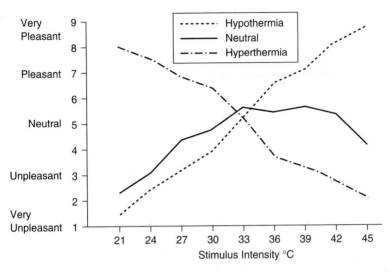

FIGURE 5–2. Body Temperature and Thermal Pleasantness. Thermal pleasantness of water baths as a function of stimulus temperature under three conditions of internal body temperature. (*Source:* From "Perceived Intensity of Peripheral Thermal Stimuli Is Independent of Internal Body Temperature" by G. D. Mower, 1976, *Journal of Comparative and Physiological Psychology,* 90, Figure 2a, p. 1154. Copyright 1976 by American Psychological Association. Reprinted by permission.)

ever, these are rare events, and animals and people survive surprisingly well in extreme environments. Polar land animals survive in subzero temperatures, and sea animals survive in subfreezing waters (because of its salt content, sea water freezes below 32° F). A combination of anatomical characteristics (such as body insulation with fat or fur), homeostatic mechanisms, and behaviors, combine to keep body temperature within the range required for survival.

Cold-blooded animals, such as fish, amphibians, and reptiles, are **poikilothermic**, which is to say that their body temperature is usually just slightly higher than that of the surrounding environment. Warm-blooded animals, such as mammals and birds, are **homeothermic**, maintaining a nearly constant internal temperature in spite of changing environmental temperature. The "constant" temperature actually fluctuates regularly with the time of day in accordance with the circadian rhythm of the animal, the so-called biological clock. Many of our body processes wax and wane with approximately a twenty-four-hour cycle. The "normal" temperature for humans is slightly higher in the afternoon (about 37°C) than during the night (about 36° C) (Kalat, 1995). A constant body temperature also permits animals to be equally active at many different environmental temperatures. Cold-blooded animals are more sluggish when the temperature is low.

Mechanisms of Temperature Regulation

One of the body's first rules of temperature regulation is to protect the brain and vital organs at the expense of peripheral parts. When the temperature goes down, peripheral blood vessels contract so that less blood is exposed to cold air and less heat is lost. We are all aware that our fingers and hands get cold before our bodies do, sometimes with frostbite resulting. About half of our body cooling occurs from exposure of the head and neck to the environment; hence, the admonishment, if your hands get cold, put on a hat. Cold hands are a signal that body temperature is going down, and covering the head slows down the loss of body heat. Other responses of the body include generation of heat by shivering and fluffing of the fur (with furry animals).

When we get too hot, the opposite reactions occur. Peripheral blood vessels expand so that more blood passes under the surface of the skin and is cooled, and we perspire so that we are cooled further as the perspiration evaporates. Cats lick their fur and cool themselves by evaporation of the saliva. Dogs cool primarily by evaporation from the mouth and tongue when they pant.

Brain mechanisms of thermoregulation. The hypothalamus plays a major role in thermoregulation, just as it does in hunger and thirst. The **preoptic area** of the hypothalamus monitors body temperature and activates homeostatic mechanisms for raising or lowering temperature. If a device called a thermode is inserted into the preoptic nucleus, thermoregulatory mechanisms can be manipulated experimentally. The thermode can be warmed or cooled, thereby fooling the preoptic nucleus into believing that the whole body is warming or cooling. The body has different receptors for detecting warm and detecting cold, and these activate different responses. If the thermode is cooled, an animal shivers; if the thermode is warmed, the animal pants or perspires. These effects occur within a constant laboratory environment. If the preoptic nucleus is damaged, animals do not show appropriate thermoregulation and have large fluctuations (e.g., 10° C) in body temperature. In addition to the preoptic nucleus, there are also temperature receptors in the skin, spinal cord, and areas of the brain other than the hypothalamus.

Eating and drinking are also affected by temperature regulatory systems. When the preoptic nucleus is cooled, animals eat more and drink less, but when it is warmed, they drink more and eat less. Reduced food intake in warm environments may occur because the digestion of food generates an increase in body temperature that may be uncomfortable.

The preoptic nucleus seems to fit the ideal model of a thermostat which is set at 37° C. If the temperature goes down, the preoptic nucleus instigates warming activities; if temperature goes up, cooling activities are instigated. A problem for this notion (Satinoff, 1983) is that when there is preoptic damage so severe that shivering, sweating, or other automatic mechanisms do not go into action, animals will still maintain body temperature behaviorally. In the laboratory, for example, they will learn to press a lever to warm or cool themselves. This means that thermoregulation is not destroyed, only that one aspect of it is changed (Satinoff, 1983).

Thermoregulatory behavior. Within limits, warm-blooded animals can maintain constant body temperature with homeostatic mechanisms, but what happens in more extreme environments? Poikilothermic animals have only their behavior to fall back on, so they protect themselves by moving to warmer or cooler environments. Fish can move to shallower or deeper water to warm or cool, and desert reptiles can move about seeking sunnier or shadier spots. Some desert animals, having to face extreme temperature differences between night and day, burrow into the ground at night and slowly come out into the sun in the morning. As the day heats up, they burrow again to keep cool.

Satinoff (1983) points out that psychologists generally think of behavior as being more complicated than homeostatic regulatory mechanisms but that physiologists often think of behavior as being simpler. In the case of thermoregulation, Satinoff says (1983, pp. 461–462), "the responses to thermal stress are many and varied, but in the beginning was behavior . . . all species tested, from insects through humans, show behavioral temperature selection." Even single-celled organisms show **thermotaxis**, moving toward or away from areas of extreme water temperatures to areas of more moderate temperatures. There is no simpler response.

Organization of Thermoregulatory Responses

Satinoff (1983) argues against the notion that there is a single "thermostat" in the preoptic nucleus because there is simply too much evidence to the contrary. What the preoptic nucleus does in the normal course of events is organize or integrate the activities of a number of different thermoregulatory responses, including behavioral. If the preoptic nucleus is made inoperative, these specific thermoregulatory responses are still available, and thermoregulation can still occur. For example, shivering may not occur, but moving to a warmer location may occur.

Satinoff also points out that thermoregulatory mechanisms did not evolve only to control temperature. Panting, for example, cools a running dog but also increases the amount of oxygen consumed, needed to sustain the effort of running. Alligators also have greater heat loss if their mouths are open than if they are closed, a variation on dog panting. Such variation suggests that there is no reason to believe that a single thermoregulatory center in the brain should have evolved. Rather, various specific responses evolved.

Individually these responses may operate at the level of the spinal cord, but they also came under the control of higher brain centers, such as the hypothalamus. Destruction of the higher control centers does not destroy the responses, it just destroys their integrated control system. Thermoregulation can and does still occur; however, it does not occur as a single response that is turned on by a hypothalamic thermostat.

Fever

When we feel sick, one of the first things we are likely to do is take our temperature to determine how serious the illness is. If oral temperature is much above 98.6°F (37°C), we consider seeking medical aid. With infants, one of our first actions is to try to reduce the body temperature, for example, by washing the baby with lukewarm water. But why does temperature go up at all when we are sick? Fever is not the illness—it is a symptom of the body's response to infections by viruses or bacteria. When foreign substances enter the body, white blood cells are mobilized to fight those substances. The white blood cells (**leukocytes**) release a protein called **leukocytic pyrogen**, which causes production of **prostaglandin E**, which acts on the preoptic nucleus to increase body temperature.

Does a fever in itself do us any good? Again, temperature is an important variable in chemical reactions, and some bacteria grow less well at elevated body temperatures (Kluger & Rottenberg, 1979). Therefore, fever may have direct value in fighting disease. From a strictly motivational point of view, however, fevers (or the conditions with which they are associated) are usually unpleasant, and we do all we can to get rid of them. At the same time, we may lose our appetite or the energy to engage in other motivated activities.

SECTION SUMMARY

1. In order for animals to survive, their body temperatures must be protected, sometimes in the face of extreme shifts in environmental temperature. **Cold-blooded animals** have the same temperature as the surrounding environment and regulate temperature by selecting temperature-friendly environments. **Warm-blooded animals** keep the same temperature in spite of changes in environment, utilizing a combination of behavioral and homeostatic mechanisms.

2. When temperature drops, heat is first conserved for the internal organs of warm-blooded animals by constriction of peripheral blood vessels. When temperature rises, these vessels expand, which facilitates heat loss through the skin.

3. The **preoptic area** of the hypothalamus monitors body temperature and activates homeostatic mechanisms for raising or lowering temperature. The preoptic nucleus seems to organize a number of different thermoregulatory responses, both homeostatic and behavioral. If there is damage to part of the system, other parts can still function. Most thermoregulatory responses (e.g.,

panting in dogs) are also parts of other functions (e.g., getting more oxygen), so that thermoregulation can be maintained in the normal course of other events.

4. **Fever** occurs when white blood cells stimulate the release of **prostaglandin E,** which acts on the hypothalamus to increase body temperature. Increased temperature may directly help fight disease by altering the body's chemical reactions to viruses or bacteria.

DRUG ADDICTION

A drug addict has an overwhelming craving for the drug to which he or she is addicted, and this craving can be a two-headed motivational monster. Initially the addict may seek the pleasure produced by the drug, but then must seek relief from the pain and torment of not having the drug. These tandem motivational factors make it difficult to break away from even a life-threatening addiction. The two primary classes of addicting drugs are the central nervous system **depressants** and **excitants.** The major addictive depressants are **alcohol, barbiturates, tranquilizers**, and **opiates**. The major excitants are **amphetamines** and the various forms of **cocaine. Caffeine** and **nicotine** are less potent addictive excitatory drugs. Although drug addictions are hardly new, the need to study and treat them has assumed a new importance because the use of cocaine in its various forms has dramatically increased. Addictions to opium, morphine, heroin, and alcohol have been around longer, but are still major problems. The brain mechanisms involved in drug addiction have a great deal of overlap with those involved in feeding. The so-called hallucinogenic drugs, which produce bizarre perceptual experiences, are not generally addictive.

One of the great paradoxes of pharmacology is that the very drugs that produce the greatest relief from suffering can themselves produce some of the greatest suffering. The opiate drug morphine not only is one of the most powerful drugs for the relief of pain but also has some of the greatest abuse potential, along with other opiates (such as heroin) that are completely illegal. This association between analgesia and abuse potential provides major clues as to the nature of pleasure and of pain and its relief.

General Principles of Drug Action

How drugs influence neural transmission.   A **neurotransmitter** is a chemical released at the synapse by one neuron to affect the activity of another neuron when it goes to a receptor site on the receiving neuron. The neurotransmitter is stored in the **axon** of the neuron until released. Following release, any excess transmitter substance is either broken down chemically in the synapse and/or reabsorbed into the axon. Of the fifty or so different neurotransmitters, the most commonly known are **adrenaline, noradrenaline, acetylcholine, serotonin, dopamine**, and the **endorphins**. The neurotransmitter effect may be excitatory (causing other neurons to "fire") or inhibitory (making it harder for other neurons to fire).

A particular drug affects the process by which neurotransmitters function in one of several possible ways. Some drugs have chemical structures similar to those of naturally occurring transmitters. These drugs mimic the effect of the transmitter and "fool" the receptor neuron into firing. Heroin may do this by mimicking the endogenous neurotransmitters, the endorphins. Or just the opposite, a drug might block out the neurotransmitter substance and prevent the neuron from being fired. Maisto, Galizio, and Connors (1991) list eight different ways by which a drug may alter normal neural activity: (1) the increase or decrease of synthesis of neurotransmitters, (2) interference with the transport of neurotransmitter molecules to the axon terminals, (3) interference with the storage of neurotransmitters in the axon terminal, (4) the production of premature release of neurotransmitters into the synapse, (5) influencing the breakdown of neurotransmitters by enzymes, (6) blocking the reuptake of neurotransmitters into the axon terminals, (7) the activation of a receptor site through mimicry, and (8) blocking a receptor site. Which of these specific actions of drugs will occur and what will be the psychological effects depend on what parts of the brain are affected.

Nonspecific Factors Affecting Drug Actions

In addition to the specific effects that different drugs have, there are nonspecific effects that apply to many different kinds of drugs. For example, drug effects may be modified by such organismic variables as age, size, sex, biological rhythms, genetics, diet, personality, or general state of health. Two drugs taken at or near the same time may interact with unexpected results. They may cancel each other out, have much more powerful effects than just adding their individual potency, have toxic effects, or have no effect at all. As a rule, drugs that have similar psychological effects add together. Central nervous system depressant drugs, for example, have additive effects.

Repeated administrations of the same drug may lead to **tolerance**, so that larger doses of the same drug are required to produce the same effect, or **cross-tolerance**, so that drugs of the same general class, such as central nervous system depressants, produce a tolerance for other drugs in the same class. For example, barbiturates would produce a cross-tolerance for alcohol.

The environmental conditions under which drugs are taken may influence the perceived effects of drugs. Lighting, music, odors, or social interactions may influence drug effects. Three beers at a party would probably have a very different effect than the same three beers in a hospital waiting room, a sterile research lab, or a police station. Our expectations of what a drug should do may have a powerful influence on its actual effect. This tendency is generally called the **placebo effect**. Virtually all drug research controls for placebo effects by the use of **double-blind procedures** so that neither the person getting the drug nor the person administering the drug know what the drug is. The subject might be getting a real drug or a placebo (e.g., a substance that looks, feels, and tastes just like the drug but that is inert—such as a sugar pill). Only if the drug shows a stronger effect than the placebo can we conclude that there is a drug-specific effect.

Through the process of classical conditioning, stimuli associated with drug administration can become conditioned stimuli for drug effects. For example, a drug addict may have addiction symptoms conditioned to environmental stimuli, people, or drug paraphenalia so that the craving for the drug is heightened in the presence of these stimuli. Such conditioned stimuli make it difficult to get addicts off a drug. A drug addict may be "cured" in a hospital and then may quickly relapse when sent back to the same cue-rich environment where the addiction originally occurred.

How Do We Identify Addiction?

Addiction is generally defined by two major symptoms, **tolerance** and **withdrawal**. Tolerance means that more of the drug must be taken to produce the same effect, usually a pleasant or exciting experience. Withdrawal symptoms are feelings and physiological effects opposite of whatever the addicting substance produces and occur if the addicted substance is withheld. If a person is addicted to a drug that excites the central nervous system, such as amphetamine, the withdrawal symptoms are a depression of central nervous system activity. Some of the most addictive drugs are central nervous system depressants, the barbiturates, once commonly used as sleeping pills. A person who had never taken the drug before would normally become sleepy with a single tablet. If the drug were taken repeatedly, however, an increasingly larger dose would be required to produce the same degree of sleepiness, the tolerance effect. If an addicted person were suddenly to stop taking the drug altogether, great central nervous system excitation—including possible seizures and death—would occur.

Theories of Addiction

Opponent process theory.   The basic principle of the theory (Solomon, 1980; Solomon & Corbit, 1974; Chapter Two here) is that when the circumstances producing a strong emotion are removed, a person does not just feel neutral, but feels the opposite emotion. If the person has been feeling joyous, then she feels sad. If the person has been feeling depressed or afraid, then she feels happy. This theory has been used to account for tolerance and withdrawal aspects of drug addictions.

Suppose a person takes a "recreational" drug that makes him feel euphoric. He gradually requires more of the drug to get the same good feeling, and then the drug supply is cut off. Without the drug he feels very bad, very depressed, and very ill. His new experience is just the opposite of that which he felt while taking the drug, but it is just as much determined by the drug as the earlier good experiences were. According to opponent process theory, with successive drug experiences, the negative effect of the drug becomes stronger and stronger until it begins to cancel out the positive emotional experience. This effect is the opponent process beginning to work. A stronger stimulus (more drug) is needed to produce the same level of positive emotion or excitement previously experienced. This is the development of tolerance. When the positive effect of the drug wears off, the opponent process, the negative effect, persists and is so strong that the addicted person feels he must have the drug to relieve this unpleasant experience, the withdrawal symptoms. So, a vicious cycle develops: The more the drug is taken, the greater the tolerance, and the more unpleasant the opponent process when the drug wears off, and more drug is taken to reduce the withdrawal symptoms, and so on. When the addict goes off the drug, the system eventually comes back into "balance," unless permanent damage has occurred. With some drugs the addict has to be weaned off the drug gradually because the effect of sudden drug removal (going "cold turkey") may produce life-threatening effects.

The dopamine depletion hypothesis.   As we have seen, the dopamine system is closely related to pleasure. **Cocaine addiction** is hypothesized to occur in relation to dopamine depletion. Dackis and Gold (1985) outline the following sequence of events as a possible explanation for cocaine addiction. If cocaine is put into the body, it quickly migrates to neuron areas where dopamine is the neurotransmitter, those same areas that underlie the pleasurable effects of reward. The cocaine triggers the release of dopamine (producing the pleasurable experience) but also blocks the normal reuptake of dopamine into the neuron from the synapse. This process is illustrated in Figure 5–3. As the drug wears off, the brain has a shortage of the dopamine neurotransmitter, and there are some withdrawal effects because the brain cannot respond pleasurably to the stimuli that are normally effective. Consequently, there is a craving for more of the drug in order to re-create even normal pleasant experience. The addict may progress from "snorting" powdered drug up the nose to "freebasing," that is, dissolving the drug and injecting it. The euphoric "rush" from freebasing occurs literally within a few seconds of injection as it is carried to the brain via the bloodstream.

If the very strong craving of the addict is to be reduced, the brain must start manufacturing more dopamine while the addict is not using the drug. Of course, it is difficult for the addict to abstain, since the craving for the drug is so intense. The addict needs considerable social support for abstaining and freedom from temptations to use the drug lest immediate relapse occur. All sorts of stimuli (such as social situations in which the drug has been taken) may become conditioned stimuli to increase the craving and

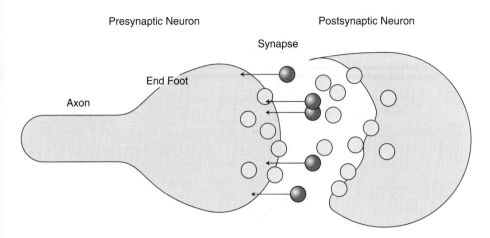

(a) Dopamine is released from the presynaptic neuron into the synapse and enters into the postsynaptic neuron. Some of the dopamine molecules are taken up from the synapse back into the presynaptic site.

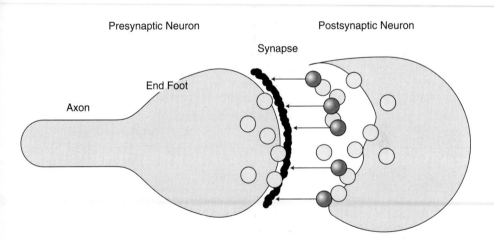

(b) Dopamine reuptake is blocked by cocaine so that dopamine remains more active in the synapse, heightening the effect of dopamine.

FIGURE 5–3.   Effect of cocaine at the synapse in the dopamine system.

lead to relapse. The power of cocaine is evidenced by several highly publicized examples of multimillion-dollar-a-year athletes whose careers have been ruined or jeopardized by cocaine addiction.

It is also likely that endorphins are involved in addictions (Kalat, 1995). In terms of brain chemistry, there may be multiple forms of addiction, but quite possibly all of them involve the endorphin system.

Sensitization theory.   This theory (Berridge & Robinson, 1995) takes into account the fact that some highly addictive drugs, most notably cocaine, do not have tolerance and withdrawal symptoms. For this reason, in spite of the great craving for the drug by people who take it, cocaine was long considered not to be addictive. Furthermore, people may not even like a drug that they work hard to get. Sensitization theory is based on the differences between liking and wanting that we have discussed. The idea is that the dopamine wanting system becomes sensitized to the drug and is more easily activated by taking the drug. In addition, cues from the addict's environment become conditioned stimuli signaling that a wanted substance is available. This further activates the wanting (craving) for the drug and behaviors to get the drug. With lesions in the dopamine system, animals do not respond to these learned signals, although they show the signs of liking. In the case of abused substances (e.g., cocaine and heroin), the brain is sensitized to the wanting cues, so that animals (or people) will do all kinds of things to get the drug (wanting) even though they may not like it after they get it. Thus, drug addiction involves an increase in wanting without necessarily involving liking.

A major point of this sensitization theory of addiction is that people are not necessarily conscious of the reasons why they seek a particular substance or why they like or dislike a particular substance. These systems operate at the level of the caudal brainstem, well below the level of consciousness. When a person says that he or she "just likes" something without knowing why, that is probably the truth. Evaluations of objects can take place, as we also saw in Chapter Two, without a person's necessarily being conscious of why.

SECTION SUMMARY

1. Drug addictions are usually defined by **tolerance** (more drug needed to obtain a particular level of effect) and **withdrawal symptoms** that are opposite to whatever the effect of the drug is. The most commonly addicted drugs are central nervous system **depressants** (including **alcohol**, **tranquilizers**, and **opiates**) and excitants (including **cocaine** and **amphetamines**). Addictive drugs operate through their effects on the dopamine and endorphin systems.

2. According to the **opponent process theory**, a drug has a particular effect (e.g., pleasurable) that is automatically followed by an unpleasant effect. With repeated exposures to a drug, the aftereffect (the opponent process) gets stronger and begins to cancel out the pleasurable experience, requiring a larger

dose of the drug. This effect is tolerance. If the drug is withheld, the opponent process is very active, producing the withdrawal symptoms.

3. According to the **dopamine depletion hypothesis** of cocaine addiction, cocaine triggers the release of dopamine (producing the pleasurable experience) but also blocks the normal reuptake of dopamine into the neuron from the synapse. The pleasurable effect produced by dopamine is therefore longer lasting.

4. According to the **Berridge-Robinson sensitization theory**, the parts of the brain involved in addiction (mainly, the dopamine system) become sensitized so that craving for a drug (wanting it) is readily aroused by environmental cues previously associated with the drug. A person can have such a craving for cocaine, for example, even though there are no withdrawal symptoms for cocaine.

REPRODUCTIVE BEHAVIOR

In terms of species survival, sex is as important as hunger or thirst. Sexual behavior, however, is not entirely "driven" by internal states any more than eating or drinking are entirely driven by internal states. Such external incentives as other people, pictures, or the written word play a major role in arousing and sustaining sexual motivation. We may presume that sex evolved into such a powerful motive because animals with higher levels of this motivation reproduced more and hence were favored by natural selection.

Sexual Arousal versus Sexual Arousability

It is important to distinguish between actually *being sexually aroused* (arousal) and the *potential to be aroused* (arousability; Whalen, 1966). Hormones or other internal factors (e.g., illness, fatigue) may set different levels of arousability at a particular time, but some stimulus triggers arousal. An animal not aroused with a particular partner may be easily aroused by a new partner. We would conclude that the animal was arousable, even though not aroused by the previous partner.

What Stimuli Are Important in Sexual Attraction?

Many different stimulus elements determine sexual attraction. Among birds, for example, there are complex courtship rituals. Male birds usually have more flamboyant plumage and coloration than females, and the males use these characteristics to attract females. Different species also have their own specific mating signals. Crickets have their calls, frogs have theirs, and mockingbirds have theirs. Obviously, however, these animals do not respond to calls of the other species. Mockingbirds are an unusual case of signaling. They have about five hundred different calls during mating season and a different five hundred calls during the "off" season. It is not clear just what they do with all the information-sending capacity, but it would seem to be sex-related.

Visual stimuli. Visual stimuli, whether from living people, photographs, drawings, or videotapes, are among the most potent sources of human sexual arousal. Many magazines, such as *Playboy* or the *Sports Illustrated* swimsuit issue, rely on the sexually exciting quality of more or less explicit nudity for their sales. The number of X-rated videotape rentals and pornography sites on the World Wide Web testify strongly to the value many people place on sexual arousal through visual stimulation. Goodson, McCormick, & Evans (2000) reported that a variety of different emotions were aroused by sexually explicit internet material.

Chemical stimuli. Some animals, such as moths, have powerful airborne chemical sex attractants called **pheromones** to entice potential mates. These are effective for distances as long as a half-mile. The effects of pheromones may depend on hormones in the recipient. For example, castration decreases a male hamster's interest in female odors (Gregory, Engle, & Pfaff, 1975). It appears that male sex hormones excite neural circuits in the amygdala so that these brain circuits respond to the odor of vaginal secretions (Carlson, 1987).

Smell plays a role in primate sexual behaviors, but there do not seem to be any pheromones that excite specific unlearned sexual behaviors in either humans or other primates (Carlson, 1987). Swabbing a female monkey with strange odors increases the interest of a male, even when the odor is like green peppers and bears little conceivable relation to normal sexual attraction. Such novel odors probably just arouse curiosity. Familiar odors may play a role in sexual attraction because they are associated with particular situations. Perfumes, for example, may be arousing to some people because (rightly or wrongly) they associate perfumes with availability for sex.

Touch. The skin is the largest sense organ of the human body, and touch is one of the most immediate triggers for sexual arousal. Being touched on any part of the body may produce arousal, but the genital areas of either sex are the most sensitive. Touching the body of a partner also triggers arousal in the person doing the touching.

Sexual fantasies. With or without the aid of pictures or other stimuli, sexual fantasies play a major role in sex. Romantic novels lacking explicit sexual passages may nevertheless produce sexual arousal because of the fantasies triggered by the story. Similarly, photographs have much of their impact because they trigger fantasies that go far beyond the photo content, such as the viewer's fantasizing having sex with the person in the picture. Such fantasies occur almost invariably with masturbation but also occur frequently during intercourse. Intercourse fantasies frequently involve a different partner than the one present at the moment or having other kinds of sex than that being engaged in at the moment (Sue, 1979).

Stimulus variation.   It is well-demonstrated with animals that stimulus variation plays a role in sexual attraction and even has a name, the **Coolidge Effect**. The story is that President and Mrs. Calvin Coolidge were taking a tour of a farm. Mrs. Coolidge observed that there was only one rooster but a hundred hens. One rooster is enough, she was told. "Tell that to Mr. Coolidge," she said. When told this, Mr. Coolidge asked whether the rooster served one hen a hundred times or a hundred hens once apiece. Informed that it was the latter, he said, "Tell that to Mrs. Coolidge." Under experimental conditions, male animals that have copulated to the point of exhaustion with a particular female partner will immediately resume their activity if a new partner is presented. In fact, Beamer, Bermant, and Clegg (1969) provided a ram with a new female after each ejaculation and found the animal able to ejaculate in less than two minutes with each of twelve different females. This response is not typical, even for a ram. What it tells us is that the "exhaustion" found with repeated intercourse is not just a physical inability to perform but that it involves a "psychological" factor, perhaps akin to boredom. Among humans, it is not uncommon to find that stimulus variation produces an increase in sexual activity. The variation may be in the form of time, place, behavior, or partner. Marriage counselors often recommend introducing variation into the love lives of clients who have "gotten in a rut" or seemed to have lost interest in each other.

Individual differences in sexual attraction.   There are individual differences in what appears sexually attractive to human males and females, and even with dogs. Frank Beach (1969) found that male beagles had reliable but different preferences for particular females but also that the females had their own preferences for certain males. Some females rejected the amorous advances of particular males even though other females accepted those same males. We do not know why the animals had the preferences they did, but it is clear that a mutual attraction between male and female had to be present before things progressed any further. We discuss interpersonal attraction in more detail in Chapter Fourteen.

Internal Factors

Among such "lower" mammals as rodents, arousability is largely determined by sex hormones, the **androgens** (primarily **testosterone**) in males and **estrogens** in females. Castrated farm animals lose their interest in sex and do not engage in sexual activity, and laboratory experiments clearly show the role of sex hormones. If castrated animals are given hormone replacement therapy (injections of testosterone), they resume sexual activity as long as the hormone lasts. Interest again wanes until further injections.

It is frequently stated that humans are less susceptible to hormone effects than other animals. Some men show considerable sexual activity at advanced ages when testosterone levels are very low. Human females are also sexually aroused and engage in sexual behavior after hormones have been reduced to very low levels, following menopause, for example. Pfaff & Ågmo (2002, p. 724), however, state that "Although it sometimes is maintained that human sexuality is less dependent on hormones than is sexuality in other animals, the truth of this idea is far from clear." Evidence suggests, for example, that females may be more sensitive to the loss of adrenal hormones whereas men are more sensitive to the loss of gonadal hormones. There may be differences in the behavior of humans and other animals that depend on such cognitive abilities as sexual fantasies for sexual arousal.

Other kinds of evidence also show that human sexual behavior is not fully determined by hormones. For example, a castrated male with female hormone replacement therapy would not act like a female just because of the particular hormone used. Conversely, testosterone treatment will not cause a woman to lose sexual interest in men (Carlson, 1987). Excessive exposure to androgens during the prenatal period has, however, been associated with somewhat different social characteristics in adult females. They consider themselves more "tomboyish" and are more athletic. But they also show the same level of satisfaction with a female sex role and its activities as control subjects not exposed to excessive androgen (Money & Ehrhardt, 1972). The interpretation of the androgen effects is itself questionable, however. Androgens may lead to greater physical activity and hence to more malelike behaviors (Carlson, 1994). None of these are "abnormal" behaviors and may be worthy of comment only because they don't fit a "feminine" stereotype. Women may engage in many nonstereotypical activities if given the opportunity and encouragement to do so. So may men.

Emotions and Sex

Positive emotion is obviously related to sex, but sometimes there are negative emotions, particularly anxiety and guilt. At some point in the history of humanity, it was apparently considered necessary to make certain sexual activities taboo, perhaps so that sex would be limited to reproduction that was necessary for social survival. Strong moral codes prohibiting such activities as masturbation, homosexuality, and artificial contraception developed. These are still major points of contention in such institutions as the Roman Catholic Church. The problems raised by these prohibitions are that situations may change, such as overpopulation rapidly overtaking the world, but the old rules are retained (Baron & Byrne, 1977). Each generation has to teach the next generation the "rules," and the teaching generation may not hold up its end of the bargain very well. For example, in its attempt to regulate sexual activities, the teaching generation may pass along such misinformation as that masturbation leads to insanity.

Because of differences in background and experience with sex, different people develop completely different attitudes about any given sexual activity. For example, Wallace and Wehmer (1972) found that people who were "sexually liberal" or "sexually conservative" were equally aroused by sexually explicit pictures of different activities. But whereas the "liberal" group considered the pictures entertaining, the "conservative" group considered them disgusting. Individuals who are more emotionally negative toward sex are also more restrictive in what they consider "permissible" sexual acts and in what they actually do in their own sex activity. The emotion of guilt seems to be particularly important; the greater the guilt associated with sex, the smaller the range of sexual activities a person is likely to engage in. People with strong negative emotions toward sex are also more likely to have difficulty in achieving successful orgasm, that is, frigidity in females and impotence in males. These are usually psychological problems rather than physical, and psychologists have devised a variety of therapies for successfully dealing with them.

Mosher & O'Grady (1979) studied sexual arousal to explicit films by subjects who were high or low in sex guilt and high or low in anxiety. High-sex guilt subjects reported fewer genital sensations and less sexual arousal, but more guilt, disgust, and anxiety than did low-sex guilt subjects. High-anxiety subjects reported more intense genital sensations and rated their sexual arousal higher following the films than did low-anxiety subjects.

The Human Sexual Response

The most dramatic breakthrough in human sexual research came with the pioneering studies by Masters and Johnson (1966). Using direct observation of behavior, as well as color cinematography and physiological recordings, they arrived at four phases of sexual responses that characterize both males and females. Not all of these occur with every individual, and some may be so brief that they are not noticed without the aid of recording instruments.

Excitement.   Sexual excitement may be produced by fantasy, looking at pictures, physical contact, or a variety of other stimuli. Nipple erection is common in females but also occurs in some males. There is sometimes a reddening of the skin of the chest and head, called a "sex tension flush." In females this may spread to lower parts of the body. Males show penile erection, which may occur in seconds (and reverse just as fast), and females have vaginal lubrication and thickening of the vaginal walls. Female breast size may begin to increase.

Plateau.   Arousal increases with sustained stimulation. There is an increased frequency of sex tension flush, general muscular tension, spasmodic movements of wrists and ankles, hyperventilation, and increased heart rate (100 to 160 beats per minute). Female breast size may increase as much as 25 percent above prestimulation baseline, along with other changes in the sex organs. The circumference of the corona of the penis may increase twofold, change to a purplish color, and emit from the Cowper's gland a fluid that deacidifies the interior of the penis, making a safer pathway for the sperm and providing lubrication.

Orgasm. At the peak of sexual excitement, there are specific muscle contractions, related to pelvic thrusting as well as to abdominal and facial muscles. In males there is contraction of the various accessory organs necessary for ejaculation. The female shows corresponding contractions of the uterus and genital area. The actual climax, expulsion of semen by the male and vaginal contraction by the female, takes only a few seconds, and once started is not under voluntary control. These are the fixed action patterns, or consummatory responses, discussed in Chapter Three. The behaviors leading up to them are highly variable, but the final responses are highly stereotyped.

Resolution. After climax there is often a sweating reaction by both male and female, but this is related to autonomic nervous system arousal and separate from physical exertion. There is also hyperventilation and high heart rate, which may largely be due to physical exertion. Males show a "refractory period," with reduced penile erection and a lower level of arousability. During this refractory period, which may last from minutes to hours, the male cannot readily be rearoused. Females, clearly showing the greater durability of their half of the species, can maintain continuously high levels of sexual arousal with no refractory period. A female may reach climax many times during a sexual episode, whereas the male climaxes only once.

The Masters and Johnson type of research has been criticized on the grounds that it deals only with the mechanical aspects of sex, ignoring the roles of love and affection. This criticism is true, and the reason is simple: Any research can deal with only a limited number of questions at a time. The Masters and Johnson research was not intended to answer all possible questions about interpersonal relations. Many other researchers have addressed those questions (Chapter Fourteen).

Sexual Orientation

Most people experience sexual attraction and arousal toward members of the opposite sex, but a significant minority (about 4 percent of males and 1 percent of females) are exclusively attracted to persons of the same sex. The percentages are higher if we include people who have a bisexual orientation (i.e., toward both sexes). Homosexuality has long been a hotly debated topic. It has been viewed as sinful, as deviant, as an illness, and as perfectly normal activity. What is clear is that the male homosexual population, for example, has a wide range of members whose only common characteristic seems to be homosexuality. The male homosexual is not necessarily effeminate. Alexander the Great of Macedonia, conqueror of the ancient world, was bisexual, and some stars of the National Football League have "come out" and reported themselves to be homosexual. Similarly, female homosexuals are not necessarily masculine in appearance or behavior. The great range of appearance and behavior among homosexuals is interestingly shown in the participants in gay parades or rallies.

The biological, psychological, and social factors that might affect sexual orientation have all been explored extensively, but thus far there is no single factor, or even a set of factors, known to produce heterosexuality or homosexuality (Kalat, 1995; Carlson, 1994). Indeed, it is just as reasonable to ask why someone is heterosexual as to ask why someone is homosexual. If the determinants of heterosexuality are found, so probably will be the determinants of homosexuality.

It contributes nothing toward answering the question to say that heterosexuality is "natural." All this tells us is that most people are heterosexual, but we already know that. It does not tell us why the majority are heterosexual. Supposed biblical exhortations against homosexuality (which may be matters of interpretation) are not much help, either. In spite of the protestations of the "moral majority," there is no evidence that homosexuality is just a "lifestyle choice" that can be "corrected" in the way that a person would shift his or her diet from French cuisine to Mexican.

What does the evidence indicate?

1. **Genetics.** Some evidence suggests a genetic predisposition toward homosexuality. In one study of male homosexuals, there were concordance ratios of 52 percent for monozygotic twins, 22 percent for dizygotic twins, and 11 percent for adopted brothers (Kalat, 1995), and similar ratios for female homosexuals. Self-reports of homosexual interest appear early in life and are not related to parental upbringing or any other known social factor. It should be noted that a concordance ratio of 52 percent for homosexuality in monozygotic twins also means that in 48 percent of twin pairs, one twin was homosexual and the other was not. Thus, there is no clear-cut biological basis in these data. In a family that had three pairs of identical twins, two pairs were homosexual, but the third pair were heterosexual. This finding would seem to eliminate environmental factors as sole determinants of homosexuality, since all the twins might be expected to be of the same sexual orientation if reared in the same family. The reason for searching for such biological factors is that social factors do not seem to account for homosexual orientation (Storms, 1983 a, b). There simply is no strong evidence that interpersonal relationships within a family, such as a domineering mother and a weak father, lead to male homosexuality.

2. **Hormones.** Homosexuality is not due to a preponderance of a particular hormone. A castrated male who is injected with female hormones does not become homosexual, nor does a female who is ovariectomized and given male hormones become homosexual. Homosexual males have normal levels of androgens, although two lines of evidence suggest the possibility of a hormonal factor. First, many homosexual men show a female type of hormonal response if injected with estrogen (Gladue, Green, & Hellman, 1984). Second, abnormally high levels of testosterone injected into a pregnant sheep at a critical time during gestation may produce a lesbian offspring (Money, 1987).

3. **Behaviors.** Carlson (1994) points out that homosexuals and heterosexuals engage in the same kinds of behaviors. It is just the sex of the object of those behaviors that is different. He speculates that there might be subtle differences in brains that are based on differences in sex hormones during prenatal development. These differences may then determine what is sexually attractive.

The best correlate of homosexuality is which sex a person says he or she is attracted to. This attraction may have partial biological (genetic) determination. Consider a couple of facts that we know about sexual behavior of animals. First, nonhumans show fluctuating interests in members of the opposite sex, related to variations in hormone level. Second, when attraction occurs, it is to members of one's own species, not to others. The latter point is so obvious as to be easily overlooked. If attraction were based solely on learning, we might expect more cross-species sexual activity than we seem to observe.

SECTION SUMMARY

1. Sex is a powerful biological motive for survival of the species. Sexual deprivation is not life-threatening but does involve complex interactions between environmental stimuli and internal states.

2. Many kinds of visual, auditory, chemical, and tactile stimuli affect sexual arousal. Chemical substances called **pheromones** which are released by many species are **olfactory** sexual attractants. **Stimulus variation** (referred to as the Coolidge effect) appears to be an important factor in sexual arousal for humans or other animals.

3. Internal factors affect **sexual arousal** and **arousability**. Arousal refers to the level of sexual motivation at the moment; arousability refers to the ease or rapidity of arousal.

4. Sexual behavior is influenced by **hormones** but not fully determined by them. Males or females injected with hormones of the opposite sex still behave much as they did before. The main effect of **androgens** (male sex hormones) on women may simply be to increase the amount of physical activity and hence give the appearance of malelike behavior.

5. Human emotional responses to sex vary from pleasure to guilt and anxiety, apparently due to cultural factors and individual differences in upbringing.

6. The **human sexual response** has been divided into four phases said to characterize both males and females: (1) **excitement**, (2) **plateau**, (3) **orgasm**, and (4) **resolution**. Each phase is described in terms of specific physiological changes.

7. Sexual preferences, especially homosexuality, have engendered a great deal of heated debate, but the basis of homosexuality is not known. Two facts do seem clear: Homosexuality is not caused by a dominance of one or another sex hormone, and it is not related to any specific family constellation, such as a weak father and a domineering mother. There is some evidence for partial genetic determination, but other factors are apparently important.

CHAPTER SIX

Drive and Activation

What do psychologists mean by the term drive?

Where did drive theory originate?

What's the difference between a need, a drive, and a goal?

How do we define drive as an intervening variable?

How does drive affect our behavior?

Is a high level of drive always "good" for behavior?

How do we tell one drive from another?

Are drives biologically determined or can they be learned?

How is activation theory similar to and different from drive theory?

Is there some level of arousal that is best for behavior?

How is level of arousal related to the environment, humor, and aesthetics?

DRIVE THEORY

Drive theory developed out of the regulatory approach to motivation, emphasizing homeostasis and a general energization of behavior. Over the years, however, it has expanded far beyond its biological origins into personality theory and social psychology although it sometimes appears under different names than drive theory. Like the homeostatic approach in general, we shall find problems with drive theory but also find instances when it continues to be useful.

Background

If our body need is so severe that we cannot compensate for a substance lost from our body by using or conserving resources (e.g., glucose) already in our body, we must actively do something to restore homeostatic balance. The critical question is, How do internal imbalances result in the particular behavioral adjustments that return us to equilibrium?

Adaptive acts. Early evolutionary approaches to psychology emphasized the *adaptation* and *adjustment* of organisms to the environment. Harvey Carr (1925) argued that the basic animal behavior was the *adaptive act*. When an organism needs food or water, there is a persistent *internal stimulus* that arouses adaptive activity until the need is satisfied. A number of key concepts emerged from this view.

1. **Need.** Need is an excess or a deficiency of some product related to homeostatic balance and survival. Need is defined on the antecedent side in terms of deprivation (such as food) or pain and on the consequent side in terms of health or survival. Needs frequently lead to activity that restores the appropriate balance, but not necessarily. Such needs as vitamin deficiencies or oxygen deficit do not stimulate compensatory activity. Therefore, the concept of drive is introduced.
2. **Drive.** The antecedents for drive could be the same as for need (e.g., deprivation), but its consequent conditions are *behaviors*. It is drive that energizes behavior, not need. Miller (1951b) suggested that any strong and persistent stimulus can have drive properties, so intensely bright lights or loud sounds can produce drive. Need and drive may be correlated, but the fact that they are not always correlated is why there are two concepts and not just one.
3. **Goal.** A goal is some commodity (e.g., food) or change (e.g., reduction of pain) that will reduce the drive that initiated the activity. A hungry animal consumes food and for a while thereafter it is inactive as far as food is concerned.

The whole sequence then is as follows:

Need → Drive → Activity → Goal → Reduced Drive → Reduced Activity

Note that according to this view, an organism is not active until there is some minimal level of need/drive to energize the activity.

Hull's Drive Theory

Clark Hull was noted early in his career for work on aptitude testing and hypnosis, but about 1930 he began to develop a general theory of behavior (Hull, 1943). Research testing his theory dominated the field of motivation until the 1960s, and although many features of the theory did not stand up to test, some are still considered to be useful. The theory was intended as a complete theory of behavior, but we shall consider only those parts most relevant to motivation. The theory is particularly instructive because of its careful use of definitions and syntax.

Drive as an intervening variable.   Hull was careful to distinguish between performance and the variables that determine performance. The two main variables were learning and motivation. He referred to learning as *habit strength* (sHr), which he considered to be the strength of association between a given stimulus and response, and referred to motivation as *drive* (D), which "activates" habit into performance. Hull argued that drive does not direct, guide, steer, or select particular responses, but instead *energizes all responses equally*. In a specific situation, the response that is best-learned in relation to the stimuli present would be the response most likely to occur.

In the more precise language of the theory, drive *multiplies* habit to produce the *excitatory potential* for a particular response. Thus,

Excitatory Potential = Habit × Drive,

or, symbolically:

$sEr = sHr \times D$, or just $E = H \times D$

E, H, and D are intervening variables, with different antecedent conditions. The strength of H is defined in terms of number of learning trials, increasing with the number of S-R associations (e.g., the number of times an animal runs in a maze to find food). The strength of D is defined, for example, in terms of number of hours of food deprivation or intensity of a noxious stimulus. The value of E is defined according to the syntax of the theory, in terms of the relation between H and D. On the consequent side, these intervening variables are measured in terms of amplitude, frequency, probability, or latency of responding. These elements of the theory are illustrated in Figure 6–1. Observable events are outside the box, and intervening variables are inside the box.

The multiplicative relationship between H and D was arrived at partly by logical considerations and partly by research. Logically it would make little sense to propose that $E = H - D$ or that $E = H/D$, since either of these statements says that performance (E) would get weaker with increasing drive. Either

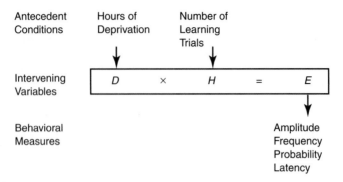

FIGURE 6–1. Antecedent conditions, consequent conditions, and intervening variables in Hull's (1943) theory.

$E = H + D$ or $E = H \times D$ makes more sense, since either of these formulations says that performance will improve with increasing drive. On the basis of data from previous experiments, Hull selected the $H \times D$ formulation. The general prediction from the multiplicative formulation is illustrated in Figure 6–2. Many subsequent researchers have used such diverging curves as illustrated in Figure 6–2 as evidence for the operation of motivational variables (e.g., Cooper & Fazio, 1984; Zajonc & Sales, 1966).

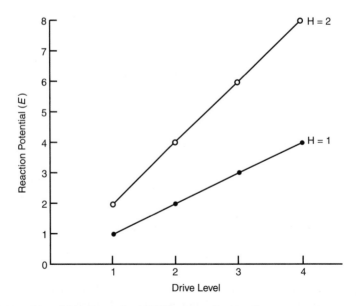

FIGURE 6–2. Habit and drive interaction in Hullian theory ($E = H \times D$).

Different predictions for simple and complex responses.   Different predictions are made depending on whether the responses to be tested are simple or complex. A simple response is a clearly *dominant* response, often a very simple one. The theory predicts that such a response will become even more dominant with a higher level of drive as Figure 6–2 indicates. If an animal has learned the simple response of running down a straight alleyway to get to food, the animal should run faster with longer deprivation (higher drive).

In a *complex response* situation, there are multiple components of the response (such as hitting a golf ball or driving a car). If not well learned, these components can conflict with each other and produce *competing responses*. When such competing responses are simultaneously activated, we would expect error and confusion. For example, to drive a car with a manual transmission, one must push in the clutch pedal, move the stick to change gears, operate the brake and gas pedals, all in a well-timed sequence. Before the *correct sequence* is well-learned, these different responses compete with each other, and in an emergency situation, the new learner may panic (a high level of drive) and make the wrong response, such as pushing the clutch pedal rather than the brake. In sum, when drive is high, dominant responses become even more dominant, but competing responses interfere with each other even more and performance gets worse. The predictions for these two situations are summarized in Table 6–1.

Why Do We Call Some Variables Motivational?

Hull defined his intervening variables carefully, but the following criteria were used to distinguish motivational (drive) intervening variables from other kinds.

1. **An increase in the level of the variable energizes a wide range of responses.** This criterion distinguishes drive from a specific stimulus that evokes a specific response, such as a reflex response. Food deprivation energizes eating, running to food, pressing a lever to get food, and so on. When such a variety of responses is energized, a specific *S-R* connection is ruled out, and a more general "motivating" variable is indicated.

2. **A decrease in the level of the variable is reinforcing.** This is the idea that response becomes "stronger" if it is followed by a stimulus called a reinforcer, such as food for a hungry animal. According to Hull, a reinforcer is effective

TABLE 6–1. Performance of simple or well-learned dominant responses and complex, nondominant responses under conditions of low and high drive, according to Hull's theory.

	SIMPLE DOMINANT RESPONSES	COMPLEX NONDOMINANT RESPONSES
Low Drive	Worse	Better
High Drive	Better	Worse

only if it reduces the level of drive present at the time. If pain is reduced following a particular response and if that same response occurs more frequently in the future under similar circumstances, the variable (pain) may be said to be drive.

3. **An increase in the level of the variable is punishing.** If a response is followed by increased pain, the response is less likely to occur; it has been punished. Pain meets this criterion for drive, but hunger and thirst have not.

Evaluating Drive Theory

Persistence in responding.   Since drive theory predicts stronger responding with higher drive, hungrier animals should respond more for food, thirstier animals should respond more for water, and so on. Research consistently shows this result. In one of the first studies of this kind, Warden (1931) studied strength of drive in an obstruction box, where an animal has to cross an electrified floor to reach food, water, or other goal. With longer deprivation, animals would cross the electrified floor more times, or would tolerate stronger shocks to get at the food.

The problem for a drive theory interpretation is that the animals were *trying to reach some goal,* and the effect of deprivation could be on responsiveness to the goal, not just an energization of behavior. For example, a thirsty animal may run more quickly to water but not necessarily to food. A less ambiguous demonstration of a drive would involve behavior where there is no clear goal. One idea is that drive energizes "random" activity which should facilitate finding an appropriate goal. Thus, a hungry animal should be more active in its search for food.

Drive and activity.   In the earliest of studies testing the drive-activity relationship, Dashiell (1925) reported that hungry rats explored a maze in the form of a checkerboard, with many paths, more than satiated rats. Confirmed in many subsequent experiments, it appeared that drive energizes activity. But does drive energize all kinds of activity, as Hull said it should? The answer is no, deprivation does not affect all kinds of activity equally. For example, Campbell (1964) used albino laboratory rats to compare food and water deprivation in three different apparatuses. The animals lived in their respective apparatuses for several days. The results, summarized in Figure 6–3), show that the amount of activity depends on the kind of deprivation (food or water), the particular measure of activity used, and the species tested (chicks, guinea pigs, hamsters, and rabbits (Campbell, Smith, Misanin, & Jaynes, 1966). An important discovery in this line of research is that animals often *learn* to become more active. If rats are fed immediately after they have been running in an activity wheel, they become more active than if their food is delayed an hour (Finger, Reid, & Weasner, 1957; Hall, 1958). In summary, what was considered a bulwark of the concept of drive, that drive energizes the activity necessary to obtain a drive-reducing substance, was not correct. The

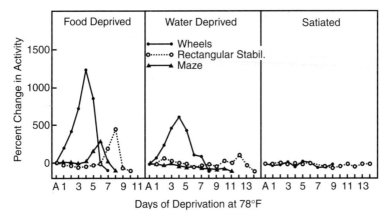

FIGURE 6–3. Percent changes in activity of food-deprived, water-deprived, and satiated rats in activity wheels, rectangular stabilimeter cages, and an automatic Dashiell maze at 78°F. (From Campbell, 1964, p. 330. Copyright © 1964 by Pergamon Press. Reprinted by permission.)

generalization that "drive increases activity" is subject to so many qualifications as to be almost useless.

Human Applications of Drive Theory

Paradoxically, drive theory has in many ways been more successful in its predictions for humans than for animals, as illustrated by the following examples.

Simple (dominant) versus complex (nondominant) responses. In classical conditioning there is a single dominant response, that which is evoked by the conditioned stimulus. In verbal learning experiments there are typically many different responses that are not dominant during early stages of learning and that can compete with each other when a particular response is called for. These two experimental settings allow for tests that predict that irrelevant drive[1] should enhance conditioned responses in classical conditioning and produce poorer performance when complex responses are involved. In one conditioning experiment a soft tone was the CS, a puff of air to the eye was the UCS, and the eyeblink was the UCR and CR (Spence, 1956). Level of drive was examined in two ways. First the intensity of the air puff was varied (high versus low), and second two levels of anxiety as measured by self-report scale were compared. Level of anxiety was considered irrelevant drive. Four groups of subjects had combinations of high versus low drive (high versus low pressure air puff) and irrelevant drive (high versus low anxiety level). Level of eyeblink conditioning increased with high levels of both these vari-

---

[1]In Hull's theory, irrelevant drive refers to any source of drive (e.g., anxiety) which is not relevant to a current reinforcer (e.g., food, water).

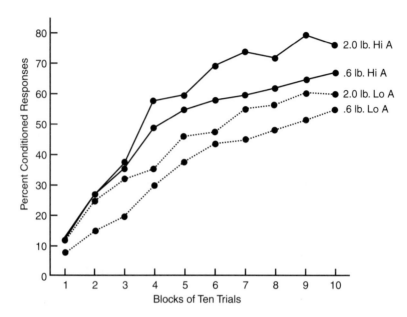

FIGURE 6–4. Eyeblink conditioning as a function of UCS intensity (pounds of pressure per square inch of the air puff) and level of anxiety (measured by the Taylor Manifest Anxiety Scale). (Originally from Spence & Taylor, 1951, adapted from Spence, 1958. Copyright 1951 by the American Psychological Association. Reprinted by permission.)

ables. The results are summarized in Figure 6–4. In verbal learning experiments, subjects with high versus low levels of anxiety are typically compared. The results of such research have been positive often enough to be provocative, although far from conclusive (see Bolles, 1967; or Byrne, 1974).

Social facilitation. Social facilitation refers to the effects that observers have on individual performance (Tripplet, 1897). Robert Zajonc (1965) proposed that an audience arouses an irrelevant drive in an actor. He correctly predicted that performance of dominant responses should be facilitated by an audience and that performance of nondominant responses should become poorer. The theory can be extended to explain a wide range of social phenomena (Guerin & Innes, 1984; Weiss & Miller, 1971). A highly trained professional athlete, whose responses to virtually every situation in his sport are well practiced, performs better in a stadium full of fans. A young child, who is just learning the same sport and has few well-learned (dominant) responses, may perform more poorly in front of an audience.

Aggression. Sexually arousing stimuli (pornographic movies), loud sounds, and the presence of weapons have all raised the level of aggressive behavior shown by laboratory subjects. Leonard Berkowitz (1974) argued that this result occurs because these conditions produce a higher level of drive.

Drive Stimulus Theory

Hull also proposed that drive-producing operations produce unique internal stimuli, which he called drive stimuli. These stimuli can operate as cues to guide behavior. Both drive and drive stimuli follow when drive is manipulated, by deprivation for example.

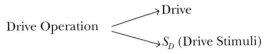

Drive Operation
→ Drive
→ S_D (Drive Stimuli)

Drive discrimination experiments. The drive stimuli are presumed to have the same properties as external stimuli: They can be *discriminated* (we can tell them apart), they can serve as *cues*, and they can be *conditioned* to responses. Thus, for example, if an animal gets food in the right arm of a T-maze and water in the left arm, it learns to go right or left according to whether it is hungry or thirsty. This is illustrated in Figure 6–5. On the very first trial on a day when the animal is thirsty, for example, it turns left to the water. Since all aspects of the apparatus are the same every day, the animal appears to be using its own hunger or thirst to guide its behavior (Bailey, 1955; Leeper, 1935). It is also found that rats easily discriminate among different levels of deprivation and use these as distinct cues (Capaldi & Davidson, 1979). In one experiment, either the kind of deprivation (food versus water) or amount of deprivation (short versus long) signaled the presence or absence of reward on a given day's tests in a straight runway. For example, a particular animal might get a food reward on days when it had short deprivation but might not get food on days when it had long deprivation. This process directly pits the "higher drive" against the internal cue for no reward (long deprivation), and vice versa. The animals did learn to run faster under low deprivation than high deprivation, if low deprivation signaled reward and if high deprivation signaled no reward (Capaldi, Vivieros, & Davidson, 1981).

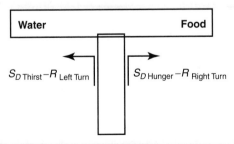

FIGURE 6–5. The general drive produced by water or food deprivation energizes both right and left turn responses. The drive stimuli, $S_{D\ Thirst}$ and $S_{D\ Hunger}$, are distinctive cues that have become conditioned to left-turning and right-turning responses. Since the maze cues themselves are the same under either hunger or thirst conditions, the drive stimuli provide the only cues for which response to make.

Mood dependent memory.   People tend to remember things better if they are in the same mood as when they learned them. For example, if a list was learned while a person was in a sad mood, there is a slight tendency to remember the list better at a later time if in a sad mood rather than in, say, a happy mood. Since moods are internal states, it appears that moods can serve as memory cues, just as drive stimuli are supposed to do. This phenomenon has been difficult to obtain in the laboratory, but appears to be real (Beck & McBee, 1995; Eich, 1995).

Learned Drives

How can drives be learned?   Hunger, thirst, and pain are often called **primary drives**, to indicate their biological primacy and to indicate there is little learning involved in their arousal. But much animal behavior, including human, is not directed toward reducing hunger, thirst, or pain. Consequently, drive theorists have postulated that behavior is also motivated by **learned drives** (also called **secondary** or **acquired** drives). A learned drive is one that is aroused by stimuli previously associated with a primary drive. For example, if a tone is paired with an aversive stimulus (e.g., electric shock or loud noise), a conditioned response to the tone will develop, often referred to as anxiety or fear. Many psychologists have believed that animal laboratory analogs for human anxiety and neurotic behavior can shed light on human clinical problems. Therefore, they have developed experimental procedures for producing animal equivalents of human anxiety, conflict, frustration, and even love and affection. These procedures allow for the experimental control necessary to determine causes, which in turn we apply to the human situation. The most widely studied acquired drive is fear.

Fear as An Acquired Drive

We treat fear as an intervening variable as indicated in Figure 6–6. A previously conditioned aversive stimulus is the antecedent condition, and verbal and nonverbal behaviors and physiological responses are consequent conditions. If fear is an acquired drive, then (1) fear should energize a variety of responses, (2) fear reduction should be reinforcing, and (3) fear increase should be punishing. There is good evidence for all of these.

Antecedent Condition	Intervening Variable	Consequent Conditions
Previously ···························· Conditioned CS	········· FEAR ············	·········Verbal Response Nonverbal Behavior Physiological Response

FIGURE 6–6.   Fear as an intervening variable.

Fear as an energizer.   Fear-drive should energize many responses, but a reflex response is of special interest because it should be inherently less variable than a learned response (Brown, Kalish, & Farber, 1951). Brown and his colleagues reasoned that fear should energize the startle response, a reflex common to all mammals that occurs when a loud, sharp sound is presented. They placed rats in a small apparatus mounted on a postage scale, so that when an animal was startled by the sharp sound of a cap pistol, it jumped. The magnitude of this startle-jump was recorded by the pressure against the scale. Over a series of trials, a tone was paired with foot shock, and periodically the animals were tested for startle when the fear-arousing tone was on. As predicted (Figure 6–7), the magnitude of startle response increased with the number of fear-conditioning trials. Control animals, on the other hand, did not show any change in the startle response, suggesting that fear was indeed energizing the startle response. Many subsequent studies (with much more sophisticated apparatus!) have supported and extended the Brown et al. results (Davis, 1986; Davis & Astrachan, 1978; Lang, Bradley & Cuthbert, 1989).

Fear reduction as reinforcement.   The reference experiment for fear reduction (Miller, 1948) is one of the most cited experiments in psychology. The apparatus is illustrated in Figure 6–8. Rats were shocked in one compart-

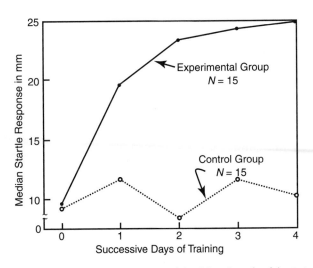

FIGURE 6–7.   Median amplitude of startle responses of fearful and nonfearful rats to a loud, sharp sound. The upper curve shows that experimental animals presumed to be fearful jumped more vigorously to the sound as the number of fear-conditioning trials increased. The responses of control (nonfearful) subjects, however, did not change progressively or significantly during the same period. (From Brown, Kalish, & Farber, 1951, p. 321. Copyright © 1951 by the American Psychological Association. Reprinted by permission.)

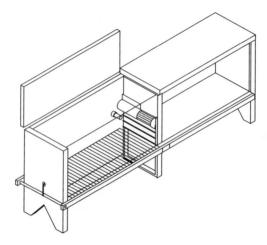

FIGURE 6–8. Acquired drive apparatus. The left compartment is painted white, the right one black. A shock may be administered through the grid that is on the floor of the white compartment. When the animal is placed on the grid that is pivoted at the inside end, it moves down slightly, making a contact that starts an electric timer. When the animal performs the correct response, turning the wheel or pressing the bar as the case may be, it stops the clock and actuates a solenoid that allows the door, painted with horizontal black and white stripes, to drop. The experimenter can also cause the door to drop by pressing a button. The dimensions of each compartment are 18 × 6 × 8½ inches. (From Miller, 1948, p. 90. Copyright © 1948 by the American Psychological Association. Reprinted by permission.)

ment of a two-compartment apparatus and allowed to escape into the other compartment. After this training, the escape route was blocked, but no more shock was given. If the animals turned a wheel mounted in the wall, the door blocking their escape was lowered, and the animals ran to the "safe" side of the apparatus. After wheel turning had been learned, the wheel was made inoperative, and pressing a lever became reinforced by escape. Wheel turning extinguished, and lever pressing increased. The conclusion was that fear was aroused when the animals were put into the shock compartment and reduced when the animals made the correct response and escaped into the safe compartment.

Many, many experiments since Miller's (see Miller, 1959; Mowrer, 1960; for reviews) point to the interpretation that fear reduction is reinforcing. Davis and Miller (1963) even found that shocked rats would press a lever more than nonshocked animals for an intravenous injection of sodium amytal, a nervous system depressant, in the situation in which they had previously been shocked. They argued that the drug was reinforcing for the previously shocked animals because it reduced their fear but that the drug did not reinforce the control animals because they had no fear to be reduced.

Fear as a punisher.   Stimuli associated with pain clearly can suppress ongoing behavior, but punishment is a broad topic and is addressed in appropriate detail in Chapter Nine.

An application of learned drive to humans.   To exemplify how learned drive could account for a human phenomenon, Brown (1961) analyzed miserliness, or "desire for money," in terms of anxiety and anxiety reduction. Brown proposed that stimuli associated with *not having money* become conditioned stimuli for fear arousal. A child may hear his parents argue about not having money, expressing anxiety over where money for food and rent is going to come from, and so on. The arguments and fears expressed by the parents are unconditioned stimuli for fear on the part of the child, and such words as "We have no money" become conditioned stimuli for arousing this fear. The child may then learn that this fear is reduced by getting and having money. Therefore, whenever the cues for not having money are presented, the adult does what she or he has learned as the means of reducing this fear (eliminating the cues): The adult gets money. This kind of fear, as well as a conspicuous consumption that serves to hold down the anxiety cues of poverty, has been described poignantly by the great American playwright Moss Hart in his autobiography, *Act One.* Other kinds of compulsions may have similar bases. Excessive sexual activity is frequently interpreted in this fashion: not being loved may serve as an anxiety-arousing cue that is temporarily removed by having sex. Such an interpretation helps the clinician account for behaviors that otherwise seem to have no common explanation.

SECTION SUMMARY

1. According to **drive theory**, disruptions of homeostatic balance energize an organism into action. The most influential drive theory (Hull's) holds that drive is a **general energizer** and energizes all responses equally. What particular response may occur is determined by learning. Responses are said to be learned if they are reinforced (rewarded) by **drive reduction**.

2. The effect of drive on behavior depends on the kind of response involved. If a response is a simple, dominant response, a high level of drive facilitates the response. If the response is complex or not the dominant response in a particular situation, high drive may make performance worse.

3. Tests of predictions from drive theory in animal research have met with variable success. Hunger and thirst do not generally produce an increase in "random" activity, as suggested by the theory. With humans, high anxiety does facilitate simple **dominant responses** but interferes with more **complex tasks**.

4. In Hull's theory, drive cannot direct or select behavior, but internal stimuli called **drive stimuli** can do so. Drive stimuli are specific stimuli accompanying particular drive-producing operations. Hunger and thirst have unique stimuli that can help direct behavior to appropriate goals.

5. **Learned drives**, such as fear, are drives that are aroused by stimuli previously associated with such primary drives as pain. Fear has been shown to energize responses, fear-reduction reinforces the learning of new responses, and increased fear is punishing.

ACTIVATION THEORY

Background

In Chapter Two we discussed activation (arousal) as a dimension of emotion, but activation theory has broader motivational implications. Like drive theory, activation theory has been used to account for the energization of behavior, but not its direction. Activation theory has been more closely related to physiology than has drive theory. Elizabeth Duffy (1934), who originally proposed activation theory under the name of **energy mobilization**, emphasized the autonomic system arousal. Subsequently, the **reticular activating system (RAS)** of the midbrain became the focus of attention (e.g., Berlyne, 1960; Duffy, 1962; Hebb, 1955; Lindsley, 1951; Malmo, 1959; Woodworth & Schlosberg, 1954). Much of the early enthusiasm for the theory occurred because it seemed to provide a physiological account of drive while at the same time solving many problems faced by drive theory. The theory expanded in various ways, however, which sharply separated it from drive theory.

RAS Activation

The reticular activating system is illustrated in Figure 6–9. The RAS receives inputs from all sensory systems except smell and then distributes these diffusely to all parts of the cerebrum via the **ascending RAS.** Specific sensory information is lost in the RAS, but the widespread distribution of RAS output "tones up" the cortex in preparation for further input and attention to the environment. Simultaneously, impulses sent to motor neurons via the **descending RAS** serve to maintain muscle tonus over long periods of time.

Increased RAS activity is seen in the **electroencephalogram** (EEG, electrical activity of the brain, or brain waves) recorded from various locations on the scalp. There is a shift from a "resting" **alpha wave** pattern (8 to 12 Hz; Hz is the abbreviation for hertz, or cycles per second) to an "activated" **beta pattern** (15 Hz and up, with lower amplitude and greater irregularity). This shift in EEG pattern, illustrated in Figure 6–10, is widely spread over the cortex and may be conceptualized as something like a fire alarm that gets people into action but does not really say where the fire is. For a determination of where to go or what responses to make, more specific environmental information must come through the sensory channels that run directly to the sensory cortex of the brain.

The alpha pattern, which has a relatively high amplitude and low frequency, is said to be "synchronized" and represents an awake but relaxed

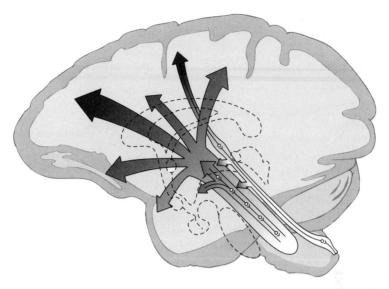

FIGURE 6–9. Schema projected upon a monkey brain showing ARAS, including the reticular formation in the central core of the lower brain stem with multisynaptic relays and its upward diffuse projections to all parts of the cortex. To the right a single afferent pathway with a relay in the thalamus proceeds to the postcentral cortex, but gives off collaterals (arrows) to the reticular formation. These are respectively the unspecified and specific sensory systems. Source: Magoun (1954). Used by permission of the publisher.

state. The beta pattern, of higher frequency and lower amplitude, is "desynchronized" and represents an aroused or excited state. Alpha and beta normally fluctuate as we go about our daily activities. Moruzzi and Magoun (1949) showed that direct electrical stimulation of the RAS through permanently implanted electrodes produces this same desynchronization.

Early research of the 1950s indicated that destruction of the RAS had effects opposite to those of stimulation. Severe RAS damage left animals comatose and unresponsive to stimulation, with a continuous highly synchronized EEG. Electrical records showed that stimuli reached the sensory cortex but that no overall desynchronization of the EEG appeared, and there was no overt response to the stimulation. Energizing drugs such as amphetamines increase RAS activity and alertness, and central nervous system depressants like barbiturates decrease activity and alertness. Such data supported the idea that the RAS is an important, if not completely critical, area of the brain for attention and consciousness.

Although EEG activity is heavily emphasized in activation theory, the more classic measures of autonomic nervous system arousal are still commonly used for practical reasons. These include heart rate, blood pressure, muscle tension, and the galvanic skin response. It is presumed that all such physiological activity should increase or decrease in unison under conditions

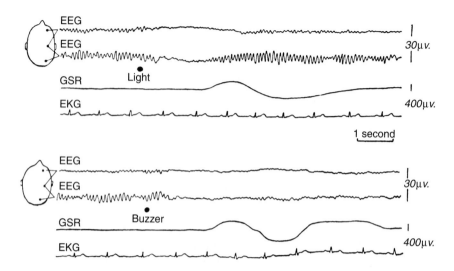

FIGURE 6–10. Arousal effects of unexpected light and sound stimuli on the electroencephalogram (EEG), galvanic skin response (GSR), and heartrate (EKG). Electrode placements for the EEG are indicated from the top of the head. Note that the posterior electrodes show a large-amplitude, low-frequency alpha wave before the presentation of light or buzzer. This is a typical, relaxed, waking record. After the light or buzzer, there is a transition to a low-amplitude, high-frequency beta wave that is typical of a more alert or excited subject. The alpha is "blocked" by activity from the brain stem reticular system following presentation of the light and buzzer. The buzzer in this illustration was obviously a more "exciting" stimulus, since the alpha blocking lasted longer and there was a larger GSR change as well. HR is not obviously faster after stimulation, but the naked eye is not a good indicator of HR records shown in this manner. Source: Lindsley (1950). Used by permission of the publisher.

of stress or relaxation, reflecting greater or lesser energy expenditure by the organism. Figure 6–9 also shows the effect of a sudden stimulus on some of these other measures.

Optimal Level of Arousal Theory

The inverted-U function.   The primary motivational proposition of activation theory is that there is an optimal level of arousal for behavior, an inverted-U function, as shown in Figure 6–11. Some intermediate level of arousal is said to be better for performance than either lower or higher levels. It is generally implicit that such a medium level of arousal is also desirable and sought (Hebb, 1955; Malmo, 1959).

The Yerkes-Dodson law.   The concept of an optimal level of arousal for performance dates back to Yerkes and Dodson (1908). These investigators reported that when a brightness discrimination problem was made more difficult for animals (they used "dancing mice" in their research), the optimal

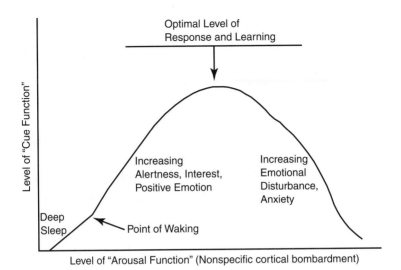

FIGURE 6–11. Relationship between level of arousal (in the ascending reticular activating system) and effectiveness of responses to cues in the environment. (From Hebb, 1955, p. 250. Copyright © 1955 by the American Psychological Association. Reprinted by permission.)

level of punishment for errors was lower. That is, more-difficult problems were learned better with lower levels of punishment. This concept is illustrated in Figure 6–12. Broadhurst (1957) deprived rats of different amounts of air by holding them under water for different periods of time. When the rats were released to swim to safety, there was an inverted-U function for a difficult brightness discrimination problem, but an optimal level was not clearly shown with problems of simple or moderate difficulty. Anderson (1994) found support for the law when she compared performance on an easy (letter cancellation) and a hard (verbal abilities) task under conditions of five different dose levels of caffeine. As predicted, performance on the easy task improved with increasing levels of caffeine. With the harder task, however, performance declined at the higher dose levels for subjects who were more easily aroused. This experiment was particularly interesting because all subjects got every dose level of caffeine, enabling a very sensitive test of the law. It has also been found, however, that almost any response can potentially be inhibited at a high enough level of arousal, not just nondominant, competing responses or difficult task behaviors. An individual may simply freeze, as with stage fright. There is a brainstem inhibitory mechanism that paralyzes motor activity when there is a high level of arousal (Morrison, 1983).

A major impetus for the optimal level of arousal view came from studies of sensory isolation (e.g., Bexton, Heron, & Scott, 1954). Following many hours of severely reduced sensory input, normal college-age subjects had difficulty in concentrating and solving problems. They showed abnormalities even in their ordinary perceptions. Printed lines refused to stay in place, walls

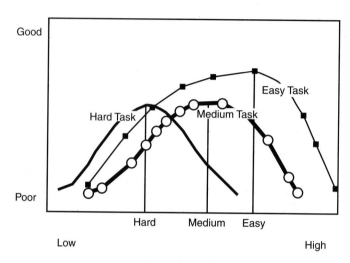

The Yerkes-Dodson (1908) Law

FIGURE 6–12. The Yerkes-Dodson law. As the difficulty of the task increases, the optimal level of arousal for performance decreases. The optimal levels of arousal for each type of task are shown by the vertical lines.

bowed outward, and objects seemed to retreat as one looked away from them. Such data suggested that insufficient sensory input had a detrimental effect on perception, which Hebb (1955) thought to be due to reduced RAS activity. Later experiments with stabilized retinal images gave further support to this conjecture (e.g., Pritchard, 1961). A tiny, high-frequency (25/sec) vibration of the eyes normally produces constantly changing retinal stimulation. By various mechanical means, such as mounting a miniature slide projector on a contact lens, the visual stimulus can be made to vibrate right along with the eye. The image is stabilized on the retina because the eye is not moving with reference to the visual stimulus. Such stabilized images disappear within a minute or so, and it is clear that stimulus change is important for normal perception. What all this says is that the lowest possible level of arousal is not a viable biological goal.

The Easterbrook hypothesis.   J. A. Easterbrook (1959) developed a perceptual hypothesis of why high levels of arousal may impair performance. He said that arousal reduces the range of cues in the environment that an organism can attend to. In a state of low arousal, all cognitive units are equally activated, but with increasing activation, there is progressively more narrow fo-

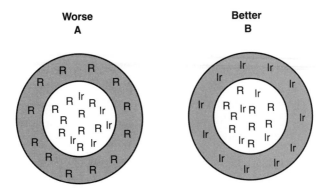

FIGURE 6–13. Easterbrook's spotlight model for the effects of arousal on attention. The whole area of the circle (dark plus light) is what is noticed under low arousal. The smaller white area is what is noticed under high arousal. R and Ir represent relevant and irrelevant cues, respectively. In A, more relevant cues (Rs) go unnoticed in the periphery, and performance is worse. In B, more irrelevant cues (Ir) go unnoticed in the periphery, and performance is better.

cusing and less attention to peripheral elements. This spotlight effect is illustrated in Figure 6–13. Reduced cue availability may either help or hinder performance. Thus,

- Arousal should improve performance if there are many peripheral stimuli that are irrelevant to the task at hand. In a noisy environment, for example, a person may become aroused by irrelevant peripheral noise but also more focused on the task. The student who claims to study better with rock music in the background may actually do so, if he becomes more focused with the music. This is no surefire way to improve studying, however!
- High arousal should impair performance if there are many relevant peripheral stimuli that should be attended to. In a problem-solving task requiring the person to be aware of all sorts of cues around her or him, narrowing the focus to just those immediately in front would impair performance. This hypothesis would account for some of the same effects that the Yerkes-Dodson law does. That is, insofar as complex tasks involve more relevant cues, some of these cues are more likely to be missed under high arousal.

The following experiment illustrates the theory. Subjects with different levels of arousal studied a list of words while also hearing an incidental (extraneous) list of words being played on a tape recorder. Subsequently, they did anagrams in which some of the incidental words were anagram solutions. The low-arousal subjects used more of the incidental words heard on the tape than did the high-arousal subjects.

In summary, our capacity to attend to environmental cues varies according to our internal state. If this capacity is reduced by arousal, stress, or emotion, we have less capacity for attending to peripheral (incidental) stimuli.

Whether performance is aided or impaired depends on the relevance of the peripheral cues to the task at hand.

Comparison of Drive and Activation Theories

Drive and activation theories both deal with an intensity dimension of motivation, but whereas drive theory assumes that the lowest possible level of drive is the "ideal" state of the organism, activation theory assumes nirvana to be at some intermediate level of stimulation. To reach this intermediate level, we may have either to increase or to decrease stimulation, depending on our momentary level. If the momentary level of arousal is low, an even lower level would be aversive. Therefore, a higher level is sought—pushing toward the optimum. Conversely, if the momentary level is very high, an even higher level would be aversive, and a lower level is sought (see Table 6–2).

Problems with RAS Activation Theory

The hope that the RAS might underlie a unitary arousal dimension was crushed soon after intense research on the RAS was begun. It was found that (1) if animals survived RAS destruction, they could show normal fluctuations in activity and responsiveness to stimuli (Lindsley, Schreiner, Knowles, & Magoun, 1950); (2) if RAS destruction is done in a series of small steps, even a temporary comatose state is forestalled (Adametz, 1959); and (3) massive lesions of sensory pathways, without direct damage to the RAS, produce many of the same overt behavioral effects as do RAS lesions (Sprague, Chambers, & Stellar, 1961). Other areas of the brain may be more important for arousal than the RAS. What appears to be likely is that there are multiple systems of arousal, as implied by evidence that EEG arousal, autonomic arousal, and behavioral arousal can be distinguished.

SECTION SUMMARY

1. **Activation theory**, like drive theory, is concerned with the **energization** of behavior, not the direction of behavior. Activation theory is more concerned with physiological arousal, in either the brain or the autonomic nervous system, than was Hull's drive theory.

2. The major behavioral prediction of activation theory is that behavior is less efficient at either very low or very high levels of arousal than at some medium level of arousal. This is the **optimal level of arousal hypothesis**, which has been influential in motivation theory. The hypothesis has received only limited support in research, perhaps because it is difficult to control or measure arousal levels accurately and because there seem to be several kinds of arousal.

3. It is generally assumed that an optimum level of arousal is actively sought when one is above or below the optimum. This differs from drive theory which assumes that one only seeks to reduce drive, not increase drive.

TABLE 6–2. Comparisons of drive theory and arousal (activation) theories. All the theories assume the importance of a motivational factor which affects a wide range of behaviors and does not in itself determine what specific behavior will occur. All the theories have some level of support.

	OPTIMAL LEVEL FOR PERFORMANCE	MOTIVATIONAL GOAL	PHYSIOLOGICAL BASIS
Drive Theory (Hull)	Low for competing responses, High for dominant responses	Reduction of drive is reinforcing and sought.	Not Specified. Drive is an intervening variable.
Activation Theory (Hebb and others)	Medium level is optimal. Type of response not specified by the theory. In practice, some behaviors found to be more sensitive to high arousal than others.	Medium level is sought. Seek to reduce high levels of arousal and increase low levels.	Reticular Activating System and/or autonomic arousal.
Yerkes-Dodson Law	The more difficult the task, the lower the optimal level.	Not specified	Not specified
Easterbrook Spotlight Theory	Task difficulty not specified. High arousal narrows range of attention. Effect depends on whether cues relevant or irrelevant to behavior are in periphery of attention.	Not specified	Not specified

4. The **Yerkes-Dodson law** is an old variant of optimal level of arousal theory, which says that the more difficult a task is, the lower is the optimal level of response.

5. The **Easterbrook "spotlight theory"** says that the focus of attention is narrower under high levels of arousal than under low levels of arousal. This tendency impedes performance if peripheral stimuli are relevant to the task at hand but improves performance if irrelevant stimuli are excluded.

Environmental Stimulation and Arousal

Stimulus intensity and stimulus complexity. Such intense stimuli as loud noises and frightening experiences produce high arousal. Our concern here, however, is with a more psychological dimension of stimuli, complexity. Daniel Berlyne (1960) used the phrase **ludic behavior** to refer to those activities we usually call "recreation, entertainment, or 'idle curiosity,'" as well as art, philosophy, and pure (as distinct from applied) science" (p. 5). The most notable characteristic of such behavior is that it is not driven by homeostatic need, it "does not have a biological function that we can clearly recognize" (p. 5). The common thread among these activities is that they involve seeking stimuli that have one or more of the following characteristics.

Novelty. This may include the characteristics of surprisingness and incongruity, both of which involve expectations that are not fulfilled, that is, we expect one thing, but something different happens.

Uncertainty. This refers to the amount of information carried by a stimulus. A plain gray sheet of cardboard, for example, is simpler and carries less information than the same cardboard painted like a checkerboard or like the face of a person.

Conflict. This is the tendency of some visual stimuli to arouse different responses from a viewer at the same time.

Complexity. This increases with the number of distinguishable elements, the dissimilarity among elements, and the degree to which the elements are responded to as a unit.

Figure 6–14 illustrates these variables. Stimuli that are more novel, uncertain, conflicting, or complex produce more arousal. Berlyne (1970) hypothesized that positive affect is aroused by stimuli that produce some medium level of arousal. Relationships between stimuli, arousal, and affect are illustrated in Figure 6–15. Here we see stimuli ranging from simple and familiar to complex and novel. Medium arousal stimuli are sought out by people or animals. Stimuli that are too far above or below the optimal level are aversive and so are escaped or avoided. We thus have approach and avoidance behavior that is "motivated" by something other than homeostatic imbalance and that is reinforced by something other than restoration of homeostatic balance. Following activation theory more generally, organisms seek some level of arousal greater than zero, not too high and not too low—just right.

Environmental load.   Environmental load refers to the amount of information an individual must use to deal with the environment. A high-load environment is a complex, changing environment, full of novelty and surprises, and it requires much effort in responding. A low-load environment is relatively unchanging and simple, with little novelty or surprise, and it requires little effort to track. The perceived amount of load in an environment has been measured by rating the environment on such stimulus dimensions as uncertain-certain, complex-simple, surprising-usual, and crowded-uncrowded (Mehrabian, 1976, p. 12). New York City is typically a high-load environment; a small rural town would typically be a low-load environment. There are, nat-

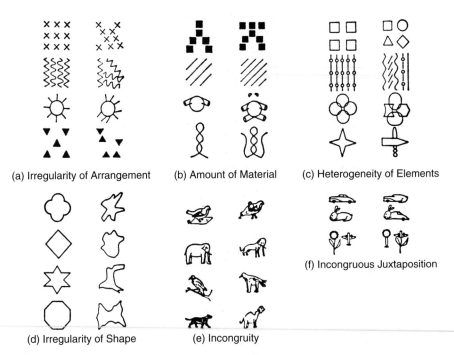

(a) Irregularity of Arrangement   (b) Amount of Material   (c) Heterogeneity of Elements

(f) Incongruous Juxtaposition

(d) Irregularity of Shape   (e) Incongruity

FIGURE 6–14.   Variables contributing to stimulus complexity and arousal. (From Berlyne, D. E., 1958. Copyright 1958 by the American Psychological Association. Used by permission.)

urally, many little pockets of variation in either the large city or the small town.

Screeners and nonscreeners.   Mehrabian distinguished what he called screeners and nonscreeners. Screeners are people who are very sensitive to selected parts of their environment and to load changes. They are quickly aroused, but their arousal also subsides quickly when the load reduces. The nonscreeners are less selective in what they respond to. They take in more stimuli, are aroused by a greater variety of things, and stay aroused longer after the load has been reduced. A screener recovers more quickly from an environmental load than a nonscreener and is ready to "take on" the environment again sooner. People try to average out situations so that over some period of time, such as a day or a week, the average load best suited to them is achieved. Even without this detailed information, however, we can understand why some people want vacations full of excitement and why others just want to have a quiet two weeks away from everything.

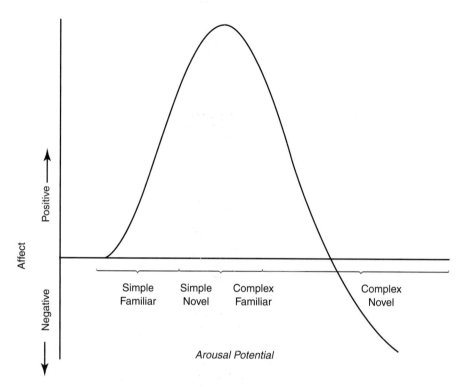

FIGURE 6–15. The hypothesized relation between affect and the arousal potential of a stimulus as proposed by Berlyne. Note that positive affect is greatest when a stimulus is moderately complex or moderately novel. (From Berlyne, 1970. Copyright 1970 by the Psychonomic Society. Used by permission.)

Humor and Aesthetics

Humor.   The importance we attach to humor can be seen in the eagerness with which we approach and pay for the privilege of exposure to variety and incongruity. Humor often involves incongruities or unexpected twists, even with very simple words. For example, Henny Youngman's "Take my wife . . . please!" first leads us to think that he is going to use his wife as an example of something, and then he switches to a very literal meaning of "take." *The Far Side*® cartoons emphasized the incongruity of animals doing what humans commonly do. The accompanying cartoon (Figure 6–16) illustrates this as well.

The "comeback line" also involves an unexpected twist. When Woodrow Wilson was governor of New Jersey, he reportedly received a phone call from a politician who wanted to be appointed replacement for a just-deceased U.S. senator. "That's perfectly agreeable with me," said Wilson, "if it's agreeable to the undertaker." Humor is, of course, a complex subject, and any explanation for all forms of humor depends on more than incongruity. Jack Benny,

FIGURE 6–16.   Courtesy of David Hills.

for example, was funniest and most famous for doing things that he was fully expected to do, such as assuming his quizzical expression and saying "Well!" He was funny because of his predictability, and his most predictable radio persona characteristic was his stinginess. His March 28, 1948, show produced the longest uninterrupted laugh in all of radio history when he was accosted by a burglar who demanded his money or his life. After a long pause, the burglar demanded an answer, to which Benny replied, "I'm thinking. I'm thinking."

Aesthetics.   The nature of beauty, as found in any sensory modality (visual art, tactual art, or music) is also a demanding topic, and our cursory treatment here is limited to the arousal aspect. Great art or music or writing is ultimately determined by its longevity, which is due in part to the technical skill of the artist or composer or writer and in part to the degree to which the art in question has "universal" appeal. That is, great aesthetic works seem to "speak" to many people, to carry messages that are attracting to many people over many years. On repeated exposure to the same work, observers or listeners see or hear different things from what they saw or heard before. People keep finding new things in a great work.

Put in psychological terms, great aesthetic works carry more information than is processed in a single viewing or listening. As different information is detected from one viewing/hearing to another, there is stimulus variation. In a very real sense, each time we hear a great piece of music, we are hearing something different from the previous times. For a particularly insightful discussion of aesthetics and psychology, Berlyne (1960, 1971) and Platt (1961) are recommended.

If medium levels of arousal are desirable, we might expect that "artistic" stimuli that produce medium levels of arousal should also be more desirable. The trick is to define stimuli so that they can be numerically scaled in terms of arousal properties. Smith and Dorfman (1975) did this by using a basic concept from information theory. The amount of information in a stimulus is defined as the amount of uncertainty about that stimulus, what has been called "surprisal value." A complex stimulus has more surprisal value than a simple one. The more information a stimulus contains, the greater its surprisal and arousal value. Smith and Dorfman used black-white checkerboard stimuli of low, medium, and high complexity. The subjects rated these for liking after one, five, ten, and twenty exposures. Smith and Dorfman also assumed that on successive exposures, subjects would adapt to the stimuli so that the stimuli would be perceived as less complex after repeated viewing.

The results are shown in Figure 6–17. The most complex stimulus (highest arousal) was least liked upon initial exposure, and the simplest stimulus (lowest arousal) was most liked. This finding would indeed provide an inverted U function for liking after the first exposure. As the subjects became more familiar with the stimuli, however, there was an orderly change. The simplest stimulus quickly became least liked, as with many popular songs that are "catchy" at first hearing but that quickly become boring. The most complex stimulus increased steadily in liking as subjects became more familiar with it, as it presumably moved from a highly arousing to a less arousing (and more optimal) position on the inverted U curve. The medium complexity

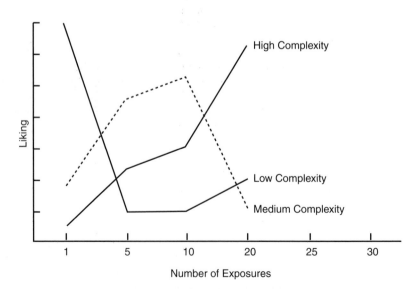

FIGURE 6–17. Liking of visual stimuli as a function of stimulus complexity and number of exposures. (From Smith & Dorfman, 1975, p. 152. Copyright © 1975 by the American Psychological Association. Reprinted by permission.)

stimulus first increased in liking, apparently shifting from highly arousing to optimally arousing and then to less liked, with further exposure to it. This experiment rather dramatically substantiates activation theory predictions taken in conjunction with adaptation principles. Vitz (1966) performed a similar experiment, but with auditory stimuli. He concocted six different tone sequences ranging from simple to complex on the basis of number of pitches, durations, and volume levels. He then had subjects of high and low musical experience rate each of the six sequences for pleasantness. The highest preference for musically inexperienced subjects was for relatively low stimulus complexity, whereas the pleasantness of the stimulus sequences was much more equal for the experienced subjects. The results of these two experiments support the idea that as we gain more experience with a particular type of stimuli, we also begin to prefer more complex stimuli.

SECTION SUMMARY

1. In addition to intensity, stimuli that are **novel, uncertain, conflicting,** or **complex** can also produce arousal. Stimuli that produce some medium of arousal may also produce positive affect and are therefore sought because of this affect.

2. Environments differ in the degree to which they produce arousal. **High-load** environments are complex and require much effort to deal with; **low-load** environments are simple and repetitive.

3. People vary in how aroused they are by the environment. **Screeners** are quickly aroused by selective stimulus events, but their arousal subsides quickly. **Nonscreeners** are aroused by a much greater range of stimulus events, and their arousal persists longer.

4. **Humor** often involves incongruities or unexpected twists, or putting ideas together in unexpected combinations, which produce pleasant arousal.

5. Great **art, music,** or **writing** survives time partly the result of the artist's technical skill with the medium, but also because it involves a degree of complexity. Great art carries some kind of **message** (information) that is not deciphered all at once; people continue to find new things in it.

CHAPTER SEVEN

Rewards as Reinforcers

What is instrumental conditioning?

What do we mean by "reinforcers" and "punishers"?

How can we use reinforcers most effectively?

What happens if we don't reinforce a behavior every time it occurs?

How do different schedules of reinforcement affect behavior?

How do we explain why reinforcers work as they do (theories)?

Are reinforcers biologically fixed or can new ones be learned?

Are some behaviors intrinsically motivating without need for external rewards?

How are reinforcers related to human economic systems?

Rewards are desirable outcomes that depend on our behavior, and rewarded behavior is more likely to be repeated. Psychologists have looked at rewards in two different ways, however: (1) as reinforcers for *learning* new behaviors, and (2) as incentive stimuli that *motivate* approach behaviors. These different accounts of rewards grow out of their use with a laboratory procedure known as **instrumental conditioning**. We therefore begin by examining some of the most basic concepts of instrumental conditioning.

INSTRUMENTAL CONDITIONING

Thorndike and the Law of Effect

The term instrumental conditioning comes from the idea that behavior is instrumental in getting rewarded or punished. Edward L. Thorndike (1913), an educational psychologist, developed what he called the **Law of Effect**. If the effect of behaving a certain way is *satisfying* (rewarding), the behavior will be "strengthened" and repeated in similar circumstances. If the effect is *annoying* (punishing), the response is less likely to occur again. These were old ideas even in Thorndike's time, but Thorndike went to the laboratory with them. He put cats inside a "puzzle box" (Figure 7–1), from which the cats learned to escape to reach food. The first time the cat made a required response (such as pressing a lever or pulling a string) it was acciden-

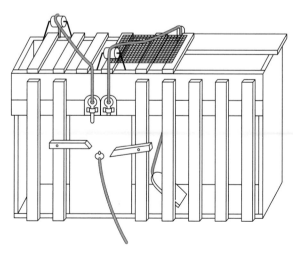

FIGURE 7–1. Thorndike's puzzle box for studying learning in cats. The box is 20 inches long by 15 inches deep by 12 inches high. The cat is put into the box, and when it pushes the pedal on the floor, the door is unlocked and the cat can get to the food. (From Thorndike, E. L. 1898. Animal Intelligence: An experimental study of associative processes in animals. *Psychological Review Monograph Supplement, 2*(8).)

tal, but the door was opened and the cat got out and was fed. On successive trials, cats got out of the box faster and faster. If we plot the time to get out of the box on each trial, we have an **instrumental learning curve**, illustrated in Figure 7–2.

Thorndike argued that learning consists of forming a *connection* between specific stimuli (e.g., the puzzle box) and a specific response (pressing a lever to escape). He called such a connection an *S-R bond.* During learning an S-R bond is "strengthened" so that the stimulus will evoke the response more readily. The evidence is now overwhelming, however, that *most instrumental learning does not consist of such S-R bonds.* We can readily illustrate why this is so. If you have never written your name in the sand with your big toe, do you think you could do it? Probably so. If you put a pencil in your mouth, do you think you could scratch out your name with it? Maybe not artistically, but probably so. If you can do these things, never having done them before, it is clear that learning to write your name using your hand involves something besides making a specific set of muscular responses to a particular stimulus. This was more systematically demonstrated in a laboratory experiment in which monkeys were taught to work mechanical puzzles with one hand literally tied behind their backs. The monkeys then proceeded to work the puzzles without difficulty when the untrained hand was freed and the trained hand was immobilized (Lashley, 1950). Since the learning transferred from one hand to the other without further training, the learning must have in-

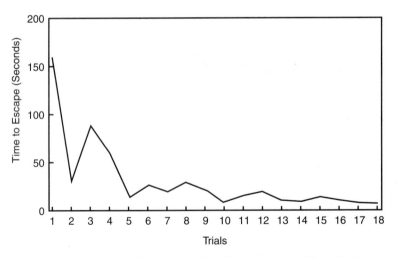

FIGURE 7–2. A typical learning curve for one cat in Thorndike's experiments. The cat is slow to get out of the box to food in early trials but finally levels off at about 8 seconds to do so. Rapid improvement in early trials followed by more gradual improvement in later trials is typical of learning. (From Thorndike, E. L., 1898. Animal intelligence: An experimental study of associative processes in animals. *Psychological Review Monograph Supplement, 2*(8).)

volved some brain activity that was not necessarily specific to each hand. Therefore, the notion of specific S-R connections to explain all learning seems to be wrong.

Skinner and Operant Conditioning

B. F. Skinner (1938, 1953) coined the phrase **operant conditioning** for his version of instrumental conditioning. Operant means that the organism operates or works on the environment. He developed an apparatus that he called the **operant conditioning chamber**, popularly known as the Skinner box, shown in Figure 7–3. Instead of putting the animal into the apparatus for each individual trial, as Thorndike did, the animal stays in the Skinner box for relatively long periods of time, and the apparatus automatically presents rewards and records responses. This makes it possible to study behavior continuously over many hours or days without disturbing the animal. The results are like time-lapse photography with which we can see the petals of a flower opening in the morning and closing at night. Psychologists can see slowly changing behavior patterns that would not be observable otherwise.

Nature of reinforcers and punishers.   Skinner used the term reinforcer rather than reward, and developed a fourfold classification of reinforcers and punishers, as follows:

Positive reinforcer. Any stimulus (such as food or praise) whose *presentation* will increase the probability of a response that it follows.

FIGURE 7–3. Skinner's operant conditioning chamber for studying behavior of the rat.

Negative reinforcer. Any stimulus (such as pain) whose *removal* will increase the probability of a response that it follows.

Punisher 1. Any stimulus, such as pain, whose presentation will *decrease* the probability of a response that it follows.

Punisher 2. Any stimulus, such as social contact or television viewing, whose *removal* will decrease the probability of a response that it follows.

What stimuli will be reinforcers or punishers must be determined by trial, not by some preconceived notion about what stimuli ought to be reinforcers or punishers. All people do not find the same events rewarding. Wise old Brer Rabbit pleaded against being "punished" by saying, "Don't throw me into the briar patch," and immediately was rewarded by being tossed exactly where he wanted to go. Even such a commonly used reinforcer as money may be ineffective, if it is less than a waitress expects as a tip, for example.

When to Deliver Rewards

Rewards are more effective the more quickly that they are given after a response because they are more easily associated. If a child does something to please her parents but they are slow to show their pleasure, the child may not even realize that the delayed approval (reinforcer) was related to her earlier behavior. She may associate the reinforcer with some irrelevant response that occurred just before the reinforcer was given. Long delays of reinforcement may therefore lead to behavior which confuses parents, who cannot understand why the child does not learn to do as they wish when they think they are rewarding that behavior. Accidental reinforcement of responses may lead to so-called *superstitious behavior,* even in adults. A coach who wins a big game while wearing his red socks may continue to wear these socks "for luck" in future games, as if wearing the socks was the behavior that won the game.

Bridging Delay between Response and Reinforcement

Long delays between behavior and reinforcement are often inevitable but can be spanned with a **secondary reinforcer**, which is a stimulus that is reinforcing only because it has been associated with some other already-established **primary reinforcer**. For example, if a distinctive sound precedes food, the sound becomes a reinforcer in its own right and can reinforce responses, but it can also bridge a delay until a primary reinforcer is received. In one experiment, poker chips were established as secondary reinforcers for monkeys by letting the monkeys trade the chips for grapes or raisins (Wolfe, 1933). The monkeys would then work for chips as people work for money, eventually trading them for what they really wanted—food. Many secondary reinforcers are acquired in a social context, such as good grades in school, high performance evaluations at work, and trophies for winning tournaments.

Extinction

Extinction means that responding declines when rewards cease coming. If you are working at a job and then stop getting paid, you might work for a while longer but would eventually stop. Working has extinguished. But extinction is not the same as forgetting how to do the work. If you get paid again, you may immediately return to your previous work level. How long an animal or a person will persist in responding without reinforcement depends on a number of factors, but the *pattern of reinforcement* is especially important. We usually persist longer during extinction if our behavior has been periodically reinforced (**partial reinforcement**) than if it is reinforced every time a response is made (**continuous reinforcement**). Under appropriate partial reinforcement training conditions, laboratory animals have made many thousands of responses without further reinforcement in extinction before finally giving up.

Generalization and Discrimination

When we reinforce a child with praise for saying "please" and "thank you" at home, we expect that the child will **generalize** this behavior to other social situations and are happy when he does so without prompting. The same behaviors should not have to be learned anew for every specific situation.

At the same time, however, the child learns the difference between situations when responses are and are not reinforced, that is, he learns to **discriminate** between the situations. Children, for example, learn that they can get favors from their grandparents more easily than from their parents, so that they ask their grandparents more often for favors (for ice cream or candy or staying up late). In our daily lives we learn many cues that tell us when or when not to respond: fire alarms, telephone sounds, traffic lights, police sirens, and clocks are all stimuli that signal that we should do something specific, but only when those stimuli occur.

Building Behavior by Shaping

It is Alice's first day in the shop, and we have to teach her how to operate the "Old No. 6" machine. Initially we may talk her through it, along with a demonstration. She then goes through the steps. First, she turns on the machine. She is reinforced twice, once when the whirring of the motor tells her that she has done it right and a second time when we say "good." The next step might require feeding a piece of wood into the machine. Alice might hold the wood improperly, making an accident likely. We immediately give her feedback about this danger and then have her do it again. When the wood is fed correctly, we immediately tell her so. It might not be fed exactly right, but we accept the approximation. Over successive practice runs, we require closer and closer approximations to the correct procedure before saying "good" or "okay" to reinforce Alice. Such selective reinforcement of **successive approximations** is what we mean by **shaping** *behavior.* Shaping is particularly important when instructions alone are not adequate, as with motor skills that are very hard to describe or with people (especially children) who cannot use language well. The instructor who is dispensing reinforcers must know in advance what behavior is finally desired and what approximations may be reinforced.

Maintaining Behavior: Schedules of Reinforcement

A **schedule of reinforcement** *is a rule for when and how often to present reinforcers.* At first, we reward children with praise every time they say "please," but we can gradually reduce the frequency of praise and the behavior will still occur, for two reasons. First, the behavior is maintained because it is *still reinforced* sometimes. Second, the behavior is maintained because it was learned on a *partial reinforcement schedule.* As noted earlier, behavior that is partially reinforced is more resistant to extinction. Saying "please" therefore does not extinguish just because it is not reinforced every time it is said.

Cumulative recording.   Animals and people learn to perform in very consistent ways on different schedules, but we may have to keep records over a period of hours or even days in order to see these consistencies. Skinner devised the **cumulative recording system** to do just this. The frequency of a given response, such as a laboratory rat's pressing a lever or a pigeon's pecking at a disk, is measured over time on a cumulative recorder, as illustrated in Figure 7–4. Every time a response occurs, a pen makes a small step across continuously unrolling paper. If the animal presses the lever rapidly, there is a steep line across the paper. When the animal is not responding, there is just a horizontal line. A blip mark shows when a reinforcer is given. Responses and reinforcers would usually be counted automatically. This process can all be done now with a computer, which is more precise and which allows for complex analyses of the data.

The basic schedules.   Each schedule of reinforcement generates a particular pattern of responding over time, illustrated by four basic schedules. A reinforcer is never given except following a response, such as lever pressing, but the schedule determines which lever presses are to be reinforced.

Fixed ratio (FR) schedule.   On an FR schedule, a response is reinforced every N times it occurs. For example, every tenth response might be reinforced, but no others. Large ratios are built up gradually so that the subject does not extinguish while waiting for a reinforcer. A shop worker paid for every twenty widgets assembled would be working on a fixed ratio schedule. The FR schedule generates a highly reliable behavior pattern over time. The person (or animal) makes a fast run of responses to get a reinforcer, and

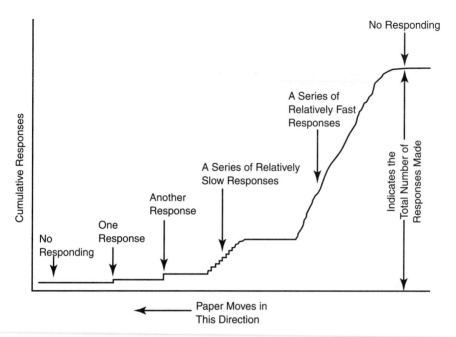

No Responding

A Series of
Relatively Fast
Responses

A Series of Relatively
Slow Responses

Another
Response

One
Response

No
Responding

Indicates the
Total Number of
Responses Made

Cumulative Responses

Paper Moves in
This Direction

FIGURE 7–4. A cumulative recording. The pen moves a step up the paper each time a response is made. The steeper the line, the faster the rate of responding. A line parallel to the baseline indicates no responding at all. (From Hergenhahn, 1976. Used by permission of Prentice Hall, Inc.)

then pauses before beginning the next run. Figure 7–5 shows this behavior pattern, along with the other basic schedules.

Variable ratio (VR) schedule. With the VR schedule, an unpredictable number of responses must be made to obtain a reinforcer. For example, a door-to-door salesperson might learn that a sale is made after an average of every twenty calls, but the actual number of calls between sales might range from one to thirty. This schedule produces a high response rate with little pause between getting a reinforcer and responding for the next one. The salesperson's very next call might be a sale. One reason why some people gamble exorbitantly is that they are on a variable ratio schedule. They get reinforced by winning unpredictably. The more they gamble, the more reinforcers they collect, so that they keep gambling even more. The schedule is demanding, however, and is often considered unpleasant.

Fixed interval (FI) schedule. Ratio schedules are defined in terms of the *number* of responses made, but interval schedules depend on *elapsed time* since the previous reinforcement. The first response made at the end of a set time, such as five minutes, is reinforced. No further response is reinforced until

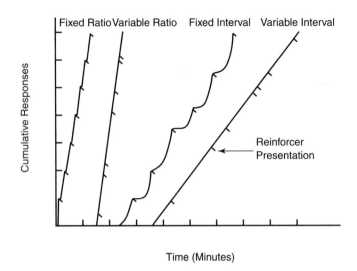

FIGURE 7–5. Stylized cumulative response records for each of the four basic schedules of reinforcement discussed in the text. Each has its characteristic pattern and relative rate of responding compared with the others. Vertical marks show when reinforcers were presented.

another five minutes has passed. The characteristic response pattern is a low response rate during the early part of each interval, gradually increasing until the end of the interval. The record of this pattern on a cumulative recorder is called a **fixed-interval scallop**. People often put things off until the last minute, then work hard to meet a reinforcing deadline. A teacher who checks work only at the end of the hour can expect to have many students on this schedule.

Variable interval (VI) schedule.   Here, the time between reinforced responses is unpredictable. Responding is steady, but slower than with the variable ratio schedule. An example might be a department store clerk's waiting for customers to appear; the time between sales is unpredictable so it is best to keep working just in case there is a sale.

By gradually increasing the number of responses required for a reinforcer, all the preceding schedules can generate many responses with few reinforcers. The author has had thirsty rats which, on a VI one-minute schedule for water reinforcers, would press a lever consistently from day to day at about Two thousand response per hour. Pigeons commonly peck thousands of times per hour with only a few seconds' access to grain every ten or fifteen minutes.

SECTION SUMMARY

1. **Instrumental conditioning** refers to the effect on a behavior when it is followed by **reward** or **punishment**. Rewards are considered **reinforcers** because they "strengthen" the likelihood that a rewarded behavior will occur again.

2. **E. L. Thorndike** argued that learning consists of forming a connection between a specific stimulus and a specific response. He called such a connection an **S-R bond**. Most instrumental learning does not consist of such S-R bonds, however, since most behaviors learned with one response to a stimulus can be transferred to other stimuli and responses without further training.

3. **B. F. Skinner** coined the phrase **operant conditioning** for his approach to instrumental conditioning. He developed an apparatus called the **operant conditioning chamber** for studying animal behavior. The apparatus automatically presents rewards and records responses, making it possible to study behavior continuously over long periods of time without disturbing the subject.

4. Skinner defined a reinforcer as any stimulus following a behavior that increases the probability that the behavior will occur again. A punisher is any stimulus following a behavior that decreases the probability that the behavior will occur again. In the terminology of this text, reinforcers are desirable outcomes of behavior, and punishers are aversive outcomes of behavior.

5. Reinforcers are most effective if given immediately after a response and are progressively less effective with longer delays. The delay between a response and a reinforcer can be bridged by a **secondary reinforcer**, a stimulus that gets its reinforcing power by previous association with some reinforcer.

6. A **schedule of reinforcement** is some **rule** for when to deliver reinforcers in relation to responses. Schedules can be **response-based**, such as delivering a reinforcer after every tenth response (a **fixed ratio** schedule) or can be **time-based**, such as reinforcing the first response after some minimum amount of time has passed since the last reinforcement (a **fixed interval schedule**).

THEORIES OF REWARDS AS REINFORCERS

Rewards are often called reinforcers because a response followed by a reward is thought to strengthen an association between particular environmental conditions and the response, Thorndike's law of effect. A *weak law of effect* says only that reinforcement is a *sufficient condition* for changing behavior, without concern for the mechanism of how reinforcers work. Skinner's approach to operant conditioning represents this view. A *strong law of effect* says that some specific feature of a reinforcer is a *necessary condition* for reinforcing effects to occur. It is such strong laws of reinforcement that we are interested in now. The various theories of rewards as reinforcers are classed as response, motivational, or stimulus theories.

Response Theories

Functional analysis. As we have seen, Skinner defined reinforcers functionally, saying that any stimulus following a response that increases the probability of that response's recurring is a reinforcer. This approach has considerable practical utility because it is often difficult to say in advance what will be a good reinforcer for a given person in a given situation. Years of experience may tell us that money and praise will be good reinforcers, but even these tried-and-true stimuli sometimes fail to modify human behavior in the way we expect them to.

The Premack principle.   David Premack (1959) proposed a more systematic functional analysis and a strong law of reinforcement. He said that any Response A will reinforce any other Response B, if A has a higher response rate than B. This says that whether a reinforcer is effective depends on the response required to get the reinforcer. Therefore, a reinforcer is only reinforcing in a relative sense, not in absolute terms. If a rat licks at a water tube at a higher rate than it presses a lever, then licking can reinforce lever pressing, but lever pressing cannot reinforce licking. This example seems trivially obvious, but consider the following experiment. Schoolchildren were given their choice of operating a candy machine or a pinball machine, and according to their choices were designated as "eaters" or "manipulators." Subsequently, getting candy reinforced playing pinball for the eaters, and playing pinball reinforced getting candy for the manipulators. Premack himself (1971) eventually concluded that the hedonic properties of reinforcing stimuli provided a simpler account of reinforcers than did the response rate theory. Nevertheless, Premack's original analysis was highly influential and was further developed. It follows, for example, that the sequencing of activities during a daily classroom routine can be arranged to advantage. Unpopular academic activities can be scheduled earlier and reinforced by popular activities that come later. Arithmetic might be followed by reading, which in turn might be followed by drawing.

Elicitation theories.   Denny and Adelman (1955) proposed that all that is required for reinforcement is that a response be repeatedly elicited by some stimulus. For example, if an animal gets food following lever pressing, it goes to the food and eats it. Going to the food reinforces lever pressing, and the response of eating reinforces going to the food. Thus,

Lever Pressing → Running to Food → Response (Eating Food)

Each response reinforces the preceding response. The only relevance of food is that food reliably elicits eating. The main weakness with the theory is that stimuli can be reinforcing even when no reliable responses are elicited by the stimuli.

A similar theory, but limited to *consummatory responses*, has also been proposed. Sheffield, Wulff, and Backer (1951) showed that male rats would learn responses reinforced by copulation (a consummatory response) without ejaculation (drive reduction). Sheffield and Roby (1950) also reported that rats would work hard for nonnutritive saccharin solution. Both of these experimental results were interpreted in support of response elicitation theory (Sheffield, 1966), but we shall see shortly that they can be cast into hedonic terms.

The Glickman-Schiff biological theory.   The preceding response theories require that the "reinforcing responses" (e.g., eating) actually occur. Glickman and Schiff (1967) suggested that a stimulus would be reinforcing if it *just activated the neural systems controlling responses,* even if an overt response did not occur. This occurs with electrical stimulation of the brain. Animals will normally eat if the lateral hypothalamus is electrically stimulated and food is available, but electrical stimulation of the lateral hypothalamus is also a powerful reinforcer for lever pressing even when food is not available. This suggests that stimulation of the feeding response system in the brain is adequate for reinforcement.

Motivational Theories

Drive reduction theory.   As we saw in Chapter Six, this theory has its origins in homeostatic theory and says that any behavioral outcome that reduces level of drive is reinforcing (Hull, 1943). Drive reduction theory directly ties reinforcement to motivation because there must be drive in order to have drive reduction. Drive theorists found it necessary to distinguish between **need reduction** and **drive stimulus reduction**, however. Miller (1951a, 1959) argued that any strong stimulus has drive properties, but not all need states produce strong stimuli. For example, oxygen deficit is not discomforting and by itself has no identifiable drive properties. By this analysis, drive stimulus reduction is the reinforcing event, whether the drive stimulation is generated by some internal need such as hunger or comes from a painful or otherwise unpleasant external stimulus. Miller and Kessen (1952) cleverly demonstrated this by showing that milk drunk by a hungry rat was a better reinforcer in a T-maze than milk injected directly into the stomach through a tube, or **fistula**. Tubed milk was more reinforcing than tubed saline solution. If need reduction were the critical factor, the milk should be equally reinforcing whether drunk normally or tubed into the stomach, but in fact it was not. Drinking milk reduced both drive stimulus intensity and need, whereas tubed milk only reduced need. Saline reduced neither. Such analytical experiments as this are important because the observation that food reinforces a hungry animal does not necessarily support the drive reduction theory. The palatability of ingested food (such as the taste of milk) might be the critical reinforcing factor, not hunger (drive) reduction. The trick is to separate palatability from need/drive reduction which tubing different solutions into the stomach does.

Evidence for drive reduction.   Drive-reduction theory is supported by research on pain reduction, fear reduction, and reward-by-fistula (as in the Miller-Kessen experiment). Pain reduction is the clearest example, however. Pain (as from electric shock) is easy to control, and its termination, like getting rid of a toothache, is a powerful reinforcer. Since there is no observable external reinforcer that corresponds to food or water, shock reduction is often considered a "pure" case of drive reduction. Termination of almost any uncomfortably intense stimulus is demonstrably reinforcing, however. Animals will also learn new responses if reinforced by opportunity to escape from a fear-arousing environment (Miller, 1948). Escape from a fear-arousing compartment increases with such variables as the intensity of the shock used to condition the fear and the number of fear-conditioning trials given before testing the escape response (Kalish, 1954).

Evidence against drive reduction.   The preceding evidence suggests that drive reduction may be reinforcing (e.g., pain reduction) but also that exciting, or drive increasing, events can also be reinforcing. For example, Sheffield's sex and saccharin studies challenge drive reduction theory by showing that events that do not reduce drive are nevertheless reinforcing. According to optimal level of arousal theory, either increases or decreases in internal arousal can be reinforcing as long as they lead to a more optimal level of arousal.

Stimulus Theories

Hedonic reinforcers.   Animals that are not under any known dietary deficiency and have never been deprived of food or water will press levers or run through mazes for sweet-tasting substances (e.g., Young, 1959). Taste, not drive reduction, seems to account for this behavior. Drive reduction theorists tried to argue that such sweet-tasting substances were drive reducing, but this is a weak argument because it simply assumes that the animals in such experiments were under some level of drive in the first place. Another argument is that sweet tastes may have become conditioned reinforcers through their previous association with drive (hunger) reduction, especially during nursing. In fact, however, sweet substances are preferred by newborn infants before there is association of the sweet substances with hunger reduction (Blass, 1992; Berridge, 2000; Lippsitt, Reilly, Butcher & Greenwood, 1976). Newborn rats and newborn humans lick at and swallow sugar solutions placed on the lips almost immediately after birth but they reject bitter solutions. Furthermore, even months of exclusive exposure to a bitter taste from birth does not change the subsequent preference for sweet substances with guinea pigs (Warren & Pfaffman, 1958). Direct evidence for genetic differences in taste preference also argues against the learning interpretation (e.g., Ramirez & Fuller, 1976). Learning can be involved in taste preferences, as shown in Chapter Four, but not all reinforcing tastes depend on previous association with drive reduction. Further, as previously noted, both sexual arousal and electrical stimulation of the brain are exciting, not drive reducing, but both are highly reinforcing. We shall reconsider hedonic reinforcers further in the chapter on incentives.

Importance of external stimuli.   Harry Harlow (1953, p. 24) said, "It is my belief that the theory which describes learning as dependent upon drive reduction is false, that internal drive as such is a variable of little importance to learning, and that this small importance steadily decreases as we investigate learning problems of progressive complexity." He then went on to point out that he usually fed his laboratory monkeys before the experimental session. The monkeys stored food in their cheek pouches and then proceeded to swallow a little food after every response they made, whether the response was right or wrong. But the animals learned the correct responses. "It would seem" said Harlow, "that the Lord was simply unaware of drive reduction learning theory when he created, or permitted the gradual evolution of, the rhesus monkey (p. 26)." Harlow contended that external stimuli are more important sources of motivation than internal drive states and suggested that the "main role of the primary drive seems to be one of altering the threshold for precurrent responses (p. 24)." That is, certain behaviors already familiar to an animal, such as eating, are simply more likely to occur when the animal is deprived.

Curiosity and exploration.   Monkeys will work for hours on puzzle-type problems without deprivation or external reinforcement. They will also work inside a dark box at a task that permits no more than a window opening so that they can see out of the box. Given the opportunity, many species are very active in exploring their environments and find this exploration reinforcing. Laboratory rats, for example, will choose the arm of a T-maze that leads to an explorable checkerboard-type maze rather than a plain box, and food deprivation actually reduces this tendency to explore (Montgomery, 1953).

Why do animals explore? The informational approach says that stimuli can be reinforcing by virtue of telling a person or animal something about the environment that it did not already know. An experiment by Bower, McLean, and Meacham (1966) exemplifies this. The question was whether information about a delay of reward would be reinforcing to pigeons even though this information could not change the delay. Pigeons were given their choice of two keys to peck at; they chose more than 90 percent of the time to peck at a key that signaled whether a short or long delay was coming (by red or green light) and less than 10 percent at a key that turned on a yellow light whether the delay was long or short. The birds clearly preferred to know what was going on. Whether good news (green light) or bad (red light), there is undoubtedly considerable value in knowing what is happening in the environment.

Spontaneous alternation.   When rats are run in a T-maze with no reward at all, they tend to alternate running to one side or the other on successive trials. That is, they tend not to go to the goal box that they entered on the previous trial. This is **spontaneous alternation behavior**. Two explanations proposed to account for alternation behavior are **response inhibition** and **stimulus satiation**. Response inhibition theory says that the animal tends not to repeat the same response, whereas stimulus satiation theory says that the animal tends not to go to the same stimulus. The animal becomes satiated for the stimulus just experienced and so goes to the alternate stimulus on the next trial because it is either more novel or more informational. Since both theories account equally well for simple alternation, the following critical test of the theories has been conducted.

Animals are run without reinforcement in a T-maze (Figure 7–6) where the left goal arm is black and the right goal arm is white (or vice versa). Assume that on Trial 1, the animals run to the right, choosing the white goal arm. On Trial 2, the animals are run in the maze with the colors of the goal boxes reversed. In which direction should they turn? According to response inhibition theory, they should go to the left, since that would be opposite their right turn on the previous trial. According to stimulus satiation theory, they should repeat the same response and go to the right, because that is now where the alternate stimulus is. A large number of experiments indicate that they go to the right and generally alternate with reference to stimuli, not responses. Interestingly, it has also been found that animals alternate with reference to absolute direction (such as east versus west), not just light versus dark. This tendency is still alternation with reference to stimuli, however.

A number of authors have proposed that exposure to complex, changing stimuli is reinforcing (Dember and Earl, 1957; Dember & Richman, 1989). Dember and Earl proposed that there is an optimal level of stimulus complexity that is reinforcing but that varies from one individual to another. Organisms tend to respond to stimuli that are just a little more complex than the optimum. These are called **pacer stimuli**. Once an individual's preferred complexity level is established, any change in stimulus preference will be in the direction of greater complexity, not less. Psychological growth—the capacity to deal with progressively more complex stimuli—is built into the theory.

Secondary Reinforcement

Just as such "primary" biological drives as hunger and thirst do not influence our behavior much of the time, neither do their corresponding primary reinforcers, food and water. The concept of secondary (acquired, con-

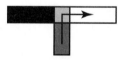

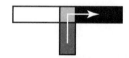

Trial 1. Animal goes right   Trial 2. Animal goes right
         to white goal box   to black goal box

FIGURE 7–6. Experiment showing that animals tend to alternate with regard to brightness rather than location. On Trial 1, the animal goes to the goal box on the right, which is white. On the next trial, it also goes to the goal box on the right, which is now black.

ditioned) reinforcement was devised to fill this void in drive reduction reinforcement theory. A **secondary reinforcer** is a formerly neutral stimulus that, through association with an already-established **primary reinforcer** (e.g., food, water), takes on some of the same functions as a primary reinforcer. A buzzer previously associated with food may reinforce lever pressing. Secondary reinforcement has been used to account for much human behavior. Money, for example, is one of the most general secondary reinforcers, useful only in relation to some other commodity.

Four different functions are ascribed to secondary reinforcers: (1) reinforcing the learning of new responses, (2) maintaining behavior during extinction, (3) mediating long delay of reinforcement by presenting a secondary reinforcer between the time a response is made and the delivery of a primary reinforcer, and (4) establishing and maintaining schedules of reinforcement (Hendry, 1969; Mowrer, 1960; Wike, 1966). If a secondary reinforcer is periodically "reconditioned" (associated with its primary reinforcer), it may retain its potency almost indefinitely (Wike, 1966; Zimmerman, 1957, 1959).

The power of a secondary reinforcer depends on variables similar to those that affect the strength of classical conditioning (Wike, 1966). These include number of associations with a primary reinforcer, the amount of primary reinforcement, close temporal association with primary reinforcement, and probability that the secondary reinforcer will be followed by the primary reinforcer.

Stimulus theories say that a stimulus becomes a secondary reinforcer if it provides reliable and unique information about a forthcoming primary reinforcer, such as a buzzer signaling that food is coming. A redundant stimulus, coming after another signal has already informed an animal that food is coming, is not a good secondary reinforcer (Egger & Miller, 1962, 1963). The most widely accepted theoretical view now is that a secondary reinforcer is a stimulus that is positively correlated with the occurrence of a primary reinforcer (Rescorla, 1987).

SECTION SUMMARY

1. A **functional analysis of behavior** involves determining what rewards are effective for changing the behavior of a given individual. No theory of reinforcement is necessary beyond saying that rewards are sufficient to produce changes.

2. **Response theories** of reinforcement say that the effective reinforcing event is the behavior itself, not the subsequent reinforcer. In this view, food is effective because it elicits the response of eating, and eating (not food) is the reinforcer for a response such as lever pressing. Actual responses may not be necessary; activation of **brain processes** that control behaviors may be adequate.

3. **Motivational theories** of reinforcement emphasize increases or decreases of drive or arousal as reinforcing events.

4. **Stimulus theories** say that stimuli that produce **positive experiences** (positive affect) or **provide information** about behavior or the environment are reinforcing.
5. **Secondary reinforcers** are formerly neutral stimuli that have gained reinforcing capacity of their own by being associated with such **primary reinforcers** as food. A good secondary reinforcer provides reliable information about a forthcoming primary reinforcer.

INTRINSIC MOTIVATION VERSUS EXTERNAL REWARDS

In the discussion of reinforcement theories, we compared *response theories*, which say that some property of the response itself is reinforcing, and *stimulus theories*, which say that some property of outside stimuli are reinforcing. A similar distinction has been made more specifically for humans in terms of **intrinsic motivation** and **extrinsic rewards**. Intrinsic motivation refers to the apparent fact that certain activities, such as hobbies, games, puzzles, and creative endeavors, are enjoyable and rewarding in themselves. They are self-rewarding. Extrinsic rewards refer to those reinforcers which are not directly under our own control, but are given us for our behavior by other people, the standard approach of operant conditioning and behavior modification. We might expect that by giving a reward for behavior that is already intrinsically motivating that we would further enhance the behavior to an even higher level of performance. Such enhancement does not always occur, however, and in some cases giving external rewards for an already interesting task may actually reduce liking or performance on the task. This is called the **overjustification effect** and described in terms of the hidden cost of reward (Lepper & Greene, 1978). The question then is: Under what conditions does this happen and how do we theoretically explain what happens?

Self-Determination Theory

Self-determination theory (Deci & Ryan, 1985) proposes that the level of intrinsic motivation in a person is determined by three psychological needs. First, there is **autonomy**. This refers to the need to feel independent, to feel that one initiates ones own behavior, to be the cause of one's own actions. In the words of deCharms (1968), a person wants to feel like an origin and not a pawn. Second, there is **competence**. A person wants to feel that he or she is good at the activity in question. The athlete wants to feel that she is a skilled performer, the teacher wants to feel that he is effective in getting across his material to his students, the small child wants to feel that he or she can build a really good block tower or draw a really nice picture. Third, there is **relatedness**, which refers to a feeling of connectedness with other people.

The more that these needs are met through some activity, the more pleasure a person gets from the activity and is motivated to continue it.

Self-determination theory says that the overjustification effect occurs when a person perceives that his behavior is being taken over and controlled by the reward (or person giving the reward) and therefore there is less feeling of autonomy. This could lead to less pleasure in the activity itself so that without the reward it would be less likely to occur again spontaneously. For example, suppose a child likes to read and then the parents decide that reading would be even more enjoyable if they paid the child a dollar for every book read—and the child reads voraciously. What would happen if the parents stopped paying the child? Would reading stay at its previously high level, would it decline to its pre-reinforcement level, or would it go down to a new low?

We can illustrate what this means in a study of nursery school children (Anderson, Manoogian, & Reznick, 1976) in which the effects of money, a "good-player" award, and verbal praise as reinforcers for an intrinsically motivated behavior were compared. The children were first pretested for the amount of time spent drawing with magic markers. They were then rewarded for drawing. Finally, they were tested again, without reward, for drawing. Both the money (pennies) and the good-player award produced a drop in amount of time spent drawing, as predicted on the grounds that both of these tangible, external rewards would lead to a change in the perception of control. The praise produced a slight increase in amount of time spent drawing, however, as would be predicted if praise is an indicator of competence. Increased competence leads to greater intrinsic motivation and enjoyment in an activity. Similar results have been produced in a variety of experiments, with both children and adults (Deci, 1975; Deci, 1980; Lepper & Greene, 1978; Notz, 1975; Sansone & Harackiewicz, 2000). Given the importance generally attached to external rewards in the control of behavior, such "hidden costs of reward" call for clarification.

There are a number of caveats to be made about the role of extrinsic rewards and intrinsic motivation, however. First, the effects are not always found and even when found do not mean that intrinsic interest in a behavior declines to zero after receiving external rewards. Amorose and Horn (2000) sampled athletes from football, field hockey, gymnastics, ice hockey, swimming, and wrestling and found that scholarship athletes derived as much enjoyment and showed as much intrinsic motivation toward their sports as did nonscholarship athletes. One can find many reasons why this is not counter to self-determination theory, but the point here is that the theory can easily be misapplied as a broad generalization. It is also easy to overlook why activities become intrinsically motivating in the first place. A child might be enticed by promise of reward to try some novel activity, only to discover after some period of time that she is competent at it and enjoys it.

Kruglanski (1978) distinguished between activities that are ends unto themselves and activities that are the means to some other goal. In his view, an activity is perceived more favorably if it is an end rather than a means to something else. It has also been argued from an operant conditioning point of view that the performance decrement that occurs after reward happens simply because reward has been omitted. In other words, it is an extinction effect. Considerable research is still needed in this area to sort out many problems.

Eisenberger and Cameron (1996) were highly critical of the idea that when rewards for intrinsically motivated behavior are removed, the behavior automatically tends to be less likely than before rewards were introduced in the first place. They note the very important practical implications of this concept, such as illustrated by an article entitled "Why Incentive Plans Cannot Work" and a book entitled *Punished by Rewards* (Kohn, 1993a, 1993b). Similarly, a report in *U.S. News and World Report* indicated that programs that reward children for reading actually were making them nonreaders by destroying their enjoyment of reading. Do the existing data actually support such strong conclusions? Or have data been magnified by some romantic idealism inherent in the American psyche, stressing the importance of self-direction and independence?

Meta-analysis of research.   Meta-analysis is a statistical technique for combining the results of a large number of studies on a topic to arrive at some conclusion about the whole set of studies. This method is preferable to comparing the numbers of studies showing positive results, no results, negative results, and so on. Several metanalyses of research on the overjustification effect have been done, with conflicting conclusions. Cameron and Pierce (1994) analyzed ninety-six studies in which a control group and an experimental group with withdrawn reward were compared. The data showed virtually no effect of removing reward on attitude toward the previously rewarded task. Eisenberger & Cameron (1996) interpreted the data to indicate that the only effects on behavior were those involving an *expected, tangible reward*. And, certainly, none of these effects are all-or-none. Deci, Koestner, and Ryan (1999) reached conclusions more favorable to cognitive evaluation theory in general.

Learned industriousness.   It has also been argued that it is not appropriate to use rewards to foster *creative behavior* because rewards only increase repetition of the rewarded responses. This argument belies the fact that one can selectively reinforce any aspect of behavior that one so chooses, including variation (Skinner, 1953). We can selectively reinforce animals for pressing a lever at a constant rate or a highly variable rate in a Skinner box, for example. Eisenberger's (1992) learned industriousness theory says that the perceived effort involved in doing a task acquires secondary reinforcing properties when the effort is successfully reinforced. It then follows that reinforcing creative behavior, such as attempts to search for unusual solutions to problems, would result in continued effort at creative behavior. One can shape creativity by shaping *the behavior that results in new ideas and behaviors.* You shape exploring new ideas, looking for sources of new information, and so on. It is not the end product that is shaped, but the behavior that results in a novel end product. Eisenberger & Rhoades (2001) found that external rewards for creative activity did in fact produce an increase in that activity. Promise of rewards also produced an increase in creativity activity, mediated by subjects' perceived self-determination. They did not find that external rewards produce a decrease in intrinsic motivation or that external rewards somehow will reduce creative activity.

SECTION SUMMARY

1. **Intrinsic motivation** refers to the fact that many behaviors, such as games and creative activities, are enjoyable and rewarding in themselves. **Extrinsic rewards** are those rewards that are given by someone else and are not under direct control of the person doing the rewarded activity.

2. According to **self-determination theory**, intrinsic motivation is enhanced by feeling of **autonomy, competence**, and **relatedness** to other people.

3. External rewards for behavior sometimes reduce intrinsic motivation to engage in those behaviors, called the **overjustification effect**. According to cognitive evaluation theory, the effect of external rewards depends on whether they are perceived as indicators of **competence** or as an outside source of **control** over behavior. Intrinsic motivation is said to decrease if a behavior is perceived to be controlled by outside forces (rewards). The generality of this effect has been challenged by some researchers.

4. Kruglanski distinguished between activities that are **ends** in themselves and activities that are **means** to ends. In this view, an activity is perceived more favorably if it is an end rather than a means.

5. It has sometimes been argued that rewards do not foster creative behavior because they only increase repetition of the rewarded responses. Rewards can be used to increase the **variability** of behavior, however, which may lead to more creative activities.

EXPANDED REINFORCEMENT THEORY: BEHAVIORAL ECONOMICS

Psychologists have traditionally developed their theories of reinforcement in laboratory settings with tight experimental control and then extrapolated their findings outside the laboratory. This process has been done most elegantly within the framework of Skinner's operant conditioning approach, where practical applications abound. Skinner's novel *Walden II* (1948) described a Utopian society based on operant conditioning principles, and small-scale "token economies" of the kind Skinner envisioned in his novel have actually been established in such institutional settings as psychiatric hospitals, prisons, and classrooms. These economies use tokens for reinforcers, which can later be traded for food, special privileges, or other commodities.

A different approach comes from viewing reinforcers as commodities or money in **open economies** as contrasted to the **closed economy** of the traditional laboratory experiment. In an open economy, there are many choices of commodities and when and how to get them, whereas in a closed economy subjects seldom have choices about what reinforcers they get or what it takes to get them. Over the past three decades, animal psychologists have begun to explore reinforcers in broader contexts than the usual Skinner box or T-maze apparatuses. One reason for this is that the standard laboratory methods have an artificiality about them, as required for experimental control. The consequence is that the concepts derived from such research may be very specific to those artificial situations. Economic theory provides a different conceptual approach. In the Skinner box, an animal gets paid (reinforced) a certain amount for a given amount of work (lever presses, key pecks). Do human economic principles apply to such behavior? For example, does an animal adjust its behavior as the price (work required) for a commodity increases?

The mathematical curve that relates the amount of a commodity sought to the price of the commodity is called a **demand curve**. For example, the number of food pellets a rat will "buy" (work for) varies with the price, such as the number of lever presses required for a pellet. The number of presses required per pellet is one characteristic of a schedule of reinforcement. A reinforcer requiring ten presses is more expensive (greater cost) than one requiring only five presses. The demand for a commodity is said to be **elastic** if the animal works less as the cost increases. Conversely, a commodity is **inelastic** if the demand remains relatively constant in spite of increasing cost. This concept is illustrated in Figure 7–7. "Luxury" items tend to be more elastic than such necessities as food, but such seeming luxuries as coffee are very inelastic. Governments also tax "sin" (such as alcohol and cigarettes) with foreknowledge that these commodities are very inelastic; they sell at nearly the same volume even at the higher prices resulting from the tax.

The effect of a price change can be divided into two parts: the **income effect** and the **substitutability effect**. The income effect is the extent to which a price change affects the real income of a person and the total amount of goods a person can buy with his or her money. If an increase in price is balanced by an increase in income (inflation), there may be no effect of price on demand. But if price goes up while income goes down, the unhappy situation with high inflation and low employment, there may be a greatly reduced demand with higher price. The substitutability effect refers to the availability of a similar commodity at a lower price. If there is no substitute, as is the case with oil for automobiles, there is a smaller effect of price increase on con-

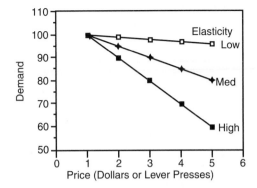

FIGURE 7–7. Demand curves varying in elasticity. A demand curve with low elasticity shows little change in demand (sales) with increasing price. A demand curve with high elasticity shows a large drop in sales when there is increasing price. In economics, cost is typically measured in monetary units, such as dollars. In animal research, cost is given by the amount of work, such as the number of lever presses required to obtain a fixed amount of food. Arbitrary units are used on both axes.

sumption than if there were a substitute. The demand for butter, however, changes with price because a number of good substitutes are available (margarine, cooking oils). In like manner, with the influx of foreign products selling at lower prices than American-made products, there is great substitutability, therefore, great elasticity in demand for American goods.

Another principle, called the **complementarity effect**, works opposite to the substitutability effect. Complementarity means that an increase in the demand for one product also produces an increased demand for another. A rise in the consumption of pretzels in a bar increases the sales of beer, and increased air travel increases the sales of flight insurance.

All these principles have been shown to work to some extent in the animal laboratory. For example, in one study, rats pressed one lever for food and a different lever for water, or one lever for Tom Collins mix and another for root beer. As the price (number of presses) required for a morsel of food increased, the animals did not switch to pressing for water (no substitutability); they paid more (pressed more) for food. When the price of Tom Collins mix went up, however, the rats readily switched their allegiance to root beer. The two commodities were substitutable (Lea, 1978).

If animals have free access to food for a certain amount of time daily in their home cages, they will still press a lever in a Skinner box for food—until the cost becomes too high. When this happens, the animals simply stop "eating out," no longer pressing the lever if free food is available elsewhere. The free food is substitutable for the food bought with lever presses. If, however, the only food available has to be bought by lever pressing, the demand for the food is much less elastic than if there is free food. The animals keep responding until they spend virtually all their time working to get food (e.g.,

Collier, Kanarek, Hirsch, & Marrine, 1976). As a final thought, it is worth considering that human economic principles may have developed as they have because they do in fact represent broad biological principles of reinforcement applicable to many species.

SECTION SUMMARY

1. **Behavioral economics** is the application of economic principles to laboratory research on rewards. **Demand curves** (effects of increasing cost for commodities) have been studied, using the number of lever presses required to obtain a reward as a definition of cost.

2. Behavioral economic studies have looked at rewards in **open economies** (where there are many choices of commodities) as compared with the traditional laboratory studies with **closed economies** (where there is usually only a single reinforcer specified by the experimenter).

3. Such economic concepts as **elasticity** have been found to apply to animal studies. A reinforcer is **elastic** if the work to get it (e.g., lever pressing) declines when the cost of the reinforcer (e.g., number of lever presses to get it) increases. A commodity is **inelastic** if the demand curve remains relatively constant in spite of cost increases.

CHAPTER EIGHT

Rewards as Incentives

What are incentives and incentive motivation?

How are incentives different from drives?

Why is the incentive concept important?

How are incentives related to performance?

How are incentives related to learning?

What are the biological and learned features of incentives?

How does incentive motivation develop?

How does incentive motivation get attached to specific behaviors?

Are incentives specific to particular responses or do they operative across many responses?

How are emotion and incentive motivation related?

Are incentives related to our fantasies?

THE CONCEPT OF INCENTIVE MOTIVATION

In Chapter Seven we explored the idea that rewards work "backward" to rein-force responses and make them more likely to occur. This approach usually starts from two assumptions, and if either is wrong, then we must look at the role of rewards differently. The first assumption is that *learning is an associa-tive process*, that is, learning depends on the formation of associations be-tween, say, stimuli and responses. The second assumption is that *the role of re-wards is to strengthen such associations*, that is, rewards reinforce learning by strengthening associations. If learning is *not* an associative process or if rein-forcers are *not necessary* for learning to occur, then we must look at other pos-sibilities for what rewards do.

As far as learning is concerned, there is cogent evidence that learning may not actually involve the strengthening of new associations (Gallistel & Gibbon, 2000, 2001). These arguments involve research in learning which is beyond our scope here, but they are not critical to examining the second as-sumption, that reinforcers are necessary for learning to occur. If we can demonstrate that rewards are not necessary for learning, then the view that rewards are *incentive motivational* determinants of performance becomes dom-inant. The **anticipation** or **expectancy** of rewards arouses incentive motivation which factor arouses us to engage in activities that lead to rewards. An organ-ism engages in behavior leading to a reward if the particular reward is valued. The anticipation of bad events, the topic of later chapters, leads us to avoid other situations.

Are Rewards Necessary for Learning?

Research over many years has produced the following kinds of data which are especially compelling in showing that rewards are not necessary for instrumental learning.

Latent learning. Tolman and Honzik (1930) were among the first to demonstrate that learning and performance are not the same thing. Perfor-mance does not always show whether learning has occurred. They had three different groups of hungry rats learn a complex maze. One group was re-warded with food in the goal box after each run and showed progressively fewer errors. A second group was never rewarded and showed no improve-ment. A third group ran the maze for several days without reward and did not improve during this time. Reward was then introduced, and the performance of the third group improved almost immediately to the level of the continu-ously rewarded group (see Figure 8–1). Rewarding the animals with food got them to perform better but was not necessary for learning the maze. The learning was latent, not demonstrated in performance until reward was intro-duced. Many subsequent experiments validated the principle of latent learn-ing (Thistlewaite, 1951).

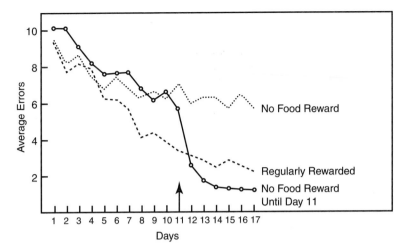

FIGURE 8–1. Evidence for the latent learning in the maze. With no food reward, there is some reduction in errors, but not as great a reduction as with regular food reward. Despite the higher error scores prior to the introduction of food, the group rewarded only from the eleventh trial immediately begins to do as well as the group that had been regularly rewarded. The interpretation is that some learning went on within the first ten days, which did not show in performance until the food incentive activated it. (After Tolman & Honzik, published in 1930 by The Regents of the University of California; reprinted by permission of the University of California Press.)

Latent extinction. Extinction of a response can occur without actually performing the response to be extinguished. Suppose we train two groups of animals to run down a straight runway with food reward. One group is then placed in the goal box a number of times without food, the other is not. Both groups then undergo the normal extinction procedure of running to the goal box and finding no food. The group previously exposed to the empty goal box extinguishes faster than the control group. Since the animals did not actually do any running during latent extinction (goal box placement) trials, they must have run more slowly than control animals because they learned *not to expect reward* in the goal box.

Incentive shifts. Research clearly shows that animals reliably perform better (faster, more vigorously, more accurately) for large rewards than for small ones (Black, 1969). This could mean either that the animals learn better the response necessary to get the rewards or that they are more motivated by large rewards. Experiments which in principle are similar to the latent learning experiments support the motivational interpretation. In these studies animals learn a response for either small or a large food reward, then are suddenly shifted from small to large or from large to small. Their performance changes appropriately to the new level of reward, but too suddenly to be accounted for by changes in response learning. The classic study was by

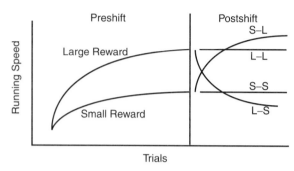

FIGURE 8–2. Idealized presentation of the Crespi shift effect. During original training (preshift) animals run faster to large rewards than to small ones. After the shift, animals switched from small to large rewards (S-L) quickly increase their speed to a level even higher than that of animals continuously trained with large rewards (L-L). Conversely, animals shifted from large to small rewards (L-S) drop below the level of animals continuing to get small rewards (S-S). Shifted animals eventually go back to the levels of animals continuously at a given reward value.

Crespi (1942), but experiments by Mellgren (1972) and many others clarified various details. Figure 8–2 shows the shift effect in a hypothetical experiment patterned after Crespi and Mellgren. Following the shift from small to large incentives, the animals immediately run faster to the new incentive and when shifted to a smaller incentive run more slowly.

Contrast effects. An important feature of incentive shifts is the occurrence of **contrast effects**. If different incentives are presented to the same animal so that the animal can compare them, the animal responds differently to each of them than if they were presented alone. In the Crespi-type experiment when the animals are shifted to a larger reward, they perform better for a while than animals that get a large reward continuously. This is an overshooting, or **positive contrast effect**. Conversely, there was an undershooting effect for downshifted animals, a **negative contrast effect** (Figure 8–2). Crespi referred to these effects as **elation** and **depression** to indicate that they were motivational effects. These shift effects are important because they show that it is not just the absolute amount of reward that is important, but also how the animal perceives the reward in comparison to previous rewards. Crespi (1944) suggested that the animals developed different amounts of anticipatory excitement, which he called **eagerness**, and said that this was related to learning only to the extent that the animal had to find out how much incentive it was getting before it exhibited the appropriate amount of eagerness.

Quality of reward. Different kinds of rewards have different incentive motivational properties. In general, more highly preferred substances are also better incentives. As early as 1924, Simmons showed that rodents performed better in a maze if rewarded with bread and milk than if rewarded

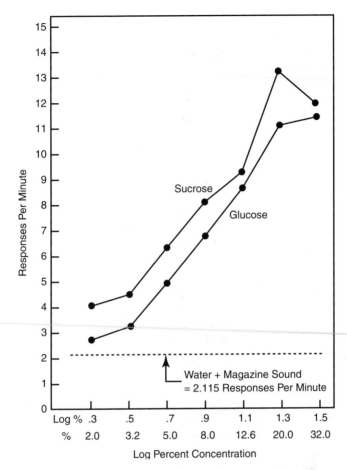

FIGURE 8-3. Rate of bar pressing as a function of concentration of reinforcing agent. (From Guttman, 1954, p. 359. Copyright © 1954 by the American Psychological Association. Reprinted by permission.)

with sunflower seeds. Guttman (1953, 1954) found that animals pressed a lever more for higher concentrations of sucrose or glucose, even though the amount of fluid was constant, as shown in Figure 8–3.

Deprivation effects.   Incentive theorists argue that deprivation does not directly energize behavior. Rather, as we saw in our earlier discussion of feeding, deprivation enhances incentives (Berridge, 2001; Bindra, 1974; Bolles, 1972). Hunger makes food a better incentive, thirst makes water a better incentive, and so on, a phenomenon called **alliesthesia** (Cabanac, 1979). Indeed, Tolman (1948) also reported that only hungry animals showed the latent learning effect when shifted from no-reward to reward, presumably because the reward had no value for nonhungry animals.

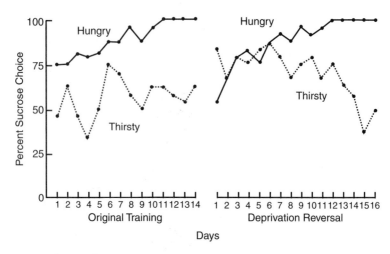

FIGURE 8–4. Preferences for 8 percent sucrose over water by hungry or thirsty rats in a maze choice situation. The animals were run six trials a day and were forced to go to the nonpreferred side, if necessary, in order to equalize number of trials to each side. Equal experience with each incentive each day was thus guaranteed. After fourteen days of original training, each group was switched to the opposite deprivation condition (deprivation reversal) for the next sixteen days of training. In each case, the animals adjusted to the new deprivation condition by responding similarly to the behavior of the other group in the original deprived condition (sucrose preference increased quickly for the now-hungry animals and declined for the now-thirsty animals). (From Beck & Bidwell, 1974, p. 331.)

Preference for a specific flavor food also increases if that food has been eaten when the animal is very hungry (Revusky, 1967, 1968). Such deprivation effects are sometimes spectacular when we compare different kinds of deprivation rather than different amounts of deprivation. For example, given the choice between 6 percent sucrose and water, hungry rats virtually always choose the sucrose, but thirsty rats are almost indifferent between the two choices. Preferences are reversed simply by making the thirsty rats hungry and the hungry rats thirsty, as shown in Figure 8–4 (from Beck & Bidwell, 1974).

SECTION SUMMARY

1. The concept of **incentive motivation** is based on the idea that rewards do not necessarily affect specific responses. Rather, the **anticipation of rewards** arouses whatever responses might be effective in obtaining the rewards.
2. A variety of experiments shows that changes in incentive value, increasing or decreasing, quickly produce appropriate changes in performance even though not associated with particular responses. In **latent learning** experiments, animals show no sign of learning a maze after many trials if they are not rewarded for running accurately, but they suddenly perform very well when reward is introduced.

3. If an animal has the opportunity to compare a particular reward with other rewards, it responds differently to that reward. This is called a **contrast effect**. This shows that it is not just the absolute amount or quality of a reward that is important, but that the perception of reward in comparison to other rewards is also important.

4. Incentive theories argue that such motivational effects as deprivation do not "drive" behavior. Rather, deprivation increases motivation by making anticipated incentives more attractive or valuable.

HOW DOES INCENTIVE MOTIVATION DEVELOP?

We have seen the evidence that consistently points to the conclusion that incentive motivation is the most important motivational determinant of performance. We now turn to theories that attempt to explain how incentive motivation works. One type of theory assumes that incentive motivation develops out of *responses* that an animal makes, the other assumes that incentive motivation is a central nervous system process that does not depend on overt responses.

Response Mediation Theory

On the basis of the Crespi's experimental results, Hull (1952) added an intervening variable for incentive motivation to his system, symbolized as the letter *K*. The new formulation then read:

Excitatory Potential = Habit $\times$ Drive $\times$ Incentive (or, $E = H \times D \times K$)

The antecedent conditions for manipulating the strength of K are the amount, quality, and delay of reward (longer delays produce weaker incentive motivation). This formulation shows how incentive motivation fits into the system, but does not specify a mechanism for how incentive motivation develops. Response mediation theory is an attempt to explain the anticipatory nature of incentive motivation in stimulus-response terms. The essence of mediation theory is that some internal event in the organism occurs between (mediates between) an overt stimulus and an overt response. Symbolically:

$S \rightarrow$ (mediating event) $\rightarrow$ Response.

The question is, What are the mediators and how do they work?

Classically Conditioned Responses as Mediators (r_g Theory)

Kenneth Spence (1956) suggested that the incentive concept in Hull's theory (K) might itself be derived from Hull's own earlier concept of the **fractional anticipatory goal response** (Hull, 1931). Very briefly, the mechanism works as follows: When an animal is rewarded with food after making a response, it eats the food. Eating is a *goal response* (R_G) and, of course, requires that there be food present. There are also, however, responses that can occur without food being present such as small chewing or licking movements, or salivation. These are *fractional goal responses* (r_g's) which can be conditioned to environmental stimuli like other responses. When the animal is put into the start box of a maze, the r_g's are aroused and are fractional anticipatory goal responses.

The anticipatory r_g's become motivational by virtue of the fact that they have *stimulus consequences*. Any response that we can "feel," for example, has stimulus consequences that feed information about the response back to the brain. The stimulus consequences of r_g's are s_g's. The s_g's in turn can become conditioned to overt responses. We then have the following sequence:

$$S \rightarrow (r_g - s_g) \rightarrow R,$$

or more specifically, for example,

$$(S) \text{ Apparatus Cues} \rightarrow (r_{\text{salivation}} - s_{\text{salivation}}) \rightarrow (R) \text{ Running to Food}$$

where S is an environmental stimulus, R is an overt response, and $r_g - s_g$ is the anticipatory goal response and its stimulus. We assume that the stronger the r_g, the stronger the s_g, and hence the stronger the effect of s_g on behavior.

Applications of r_g theory to incentive phenomena. The $r_g - s_g$ mechanism accounts for some of the major incentive phenomena as follows.

Incentive shifts. When rewards are shifted from small to large, there is a larger R_G, and therefore a larger $r_g - s_g$. Since $r_g - s_g$ was already conditioned to responses in earlier training, a sudden increase in the intensity of $r_g - s_g$ could produce a sudden "improvement" in behavior.

Latent learning. Incentive motivation could not develop in nonrewarded animals because there is no R_G (eating) and hence no $r_g - s_g$ related to eating. When food is introduced, $r_g - s_g$ occurs and can be conditioned to various maze stimuli, and performance improves.

Quality or quantity of reward. A better or larger reward arouses a stronger R_G and hence a stronger $r_g - s_g$. The stronger $r_g - s_g$ stimulates more vigorous performance.

Problems with r_g theory. Few psychologists would doubt that there are mediating events, but r_g theory is beset with serious problems. The main empirical problem is the lack of tangible evidence that fractional responses of the kind demanded by the theory actually do occur or are conditioned to environmental cues. For example, vigor of consummatory and instrumental responses should be highly correlated if stronger r_g's stimulate stronger responses. Such correlations are small at best, however (e.g., Black, 1969; Robbins, 1969). Furthermore, the r_g's should be conditioned to start-box cues if the theory is to account for the well-documented fact that with "better" rewards animals are much quicker to leave the start box of the apparatus. This conditioning simply has not been observed (Sheffield, 1966).

In conclusion, r_g theory was an ingenious but inadequate attempt to account for mediation in response terms because of lack of evidence that responses occur or function as the theory requires. In fairness to Hull's theory, the addition of incentive motivation to his basic formulation ($E = H \times D \times K$) does not require response mediation. Other theorists have specifically considered incentive motivation to be a *central brain process*.

Central Processes: Emotional Mediation

Clifford Morgan (1943, 1959) proposed that a variety of circumstances lead to central nervous system changes that he called **central motive states (CMS)**. Central motive states can be aroused by external stimuli but can also persist after the initiating stimuli have disappeared. They may be maintained by hormonal activity, for example. Elliot Stellar (1954) proposed more specifically that the hypothalamus was the brain structure most intimately involved in central motive states.

Dalbir Bindra (e.g., 1969, 1978) elaborated the CMS concept, saying that the CMS is generated by the interactions of "neural representations of organismic state and incentive object" (1969, p. 12). For example, the neural activity occurring when an animal is hungry interacts with the neural representation of food. The brain combines this information to produce a motivational state that directs behavior toward a relevant incentive, such as food. From this incentive motivational perspective, a reward does not strengthen (reinforce) a particular response; it arouses a *motivational state that influences many subsequent responses*. The CMS alters the value of incentive objects and changes the likelihood of many possible approach responses.

An experiment by Bindra and Palfai (1967) illustrates how internal states interact with external stimuli. Thirsty rats were confined in a small cage where they could not move around. All of them heard the click of a metronome when water was presented. The animals were then divided into three groups (low, medium, and high water deprivation) and, in a larger cage, the activities of locomotion, sitting, and grooming were recorded before, during, and after the metronome was clicking. Locomotion was generally higher under medium or high deprivation, but the click of the metronome, signaling water, increased locomotion to an even higher level only under medium or high deprivation. In other words, the conditioned stimulus signaling water only produced motivational excitement when the animals were also thirsty.

Incentive Valence

Toates (2001) has used the term **incentive valence** to describe the capacity of an incentive to evoke approach behavior. He and others have also asked how this develops. As we have seen, hungry animals like food more and work for it more persistently than do satiated animals. Some authors, such as Bindra (1974), have considered this process to be automatic. Simply making an animal hungry will increase the attractiveness of food (see Berridge, 2001, for an historical review). Recent research suggests a different answer, however (e.g., Balleine, 2001).

Dickenson and Balleine (1995) asked whether the incentive values of a given food reward in different motivational states (e.g., deprived versus non-deprived) are hard-wired and automatic, as suggested by Bindra, for example. Or do they have to be learned? Their procedure was to shift animals' motivational states following training with food reward, but to test the animals without allowing them to actually taste the food during the testing process. If the animal's current motivational state automatically confers a particular incentive value on food then an animal should immediately shift its responsiveness to food appropriate to the new deprivation level. They trained animals to press a lever for food pellets while hungry, then satiated them with food prior to testing them. They tested the animals for lever pressing in extinction so that the animals could not directly experience the reward. Surprisingly, they found that their satiated animals responded just as much during extinction as did food deprived animals. The animals' behavior was being controlled by the previous high incentive value of the food when they were deprived, not its current low value. If, however, the animals were allowed to eat food pellets after the deprivation shift, but before lever pressing, they did show a much lower level of lever pressing in extinction. In this case they had opportunity to learn about the lower incentive value of the pellets and carried this back into the lever pressing situation. The conclusion from this and similar experiments is that the animals' level of incentive motivation does not automatically change with a change in deprivation; they have to experience the incentive under the new deprivation condition first.

In another experiment getting at the same problem, Hall, Arnold, and Myers (2000) studied drinking in young rats. Adult animals are readily induced either to drink water or to work for water by injecting them with an appropriate amount of salt solution (e.g., 2 percent body weight of 15 percent sodium chloride, table salt). Is this drinking also subject to learning? Hall et al. reported that 35-day-old rats drank water avidly (4 percent of their body weight) in an hour immediately following such an injection However, 21-day-old rats, which had been weaned only three days earlier, drank only about

0.5 percent of their body weight. The authors speculated that the younger animals had not yet experienced the effect of drinking after the dehydration induced by eating dry lab food. In a second experiment, then, one group of animals was weaned at 18 days but was put on a liquid diet instead of getting dry food so that they were not dehydrated by feeding. When tested for intake following saline injections at 35 days of age, these animals did not drink any more water than 18-day-old animals. The conclusion was that water is not a positive incentive until it has been experienced in the context of dehydration, which, of course, is a normal occurrence in the lives of most animals.

Such experiments as the above indicate that food or water are not automatically rewarding until there is opportunity to experience them in the contexts of deprivation and satiation. Other research even shows that when an incentive is revalued (e.g., by deprivation or satiation) for one response it is not necessarily revalued for other responses (Rescorla, 1987). Therefore, it appears that incentive value depends not only on specific experiences with incentives, but also may even be specific to the particular behaviors used to obtain the incentives.

SECTION SUMMARY

1. Spence proposed that incentive motivation grows out of goal responses. A fraction of the eating response (salivation, for example) can be conditioned. This **fractional goal response**, $r_g - s_g$, is conditioned to environmental cues and has incentive motivational properties when activated by these cues. The theory accounted for many facts of incentive motivation, but there is little evidence for the existence of such responses

2. Current theory views incentive motivation as a brain process, or **central motive state**. Such a process involves neural activity related to internal states (e.g., hunger, thirst) and neural activity related to specific external stimuli (e.g., food, water). The central motive state influences many different responses.

3. **Incentive valence** refers to the capacity of an incentive to evoke approach behavior. Research suggests that the development of incentive valence depends on the experience an animal has with a particular incentive under a particular deprivation condition, and that this may even be specific to particular responses occurring under those conditions.

GENERAL THEORETICAL APPROACHES

Tolman's Purposive Behaviorism

We previously looked at the very general theory of behavior espoused by Clark Hull and his followers. This theory assumed that learning involves specific stimulus-response associations, that these associations (habits) are reinforced by drive reduction, and that habits are activated by drives. Edward Chace Tolman and his advocates had a more cognitive orientation and were the primary theoretical antagonists to Hullian theory. Tolman was nevertheless a strict behaviorist, and in fact it was Tolman who introduced intervening variables into psychological theory, insisting on the importance of tying theoretical concepts to observable events (Tolman, 1938). At the same time, however, Tolman was concerned with what he called **molar behavior**, not with specific "muscle twitches" that make up **molecular behaviors**. If an animal turns to the right in a maze, "turning right" is the molar behavior. It makes little difference which exact muscles contract in order to make the correct turn.

Tolman's concepts had more mentalistic-sounding names than Hull's because Tolman did not believe that learning consists of establishing S-R associations (Tolman, 1932, 1938). Tolman's use of the concepts of **expectancy** and **demand** illustrates the difference. An expectancy is the anticipation that under given circumstances a particular behavior will lead to a particular outcome. Going to the store will result in getting food. A demand is the motivation for food. Whereas Hull had an S-R concept to explain instrumental learning, Tolman had an $S_1 R_1 - S_2$ theory. $S_1 R_1 - S_2$ is an expectancy that in this situation (S_1) if I make a particular response (R_1), then some event (S_2) will follow. For Tolman, the S's were environmental places or events, and behavior was simply how a person or an animal got from one place or event to another.

Tolman believed that expectancies were central brain processes, not requiring responses. What distinguished his approach from the "mentalistic" approach of some earlier psychologists was that he worked only with observable events and *inferred* underlying expectancies and demands from his objective observations. Studying laboratory rats, he showed that it was possible to discuss purpose, foresight, and expectation with objective events as the primary data, not depending on human introspection. Purpose, foresight, and expectation were intervening variables

Demand, the motivation component, is related to the outcome of behavior. I might expect that if I go to the refrigerator there will be a piece of chicken to eat, but unless I have a demand for food, the chicken will have no value for me and I will not go to the refrigerator. Demands are determined jointly by internal and external events, such as being hungry and liking the taste of chicken. We have demands for desirable outcomes and against aversive outcomes.

Cognitive maps.   If a person or an animal has expectancies about "getting from here to there," the person or animal must have some notion, or mental (brain) representation, about where "here" and "there" are. Tolman (1948) argued that animals have environmental "maps" in their heads and their behavior is guided in accordance with what maps they have learned. The cognitive map concept has been important to modern environmental psychologists, who are much concerned with how people perceive, learn about, and locomote through their environments.

Tolman's systematic theory.   The following formula is modified from Tolman's final presentation of his theory (1959, p. 134), but neither his symbolism nor the entire formula is used.

$$\text{Performance Tendency} = f\,(\text{Expectancy, Drive Stimulation,}$$
$$\text{Incentive Valence)}$$

Each of these is an intervening variable that has a rough equivalent in Hull's theory. The basic concepts in the two theories are compared in Table 8–1. Tolman defines his concepts differently, of course, and attributes different characteristics to them.

Performance tendency is the tendency for an expectancy $S_1 R_1 - S_2$ to be expressed in behavior, just as sEr in Hull's theory is the tendency for sHr to be expressed in behavior. The strength of performance tendency is a function of many variables, as is sEr.

Expectancies were of two kinds. Tolman considered the $S_1 R_1 - S_2$ expectancy more important, since it involves behavior. The second kind was an $S_1 - S_2$ expectancy, that one stimulus event will follow from another. This is the general form of classical conditioning, where S_1 and S_2 correspond to CS and UCS.

A concept closely related to expectancy is *means-end-readiness,* or *belief.* When a particular S_1 occurs, there is "released" an expectancy that a particular response will lead to a particular outcome, or that an S_2 will follow. A belief is more enduring than an expectancy. For example, I may always *believe* that with certain temperature and cloud conditions, it will snow. However, it is only when these conditions actually prevail will I *expect* it to snow.

Incentive valence refers to the value of S_2 to the organism. If a tasty food has a high positive value now, I expect it to have a high value in the future. This expected value is the valence of the food. Valences are learned from experiences with objects of particular values. The combination of drive stimulation and valence is what Tolman had earlier called demand.

Criticism of Tolman's theory.   Tolman (1959) saw evidence for the correctness of his theory throughout all experiments in instrumental learning. His approach simply looks at everything differently from an S-R approach

TABLE 8–1.   Comparisons of concepts in Hull's and Tolman's theories.

CONCEPTS	HULL	TOLMAN
Performance	Excitatory potential	Performance tendency
Learning	Habit (H)	Expectancy
Internal state	Drive (D)	Drive stimulation
Incentive motivation	Incentive (K)	Incentive valence

like Hull's. Problems that nagged at Hull's theory simply dissipated in Tolman's. Such issues as drive reduction reinforcement and the possibility of whether learning can take place without responding did not bother Tolman. He also believed that his view was more likely to be a fruitful approach to human cognition than was S-R theory, a view vindicated in modern cognitive theory and research.

One of the major criticisms of Tolman's approach was that it seemed to have no "action principle." Whereas Hull's theory had an action principle, that stimuli arouse responses, Tolman's expectancy theory did not. As Edwin Guthrie, a well-known critic of Tolman's theory put it, Tolman's rats are left buried in thought. Bolles (1972) gave a spirited rejoinder to this criticism, pointing out that the action principle in Hull's theory really only existed in words. Except for the case of simple reflexes, there was no direct link demonstrated between incoming stimuli and particular learned behaviors by which one could say that "this stimulus arouses that response." One can just as readily say that expectancies arouse behavior as one can argue that S-R connections are responsible for behavior.

SECTION SUMMARY

1. In **Tolman's** system of **purposive behaviorism**, organisms are said to learn **expectancies** about incentives. Incentives have **positive** or **negative valence**, which is their motivational power to attract or repel organisms.

2. Tolman's concepts had mentalistic sounding names, but were intervening variables defined by antecedent and consequent events. He was behavioristic in his approach.

3. There are two types of expectancies, corresponding to classical and instrumental conditioning. An **instrumental expectancy** is the anticipation that under given circumstances a particular behavior will lead to a particular outcome. That behavior will occur, however, only if there is a **demand** (motivation) for the outcome (e.g., food).

4. **Cognitive maps** refer to the idea that organisms have mental representations of the environment in the brains and that as an animal locomotes through its environment its behavior is often guided by these representations.

5. A major criticism of Tolman's approach was that it had no **action principle**, such as S-R connections energized by drive. Bolles argued that, given our ignorance of the neural activities underlying specific behaviors, it is just as reasonable to argue that expectancies arouse behavior as to say that stimuli arouse behavior.

Young's Experimental Hedonism

America's foremost hedonic incentive theorist for many years was Paul Thomas Young (1959, 1966, 1968). His early work did not initially attract a great deal of attention, but as the flaws of drive theory were gradually exposed, more and more psychologists were attracted to his ideas, especially workers in hunger, thirst, and taste. As we saw in Chapter Four, organisms do not often seem to eat and drink just to restore homeostasis. Instead, they eat foods according to whether they do or do not like them. Young assumed the existence of a hedonic continuum and the hedonic axiom, as were discussed in Chapter One.[1] Although some researchers tried to interpret Young's research results in terms of drive theory (e.g., Mowrer, 1960), Young repeatedly pointed out that the animals in his experiments were sleek and healthy and eagerly sought the tasty solutions he provided them in his experiments, even though they were never deprived of food or water. Where was the homeostatic imbalance or any other source of drive?

Principles of experimental hedonism. Young proposed a number of specific hedonic principles, some of which we summarize here in abbreviated form. He assumed that certain stimuli produced positive or negative affective arousals, and that motives grow out of these arousals. **Primary affective arousals**, positive or negative, are directly produced by stimuli (e.g., taste of food in the mouth). **Conditioned affective arousals** are *anticipatory* arousals produced by stimuli previously associated with primary arousal through classical conditioning. A **motive** is the anticipation of future primary hedonic arousal with the power to arouse behavior. Berridge's distinction between liking and wanting, which we also saw in Chapter Four, seems similar to Young's distinction between primary and conditioned affective arousals. Liking refers to the immediate affective experience of a stimulus, such as primary arousal. Wanting is the motivation to approach a stimulus, produced by conditioned affective arousal. In general, behavior is organized according to the basic hedonic principle of maximizing positive and minimizing negative hedonic arousal, the hedonic axiom. The affective value of stimuli is modified by internal states. Young (1966, p. 60) defined **palatability** as "the hedonic characteristic of a food" dependent upon a variety of other factors besides just taste. The hedonic quality of food changes with deprivation and satiation, for example. Palatability seems to be much like Toates's concept of *incentive valence.*

In summary, Young's principles are still solid, but the addition of some new principles uncovered since his last writings on the topic make them even more potent. Much of what we know about the facts of motivation can be encompassed within his framework.

Two-Process Learning Theory

Two-process learning theory combines principles from classical and instrumental conditioning as they are jointly involved in the development of incentive motivation and control of behavior by incentive motivation. The the-

---

[1] In correspondence with Professor Young, shortly before his death in 1978, I pointed out that I had defined motivation in terms of the concepts of desire and aversion in the first edition of this book (Beck, 1978). He replied that it was interesting that I considered them concepts, because he considered them empirical facts.

ory asserts that Pavlovian **conditioned emotional responses** (**CER**s) can directly affect instrumental behavior (Bolles & Moot, 1972; Mowrer, 1960; Rescorla & Solomon, 1967). The conditioned emotional responses are what we previously saw in Chapter Six as types of reinforcers. Consider an animal that runs down a runway to get food. The animal's running is rewarded when it obtains food (instrumental conditioning), but the various runway cues also come to predict that the food will follow (classical conditioning). These cues to food (CSs) arouse a conditioned response (CR), which is a central emotional state labeled **hope**. If the animal anticipated getting shocked, the CS would arouse an emotional state commonly called **fear**. If the animal anticipated a positive event that did not occur, an aversive state of **disappointment** would be signaled. Finally, a signal that an aversive event is about to end produces a positive state of **relief**. These are summarized in Table 8–2.[2] What makes the theory interesting is how these emotional states affect other behaviors beyond those in the situation in which they may have been learned.

Transfer of control experiments.   Classically conditioned emotional responses which have been developed in one situation can gain control over behaviors in entirely different situations. Again, we apply a theory to our animal running down the alleyway to food. The animal runs because the runway cues trigger a positive conditioned emotional response (hope) in anticipation of getting food. But now suppose that we put the animal into an entirely different situation and classically condition a novel tone by pairing it with food. The tone CS comes to arouse the positive emotion of hope. Finally, we put the animal back into the runway and sound the tone just before it starts to run. The theory predicts that the animal should run more vigorously because its hope is aroused by the runway apparatus cues *plus the hope*

TABLE 8–2.   Emotional states involved in classical conditioning.

CONDITIONED STIMULUS	UNCONDITIONED STIMULUS	
	APPETITIVE (FOOD)	AVERSIVE (SHOCK)
CS+	Hope	Fear
CS−	Disappointment	Relief

[2]This terminology was first used by Mowrer (e.g., 1960), but to help keep the historical record straight, Mowrer himself never thought of hope as anticipation of a positive event. Rather, he considered hope to be the anticipatory reduction of fear. Mowrer never considered pleasure as a source of motivation separate from fear. In one of Mowrer's 1950s seminars on "revised two-factor theory" in which the author participated, Mowrer was challenged on this point by a student who asked why fear was necessary in order to explain all approach behaviors. Mowrer's answer was enlightening, both theoretically and clinically. "Why," he replied, "I wouldn't know what to do without my fear." Mowrer's personal history of depression is well known.

aroused by the tone. And the animal does run more vigorously following the tone. As a generalization we can say that if the classically conditioned hedonic arousal has the same valence (positive or negative) as the instrumental outcome, the classical CR will facilitate the instrumental response.

If the emotional response conditioned to the tone has valence *opposite* that of the response outcome, however, it will tend to inhibit behavior. For example, if the animal were running to food and had a CS for fear imposed on it in the apparatus, this would inhibit running to food. The general rule is that if emotional states are of the same valence they will be mutually excitatory but if they are of the opposite valence they will be mutually inhibitory. Hope quells fear, and fear dashes hope. Table 8–3 summarizes eight different combinations of unconditioned stimuli and type of reinforcement.

Table 8–3 shows us that appetitive (approach) responses are facilitated by appetitive CRs and inhibited by aversive CRs. Conversely, escape and avoidance responses are facilitated by aversive CRs and inhibited by appetitive CRs. Thus, for example, when a stimulus previously paired with food is presented while a dog is responding with regularity for food in a Skinner box, presentation of the food signal will increase the rate of responding (#3 in Table 8–3). If a signal for shock is presented, however, responding will decrease (#4). If an animal is engaged in an avoidance response, however, the food signal reduces the rate of responding (#6) (Bolles & Moot, 1972; Rescorla & Lolordo, 1965). Conversely, if a signal associated with shock is presented while the subject is making avoidance responses, the rate of responding increases.

Lang's Affect Modulation Theory

Lang's theory (Lang, Bradley, & Cuthbert, 1989) has many similarities to two-process learning theory, and research growing out of Lang's theory is compatible with two-process theory. Lang's approach defines emotions as action dispositions, founded on brain states that organize behavior along a basic approach-avoidance dimension. All affects are assumed to be associated with behavioral tendencies to approach (movement toward, attachment, and consummatory behaviors) or to escape, avoid, or defend against aversive stim-

TABLE 8–3.   Effects of classically conditioned stimuli on rate of instrumental behavior.

	AVERSIVE UCS		APPETITIVE UCS	
CONDITIONED STIMULI	CS + (FEAR)	CS − (RELIEF)	CS + (HOPE)	CS − (DISAPPOINTMENT)
Instrumental Schedule				
ositive reinforcement	1. **Decrease**	2. Increase	3. **Increase**	4. **Decrease**
Negative reinforcement	5. **Increase**	6. **Decrease**	7. **Decrease**	8. Increase

Note: **Boldface** means that there is good evidence for the prediction.

uli. The whole motor system is "tuned" in terms of the central affects. Thus, reflexes associated with appetitive behaviors (e.g., the salivary reflex to food) would be enhanced if activated when a subject was already in a positive emotional state. Conversely, the startle reflex to a sudden loud noise is viewed as an aversive or defensive response and would be enhanced if the organism was already in a negative emotional state when the startle was elicited.

The reflex eye blink has been studied extensively in humans and found to be modifiable by positive and negative toned "foreground" stimuli, such as hedonically positive or negative pictures. In the context of aversive foreground stimuli (e.g., while looking at unpleasant slides), the defensive startle reflex would be enhanced, but with pleasant slides would be inhibited. These predictions, much like those that two-process theory would make, have been repeatedly confirmed. The startle response has been reduced or augmented with pleasant versus unpleasant slides, pleasant versus unpleasant mental imagery, and pleasant versus unpleasant music. Figure 8–5 shows some illustrative results. Furthermore, subjects have been induced into positive or negative moods, and the startle reflex tested during the mood. Pleasant moods inhibit the startle, and negative moods facilitate it.

We then have the model shown in Figure 8–6, which summarizes both two-process theory and affective modulation theory.

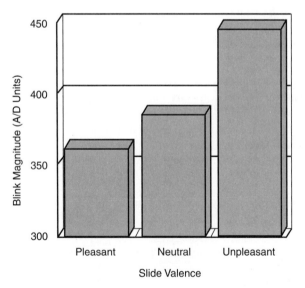

FIGURE 8–5. Magnitude of startle response to auditory stimulus while watching slides with different valences. Unpleasant slides increase the startle magnitude as compared with control (neutral), and pleasant slides reduce startle magnitude. See text for details. (Source: Vrana, S. R., Spence, E. L., & Lang, P. J. 1988. Copyright 1988 by the American Psychological Association. Used by permission.)

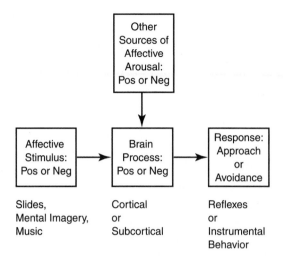

FIGURE 8–6. Model for affective modification of stimulus input. A stimulus arouses positive or negative affective brain process and leads to approach or avoidance behavior. Independent sources of affective arousal can either enhance or inhibit the stimulus-aroused emotional process and thereby facilitate or impede behavior, even though never previously associated with that behavior.

Extension to moods. Two-process learning theory has other potentially powerful extensions to human research on moods. The theory would predict, for example, that positive or negative moods should have different effects according to the kind of stimulus situation in which they occur. Thus, if a particular behavior (e.g., prosocial) is normally rewarded, a positive mood will facilitate such behavior in the future because it has the same valence as that produced when the behavior was rewarded. More generally, the theory would predict the following:

- Positive mood should facilitate rewarded behavior.
- Negative mood should facilitate avoidance or escape.
- Positive mood should inhibit avoidance or escape.
- Negative mood should inhibit rewarded behavior.

Two-process learning theory can serve as a guide for many predictions about the effects of mood that might not otherwise be obvious. Two-process theory suggests that good mood should automatically increase the likelihood of any behavior previously rewarded in similar circumstances. This prediction is independent of the usual cognitive interpretations that accompany explanations for mood and prosocial behavior.

INCENTIVES AND FANTASY

Commitments and Concerns

The final approach to incentives that we review was developed by Eric Klinger (1975, 1977). Klinger's basic concepts are commitment to goals and current concerns about achieving goals. Current concerns are considered to persist over time, even when there are numerous interruptions in striving for a particular goal. For example, as I write, I am interrupted by the telephone and then return to the computer. Then there is a meeting, a different concern, after which I again resume writing. This behavior persists intermittently for perhaps a year or two, at which time I become disengaged from the particular writing goal and have a different set of concerns. Once there is commitment to a goal, Klinger (1975, p. 4) suggests, there are at least four kinds of consequences.

1. **Actions.** The anticipation of obtaining incentives (commitment to goals) is vital in instigating, directing, and maintaining action.
2. **Content of thoughts and dreams.** A person is most likely to think or dream about something while it is related to one of the person's current concerns. These thoughts, dreams, or fantasies may involve achievement, power, affiliation, fear, sex, aggression, and so on. If you know what someone's current concerns are, you can likely predict rather well that person's fantasy life.
3. **Sensitization to goal-related cues.** People are more sensitive to stimuli associated with themselves and their current concerns. For example, people hear their own names when they do not detect other stimuli.
4. **Perceptual qualities of goal-related stimuli.** Stimuli related to current concerns are more prominent or noticeable.

Disengagement from Incentives

The value of incentives and commitment to them is, of course, not permanently fixed. The value of a graduate degree may change with the economy or the availability of jobs for people with that degree, and our commitment stops after a goal has been achieved. But what happens when commitment to a goal ends?

First, even if a goal is achieved, we may feel let down, and perhaps somewhat depressed, unless we have other ongoing concerns and incentives. Indeed, this is said to be a major problem with retirement.

Second, more devastating circumstances may come when we fail to achieve the incentive that we are committed to. Klinger sees five phases of the incentive disengagement cycle.

1. There is invigoration, a stronger attempt to achieve the goal, as also may happen in other frustrating situations.
2. Second, there may be aggressive behavior, as when aggression follows frustration.

3. Third, there is a downswing into depression, a giving up when an important incentive, or incentives, is not achieved.
4. Fourth, there is depression, characterized by apathy toward a great many normally attractive incentives.
5. Fifth, there is recovery, which seems to occur commonly after reactive depressions (those related to specific life events).

One may find other concepts to explain this cycle. The opponent process theory, for example, can explain many of these phenomena, such as depression following the pursuit of exhilarating goals. Our concern at this point, however, is to emphasize the role of cognitive processes, including fantasy and perception, in relation to incentive motivation. The kind of cognitive theory that Tolman applied to rats can be considerably expanded when applied to humans.

SECTION SUMMARY

1. Young's experimental hedonism says that organisms act to "maximize delight and minimize distress." **Delight** and **distress** are central brain processes activated by both unlearned and conditioned stimuli.
2. **Two-process learning theory** concerns the interaction between classical and instrumental conditioning. It asserts that Pavlovian conditioned emotional responses (CERs) can directly affect instrumental behavior. For example, in a **transfer of control experiment**, a tone associated with food can stimulate lever pressing for food even though the tone was never previously associated with lever pressing.
3. Two-process theory postulates four kinds of conditioned emotions, called **hope, fear, relief**, and **disappointment**. Two of these involve positive affect, and two involve negative affect. These are aroused by stimuli associated with the presentation of (a) a positive stimulus (hope) or (b) a negative stimulus (fear) or by the removal of (c) a negative stimulus (relief) or (d) a positive stimulus (disappointment).
4. Simultaneous arousal of emotions of the same valence (either positive or negative) by more than one cue facilitates the related behavior, but simultaneous arousal of opposing emotions (e.g., fear and hope) inhibits corresponding behaviors. This has been demonstrated with the **startle reflex** in humans, as well as instrumental behavior in animals. This line of theory can be extended to the study of human moods.
5. Human incentives are also related to **fantasy**. Klinger has proposed that we have **commitment** to goals (incentives) and that this commitment is reflected in our **current concerns** that persist over time. Current concerns are shown in fantasy, dreams, and thoughts

CHAPTER NINE

Escape, Fear, Avoidance, and Punishment

Why is it important to study such aversive motives as fear?

How is escape learning similar to reward learning?

Are some fears determined genetically?

What is required for fears to be learned?

Are we necessarily aware of the conditions that produce fear learning?

How are phobias different from "normal" fears?

How can we reduce or eliminate fears?

How is avoidance learning different from escape learning?

What is the role of fear in avoidance learning?

What do we mean by punishment?

What factors determine the effectiveness of punishment?

What are some of the major pitfalls in the use of punishment?

In the previous two chapters, we looked at behavioral outcomes that are desirable and sought. In this and the next chapter, we look at events that lead to escape and avoidance and produce the experiences of frustration, fear, and anxiety. The importance of the responses to such events is witnessed by the fact that the entire fields of clinical psychology and psychiatry have in large part developed as a means of helping people modify the distress of their negative experiences and responses to aversive situations. This is not easy, perhaps because there is a strong *negativity bias* such that negative events tend to have more powerful effects than positive events (Rozin & Royzman, 2001). Indeed, we have seen the rapidity with which taste aversions are learned and their endurance over years. Aversions are adaptive, however, because survival does depend on our avoiding dangers. If aversions produce problems, it is because adaptive mechanisms do not always work in quite the way we wish they would, especially since they evolved under very different circumstances than those in which we now live. It is important to understand how they do work, however, if we wish to allay the problems they might produce.

INSTRUMENTAL ESCAPE LEARNING

Instrumental escape learning refers to any response that is reinforced by a reduction of aversive stimulation. An obvious escape response is running away. It is also escape if we end an unpleasant conversation by turning our back. Although electric shock has been the most-used aversive stimulus in the animal laboratory, cold water, loud noises, and bright lights are also effective aversive stimuli. The most commonly used aversive stimuli with human research now are loud noises and threats of various kinds, such as threat of shock or some kind of negative personal evaluation.

Variables Affecting Animal Escape Learning

Amount of reinforcement. Amount of reinforcement is just as important in escape learning as it is in reward learning. For example, Campbell and Kraeling (1953) had rats run in a straight alley to escape from 200, 300, or 400 volts of grid shock to a lower level of shock. Early in training, higher shock produced faster running, although all groups eventually converged to the same level of rapid escape. It was also found that running speed depended on the *proportion* of shock intensity that was reduced, not the absolute amount of reduction in the goal box. For example, a 100-volt reduction was very effective if the change was from 100 volts to no shock, but less effective going from 200 to 100 volts, and still less effective going from 400 to 300 volts. The data were an approximation to Weber's law in perception:[1]

---

[1]According to Weber's law, the minimum amount of stimulus intensity change which is just noticeable is some constant proportion of the reference stimulus. For example, if the value of the proportion were .10, it would take a change from 10 to 11, or from 100 to 110, to be noticed.

amount of reinforcement depends on percentage change, not just absolute change (Campbell & Masterton, 1969).

There is an even more important implication of these data from a motivational point of view. If animals are running faster from 400 volts to 100 volts than from 400 volts to 300 volts, then they must be *anticipating* the amount of shock reduction to come. If their running speed were determined only by the shock in the alleyway that they were escaping, they would have run at the same speed. Thus, there seems to be an incentive effect with escape learning just as there is with reward learning.

"Drive" and "incentive" effects have been studied in some detail with rats swimming to escape cold water (Woods, Davidson, & Peters, 1964). Drive was manipulated by varying temperature in a "runway" tank, and incentive was manipulated by adjusting temperature in the "goal" tank. Goal tank temperature turned out to affect swimming speed much more than runway tank temperature, further lending emphasis to the incentive aspects of escape learning. Other investigators have reported similar results (Stavely, 1966).

Delay of reinforcement.   Immediacy of reinforcement after a response is also important for escape learning, as it is with reward learning. Fowler and Trapold (1962) had rats run from a 250-volt runway shock to a goal box where shock termination was delayed between 0 and 16 seconds for different groups. Running speed was faster with shorter delays of reinforcement (Figure 9–1). When shock levels are high, however, long delays are less detrimental to running (Bell, Noah, & Davis, 1965).

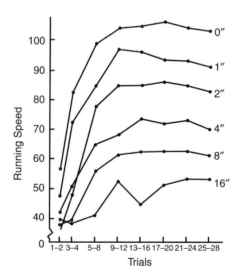

FIGURE 9–1.   Running speed (100/time in seconds) as a function of the delay (in seconds) of shock termination in the goal box. (From Fowler & Trapold, 1962, p. 465. Copyright © 1962 by the American Psychological Association. Reprinted by permission.)

Incentive shifts. The pièce de résistance for an incentive interpretation for shock reduction reinforcement would be to show incentive shift effects like those found by Crespi for amount of food. Bower, Fowler, and Trapold (1959) did exactly this. They had rats run from a 250-volt alleyway shock to a goal box where shocks of 200, 150, or 50 volts were continued for 20 seconds after the animal had entered. The animals escaped faster when there was greater shock reduction, and when the goal-box shock level was adjusted upward or downward, the animals rapidly adjusted their running speeds accordingly. The results (Figure 9–2) look very much like those found in the positive incentive shift experiments discussed in Chapter Eight. Woods (1967) reported similar results when goal-tank water temperatures were lowered or raised for escape from a cold-water alley tank.

Unlike results with positive incentive shifts, however, the elation and depression effects were not found with escape. For example, animals going from a lower amount of reinforcement to a larger one did not run faster than animals continuously on larger reinforcement. In general, contrast effects have not been reported for escape learning.

Theories for Escape Learning

Drive theory. For a long time, drive theory seemed such an obvious interpretation for escape learning that alternatives were not seriously considered. An intense stimulus produces drive; the more intense the stimulus, the harder an animal will work to escape, and the greater is the reinforcement when the animal does escape. Thus, shock produces a drive, and shock reduction is the reinforcer. In the experiments just reviewed, however, in which animals ran to different amounts of shock in the goal box, the animals were

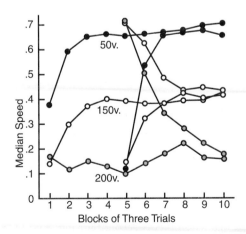

FIGURE 9–2. Group median speed (1/time in seconds) as a function of goal-shock voltage. (From Bower, Fowler, & Trapold, 1959, p. 483. Copyright © 1959 by the American Psychological Association. Reprinted by permission.)

clearly responding to anticipated shock levels in the goal box, as well as to the shock they encountered in the alleyway. At the very least, then, we need to supplement a drive interpretation with an incentive interpretation.

Incentive theory.   When a painful stimulus ends, there is an internal change that can be conditioned to stimuli preceding the end of the stimulus (Denny, 1971; Mowrer, 1960). We shall denote this conditioned change as **anticipatory relaxation**. When an animal finds its way to the shock-free goal box, the "goal response" is relaxation, and the conditioned component of the goal response is anticipatory relaxation. Anticipatory relaxation is stronger as the animal gets closer to the goal box, and the animal makes responses that increasingly maximize anticipatory relaxation until it obtains "real" relaxation.

What is the role of shock intensity in an incentive theory of escape learning? Just as deprivation increases the incentive value of food, intense stimulation should increase the amount of anticipatory relaxation: the stronger the shock, the greater the anticipatory relaxation. Without shock, there should be no anticipatory relaxation, so that "poor" performance should result. Increasing or decreasing either alley shock or goal shock changes the amount of anticipated relaxation, and behavior changes appropriately. This is the incentive shift effect.

An exception to the previous predictions can occur as a result of fear learning. The alleyway stimuli could become conditioned stimuli for fear because they have been paired with shock. Even without shock in the alleyway, the animal would be fearful, and anticipatory relaxation would still occur as long as this fear persists. The fearful subject would continue to escape at least until the fear extinguished to a low enough level that anticipatory relaxation was too weak an incentive to motivate behavior. Fear in such situations may persist for a long time (McAllister, Scoles, & Hampton, 1986).

SECTION SUMMARY

1. **Instrumental escape learning** refers to any situation in which responses are reinforced by reducing the level of aversive stimulation. Almost any intense stimulus is potentially aversive, and any response that reduces the aversive stimulation is escape.

2. The rewarding effects of such escape follow the same general rules as food or other positive rewards: The greater the reduction of the aversive event, or the more immediate the reduction, the greater the rewarding effect. **Incentive shift effects** are also found when the amount of aversive stimulation following escape is varied.

3. Drive and drive reduction theory account for much escape learning but fail to account for the anticipation of the amount of stimulus reduction shown by animals in escape learning situations. The concept of **anticipatory relaxation**, an incentive point of view, does account for such anticipatory responses.

CONDITIONED AVERSION: FEAR

Historical Background and Clinical Importance

In 1920, Watson and Raynor reported their classic study of Little Albert. An eleven-month-old child, Albert, was initially exposed to a series of objects, including a white rat, a rabbit, a dog, a monkey, masks with and without hair, cotton, wool, and so on. "Manipulation was the most usual reaction called out. At no time did this infant ever show fear in any situation" (Watson & Rayner, 1920, p. 2). Albert was then shown a white rat while a steel bar behind him was struck with a hammer. The rat was the conditioned stimulus (CS), and the loud noise the unconditioned stimulus (UCS). After seven trials that were spread over several days, "the instant the rat was shown the baby began to cry" and to try to get away. Five days later Albert was fearful not only of the rat but also of the rabbit, the dog, a seal-fur coat, and a Santa Claus mask. A fear response had been classically conditioned and generalized to other stimuli. Watson pointed out that the results demonstrated that not all anxiety was related to sex or unconscious conflicts, as he said that Freud claimed.

Shortly thereafter, another of Watson's students, Mary Cover Jones (1924), studied the elimination of children's preexisting fears rather than fears experimentally induced in the laboratory. Describing her most effective technique for doing this, she said, "By the method of direct conditioning, we associated the fear object with a craving object and replaced the fear by a positive response" (p. 390). Food, for example, was presented along with the feared object. In contemporary terminology, this process is counterconditioning.

In these two experiments, the foundations of contemporary behavior therapy could well have been laid, and we might have expected an outpouring of further research of this type. Instead, the Freudians held the day, and it remained for Mowrer (1939), fifteen years later, to focus on the problem of aversive conditioning and neurosis in a way that was to have real impact on psychological research and theory. We have already seen part of this development in the study of learned drives (Chapter Six), but the study of fear has not been limited to drive theory. Because of the clinical importance of fear, anxiety, and phobias (intense fears of specific objects), fear has been approached from many different directions.

Unlearned Sources of Fear

It is difficult to demonstrate unequivocally that any phenomenon is genetically determined, but a number of stimulus characteristics have been proposed to be genetically based sources of fear because of their apparent universality and early appearance in life. These include (1) *intense stimuli,* such as pain or loud noise; (2) *sensory loss,* such as loss of physical support (e.g., being dropped), darkness, solitude; (3) *looming stimuli* (stimuli that rapidly grow larger, like a predator approaching); and (4) snakes, furry objects, dragons, some birds. If not genetic, these stimuli seem to be more readily learned as fear-objects. A common phobia, for example, is fear of snakes. Jones and Jones (1928) reported that young city children who had never encountered snakes in the wild did not have a fear of snakes, but that a large percentage of adults reared in the city did have this fear, leading Hebb to conclude that snake phobia is the result of maturation and does not require specific experience with snakes for its occurrence. Hebb also claimed that "psychologically" there is little in common among the many events that arouse fear, but it seems reasonable to conjecture that these are all stimulus conditions in which emotional responses have enhanced survival (Gray, 1971). For example, loud noises call for attention and make us wary, and we may need to be more attentive in the dark because we do not have the use of vision, our major source of information about the environment.

The fear of snakes (as well as insects, lizards, and other "creepy, crawly" animals) may be a kind of species-specific reaction left over from a period of evolutionary development when it was adaptive to avoid snakes without having to be bitten first. Ancestors who ran first and asked questions later may have lived to love more frequently than those who waited around for attack. Such genetically determined fear might indeed account for the evil attributed to the serpent and for the worldwide use of dragon and serpent symbols in mythology. Research has indicated that it is in fact easier to condition fear to pictures of snakes and spiders than to pictures of bunnies and flowers (Öhman, 1986; Öhman & Mineka, 2001). Furthermore, such conditioned fear responses as the galvanic skin response to snake/spider pictures are also more resistant to extinction.

Fears can also occur because of direct changes to the nervous system. For example, people affected by the nutrition-deficit disease pellagra show psychotic fears that disappear on treatment with nicotinic acid. The individual may recall the fears that he or she had while sick and be at a loss to explain them. Hormones can also produce unexpected emotional responsiveness. For example, pregnant women or women getting injections of estrogens may inexplicably break into tears. Such responses disappear after the pregnancy is completed or hormone treatment is discontinued.

Learned Sources of Fear

Fear of the unfamiliar.   At about three months of age, human infants begin to make positive responses to people by smiling and cooing. But at six months, they often show a strong negative reaction toward strangers (or even toward people to whom they have previously shown positive responses, such as grandparents). Hebb (1946) suggested that this reaction is based on experience but not on classical conditioning. Rather, the child becomes familiar with certain people, and therefore when an unfamiliar face appears, the child is afraid. This kind of fear involves the violation of an expectation. As an example of such an expectancy violation with an adult, the author was startled one morning when he got off the elevator at his accustomed floor, and the hallway was not there! It took a few troubled seconds to realize that earlier that morning, physical-plant employees had placed a number of tall metal cabinets in front of the elevator door, where they blocked off all the familiar signs of the hallway. Had this been the first trip ever to this floor, there would have been no startle, since the author would have had no expectation about what the hall should look like when the elevator door opened.

Classical Conditioning of Fear

Methods.   The standard technique for fear conditioning is to present a neutral stimulus (CS) followed by an aversive stimulus (e.g., electric shock or loud noise), recording the change in some appropriate response as a measure of conditioning. Many fears seem to be learned in a social context, however, not necessarily based on direct experience with the feared stimulus: We *vicariously learn* to be afraid by watching other people being afraid in particular situations. Mineka and Cook (1993) explained this in classical conditioning terms, based on research with the observational learning of fear of snakes by rhesus monkeys. Some of the monkeys (the *observers*) were laboratory reared and not initially afraid of snakes. Others (the *models*) had been reared in the wild before being brought to the lab and were afraid of snakes. In the experiment, the observers watched a snake (a 40-inch live boa constrictor) being presented to a model. A set category of fearful responses was observed, such as vocalization, sudden withdrawal to the back of the cage, staring at the stimulus, and piloerection. When the model became fearful, the observer also became fearful in response to the model. If the snake was in view, the observer became fearful of the snake. In classical conditioning terms, then, (1) the snake was the conditioned stimulus, (2) the model and its response to the snake was the unconditioned stimulus, (3) the observers fearful response to the model was the unconditioned response, and (4) the observers learned fear response to the snake was the conditioned response.

Is awareness necessary for fear conditioning?   A long-standing question about human classical conditioning is whether a person has to be aware of the stimuli, or the relationships among them, in order for conditioning to occur. Nothing about classical conditioning says that one has to be consciously aware of such relationships, but this often seems to be the case. For example, Fuhrer and Baer (1965) presented one stimulus as a CS+ (followed by shock) to human subjects and a different stimulus as CS− (not followed by shock). This process is a **differential conditioning paradigm**, which controls for such factors as individual differences in subjects' responsiveness to aversive stimuli and **sensitization**, an increased responsiveness to all stimuli as a result of an aversive UCS being presented. If the response being measured is elicited more strongly by CS+ than by CS−, there is evidence of conditioning. In the Fuhrer and Baer experiment, differential galvanic skin response (GSR) conditioning occurred only with those subjects who reported that the CS+ meant that shock was coming. If they were not aware of this relationship, differential conditioning did not occur. Other experiments have reported similar results, but there is now also research reporting conditioning without awareness, especially with **fear-relevant stimuli** (such as pictures of snakes and spiders) as the CSs. This is called **preattentive conditioning**, meaning that the person being conditioned makes emotional responses without being consciously attentive to the stimuli involved.

Preattentive Conditioning

Methodology.   Research on conditioning without awareness obviously requires that stimuli be presented in such a way that the subject is not aware of them. This can be done by presenting them very rapidly with a device called a **tachistoscope**. This can be accomplished by mounting a cameralike shutter mechanism in front of the lens on a slide projector. The shutter is set to a very rapid speed (e.g., 4/1000 sec) so that a slide image is flashed onto a screen so rapidly that it cannot be consciously identified by the subject. Another method, now more cheap and advantageous because of the wide availability of computers, utilizes a phenomenon called **backward masking**. The procedure here is to present a stimulus (e.g., a word or picture) on a computer screen long enough that the word is easily recognized (e.g., 40/1000 sec). This stimulus is then immediately followed by a **masking stimulus** in the same position on the screen as the word. The subject is then unaware of the word, seeing only the masking stimulus, even though the word would otherwise be identifiable. Thus, for example, if a word, such as *dog*, is briefly displayed, the subject correctly reports that the word was "dog." But if the word is immediately followed by a string of Xs overlaying the screen position where the word appeared, the subject is unable to report the word. Obviously, the word got into the brain, since without the backward masking, it could be identified. The question then is this: Can such a masked word, or other visual pattern, play a role in conditioning?

Öhman's research.   Arne Öhman and his colleagues asked whether a backward-masked conditioned stimulus would evoke a conditioned GSR response (e.g., Esteves, Parra, Dimberg, & Öhman, 1994; Öhman, 1986). Their general procedure is outlined in Figure 9–3. Subjects were first trained with the differential conditioning procedure just described, but during training *neither* CS+ nor CS− was masked. The CS+ was a slide of a person smiling and the CS− was a slide of a person frowning (for some subjects these were reversed). Differential conditioning was successfully established, with larger

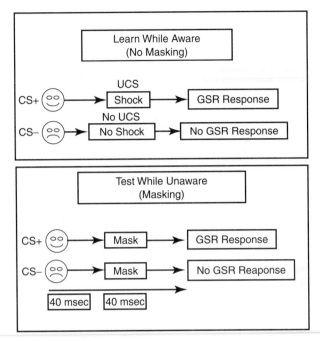

FIGURE 9–3. Öhman's backward masking paradigm for classical aversive conditioning. In the learning phase, one facial stimulus (CS+) is paired with shock, but the other (CS−) is not. There is a greater GSR response to the CS+ than the CS−. In testing, CS+ and CS− are presented but immediately followed by a masking stimulus so that the subject does not consciously recognize them. Nevertheless, the subject shows a greater GSR response to the CS+ than to the CS−, indicating that at some preattentive (unconscious) level, the two stimuli were recognized and distinguished.

GSR responses to the face preceding the shock. The subjects were then tested when *both* CS+ and CS− were masked so that the smiles and frowns could not be consciously distinguished. The results indicate that the backward-masked CS+ (smiling face of frowning) evoked the GSR but that the backward-masked CS− did not do so. At a level below conscious awareness, subjects were able to tell the difference between CS+ and CS− and give different autonomic responses to the CS+. Similar results have also been found in experiments where the smiling and frowning faces were back-masked during conditioning and then tested without backward masking. Such experiments lead to the tentative conclusion that a conditioned emotional response can be evoked without the subject's being aware of the conditioned stimulus. Some authors believe that these effects may be limited to stimuli that are genetically prepared, fear-relevant stimuli to be fearful, as of snakes and spiders (Öhman & Mineka, 2001). As discussed in Chapter Two (Emotion), it appears that the *amygdala* plays an important role in such conditioning.

Phobias

Phobias are intense, irrational fears of specific stimuli, such as a fear of high places, open or closed spaces, flying, or such objects as snakes or insects. Phobias are resistant to change and may have such debilitating effects as keeping a person from going outside or always having to avoid animals. According to classical psychoanalytic theory, a phobia is nonspecific anxiety attached to some specific object. Anxiety is vague and difficult to deal with by the person experiencing it, whereas a phobia can be dealt with, for example, by avoiding the situation that arouses the phobia. The *psychoanalytic treatment* would be to try to find the underlying conflict, or source of anxiety, leading to the phobia and then to reduce that anxiety.

Behavior theorists, on the other hand, argue that phobias are acquired through classical conditioning (McNally, 1987; Wolpe & Rachman, 1960). An important question, however, is whether phobias presented to clinicians by their patients really are the same kinds of fear as those established by laboratory conditioning. Seligman (1971) pointed out that phobias differ from conventional conditioned fears in that they (1) are acquired very quickly, (2) persist in spite of the patient's "objective knowledge" that the phobic object is harmless, (3) relate to objects (such as animals) that rarely pose a threat in modern life, and, finally, (4) are resistant to extinction by normal Pavlovian procedures.

Seligman's preparedness theory (Seligman, 1970, 1971) maintains that organisms are "prepared" or "predisposed" to learn associations that have had survival value in past millennia but that are no longer appropriate. The common phobias of snakes, lizards, spiders, insects, and the like represent stimuli whose forms are supposedly readily conditionable to humans. McNally (1987) concludes that there is not a great deal of empirical support for the preparedness theory of phobias. Some experiments have shown faster GSR conditioning with "phobic" (fear-relevant) stimuli as CSs than to such neutral stimuli as triangles (e.g., see Davey, 1995; Öhman, 1986), but many experiments have not done so. The best evidence for preparedness theory is that extinction of the GSR conditioned to such prepared phobic stimuli as snakes is consistently slower than extinction to neutral stimuli. Upon examination, however, the difference is a mere handful of trials. Evidence for other aspects of preparedness theory and phobias is ambiguous at best.

Modifying Fears

Several approaches to modifying fears (or phobias) have been utilized in behavior therapy, the application of learning principles to therapeutic problems.

Extinction.   One treatment, called **systematic desensitization**, is to present a phobic stimulus repeatedly to a patient, showing that it has no ill effects and, hopefully, producing extinction. This treatment is often done in conjunction with a **fear hierarchy**, gradually presenting a client with stimuli that are progressively more similar to the phobic stimuli. When the client's fear of the weak fear-producing generalized stimulus has extinguished, another stimulus more like the phobic stimulus is presented until fear of that stimulus extinguishes, and so on. For example, the word snake may be presented first, followed in progression by a picture of a snake, a model of a snake, a real snake at a distance, and finally a real snake to be touched and held. This kind of treatment has been found to be quite effective (Rimm & Masters, 1979).

Counterconditioning.   A phobic stimulus, which arouses a fearful response, is presented in conjunction with a stimulus that arouses a response that is incompatible with the fear response. For example, a phobic stimulus arousing negative affect might be presented along with food that arouses positive affect, so that the phobic stimulus becomes associated with the food. This result has also been reported for pleasant music played in a fearful situation (Eifert, Craill, Carey, & O'Connor, 1988). It is also common practice to do extinction in conjunction with relaxation exercises, the relaxation presumably being incompatible with fear-related tension.

Flooding.   Flooding refers to presenting repeatedly or intensely a fear-arousing stimulus to a client. Thus a person with a snake phobia might be "bombarded" with pictures of snakes. Fear responses may extinguish when no harm follows the phobic stimuli.

Cognitive changes.   Foa and Kozak (1986) argue that emotional changes, such as reduction of phobic responses, result from exposure to emotional stimuli because of changed meanings of the phobic stimuli. The therapeutic tactic then is (1) to activate the fear by facing the client with those stimuli/situations that arouse fear, and (2) while the fear is still aroused, to incorporate information about a stimulus that is incompatible with the fear-arousing elements. The phobic stimuli may be imagined by the client or be real stimuli. Just presenting a phobic stimulus repeatedly may not in itself be sufficient to produce change (because adequate new information may not be conveyed), and just giving new information may be inadequate (if the fear is not aroused at the time). The new information may be both cognitive (such as a different interpretation of the stimulus that arouses the fear) and emotional (fear-reducing, pleasure-arousing) at the same time.

SECTION SUMMARY

1. **Fear**, an aversive emotional state, may be aroused by intense or painful unconditioned stimuli, sensory loss, suddenly changing stimuli, or by such specific stimuli as snakes or insects. Unlearned fearful responses to some stimuli might

have evolved as an adaptive survival mechanism. Some fears are also related to direct changes in the nervous system, such as during illness.

2. Fear is readily conditioned in accordance with Pavlovian principles with either humans or animals. Such conditioning may occur from direct experience, or by observation of other animals or people acting fearfully.

3. **Human fear conditioning** appears to be possible when subjects are **not aware** of the conditioned stimuli. This seems to occur with conditioned stimuli which in themselves tend to be emotion-arousing, such as pictures of angry faces or of spiders.

4. **Phobias** are intense fears of specific stimuli, which are quickly acquired, difficult to eliminate, and often unrelated to objects that pose a real threat. According to **preparedness theory**, organisms are genetically prepared to learn quickly to be afraid of such stimuli as snakes.

5. Treatments for the elimination of phobias have involved **extinction** and **counterconditioning** procedures. **Flooding**, intense exposure to feared stimuli, has also been effective in reducing or eliminating phobias, as clients discover that their fears are unfounded.

6. Fears may also be reduced by various procedures that change the **meaning** of stimuli to a fearful person. Meaning may be changed by a reinterpretation of stimuli or attaching a new emotional response to a stimulus.

AVOIDANCE LEARNING

Have you ever compulsively checked and rechecked your alarm clock on the night before you have to catch an early flight? Or checked to make sure you had your ticket? Almost everyone goes through some such compulsive ritual when there is anxiety about some forthcoming event, such as missing an airplane or an important appointment. There are also less fortunate individuals whose lives are consumed by obsessive thoughts or compulsive rituals, of which *checking* and *washing* are the most common (Barlow, 1988). Compulsive washing is familiar to all of us in the behavior of Shakespeare's Lady Mac-Beth. The puzzle is, Why does such compulsive behavior occur? The clue to the answer lies in our everyday experience. We check and recheck our alarm clocks or tickets the night before a trip because these checks temporarily allay our fear that we might miss our flight. We want to avoid that unfortunate outcome. At the same time, the very process of checking may interfere with other activities (such as sleeping!). The dilemma of why such behavior persists, even though it may be maladaptive, has been called the **neurotic paradox** (Levis & Brewer, 2001; Mowrer, 1948). To understand how all this comes together, we must turn to laboratory research on the phenomenon of avoidance learning.

Laboratory Avoidance

If we put a rat into a grid-floor shock apparatus and sound a buzzer, the animal will make little noticeable response to the buzzer. If we electrify the grid sufficiently five seconds later, however, the response to the shock is vigorous and immediate. The rat may jump about and will probably urinate or defecate, all signs of strong emotional arousal. In a few seconds the animal crosses the midline of the box to the other side, where there is no shock. The animal has *escaped* the shock. The next time we present the buzzer, the animal makes a noticeable response—most likely freezing—indicating it has learned something about the buzzer. The animal quickly escapes when the shock comes on. With repeated trials, the escape response becomes swift and precise.

After about thirty trials or so, however, something new happens. The animal crosses the midline of the box in less than five seconds after the buzzer is turned on and does not get shocked. It has made its first *avoidance* response. On an increasing percentage of trials, the animal responds before the shock comes on, thus becoming a proficient avoider. Figure 9–4 illustrates the performance of a single animal during the course of avoidance training. Two important elements seem to be involved in this situation: (1) The animal learns to become afraid when the buzzer sounds, and (2) the animal learns to run to the other side of the box before it gets shocked. These events have been quantified in a number of experiments (e.g., Hoffman & Fleshler, 1962).

Many factors determine just how fast an animal learns to avoid and how proficient it becomes, but a basic question has always been, What keeps the animal avoiding? Fear seems to be involved, but if the animal successfully avoids getting shocked, why doesn't the fear extinguish and the animal stop avoiding? Under specific conditions, dogs in such a situation have been found to keep on avoiding for literally hundreds of trials without getting shocked (Solomon & Wynne, 1954), a dramatic illustration of the neurotic paradox.

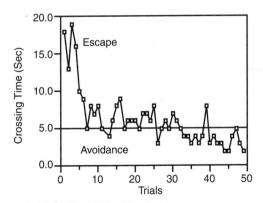

FIGURE 9–4. The course of avoidance learning. A five-second signal forewarns the animal of impending shock. Early in learning, the animal escapes from shock, taking more than five-seconds to make the appropriate response. Later, it avoids shock by responding in less than five-seconds after the signal is presented.

Interpretations of Avoidance Behavior

The most popular interpretation of active avoidance has been **two-factor learning theory**. The two factors are (1) *classical conditioning of fear* to the CS as a result of shock coming on after a buzzer sounds, and (2) *instrumental conditioning of the escape and avoidance behaviors,* with pain reduction and fear reduction as reinforcers. A two-factor theory seems to be demanded because neither classical nor instrumental conditioning alone provide adequate explanation of avoidance (Mowrer, 1960; Rescorla & Solomon, 1967). Let us see why.

Avoidance is not just classical conditioning. Brogden, Lipman, and Culler (1938) studied classical conditioning with guinea pigs in a revolving cage, where a buzzer (CS) sounded and was followed by shock (UCS). For one group, the buzzer was always followed by shock, which typically evoked running. According to classical conditioning principles, this group should have run reliably when the buzzer came on. In fact, however, the animals never ran in response to the buzzer more than about half the time it sounded (Figure 9–5). For a second group, however, shock was delivered only if an animal *failed* to run when the buzzer sounded. This avoidance group quickly learned to run on every trial when they heard the buzzer. The results of this experiment were thus contrary to what was predicted by classical conditioning theory. The reason for the poor performance by the classical conditioning group was clarified by Sheffield (1948) who found that the animals were frequently already moving when the shock came on. The shock actually punished their moving; therefore, they ran inconsistently. The death knell to the

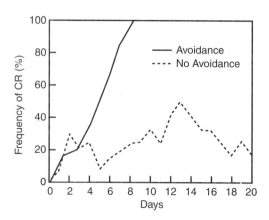

FIGURE 9–5. Learning curves showing the performance of animals for whom the response to the CS was not followed by shock (avoidance) and those for which the CS was always followed by shock (no avoidance). These results show that avoidance learning is not just classical conditioning. (From Brogden, Lipman, & Culler, 1938, p. 110. Reprinted by permission of The University of Illinois Press.)

classical conditioning interpretation was sounded in an experiment by Mowrer and Lamoreaux (1946). They trained rats to escape shock by *running* and to avoid shock by *jumping off the floor,* both in the same situation. The escape and avoidance responses were very different, and the avoidance response was not even the same as the unconditioned response to shock. Classical conditioning of the avoidance response was thus ruled out as an explanation for avoidance when the same animals learned both responses without difficulty.

Avoidance is not just instrumental conditioning.   The inadequacy of just instrumental conditioning as an explanation for avoidance is brought out in the question, What is the reinforcer if the animal is successfully avoiding the shock? It cannot be shock reduction, since the animal is not getting shocked. We can postulate that fear reduction is the reinforcement, but then we would also have to postulate that fear had been conditioned. If fear has been conditioned in such a situation, we are led back to the two-factor theory of avoidance.

Two-factor interpretation of avoidance.   According to two-factor theory, an animal first learns to become afraid of the buzzer through classical conditioning (buzzer paired with shock). Simultaneously, the animal learns to escape from shock. The animal then transfers the running responses from the shock stimulus to the fear stimulus. This transfer is easy because the shock also aroused fear (along with pain) in earlier training, and the fear also was a cue for running at that time. The animal is reinforced on successful avoidance trials because the fear-arousing buzzer is turned off when the avoidance response is made. The fear therefore is both a drive and a cue, and fear reduction is the reinforcer for running. This theory solved many problems, but has also raised questions about the role of both fear and the CS. Specifically, is it necessary to have fear and is it necessary that there be a CS to arouse it? All available evidence would indicate that avoidance learning does involve fear (Mineka, 1979), but beyond this, the evidence on the role of fear is less certain. If the role of fear is questionable, then any theory requiring fear (such as two-factor theory) is equally in doubt.

Evidence for Fear in Avoidance

Cutting the sympathetic nervous system.   If we reduce the autonomic aspects of the fear response by cutting the sympathetic nervous system, we would expect avoidance behavior to be disrupted. The results of such an experiment (Solomon & Wynne, 1950) are even more intriguing than this, however. If the operation is done *before* avoidance training, avoidance learning is much poorer. This supports the theory that fear is important to avoidance. If the operation is performed *after* the animal has already learned to avoid, however, performance is not affected; the animals continue to avoid quite adequately. This suggests that once the behavior is well learned, the CS may be only a cue to make the response and does not have to arouse fear the same way as it does in the early training. This conclusion is also supported by research showing that fear is greatly reduced in animals that have learned an avoidance response well.

Curare experiments. Suppose that we conditioned fear when no overt response could be made. If fear arousal facilitated avoidance at a later time, we would have to conclude that fear was important to avoidance. In such an experiment, dogs were first given standard avoidance training with a light as the CS. Then, while immobilized by the paralyzing drug curare, the animals were given differential classical conditioning with one tone as CS+ and a different tone as CS−, and shock as the UCS. Subsequently, these stimuli were presented as CSs in the avoidance apparatus. The animals made avoidance responses to CS+ but not to CS−. Since the fearful CS+ had never before been paired with the avoidance response, we conclude that the fear aroused by CS+ is important to avoidance (Black, Carlson, & Solomon, 1962; Leaf, 1964; Solomon & Turner, 1962). At the very least, fear seems to increase the likelihood of avoidance responding.

Tranquilizing drugs. Tranquilizing drugs, such as **Valium** (diazepam), operate selectively to suppress avoidance and other fear-related behaviors, but they have little effect on behavior rewarded by food (Gray, 1982a, b; Ray, 1963). This finding indicates that fear is involved in avoidance.

Dissociation of fear and responding. As we observed earlier, animals become less fearful as avoidance learning progresses (Mineka, 1979). The reduction in fear by animals that have learned to avoid very well is clearly demonstrated when fear and avoidance responding are measured simultaneously, but independently of each other (Hoffman & Fleshler, 1962). Even if fear declines, however, it is possible that even a very slight amount of conditioned fear might be sufficient to trigger an avoidance response (Solomon & Wynn, 1954). If the fear response does not occur fully on such trials, it is "protected" from extinction. This hypothesis was supported by research showing that conditioned fear could motivate escape responding for literally hundreds of trials after the last fear-conditioning trial had been completed (McAllister, McAllister, Scoles, & Hampton, 1986). In this experiment, animals had twenty-five pairings of a light and an electric shock prior to any escape. The animals then had hurdle-jumping escape trials in response to light onset, without any further shock. Speed of escape increased sharply in the first fifty escape trials, then slowly declined over the next 250 trials, illustrated in Figure 9–6. Behavior motivated by fear can be very resistant to extinction.

During avoidance, the decline in fear is related to responding, because control animals getting the same shocks (but not allowed to avoid) do not

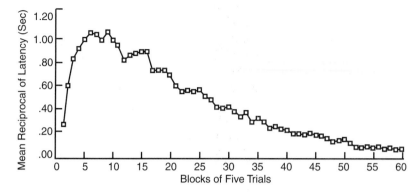

FIGURE 9–6. Mean speed of hurdle jumping over sixty blocks of five trials. (From McAllister, McAllister, Scoles, & Hampton, 1986. Reprinted by permission of the American Psychological Association.)

show the fear decrement (Starr & Mineka, 1977). This suggests that the fear may decline when animals gain *control* over the situation, a topic we take up in detail in Chapter Ten. Furthermore, animals that show significant extinction of avoidance responding have been found to be just as fearful as animals without extinction trials at all (Kamin, Brimer, & Black, 1963). Why then do animals extinguish if fear is not being reduced during extinction? Some insight on this problem is found with response prevention and flooding.

Response prevention and flooding techniques.   Two-factor theory predicts that if animals had extensive nonreinforced exposure to the CS, fear should extinguish, and avoidance responding should decline. Flooding refers to forced exposure to fear stimuli with no way for the subject to get rid of the stimuli, presumably a condition under which extinction should occur. Page (1955) had animals learn an avoidance response, then prevented them from making this response when put into the apparatus without shock (response prevention). This procedure did facilitate the regular extinction of avoidance that followed, apparently supporting the extinction prediction. After avoidance responding extinguished, however, animals refused to go back into the avoidance apparatus when given the opportunity to do so. The fact that they were still fearful of the apparatus, even though they had stopped avoiding, indicates that their extinction of avoidance was not due to extinction of fear. The continued presence of fear in such situations was also shown in an experiment in which rats had been kept from responding and stopped avoiding, but their heart rates were still as elevated as when they were avoiding (Werboff, Duane, & Cohen, 1964). In short, when animals undergo extinction of an avoidance response, they do not necessarily become free of fear.

Flooding results are further complicated by the fact that extinction of avoidance is facilitated by simply confining animals in either a novel or a fearful place that is not related to the place where avoidance learning occurred. Crawford (1977) suggested that this result was due to the emergence of a freezing response. Specifically, when an animal is fearful during the course of confinement, it may engage in what Bolles (1972) called a **species-specific defense reaction** (SSDR), which for the rat in such a situation is freezing. When it is placed back into the avoidance apparatus, the animal might now show this new dominant response. This response interferes with avoidance without eliminating fear.

Is a CS Necessary for Avoidance?

In the early avoidance learning experiments, the CS was left on until the animal made an avoidance response, at which time the CS was terminated. It was argued that onset of the CS aroused fear and the avoidance response, which was then reinforced by turning off the fearful CS. With this experimental procedure, however, shock avoidance and CS termination both occurred at the same time, and hence the interpretation was confounded. Kamin (1956) tried to separate the effects of CS termination and UCS avoidance, but concluded that both were important aspects of avoidance learning.

A variation on the theme that the CS arouses fear is one that we saw in Chapter Seven under the discussion of two-process theory which is a much more general theory than the two-factor theory of avoidance. This is the notion of fear as conditioned excitation (Rescorla & Solomon, 1967). A CS signaling the onset of shock will increase the rate of avoidance responses even though it has never been specifically paired with those responses, as was shown in the curare experiments. The CS presumably increases fear. Conversely, a signal that indicates that no shock is forthcoming produces conditioned inhibition of fear, and reduces the rate of avoidance responding.

A third idea is that the CS for avoidance is a *discriminative stimulus,* or cue, for responding. Herrnstein (1969) argued that a CS is not necessary for avoidance learning. All the animal has to learn is that it gets shocked less often when it makes the avoidance response than when it does not make the response. The CS just tells the animal when to respond in order to minimize the amount of shock it gets. If this view is correct, then it should be possible for an animal to learn avoidance without any external signal as a CS.

Unsignaled avoidance. An avoidance learning experiment without an external signal is conducted in the following manner (Sidman, 1966). Animals in a Skinner box with an electrifiable grid floor are given brief shocks (0.5 second) that cannot be escaped. These shocks are programmed according to two different schedules. If the animal never responds at all, it is automatically shocked every so often (say, 20 seconds). This is the *shock-shock interval.* If, however, the animal presses the lever during the shock-shock interval, the clock is reset, and the next shock is postponed for a set length of time (say, also, 20 seconds). This is the *response-shock interval.* If the animal were to press the lever just once every 20 seconds, it would never get shocked. But, pity to say, animals never respond quite this way.

If the shock-shock and response-shock intervals are equally long, there is great variability in how rapidly and well animals learn unsignaled avoidance. Figure 9–7 shows the performance of one "typical" learner and one "fast" learner. Note that the sessions are eight and six hours long, respectively, and that each blip represents a shock. Even the fast learner gets many, many more shocks than is typical for the shuttle box situation. The animals never seem to "wait out" an interval and respond just before the next shock is due. To the contrary, the animals are as likely to respond in the first half of an interval as in the last half. By special training procedures, animals can be taught to wait until the last part of the response-shock interval to respond, but they do not seem to learn this spontaneously. The animals' overall rate of responding can be manipulated by changing the length of the intervals, how-

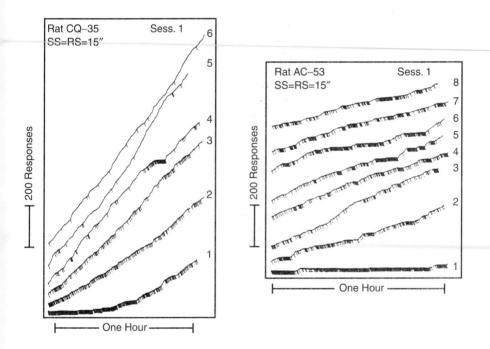

FIGURE 9–7. Cumulative records for two rats in their first sessions of Sidman avoidance learning, about six and eight hours long, respectively. To condense the figures, the records have been cut into segments of approximately one hour each and are numbered in temporal order. The oblique "pips" on the record indicate shocks. Rat CQ-35 learned more rapidly than did Rat AC-53, but CQ-35 had a few minutes in the fourth hour when it got a large number of shocks. (From Sidman, 1966, pp. 451, 452, 453. Reprinted by permission of Prentice Hall, Inc., Englewood Cliffs, New Jersey.)

ever. If the response-shock interval is much longer than the shock-shock interval (responding produces a longer shock-free period), they learn to respond more readily. If the response-shock interval is much shorter than the shock-shock interval, however, animals learn *not* to respond quickly because, in effect, they are punished for responding by getting a shorter shock-free period.

Since there is no external CS in Sidman's situation, the importance of a CS in avoidance is questioned. It has been argued, however, that the CS for responding is an internal **stimulus trace** from the previous avoidance response (Anger, 1963; Mowrer, 1960). When the animal makes an avoidance response, there is strong feedback from the muscles, and this feedback gradually gets weaker after the response is made. This is the stimulus trace. A strong feedback trace is thus associated with no-shock because the animal is never shocked immediately after responding. As the trace weakens, however, shock becomes more likely, and a weak trace becomes a CS for fear. Over the course of the response-shock interval, then, fear builds up to a level where it triggers the animal to respond. This response is followed by fear reduction, and the whole cycle starts up again. Furthermore, if fear is conditioned to a CS in a different situation and this CS is then presented while the animal is engaged in unsignaled avoidance, the rate of avoidance responding increases. Clearly, then, fear is playing a role in unsignaled avoidance, and it is quite possible that there is a CS in the form of muscle feedback (the stimulus trace). The "unsignaled" avoidance may, in fact, have a signal.

Cognitive Interpretations of Avoidance

At the time that research on avoidance learning was undertaken, the primary researchers were strongly behavioristic and wary of cognitive concepts. Therefore, they emphasized classical and instrumental conditioning. Quite early, however, Osgood (1950) proposed a cognitive interpretation based on Tolman's theory. Osgood said that the buzzer becomes a signal of shock and that the animals have a demand against shock and do whatever is required to avoid it. If this is true, however, why should avoidance ever decline? Unless the animal *fails* to make the avoidance response, how will it find out that shock will not follow the buzzer? Osgood simply assumed that the demand against shock declines with successful avoidance. Occasionally, the animal will fail to respond in time to avoid shock. Then, either (1) it will get shocked and its expectation of shock will be reconfirmed, and it will start avoiding again; or (2) it will not get shocked (as with extinction) and a new expectation of no-shock will be established, and avoidance will cease.

Seligman and Johnston (1973) also proposed a cognitive theory of avoidance, but based on Irwin's (1971) theory of intentional behavior, as follows. At the peak of avoidance learning, an animal acquires two expectancies: (1) If it responds in a given time after CS onset, it will not get shocked; and

(2) if it does not respond fast enough, it will get shocked. The animal prefers not getting shocked and therefore makes the avoidance response.

These cognitive interpretations have a certain appeal, but neither of them has been fruitful and generated any research. Therefore, these theories have contributed little to our understanding of avoidance and are rarely referred to in the avoidance literature.

SECTION SUMMARY

1. **Avoidance behavior** consists of any response that prevents the occurrence of an anticipated aversive event. A major question is why animals or people continue avoiding, since they do not experience the aversive stimulus if they successfully avoid it.

2. The most widely used interpretation of avoidance is **two-factor learning theory**. This says that organisms first learn to be fearful in the situation according to classical conditioning principles and then learn to reduce fear according to instrumental conditioning principles. Neither process alone accounts for avoidance. Various fear-reducing drugs reduce avoidance and show that fear is important in avoidance.

3. Fear is clearly important in the initial learning of avoidance responses but is less clearly involved in their long-term maintenance. Fear declines during avoidance even as avoidance responses become better learned. The decline of fear may be due to animals gaining **control** over the situation as they learn the avoidance response. Avoidance responses can also be extinguished, but without apparent reduction in fear. Therefore, there is some degree of **dissociation** between fear and avoidance behavior which has been challenging to two-factor theory.

4. The CS for avoidance generally has been considered important because it arouses fear and because CS termination is reinforcing. Using a procedure called **unsignaled avoidance**, animals can learn to avoid without any external stimulus to signal oncoming shock, and the CS may serve only as a cue to tell the organism when responding will prevent an aversive stimulus.

5. **Cognitive interpretations** for avoidance learning have been proposed but have not generated significant research and are rarely discussed.

PUNISHMENT

Punishment takes such varied guises as physical pain or its threat, social sanctions, isolation, and withdrawal of privileges. All these are supposed to suppress "undesirable" behavior. Events that are supposed to be punishing are often ineffective, however. Sometimes "punishment" increases the very behavior it is expected to eliminate and sometimes suppresses many different behaviors indiscriminately. Thus, while it is true that "punishment suppresses behavior," our understanding of exactly what is involved requires more detailed study (Campbell & Church, 1969; Dunham, 1971).

Defining Punishment

Stimulus definition.   According to a stimulus definition, punishment is the delivery of an aversive stimulus to an organism following a response. The organism is expected to suppress the response as a means of avoiding punishment. This behavior is sometimes referred to as passive avoidance, as compared with the active avoidance that we discussed earlier. This definition would require that in the study of punishment, we must use stimuli that are demonstrably aversive; otherwise, the definition cannot apply.

Response definition.   A response definition of punishment says that punishment is the delivery of any stimulus that effectively suppresses the preceding behavior, whether or not the stimulus is demonstrably aversive otherwise. Such a stimulus could be punishing in some situations but not others. This explanation does not define for us in advance whether a particular stimulus will be a punisher, but it does encourage us to look for effective punishers. For example, a retarded child who stuck out her tongue several times a minute was resistant to all kinds of attempted punishment until the therapist hit upon putting lemon juice on the child's tongue whenever she stuck it out. Doing this was an effective punisher; it suppressed the behavior. For the sake of consistency, we will hereafter assume a response definition of punishment unless otherwise indicated.

Suppressive Effects of Punishment

It is clear from much research and practical experience that *punishment does not eliminate behaviors;* it *suppresses* behaviors in certain situations. According to **alternative response theory**, punished behaviors are less likely to occur because they have been replaced at least temporarily by other, alternative behaviors. Skinner (1938), in one of the earliest laboratory reports of punishment of free operant behavior (lever pressing), slapped a rat's paw when it touched the lever to get food. Lever pressing was suppressed for a while but came back, presumably because there was no other way the animal could get food. Estes and Skinner (1941) went on to show that even electric shock following a response suppressed lever pressing only temporarily, and for the same reason: The only way to get food was to press the lever. Dunham (1971) explicitly tested the alternative response hypothesis with Mongolian gerbils as subjects. Given the opportunity, isolated gerbils will spend most of their waking time doing just three things: shredding paper, eating food pellets, and drinking water. Each of these is easily measured (amount of paper pulled from a roll can be recorded automatically), so it is possible to get normal baseline measures for each and then to see how all the responses change when one of them is punished. As predicted by the alternative response theory, if any one of the responses was punished, one of the other two responses would increase. That is, the animal performed an alternative response in place of the punished response.

Response Factors in Punishment

The nature of the response elicited by punishment is very important, since the elicited response may either interfere with or facilitate the punished response. We saw this outcome with the guinea pigs in avoidance learning. If an animal is punished while running, the automatic response is to stop. If an animal is punished while standing still, the response is to move. In order to predict the effects of punishment, then, we have to know what response the punishment evokes. Fowler and Miller (1963) studied this by having animals run down a straight runway to get food. They found that when animals had their hind paws shocked just as they entered the goal box (thereby facilitating forward movement), they ran faster. On the other hand, animals that had their forepaws shocked as they entered the goal box (thereby facilitating backing up) ran slower. Shock by itself did not determine how the animals responded; the response elicited by the shock determined how they would respond.

Stimulus Factors in Punishment

Immediacy of punishment.   If one has an effective punisher available, the single most basic rule for using it is that the punisher should follow an undesirable response as quickly as possible so that the punishment is **response-contingent**. The longer the delay between response and punishment, the less effective the punishment is. Figure 9–8 shows the results of an experiment in which punishment of lever pressing by electric shock was delayed from zero to thirty seconds (Camp, Raymond, & Church, 1967). The zero-delay group was most suppressed, and the 30-second delay the least. Note also in Figure 9–8 that even a **noncontingent punishment** group (NC), which received shocks randomly, showed less suppression than the 30-second-delay group.

What is meant to be response-contingent punishment may, because of bad timing, become either noncontingent or **stimulus-contingent**. By stimulus-contingent we mean that the punishment is associated with a particular stimulus (as in classical conditioning) rather than with a particular response. For example, instead of punishing a child immediately for some indiscretion, suppose a parent waits until the spouse comes home to have the spouse punish the child. Instead of the bad behavior becoming associated with the punishment, the punishing parent becomes associated with the punishment. The expected result would be fear of the parent but little suppression of the undesired behavior. With older children or adults, long delays between response and punishment may be mediated by verbal warning, such as discussing the behavior to be punished and the reason for punishment.

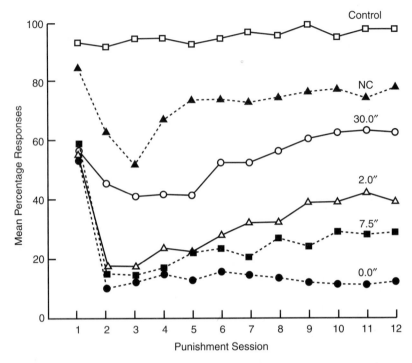

FIGURE 9–8.   Mean percentages of responses as a function of sessions for groups with .0, 2.0, 7.5, 30.0 seconds delay of punishment, noncontingent shock, and unpunished control group. (Failure to press the lever within 10 seconds of stimulus onset was defined as a nonresponse.) (From Camp, Raymond, & Church, 1967, p. 121. Copyright © 1967 by the American Psychological Association. Reprinted by permission.)

Effects of noncontingent punishment.   A noncontingent punishment procedure called the **conditioned emotional response** (CER) procedure has been used to study punishment of free operant behavior. The punishing stimulus follows some signal, rather than a response, but such behavior as lever pressing is suppressed when the signal is turned on. The CER procedure has a number of different effects from those of response-contingent punishment, however (Church, 1969; Hunt & Brady, 1955). For example, the CER procedure suppresses many different behaviors, is slower to extinguish, and is harder to counter condition with positive reinforcement. And, as we have seen, even delayed response-contingent punishment is more effective in suppressing specific responses than is noncontingent punishment.

Stimulus intensity and adaptation.   More intense punishing stimuli have greater suppressive effects (Azrin & Holz, 1966), and if the punishing stimulus is strong enough, the effects may be nearly irreversible. For example, cats that had received strong punishment for eating refused thereafter to eat in the experimental apparatus (Masserman, 1943). If experimental animals are gradually adapted to increasingly strong shocks, however, the suppressive effect is considerably weakened (Miller, 1960). This weakening is not due to simple sensory adaptation to the shocks, however. Control animals that were exposed to the same intensities of shock outside the primary experimental apparatus did not show the effects of this adaptation when they were inside the apparatus. The adaptation in some sense was "psychological" in the sense that it was specific to the apparatus in which it occurred. Possibly, when shock was increased gradually in the apparatus, the animals may have learned to cope with it by responding in particular ways that lessened the shock intensity. Increasing shock levels outside the apparatus would not have allowed this kind of learning. Therefore, the shock was more suppressive when the animals were introduced into the apparatus. This phenomenon may be related to the learned helplessness phenomenon, discussed in detail in Chapter Ten.

Potential Problems Using Punishment

Since punishment is used widely, if not wisely, it is worthwhile to point out some very specific general rules for its effective use.

1. **Make sure that the punishment is associated with the undesirable behavior.** Punishment should be delivered promptly, whether in the form of a reprimand, a slap on the wrist, or withdrawal of privileges. This advice is especially true with small children or nonverbal organisms. With older children, one can make the association verbally after a delay, but it still is more effective if made immediately.

2. **Make sure that the punisher is punishing.** A slight word of discouragement that may stop one child from an activity may be completely ineffective with a different child. It may be necessary to work at finding what is punishing for a particular individual.

3. **The punishment should not contain concealed rewards.** For example, if a child is sent to his room as punishment, where he plays his stereo, watches TV, and phones his friends, the "punishment" is not likely to have much effect.

4. **Watch out for side effects of punishment.** Strong punishment may produce excessive emotional responses and/or escape behavior. These are minimized by careful response-contingent punishment, which is more effective and less disturbing than delayed or stimulus-contingent punishment.

5. **Reinforce alternative behaviors.** The problem is to change behavior, not just to deliver punishment. The role of punishment may then be just to suppress undesirable behavior long enough for desirable behavior to occur (possibly with encouragement) and be rewarded. If desirable behaviors are rewarded at the same time that undesirable behaviors are punished, then the effects of punishment are likely to be more satisfactory. In the same vein, undesirable behaviors that are not rewarded are more likely to extinguish. Thus, the twin technique of rewarding alternative behaviors and extinguishing undesirable behaviors may render punishment unnecessary. If a child gets hold of a dangerous kitchen utensil

to play with, the child may be praised for giving the utensil to the parent, who at the same time gives the child a toy to play with. The child can learn alternative behavior without punishment.

SECTION SUMMARY

1. Punishment involves the **inhibition** of responses by presenting aversive stimuli when such responses occur. As a practical matter, whatever stimuli suppress behavior may be considered punishers. Removal of some stimuli, such as withdrawing privileges, is also punishing.

2. **Response factors** are important in punishment, because a punisher may arouse responses that either **compete** with or **facilitate** a punished response. To be effective, punishment should arouse responses that compete with the punished response.

3. The **alternative response theory** says that punishment stimulates organisms to make some response other than the punished response, and this alternative response is reinforced.

4. **Stimulus variables** affecting power of punishment include **delay** between response and punishment, **intensity** of the punishment, and **adaptation** to the punishing stimulus.

5. **Effective use** of punishment involves making sure that (a) the punishment is associated with the undesirable behavior, (b) the punishing stimulus is in fact punishing, (c) the punishment contains no concealed rewards, (d) the side effects of punishment are not worse than the behavior being punished, and (e) alternative behaviors are reinforced.

CHAPTER TEN

Frustration, Anxiety, Stress, and Coping

How do we define frustration?

What determines how frustrated we are?

What effects does frustration have on our behavior?

Can we make frustration work for us?

What kinds of internal conflicts do we have?

How do conflicts get resolved?

How is anxiety different from fear?

How does anxiety affect the way we think about things?

What is stress and how does it affect us?

What are the causes of stress?

What experiences or personality factors protect us from stress?

How can we cope with stress?

Is stress always bad for us or is it a necessary part of life?

FRUSTRATION

Many years ago a psychologist named Tinklepaugh (1928) was training a monkey with standard monkey rewards—raisins and grapes—which the animal came to expect for its efforts. Tinklepaugh then substituted a piece of lettuce for the expected reward, and this substitution obviously disturbed the animal. This observation has three important elements. First, the monkey had learned to expect a particular reward. Second, the monkey got something less than expected. Third, the change in reward produced a disturbance in the animal's behavior, from which an emotional response—frustration—is inferred. Presumably, Tinklepaugh's monkey felt something like an upset student who has gotten a C after expecting an A.

Here is a second example, quite different from the first, but embodying the same principles. A student told me about a friend who had gone to the airport in a rented car to meet his wife before she left on a flight. He was delayed and arrived too late for the meeting. He thereupon beat in the hood of his rented car, and had to pay for the damage out of his pocket. This example again indicates rather extremely what we mean when we say that frustration is a negative emotion aroused when an anticipated desirable goal is not attained. Frustration is an important explanatory concept because it involves the reactions to aversive states when there is no prior aversive stimulus. Frustration grows out of positive expectations that are not fulfilled. Papini and Dudley (1997) point out that when there is "surprising nonreward" (or reduction in expected reward) many species of animals show many different types of behavioral and physiological responses "that could collectively be referred to as aversive and emotional" (p. 195). Some of these effects have been demonstrably reduced by antianxiety drugs. The behavioral effects of frustration depend on an intact amygdala, a structure we have previously seen to be involved in aversive emotion.

Frustration Defined as an Intervening Variable

Failing to reach the airport on time to see his wife (which he really wanted to do and just missed) was the antecedent condition for the woebegone spouse, and beating in the car hood was the consequent condition. Had we only seen him beating in the car hood, we would have no firm justification for saying he was frustrated because there might be other reasons for this behavior (maybe he wanted to collect insurance). Knowing what had transpired previously, however, we have better grounds for saying frustration was involved. We can define frustration as an intervening variable. The antecedent condition is not obtaining an expected goal or reward. Commonly, this may occur as the result of failure to reach a goal, but as we shall see, unfulfilled expectations aroused even without working toward a goal may induce frustration. The consequent conditions fall into the usual categories: cognitive (in-

Antecedent Conditions	Intervening Variable	Consequent Conditions
Not Getting Expected Reward	Frustration Negative Emotion (Disappointment) (Anger)	Cognitive Behavioral Physiological

FIGURE 10–1.   Frustration as an intervening variable.

cluding self-report), behavioral, and physiological. This is illustrated in Figure 10–1.

The frustration situation not the same as frustration.   We need to distinguish between the effects of the situation per se on behavior and the effects of *frustration* on behavior. For example, a problem-solving situation is a circumstance in which frustration might occur. However, a particular behavior may simply be a response to the situation without strong frustration being involved. For example, I once had a TV set that in its declining years had a very snowy screen. The temporary cure was to hit the set until the screen cleared. This cure usually worked and was cheaper than repairing the set. But how would a stranger interpret my behavior? She might infer that in response to frustration, I became emotional and lashed out angrily at the TV set. My interpretation, however, is that I just did what I had previously been rewarded for doing—I hit the set because that got rid of the snow. To infer that there was *necessarily* strong emotion would be overinterpreting the situation. Knowing that our friend beat his car hood just after he had failed to reach an important goal, however, we are justified in inferring frustration to explain the behavior.

There are no responses specific to frustration.   We must also be aware that responses to frustration are as varied as responses to any other motivational condition. The responses depend on what an animal or a person has learned to do in such a situation, as well as upon the motivation (Brown & Farber, 1951). Considerable effort has been spent trying to find specific responses unique to frustration, but such responses have not been found (Lawson, 1965; Yates, 1962). For example, aggression has been thought to be a specific frustration response (Dollard, Doob, Miller, Mowrer, & Sears, 1939), but this is not always the case.

Frustration as Emotion

As Figure 10–1 suggests, however, the negative emotional arousal following the thwarting of a goal may range from *disappointment* to *anger*. In some instances frustration may be mildly disappointing, but in the opening examples in this chapter, the emotional responses were more akin to anger.

How is it, however, that the unfulfilled anticipation of something positive can so quickly turn sour? One answer to this is in terms of opponent process theory of emotion.

Frustration and Opponent Process Theory

You may recall from earlier discussions that this theory accounts for negative contrast effects by assuming that the positive emotion aroused by some stimulus event is automatically followed by its opponent process, a negative emotion. Over repeated experiences with the positive emotion, the negative emotion becomes progressively stronger and tends to neutralize the positive emotion. If the stimuli anticipating the positive emotion are presented and then removed, the opponent process becomes dominant, and strong negative emotion is experienced. So, based on previous experience getting rewards a person may work with the expectation of getting more rewards and positive emotional experiences. If the expected reward fails to materialize, the opponent negative emotion is strong, and we may call the experience frustration.

Variables Affecting the Intensity of Frustration Responses

Exactly what response to frustration will occur depends in part on what behaviors a person has learned in the frustrating situation. The response also depends on a variety of factors that determine the intensity of frustration, such as the following:

1. **The number of prior frustrations.** The expression "the straw that broke the camel's back" means that the last in a sequence of many small frustrations may produce a response that appears to be completely out of proportion to the immediate circumstances, such as a violent outburst. Domestic violence, for example, may result from many accumulated frustrating experiences, not just a seemingly insignificant one that finally triggered violence.

2. **The size and value of the goal.** Other things being equal, the larger or better the anticipated goal, the greater the frustration when the goal is not obtained.

3. **The perceived probability of actually obtaining the goal.** How many of us have bought a lottery ticket that did not win. This happens to 99+ percent of ticket buyers. But how many of them actually feel very emotional about not winning millions of dollars? Probably very few of them. Why? It is probably safe to assume that they did not actually expect to win. The frustration would be greater for a much smaller goal for which the probability of winning is much higher.

4. **The importance of the goal to the individual.** The *subjective value* of a goal to a particular person may not be highly correlated with any measurable objective value. The frustration is proportional to the importance to the individual (otherwise, how could we explain why amateurs get so upset about bad golf shots?).

5. **Investment expended to reach a goal.** The more we put in to reach a goal, the more frustrating it is not to achieve it. The investment may be time, effort, loss of other pleasures (e.g., family life), and so on.

6. **Previous experience in dealing with frustrating events.** A concept called **frustration tolerance** is sometimes used to account for the fact that different individuals respond to frustrating circumstances with different degrees of emotional intensity. Some people maintain great equanimity and others become highly emotional. This may in part be due to differences in a stable personality characteristic, such as neuroticism (see Chapter 12, Personality) which has a genetic component. But it is equally clear that such differences may be due to past experiences. For example, if a person has survived many frustrating experiences and learned that "things work out," it is easier to remain calm. If a person is experiencing his or her first major frustrations (e.g., as a freshman in college not getting the same grades as in high school), the experience may be very upsetting. Imagine a child who has grown up getting his or her every desired fulfilled simply by asking, and then is denied further requests. What would we call such a child? What would we predict its reactions to the answer "no" to be?

Frustration as Drive

Nonreward frustration. The bulk of frustration research in the past thirty years has been research on animals and largely in the Hullian tradition, where frustration has been considered a drive aroused when an expected incentive is not obtained. This is called nonreward frustration. The antecedent condition for nonreward frustration is like that just described, except that no expected reward at all is given. Amsel's (1992) nonreward frustration theory is the prime example of this approach.

Amsel's theory. Amsel assumed that nonreward frustration has the properties that have been used to identify drive: Frustration energizes a wide range of responses, its onset is punishing, and its termination is reinforcing. For example, rats frustrated by nonreward (after having been rewarded) in an apparatus goal box subsequently learned to escape faster from the goal box than did nonfrustrated control animals (Daly, 1974). Similarly, pigeons learn to peck at a key to remove a stimulus signaling nonreinforcement (Rilling, Askew, Ahlskog, & Kramer, 1969). Speed of escape from such a situation is a function of variables that should produce greater frustration, variables involving stronger, more desirable expectations of reward. For example, large rewards produce more nonreward frustration than small rewards, and very sweet sugar rewards produce more frustration than not-so-sweet rewards. In both cases, rats trained with the "better" reward learn to escape faster from the goal box when the reward is omitted than do animals trained with the lesser reward.

As we noted earlier, frustration theory does not say that instrumental responses are *necessary* for frustration, only that the *expectation* of reward be frustrated. Therefore, the frustration effects that follow nonrewarded instrumental responding should also be found after simply consuming food in a particular environment. Daly (1974) demonstrated such frustration by directly placing animals into a goal box with food, and without their running during training. Then, when the animals were placed in the goal box without food, the animals learned to escape from the goal box faster than animals never fed in the goal box at all. You can frustrate humans by telling them that they are going to get something they want and then not giving it to them. The person who has made a promise and not kept it, who arouses hopes and then dashes them, may become aversive and disliked because of association with aversive frustration.

Frustration also serves as a cue because it has drive stimuli ($S_{D\,\text{frustration}}$). Recall that in Hullian drive theory, the drive itself does not give direction to behavior; it is drive stimuli that do this. Frustration may thus motivate behavior or guide behavior. These stimulus properties are very important, as we shall shortly see.

Energizing effect of nonreward frustration.   Suppose that we put an animal into an apparatus called a double runway, two separate runways strung together so that the goal box for the first runway is also the start box for the second runway. This apparatus is illustrated in Figure 10–2. The animal runs down the first runway to get food in the first goal box; then when a door is opened, it runs down the second runway to get food in the second goal box. After the animal has thoroughly learned the task, we ask this question: If food is omitted in the first goal box, what will be the effect on running speed in the second runway? Frustration theory predicts that the animal should run faster than usual because nonreward in the first goal box is frustrating and produces a higher level of drive. This increased drive should energize running in the second runway. And that is exactly what happens. The increase in running speed following nonreward is called the **frustration effect** (Amsel & Roussel, 1952). Control subjects that were never rewarded in the first goal box run slower in the second runway than do frustrated animals (Wagner, 1963). Amsel proposed that during training, an anticipatory goal response is conditioned to apparatus cues during training. As this response becomes stronger, there is more frustration if the reward is omitted. The frustration is a source of drive, and hence the animal runs faster.

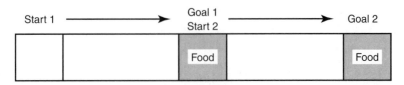

FIGURE 10–2.   The double-runway apparatus for studying nonreward frustration. The animal is placed in start box 1 and runs to goal box 1 for food. It then runs from goal box 1 to goal box 2 for food. The animal learns to run quickly from each point to the next. If food is then omitted in goal box 1, the animal runs faster to goal box 2. It is "energized" by omission of food in goal box 1, the frustration effect.

Frustrative nonreward and extinction.   If an animal is trained in a simple runway with one goal box, it learns to expect reward and then is frustrated when the reward is omitted. This is the same frustration effect that occurs in the double runway. In this case, however, the goal box cues are associated with the aversive frustration and arouse conditioned frustration, which is aversive. As the animal approaches the goal box, the conditioned aversion gets stronger, and the animal slows down. The animal extinguishes running to the goal box both because it learns that food is not there and because it is frustrated. How do we know that frustration is involved? Experiments that manipulate the level of frustration reveal this tendency. For example, suppose that one animal is trained with a large reward and another with a small reward. Since a large reward is a better incentive, we might expect the large-reward subject to extinguish more slowly. But according to frustration theory, omission of a large reward should be more frustrating (more aversive) than omission of a small reward. Therefore, the large-reward animal should extinguish faster. The results are as predicted. A similar result occurs when animals are shifted from a larger to a smaller reward, as we saw with the Crespi effect in Chapter Eight. The animals run more slowly than do animals that have been continuously trained with a small reward. Crespi's "depression effect" is usually interpreted in terms of frustration.

Persistence following frustration: partial reinforcement effects.   One of the more puzzling effects of rewards is that they produce greater resistance to extinction if not given for every response. Animals rewarded after every trip down a runway or after a lever press (100 percent reinforcement) extinguish faster than animals rewarded only part of the time (partial reinforcement). This is called the **partial reinforcement extinction effect (PREE).** The obvious question is, How can a response rewarded part of the time be "stronger" than one rewarded all the time?

According to frustration theory, following 100 percent reinforcement during training, omission of reward in extinction produces the animal's first nonreward frustration in the situation. This is the same as the interpretation of extinction previously given. With partial reinforcement training, however, the animal is frustrated on each nonreinforced trial during training. This primary frustration (R_F) also has a conditionable component (r_f) that has a stimulus component (s_f). How does this affect behavior? Early in training, partially reinforced animals run more slowly than 100-percent-reinforced animals, because the partially reinforced animals have some frustration conditioned to the goal box (Wagner, 1963). As frustration (and r_f-s_f) occurs more often, however, s_f becomes one of the stimuli to which running is conditioned. Eventually, r_f-s_f facilitates running:

Apparatus Cues $\rightarrow$ (r_f-s_f) $\rightarrow$ Running.

As a consequence, when extinction is begun and reward is omitted altogether, the animal's performance does not suddenly fall apart. The animal has learned to run and be reinforced when the frustration cues (r_f-s_f) are aroused on nonreinforced trials. Such an interpretation accounts for persistence of behavior in many situations in which there is emotional arousal (Amsel, 1992).

Some athletes, for example, seem to thrive on emotional outburst and controversy when they are frustrated. The frustration interpretation is that their performance has become conditioned to the emotional arousal and that the emotional arousal is a "support stimulus" for their performance. In addition, of course, their motivational arousal may be a drive that energizes their performance. The partial reinforcement effect also accounts for what is called frustration tolerance in humans. People who have learned to persist in the face of frustration use frustration as a cue to keep on working. If they keep on working, they are more likely to succeed. Instead of having nonproductive emotional responses to frustration (as a "spoiled" child might have), they engage in productive behavior. We often consider the development of such frustration tolerance to be a sign of maturity. Amsel (1992) has shown a number of instances in which frustration theory applies to human behavior.

SECTION SUMMARY

1. **Frustration** is generally considered an **aversive state** that occurs when an anticipated desirable goal is not attained. It is particularly interesting because a negative emotional response is occurring in the context of positive expectations. There are no responses that are unique to frustration.

2. One explanation for the negative frustration response is in terms of **opponent process theory,** which says that when positive affect is aroused (as with positive anticipations), an opponent process is also aroused (negative affect). If the anticipation is not fulfilled, the positive affect declines, but the opponent process remains longer.

3. The amount of frustration experienced is a function of such variables as **number** of prior frustrations, **size** and **value** of the anticipated goal, the **probability** of getting the goal, the **importance** of the goal, and **previous experience** in dealing with frustrating situations.

4. The most developed area of research on frustration treats **nonreward frustration** as an **aversive drive** that energizes behavior. A frustration interpretation of extinction is that when a behavior is not rewarded, after previously having been rewarded, the animal avoids the aversive conditions associated with the nonreward.

5. If an animal is not rewarded after every response, it takes longer to extinguish than if it is rewarded after every response. This is the **partial reinforcement effect.** The frustration interpretation for this is that the animal learns that rewards follow nonrewarded (frustrating) trials and nonrewarded trials become a cue to keep responding because reward will follow.

CONFLICT THEORY

Conflict as a Source of Frustration

A conflict situation produces frustration when one goal is "blocked" by a competing goal. Virtually all behavior involves some degree of conflict because we are always making choices among competing goals. Conflict has long been considered a basic problem in neurotic behavior. In Freudian theory, for example, conflicts between the id (such biological "drives" as sex or aggression) and the superego (socialization) are particularly important. Clinical problems have been a rich source of research ideas about conflict, and the most dominant theory of conflict in this tradition has been that of Neal Miller.

Miller's Theory of Conflict

The theory.   Miller and his associates (e.g., Dollard & Miller, 1941; Miller, 1959) progressively developed the theory of conflict. Miller (1959) begins with six assumptions:

1. The closer an organism is to a positive goal, the stronger the motivation to approach that goal. This is called an approach gradient.
2. The closer an organism is to an aversive goal, the stronger the motivation to escape or avoid the goal. This is called an avoidance gradient.
3. The avoidance gradient is steeper than the approach gradient. It drops off more rapidly than the approach gradient as the organism is further from the goal.
4. The level of either approach or avoidance gradients can be raised or lowered by appropriate manipulations of approach and avoidance motivation (such as changes in degree of hunger or level of fearfulness).
5. The approach or avoidance tendencies increase in strength with number of trials.
6. When two incompatible responses are in conflict, the one with the stronger motivation (approach or avoidance) will occur.

Figure 10–3 illustrates the typical conflict situation in laboratory research. The strength of approach or avoidance is a function of both learning and motivation, so Miller's concepts are more like Hull's excitatory potentials (Chapter Six) than just motivational concepts.

Evidence for Miller's theory.   Judson Brown (1948) tested the first four assumptions. He tethered rats to a calibrated spring with a harness so that he could record the strength of the rats' pull toward or away from a goal. Some animals were trained to run down an alleyway to food and then were stopped by the tether either "near" (30 cm) or "far" (170 cm) from the goal. The results, which are shown in Figure 10–4, were that

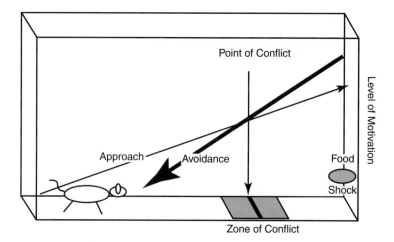

FIGURE 10–3. Conflict situation. The animal is first trained to run down the apparatus (left to right) to get food. Doing this establishes the approach motivation gradient. It then receives a shock at the food source. This establishes the avoidance motivation gradient and produces an approach-avoidance conflict. The "point of conflict" is where the two gradients intersect. See text for further details.

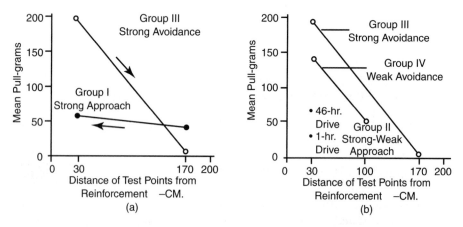

FIGURE 10–4. (a) The approach gradient represents the mean force exerted by forty-six-hour motivated rats when restrained at two points in the alley. The avoidance gradient reveals the force exerted by rats in their efforts to avoid a region where strong shock has been given. Although the experimental points in this figure and in (b) have been joined by straight lines, no assumption is intended with respect to the linearity of the gradients. (b) This section illustrates the effect of reduced shock and reduced hunger upon the strengths of the avoidance and approach responses, respectively. (From Brown, 1948, pp. 457 and 459. Copyright © 1948 by the American Psychological Association. Reprinted by permission.)

1. The rats pulled harder when they were in the near position.

2. Other animals, shocked but not fed at the end of the runway, pulled away from the shock area harder when in the near position.

3. The slope of the escape gradient was steeper between the two points than was that of the approach gradient. The results, which are shown in Figure 10–4(a), are as predicted, but the gradients are not necessarily linear (it's just that two points can define only a linear function). The only real requirement of the theory, however, is that the gradients cross.

4. Figure 10–4(b) shows the results of testing the animals under strong versus weak avoidance. The overall gradient is lower with weak avoidance. Other animals, tested at forty-six hours of deprivation, showed stronger approach than animals deprived for one hour. However, since these animals were tested only at the near distance, we can only assume that the overall approach gradient was lower for one group than the other.

5. Kaufman and Miller (1949) supported the fifth assumption by showing that with more approach training trials, the animals were more likely to go to the goal after having been shocked there.

6. The primary evidence for this assumption is the fact of conflict resolution. That is, animals do ultimately approach or avoid.

Types of conflict.   Psychologists generally distinguish four kinds of conflict, diagrammed in Figure 10–5, in terms of Miller's gradient theory.

- **Approach-Approach.**   This involves two discrete positive alternatives, Goal A and Goal B. As the animal moves toward A, the tendency to approach A is even stronger, and the tendency to approach B is less. Therefore, the conflict is easily resolved. The fable of the indecisive jackass that starved to death between two bales of hay is charming but unlikely.

- **Avoidance-Avoidance.**   This involves two aversive goals. As the animal moves away from one, it necessarily moves toward the other and then is forced back toward the first, and so on. Such conflict gives rise to sayings such as "between the devil and the deep blue sea." If the animal has to stay in the situation, it should eventually become more or less immobile at the point of minimal aversive stimulation, where the two gradients intersect. This behavior is commonly seen in the laboratory when an animal (e.g., a rat) is shocked at either end of a runway and settles down in the middle.

  Given the chance to get away from such a totally disastrous situation, animals will attempt to get out of the situation, either physically or psychologically. Amnesia is often thought to have this motivational basis: A person in an intolerable situation may escape by "forgetting." Such forgetting is not consciously intentional but nevertheless serves the purpose. Some people escape by sleeping, others by taking drugs.

- **Approach-Avoidance.**   This conflict involves goals with both desirable and aversive features. As in Brown's experiment, an animal is trained to run down an alleyway to food, and then the food container is wired so that the animal gets shocked if it touches the food. The animal then vacillates in the runway because of its simultaneous motivation to approach and to avoid the same goal. The area in which vacillation occurs is the "conflict zone," the region in which the approach and avoidance gradients intersect. Approach-avoidance conflicts have

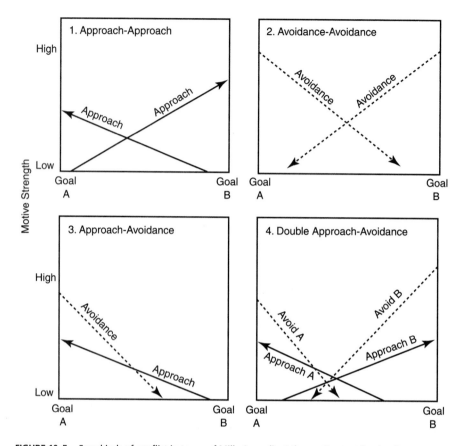

FIGURE 10–5. Four kinds of conflict in terms of Miller's gradient theory. See text for details.

received considerable experimental attention because they are so common. Usually such a conflict is resolved in some way, and we must assume a shift in the relative strengths of approach and avoidance so that the individual goes either all the way to the goal or so far away that the approach motivation is no longer effective.

- **Double Approach-Avoidance.** This conflict involves two goals, each having positive and negative features. The choice of one goal results in the loss of another, and this loss is a negative feature of the chosen goal. For example, you might have the choice of buying a large, comfortable, and expensive car or of a smaller, less comfortable car that costs less. To gain the good feature of one, you inevitably lose the good feature of the other. This type of conflict, perhaps better called multiple approach-avoidance because the alternatives may be more than two, is more typical of real-life situations but is also more difficult to analyze experimentally.

SECTION SUMMARY

1. **Conflict** may be considered a special category of frustration, involving choices among **incompatible responses** so that achieving one goal precludes achieving another.

2. The best developed experimental theory of conflict is that of **Neal Miller,** which assumes that the closer one is to a positive or negative goal, the stronger is the tendency to approach or avoid. These increasing tendencies are called **approach** and **avoidance gradients,** with the avoidance gradient being steeper than the approach gradient.

3. Four basic kinds of conflict are (1) **approach-approach,** where there are two positive goals; (2) **avoidance-avoidance,** where there are two negative goals; (3) **approach-avoidance,** where the same goal has both positive and negative features; and (4) **multiple approach-avoidance,** where there is more than one goal and each has both positive and negative features.

4. Conflict behavior is characterized by **vacillating** back and forth between goals or between approaching and avoiding a goal. Conflicts are **resolved** when an organism moves past the point of conflict, or pulls away from the point of conflict.

5. Most research has been done on approach-avoidance conflicts, where it is assumed that conflict occurs at the point where approach and avoidance gradients intersect. Theoretically, conflicts may be resolved by increasing or decreasing approach or avoidance gradients so they do not intersect.

ANXIETY

Most psychologists would agree that strong anxiety is an unpleasant emotional experience, that it is strongly motivating, sometimes pushing people to extreme thoughts and behaviors to control it, and that long periods of anxiety can be bad for your health, producing so-called stress disorders. For these reasons, anxiety has probably received more attention than any other emotion in terms of both research and theory. Anxiety disorders are "shockingly common" (Barlow, 2000), exceeding substance abuse disorders, for example, and may last almost literally for a lifetime. Let us begin by making some basic distinctions and then look at anxiety in more detail.

Anxiety versus Fear

Freud distinguished between *objective anxiety* (what we usually call fear) and *neurotic anxiety*. Objective anxiety is directed toward some specific object that causes it, whereas neurotic anxiety is fear without a (recognized) cause. Neurotic anxiety has also been characterized as out of proportion to the actual threat to the individual.

S. Epstein (1967, 1986) has distinguished between fear and anxiety based on *perception of control* rather than recognition of the cause. Anxiety, he says, is a qualitatively different experience from fear and arises when a person cannot cope with threat. Such an inability to cope might occur because a person does not recognize the source of the threat, as Freud would have it, but may also occur when a person knows exactly what the threat is but can do nothing about it. For example, a soldier might specifically be afraid of the mortar shells he sees and hears dropping around him but might also be anxious because he cannot cope with them. The critical element is ability to cope with, or have some control over, a fearful situation, not whether the cause is recognized. Barlow makes a similar distinction but adds an element of time. Fear occurs when a danger is present and imminent whereas anxiety is a "sense of uncontrollability focused largely on possible future threats" (Barlow, 2000, p. 1249). Barlow suggests that the phrase *anxious apprehension* might capture his meaning better than the word anxiety.

State versus Trait Anxiety

State anxiety (A-state).   State anxiety is that which an individual experiences in a specific situation at a specific time (Cattell & Scheier, 1961; Spielberger, 1966, 1976). For example, a person who is fearless in many danger situations might become highly anxious when giving a speech to a group. Or, an otherwise nonanxious student might be highly anxious only when taking tests.

Research has repeatedly shown that whether a person reports being anxious depends on the person, the situation, and the type of "anxious response" being reported (Endler, 1998; Endler, Hunt, & Rosenstein, 1962). Endler et al. devised the S-R Inventory of Anxiousness, consisting of eleven different situations (such as starting on an auto trip or climbing on a mountain ledge) and fourteen kinds of responses (such as heart beats faster, feels uneasy). A given person tends to rate himself or herself as more or less anxious according to the situation *and* the response, that is, in Situation A my heart beats faster and in Situation B I feel very nervous. This tendency carries the important implication that if anxiety is specific to situations and responses, then treatments may have to be equally specific. For example, test anxiety would be treated differently from fear of heights or fear of snakes. This has been the approach taken by behavior therapists.

Trait anxiety (A-trait).   Trait anxiety is a relatively enduring personality trait, a disposition to be anxious in many different situations. It is commonly distinguished from state anxiety by means of the State-Trait Anxiety Inventory (STAI; Spielberger, Gorsuch, & Lushene, 1970). In personality theory, trait anxiety may also be referred to as *neuroticism* or *negative affectivity* and is one of the most commonly described personality traits (see Chapter Twelve). It is generally considered a "basic" emotion (i.e., fear), and is a major concern in clinical psychology (M. Eysenck, 1997). Twelve different anxiety disorders are identified in DSM-IV (1994).

Panic.   Barlow (2000) refers to panic attacks as false alarms, which is to say that they are intense fears that have a sudden onset, but do not have an identifiable cause. This is different from anxiety which is usually more enduring. It is estimated that about 12 percent of the population experiences such an uncued attack during a year, and these often occur during sleep.

General Theories of Anxiety

Biological approaches to anxiety.   Biological theories of anxiety (e.g., H. Eysenck, 1967; Gray, 1982a, b) assume that physiological differences account for the difference in anxiety levels that people experience, and that there is a genetic basis for individual differences in anxiety. A number of genetic studies, especially of twins, indicate that perhaps 30 percent to 50 percent of the variance in trait anxiety may be genetic (M. Eysenck, 1997). It is also true that over 90 percent of people suffering insect phobias (strong, irrational fears) are female, and by the age of six twice as many girls as boys are likely to have experienced anxiety (Barlow, 2000). Although 50 percent genetic variance is far from trivial, it still leaves the other 50 percent to be accounted for. There are no biology-only theories of anxiety; all current theories assume that perception, learning, and cognition are important in the development and functioning of anxiety.

Barlow's theory.   Barlow (2000) proposes a general theory of anxiety that follows approaches to emotion. He suggests that the following sequence of events occurs.

    a. Some event arouses negative affect, along with a sense of uncontrollability and some preliminary coping activity;

TABLE 10–1.   Barlow's theory of anxiety.

ANTECEDENT CONDITIONS	INTERVENING VARIABLE	CONSEQUENT CONDITIONS

		Perceptual/Cognitive
		   Lack of Concentration
		   Attention to Self
		   Hypervigilance to Threat Cues
		   Worry

Stimulus Event	Negative Affect
	Uncontrollability
		Behavior
		   Dysfunctional Behavior
		   Escape/Avoidance
		Physiological
		   ACTH Release
		   Gray's Behavioral Inhibition
		   System (See text.)

b. There is increased vigilance for cues of danger and cognitive biases in overestimating future dangers, remembering past dangers, and so on.

c. There are attempts to deal with the perceived threat, such as *escaping* or *avoiding* the danger situation or *worrying* about the situation. The shift in attention toward threat cues may also make behavior more dysfunctional, thereby further increasing a sense of uncontrollability and further increasing anxiety. These are summarized in Table 10–1.

Gray's behavioral inhibition system (BIS).   Gray (1982a, b) proposed a theory that relates "anxious behavior" to particular brain locations and neurochemistry. He argues that there is a **behavioral inhibition system (BIS),** which is located in a **septal-hippocampal system** (part of the limbic system) in the brain. In Gray's theory, activation of the BIS *is* anxiety. The BIS responds to several kinds of stimulus inputs with several kinds of response outputs, illustrated in Figure 10–6.

When a person is engaged in some goal-oriented behavior and faces *threatening (punishing) stimuli, frustrative nonreward,* or *unexpected (novel) stimuli,* the BIS is activated. This activation inhibits the ongoing behavior and produces increased arousal, and the organism attends to the disruptive elements. Anxiety is experienced. Much of the evidence for Gray's theory is from research with antianxiety (tranquilizing) drugs. These drugs reduce each of these three kinds of responses. Gray suggests that these drugs reduce anxiety because they facilitate the effects of **gamma aminobutyric acid (GABA),** an inhibitory neurotransmitter.

Gray also brings cognitive factors into the theory, saying that an organism is continuously comparing its plans for the future, its predicted outcomes of its present behavior, and stored information about the way the world works. The septal-hippocampal system (known to be involved in memory) compares internal plans, predictions, and stored information with what is going on in the environment. As long as plans and expectations are being met, there is no anxiety and no behavioral inhibition. If progress toward an expected outcome is interrupted by threat, frustration, or novel event, however, the BIS becomes active, and anxiety is experienced.

In Gray's theory, signals of punishment or nonreward are anxiety-provoking but the perceived threat depends on the individual's interpretation of environmental signals. A person has to perceive that a particular signal means danger before responding to it as a threatening stimulus. Clinical

Input		Output
Signals of Punishment		Behavioral Inhibition
Signals of Nonreward $\rightarrow$ Behavioral Inhibition System $\rightarrow$		Increased Arousal
Novel Stimuli		Increased Attention

FIGURE 10–6.   Gray's behavioral inhibition system. See text for details.

patients with anxiety disorders express exaggerated thoughts about danger and exaggerated fear of the consequences of their behavior. They appraise life events as more dangerous and threatening than a more objective observer would (Beck & Rush, 1980). Recall from Chapter Two, however, that not all appraisals are necessarily conscious; people can discriminate between "good" and "bad" stimuli without consciously recognizing them.

Cognitive Aspects of Anxiety

Cognitive approaches to anxiety emphasize environmental factors, changes in personality over time, the multidimensional nature of trait anxiety, and individual differences in cognitive functioning (M. Eysenck, 1997; Williams, Watts, McLeod, & Mathews, 1997). For example, there are individual differences in the ways that people characteristically interpret events. Some people are more prone than others to see stimuli as dangerous or threatening, and hence they are biased in the way they attend to events. An "emotional" stimulus triggers cognitive appraisal, but a person high in trait anxiety is more likely to perceive an event as dangerous. This biased cognitive appraisal determines the level of physiological activity (e.g., sympathetic arousal), action tendencies (e.g., to run away or otherwise be defensive), and cognitions (e.g., likelihood of worrying about the situation).

Selective attention. M. Eysenck (1997) studied bias in attention by high and low trait anxious subjects. He used a standard **dichotic listening task,** in which subjects have different messages sent to the two ears through stereo headphones. Subjects had a mix of emotionally neutral and threatening words presented to the ear which they were instructed to pay attention to (the *attended ear*), and were supposed to "shadow" the words by repeating them as they heard them. Emotionally neutral words were presented to the *unattended ear,* and subjects were instructed to ignore these. The measure of attention was how fast a subject responded to a tone presented to one of the ears. A faster response when the tone is presented to one ear rather than the other indicates that the subject is paying closer attention to that ear. High anxious subjects responded more quickly to the emotional stimuli in the attended ear, whereas the low anxious subjects responded more rapidly to the neutral stimuli in the unattended ear. The high anxious subjects were more attentive to threatening stimuli than were low anxious subjects.

Interpretive bias. High anxious subjects make more threatening interpretations of what they hear than do low anxious subjects. For example, Eysenck, MacLeod, and Mathews (1987) orally presented subjects with *homophones,* words with the same sound but different meanings, such as pain and pane, or die and dye. The subjects' task was simply to write down the word they heard. Anxious subjects were more prone to make negative interpretations of what they heard (e.g., writing down "pain" rather than "pane").

There was a strong correlation ($r = +.60$) between level of anxiety and number of threat-related interpretations.

Negative memory bias.   High anxious subjects tend to remember negative words that they had previously used to describe themselves rather than positive words. A general account of such memory bias is called **mood congruent memory** (Blaney, 1986). People tend to remember events that are congruent with their present mood regardless of what their present mood is. People in a sad mood remember sad events, people in a happy mood remember happy events, and so on. Such biased memories are thought to perpetuate whatever mood a person is in. Thus, a person in a sad mood is more likely to remember sad events, which tends to make her more sad yet.

SECTION SUMMARY

1. Fear and **anxiety** are similar, but have been distinguished in terms of anxiety involving a perception of **lack of control** over the fearful situation and/or being more focused on possible future threats.

2. **Trait anxiety** is an enduring disposition to be anxious in many situations. **State anxiety** refers to anxiety aroused in a very specific situation. People are highly variable in terms of the situations that produce anxiety for them and for the particular kinds of responses they make in anxiety situations.

3. **Biological approaches** to anxiety emphasize the physiological aspects of emotional responses. Anxiety has a strong genetic component. Gray has proposed a biological theory of anxiety, which he calls the **behavioral inhibition system.** This says that when ongoing behaviors are interrupted by signals of **punishment,** signals of **nonreward,** or by **novel stimuli,** activity in the behavioral inhibition system is aroused. This activity is anxiety and produces **inhibition** of the ongoing behavior, **increases physiological arousal,** and **increased attention** to the threatening stimuli.

4. **Cognitive approaches** to anxiety are not incompatible with biological approaches, but emphasize the importance of **environmental** and **personality** factors and **individual differences** in cognitive functioning in anxiety.

5. Three cognitive factors related to anxiety are **selective attention** to threatening stimuli, putting **bad interpretations** on ambiguous situations, and tending to **remember bad events** disproportionately more often than good events. All these tend to sustain an individual's anxiety.

STRESS

Historical Background: The General Adaptation Syndrome

The concept of stress has subsumed much of the subject matter once covered under the topics of frustration, conflict, and anxiety. This focus is largely due to the prodigious efforts of Hans Selye and his concept of the

general adaptation syndrome (GAS). Selye (pronounced Sel-yea) considered the GAS to be common to many different "stress situations" and characterized it in three stages (Selye, 1956). First is the **alarm reaction.** When an organism faces a stressor, such as disease, extreme temperature, or injury, the body shows an alarm reaction, such as a sudden drop in blood sugar level followed quickly by a counterreponse, such as an increase in blood sugar. Other typical changes are in blood pressure, heart rate, and release of adrenal hormones. This is followed by a **stage of resistance,** in which the body uses its resources to keep its physiology on a normal course during stress. Since the body has to work harder than usual to maintain itself, it is especially susceptible to the effects of additional stress. If this effortful resistance continues long enough, the body may "wear down" and go into **stage of exhaustion.** This stage, possibly life threatening, is characterized by enlarged **adrenal glands,** *shriveling of the* **thymus** *and lymph glands* (necessary to fight disease), and **gastrointestinal ulcers.** Other effects specific to particular stressors may also occur, but the three described here are widely found, hence the name "general adaptation syndrome."

The concept of stress has been advantageous in that it provides medical and psychological researchers a common theoretical framework. So-called psychosomatic disorders, illnesses sometimes said to be "in the head" and therefore not "real," make sense in terms of stress. We need only assume that stress disorders have both psychological and physical origins. This assumption also forces a more psychologically oriented definition of stress than that originally provided by Selye. Selye's approach was too limited in the sense that his *response definition* of stress did not take into account many factors that determine individual differences in response to stress situations.

Definitions of Stress

As we look at stress more closely, we see that there have been three kinds of definitions.

1. **Stimulus definition.** Stress is defined in terms of specific environmental (stimulus) conditions that produce arousal, such as danger or loud noise. These same conditions are not equally stressful for all individuals, however, so that the stimulus definition has limited value.

2. **Response definition.** Selye (1956) said that stress is a state manifested by the pattern of symptoms (responses) that characterizes the emotional fight-flight reaction. We infer stress from these symptoms (responses). This definition does not tell us what situations will produce stress, however, and easily becomes circular: "This must be stress because the person/animal is showing stress responses." Experience tells us that some stimulus events frequently produce stress, such as surgical anesthesia, pain, cold, or loss of blood, but this knowledge does not define stress for us.

3. **Interactive definition.** Most psychologists now define stress in terms of stimuli and responses, an organism-environment interaction. Stress occurs when the demands of the environment are too great for the organism to cope with (Mc-

Grath, 1970, p. 17). This definition includes the element of uncontrollability, but the imbalance is partly subjective, depending on whether a person perceives that he or she can respond effectively to the environment and on whether it is important to do so. A person perfectly capable of responding effectively may not perceive that she or he can do so and is therefore "stressed," or a person may perceive that he or she is "invincible" and is therefore not stressed, even though objectively no more capable than the person who is stressed.

Sources of Stress

Traumatic events.   Being caught in a fire, being raped, witnessing a gory crime, or being held prisoner of war are examples of traumatic stressors. Sometimes, even though a victim seems to be coping with the immediate situation, a delayed stress reaction, called **posttraumatic stress disorder** (**PTSD**), may appear weeks or months later. A victim may begin to feel depressed and have nightmares about the event, or may have flashbacks and briefly relive the horror of the earlier experience.

Recent life changes.   Holmes and Rahe (1967) devised a scale to quantify the degree of stressfulness of many different life changes, such as getting married, getting divorced, a family member dying, changing jobs, and so on. Different numbers of points are assigned to different changes according to their severity, and the authors suggested that the effects of life changes cumulate so that if the total number of points exceeds a threshold (300 points on their scale), illness is more likely to occur. Such details are controversial, however, for several reasons. Life changes can mean different things to different people; some of the changes in the scale are themselves illnesses and hence would probably contribute more to stress; and the scores often depend on memory and may not be entirely reliable. Research also suggests that it is predominantly negative events that contribute to stress, not positive ones. Details aside, however, life changes do contribute to stress.

Hassles.   The stresses we face most often are the hassles of everyday life (Lazarus, 1981), which may cumulate to high levels of stress just as they contribute to frustration. Many parents spend hours weekly getting children to and from school, parties, and lessons; taking care of the family; and dealing with countless small family emergencies. As such hassles continue, stress increases, and ability to cope with stress may go down. Long-term accumulation of small frustrations, hassles, and stress may occur in any occupation, for either men or women. People do lead lives of quiet desperation, and all their stresses may not be obvious to the outsider.

Stress and the Environment

Environmental load.   We saw the concept of environmental load in Chapter Six in the discussion of arousal. A high-load environment is complex and changing, a low-load environment is simple and unchanging. A high load makes more demands on the individual, with greater chance of stress. Crowding and noise, among many other factors, add to environmental load.

Crowding and stress.   Animals and people tend to distance themselves from each other, maintaining personal space, which is often described as a "protective bubble" around the individual. Other individuals are kept at distances appropriate for certain kinds of activities: close for intimate activities, further away for business activities, and so on. A person moving too close to conduct business would be violating personal space, producing discomfort and stress. Personal space is said to be maintained for protection from overstimulation and for communication about the relationships between people (Bell, Fisher, & Loomis, 1978).

1. **Protection.** We try to protect ourselves from overstimulation produced by too-close contact with others. Although animal research is not always directly applicable to human situations, animal populations are thought to rise and fall because population growth produces greater stress from excessive interanimal contact. Calhoun (1962) showed that if rodents are allowed unlimited food and water but have limited space in which to live and breed, the population will level off at a number well below the limit to which it could rise. There is a disastrous drop in birthrate, high infant mortality rate, homosexuality, greater aggressiveness, and cannibalism. A **behavioral sink** is established, usually around a food source, where there is a high density of animals and where many social problems occur. In the wild, heavily crowded conditions can also produce population decrements.

2. **Communication.** The communication function is that by maintaining a distance between ourselves and others, we send the message that we are controlling our space. Schmidt and Keating (1979) suggested that the term crowding is a label we put on a situation when density results in a loss of personal control, where we perceive we are losing freedom because of the number of people. Studies in prisons, for example, indicate that the greater the crowding, the higher the blood pressure and the greater the number of illnesses reported by inmates (Cox, Paulus, McCain, & Karlovac, 1982). Individuals in dense urban environments seem to maintain control partly by ignoring much of the environment, thereby reducing the amount of stimulation to be responded to. It is harder for prisoners to ignore each other.

Noise and stress.   About one American in three lives in a neighborhood so noisy that there is general annoyance and interference with communication (Cohen, Krantz, Evans, & Stokols, 1982). The noise comes from traffic, aircraft, construction, neighbors, children, pets, and so on. High-intensity noise can impair hearing, increase cardiovascular risk, and produce disturbing psychological symptoms (Cohen & Weinstein, 1981). Laboratory research indicates that high-intensity noise narrows the focus of attention, reduces perceived control, and increases physiological arousal. In the *Los Angeles Noise Project,* Cohen et al. (1982) compared the academic performance and blood pressure of children attending school near the Los Angeles International Airport with children at more distant points. Aircraft took off and landed an average of every two-and-a-half minutes during school hours, with peak noise intensities as high as 95 db. Mean systolic and diastolic pressures for the high-noise subjects were two to four points above the low-noise subjects, although still well within a normal range. The high-noise subjects were also poorer at solving puzzles than the low-noise subjects. The effects of the noisy environment were (to this reader, at least) surprisingly small, a testimonial perhaps to the resilience of children. Unwanted noise is nevertheless a great irritant to many people.

In a similar study, third- and fourth-grade children living near the Munich (Germany) International Airport were compared with those living in a quiet suburban neighborhood (Evans, Hygge, & Bullinger, 1995). Their results were compatible with those of the earlier Los Angeles study but added to it by showing that the children living near the airport had higher levels of **catecholamines** (epinephrine and norepinephrine) in urine which was collected overnight at home. There was little difference in blood pressure, but the differences in catecholamines indicated a higher stress level. The children near the airport also performed significantly poorer on both memory and reading tests.

Individual Differences in Susceptibility to Stress

Genetic differences.   In both applied and experimental settings, people have bred animals of very different temperaments. Some dogs (e.g., retrievers) are normally calm and relatively unresponsive to stimulation, whereas others are highly excitable (e.g., Pekingese). Laboratory mice have been bred for high or low levels of emotional reactivity, indexed by both physiological arousal and behaviors (e.g., crouching in a corner).

Early experience.   Early experience may be either prenatal or postnatal, exemplified in the research of Seymour Levine and Victor Denenberg.

Levine's research.   According to psychoanalytic theory, early infantile trauma should result in later emotional disorders. Levine (1960) put this hypothesis to the test with rat pups in their first ten days of life. Contrary to expectation, he found that pups that were left entirely in the care of their mothers were more anxious as adults in new situations than were pups that had been either "traumatized" by being shocked or handled ten minutes a day by the experimenter. Levine argued that either the mild shock or the daily handling provided stimulation that facilitated emotional stability. It was also found that escape learning was faster with nonhandled animals but that avoidance learning was faster with handled animals. This finding is explained in terms of the kinds of behaviors required. Escape is usually a simple response, and the greater the fear arousal, the faster the escape. Avoidance, on the other hand, requires a more delicately timed response in the presence of a cue. Nonhandled animals might be too emotional to respond efficiently.

Furthermore, the **adrenalcorticosteroid** levels of the nonhandled animals rise and fall more slowly when shock is presented and terminated than the levels do with shocked or handled animals. The autonomic nervous systems of the nonhandled animals simply did not respond very efficiently to environmental changes.

Denenberg's research: genetics-experience interactions. Different animals with the same genes may develop different degrees of emotionality because they have different social interactions. Denenberg (1963) made female rats emotional or nonemotional by Levine's procedure of differential early handling. He then reared some offspring of these animals with surrogate emotional or nonemotional mothers. Birthing and parenting by emotional mothers produced the most emotional offspring, and birthing and parenting by nonemotional mothers produced the least emotional offspring, the other two combinations falling between. Being born to an emotional mother is thus different from being born to a nonemotional mother, but either of these can be modified by subsequent parents. The fetus of the emotional mother may become more emotional because it is "sensitized" by maternal adrenal hormones, for example. It was also found that the offspring affected the mothers. Babies of nonemotional mothers had a calming effect on an emotional foster mother, whereas offspring of emotional mothers had "upsetting" effects on a calm mother (Gray, 1971).

Emotional conditioning. As we saw in Chapter Nine, emotional responses can be classically conditioned. Many internal "stress responses" can be conditioned to external stimuli (e.g., Bykov, 1957; Razran, 1961). This being the case, then stress responses can be aroused in otherwise nonstressful situations if the appropriate conditioned stimuli are present. For example, a person who as a child was punished by an authority figure (e.g., parent) may experience stress and anxiety in dealing with authority figures in entirely different situations in later life.

Stress and Control

The concept of control has been pursued with considerable success in research on both human and animal subjects. The physiological effects of lack of control are especially noteworthy.

Decision making and ulcers. Folklore has it that the conflict of making decisions takes its toll through the ulcerated stomach if not the palpitating heart. Research has repeatedly shown, however, that animals that do not have control over aversive events are the ones that develop ulcers (Weiss, 1972, 1977). If two animals are simultaneously hooked up to an apparatus in such a way that only one of the animals controls the amount of shock received by both of them, the animal in charge does not develop ulcers. The animal with-

EXP   Yoked
             Control

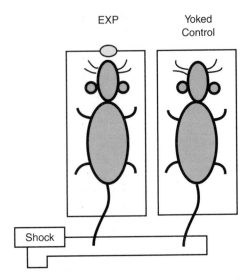

Shock

FIGURE 10–7. Experimental arrangement for yoked-control procedure. Both animals receive shock through the tail simultaneously, but only the experimental animal (EXP) can turn off the shock for itself and for the control animal by pushing a button at the front of the apparatus. The yoked control animal is helpless.

out control gets them. Figure 10–7 illustrates such an experimental arrangement.

Control in human research.   In animal research it is relatively easy to say what we mean by control: An animal can or cannot terminate or postpone shock by its behavior. In human situations it is more difficult to determine what constitutes control. Humans devise many methods to gain what they perceive as control, and perceived control is often the critical factor in stress.

Perceived control is not a simple idea, however; because even being helpless may be a kind of control (Rothbaum, Weisz, & Snyder, 1982). The stereotypical Southern belle of the *Gone with the Wind* genre tyrannizes others with her "helplessness" just as some babies tyrannize their parents. Rothbaum et al. argue that people first try to control events (primary control), and if this fails, they adjust themselves to events (secondary control), with much of life being a compromise between the two. Secondary control takes on many guises.

- **Predictive control** is achieved even in failure situations; failure becomes a predictable outcome and can be dealt with.
- **Illusory control** is achieved even in chance situations; a person may attribute chance outcomes to personal skill. Even the luck that one might have at throwing dice becomes a kind of personal skill.

- **Vicarious control** can be gained by identifying with powerful others. The most intolerable situations, including prison camps, can be tolerable to a person who believes that God is on his or her side.
- **Interpretive control** can be gained if a person can find meaning in uncontrollable events, such as "This is a test of my faith, so I shall accept it." All these variations on control help alleviate the stressfulness of a situation.

Thompson (1981) sees *meaning* as the unifying element in many different kinds of control in aversive situations. She defines control as the belief that one can do something to reduce the aversiveness of an event. Meaning may affect a person's perception of control by making events seem more endurable, by interpreting bad events as forerunners of future good events, or by perceiving misfortune as a part of some greater plan. One lesson to be learned from the preceding recitation of kinds of control is that methods of gaining control are just as variable and idiosyncratic as methods of getting food or of getting rid of pain.

Predictability and control.   If a person or an animal has control, it has "mastery" or "power" over the environment. If an organism has power, it can *predict* the outcome of its actions because its expectancies are fulfilled. We may, then, ask whether predictability alone is sufficient to confer the perception of control and thereby reduce stress (Arthur, 1986; Fisher, 1984; Mineka & Henderson, 1985). Considerable evidence shows that animals prefer to know that an aversive event is coming. Specifically, they prefer signaled shock to unsignaled shock. Miller, Greco, Vigorito, and Marlin (1983) even found that animals preferred a strong, signaled shock to a weaker shock that was unsignaled. An *anticipatory response* interpretation for this is that the foreknowledge gives an animal a chance to prepare for the oncoming aversive event, such as by assuming a body posture that will make the shock less painful. An *information theory* interpretation says information is reinforcing, even when it is about bad events. In line with this interpretation, D'Amato and Safarjan (1979) found that animals preferred a situation in which one signal predicted the inevitable occurrence of a long shock and a different signal predicted a brief shock, rather than signals that did not say which shock was coming. There are alternative interpretations for such phenomena (Mineka & Henderson, 1985), but the basic facts remain the same.

A particularly poignant experiment on control was conducted in a nursing home environment (Rodin and Langer, 1977). Using standard institutional procedures as a baseline condition, a series of additional small responsibilities were given to the residents of one floor of the home. For example, they had more responsibility for room arrangements and had a houseplant to take care of if they wanted one. These residents then had a greater feeling of enjoyment in this environment than did residents who had less control over their lives.

Lack of Control and Learned Helplessness

Many experiments show that inescapable shock greatly interferes with later escape and avoidance learning (Overmier & Seligman, 1967; Seligman & Maier, 1967). Because this is due to particular experience, it is commonly called **learned helplessness.** Specifically, dogs shocked helplessly while in a harness would subsequently just sit and take shocks in a shuttle box. They did not even learn to escape from shock, much less avoid it. Figure 10–8 shows the escape latencies for "helpless" animals in the shuttle box compared with animals without earlier exposure to shock (Maier, Seligman, & Solomon, 1969). Two-thirds of the eighty-two dogs given inescapable shock did not learn to escape from shock in the shuttle box, as compared with only 6 percent of animals not shocked previously. Lack of control over shock while in the harness is the critical element, because animals that can turn off the shock while in the harness later learn escape and avoidance responses normally (Seligman & Maier, 1967). Learned helplessness is found with many species (cats, dogs, mice, monkeys, and humans), with several forms of aversive stimulation (electric shock, loud noise, forced swimming), and with different tasks (lever pressing, shuttle box avoidance, or, for humans, solving anagrams). It is not an isolated phenomenon.

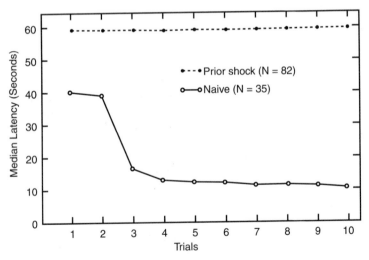

FIGURE 10–8. The effects of inescapable shocks in the Pavlov harness on escape responding in the shuttle box. This figure shows that there is rapid escape learning by thirty-five naive dogs that received no shocks in the harness. In contrast, the median for eighty-two dogs that received inescapable shocks in the harness, prior to escape training in the shuttle box, shows failure to escape shock. The arbitrary failure criterion was 60 seconds a shock (a latency of 60 seconds after onset of the S+). (From Maier, Seligam, & Solomon, 1969, p. 321. © 1969. Reprinted by permission of Prentice Hall, Inc., Englewood Cliffs, New Jersey.)

The role of serotonin. Mowrer and Viek (1948) reported what they called *fear from a sense of helplessness.* Some subjects (laboratory rats) experienced a tone followed by an electric shock to the feet, which they could terminate by jumping off the floor. Other subjects could not end the shock by their own responses. The tone was a conditioned stimulus for fear and found to suppress behavior more effectively for animals previously unable to escape the shock. Mowrer and Viek suggested that the tone aroused greater fear for these animals because of their helplessness in the previous shock situation. **Serotonin** is an inhibitory neural transmitter which has been found to rise following uncontrollable shock but not following controllable shock. The level may stay high for several days. The importance of this is that while the level is high, animals show much greater fearfulness in a novel situation (e.g., freezing in a novel environment) and are more readily fear-conditioned to a novel stimulus. Injections of a drug that facilitates serotonin increase has behavioral effects similar to those of uncontrollable shock in producing helplessness. This suggests that the "learned" helplessness effect may not be due to learning that "nothing can be done," but is instead the result of an excessively high level of fear produced by serotonin. As yet, however, we do not know why helplessness leads to an increase in serotonin (Maier & Watkins, 1998).

Learned helplessness in humans. The procedures used to establish learned helplessness in laboratory animals quickly caught the attention of researchers interested in human clinical problems. Hiroto (1974) pointed out the similarity of the learned helplessness concept to that of locus of control (Rotter, 1966) and studied learned helplessness in subjects with high versus low external locus of control. Using an analog of the animal procedures, Hiroto exposed his subjects to loud bursts of aversive noise. Some subjects could stop the noise by pushing a button, while others could not. Subjects could then move a knob to avoid a signaled noise, simulating the shuttle box.

The subjects with previous uncontrollable noise learned to avoid more slowly and had more trials without responding at all. In addition, subjects with external locus of control performed more poorly than those with internal locus, and subjects led to believe that their success was due to chance did less well than those who believed that skill could be effective. Hiroto and Seligman (1975) subsequently reported similar results using solutions to anagram problems as the response. Other investigators have not always been able to replicate these results, but these experiments were important to the development of learned helplessness theory.

Helplessness and depression. Seligman (1975) proposed that learned helplessness might be a cause of depression. The difficulty with this interpretation is that many individuals in a "helpless" situation do not become depressed, whereas many individuals who are not in "helpless" situations do become depressed. This tendency suggests that whether a situation is "helpless" depends on a person's perception of whether she is in control of the situation and thus led to the **attributional theory of depression** (Abramson, Seligman, & Teasdale, 1978). The new theory was also intended to account for the observations that (1) lowered self-esteem is a common symptom of depression, (2) depressed individuals frequently blame themselves for their failures, and (3) helplessness generalizes across many situations and times.

Attribution theory (Heider, 1958) is an account of how people search for causes for their own behavior or that of other people. A particular cause is attributed to some person, thing, or event. Within their theory, Abramson et al. (1978) defined the following three major dimensions of attribution that would be related to helplessness:

1. **Internal versus external locus of control.** A particular event, such as success or failure at a job, is attributed to oneself (internal) or to some outside event (external), such as to another person or to the difficulty of the job at which one succeeded or failed.

2. **Stable versus unstable causes.** A stable cause is one that is enduring, such as a person's intellectual ability. An unstable cause is one that can vary from time to time, such as how much a person is motivated to study for an exam or whether the questions on the exam happen to match what has been studied. Stable factors can be either internal or external.

3. **Global versus specific.** An attribution may apply to a wide range of events or to a particular event. Thus, I might attribute my failure on an exam to such a global factor as "I always fail exams" or to some specific characteristic of this particular exam, such as "I did not study for this exam."

Table 10–2 summarizes the preceding dimensions and the type of attributions that might be given for failing an examination. The attributional dimensions relate to depression as follows: (1) Lowered self-esteem occurs when a person attributes failure, which is a lack of control over the situation, to an internal dimension, such as lack of ability; (2) attributing lack of control to stable factors produces a generalized expectancy of no control, thus extending helplessness and depression to other times and situations; and

TABLE 10–2.   The attributional model of depression in relation to examination failure.

	INTERNAL		EXTERNAL	
DIMENSION	STABLE	UNSTABLE	STABLE	UNSTABLE
Global	I always fail examinations.	I often don't study for exams.	Exams are always too picky.	I usually get the hard exam questions.
Specific	This subject is too hard for me.	I did not study for this exam.	This exam was too hard.	The questions on this exam weren't what I studied.

(3) global attributions extend helplessness over situations, just as stability extends helplessness over time. The most helpless and depressing attribution should then be an internal, stable, global attribution for lack of control (failure).

Seligman and his colleagues developed the Attributional Style Questionnaire, a self-report measure designed to score attributions in terms of the three attribution dimensions (Seligman, Abramson, Semmel, & von Bayer, 1979). As predicted, undergraduate students who were more depressed according to the Beck Depression Inventory (Beck, 1967) attributed bad outcomes more to internal, stable, and global factors than did the less-depressed students. Seligman and his colleagues argue that the depressive attributional style is a cause of depression, but attributional style may be more involved in the maintenance of depression after it has been initiated by some other factor (Munton, 1985–1986). Robins (1988), noting the inconsistent conclusions about attributional style in previous reviews (Coyne & Gotlib, 1983; Hammen, 1985; Sweeney, Anderson, & Bailey, 1986), concluded that in studies in which there were enough subjects to obtain significant results with a "medium-size" difference between depressed and nondepressed groups, there were fairly consistent attributional differences between the groups. The question of causality is not yet answered, however.

The attribution model assumes, of course, that an individual has experienced negative life events so that depressive attributions can be made. The question is whether people with depressive attributional styles are more likely to become depressed after such events than are individuals with different attributional styles. Several studies of real-life negative events provide only modest support for the attributional style interpretation (Munton, 1985–1986, p. 339). Feather and Barbor (1983), for example, found that attributional style accounted for less than 10 percent of the variation in depression inventory scores of unemployed young Australians. The attribution model might be correct in the kinds of attributions important for depression, but data demonstrating the attribution-depression relationship are not very reliable (Munton, 1985–1986).

Personality Moderators of Stress

Type A behavior pattern. Friedman and Rosenman (1974) distinguished between what they called the Type A and Type B behavior patterns. The Type A person is characterized by anger or hostility, and excessive achievement striving. Type A has also been called the "hurry sickness," trying to get more and more done in less and less time and responding aggressively when there is frustration. The Type B is defined by the absence of Type A characteristics. The distinction between Type A and Type B caught the fancy of researchers because it appeared that Type A people might have greater susceptibility to coronary heart disease. Coronary heart disease includes the building up of fat deposits in the arteries (atherosclerosis) and high blood pressure.

The evidence linking Type A behavior and heart disease is not nearly so strong as commonly reported in the popular press or even in many textbooks. Moreover, to the extent that such a link does exist, all the evidence points to the anger/hostility component of Type A behavior, not to the time orientation or achievement components (e.g., Hecker, Chesney, Black, & Frautschi, 1988). One investigator (Williams, 1994) suggests that people who are generally cynical (distrusting the motives of others or tending to attribute malicious motives to others) are more likely to develop coronary heart disease. For example, if caught in a line at the checkout counter of the supermarket, a person with a "cynical heart" might take the delay as a personal affront and react physiologically with an "aggressive" cardiovascular response.

Hardiness.   Another personality type that supposedly buffers the effect of stress is the *hardy personality*. Proposed by Suzanne Kobasa (1979), the hardy personality is said to be *committed* to goals rather than alienated from life, to treat life's frustrations as *challenges* rather than threats, and to feel in *control* of his or her own life. Kobasa and others have reported some evidence that "hardy" individuals show less illness of various kinds (Kobasa, 1979). Other research indicates some problems with the concept, however. First, factor analyses of various test scores have not produced the three dimensions of hardiness (challenge, commitment, control) postulated by Kobasa (Funk & Houston, 1987; Gainer & Beck, 1987). Second, there is a high negative correlation between hardiness scores and measures of neuroticism. This suggests that hardiness is not really a new concept but is simply a different way of getting at the personality trait of neuroticism. People who are said to be high in hardiness are low in neuroticism, and vice versa. People who score high on tests of neuroticism have long been known to have more health problems than people low in neuroticism (Funk and Houston, 1987), which may be the same thing as saying that people low in hardiness have more health problems. "Hardiness" is a warmer, fuzzier sounding word than "low neuroticism," but both terms appear to refer to the same personality dimension.

Extraversion and optimism.   Extraversion is characterized by a person being open, talkative, adventurous, and sociable as opposed to being secretive, silent, cautious, and reclusive. Extraverts are generally happier and more optimistic than introverts. Optimists appear less prone to stress problems than pessimists (Taylor, 1989). In part, extraversion and optimism are inherited traits, with about 50 percent of the variation of either characteristic being genetic. Studies showing greater resilience to stress of optimistic individuals may therefore be mirroring the genetic differences, since such studies are correlational.

A Brighter Outlook on Stress

The present discussion, as with most discussions about stress, has emphasized the bad effects. There are other considerations, however. First, depending on the exact definition of stress, some amount of stress is probably good. If we never had any stress, how would we learn to cope with it? Recall the notion of frustration tolerance, which develops out of experiences with frustration. We could talk about stress tolerance in the same way. Second, even highly traumatic stress events may have long-term good effects. Suedfield (1998, p. 164), having interviewed many survivors of stressful situations, including concentration camps, says, "The fact is that most survivors have demonstrated surprising ability to endure, recover from, overcome, and even be strengthened by, events that to outside observers seem overwhelmingly destructive. We must recognize that trauma and damage are not inescapable consequences of the many vicissitudes that life can put in our way."

We should make a couple of points here. First, going to a concentration camp would not be the recommended way to build emotional stability. Second, many of the examples that Suedfield gives are indeed from survivors or sometimes from people who volunteered themselves into such situations as wintering over in the arctic regions. In either case, the examples given are from highly selected subjects who may not be at all typical of the general population. Describing the horrors of World War II prisoner-of-war camps, Bettleheim (1960) observed that when new prisoners were brought to a camp, it was obvious to the "old" inmates who among the newcomers were going to be survivors and who were not. The nonsurvivors had a look of hopelessness about them—they had already given up—whereas the "survivors" showed more of a fighting spirit.

Having said this, however, we would completely agree with the point that moderate stress, especially in early life, promotes successful coping later. Neither children nor adults should be protected from all frustration, conflict, or stress but should be given the opportunity to learn how to cope with limited stress. Suedfield's point is not that we should be unsympathetic toward people with problems, rather it is that in recent years, society seems to have taken the view that "human beings are predominantly weak and vulnerable creatures, who need protection from, and professional intervention after, almost any unpleasant experience" (1998, p. 169). Instead of thinking about how getting through a stressful situation might strengthen someone (and researching that possibility), we emphasize posttraumatic stress disorder as a clinical entity to be cured or prevented. Reiterating the earlier point, people are made stronger by facing and overcoming limited-stress situations. They should not be deprived of the opportunity and benefits of this experience.

SECTION SUMMARY

1. The **interactive definition** of stress says that stress occurs when the environment makes demands on an organism that the organism cannot meet. This definition accounts for individual differences in susceptibility to stress when organisms are in the same situation.

2. Stress may occur as a result of **traumatic events, accumulated life changes,** or accumulated **daily hassles.** Noise and crowding are also stressful. Animals and people try to maintain **personal space** between themselves and others, **protecting** the individual from overstimulation and **informing** others that the "owner" of the space is in control.

3. Individual differences in susceptibility to stress depend on genetics and early experiences, both prenatal and postnatal. Early exposure to changing stimulation is important in developing resistance to stress. Emotional conditioning also occurs.

4. **Lack of control** in aversive situations can produce such stress disorders as gastrointestinal ulcers. Humans develop many strategies for gaining **perceived control** in situations in which there may be no real control. Such strategies help to reduce the stressfulness of uncontrollable aversive events.

5. If an organism is repeatedly unable to be effective in its interactions with the environment, **learned helplessness** may result. This failure to respond is often presumed to occur when the organism perceives that it has no control over the environment. The inhibitory neurotransmitter **serotonin,** associated with strong fear, also increases in such situations.

6. The **attributional theory of depression** says that human depression occurs when a person perceives that his or her failures are due to causes that are **internal** to the person, are **global** (occurring across many situations), and are **stable** across time.

7. A number of personality characteristics are thought to moderate the effects of stress, including the **Type A** behavior pattern, **hardiness,** and **extraversion.**

COPING

Nature of Coping

Coping refers to any way that we may voluntarily try to control stress or anxiety in ourselves. Coping activities are self-regulatory. The individual consciously does something to deal with his or her own situation. Historically, psychologists have talked a great deal about defense mechanisms (such as repression, reaction formation, projection, and denial), whose function is also to reduce anxiety, but not consciously. One important aspect of newer approaches is that in contrast to the classic mechanisms, there is no hint of "abnormality" in their use.

Classification of Coping Mechanisms

Lazarus and Folkman (1984) distinguished the two kinds of coping noted earlier. **Problem-focused coping** seeks to improve a stress situation by working on the cause of the stress. A person feeling the stress of overwork might try to reduce the workload, go on a vacation, use time more efficiently, and so on. **Emotion-focused coping** (palliative coping) activities do not change the situation, but instead just aim to make one feel better. These might involve denying that there is a problem, engaging in vigorous exercise, or taking drugs or alcohol. Obviously, some emotion-focused behaviors (e.g., taking drugs) may produce worse problems than those that initiated the coping in the first place. As Monat and Lazarus (1985) also point out, people do not exclusively employ one form of coping response.

Stress Management Techniques

Monat and Lazarus (1985) summarize stress-management techniques in three categories: changing environment and lifestyle, changing personality and perceptions, and directly modifying biological responses.

Changing environment and lifestyle. This includes such activities as time management, getting proper nutrition, exercising, stopping smoking and drinking, finding alternatives to frustrated goals, and so on. Many of the activities in this category are things that our grandmothers might have advised, but in the more technical jargon of modern health psychology, many of these are **immunogenic behaviors.** That is, they immunize us from the potential ravages of too-severe stress. Other stress management techniques may be **pathogenic behaviors** (such as alcohol consumption or poor sleeping habits) that have ill effects.

Changing personality and perceptions. These might include such activities as assertiveness training (to achieve goals more successfully) or changes in how we think about things or appraise situations. If two people are in a sinking boat, one may appraise the situation as dangerous (he cannot swim and believes the water to be deep), but the other appraises the situation as safe (she knows the water is only 3 feet deep). One effective way to cope with dangerous situations sometimes, then, is to change our appraisals of them. Throwing out the anchor would indicate the depth of the water and lead to a reappraisal of the situation (if the water is in fact shallow). Changes in appraisals are not always effective, but it is useful to explore different appraisals to find out whether new ones might be more appropriate.

Lazarus (1968) showed how different appraisals of a situation can affect emotional responses. He recorded the GSR of subjects before and during a movie showing a primitive male puberty rite known as subcision, which consists of making several cuts on the underside of the initiate's penis. The movie uniformly produces emotional reactions in the viewers, with GSR peaks corresponding to each of the cuts. Lazarus asked whether different kinds of cognitive appraisals of the situation would diminish the emotional reactivity of different kinds of subjects. In one experiment, college students and relatively uneducated middle-management businessmen were compared.

Three different soundtracks accompanied the otherwise silent film. In the first, there was no sound. In the second, the narrator said that the operation was not really unpleasant or painful and that the young man looked forward to it. In the third, a narrator described the scene objectively as just an interesting bit of anthropological data. The first narration involved the defense mechanism of denial, whereas the second involved the mechanism of intellectualization. Lazarus predicted that the college students would cope better (as indicated by lower GSR) by intellectualizing along with the soundtrack but that the businessmen would show less stress with the denial. The results came out as predicted. Another experiment showed that just presenting different introductions to the film was about as effective as narrations that continued throughout the film.

Modifying biological responses.   A person might try to control stress responses through the use of relaxation exercises, meditation, hypnosis, or biofeedback. The difference between this overall approach and those listed earlier is the emphasis on directly modifying the physiological responses to stress, without necessarily changing the stressful situation or the perception of it.

1. **Meditation.** There are many different forms of meditation (Ornstein, 1986), but the best known in the United States is **transcendental meditation** (TM), a simplification of Zen Buddhism. Its primary guru (teacher) is Maharishi Mahesh Yogi. Under the guidance of a trained teacher, the initiate is given a **mantra,** a particular word or phrase that is said repeatedly. The mantra is a word or syllable, like "om," which has a soft rolling sound to it. The individual relaxes as much as possible in nondistracting conditions and concentrates on the mantra to the exclusion of other stimuli or thoughts. Two 20-minute periods of meditation a day are claimed to make one happier, healthier, more loving, more energetic, and more able to use one's mind creatively. Many devotees are satisfied that they have indeed become better people through the use of TM, and quite possibly this is so. The question is whether TM does any of these things, and, if so, is there anything unique about TM to account for the effects?

There is no compelling evidence that meditation is associated with any cognitive or physiological state that is unique to meditation. The effects of meditation are comparable to those produced by relaxation (Delmonte, 1984). Moreover, Holmes (1984) found that subjects who meditated showed just as strong somatic responses to stressful situations as did nonmeditators. Speech-anxious subjects assigned to a meditation condition did not show any lower heartrate during a subsequent speech than did subjects in three different control conditions (Kirsch & Henry, 1979). Meditation may be an especially effective way for some individuals to achieve relaxation, and it has some merit in that regard. Our existing knowledge does not show that TM (or any other form of meditation) produces a clearly different physiological state than other methods of achieving relaxation, however, and other relaxation techniques may be better for some people.

2. **Biofeedback.** Biofeedback instruments are amplifiers specialized to convert such physiological signals as skin temperature, blood pressure, heartrate, muscle tension, or EEG into readily identifiable visual or auditory stimuli that tell us what is happening. For example, a light may come on only when our brain is producing alpha waves, or a tone may change pitch upward or downward as muscle tension increases or decreases.

The therapeutic logic behind the use of biofeedback is generally that high levels of physiological activity are associated with tension (beta waves in the EEG, low skin resistance, high blood pressure and heartrate, and tense muscles). Biofeedback techniques can help us to learn what it feels like to relax by telling us when we relax even a tiny bit. Muscle tension, for example, often creeps up on us over a period of time so that we do not notice that we are getting tense; then suddenly we have headaches, muscle aches, or tics, or we grind our teeth. From electrodes placed on the appropriate muscles, we can see or hear from the biofeedback instrument when there is an increase or decrease in tension. We may thereby learn to discriminate tension from relaxation and be able to control tension. The 1970s wave of almost uncritical enthusiasm for biofeedback has now subsided as the limitations of the technique have become apparent. Biofeedback works well for some kinds of problems but not so well for others. For example, it has been difficult to obtain reductions of heartrate or blood pressure of clinically significant magnitude that will last outside the laboratory setting. Feedback is very effective, however, for any problem (including headaches) that is related to muscle tension.

SECTION SUMMARY

1. **Coping** refers to any way in which we more or less consciously try to control stress or anxiety in ourselves. **Problem-focused coping** seeks to change the cause of the stress. **Emotion-focused coping** tries to change the emotional response to the stressful situation.

2. **Stress management techniques** include changing the environment or one's lifestyle, changing one's perceptions (especially by reappraising the stressful situation), and changing biological responses (physiological arousal).

3. **Meditation** is a way of reducing physiological responsiveness by producing relaxation. In spite of popular claims to the contrary, there is little evidence that meditation does anything beyond producing general relaxation.

4. **Biofeedback** involves electronic amplification of physiological responses as a technique to aid learning how to control those responses. Biofeedback works best for relaxation of specific skeletal muscle groups and for disorders resulting from muscle tension, but has not been found to be effective for reducing blood pressure.

CHAPTER ELEVEN

Aggression and Altruism

What do we mean by aggression?

Is there more than one kind of aggression?

How is human aggression different from animal aggression?

What factors make it more or less likely that aggressive behavior will occur?

Can we bring aggression upon ourselves?

Is aggression inevitable or can it be eliminated?

What role does emotion play in aggression?

Can we account for war by the same principles we explain individual hostility?

How can we account for the occurrence of apparently selfless altruistic behavior?

AGGRESSION

The simultaneous presence of aggressive and altruistic behaviors within at least one species, *Homo sapiens,* provides an interesting biological and social puzzle. From the point of view of natural selection, aggressive behavior in some situations would seem to have great value. Aggressive males typically have access to more females and hence disseminate their genes more widely. Among humans, unfortunately, aggressive behavior can literally lead to "overkill." Most of us are familiar with the German and Soviet atrocities under Hitler and Stalin during the 1930s and 1940s, but the 1990s attempts at genocide occurring between the Hutu and Tutsi tribes in Africa, warfare between the Serbians and Croatians in deconstructed Yugoslavia, and terrorist destruction of the twin towers of the World Trade Center on September 11, 2001, remind us that such events can happen anywhere at any time. These examples seem to lend credence to the philosophical view held by the British philosopher Thomas Hobbes (1962 [1651]), who said that men are inherently evil and that it is the duty of the state to keep their violent impulses in check. The other side of the coin is Jean-Jacques Rousseau's eighteenth-century view of the "noble savage," that men are inherently good but are corrupted by society (Hergenhahn, 1997). People do engage in apparently selfless acts of heroism, as well as everyday kindnesses to others, which would not seem to promote self-interest. Why, for example, would a person donate his or her own blood to a faceless blood bank? It is to such questions of "good" and "evil" that we turn in this chapter.

What Do We Mean by Aggression?

No amount of definition seems to cover what everyone means by aggression. What has been called aggression ranges from attack and killing to verbal descriptions of Rorschach inkblots. Table 11–1 is a list of examples that may or may not be considered aggressive. Check the ones you think represent aggression. If you compare notes with someone else, the difficulty soon becomes obvious. It is hard to find consistent rules that seem to apply to every situation and provide an unambiguous decision about whether a behavior is aggressive. This point is further emphasized when we look at cross-cultural definitions of "crime." In some societies killing a newborn child is an aggressive act punishable by law, as is abortion. In other societies, "infanticide" is taken for granted and justified on the same grounds that abortion may be justified, such as having too many children or being unable to afford to take care of a child (Segall, Ember, & Ember, 1997). Behaviors that are called aggressive may represent many different underlying processes, as well as being subject to differences in definition. To help clarify such issues, we first look at animal aggression and then human aggression.

TABLE 11–1. Behaviors that might be considered aggressive.

1. A Boy Scout helping an old lady across the street accidentally trips her, and she sprains her ankle.
2. An assassin attempts to kill a presidential candidate, but his shot misses.
3. A housewife knocks a flowerpot off a fifth-story window ledge, and it hits a passerby.
4. A farmer kills a chicken for dinner.
5. In a debate, one person belittles another's qualifications.
6. A soldier presses a button that fires a nuclear missile and kills thousands of people whom he cannot even see.
7. A policeman trying to break up a riot hits a rioter on the head with a club and knocks him unconscious.
8. A cat stalks, catches, tosses around, and eventually kills a mouse.
9. A wife accuses her husband of having an affair, and he retorts that after living with her, anyone would have an affair.
10. A frightened boy, caught in the act of stealing and trying to escape, shoots his discoverer.
11. One child takes a toy away from another, making him cry.
12. A man unable to get into his locked car kicks in the side of the door.
13. A man pays 25¢ to beat an old car with an iron bar, which he does vigorously.
14. A football player blocks another player from behind (clipping) and breaks his leg.
15. A businessman hires a professional killer to "take care of" a business rival.
16. A woman carefully plots how she will kill her husband, and then does so.
17. Two students get into a drunken brawl, and one hits the other with a beer bottle.
18. A businessman works vigorously to improve his business and drive out the competition.
19. On the Rorschach inkblot test, a hospitalized mental patient is scored as being highly aggressive, although he has never actually harmed anyone.
20. A young boy talks a lot about how he is going to beat up others, but he never does it.
21. A hired killer successfully completes his job.

ANIMAL AGGRESSIVE BEHAVIOR

Multiprocess Views of Aggression

Biologists generally talk about **agonistic behaviors** rather than aggression. Three common types are **predatory behavior, attack behavior,** and **defensive fighting.** Predatory behavior is seldom considered aggressive because it is not between members of the same species and is usually unemotional, such as the quiet behavior of a cat stalking a bird. Attack behavior between cats, on the other hand, involves a lot of noise, back arching, and hair fluffing. Defensive fighting also has a desperate and highly emotional quality.

Moyer (1971) identified eight forms of aggression, differentiated by specific behaviors and different physiological bases. These are (1) predatory, (2) intermale, (3) fear induced, (4) irritable (such as pain induced), (5) territorial defense, (6) maternal, (7) sex related, and (8) instrumental (rewarded). Moyer argued that each form of aggression in lower animals has a different brain circuitry but that the circuits may overlap—as they obviously must, if they result in common behaviors. With people, however, there is no good evidence for differences in brain circuitry for different kinds of aggressive behavior. The human's refined capacity for learning and using symbols provides an indefinitely wide range of possibilities for arousing aggressive behavior through the same circuitry. For example, a simple contraction of a finger can be a highly aggressive act—if the finger is on the trigger of a gun.

Environmental Causes of Animal Aggression

Aversive stimuli. We can arouse fighting behavior in laboratory animals by application of a variety of aversive ("irritating") stimuli (Vernon, 1969) and reward it by removing these conditions (Hutchinson, 1972). A mouse tries to bite anything that pinches its tail, and when a monkey in a restraining chair is struck on the tail, it will bite a ball held in front of its head. The delivery of physical blows, tail shock, intense heat, noxious brain stimulation, air blasts, foot shock, loud noise, and aversive conditioned stimuli, or the withdrawal of food, morphine, mobility, rewarding brain stimulation, money, and conditioned stimuli for rewarding events will produce attacks on conspecifics, rubber hoses, toy animals, real animals, response panels, and tennis balls.

Proximity and crowding. Proximity is one of the most important antecedents for aggression (Marler, 1976). Crowding results in fighting with either birds or mammals, and the closeness of a same-sex member of the same species is especially important. Male chaffinches start fights with other males when they are at a greater distance than they do with females. But if the females have their breasts dyed red like the males, the females are attacked when further away. There may have been selection for fighting with same-sex conspecifics because they are the strongest competitors for resources and mates. Among rats living under group conditions, crowding has produced disastrous consequences, including low birthrate, high infant mortality rate, homosexuality, heightened aggressiveness, and cannibalism (Calhoun, 1962).

Dominance, rituals, and peaceful coexistence. Many animals develop dominance hierarchies, usually with one male at the top that gets first chance at food and his choice of females. Positions in the hierarchy are sometimes determined by actual fighting and sometimes by ritual fighting—aggressive displays such as spreading out feathers, baring teeth, or making noise. High rank may also be attained "by cunning or even by accident if the critical encounters with opponents occur at a time when something else in their recent past predisposes them to be subordinate to whomever they meet" (Marler, 1976, p. 239). One can be born into a high-status position, even among monkeys. If one's mother is of high status, then the offspring enjoys the same status. A hierarchy remains stable until some animal is challenged for its place. Actual fighting also may be reduced by establishment of territories. Some species fight at territorial boundaries, but others tend not to. Shrews, for example, "give a chirp of alarm, turn tail, and run" when they meet at the common boundary of their territories (Marler, 1976, p. 240).

Ritualized aggression, dominance hierarchies, and territorial control have been said to be nature's way of preserving life. The apparent calm may mask the destruction of uncountable numbers of animals forced to live in marginal habitats, however. Ritualized aggression still favors the victor. The loser has fewer chances at food or mates, and in evolution it matters not how you play the game but whether you win or lose.

Inhibition to aggression.   Animals can do many things to avoid aggressive encounters, some of which are under social control. These include

- Keeping a distance from the antagonist.
- Arousing a noncompetitive response, such as making a sexual display so that the antagonist is distracted.
- Avoiding provocation of others, including not fighting back.
- Producing rapid familiarity, which includes making the animal's own smell, taste, sight, and sound as familiar as possible to the other animals with which it must remain in close contact. Animals are more likely to attack "strangers" than "friends." Animals sprayed with deodorants to hide a familiar smell, for example, are attacked by normally friendly members of their living group.
- Diverting attack elsewhere. A victim might attack a third animal and have its own attacker then become an aggressive partner. Such coalitions are found among both human and nonhuman primates. Lorenz (1965b) has repeatedly claimed that defeated wolves inhibit further aggression by baring their throats to their victors. Other authors (e.g., Scott, 1958) strongly disputed this claim, however.

Biological Conditions

Here we consider both nonhuman and human biological factors. Often we must extrapolate from nonhumans because of limitations on human research.

Genetics.   Genetics plays a role in aggressive behavior as shown by selective breeding in animal husbandry and in laboratory research. An interesting example is the Norway gray rat (*Rattus norvegicus*) so commonly used in psychological research. An albino strain of this species has been selectively bred for ease of handling by researchers who must frequently pick up and move the animals. These animals are gentle, rarely bite, and are relatively nonresponsive to stimuli. As a rule, only a female with a litter is likely to bite. A wild gray rat brought into the laboratory is an entirely different story. It is highly responsive to the slightest noise and ready to bite at anything. Only a daring experimenter wearing heavy gloves would think of handling one of these beasts. In a similar vein, some dogs have been bred to be attacking watch dogs and others to be gentle children's pets.

Brain mechanisms.   The limbic system and hypothalamus are particularly important for the arousal or modulation of aggressive behavior. Stimulation of some hypothalamic and midbrain areas can produce attack behavior, such as mouse-killing behavior by rats or cricket-killing behavior by mice. Extensive research by Flynn (1972) has shown how stimulation of very specific brain sites can produce parts of the attack sequence or the entire attack. Aggressive behavior is organized hierarchically, as illustrated in Figure 3–1 of this text. Stimulation of one part of the amygdala facilitates attack behavior, but the general function of the amygdala seems to be to modulate the effects of hypothalamic arousal. The septal area of the brain seems to work opposite to the amygdala. Septal stimulation has a calming effect, and septal lesions produce a more vicious animal (Carlson, 1987).

Hormones and Neurotransmitters

Testosterone.   In many species, males are more aggressive than females. The hormonal basis for this (testosterone) is indicated by the fact that males are more aggressive during the mating season when their hormones are at their highest level and are least aggressive after castration (as with a gelding steer or horse). Testosterone is related to a variety of competitive activities in humans. Testosterone levels are higher in the winners than the losers of competitions, whether among humans or other animals. There is also the phenomenon of steroid rage, shown by athletes' taking hormones in order to "bulk up" their bodies. The testosterone increases muscle size but also increases aggressive behavior. The aggressive effect may have some on-field advantage in a contact sport like football, but the effect is unfortunately not limited to on-field activities. Since the research is correlational, we cannot be certain that the steroids cause more aggressive behavior (Carlson, 1994), but given the dangerous health side effects of such hormones, it seems wise to refrain from their use.

Serotonin.   Low levels of serotonin, an inhibitory neurotransmitter that we saw in Chapter Ten are related to fear, have also been implicated in higher levels of aggressive behavior in both animals and humans. Serotonin deficits have been associated with antisocial traits, suicide, aggressive/hostile traits, and impulsive violence (Berman & Coccaro, 1998; Finn, Young, Pihl, & Ervin, 1998). Experimentally raising or lowering the amount of **tryptophan** (an amino acid precursor of serotonin) in the diet also leads to lower or higher levels of aggressive behavior in animals and mood changes in humans. People who are normally high in trait hostility may be more responsive to manipulation of tryptophan treatment.

SECTION SUMMARY

1. Biologists commonly talk about **agonistic behaviors** (attack, fighting, escape, fleeing) rather than aggression. As many as eight different kinds of animal aggression have been distinguished, each with its own brain circuitry.

2. Animal attack/fighting behavior is aroused by a variety of aversive stimuli, including pain. Other animals, especially male conspecifics, provoke fighting with each other. Actual fighting is reduced by the establishment of dominance hierarchies or by ritualized fighting.

3. Aggressive behavior in animals is heightened by the **proximity** of other animals, especially in crowded conditions.

4. Aggressive behavior from other animals may be **inhibited** by such behaviors as keeping a distance from the other animal, by not responding to aggressive overtures in a hostile manner so that there is an escalation of hostility, or by distraction.

5. Important biological factors in aggressive activities are **genetics,** brain structures (especially the **hypothalamus** and **amygdala**), hormones (including **testosterone** and **serotonin**).

HUMAN AGGRESSION

The Role of Intent

Intent is a nebulous concept in the discussion of animal aggression but is widely accepted in definitions of human aggression. We may say that *aggressive behaviors are behaviors intended to do physical or psychological damage to someone.* Let us clarify this definition.

First, there is intent to harm. Did the defendant, with malice aforethought, intend to kill the victim? The jury's answer to that question is of vital interest to the defendant, but how can intention be determined? Francis Irwin (1971) illustrated a way to determine intent with an episode from Bullivant and the Lambs (Compton-Burnett, 1949). The father of two young boys walks by a place in a garden where the boys are building a hutch, speaks with them, then continues walking on a path toward a footbridge over a deep ravine. The bridge had been so weakened by a storm the previous night that it would not support a man's weight, but this danger was not immediately visible. A warning sign had been posted, but the father (in the context of the story) concludes that his sons wanted him to die because they knew of the danger but did not tell him about it. Irwin analyzes the episode in terms of his criteria for intentional behavior, which were discussed with regard to desire and aversion in Chapter One. The father realized that the sons expected that (1) he would not be hurt if they told him of the danger, and (2) he would be hurt if they did not tell him, and they preferred (2) over (1). The sons preferred his being hurt to his not being hurt. Intent is inferred from the choice of one act over another when the expected outcome of each act is known. In the list in Table 11–1, we assume that the Boy Scout does not expect that helping the old lady will harm her, so the unfortunate result is neither intentional nor aggressive. The man who employs an assassin, however, expects that this act will result in harm, and the employment is therefore an aggressive act.

The distinction between physical and psychological harm is straightforward. We may harm people by physically hitting them or by damaging their self-esteem. We make "cutting remarks" with "sharp tongues," verbal barbs as ruthless as metal ones.

Much "aggression" research does not meet these definitional criteria, however. Tedeschi, Smith, and Brown (1974) even challenge the usefulness of intent as a research criterion because laboratory studies almost never establish aggressive intent in their subjects and frequently involve elaborate cover stories to seduce subjects into harmful behaviors. Laboratory subjects generally intend to carry out the experimenter's wishes, not to harm someone. This disclaimer should be kept in mind while reading the pages that follow.

VARIABLES INFLUENCING HUMAN AGGRESSION

Environmental Factors

Impulsive aggression. Impulsive aggression refers to aggressive acts that were not preplanned. Berkowitz (1988) maintains that environmental situations (including the actions of other people) provoke impulsive attack behaviors. A variety of stimulus events may facilitate, if not entirely provoke, impulsive aggressive behaviors.

Painful stimuli. In general, people are like animals when it comes to painful irritation and aggression.

Temperature. The weather provides a good example of a nonarbitrary source of aggressive acts because the weather does not select particular individuals to treat unfairly. Working under the dashboard of a car on a hot summer day, head upside down, glasses falling off, and perspiration flooding into one's eyes, can lead to frustration and hostility quite apart from any culpability of the weather. Crime rates are apparently higher during long sieges of hot weather, a phenomenon known as the "long hot summer effect." This effect has been used to account in part for urban riots (Carlsmith & Anderson, 1979), and such violent crimes as homicides and assaults (Anderson & Anderson, 1984). Laboratory studies have also indicated that high temperatures, smoke, and bad odors heighten aggressive activities (Berkowitz, 1983). Figure 11–1 illustrates the effect.

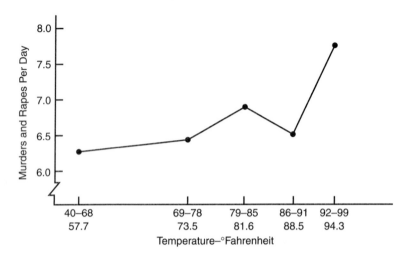

FIGURE 11–1. The long hot summer effect. In this study, the numbers of rapes and murders were correlated with temperature in Houston, Texas, over a two-year period. There were more of these crimes during very warm weather, but this fact does not necessarily mean that high temperatures caused the crimes. There may have been other important factors that were not recorded. (From Anderson & Anderson, 1984, pp. 91–97. Copyright 1984 by the American Psychological Association. Reprinted by permission.)

The weapons effect. Suppose you were asked to serve in an experiment studying physiological reactions to the stress produced by mild electric shocks. You and another subject are to evaluate each other's performance on a problem-solving task by giving each other electric shocks. You get evaluated first and receive seven shocks out of the ten possible—not very good. In your experimental room, there is a telegraph key for delivering shocks to your partner, along with a rifle and a pistol left by a previous experimenter from an unrelated experiment. You deliver six shocks to your partner as your evaluation of his performance.

You, of course, were in just one of a number of experimental conditions, and your "partner" was really the experimenter's assistant. Your treatment was intended to anger you by giving you a large number of shocks and to provide aggression-arousing cues (the guns). Both of these factors were expected to make you more aggressive so that you would give more shocks than if you were less angry or did not have cues for aggressive behavior. Table 11–2 summarizes the results of this classic experiment by Berkowitz and Le Page (1967). Subjects getting seven shocks gave back more shocks than subjects getting only one shock, supporting the anger-arousal part of the hypothesis. Subjects seeing the guns gave more shocks than those not seeing the guns, supporting the cue-arousal part of the hypothesis.

Berkowitz originally described this cue property in terms of classically conditioned aggressive responses. By prior association with anger, weapons

TABLE 11–2. Mean number of shocks given in each condition of the Berkowitz and Le Page (1967) experiment.

	NUMBER OF SHOCKS RECEIVED BY THE SUBJECT	
CONDITION	1	7
Associated weapons	2.60	6.07
Unassociated weapons	2.20	5.67
No object	3.07	4.67
Badminton rackets[a]	—	4.60

[a]There was no one-shock group with badminton rackets.

Source: From Berkowitz & Le Page, 1967, p. 205. Copyright © 1967 by the American Psychological Association. Reprinted by permission.

become conditioned stimuli for anger. The anger then serves the twofold function of being a *cue* for making particular responses and of being a *drive* to intensify responses. More recently, Berkowitz suggests that weapons tap into an *associative network* that can trigger any behavior that might be associated with anger. In some situations, anger may be a more direct cue for a particular response. If someone has previously learned to fire a gun while angry, the sight of the weapon might be a conditioned stimulus to anger, and the anger might be a cue for firing the weapon. Diagrammatically:

Gun → Anger Response → Anger Stimulus → Firing Gun

Other factors in the situation, such as fear of retribution, would also help determine whether the gun will be fired.

Many factors can heighten aggressive responses toward the target (the fictitious other subject). For example, when the target was said to be a college boxer and subjects had been shown a boxing film, the target got more shocks. Subjects shown an exciting, but nonaggressive, track race did not give more shocks to the target. Subjects seeing Kirk Douglas beaten up in a fight movie (*The Champion*) subsequently delivered more shocks to the confederate if told that the beating was justified, as if this information provided justification for aggressive actions. There is also evidence that *generalized arousal* may facilitate aggressive response, in line with Zillman's excitation-transfer theory, discussed in Chapter Two. Thus, subjects frustrated when working a jigsaw puzzle subsequently delivered more shocks to the confederate (Geen & Berkowitz, 1967), a loud noise made subjects more aggressive (Geen & O'Neal, 1969), and a sex film led to more punishment of an antagonistic partner (Tannenbaum & Zillman, 1975).

The research just described is dramatic and obviously bears on such important issues as gun control and television violence. Nevertheless, serious reservations have been raised about its meaning. First, in at least two sets of experiments, the effects could not be repeated. Buss, Booker, and Buss (1972) reported five experiments in which neither firing guns nor the presence of guns enhanced shocking a confederate. Page and Sheidt (1971) could not reproduce the weapons effect and suggested that the effect is due to an experimenter demand to behave aggressively. Given the situation, they suggest that the subject does what the subject thinks he or she is supposed to do—act aggressively. Page and Sheidt report that subjects receiving seven shocks were no more angry than subjects getting one shock. On many occasions the present author has outlined the experimental procedure to a class and then asked how many shocks class members would give back after receiving one shock or seven shocks. The class estimates are very close to the results obtained with real subjects getting real shocks, suggesting that under these experimental conditions, subjects do have some expectations about what is appropriate.

Berkowitz (1974) argued in defense of the weapons effect by saying that the way in which weapons are perceived and interpreted by subjects is critical. If a subject thinks a gun is terrible and frightening, it might arouse more anxiety than aggression and even lead to fewer shocks being delivered. Even granting the validity of this argument, however, it is difficult to see why the meaning should have been so different in Berkowitz's experiments from those reported from other laboratories.

Social Factors

Crowding.   Human research does not bear out all the pessimistic implications of the animal research previously described. The fact that some cities of very high population density (e.g., Hong Kong, Tokyo) have much less crime than cities of lower density indicates that the aversive consequences of crowding can be overridden or inhibited by social controls. For example, in the Far East there is a greater emphasis on **collectivism** than on **individualism.** The amount and/or kind of aggressive behavior may vary according to this emphasis (Triandis, 1994). Members of collectivist cultures find aggressive behavior more tolerable when it comes from an in-group authority than when it comes from a low-level in-group member or an outsider. Overall, there are wide cultural differences in the prevalence of crime. Some indications of the aversive consequences of crowding, which might lead to more hostile behaviors, are the following (Bell, Fisher, & Loomis, 1978):

- People working under crowded conditions report more discomfort, and males more so than females.
- Males show increased physiological arousal under crowded conditions, but females do not.
- People living under crowded conditions are less attracted to others, again more true for males than females.
- People tend to withdraw from high-density situations.

- The greater the population density, as in an apartment building, the less likely people are to help each other.

What makes crowding unpleasant? One possibility is that crowding produces a very high level of arousal, which is aversive. Another is that personal freedom is restricted and that this reduced freedom is aversive.

Victims may provoke attack upon themselves.   Most murders are committed by people who know the victim well, the victim is often a relative, and the homicide is likely to have been preceded by an argument that escalated into a killing. The well-known popular singer Marvin Gaye was killed by his own father under such circumstances. In one study, 25 percent of six hundred homicides were at least partly provoked by the victim (Wolfgang, 1957). Toch (1970) also found from interviews with police, from prison inmates, and from police records that about 40 percent of violent sequences were initiated when an arresting officer notified a person of his or her arrest and was treated contemptuously. In about a quarter of the cases, violence already existed, and police action tended to inflame it. The moral seems to be clear: One of the most effective ways to avoid being attacked is not to provoke attack on oneself by returning hostile actions. An argument for gun control is that even a robbery victim is less likely to get shot if the victim does not have a gun to provoke attack by an intruder. An acquaintance of the author, a night manager of an all-night market, was killed when he picked up a gun and followed a robber out into the night. In another instance with which the author has some firsthand knowledge, a man asked his neighbor, over the back fence, for a cigarette but was refused. This refusal escalated into an argument, culminating in the shooting death of the man who had refused the cigarette.

Obedient aggression.   As noted earlier, in this century alone many major atrocities have been well documented. When such activities come to trial, as with the high-documented Nuremburg trials for World War II crimes, however, it is very difficult to fix blame. It is often said that the "little guys" who pull the triggers are the scapegoats for the "big guys" who give the orders. But what are these little guys like that they follow such orders? Stanley Milgram (1974) made this question into a laboratory experiment.

How far, asked Milgram, will a normal person go in following repugnant orders? Using a good cross-section of the adult population, Milgram set up a situation in which subjects were supposed to give a "learner" increasingly strong electric shocks every time the learner made a mistake in memorizing a list of words. The "learner," an experimental assistant, was a friendly, middle-aged man whom the subjects met prior to the experiment. The fake shock apparatus was clearly marked in thirty levels, ranging from 15 to 450 volts,

and with such written labels as "Slight Shock" (15 to 60 volts), "Danger: Severe Shock" (375 to 420 volts), and "XXX" (435 to 450 volts). The learner followed a set routine: He was wrong about 75 percent of the time and com-
plained of how painful the ever-increasing shocks were. The learner and
subject were in different rooms. The subjects looked to the experimenter for
guidance as they became unsure about what they were doing, but they were
told to continue and even to treat failure to respond as an error and to give
another shock.

Milgram had estimated that only about 3 percent of subjects would continue to shock the learner up to the maximum. But in the first experiment,
26 or 40 subjects went all the way to 450 volts and none stopped below 300
volts. Various checks indicated that the subjects really did believe they were
delivering highly painful, perhaps dangerous, shocks to the learner. For example, subjects judged the intensity of the strongest shock as 13.4 on a 14
point scale. These results are astonishing in their suggestion of how easy it is
to get one human to hurt another, especially since the subjects came from all
walks of life, varied in age from 20 to 50 years, and (perhaps unlike college
students) were likely to believe what they were told about their participation
in "an experiment on learning and memory" conducted by Yale University. In
another experiment (Sheridan & King, 1972), the learner was a puppy. The
stated shock levels were highly exaggerated, but they were sufficient to evoke
obviously negative responses from the puppy. Most subjects, male or female,
shocked the puppy all the way to the top of the shock scale. Milgram subsequently found some important modifying variables. For example, the closer
the contact between subject and learner (having complete isolation of the
two from each other, hearing the learner's voice, being in the same room,
and touching), the less likely the subject was to give the strongest shock. It
does seem clear that people get themselves into situations in which they feel
compelled to carry out orders and do highly repugnant things, either
because of their commitment or because of fear of punishment for not
doing so.

Television Viewing and Aggression

Because of the great amount of exposure that people (especially children) have to television and the violence it portrays, much concern has been
expressed about TV as a contributor to real-life violence. There are individuals and groups who claim that it is obvious that the massive amount of violence shown on TV produces an increase in violence outside the box. This
belief reflects the social learning view. The cathartic view (see later) would
say just the opposite, that TV violence may protect society by providing a
harmless outlet for aggressive tendencies. There certainly is no dispute that
there is a large amount of wanton killing, fighting, and property damage

shown on TV. We then have two questions to face. First, what data are there to show that TV violence is related to real-life violence? And second, if there is such a relationship, how do we interpret the data that show it? For example, are the data only correlational, or do they indicate a causal relationship? One important point we can make in advance is that there is no evidence that observing aggressive television *reduces* violent behavior or crime. The cathartic point of view gains no support from television research.

Correlational studies of TV viewing and violence.   In one of the major studies of the effects of TV violence, data relating TV viewing and aggressive behavior were collected for 427 children over a period of ten years (Eron, Lefkowitz, Huesmann, & Walder, 1972). In Grade 3, the original group of 875 children (every third-grader in town) were judged by their peers as to how aggressive they were. At the same time, data on other variables potentially related to aggressive behavior of the children were collected from parents, such as children's preferences in TV viewing. Each parent was asked the child's three favorite TV shows, and these were given violence ratings based on an independent judge's ratings of all the TV shows mentioned.

The ten-year follow-up data are referred to as Grade 13. At this time, there were three measures of aggressiveness: peer ratings, subjects' self-reports, and a personality test. Other data, such as favorite programs, were also collected by self-reports. It is important to note that all the Grade 13 measures were obtained independently of the Grade 3 measures. The results for boys are shown in Figure 11–2; the data for girls showed no significant trends.

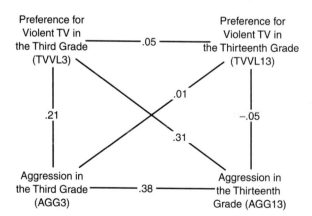

FIGURE 11–2.   The correlations between a preference for violent television and peer-rated aggression for 211 boys over a ten-year-lag. (From Eron, Lefkowitz, Huesmann, and Walder, 1972, p. 257. Copyright © 1972 by the American Psychological Association. Reprinted by permission.)

Figure 11–2 shows a cross-lagged correlation, a method for using correlational data to get at causal relations. First, there was a low (.21) but significant relation between TV preference and aggressive behavior in Grade 3. This finding, of course, is ambiguous as regards causality. There was an even higher correlation between Grade 3 and Grade 13 aggressive behavior, which tells us only that the same people were violent ten years later. Two other correlations tell us more about the effect of TV viewing on violence: Grade 3 aggressiveness did not predict Grade 13 TV preference ($r = .01$), but Grade 3 TV preference did predict Grade 13 violence ($r = .31$). From this it appears that Grade 3 TV preference played a causal role in Grade 13 violence, but not the other way around. Television viewing habits are obviously not the only factor involved in Grade 13 aggression, since the correlations are not tremendously high, but it is remarkable that there are any significant correlations at all over a ten-year period. The data are, however, weakened by the lack of any relationship for the females.

Reviewing all the published literature to date, Freedman (1984) concluded that there is a small but consistently positive correlation (somewhere between .10 and .20) between viewing TV violence and aggressiveness. This conclusion was based on research involving thousands of subjects, in several different countries. At the same time, it should be noted that this finding means that only about 4 percent of the variation in aggressive behavior can be accounted for by variation in television viewing. The most generous interpretation possible, based only on the highest of such correlations (on the order of .30), would account for only about 10 percent of the aggression variability in terms of TV viewing. It is important to note, however, that similar results have been found in several other countries, lending credibility to the research conducted in the United States (Segall, Ember, & Ember, 1997).

Field experiments on TV viewing and violence.   These are studies in natural settings, with some degree of experimental control over television or movie viewing so that the effects of the kind or amount of viewing on behavior can be interpreted causally. Residential schools have been one of the more-used settings. There have been a number of reviews of such studies, with the reviewers not always in agreement. Freedman (1984) concluded that there were found at best only a few modest relationships between TV viewing and aggressiveness. Friedrich-Cofer & Huston (1986) argued that there is a more consistent relationship between violent TV viewing and aggressive behavior than Freedman's analysis would make it appear. Wood, Wong, and Chachere (1991) analyzed the results of twenty-eight laboratory and field experiments in which children or adolescents were randomly assigned to groups exposed to violent or nonviolent presentations of movies, and their subsequent spontaneous social interactions were analyzed for aggressive acts. The results showed with statistical reliability that groups watching violent films were more aggressive in their social interactions than were control subjects.

SECTION SUMMARY

1. Human aggression is typically defined in terms of **intent** to do physical or psychological harm to someone. **Impulsive aggression** has intent to harm as a goal whereas **instrumental aggression** has some other goal.

2. **Environmental factors** that facilitate impulsive aggression are such aversive stimuli as pain, extreme temperature, or presence of cues to aggression (such as guns).

3. **Social factors** influencing human aggression include crowding, bringing attack upon oneself by initiating aggressive action, obedience to authority which calls for aggression, and viewing aggressive television.

4. Taken as a whole, the results of a large number of studies (both correlational and experimental) indicate there is a causal relation between viewing violent television and behaving violently.

THEORIES OF HUMAN AGGRESSION

Several theories of aggression have been developed. Anderson and Bushman (2002) refer to such theories as domain-specific, meaning that each is focused on some particular aspect of aggression.

Drive Theory

The frustration-aggression hypothesis.   This theory postulates that frustration arouses an aggressive drive which triggers aggressive behavior. Dollard, Doob, Miller, Mowrer, and Sears (1939) illustrated the theory with the following example. Four-year-old James hears the ice-cream-truck bell and says he wants some ice cream. He is refused and so becomes aggressive. The following concepts are used to explain James's aggressive behavior: The bell **instigates** the goal response of getting ice cream, but **interference** with this response produces **frustration.** Frustration instigates aggressive behavior that is intended to harm someone. If the instigated aggressive behavior is itself interfered with, this interference is further instigation to aggressive behavior. Aggressive behavior may be **inhibited** by fear of punishment. Aggressive behavior may be **direct** (aimed at the source of the frustration) or **indirect** (also called **displaced aggression**), especially if there is fear of punishment from the source of the frustration. Indirect aggression may involve a change in the **object** of aggression (perhaps a more vulnerable target than the direct object) or a change in the **form** of aggression (such as from physical to psychological). Finally, according to the concept of **catharsis** (from the Greek word for "cleansing" or "purging"), aggressive acts are assumed to reduce further instigation to aggression.

Role of anger. The frustration-aggression hypothesis says that blocking a goal instigates the intention to harm someone. Many theorists say this may be correct, however, only when the frustration produces the negative emotion of anger. But why should the negative emotion of anger lead to aggression when the negative emotion of fear does not? The answer may lie in differences in the *controllability* of events producing negative affect, as well as neural mechanisms for approach and avoidance. The following lines of research support this line of argument.

First, Harmon-Jones and Allen (1998) found that self-report measures of anger were correlated with *left frontal EEG activity,* usually considered the hemisphere involved in positive emotion and approach behavior. Anger often is related to approach behavior, for attack. It is possible, therefore, that anger has a positive aspect which is related to approach behavior, which fear does not have.

Second, Lerner and Keltner (2001) found a major difference in risk assessments between fearful and angry people. Fearful people were more pessimistic about risky outcomes than were angry people. Moreover, the risk assessments of angry people were almost identical to those of happy people. The angry and happy people both expressed feelings of greater certainty and *control* than did the fearful people.

Third, Bushman, Baumeister, and Phillips (2001) suggested that acting aggressively may not actually reduce aggressive tendencies, as the catharsis hypothesis says it should, but that aggressive activity may nevertheless *feel good.* They described research showing that angry people may engage in aggressive behavior because it improves the negative mood associated with anger. The research indicated that people must *believe* that acting aggressively will make them feel better. Therefore, the incentive for aggressive actions is the goal of feeling better, reducing the negative affect of anger. There is also an element of control, because if people believe that their actions will have a desired outcome, they are also experiencing some degree of perceived control.

Why does frustration produce negative affect? Earlier, we observed that not obtaining an expected positive goal might arouse the opponent process, the negative affect we associate with frustration. This would be a direct response to the unfulfilled expectation. In addition, however, a person's anger in a frustrating situation may depend on whether the interference is perceived to be *justified* or to be *arbitrary* (Averill, 1983; Berkowitz, 1988). People tend to become angry when they perceive that someone has unjustly or arbitrarily deprived them of some anticipated gratification. Pastore (1952), for example, presented research subjects with various frustration scenarios, and the subjects reported they would not become angry if interference were appropriate to the situation. A person might be disappointed at 12:15 if a store had closed at its usual 12:00 time and thus desirable refreshment could not be obtained, but would not be angry. If admittance were refused at 11:55, however, a person might become angry at this arbitrary frustration of closing five minutes before the stated time.

Arbitrary frustrations produce stronger anger than justifiable or uncontrollable frustrations, but the latter can produce anger. In one study, research subjects imagining themselves caught in a traffic jam on the way to a job interview reported that they would become very angry (Berkowitz, 1988). In another study, subjects overtly indicated hostile reactions toward a person who frustrated them by repeatedly misunderstanding and asking questions. Subjects did not show overt hostility toward a person who was said to be hard-of-hearing but who engaged in the same behaviors. Subsequently, however, the same subjects indicated disliking for the hearing-impaired person if they could do so privately (Burnstein & Worchel, 1962). In short, a nonarbitrary frustration produced hostility that was not publicly expressed. This finding presumably reflects social rules about when it is appropriate to become angry.

Does acting angry reduce subsequent aggression? The "ventilationist" point of view holds that anger will be reduced faster if it is expressed. Holding in anger is said to be bad because we are stuck with the emotional arousal of anger, including autonomic arousal. Tavris (1983), however, argues that venting anger simply makes people angrier, raises the noise level of our lives, and seldom does any good.

How fast anger subsides depends on many factors, and venting anger may indeed sustain or increase anger rather than reduce it. Hokanson (1970) found that male laboratory subjects intentionally angered by the experimenter tended to show a quicker drop in blood pressure if they responded in an angry manner but that female subjects showed a more rapid drop if they responded in a conciliatory manner. Hokanson then went on to show that male subjects could be taught to respond in a more conciliatory manner and females in a more aggressive manner, and that blood pressure came down more quickly with the new mode of responding. Either angry or friendly responses could be "cathartic," if properly learned.

Tavris also argues that "talking out" anger does not reduce anger, it rehearses it. Couples who yell at each other usually get more angry, not less. In a study of aerospace engineers and technicians who had been laid off from their jobs, interview responses were compared with those of other employees who had voluntarily resigned. When fired employees targeted the company or a particular supervisor whom they could blame for their predicament, they became more angry and hostile toward their target as a result of talking about the target. If they picked on a supervisor, they became more angry at the supervisor but not at the company in general, and vice versa. Tavris suggests that getting angry is cathartic only if you get a sense of control from the anger, whether control of your own internal arousal or of the anger-provoking situation.

Criticisms of the frustration-aggression hypothesis.   The first criticism of the hypothesis was that it simply is not always correct. Aggression has other causes, and frustration has other effects. A second difficulty is that the hypothesis seems to require two unseen processes: frustration and tendency to aggression, but without independent operations for each. If aggressive behavior occurs, we have to speculate that there was prior frustration. A frustrating situation, however, may simply arouse an aversive state. As we saw in Chapter Ten, there are no behavioral effects specific to frustration. The frustration-aggression hypothesis has faded as a major theory in its own right, but its terms are still found in many discussions of aggression.

Social Learning Theory

The difficulties with the frustration-aggression drive theory approach to aggression led to the development of social learning theory (Eron, 1994). Social learning theory (e.g., Bandura, 1973) tries to take into account all the possible sources of stimulation and reinforcement for behaviors that a social environment provides. It assigns special importance to **imitation** and **modeling** with humans, however. A child sees another person doing something ("modeling") and copies the behavior ("imitation").

In a classic study, Bandura, Ross, and Ross (1963) compared aggressive behaviors of nursery school children after the children had observed aggressive behavior by live adults, in a film of adults, or in a film of cartoon characters (adults dressed in cat costumes). Control subjects were not shown any of the aggressive sequences. The groups were further subdivided according to whether models were the same or opposite sex of the child. The main aggressive behavior was hitting a three-foot-tall inflatable rubber doll. The model sat on the doll, hit it with a fist or mallet, threw it up in the air, and kicked it about the room. The model also said such things as "Sock him in the nose" or "Hit him down." Such specific behaviors by the model were intended to be behaviors that could clearly be identified as imitative on the part of the child. Each child was then mildly frustrated by being allowed to play for a little while with an attractive toy and then being told that he or she could not play with it anymore. Toys in a different room, including a Bobo doll, could be played with, however. In each 5 seconds of a 20-minute test period, the child was scored for aggressive responses, a total of 240 possible scores. The response categories were imitative aggression, partially imitative aggression, mallet aggression, sitting on the doll, nonimitative aggression, and aggressive gun play (a gun was among the toys in the test room). Certain results were clear-cut:

1. Aggressive-model groups were more aggressive than the control group.
2. Boys were more aggressive than girls.

3. Girls were more aggressive with female models, and boys more aggressive with male models.
4. Live models or film models, real people or cartoon characters, were equally effective models.

In a related study (Bandura et al., 1963), children who saw an aggressive model rewarded were subsequently more aggressive than control subjects, but children who saw the aggressive model punished were less aggressive. The children later identified the models as "good" (nonaggressive) or "bad" (aggressive), but they preferred the aggressive model when he succeeded but not when he failed. Their reasoning was quite frank: The aggressive, rewarded model got what he wanted. Aggressive behavior was therefore viewed as a successful behavior.

Modeling and imitation are particularly important when we look at the role of television as an instigator or inhibitor of aggressive behaviors. Television is obviously a source of information about aggressive activities, although it is less clear that television viewing directly instigates aggressive behaviors. For example, a hoax following the story line of a television program was perpetrated on an airline. A bomb was said to be planted on an airliner and set to go off at any altitude less than 5,000 feet. The plane was rerouted to Denver, Colorado, which has an airport above 5,000 feet. Even more violent instances of imitation have been reported, such as dousing an innocent victim with gasoline and striking a match, after having seen such an act on television. Berkowitz (1984) has recorded many instances of epidemic violent behavior that were apparently copied. One such example during the Vietnam War was a brief flurry of self-directed aggression, setting oneself on fire in protest of the war. It is not clear, however, whether such individuals were stimulated to imitate aggressive acts when they would not have been aggressive otherwise or whether they have simply been provided with information that helps them do something they were already motivated to do for other reasons.

Social Cognitive Theory

As problems arose with the notion that external events solely control behavior, there was a movement toward more cognitive theories of aggressive behavior, which built on previous motivational and reinforcement theories. These cognitive theories differ in detail, but all agree that the way the individual *perceives* and *interprets* environmental events determines whether he or she will respond aggressively (Eron, 1994, p. 7). Three of these social cognitive theories are neoassociation theory, attribution theory, and script theory.

Neoassociation theory.   Berkowitz (1984) argued that television or other media events can instill ideas into an audience that are then carried into action—the contagion of violence. Gabriel Tarde, a French sociologist writing in 1912, said that "epidemics of crime follow the line of the telegraph." Tarde reported that the infamous Jack the Ripper murders in London led to eight imitations in London itself, and others elsewhere. According to **associative network theory** (e.g., Bower, 1981), memory is a series of networks that consist of *nodes* (representing thoughts, feelings, and actions) that are interconnected by **associative pathways.** It is assumed that these nodes and pathways are represented in brain structures, but there is no specific brain reference. Such a network is illustrated in Figure 11–3. Memories are aroused when a stimulus activates a particular node and this activation *spreads* to other nodes. The more nodes that are interconnected, the more memories that this **spreading activation** will arouse.

According to this theory, then, when an aggressive idea is suggested by a violent movie, the idea spreads from its particular node to other nodes. The associative strength will be greater among aggressive nodes, so that other aggressive thoughts, feelings, or actions are more likely to occur. For example, different groups of subjects in an experiment constructed sentences out of either aggressive words or nonaggressive words. Subjects exposed to the aggressive words were subsequently more likely to give a negative evaluation to a person on the basis of a brief description than were subjects who had made sentences from nonaggressive words (Wyer & Hartwick, 1980). The aggressive nodes aroused negative affect, which then became associated with the target of the evaluation.

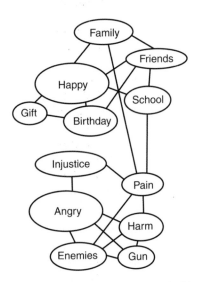

FIGURE 11–3. An associative network. The closer together two nodes (shown as ellipses) are, the more likely that when one is activated, the other will also be activated. A happy mood is more likely to activate happy thoughts and actions, and an angry mood is more likely to activate angry thoughts and actions.

Berkowitz points out that a difficulty for a social learning theory is that aggressive (or other) acts ought to be physically similar to the portrayed behavior (e.g., a knifing) but in fact rarely are. Associative network accounts for this by saying that portrayed violence would activate a node in an associative network and that the spreading activation from this node could reach nodes for several aggressive behaviors, not just the one depicted. Thus, a subject in a laboratory, seeing a gun, would have the "gun node" activated. The activation would spread to other associated nodes, such as to a node for "hurting" someone. This event could then facilitate the subject's pressing a button to deliver shocks.

This line of theory leads to another possibility, namely, that what we see on television does not just activate a preexisting associative network, it actually becomes part of a person's associative network. Television violence may become part of the reality of the viewer, so that the viewer "gets used to it" and thinks that the TV viewing should be treated as part of reality. This is the argument used in connection with pornography and violence against women, that there is a kind of desensitization because pornography and violence are accepted as reality.

Attribution theory. We saw earlier that whether a person becomes angry in response to frustration depends partly on whether the frustrated party attributes intent to the frustrating agent. Thus if I am walking down the aisle of a theater and someone inadvertently trips me in the dark, I am less likely to be angry than if I think the trip was intentional.

Script theory. Huesmann and Eron (1984) hypothesized that social behavior is to a large extent controlled by "programs" for behavior that have been learned during early development. These programs, or scripts, are used to guide behavior and to solve social problems. On the basis of his experience, a child may develop the script that whenever he doesn't get what he wants, he should become aggressive. Therefore, an innocuous situation might evoke aggressive behavior on the part of an individual whose script for dealing with most situations is to be aggressive. The typical "aggression-inducing variables" would not need to be present because the child has learned to be aggressive regardless of the details of the situation. To the extent that the aggression script continues to be reinforced, the individual continues to behave aggressively.

Social Interaction Theory

Aggressive behavior may be considered a way by which one person or group gets another to behave in a certain way. Such social interactions may or may not involve intent to harm as the goal. Tedeschi and his colleagues (Tedeschi & Felson, 1994; Tedeschi, Smith, & Brown, 1974) view what is called human aggression as just another way that people try to get what they want, such as information, money, goods, or services. The standard Godfather-like crime movie, for example, depicts people who use violent behavior as a way of conducting business. When other methods fail, people threaten violence and sometimes back up the threat. It may thus be important to determine conditions under which society says behavior is aggressive. Socially justified acts are typically not considered aggressive but unjustified acts are. Many people seem to believe that it is justifiable to shoot (and possibly kill) an intruder into one's home, but the law is more likely to treat this as punishable aggressive behavior.

The scientists' labeling of a particular behavior as aggressive may ignore *negative reciprocity* and *equity* (Kane, Doerge, and Tedeschi, 1973). Negative reciprocity is a social norm that gives a person the "right" to retaliate for harm done. Equity is a social norm that says you can have an eye for an eye, but no more. Kane et al. illustrated this point by having subjects rate the aggressiveness of participants in various conditions of a hypothetical Berkowitz-type experiment. The result was that someone receiving seven shocks was not considered aggressive for giving back seven—that number was perfectly equitable. Only if a person gave back more shocks than received was she or he considered aggressive. On average, subjects in the Berkowitz experiments never gave back more than they received. Therefore, it may have been equity that was demonstrated, not aggression.

Negative reciprocity and equity have considerable social importance, for if a person can change the meaning of his or her action, it may be judged nonaggressive. For example, German troops dressed as Polish soldiers "attacked" German installations along the Polish-German border in 1939. Hitler then "justified" the invasion of Poland as a countermeasure. Most of us try to make our "aggressive" actions look necessary or defensive so that they will be labeled nonaggressive.

SECTION SUMMARY

1. The **frustration-aggression hypothesis** is a **drive theory** account of aggression which states that aggressive acts are directed toward the agent who blocks the attainment of a goal. Aggressive behavior reduces instigation toward further aggression, called **catharsis.** Direct aggressive acts may be inhibited by threat of punishment and hence may be directed toward other objects or take different forms. Frustration may lead to aggression only if a person becomes **angry.**

2. **Social learning theory** assigns especial importance to **modeling** and **imitation** in the development of aggressive behavior. A child sees someone else (e.g., an adult) act aggressively and imitates that behavior, especially if the behavior is seen to be rewarded. Television is thought to be a particularly important source of modeling.

3. **Social cognitive theories** emphasize individual differences in the ways people perceive and interpret environmental events. **Neoassociation theory, attribution theory,** and **script theory** emphasize different reasons for such individual differ-

ences. An important fact addressed by these theories is that people do not use exactly the same aggressive behaviors that they have seen modeled.

4. **Social interaction theory** maintains that much aggressive behavior is a means by which one person or group coerces another in order to get what it wants. This may work at the level of individual behavior (a child taking candy from another) or international activity (one country attacking another in order to get land or other resources).

Control of Aggression

Biological control. We first of all have major definitional problems. Behavior that is called "aggressive" (1) may be socially defined, and hence vary from one culture to another, (2) is often hard to identify as unambiguously aggressive, (3) is affected by noxious events in the immediate environment, and (4) is heavily influenced by the specific ways in which an individual has learned to deal with situations. Given all these caveats, do we know enough about brain mechanisms to justify doing anything permanently to the brain when there might be serious side effects? In some cases the answer is clearly yes. Surgeons operate on the brain for tumors, for extremely severe epilepsy, or other physically definable pathologies in which the benefits to the patient outweigh the risks. Aggressive behavior might be secondary to these brain disorders and reduced by their treatment. Without a clearly defined brain pathology, however, there is little justification for surgical intervention to modify aggressive behavior (Valenstein, 1973). It has also been proposed seriously, though hardly taken that way, that world leaders should take drugs which would reduce their aggressive tendencies and therefore reduce the likelihood of war (Clark, 1971). By now, just from the evidence cited throughout this chapter, it should be clear that this is most unlikely to have the desired effect—a point not lost on the host of immediate critics of this proposal.

Catharsis versus social learning. Konrad Lorenz (1965b), among others, considered aggression to be instinctive, following the water-tank (hydraulic) model. Aggressive "energy" is said to well up inside the individual, like water in a tank, until it overflows spontaneously into aggressive behavior unless "drained off" harmlessly (catharsis). Lorenz also claimed that animals have instinctive inhibitions to aggression, so that a species does not kill itself off. For example, a dog defeated in a fight stops fighting and adopts a vulnerable position that tends to inhibit further attack by the winner. Humans, on the other hand (says Lorenz), do not have these inhibitions. Therefore, without some other outlet for the spontaneously building aggressive energy, humans will inevitably fight among themselves. Lorenz's solution was to provide alternative aggression outlets so that aggressive energy does not build up too much. Such displacement (indirect) activities as athletic events would presumably be cathartic because they would drain off aggressive energy harmlessly and hence reduce the likelihood of serious aggressive activity. This view is the same as the ventilationist view of anger.

The instinct model has not been taken seriously by either biologists or psychologists for many years (e.g., see Bandura, 1973). There is no known physiological mechanism by which there could be a buildup of instinctive energy as described by the model. Energy can be stored, of course, but it is in the form of fat or glycogen that is available for all behaviors, not just aggressive behaviors. As Scott (1971) pointed out, anger is aroused by external stimuli, not by some aggression-specific energy. Furthermore, internal arousal eventually dies out in the absence of further stimulation. It does not accumulate indefinitely, as the hydraulic model says. Neither is there real evidence that animals are kept from fighting by inhibitions that humans do not have. We saw earlier that either aggressive or nonaggressive responses may lead to a reduction of emotional arousal, depending on previous experience. Further, in the face of such events as a 1964 soccer championship in Peru where fans got into a riot resulting in three hundred deaths and five hundred injuries, it is difficult to believe that vicarious participation in violence is cathartic. Indeed, fan violence is some of the most visible evidence against the cathartic view. Finally, research on the effects of television viewing have consistently shown positive correlations between watching violent television shows and aggressive behavior. Sometimes the results are negligible. But from the point of view of catharsis, it appears that no research has shown a negative correlation between watching violent television and aggressive behavior. Yet, this is exactly what the catharsis hypothesis would predict.

Social learning.   The alternative view from social learning theory, however, is exactly the opposite of the cathartic view. The learning view says that aggressive behavior occurs because it is rewarded and that successful aggression is more likely to occur again, not less likely. If either of these views were entirely correct, it would obviously be socially disastrous to try to control aggression on the basis of the wrong one, either instinct or social learning. It becomes critical, then, to evaluate as best one can the evidence pro and con on these views. It is also possible that both views have some validity under particular circumstances. If so, the circumstances should be clarified.

The Institution of War and Other Evils

The events of September 11, 2001, have forever changed Americans' views of terrorist activities. Suicide bombings are no longer distant events in Europe, the Mideast, or Asia, but are a reality and a threat everywhere in the United States. But the World Trade Center attack, with its wanton destruction of almost three thousand human lives and billions of dollars of property loss, did not occur because somebody just got angry at the moment. The attack was well-coordinated and years in the planning. Aggression on such a grand scale is simply something different than individual aggression and the question is, How does such aggression get propagated?

Robert Hinde (1998), an eminent student of animal behavior, raised the following provocative question: Is war a consequence of human aggression? His conclusion is just the opposite, that aggression is a consequence of war. Wars are activities maintained by social institutions. Hinde provides three categories of forces that maintain war as an institution.

1. **Continuously acting everyday factors.** These are the common expressions, games, films, language and so on that romanticize war. Such films as *Saving Private Ryan* are the exception in their more accurate portrayal of the horrors of war.
2. **Pervasive cultural factors.** Some countries are more likely to go to war than others. The Balkan countries, for example, have a history of military strife going back hundreds of years. This may be contrasted with the pacifistic Switzerland. Religions differ along the dimension of pacifism-militarism and also change over time. Early Christians were pacifists and did not accept militarism until the fourth century (Hinde, 1998, p. 180). St. Augustine founded the "just war" tradition which provided moral justification for war. Unrelated to any particular religion, patriotism (devotion to country) and nationalism (belief in the superiority of one's own country) have contributed to the willingness of individuals to go to war.
3. **War as an institutionalized set of institutions.** Hinde sees the military-industrial-scientific complex as a complex set of institutions, each maintaining itself for its own reasons, but all contributing to the likelihood of war. The military does its job, with individuals playing their roles and working to advance themselves. The airman who presses the button that fires the missile is not angry and impulsive at the time he does his job. He just does his job because that is his role in the military institution. Industrial firms, admirably providing jobs for citizens, must maintain arms output and have customers for those arms in order to survive. Finally, science marches on, often supported by "defense contracts" both to industry and universities. Each of these institutions works to maintain itself and interacts with the others in doing so. Hinde summarizes by saying that ". . . although making war can be described as an aggressive act, individual aggressiveness plays only a very limited role in either the causation of war or the behavior of the individuals involved" (p. 182).

Massacres. Robert Zajonc (1999) makes a similar argument in reference to massacres, most notably those which took place during the twentieth century, with as many as 100 million civilian casualties. In Rwanda (Africa) in 1994, 800,000 Tutsis were killed in 100 days. In Europe, an estimated 5 to 6 million Jews were killed in the Holocaust, and in Russia about 14 million people were killed in government purges of the opposition. Such atrocities, costing hundreds of thousands of lives in a short time, are not spontaneous outbursts. Rather they are well planned and organized. You can't kill a quarter-million people a month, as was the case in Rwanda, without organization, availability of weapons, and so on. This requires a large amount of money to buy weapons, the weapons have to be ordered in advance from a manufacturer, and then they have to be distributed in a timely manner to their end-users. In Rwanda most of the weapons were machetes and the victims were hacked to death. Zajonc calls it a "striking paradox" that some of the most appalling atrocities of our times were, to their perpetrators, actions in pursuit of virtue. They were moral imperatives, murder in the name of God and country. In other words, such acts were not the acts of individuals consumed in anger at the time they were initiated. They were "instrumental" acts done for reasons other than individual aggression.

Feshbach (1997, p. 227) reports that in his research "various indices of individual aggression proved to be negligibly or weakly correlated with militaristic, hawkish views concerning armaments and war. Individual hostility or physical aggressiveness were poor predictors of attitudes toward war. Much stronger correlates of the readiness to engage in war are nationalistic attitudes reflecting the importance of national dominance and power. War is an action in which pacific as well as aggressive individuals engage. It is a form of group aggression that bears little relationship to individual aggressiveness." Preventive measures against hostile actions resulting from such fundamental beliefs as the moral righteousness of nationalism are the obvious major challenge to our existence.

SECTION SUMMARY

1. **Biological control** of aggression on any large scale appears to be implausible for a variety of reasons. The most notable reasons are that (a) we really do not know enough about the biology of aggression to institute any meaningful controls, and (b) to the extent that aggressive behavior is instrumental and aimed to achieve nonaggressive goals, it would be virtually impossible to distinguish aggressive from nonaggressive behavior.

2. Two major and opposing psychological approaches to the control of aggression are (a) **catharsis theory,** which says that vicarious aggression will reduce the occurrence of truly harmful behavior, and (b) **social learning theory,** which says that social acceptance of aggressive acts rewards such acts and that aggressive acts will lead to further aggression. There is no evidence that watching violent television or other violent events **reduces** the occurrence of everyday violent behavior.

3. Such large scale instances of violent behavior as **wars** and **massacres** require a high level of organization for their conduct and may be carried out in the name of God or country. Such activities may be propagated by a general culture and by specific cultural institutions (e.g. military, industrial). This makes the problem of control extremely difficult.

ALTRUISM

Altruism, helping, and prosocial behavior are equivalent terms referring to behavior intended to benefit others without obvious benefit in return. This seems to run contrary to the motivational themes which characterize psychology. Do people really engage in totally selfless behavior, or are there (hidden?) rewards for helping others? What specific factors promote or diminish helping behavior?

Bystander Apathy

The single event that more than any other sparked interest in helping behavior was the 1964 case of Kitty Genovese. As she returned to her home in Queens (New York City) about 3:00 A.M., she was attacked and repeatedly stabbed over a half-hour period, all the while screaming until she was finally killed. Thirty-eight neighbors watched the gory episode without so much as calling the police. The horror of this scene highlighted the dramatic failure of people to help a fellow person. An immediate interpretation was that "big city people" had become callous and indifferent to the plight of anyone else. At best, however, this is just one of many factors that determine when someone will help. We may divide these factors into characteristics of the situation, of the helper, and of the victim.

Situational Influences

Latane and Darley (1970) argued that the presence of other bystanders makes it less likely that any one person will help. They staged elaborate "emergencies" in laboratories and public places, and observed bystander behavior. For example, they had smoke pour into a room where students were working, arranged for subjects to hear an apparent accident over an intercom, staged an epileptic seizure, and pulled a fake robbery in a liquor store (with the manager's permission). Their results consistently indicated that people were more likely to help if they were alone than if someone else were present. Latane and Darley proposed three complementary explanations for this behavior:

1. **Audience inhibition.** If others are present, we are slower to act because we are concerned about their evaluation of our behavior. Perhaps the smoke is not really an emergency, and we would look foolish if we treated it as such.
2. **Social influence.** We watch others to see how they are acting. If everyone is trying to be cool and nonchalant, then a whole group may fool itself into believing there is no emergency.
3. **Diffusion of responsibility.** Psychologically we may feel that if there is a single person present at an emergency, it is more imperative to help. When more people are present, there is less pressure for any single individual to help. Hence, nobody may act.

Latane and Darley found that a person alone would help someone about 95 percent of the time, but helping dropped to 84 percent if a second person were present. The percentage dropped to 50 if another person present failed to respond to the emergency. Fortunately, people will sometimes help in the presence of others. Piliavin, Rodin, and Piliavin (1969) faked the collapse of a person on a subway train and found that 70 percent of the time bystanders helped immediately. The authors believed that this response occured because the emergency was unquestionable to the bystanders and that there clearly was no one else to help except them.

The diffusion of responsibility phenomenon has subsequently been studied under the rubric of social loafing and turns out to be a very general phenomenon (Latane, 1981). The idea here is that people will generally work less hard if the work is shared than if they are working alone. For example, in a tug of war, each individual on a team works less hard than if just one person on each team were pitted against one person on the other team.

Costs and benefits of helping.   In an informal manner, people weigh the relative costs and benefits of getting involved with any particular activity. The potential costs of intervening in a situation are inconvenience, unpleasantness, and possible danger. The costs of not helping may be feelings of guilt and possible scorn from others. Benefits of helping may be feeling greater self-esteem, being praised by others, or receiving thanks. Sometimes people do jump in and help without thinking at all, as did a bystander when a plane crashed into freezing waters in Washington, D.C. Research shows that

- Bystanders are more likely to help someone neat and well dressed than an apparent derelict or drunk or troublemaker.
- Bystanders are more likely to help someone with a cane rather than an apparent drunk carrying what appears to be a bottle in a brown bag.
- Bystanders are less likely to help if there is some person apparently more capable present (such as someone in a hospital uniform).

Modeling.   Bryan and Test (1967) had two disabled cars with women as drivers along the side of a busy street. Under one condition someone was helping the first woman driver, but under another condition not helping. Fifty-eight motorists stopped to help the second driver when they saw the first driver being aided, as compared with thirty-five when the first driver was not being aided. Similar results were obtained with people who saw another person donate to Salvation Army solicitors. If the model is too generous, however, potential donors might be scared off because they might be embarrassed by their own small contributions.

Being a Good Samaritan may be discouraged for many reasons. Physicians may refrain from spontaneously helping accident victims for fear of malpractice suits. Within large cities there is also an element of trying to keep a certain amount of social distance between oneself and others. The hurried activity in a city may also make it more difficult to attract attention for help. Darley and Bateson (1973) found that if subjects were told to be someplace in a hurry, they were less likely to stop and help someone in apparent difficulty. The subjects were theology students told to go to a lecture on Good Samaritanism!

Severity of the emergency. Severity is not an overriding factor, else Kitty Genovese would have gotten help. The costs associated with helping seem particularly important in such situations. For example, in one study a bloodied victim was less likely than a nonbloodied victim to receive direct help. The bloodied victim did get more help indirectly, however, such as by a phone call.

Characteristics of the Victim

A reputable looking victim has a better chance of getting help than a disreputable victim, but people are also more likely to help others who are like themselves. For example, in the early 1970s a "hippie-looking" person and a more conservative-looking person solicited money from "hippies" and "straights" on the street. The person-on-the-street was more likely to help the solicitor who was more like himself or herself (Enswiller, Deaux, & Willits, 1971).

There is also the so-called just world hypothesis, which says that people bring their problems on themselves and that they get what they deserve. Some people are unwilling to help others because they believe, rightly or wrongly, that people in trouble are getting what they deserve. The "just world" belief has strong implications for such social issues as welfare, and it has certainly played a role in attitudes towards AIDS. Since AIDS has been more widespread among homosexuals and among intravenous drug users sharing needles, there have been people (including public figures such as the Reverend Jerry Falwell) who have proclaimed the disease a just retribution for a sinful lifestyle.

Finally, the norm of reciprocity comes into play. If a person has given help to someone in the past, this "helping person" is more likely to get help in the future. Goranson and Berkowitz (1966) found that experimental subjects were more likely to help a laboratory supervisor if they believed that the supervisor had previously volunteered to help them than if the supervisor had refused to help or if the help had been mandatory.

Characteristics of the Helper

Personality variables. Several personal characteristics distinguish helpers from nonhelpers. Schwartz found that high scorers on his Ascription of Responsibility Scale (those who tended to ascribe responsibility to themselves rather than others) were more likely to take action in a fake emergency situation (Schwartz, 1968; Schwartz & Clausen, 1970). Similarly, people who feel competent are more likely to help, even if this feeling has only just been engendered in an experimental situation by success at an experimental task.

Conversely, it has also been suggested that people with low self-esteem may be more likely to help if they can thereby raise their self-esteem.

Mood.   A large amount of research shows that people in a good mood are more likely to help than are people in a bad mood (Morris, 1989; Salovey, Mayer, & Rosenhan, 1991). For example, a person in a shopping mall is more likely to help a stranger pick up a spilled bag of items after the helping person has just received a small gift. There are a number of explanations to account for this behavior. According to mood maintenance theory, people in a good mood are more likely to help others because it helps maintain the good mood that they are in. It has also been reported, albeit less often than with positive mood, that people in a negative mood are also more likely to help someone. This behavior is accounted for in terms of mood restoration. Helping someone else gets a person out of a bad mood into a more neutral or positive mood. Both theories are incentive theories, saying that people engage in activities that they anticipate will make them happier (by maintaining or improving their good mood) or less unhappy (by getting rid of a negative mood). Both these hypotheses seem to assume that people are thoughtful and calculating about helping others. Although this may be true for some situations, the little helpful things that people do every day do not seem to involve much forethought.

Theories of Prosocial Behavior

Reinforcement theory.   Reinforcement theory emphasizes the rewards and punishments accompanying specific behaviors. Altruistic behavior would in this view occur because it has been rewarded in the past and occurs again because there is anticipation of future rewards. The rewards, or benefits, of helping may not be obvious. One such benefit is simply feeling good because we have helped someone. This may develop because we have been rewarded in the past for helping people and we associate the good feeling with the behavior. In line with either reinforcement theory or hedonic theory, there are two sides to this coin. We may have a positive feeling because we have donated blood, given money to support a cause, or jump started a stranger's car with a dead battery, or we may head off a feeling of discomfort that would occur if we did not help.

Moss and Page (1972) studied the effect of reward for helping on future helping. They approached passersby on the street and asked directions to a particular department store. The strangers were either rewarded with a smile and a thank you, were punished by being rudely told the direction did not make sense, or were left neutral (with just an "okay"). Farther down the street, a female confederate dropped a small bag as the same passerby approached. Only 40 percent of the just-punished individuals picked up the bag for her, but 82 percent of the neutral subjects and 85 percent of the rewarded subjects did so. The rude response clearly had a detrimental effect, but the neutral subjects were about as helpful as the rewarded.

Social exchange theory.   This is an "economic" analysis in which people judge the costs as well as the benefits of various social interactions and behave accordingly. The costs of helping might be money, time, effort, pain (e.g., from the needle prick of giving blood) and the benefits are such rewards as those described above (Myers, 2002). If the perceived costs outweigh the perceived benefits helping will occur, but if the costs are too high helping will not occur. People do not necessarily spend a lot of time consciously weighing such factors, but may make quick judgments involving them. A person might readily give some pocket change for a charitable cause at the entrance to a grocery store, but would probably think about it awhile before donating $10.

Freud's psychoanalytic theory.   Freud divided personality into three parts—id, ego, and superego. The id refers to such "basic" drives as hunger, thirst, sex, and aggression. Superego is equivalent to "conscience." Ego is the rational part of the personality that tries to "referee" between the demands of the id for immediate gratification and the hesitancy on the part of the superego. These are not separately identifiable parts of the brain but are Freud's metaphorical way of looking at the mind. Our interest here is in superego, or conscience.

According to Freud, the superego develops as a child learns values (what is good and what is bad) from his or her parents and culture. These values are "internalized" and become part of the individual, serving as ideals and internal sources of reward and punishment. In a sense, the child develops a set of imaginary parents who, like Jiminy Cricket in *Pinocchio,* direct the child's behavior. If we do something we have learned is "wrong," we may be punished by feeling guilt and anxiety. If we do something that is "right," we are rewarded by feeling good. If certain ideals are strongly internalized, we may, for example, do almost anything rather than lie or cheat. Martyrs appear to be people who would give up their lives rather than their ideals.

Kohlberg's theory of moral judgment.   Kohlberg (1964) proposed a theory of moral judgment that depends on the increasing ability of a child to understand complex situations. At the preconventional level, the child is primarily influenced by the consequences of her or his actions. That is, the child's behavior is determined by rewards and punishments, just as reinforcement theory says. The young child obeys adults because adults mete out punishment. At the conventional level, the older child becomes concerned with what others expect of her or him and tries to behave in a conventional way. This is a kind of conformity for the sake of conformity, having respect for authority because such respect is right and proper. At the postconventional level, which some adults never achieve, there is a mature level of conscience that is more influential than society's laws. The individual becomes concerned with moral values and the basis for laws. This level is important for any change in a system of justice. It does not represent a flagrant disregard of all of society's rules, but it is concerned with the basis of these rules and their moral correctness. For example, someone may intentionally break a law in order to test its constitutionality in court. Nonviolent methods of breaking the law as a matter of principle have been effective around the world, such as in bringing discriminatory laws to test in the civil rights activities starting in the 1960s.

The Role of Empathy

Empathy refers to sharing the same feelings as another person, to be sad when they are sad or happy when they are happy. The empathic view of helping, then, is that we feel the unhappiness of someone in distress and helping them makes them (and us) feel better. We focus on the distress of the victim, however, not on our own. This apparently is not limited to humans. Frans de Waal, a well-known primate researcher, has reported instances of one ape coming to the aid of another in a fight or comforting another ape and of an eight-year-old female gorilla coming to the aid of and comforting a three-year-old child who had fallen into the gorilla enclosure in the Brookfield Zoo. Individuals of many species (from rat to primate) "are distressed by the distress of a conspecific and will act to terminate the object's distress" (Preston & de Waal, 2002).

Preston and de Waal (2002) propose what they call the perception-action model (PAM) to account for empathic behavior. The substance of this model is that the perception of another organism's state (e.g., happiness, distress) automatically activates a representation in the observer's brain of the state and other characteristics of the situation. The representation automatically primes or generates the associated autonomic and behavioral responses, unless something occurs to inhibit these. To the extent that the observer's representation is similar to that of the object of the observation, the observer is empathic and responds in a appropriate way. For example, if the observer's observation of distress in another animal generates a mental representation like that of the distressed animal, the observing animal will both experience distress and act to reduce the distress, as if it were its own. As another example, one primate may stroke another in a calming way. An important factor is the similarity of the observer and the observed. Thus, there is greater empathy for one's kin than for strangers, partly based on the familiarity one kin has with another's movements, facial expressions, and vocalizations. The greater the familiarity the more accurate the representations and more appropriate the actions.

SECTION SUMMARY

1. **Altruism** (also called **prosocial behavior**) refers to behaviors intended to benefit others without obvious return benefit to oneself.

2. **Bystander apathy** is the failure of people to help others in emergencies. Important variables are the presence of others, costs and benefits of helping, characteristics of the helper and the victim, and situational factors. Helping behavior can be facilitated or hindered by situational variables.

3. **Reinforcement theory** emphasizes the rewards and punishments accompanying specific behaviors. Altruistic behavior would in this view occur because it has been rewarded in the past and occurs again because there is anticipation of future rewards. The rewards, or benefits, of helping may not be obvious.

4. **Social exchange theory** is an **economic analysis** in which people judge the **costs** as well as the **benefits** of various social interactions and behave accordingly. If the perceived benefits outweigh the perceived costs helping will occur, but if the costs are too high helping will not occur.

5. **Psychoanalytic theory** says that a child learns values (what is good and what is bad) from his or her parents and culture. These values are "internalized" and become part of the individual, serving as ideals and internal sources of reward and punishment. In this way, people internalize social values that influence helping.

6. Kohlberg's **theory of moral judgment** is based on the increasing ability of a child to understand complex situations as it grows older. It assumes that people pass sequentially through stages of moral development that he named **preconventional, conventional,** and **postconventional.** The last of these is a level of individual morality which transcends social custom or law and which is rarely achieved.

7. **Empathy** refers to the capacity to experience events in much the same way that another individual does, to put oneself in the other's place. The more closely one individual empathizes with another, the more likely that helping an individual in distress will occur.

CHAPTER TWELVE

Personality and Individual Differences

How is motivation related to personality?

How do people differ in the kinds of goals they have?

How does high achievement motivation affect behavior?

Is there more than one kind of achievement motivation?

Are we born with high achievement motivation or is it learned?

How does motivation for power affect our actions?

How do feelings of competence or incompetence affect us?

Why do some people seek out thrills and others do not?

Is there a biological aspect to sensation seeking behavior?

Do we have a basic motive to seek knowledge?

Personality refers to those enduring characteristics by which we distinguish one person from another. It is the study of individual differences in people. Personality theories vary, however, in what aspects of people to emphasize. For example, some theories specifically emphasize differences in motivation but other theories emphasize nonmotivational aspects as well. In this chapter we selectively look at a number of human motives that have particularly interested personality theorists.

THEORIES OF PERSONALITY

Trait Theories

Trait theories assume that every individual can be described in terms of some relatively small number of personal characteristics (such as friendliness, anxiousness, aggressiveness) and that every individual "possesses" these in some measurable degree. For example, George might be a "7" on a ten-point scale of "aggressiveness," whereas Susan is only a "3." Susan might be an "8" on independence, however, whereas George is a "4." Traits, however, are just convenient ways of describing individuals and we do not assume that traits are "things." The number of traits in different well-known theories has varied from three (Eysenck, 1967) to sixteen (Cattell, 1965). The first modern trait theory is attributable to Gordon Allport (1937) but the theory now in ascendance is **Five Factor Theory,** or just "The Big Five."

Five factor theory. Extensive research has consistently uncovered five personality characteristics that some researchers believe represent the basic "structure" of personality (McRae & Costa, 1987; McCrae & John, 1992). The five traits are **extraversion, neuroticism, conscientiousness, agreeableness,** and **openness.** A number of more specific characteristics are subsumed under each of the five general traits, as illustrated in Table 12–1. The two traits most obviously having motivational properties are extraversion, which has a large element of positive affect, and neuroticism, which is characterized by negative affect (e.g., feeling anxious, worrying).

The primary criticisms of trait theories hinge on whether there are such permanent characteristics of people as traits or whether people just respond consistently to situations in which they repeatedly find themselves. The latter point of view is called **situationism** or **interactionism** (Endler, 1998; Mischel, 1973). For example, we saw in Chapter Ten that psychologists frequently distinguish between "permanent" trait anxiety and "situational" state anxiety. We may then ask whether trait anxiety means that a person is always anxious or just tends to be anxious in many (but not all) situations. A person who is anxious in many harmless social situations might be fearless in the face of real danger. Similarly, we might ask whether an agreeable person is one who is always agreeable or who is agreeable in most situations but might be dis-

TABLE 12–1.   Illustrative adjectives characterizing each of the Big Five personality traits. The adjectives are shown in pairs of opposites indicating high versus low on the trait in question. There are up to two dozen adjectives related to each trait.

Neuroticism	Extraversion	Openness	Agreeableness	Conscientiousness
Calm-Worrying	Retiring-Sociable	Conventional-Original	Irritable-Good Natured	Careless-Careful
At Ease-Nervous	Sober-Fun Loving	Uncreative-Creative	Ruthless-Soft Hearted	Undependable-Reliable
Relaxed-High Strung	Quiet-Talkative	Unadventurous-Daring	Critical-Lenient	Disorganized-Well Organized

Source: McCrae, R. R. & Costa, P. T. (1987) Validation of the five-factor model of personality across instruments and observers. *Journal of Personality and Social Psychology, 52,* 81–90, Table 3, p. 85. Copyright: American Psychological Association, 1987. Used by permission.

agreeable in some. The trait versus situationism controversy seems likely to remain with us for a while.

Dynamic (Motivational) Theories

Nature of dynamic theories.   A dynamic theory of personality is specifically a motivational theory. Freud's psychoanalytic theory was a dynamic theory, abounding with unseen conflicting forces wreaking mental and behavioral havoc. Kurt Lewin's (1935) dynamic theory incorporated conflict but also had **tensions** produced by such events as uncompleted goal activities. A person was considered prone to continue a behavior until a goal is completed and the tension reduced. Dollard and Miller's (1941) behavioral approach to personality was based on drive theory. McAdams (1997) notes that the trend has been away from the tension reduction (regulatory) theories to more cognitive (purposive) theories, but that does not make them less dynamic. Emmons (1997, p. 485) observed that there was a decline in interest in motivational concepts in personality theory as interest in drive theory declined, but that the "revitalization of the field of personality has been due in large part to a resurgence of interest in motivational concepts, especially goals." For example, we might describe one person as "power hungry" to mean that she consistently strives to put herself into a position of power, to control others, to promote herself, and so on. Another person might be described as a high achiever, to mean that he persistently and energetically strives to meet his goals. Such goals may be termed **needs,** like the need for power or need for achievement, but these are not the same as such life-threatening biological needs as hunger and thirst.

Goals.   Goals are theoretically the same as incentives. They are behavioral outcomes that we strive to achieve or avoid. Psychological needs, then, are just the goals that people strive for and the motivation is incentive motivation as we discussed in Chapter Eight.

The question for personality theory is, What kinds of goals impel particular people to action? In practice, there are so many possible goals that a major problem is how to organize goals in ways that are theoretically meaningful. Emmons (1997) suggests two complementary approaches. The **nomothetic** approach looks for general laws, and *nomothetic goals* are those that characterize "people in general." The ***idiographic*** approach looks for those goals that characterize a particular person. Which approach is preferable depends on what we want to do. For example, when we do research we usually take a more nomothetic approach because we want to generalize our results and theory beyond the specific subjects in the research. If, however, we are concerned about the problems of a particular clinical patient, we would take a more idiographic approach because we are concerned with the details of a particular person's life.

Nomothetic goals.   To find out what are the typical goals for a group, we might ask people to rate lists of goals for their degree of importance, relevance, and other characteristics. The goals are then grouped into clusters according to their similarity, using special statistical techniques. Five general groupings have emerged from various studies (Emmons, 1997).

1. **Enjoyment:** relaxation, fun, sensation-seeking, exploration, play
2. **Self-Assertion:** aggression, power, achievement, competition
3. **Esteem:** self-esteem, personal growth
4. **Interpersonal:** affection, support, affiliation, social relationships
5. **Avoidance of negative affect:** anxiety reduction, stress avoidance

Idiographic goals.   These have been described by various researchers as *current concerns* (Klinger, 1977), *personal projects* (Little, 1983), *life tasks* (Cantor & Langston, 1989), and *personal striving* (Emmons, 1986). In each case, however, they are goals related to a particular person in a particular situation or point in his or her life. Some examples of such goals are:

1. **Current concerns:** travel, family, job, religion, health
2. **Personal projects:** interpersonal, academic, recreational, family
3. **Personal striving:** interpersonal, achievement, affiliation, power, growth
4. **Personal goals:** work, school, social life, leisure

Thus, for example, enjoyment is a nomothetic category of goals shared by many people, but travel, recreation, and social life are more specific idiographic goals by which different individuals might obtain enjoyment.

Henry Murray's theory.   Henry Murray (1938), along with Allport, a pioneer in personality research, distinguished between what he called **presses** and **needs.** A press is an environmental feature that is appraised as harmful or beneficial by a person, and hence it is avoided or approached. In our terms, it is an incentive. A need is a hypothetical internal state inferred from observation. Murray considered needs to represent states of disequilibrium in the organism. These needs orient the organism toward certain ends (goals) that will reduce the needs. These needs are thus like drives.

Murray further distinguished between what he called **viscerogenic** and **psychogenic** needs. Viscerogenic, or primary, needs are due to periodic body changes and have readily identifiable localization in the body. These are needs for air, water, food, sex, lactation, urination, defecation, harm avoidance, nox avoidance (unpleasant stimuli), heat avoidance, cold avoidance, and sentience (pleasant stimulation). Some of these needs involve approach (e.g., sex), whereas others involve avoidance (e.g., heat). Psychogenic, or secondary, needs are not localized in any particular body place outside the brain, but Murray thought that they are derived from the primary needs. Among the many psychogenic needs he listed are needs for achievement, power, recognition, exhibition, dominance, aggression, and autonomy, and possibly play and curiosity. Murray proposed that hedonistic principles govern behavior. Because the need states are unpleasant, we try to rid ourselves of them, either by getting away from a noxious situation or approaching a pleasant one.

Three motives from Murray's list have received a great amount of attention from subsequent personality researchers. These are needs for **achievement, power,** and **affiliation.** We look at achievement and power in this chapter, but defer affiliation to Chapter Fourteen.

SECTION SUMMARY

1. **Trait theories** of personality assume that people can be described in terms of some relatively small set of personal characteristics. The **Five Factor Theory** establishes the following traits: extraversion, neuroticism, conscientiousness, agreeableness, and openness.

2. **Dynamic theories** of personality are motivational theories, especially emphasizing the **goals** people have. **Nomothetic** goals are those which characterize groups of individuals. **Idiographic** goals are those which distinguish individuals.

3. Henry Murray distinguished between **presses** (environmental features appraised as harmful or beneficial) and **needs** (internal states). He further distinguished between **viscerogenic** needs due to periodic body changes (such as hunger or thirst) and **psychogenic** needs (which do not have a clear physiological basis outside the brain, such as achievement motivation). Three of Murray's psychogenic needs most widely studied are need for **achievement,** need for **power,** and need for **affiliation.**

ACHIEVEMENT MOTIVATION

McClelland's Theory

Definition of the need for achievement (nAch). Murray (1938, pp. 80–81) defined need for achievement as a desire or tendency "to overcome obstacles, to exercise power, to strive to do something difficult as well and as quickly as possible." Murray also devised the Thematic Apperception Test (TAT) as a means of studying personality and needs. This test consists of a series of pictures about which the individual tells a story to answer these questions: (1) What led up to the scene being depicted? (2) What is now happening in the scene? (3) How do the characters feel? (4) What will be the outcome? The relatively ambiguous pictures are intended to evoke themes which will be characteristically different for different individuals.

Various scoring schemes are used to detect themes which characterize the needs of the individual telling the story. For example, one card shows a boy with a violin lying on a table in front of him while he looks into space. If the story is about a boy working hard to achieve the goal of becoming a world-renowned violinist, the interpretation would be different from a story about a boy who is forced to practice but whose goal is really to be outside playing with his friends. The former story would indicate need for achievement, and the latter would indicate need for affiliation. In achievement research there are usually four pictures, with a time limit of five minutes for telling each story (Atkinson, 1958; McClelland, Atkinson, Clark, & Lowell, 1953). A more direct or objective test might seem better, but the fantasy measures have been successfully used for many years.

People high in need for achievement are more persistent in goal striving, work harder and tend to be medium risk takers (McClelland, 1985). Medium risk taking is often described as a balance between the likelihood of gaining the "pride of success" from doing a reasonably difficult task well but still avoiding the "shame of failure" that would occur if a task were too difficult. The obvious questions are, What produces higher nAch? and Why does nAch lead to better performance?

Development of achievement motivation. David McClelland and his associates offered a hedonic interpretation of nAch (McClelland, Atkinson, Clark & Lowell, 1953). They proposed that cues previously associated with hedonically positive events also arouse the previously experienced affect. When this positive affect has been aroused, a person is more likely to engage in achievement behaviors that would in turn lead to more achievement and positive affect. Thus, a person who has found test taking to be a rewarding experience is more likely to try hard on tests in the future. Conversely, if a person were punished for failing, a fear of failure could develop, and there would be a motive to avoid failure. If a competitive situation is a cue for rewarded achievement striving, then in competitive situations, the individual will work harder. In brief, this theory says that under appropriate conditions, people will do what they have been rewarded for doing and is obviously like contemporary incentive motivation theory. Men with high nAch tend to come from families in which achievement striving is rewarded and young adults with high nAch often report that their parents were not particularly warm individuals, who emphasized achievement rather than affiliation.

Robert Eisenberger (1992) has proposed the concept of **learned industriousness** to account for some of the individual differences in the amount of
work that people are willing to do to reach a goal. Eisenberger argues that
the experience of effort (normally considered aversive) may be associated
with rewards and become a secondary reinforcer. That is, the effort becomes
a cue which arouses anticipatory pleasure and facilitates the achievement-
oriented behavior. Hence, rather than being punishing, increased effort becomes rewarding in itself. Research with both animals and humans lends
strong support to the concept, and its relation to the development of achievement motivation seems clear.

Occupational preferences. Individuals in "entrepreneurial" occupations should also have high nAch scores. Accordingly, research showed that
83 percent of Wesleyan graduates in entrepreneurial occupations fourteen
years after graduation had high nAch scores when they were students, as
compared to only 21 percent of those in nonentrepreneurial occupations
(McClelland, 1965). McClelland came to view the "managerial type" in business as being a medium risk taker, wanting immediate feedback for behavior,
and working harder under conditions of achievement arousal.

The achieving society. McClelland's interests broadened from laboratory tasks to complex social activities, and he tried to determine whether
nAch was related to the rise and fall of cultures (McClelland, 1961). This was
related to Max Weber's thesis in *The Protestant Ethic and the Spirit of Capitalism*
([1904] 1930), that the Protestant Revolution had infused a more vigorous
spirit into both workers and entrepreneurs. The Protestant Reformation was
a liberation movement, a break from the authoritarianism of the Catholic
Church that led to a greater social, as well as ecclesiastical, freedom. Since
freedom also carries with it a greater stress on individual responsibility and
independence, McClelland argued that Protestant individuals and countries
should therefore show greater nAch than Catholic individuals and countries.
As predicted, Protestant families stressed independence in their children earlier than Irish or Italian Catholic families and Protestant children scored
higher on nAch tests. Protestant countries were more advanced economically, as shown by comparing such measures of economic development as per
capita use of electricity and amount of shipping (McClelland, Rindlisbacher,
& de Charms, 1955). Children's books have also been scored for achievement
themes and related to subsequent economic growth. For example, between
1800 and 1850, there was an increase and then a decrease in number of
patents per 100,000 people in the United States. This was closely paralleled
by a rise and fall in achievement imagery in the children's books in the
preceding fifty years, with a correlation of .79 between the two measures
(de Charms and Moeller, 1962) Although some other factor(s) might be affecting patents, the correlation is impressive.

Atkinson's Expectancy-Value Theory

John Atkinson (e.g., 1964), a student of McClelland's, went a different direction with achievement motivation research. First, he put the theory into the framework of **expectancy-value theory.** Second, he emphasized the role of conflict, especially between need for achievement and fear of failure. To understand Atkinson, however, we must first review expectancy-value theory.

Expectancy-value in economic theory.   Expectancy-value theory is a theory of rational economic choice dating back to the early eighteenth-century mathematician Daniel Bernoulli. The idea is that people act in such a way as to make the best future deal they can based on current information about what they consider valuable and the odds of being successful. For example, we might have to decide whether to invest money in a risky stock that is potentially very valuable or putting our money into a savings account with a guaranteed income, but at a low rate of return. How would we decide which to choose? There are obviously many considerations, but the following concepts are basic to the economic decision-making choice:

Expected Value (EV) of an Outcome = Outcome Probability $\times$ Outcome Value, or in abbreviated form: $EV = P \times V$.

Suppose we have $1000 to invest. We can put it into a savings account that has a 100 percent chance of returning 16 percent (at compounded interest) over three years or put it into a stock that has a 25 percent chance of returning 25 percent over three years. Which should we choose? The expected value of the savings account is $1.0 \times (16\% \times \$1000) = \$160$. The expected value of the stock is $.25 \times (25\% \times \$1000) = .25 \times \$250 = \$62.50$. Obviously, the savings account is the choice. In other situations, the stock might be a better choice (if we are willing to gamble at all).

Unfortunately, we often have no grounds for stating an objective probability for an event, such as a stock going up or down. Or, what is the probability that one fighter will beat another if the two have never fought before? There is no history to give us a probability, such as "He has beaten him eight out of ten times." The only meaningful probability in such cases is called **subjective probability,** our "feeling" that one outcome has greater likelihood than another.

Similarly, we may not have an objective measure of value. What objective value do we attach to winning a trophy or attracting a particular mate? We can seldom put real numbers to such events, but some things are almost without question more valuable than others. In such cases, we use a subjective measure of value, called **utility.** However, we still use the same basic formula: **subjectively expected utility** = subjective probability $\times$ utility (subjective value). Economists and psychologists have spent considerable effort in devising ways of estimating utility.

Atkinson's modification of achievement theory.   Atkinson's modification of achievement theory says that the tendency to engage in any particular achievement-oriented behavior depends on the probability of success and the incentive value of success, as well as need for achievement in McClelland's sense. The theory is distinguished from other incentive theories by the fact that it is concerned with the incentive value of succeeding for success' sake, rather than for external rewards. This distinction is like the distinction between intrinsic motivation and external rewards discussed in Chapter Seven. The theory assumes that there is greater incentive value in achieving something difficult (where there is a low probability of success) than there is in achieving something easy (where there is a high probability of success). The **incentive value of success (Is)** is defined as **1 − probability of success (1−Ps).** Since probabilities range from zero to one, the lower the probability of success the greater the incentive value of success.

The tendency to success (T_s).   The tendency to engage in achievement-oriented behaviors (tendency to success, or T_s) is a multiplicative function of

1.   the motivation for success (M_s), which is the same as nAch;
2.   the probability of success (P_s); and
3.   the incentive value of success ($I_s = 1 - P_s$).

The formula reads $T_s = M_s \times P_s \times I_s$

The higher the level of T_s, the greater the achievement striving, but if any of the components is zero, then there will be not be a tendency to strive for success in a particular situation. When there is competition between two activities, the one with the higher level of T_s is chosen. The formula is similar to Hull's formula ($E = H \times D \times K$), both in being multiplicative and in what the concepts refer to. Both theories assume that the tendency to engage in a particular behavior is a function of learning, an internal motivational state, and an incentive. Thus, T_s is like E, M_s is an internal state like drive, P_s is a learning component corresponding roughly to habit, and I_s corresponds roughly to Hull's incentive, K. The details, of course, differ.

There are obviously important differences from Hull, however, particularly with regard to P_s and I_s. As noted earlier, high nAch people tend to be medium risk takers. Given a choice of activities with different chances of being successful, they tend to choose activities with a medium level of P_s. The Atkinson model accounts for this as follows: Since P_s ranges from 0 to 1, and I_s ranges from 1 to 0, the maximum possible value of $P_s \times (1 - P_s)$ occurs when $P_s = .50$. Plugging some numbers into the formula, if $M_s = 1$, $P_s = .50$, and $I_s = .50$, then $T_s = 1.0 \times .50 \times .50 = .25$. Any other value of P_s will give a lower value of T_s. Table 12–2 illustrates some calculations, and the upper part of Figure 12–1 graphically illustrates the results for different values of P_s and I_s, which give us an inverted U curve for values of T_s. If the task

TABLE 12–2. Calculations of T_s and T_{af} for five different difficulty level tasks and different values of M_s and M_{af}.

			$T_s = M_s \times P_s \times I_s$ WHEN		
TASK	P_s	I_s	$M_s = 1$	$M_s = 3$	$M_s = 8$
A	.90	.10	.09	.27	.72
B	.70	.30	.21	.63	1.68
C	.50	.50	.25	.75	2.00
D	.30	.70	.21	.63	1.68
E	.10	.90	.09	.27	.72
			$T_{af} = M_{af} \times P_f \times I_{-f}$ WHEN		
	P_f	I_{-f}	$M_{af} = 1$	$M_{af} = 3$	$M_{af} = 8$
A	.10	−.90	−.09	−.27	−.72
B	.30	−.70	−.21	−.63	−1.68
C	.50	−.50	−.25	−.75	−2.00
D	.70	−.30	−.21	−.63	−1.68
E	.90	−.10	−.09	−.27	−.72

is too difficult, there is little chance of succeeding; and if it is too easy, there is little incentive to succeed. Therefore, middle-level tasks are the most likely to be chosen. Consider how we divide up teams in pickup games of basketball. We elect two captains, who then proceed to choose players alternately. The whole idea is to get teams as evenly matched as possible so that the chances of winning are as near as possible to fifty-fifty.

As one test of the theory, Atkinson (1958) told female subjects that they were to compete for a prize of either $1.25 or $2.50, drawing X's inside small circles for twenty minutes. Four probabilities of winning were stated: .20, .33, .50, and .75. The high-reward group performed better than the low-reward group, as expected for the external reward. Performance declined for both groups, however, when P_s was said to be .75 rather than .50. This outcome confirmed the prediction of an inverted U function for performance when one probability of success was greater than .50.

The tendency to avoid failure (T_{af}). Besides the "satisfaction" or "pride" that comes from success, there is "shame" from failure, sometimes called a fear of failure. There is also a tendency to avoid failure. The fear of failure depends on one's previous experience with failure, whether one was punished or ridiculed for failing, for example. A multiplication formula is also used to determine the strength of the tendency to avoid failure. The components are

1. The motive to avoid failure (M_{af}), the fear of failure, commonly measured by a test anxiety questionnaire;

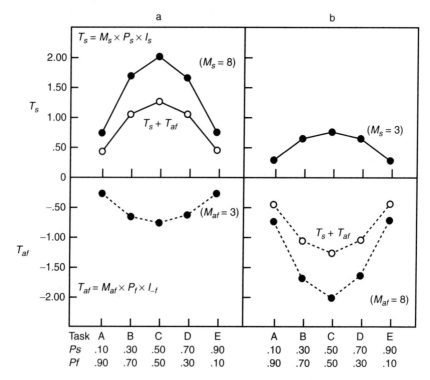

FIGURE 12–1. Illustrations of T_s and T_{af} and resultant tendencies to approach or avoid when M_s = 3 or 8 and when M_{af} = 3 or 8. In (a), the tendency to success is greater than the tendency to avoid failure; therefore, the resultant tendency, the algebraic summation of T_s and T_{af}, is positive. In (b) the situation is just reversed, with the resultant tendency being negative. Note also that T_s is a steeper function in (a) (M_s = 8) than in (b) (M_s = 3). This indicates why high n Ach individuals are medium-risk takers; medium probabilities of success produce much higher relative values of T_s when M_s is high.

2. The probability of failure (P_f), which for any given task is $1 - P_s$; and
3. The negative incentive value of failure (I_{-f}) is $- (1 - P_f)$, which is the same as $- P_s$.

If the probability of failure is .90, then I_{-f} is $- (1 - .90) = -.10$. Since P_s for this example is $1 - .90 = .10$, then $I_{-f} = -P_s = -.10$. The tendency to avoid failure is thus given by the formula

$$T_{af} = M_{af} \times P_f \times I_{-f}$$

Table 12–2 and Figure 12–1 show more detailed illustrations. This formula says that if a person has motivation to avoid failure, there will be some tendency to avoid tasks that could potentially lead to failure. Furthermore, the maximum value of T_{af} will also occur with medium-probability tasks because the maximum value of $P_f \times I_{-f}$ occurs when $P_f = .50$. In this case, however, the product is a negative value. The tendency to avoid failure will therefore be the strongest for tasks having a medium expectancy of failure, which is just the opposite of the prediction for individuals with high nAch. In everyday language, the person afraid of failing may choose a task that is so easy that he or she almost cannot fail or one that is so difficult that there is no shame in failing. The medium level task is avoided.

The combination of T_s and T_{af}.   The values of I_s, P_f, and I_{-f} are all determined once we know the value of P_s. What differentiates T_s and T_{af}, then, are the relative strengths of M_s and M_{af}. The resolution of the conflict between T_s and T_{af} is then represented as follows:

$$T_s + T_{af} = (M_s \times P_s \times I_s) + (M_{af} \times P_f \times I_{-f})$$

This says that we calculate the positive values of T_s and the negative values of T_{af} using their respective formulae, and then add them together. If the $M_s > M_{af}$, the individual should choose medium-probability tasks, but if $M_{af} > M_s$, the person should tend to avoid medium-probability tasks. This guideline is illustrated in Figure 12–1. The theory, then, is like any other approach-avoidance conflict theory, where the resolution depends on the relative strengths of approach and avoidance tendencies. Atkinson's theory, with its special assumptions about positive and negative incentives for achievement, makes interesting and unique predictions, however, which we can illustrate with task preference and level of aspiration.

Task preference.   McClelland (1958) showed that high nAch children preferred to toss a ring at a peg (the ring toss game) from a medium distance, as compared with low nAch children, who tended to choose either near or far distances. Atkinson and Litwin (1960) divided subjects into four groups of all combinations of high and low nAch and of high and low anxiety. They predicted that high M_s, low M_{af} subjects would show the strongest tendency to choose medium distances in the ring toss game and that high M_{af}, low M_s subjects would avoid the middle range. The other two groups should fall between. The predictions were somewhat confirmed, as shown in Figure 12–2. The high M_{af}, low M_s group tended to choose a middle range, but their preferences were spread across a wider range of distances than for any other group. To obtain results exactly as predicted for the group where $M_{af} > M_s$ would depend on very exact measurements of M_{af} and M_s. It may not really be in the present situation that M_{af} was greater than M_s.

Level of aspiration.   Suppose a high M_s person chooses a task that she perceives to be of medium difficulty. By experimental prearrangement, she then either succeeds or fails. What difficulty level should she subsequently

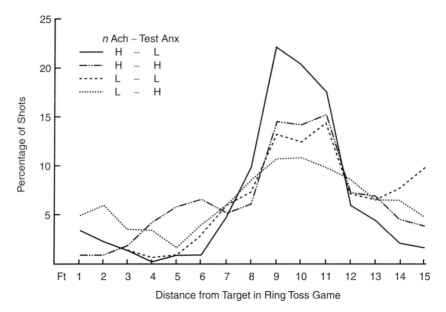

FIGURE 12–2. Percentage of shots taken from each distance by college men in a ring toss game. Graph is smoothed according to the method of running averages, for Ss classified as high or low simultaneously in n Ach and test anxiety, H-L (N = 13), H-H (N = 10), L-L (N = 9), L-H (N = 13). (From Atkinson & Litwin, 1960, p. 55. Copyright © 1960 by the American Psychological Association. Used with permission.)

choose? One of the commonest results of such level of aspiration research is that people tend to change their goals realistically on the basis of experience (e.g., Lewin, Dembo, Festinger, & Sears, 1944). After failure, the goal is lowered but after success it is raised. Atkinson's explanation is that after easy success, a person would perceive P_s as higher than previously expected. He therefore sets the next goal higher because that would bring P_s of this goal closer to his newly adjusted concept of a $p = .50$ goal. Conversely, if he failed, he would assume that P_s was lower than he had expected and hence would choose a simpler task to bring P_s up more nearly to .50. These are typical shifts in level-of-aspiration research.

There are sometimes peculiar atypical shifts, however. Some individuals raise their goals after failure and lower them after success. According to the theory, if $M_{af} > M_s$, then the individual should avoid medium-difficulty tasks. If a high M_{af} subject is told she has a task where $P_s = .50$ and fails it, she may then believe that P_s was lower than she initially had thought, .35, for instance. An easier task would put her closer to $P_s = .50$, which should be aversive for her. She may therefore select a more difficult task (for example, $P_s = .25$) than the one she failed at. Conversely, if successful at a task she believes to be $P_s = .50$, the subject may think that the task was easier than she had believed, such as P_s = .65. Therefore, she would next choose an even easier task because she wants to keep away from the P_s = .50 task. Moulton (1965) obtained such results, for high M_{af}, low M_s individuals, as well as showing that high M_s, low M_{af} subjects and M_s = M_{af} subjects made typical shifts more frequently. This finding is rather remarkable support for the theory.

There have been a number of serious problems with both the McClelland and the Atkinson versions of achievement theory, however. First, there seem to be more dimensions of achievement motivation than just motivation for success and fear of failure. Second, much of the early research with nAch was restricted to males, raising the question whether men and women are different in achievement motivation. Research with different measures of achievement motivation than the TAT measures generally shows no sex differences, however. Third, many studies did not find differences between high and low nAch people. See Beck (1990) for more detailed criticisms.

Attribution Theory and Achievement Motivation

One of the complications for achievement theory is that not all people respond the same way to success and failure. Some people respond to failure by trying harder, whereas others respond to initial failure by giving up. One reason for such behavioral differences is that people may view the causes for success and failure differently. For example, people who attribute failure to bad luck may respond differently in the future than do people who (correctly or not) attribute failure to their own stupidity. The attributional approach to achievement motivation deals with just such questions.

Nature of attribution theory.   Attribution theory is concerned with (1) how and why people search for the causes of their own behavior or that of other people, (2) the kinds of causes that are found, and (3) the effects of such attributions on emotion, motivation, and subsequent behaviors.

Why search for causes?   Kelley (1967) suggested that people are motivated to obtain a cognitive mastery of the "causal structures" in their environment. They want to understand and make sense of how their environment works. Finding such relations is rewarding because knowing causal relations increases our expectancy of success in future behaviors and in setting future goals.

Fritz Heider, generally considered the founder of attribution theory, categorized attributions into internal (personal force) and external (environmental force).

Personal Force = effort and ability
External Force = Task Difficulty and Luck

How do we make attributions?   We tend to make internal attributions if a person consistently does the same thing in the same situation (**consistency**) or does the same thing across many different situations (**distinctiveness**) but is different from other individuals (**lack of consensus**) in the same situations. If everybody gets angry in a particular situation, we would be likely to attribute anger to the situation (external). If only one person gets angry, but always gets angry, we would be likely to attribute the anger to the person (internal) and not the situation.

Weiner's attributional theory of achievement.   Bernard Weiner (1985) has presented the most ambitious attributional theory of achievement motivation. The theory deals with all three of the attribution questions posed above: What are the perceived causes of success and failure, what are the characteristics of causal thinking, and what are the subsequent emotional experiences in relation to achievement behaviors. There are, of course, many possible causes for any specific success or failure, but these can be reduced to a relatively small number of categories that appear repeatedly in relation to many situations. Weiner (1985) expanded on Heider and categorized these causes as **internal** versus **external, stable** versus **unstable,** and **controllable** versus **uncontrollable.** Table 12–3 summarizes these attributions, with examples.

1. **Internal versus external attributions.** de Charms (1968) put the internal-external distinction in terms of what he called **origins** and **pawns.** Some individuals feel that they originate their own activities and are responsible for their own rewards and punishments (internal attributions). Others feel that, like chess pawns, they have little freedom and that the limited freedom they do have is at the service of more powerful outside sources (external attributions). A per-

TABLE 12–3.   Different classes of attributions for success and failure in playing tennis.

	SUCCESS/FAILURE ATTRIBUTIONS IN TENNIS			
	STABLE		UNSTABLE	
	CONTROLLABLE	UNCONTROLLABLE	CONTROLLABLE	UNCONTROLLABLE
Internal	**My Experience** S: I'm well practiced F: Poor coaching	**My Ability** S: I'm a natural F: I'm uncoordinated	**My Effort** S: I tried hard F: I didn't concentrate	**My Fatigue/Illness etc.** S: I felt good F: I was too tired
External	**Skill of Others** S: Opponent had no lessons F: Opponent had good coaching	**Task Difficulty** S: Poor opponents F: Tennis is too hard for me	**Effort of Others** S: Opponent took me too lightly F: Opponent worked very hard	**Luck** S: My serves got in F: Line calls were bad

son may make internal attributions for success, such as "I have a lot of ability and work hard." On the other hand, the same person might make external attributions for failure, such as "I had some bad luck" or some other uncontrollable event.

2. **Stable versus unstable attributions.** A person might attribute success to *ability* (which is a relatively enduring characteristic) or to *effort* (which may be more fluctuating). Task difficulty is described as being stable, but chance (luck) is unstable. For example, "I had difficulty with the test because this is a very hard course" (task difficulty) or "I just didn't study the right things" (chance).

3. **Controllable versus uncontrollable attributions.** Lack of effort and being ill are internal and unstable causes for failure, but there is an obvious difference between them. Lack of effort is considered to be controllable ("I could have tried harder"), but the illness is not ("I couldn't overcome the flu the day of the test").

More specific attributions can be found, but the preceding three classifications of attributions cut across considerable research. In addition, detailed statistical analyses of the causes given by people to account for their actions have indicated that these categories are those used by real people and are not just figments of attribution theorists' imaginations.

Attribution training.   Are some attributions better than others and, if so, Why? Attributions that are controllable are considered better, in terms of future behavior. I may not be able to change the difficulty of the job to be done, or to control the behavior of others, but I can work harder and practice more. Both of these, effort and skill, improve my chances of success in future endeavors. If a person has attributions for failure that are internal and stable ("I'm not any good at this and never will be") the future is bleak. But, if a person is taught to use different attributions, the future may be better because the person will try. The obvious problem is that my ability may be limited (e.g., weight lifting, jumping, running). However, there is no way to know the limit of my ability unless I push the limits of effort and practice. In short, attribution training is a good place to start in the effort to increase one's success, but there is no guarantee that it will be work.

Emotional consequences of attributions.   Causal attributions influence the expectancy of success, a cognitive effect. Goal expectancies are not sufficient, however, unless the goals have some positive or negative valence. Expectancy and value are independent determinants of behavior which are combined multiplicatively. However, the attributions of causality that occur may influence emotions as well as expectancies.

Weiner (1985) suggests that there are two kinds of appraisals of the goodness or badness of a behavioral outcome.

1. **Primary appraisal: outcome-dependent but attribution-independent.** The outcome of a situation may be evaluated as good or bad regardless of the reason (e.g. we win the lottery or we lose money by a bad investment). We are happy

for success and sad or frustrated for failure. These are *outcome-dependent* but *attribution-independent*. They are determined by getting or not getting a desired goal, not by the cause of the outcome. We may be equally happy to get a million dollars, whether in the lottery or by a shrewd investment.

2. **Secondary appraisal: attribution-dependent.** Following the outcome, win or lose, there may be a causal search which generates a more specific emotion. Winning the lottery generates *surprise* and happiness, but a shrewd investment from which we expected to have a good outcome may generate *calmness* or *serenity*. Such secondary emotions are *attribution-dependent* because they follow upon causal ascriptions.

$$/ \rightarrow \textbf{immediate positive or negative affect}$$
$$\textbf{OUTCOME} \rightarrow \textbf{OUTCOME EVALUATION}/$$
$$\backslash \rightarrow \textbf{causal attribution} \rightarrow \textbf{distinct emotions}$$

A sports example of attribution-independent emotion would be that immediately following a win there is happiness, whether the win occurred in regulation time or overtime, whether it was due to the winner's good play or the loser's poor play, and so on. How many times have winning athletes told reporters after winning a game "Right now I'm just enjoying the moment, I'll think about it later." Upon reflection about causes, the emotion may indeed change. If the win was in overtime against a clearly inferior opponent the happiness may be considerably dampened and possibly turn to unhappiness because it is perceived as a failure of expectation.

Attribution biases. Attribution theory is presented as if causes were arrived at rationally, in a scientific manner. It is well-known, however, that people have certain consistent biases in the causes they arrive at. Two of these are the **fundamental attribution error** and the **self-serving bias.**

The fundamental attribution error. People tend to make external attributions for their own behavior and internal attributions for the behavior of others. For example, I made an error fielding a baseball because I slipped on the wet grass (external). He made an error because he is not a very good player (internal). There are two main reasons for making internal attributions about others. First, we tend to pay more attention to the person than the situation as a whole. Second, it takes less effort to make an internal attribution because we don't have to look at all the situational details.

The self-serving bias. We tend to make internal attributions for our success and external attributions for our failures. The internal attribution is **ego-enhancing** (giving oneself the credit) and the second is **ego-protecting** (giving someone else the blame).

Behavioral consequences of attributions. Attributions for success and failure are ultimately of interest only to the extent that they will predict future achievement behaviors. Unfortunately, the evidence is not entirely compelling. Heckhausen (1975), for example, reported that even though subjects high in need for achievement attributed failure to their own lack of effort, they did not subsequently show increased effort in another task. The attribution was as expected, but it did not predict subsequent behavior. The most general conclusion that can be drawn about attributions and achievement, said McClelland (1985), is that subjects high in need for achievement tend to attribute success to ability and failure to lack of effort, whereas subjects low in need for achievement tend to attribute failure to lack of ability. He does not consider it to be empirically demonstrated that attributions for past performance will predict future achievement behavior very well.

The Spence-Helmreich Achievement Theory

Spence and Helmreich (1983) developed a theory of achievement motivation that has three achievement dimensions that are undoubtedly familiar to the typical student.

1. **Satisfaction in work itself,** in a job well done. When a student writes a term paper, she may well be concerned with the grade but also with the satisfaction of having turned out a good piece of work.
2. **A sense of completion,** of satisfaction with getting a job done. Sometimes we are pleased to get a job done at all. If we run the Boston Marathon, we are probably proud just to have completed the twenty-six-mile race in spite of coming in at Number 15,000.
3. **A sense of competitiveness,** as well as enjoyment of competition and winning that may come with schoolwork, job success, games, or any other competitive situation.

Spence and Helmreich devised an objectively scored test for these three aspects of achievement called the *Work and Family Orientation* (WOFO) *Questionnaire.* Research in a rather impressive array of situations, ranging from grades in college to salaries in business organizations, regularly shows a consistent pattern of results illustrated in Figure 12–3. Grades and salaries are higher for people who have high levels of motivation for work and mastery if they are also low in competitiveness. If they are high in competitiveness, performance suffers. One explanation is that highly competitive people may focus so much on the competition rather than on doing a good job that they do less well than they would otherwise.

SECTION SUMMARY

1. **Need for achievement** (nAch) is defined as a desire or tendency "to overcome obstacles, to exercise power, to strive to do something difficult as well and as quickly as possible." McClelland argued that achievement need develops out of previously rewarded achievement behavior and the positive affect associated with achievement.

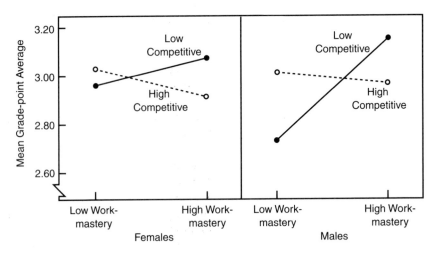

FIGURE 12-3.   Mean grade-point averages in low competitive and high competitive male and female undergraduate students. Work and mastery are put together on the same horizontal axis because the effect of competitiveness is the same whether low or high work or low or high mastery are compared. (From Spence & Helmreich, 1983. Copyright © 1983 by W. H. Freeman and Company. Used by permission.)

2. A more **mathematical theory** developed by Atkinson says that the tendency to engage in achievement behaviors (T_s) is the product of the **motive** for success (M_s), the **probability** of success (P_s), and the **incentive value** of success (I_s). P_s and I_s are inversely related: $I_s = 1 - P_s$. There is also a **tendency to avoid failure** (T_{af}), based on a **fear of failure.** T_s and T_{af} are additive, with behavioral predictions based on which one is greater.

3. **Attributional approaches** to achievement account for many individual differences in achievement motivation in terms of the **attributions** that people give for **success** or **failure.** Weiner's attributional theory has three attributional dimensions: (a) internal versus external locus of control, (b) stable versus unstable factors, and (c) controllable versus uncontrollable factors. It is assumed that each specific causal attribution for success or failure has particular emotional consequences, which in turn influence future achievement-oriented behaviors.

4. Spence and Helmreich developed an achievement theory with the dimensions of **mastery, completion,** and **competitiveness.** People high in competitiveness often do not perform as well as people who are less competitive.

POWER AND CONTROL MOTIVES

Power Motivation

Definition and measurement.   Need for power is measured in the same general way as the need for achievement. Winter (1973) developed a TAT scoring system for three categories of power imagery: (1) strong vigorous action that expresses power, (2) actions that arouse strong emotion in others, and (3) explicit concerns about reputation or position. Collectively, these define what is meant by power.

Energizing effects of power motivation.   It is assumed that like achievement, power is a *dispositional motive* that has to be "engaged" by circumstances before it influences behavior. It is a latent (dormant) motive until aroused. Steele (1977) examined the arousal of power motivation by having subjects write TAT stories after listening to tape recordings of famous inspirational speeches. Power scores were significantly higher after the inspirational speeches than before, but they were unchanged by listening to travelogues (McClelland, 1985, p. 272.). Steele also obtained self-reports of perceived arousal as well as a physiological measure, the amount of adrenaline in the urine. Both measures were significantly higher after the inspirational speeches than after the travelogue, with power scores and adrenaline increase correlating +.71. The adrenaline change seems to rule out experimenter demand as an interpretation for the self-report changes. A person might report feeling more aroused after an inspirational speech because he thinks that he should be aroused under such circumstances, but it would seem more difficult to increase urinary adrenaline on demand. Furthermore, adrenaline increase was not correlated with achievement motivation scores obtained from the same subjects, meaning that the speeches did not arouse all forms of motivation, but selectively aroused power motivation.

Selective effects of power motivation.   Power motivation may selectively tune us into power-related cues in the environment. McAdams and McClelland (1983) had subjects high and low in need for power listen to a tape recording of someone telling a story about a picture. The story had fifteen power-related facts, fifteen neutral facts, and fifteen facts related to intimacy. Subjects high in need for power recalled a significantly greater proportion of power-related facts than neutral facts. In a different experiment, subjects high in need for power learned power-related stimulus materials faster than subjects low in need for power (McClelland, Davidson, Saron, & Floor, 1980).

Power and behavior.   McClelland distinguished between *personal power* and *social power*. Personal power was considered to be more "primitive" than social power, and characterized by dominance over others. Social power is more subtle and has the aim of benefitting others. Persons high in either of these kinds of power might seek political office, but for the different reasons related to their kinds of power need—controlling or benefitting.

Need for personal power is related to competitiveness and aggression. Men high in need for personal power have been found to do more fighting, drinking, gambling, and speeding than men low in need for personal power (McClelland, 1985). This finding is not true for women, however, possibly because women are taught to suppress aggressive tendencies more so than men.

Such apparent socialization differences have also been found among men, however. Working-class men with high need for power have been found to be more aggressive than middle-class men with equivalent levels of power motivation. Middle-class men presumably have learned to suppress aggressive tendencies more than lower-class men.

People high in need for power also act in many ways so as to appear powerful. For example, they collect such symbols of power as prestige possessions, including certain types of cars, wristwatches, jewelry, and so on (Winter, 1973). They are more willing to take risks, drink more, and are more likely to surround themselves with lesser-known people who can be led. Power scores have actually been found to change with drinking, but the nature of the change depends on the type of power involved. Individuals high in personal power show progressively higher power scores with increased drinking. Individuals high in social power, on the other hand, show a decline in need-for-power scores when they drink heavily (Figure 12–4; McClelland, Davis, Kalin, & Wanner, 1972). Women appear to respond differently to alcohol, feeling more friendly after drinking rather than more powerful (McClelland, 1985, p. 299). The social implications of this difference are obvious and sometimes disastrous.

Need for power may express itself in what appear to be unusual occupational choices. For example, students with high need for power were most in-

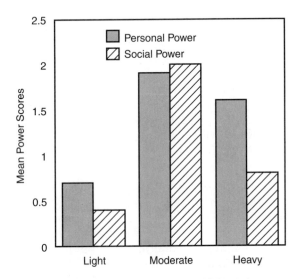

FIGURE 12–4. Mean social power and personal power scores with increasing consumption of 86 proof alcohol (light = 0.1 to 3.9 oz.; moderate = 4 to 6 oz.; heavy = 6.1 to 12 oz.). Social power scores show a sharp decline with heavy alcohol consumption. (From McClelland, Davis, Kalin, & Wanner, 1972. Copyright 1972 by David C. McClelland, William N. Davis, Rudolf Kalin, and Eric Wanner. Reprinted by permission of The Free Press, a Division of Macmillan, Inc.)

terested in teaching, psychology, ministry, business, and international diplomacy. Students low in need for power were more interested in government and politics, medicine, law, creative arts, and architecture. These seem like strange occupational preferences but when we think about it there is a pattern. Teachers, psychologists, and ministers, for example, have occupations in which they normally exert considerable control over others in their day-to-day work. Politicians, on the other hand, spend a great deal of time bargaining and compromising in order to get things done.

Power and physical health.   Research by McClelland and his associates indicates that power motivation can have bad effects on health, depending on patterns of different motives. Two such patterns are the *inhibited power motive syndrome* and the *relaxed affiliative syndrome*. The inhibited power syndrome is characterized by need for power being greater than need for affiliation, but with inhibited expression of the need for power. This syndrome has been linked with high blood pressure, increased stress responses, and other physical illnesses (Jemmott, 1987). The relaxed affiliation syndrome is characterized by the need for affiliation being greater than the need for power, coupled with a low level of inhibition of the affiliation motive. The syndrome is generally associated with less stress and better health.

Competence and Effectance

Robert White (1959) argued that striving for competence is a major motive and that success produces feelings of effectance. Bandura (1977, 1982) proposed the concept of **self-efficacy,** which is the expectation that one can perform any particular action successfully. This is called an **efficacy expectation.** People with greater perceived self-efficacy actually do perform better on many kinds of tasks. Efficacy is not just a matter of "will power" or determination to try harder, however. Self-efficacy is established through actually having successes, just as the development of an internal locus of control is learned through successful behavior. Bandura (1977) lists the following principles.

1. Self-efficacy increases with personal accomplishment. Perceived efficacy is greater if we have more accomplishments, and efficacy expectations generalize across situations. This factor is important because it means that efficacy training is possible. We can, for example, set up situations that guarantee that children have some degree of success.

2. Self-efficacy can increase or decrease if we see others similar to ourselves succeeding or failing at a task. This principle is important with regard to modeling as a method of teaching, suggesting that a model similar to the subject be used, such as one child modeling for another. If a person does try to imitate a model, however, the degree of perceived success is determined by the actual degree of success. A person who tries to imitate the model and fails is not going to develop a sense of self-efficacy. The model simply provides a direction for behavior.

3. We can be persuaded that we are capable of coping with a difficult situation, but this process breaks down if we actually fail in such situations. Like modeling, persuasion may serve to get a person to try some activity, but the effort must be followed by perceived success at the actual task.

4. Emotional arousal can affect our feeling of self-efficacy. If we are upset, depressed, or overly anxious about some activity, such as giving a speech, we do not perceive our self-efficacy as high as when we are in a better mood. We may learn to use our emotion as a cue for lower self-efficacy, as in "I just cannot cope today," as a result of some particular emotional experience.

Desire for Control

Discussions of personal control always seem to assume that such control is good and sought by everyone. But this is not necessarily so. Indeed, if a person does not care about having control, then lack of control should pose no threat, and control might even be aversive and avoided. The first step in getting at such questions is to measure desire for control.

Burger and Cooper (1979) developed the **Desirability of Control (DC) Scale,** consisting of twenty items, such as "I try to avoid situations in which someone else tells me what to do." The scale does not correlate with Rotter's locus of control scale, so it is not just another measure of perceived locus of control. Males generally score higher than females, a finding that fits much data indicating that males are generally more assertive than females. Burger and Cooper also showed that people with high desire for control are also more likely in ambiguous situations to perceive that they do have control. In a gambling game, for example, subjects were given the illusion of control by letting them believe that their own actions determined the outcome of a random bet. The high DC subjects bet more than subjects not given the illusion of control, but low DC subjects were not affected by the illusion of control manipulation. A variety of predictions about differences between people who are high and low in desire for control have been supported by research (Burger, 1989).

SECTION SUMMARY

1. **Power motivation** is defined as the desire to have control over others and is measured by scoring imaginative stories for imagery relating to strong, vigorous actions that arouse strong emotion in others and that demonstrate explicit concerns about reputation or position.

2. People high in need for power show increased internal arousal when power need is engaged and tend to respond more selectively to environmental cues related to power, such as better remembering power-related stimuli.

3. **Personal power** is distinguished from more altruistic **social power.** Men high in personal power tend to be aggressive and competitive, but women are not. Socialization seems partly to determine such behaviors, since middle-class men are less aggressive than lower-class men with equal power scores.

4. Bandura's **theory of self-efficacy** says that people who believe that their behavior will be more effective also perform more effectively. There are several ways to enhance self-efficacy, but personal accomplishment is the most powerful and enduring.

5. People differ in their **desire for control** (DC). Low DC individuals with control are not as affected by perceived loss of control as are high DC individuals. Conversely, the "good effects" that accrue to people with control may not be so perceived by people with low desire for control.

SENSATION SEEKING

Are bungee jumping, skydiving, and riding on world-class roller coasters your idea of a good afternoon's fun? If so, you may wonder why other people fail to see the enjoyment in these activities. The individual differences in the extent to which people seek out and enjoy exciting experiences have been captured in the measurement of a personality trait called **sensation seeking.**

Description and Measurement of Sensation Seeking

Zuckerman (1994) states that "Sensation seeking represents the optimistic tendency to approach novel stimuli and explore the environment" (p. 385). Approach may be manifest in many different specific behaviors, and Zuckerman (1979) distinguishes four different kinds of sensation seeking, which are defined by his **Sensation Seeking Scale,** shown in Table 12–4.

Thrill and adventure seeking (TAS).   Bungee jumpers and sky divers fit into this class of sensation seekers. Other activities might involve such job choices as working high iron in construction or law enforcement rather than an office job.

Experience seeking (ES).   This is seeking sensation through the mind and the senses or through a nonconforming lifestyle. Not all sensation seeking has to involve dangerous or exciting physical activity.

Disinhibition (Dis).   Sensation may be sought through social stimulation in such a way that normal inhibitions are released, such as at wild parties. Social drinking may serve the same function, to "loosen up" oneself.

Boredom susceptibility (BS).   This is characterized by an aversion to monotonous, unchanging situations and by restlessness while in such situations.

TABLE 12–4. Items from the subscales of Zuckerman's Sensation Seeking Scale.

Thrill and Adventure Seeking

_____ I often wish I could be a mountain climber.
_____ I sometimes like to do things that are a little frightening.
_____ I would like to take up the sport of waterskiing.
_____ I would like to try surfboard riding.
_____ I would like to go scuba diving.
_____ I would like to learn to fly an airplane.
_____ I would like to try parachute jumping.
_____ I like to dive off the high board.
_____ I would like to sail a long distance in a small but seaworthy sailing craft.
_____ I think I would enjoy the sensations of skiing very fast down a high mountain slope.

Experience Seeking

_____ I like some of the earthy body smells.
_____ I like to explore a strange city or section of town myself, even if it means getting lost.
_____ I have tried marijuana or would like to.
_____ I would like to try some of the new drugs that produce hallucinations.
_____ I like to try new foods that I have never tasted before.
_____ I would like to take off on a trip with no preplanned or definite routes or timetables.
_____ I would like to make friends in some of the "far-out" groups like artists or "hippies."
_____ I would like to meet some people who are homosexual (men or women).
_____ I often find beauty in the "clashing" colors and irregular form of modern painting.
_____ People should dress in individual ways even if the effects are sometimes strange.

Disinhibition

_____ I like wild, "uninhibited" parties.
_____ I enjoy the company of real "swingers."
_____ I often like to get high (drinking liquor or smoking marijuana).
_____ I like to have new and exciting experiences and sensations, even if they are a little unconventional or illegal.
_____ I like to date members of the opposite sex who are physically exciting.
_____ Keeping the drinks full is the key to a good party.
_____ A person should have considerable sexual experience before marriage.
_____ I could conceive of myself seeking pleasures around the world with the "jet set."
_____ I enjoy watching many of the "sexy" scenes in movies.
_____ I feel best after taking a couple of drinks.

Boredom Susceptibility

_____ I can't stand watching a movie that I've seen before.
_____ I get bored seeing the same old faces.
_____ When you can predict almost everything a person will do and say, he or she must be a bore.
_____ I usually don't enjoy a movie or play where I can predict what will happen in advance.
_____ Looking at someone's home movies or travel slides bores me tremendously.
_____ I prefer friends who are excitingly unpredictable.
_____ I get very restless if I have to stay around home for any length of time.
_____ The worst social sin is to be a bore.
_____ I like people who are sharp and witty even if they do sometimes insult others.
_____ I have no patience with dull or boring parties.

The Sensation Seeking (SS) Scales correlate with behaviors across many different domains of activity, including the following (Zuckerman, 1994). Males are higher SS than females, especially regarding physical risk and permissive attitudes toward sex, but SS for both declines with age. In spite of the fact that high SS people engage in riskier behaviors, they also take precautions to reduce the risk. For example, they may engage in sex with more partners but protect themselves against disease or unwanted pregnancy as much as low SS individuals do. Interestingly, anxiety is generally not correlated with sensation seeking, which indicates that high SS people are not simply less fearful than others. Finally, high SS people tend to be more aggressive and politically liberal.

Theory of Sensation Seeking

Optimal level of arousal.   As we saw in Chapter Six, this theory says that there is an optimal level of stimulation that is best for performance and is desirable. People seek out situations and activities that will lead to and maintain this optimal level. One of the great perceived advantages of this line of theory was that it accounted for why people seek increases in stimulation as well as decreases. Tension reduction theories, including Hull's drive theory, seemed only to account for why organisms seek lower levels of drive or stimulation. Individual differences in sensation seeking would be explained in terms of different people's needing different levels of stimulation to achieve an optimal level of arousal. Low SS people would be readily aroused by low levels of stimulation and be easily over-aroused, leading them to seek less stimulating situations. High SS people would require a great deal of stimulation to reach their optimal level of arousal. Figure 12–5 shows how three different people might respond to the same levels of stimulation.

The problem with optimal level of arousal theory is that high and low sensation seekers do not always show predicted differences in arousal (Zuckerman, 1994). For example, measures of EEG and skin conductance have shown that high sensation seekers react more strongly to stimulation than do low sensation seekers, just the opposite of what the theory predicts. Also, high sensation seekers show greater use of stimulant drugs, as predicted, but they also show greater use of depressant drugs, a result that runs counter to the theory. This led Zuckerman to a new theory.

Monoamine oxidase theory.   The monoamines are a class of neurotransmitters that include **noradrenaline** and **dopamine,** both of which are associated with pleasure and excitement. **Monoamine oxidase** (MAO) breaks down the monoamines in the synapse or upon reuptake into the neuron from which the neurotransmitter was released. This process keeps the transmitter from cumulating in the synapse and continuing to act after the neuron has stopped firing. Drugs (called **MAO inhibitors,** used as antidepressants) or natural chemicals in the body that inhibit MAO produce greater

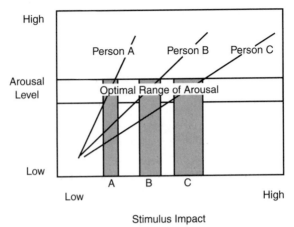

FIGURE 12–5. Optimal levels (ranges) of arousal for three different people: A, B, and C. Person A is easily aroused by stimuli and reaches his optimal level with a low level of stimulus impact. Person C takes a higher level of stimulus impact to reach her optimal range of arousal. Person B falls in between. In this example the optimal ranges are nonoverlapping. The optimal range for Person B is too high for A and too low for C.

activity in the dopamine reward systems (Zuckerman, 1994). The level of MAO is partly determined by genetics so there are heritable individual differences in the degree to which our dopamine reward systems are aroused by stimulation. Activation of the reward system may also inhibit activity in the punishment system (Gray's behavioral inhibition system), suggesting that there is an interplay between relative levels of arousal in reward and punishment systems that is crucial for sensation seeking.

SECTION SUMMARY

1. Zuckerman defines **sensation seeking** in terms of the optimistic tendency to approach novel stimuli and explore the environment and there are large individual differences in this tendency.

2. Zuckerman's **Sensation Seeking Scale** distinguishes four different dimensions of sensation seeking: thrill and adventure seeking, experience seeking, disinhibition (e.g., wild parties), and boredom susceptibility.

3. People vary widely in how much they enjoy sensation-seeking. One theory to account for this says that there are individual differences in **optimal level of arousal,** requiring some people to seek more sensations to reach their optimal level. Zuckerman has proposed what he calls the **monoamine oxidase theory,** which says that people higher in sensation seeking tend to have higher levels of the neurotransmitter **dopamine** released in exciting situations.

INFORMATION PROCESSING MOTIVES

Loewenstein (1994, p. 94) described research on problem solving in the last quarter century thusly: "Virtually all of this research has examined the cognitive strategies that people use to solve problems. Amazingly there has been almost no research on why people are so powerfully driven to solve such problems." It would seem to be true that people or animals engage in activities that are driven neither by hunger nor pain, nor rewarded by food or solace. This view takes us back to the stimulus theories of reinforcement in Chapter Seven, where we saw that monkeys would work to see a toy electric train travel in circles, that rats would run mazes without reward, and that pigeons would choose to peck at a colored disk that only informed them whether or not food was coming. Humans work puzzles, read, and do research "for fun." It is this "motivation inherent in information processing" (Hunt, 1965) to which we turn now. The question is, Why should people be so attracted to situations that confer no other benefits than to help make sense of the world?

Curiosity has been characterized as an internally driven desire for information, as a passion for learning, and as a longing or appetite for knowledge (Loewenstein, 1994). It is clearly motivational in that it directs and energizes behavior and people obtain pleasure from the activities involved. But what fundamental process or processes underlie all the activities we include under curiosity? In order to understand some of the answers to this question, we must first know a little about **control theory** and **negative feedback systems.**

Control Theory

Control theory in engineering is concerned with machines that engage in "purposive" behaviors aimed at some precisely defined goal (Hyland, 1988). The basic concept is that deviation from some norm sets a system into action. For example, in order to control room temperature, we set the thermostat at a point called the **reference criterion,** such as 72 degrees F. A sensor (called a **comparator**) detects a **difference** between the thermostat reference and the actual room temperature. When the difference (**detected error**) is large enough (e.g., 2 degrees), a heater is turned on. The rising temperature provides a **negative feedback signal,** and when the detected error is reduced to zero (room temperature = thermostat setting), the system turns off. The "purpose" of the system is to keep the room temperature at a certain level, but the "purposefulness" is entirely within the physical properties of the feedback system. Figure 12–6 illustrates the system.

In living organisms we also speak of feedback systems that reduce discrepancies, including a temperature system. Departure from an internal body temperature of 98.6 degrees F stimulates homeostatic mechanisms to return temperature to "normal" (Chapter Five), or departure from an optimal level of arousal may instigate activities to restore arousal to the optimal level. In

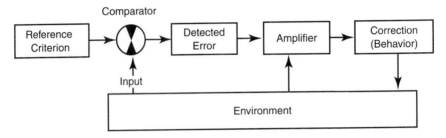

FIGURE 12–6. Basic control system. Using the system as a thermostat, a reference criterion of some temperature would be set, such as 72°. A comparator within the thermostat would detect any error between the reference criterion and the surrounding environment, such as when the temperature drops too low. The error signal would be amplified so that corrective action (turning on the furnace) would occur.

each of these instances, we can conceive of a thermostat-like mechanism that triggers appropriate activities to reduce the discrepancy between some reference condition and an actual condition.

Sokolov's model of attention.   E. N. Sokolov (1960) proposed a widely accepted motivational theory of attention based on control theory concepts, which applies to something we have all experienced. This is situations in which attention-getting stimuli go unnoticed after a while. For example, we notice when an air conditioner turns on, but we stop noticing the sound after a while. This phenomenon is called **habituation** and is readily demonstrated in the laboratory. A simple *change* in sound, however, may immediately command our attention. Thus, we also notice when the air conditioner goes off. Experimental subjects show an aroused EEG if just the pitch, but not the loudness, of a habituated tone is slightly changed. This tells us that there must be processing of the habituated stimulus inputs somewhere in the brain or we could not be aroused by a change in the stimulus. Sokolov's theory says that repetitious inputs are stored in the nervous system as a reference against which new inputs are compared. If input and storage are the same, then attention is not aroused. If an input signal is different from those previously stored, there is arousal (see Figure 12–7). Pavlov called such behavioral arousal the **orienting reflex.** We "perk up" at a novel stimulus, and by paying attention, we are more prepared to cope with either beneficial or dangerous events. If the stimulus occurs repeatedly and is benign (neither good nor bad), we habituate to it.

These illustrations of control theory tell us that across a wide spectrum of human events, we are aroused physiologically and behaviorally by incongruous events and that our arousal is reduced when the incongruity is reduced. When we solve a problem, we understand something that we did not understand before. Uncertainty about a situation produces tension and we stay with a problem until the uncertainty disappears and the tension is re-

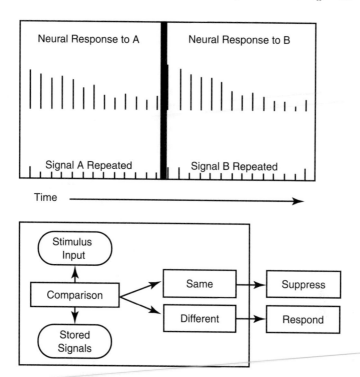

FIGURE 12–7. Sokolov model for habituation of orienting responses. The magnitude of neural responses to repetitious Signal A (such as a tone) gradually declines. If a new Signal, B, only slightly different from Signal A, is presented, there is once again a large response. According to Sokolov, stimulus inputs are compared with stored signals. If the stimuli are the same as the stored signals, there is suppression of responses to the stimuli. If the incoming stimulus is different from the stored signal, there is a neural response. The brain responds to changing stimulation.

duced. This model faces the same problem of other drive-reduction theories (Chapter Six), however, in failing to account for why we seek out problems and puzzles in the first place? Is it not this feature of curiosity that sets it apart from other behaviors?

Hunt's Information Processing Model

J. McV. Hunt (1965) championed a discrepancy view of curiosity that leaned heavily on control theory concepts but also fell back on optimal level of arousal theory to explain why people put themselves into incongruous situations. Hunt proposed that there is an optimal level of arousal, neither too high nor too low, that people seek. As a person deals intellectually with the environment, the person learns about it, and incongruities are reduced to such a low level that they are no longer arousing. However, if the environment becomes so predictable that there is no incongruity between expectation and occurrence, the person seeks out stimuli that produce incongruity. Hence, we seek out new situations, puzzles, games, problems, reading, and other sources of arousal. We may recall from Chapter Seven that Dember and Earl (1957) proposed that when we have learned to cope with a particular level of incongruity in the environment, we seek more complicated situations, so that we are always growing in our capacity to deal with events.

Loewenstein's Information-Gap Theory

Loewenstein (1994, p. 90) says that curiosity is aroused when one becomes attentive to a gap in one's knowledge. An **information gap** is the difference between what one *does* know and what one *wants* to know. What one wants to know is the reference point in a control system. We compare what we want to know with what we do know. This is the comparator in the model. If there is a discrepancy, we are aroused to do something to reduce the discrepancy (make a correction) and then we compare again. When we have corrected enough to reduce the discrepancy, we quit and move on to something else. Whether a fixed amount of new knowledge may satisfy curiosity depends on how much we want to know. For example, most people's curiosity about computers seems to be satisfied when they can run the specific programs they want to use, whether games, e-mail, word processing, browser, instant messaging, downloading MP3 files, or whatever. They are "driven" to learn what they must know to run their software, but they don't really want to know the details about ROM, RAM, gigs or megahertz. Their curiosity about computers is satisfied relatively easily because their information gap is relatively small. Other people want to know more about how computers work and actually read manuals to satisfy their curiosity.

Information-gap theory makes a variety of predictions. For example, the degree of curiosity about a piece of information should be related to the capacity of the information to close a person's information gap. This was supported in an experiment by Loewenstein, Adler, Behrens, and Gillis (1992; described in Loewenstein, 1994). Subjects were shown two lists of states and asked to guess the rule by which each list was generated. The first list had ten states and the second list had five states, but the actual rule was the same in both cases. After guessing a rule for each list, the subjects were asked to choose which rule they would like to learn. Seventy percent of the subjects chose the rule for the longer list. This result had been predicted on the grounds that the subjects would perceive that the rule for the long list would give them more information than would the rule for the short list.

The question of why people seek out discrepancies arises for Loewenstein's theory, however, just as it did for Hunt's. Why do people voluntarily put themselves into such information gaps as problem-solving situations? Loewenstein (1994, p. 90) assumed that curiosity is always aversive but that the process of satisfying curiosity is more pleasurable than the curiosity itself is aversive. A person who voluntarily puts herself into a puzzle situation must anticipate that the pleasure of solving the puzzle will be greater than the aversion of the puzzle itself. The theory postulates that curiosity satisfaction is pleasurable but offers no mechanism for the pleasure. Loewenstein rejected an optimal level of arousal explanation. We might speculate, however, that reduction of the information gap arouses the same dopamine/endorphin pleasure system that underlies other rewards. In this case we would not need to assume that curiosity is aversive.

The Need for Closure

Kruglanski and Webster (1996) propose a theory in which **need for cognitive closure** is the key construct. Need for closure is defined as a desire for an answer on a given topic, any answer, rather than continued confusion and ambiguity. It is a motivational concept similar to the information gap concept. According to the theory, people who have a high need for closure tend quickly to **seize** upon an answer to their question or problem and then to **freeze** on that answer, closing themselves to further information. Individual differences are measured by the **Need for Closure Scale** (Webster & Kruglanski, 1994). This scale has five dimensions, which are shown in Table 12–5 with a sample item for each subscale. The total scale correlates about −.28 with the Need for Cognition Scale (which is discussed shortly) and positively about .28 with scales of dogmatism, authoritarianism, and intolerance of ambiguity. Authoritarianism is related to prejudice, discrimination, desire for law and order, and unwillingness to entertain alternative views (Adorno, Frenkel-Brunswik, Levinson, & Sanford, 1950).

Need for closure is a traitlike personality characteristic but it can also be aroused by particular situations. For example, as the deadline for turning in a paper for a course approaches, there is a strong situational demand for closure on the paper. People with a high need for closure should respond more strongly to situations calling for closure than individuals with a weak need for

TABLE 12–5.　Dimensions and sample items from the Need for Closure Scale.

DIMENSION	SAMPLE SCALE ITEM
1. Preference for order	"I enjoy having a clear and structured mode of life."
2. Preference for predictability	"I dislike unpredictable situations."
3. Decisiveness	"I usually make important decisions quickly and confidently."
4. Discomfort with ambiguity	"I dislike it when a person's statement could mean many different things."
5. Closed-mindedness	"I do not usually consult many different opinions before forming my own view."

Source: Kruglanski, Webster, & Klem (1993). ©American Psychological Association, 1993. Used by permission.

closure. They should tend to base their final judgments of a problem on early cues that they are given, achieving closure quickly. Webster and Kruglanski (1994) tested this by having subjects high or low in need for closure form impressions of a hypothetical candidate for the presidency of a company. Positive and negative information about the candidate was presented in opposite orders for two groups. The usual **primacy effect** (Asch, 1946) obtained with this procedure is that the positive-then-negative group rates the candidate more favorably than the negative-then-positive, even though both groups get exactly the same information. Table 12–6, summarizes the results. The usual effect of order of information was found only for those subjects who were high in need for closure. Subjects low in need for closure did not show the classic primacy effect at all.

What are the origins of individual differences in need for closure? Kruglanski and Webster (1996) suggest only that there may be differences in personal histories or social norms. The differences may run deeper than this, however. Recall that need for closure is correlated with, among other things, authoritarianism. Some aspects of authoritarianism have been found in twin studies to have estimated heritability coefficients in the 40 percent to 50 percent range (Tesser, 1993). Thus differences in need for closure may be partially inherited just as many other personality differences are.

The Need for Cognition

Cacioppo and Petty (1982) argued that people differ in their **need for cognition** or for information and devised a "need for cognition" scale to measure such differences. They defined need for cognition as "the tendency for an individual to engage in and enjoy thinking." The scale has such items as "I really enjoy a task that involves coming up with new solutions to problems" and "When something I read confuses me, I just put it down and forget it" (scored negatively). They then had high- and low-scoring subjects do a simple or complex number-circling task for ten minutes. In the simple task, subjects were told to circle as many 1s, 5s, and 7s as they could from a list of 3,500 random digits. In the complex task, the subjects circled all 3s, any 6 that pre-

TABLE 12–6. Mean ratings of job candidate's personality as a function of need for closure and information sequence. Higher numbers are more positive evaluations.

INFORMATION SEQUENCE	NEED FOR CLOSURE CLASSIFICATION	
	HIGH NEED FOR CLOSURE	LOW NEED FOR CLOSURE
Positive-Negative	112.2	88.5
Negative-Positive	61.1	90.2

Source: Webster & Kruglanski, 1994, pp. 1049–1062, Table 5. Copyright American Psychological Association. Used by permission.

ceded a 7, and every other 4. Subjects reported enjoyment of the task on a seven-point scale. Nobody was terribly thrilled by such a boring task, but the subjects with a high need for cognition did enjoy the complex task more than the simple one, and the low-need subjects enjoyed the simple task more. It thus appears there are individual differences in the degree to which information processing activities are found pleasant and, presumably, reinforcing.

SECTION SUMMARY

1. **Information processing** theories of motivation assume an inherent motivation to learn more about or gain information about the environment. Curiosity is one such motive.

2. According to **control theory,** derived from engineering, **discrepancies** of various kinds motivate action to reduce the discrepancies. The classic example is the thermostat, which turns on a furnace or air conditioning when there is a discrepancy between room temperature and thermostat setting.

3. Sokolov proposed a motivational theory of attention which says that we **habituate** (stop responding) to repetitive stimuli but respond when there is a **stimulus change** which captures our attention.

4. According to some theories, when there are discrepancies in our information about the environment (e.g., puzzles, problems) we are motivated to fill in the gaps in our information. A problem for such theories is why we voluntarily seek out puzzles and problems.

5. **Need for Closure** refers to the desire to have an answer to a question. Sometimes people quickly "seize" on the first answer available and then "freeze" on that answer, closing themselves off to further information.

6. People also vary in their tendencies to engage in and enjoy thinking, measured by the **Need for Cognition Scale.** Differences here are relevant to the kinds of work and leisure activities that people choose.

CHAPTER THIRTEEN

Attitudes and Cognitive Consistency

What is an attitude?

How can we know what a person's attitudes are?

Are we always aware of what our own attitudes are?

Is there a genetic component to attitudes?

Is there more than one process for producing attitude change?

How does conditioning produce attitude change?

How do inconsistent thoughts or behaviors lead to attitude change?

What happens to people who depart from group standards?

THE NATURE OF ATTITUDES

What Do We Mean by Attitude?

Throughout the previous chapters we have approached motivation in terms of desire and aversion. We now define attitudes in those same terms. An attitude is a positive or negative affective response directed toward a specific person, object, event or situation. The object of the attitude lies on the hedonic continuum as illustrated in Figure 13–1, which shows a negative attitude (aversion) toward Person A and a mildly positive attitude (attraction) toward Object X. Attitudes were initially conceived as affective responses in the manner just described (Thurstone & Chave, 1929), but subsequent theorists began to argue that attitudes have three distinct components: affect, cognition, and conation (action).

Affect. This is the basic positive or negative feeling with regard to a particular person, object, or thing.

Cognition. This refers to ideas and perceptions about the attitude object. For example, what do you *think* about Republicans versus Democrats or Candidate A versus Candidate B? How does your knowledge of a candidate influence your feelings toward her? Conversely, how do your feelings influence your beliefs about people? Are you more likely to believe bad things about people you like or about people you dislike?

Conation (action). How does your attitude affect the way you behave? Are you more or less likely to vote or work for (or against) a candidate because of your attitude toward him or her? If you are highly frustrated and unhappy about the economy, how does this attitude affect your voting behavior? Are you more likely to vote against whoever you think is responsible?

In fact, however, these three components fit just about any topic in psychology and do not set attitudes off from other concepts. Attitude theorists have now moved back to the affect concept of attitude. Baron and Byrne (1997), for example, accept the definition that "attitudes are associations between objects and evaluations of those objects." It is recognized, however, that the affective component (attitude) influences cognition and action, and is reciprocally influenced by them.

Multiple attitudes. We frequently speak as if a person can hold just one attitude toward a particular attitude object, but more than one is possible. The approach-avoidance conflict (Chapter Ten) is a well-worn example of two attitudes held simultaneously. One is positive (evoking approach), the other is negative (evoking avoidance). Similarly, we may hold different attitudes toward the same person in different contexts. We might have a positive attitude toward a particular person in a work context, but a less positive or

Object:	Person A	Object X	
Attitude:	−5	0	+5
	Aversion	Neutrality	Desire

FIGURE 13–1. Objects of attitude (Person A, Object X) lying along the hedonic continuum.

negative attitude in a social context. Finally, there is increasing concern with the difference between **explicit attitudes,** as shown on standard attitude scales, and **implicit attitudes,** which a person may not consciously recognize in himself (Ajzen, 2001; Greenwald, McGhee, & Schwartz, 1998; Wilson, Lindsey, & Schooler, 2000).

Attitude Measurement

If an attitude is an emotional reaction to an attitude object, then any visible sign of that emotion could be an indicator of attitude. If I smile when a particular person enters the room, that surely says something different about my attitude toward that person than if I frown. In general, signs of positive affect and approach behaviors are indicators of positive attitudes, and signs of negative affect and escape/avoidance behaviors are indicators of negative attitudes.

For many practical reasons such behavioral indicators are not widely used. Those measures that are used, however, are intended to locate an attitude object on an hedonic scale ranging from favorable to unfavorable. We discuss three different approaches to measurement: **Likert scales,** the **semantic differential,** and the **automatic activation of attitudes,** particularly as exemplified by the **Implicit Attitude Test (IAT).** The first two are widely used, but the IAT is more a research tool at the moment. In addition to these, in public polling procedures there are often simple "yes" or "no" (or, "for" or "against") alternative answers to questions. For example, "Do you think the President is doing a good job, Yes or No?" For detailed discussion of attitude measures, see Eagly and Chaiken (1993).

Likert scale. On a Likert scale you indicate the extent to which you agree or disagree with a strongly positive or negative statement about an attitude object, typically on a 5-point scale as illustrated in Figure 13–2. Note,

---

Democracy is the best form of government possible

Agree: 1 2 3 4 5: Disagree

FIGURE 13–2. Example of a Likert scale, recording agreement of disagreement with extreme statements. If the statement were worded negatively (e.g., democracy is the worst form of government possible), strong disagreement would indicate a positive attitude toward democracy.

however, that not all numbered scales are Likert scales. Likert scales are uniquely characterized by measuring agreement with extreme statements.

Semantic differential. With this procedure, an attitude object is located at one of seven locations between sets of bipolar adjectives, illustrated in Figure 13–3. Statistical analyses consistently show that three underlying dimensions account for the **connotative meaning** of such polar opposite words. Connotative meaning is the subjective (in this case emotional) meaning of words, as contrasted with their **denotative meaning** (dictionary meaning). These three dimensions, along with sample bipolar adjective pairs as specific illustrations, are (1) **evaluation:** good-bad, pleasant-unpleasant, foul-fragrant; (2) **activation:** fast-slow, active-passive, sharp-dull; and (3) **potency:** heavy-light, strong-weak (Osgood, Suci, & Tannebaum, 1957). We can diagram a three-dimensional **attitude space** into which we can put various attitude objects and see their similarities and differences. For most purposes, a two-dimensional space works well, just using the evaluative and activity dimensions.

Automatic activation of attitudes. A continual problem in the use of attitude measures is the extent to which such direct measures as Likert scales may be influenced by nonattitudinal factors. For example, it may be socially undesirable or politically incorrect to express one's true attitude with regard to some issue. Therefore, researchers have attempted to assess attitudes by more indirect procedures, such as the automatic activation method. This is an indirect method that relies on the fact that stimuli can automatically activate evaluative responses even though we may not be aware of them. These evaluative responses can then affect our behavior in measurable ways. Suppose that we have as an attitude object the word "vodka," which an individual evaluates positively. If this word is used as a **prime** (being presented before another word), it automatically activates a positive evaluation. If a *target adjective* following the prime is also positive (e.g., the word "happy"), a subject indicates more quickly that the target adjective has a positive connotation than if there were no prime or if the prime were just a meaningless string of letters (e.g., XXXX). Conversely, a negative prime facilitates identification of a negative adjective (Fazio, Sanbonmatsu, Powell, & Kardes, 1986). Since this is a

---

Chili Peppers

Good	___:___:___:___:___:___:___	Bad
Active	___:___:___:___:___:___:___	Passive
Strong	___:___:___:___:___:___:___	Weak

FIGURE 13–3. Semantic differential. A check mark is made in one of the seven spaces between each pair of polar opposite adjectives.

relatively complicated procedure, it is interesting only if it produces espe-cially interesting results as compared with simpler measures. In fact, the re-sults sometimes are interestingly different.

The Implicit Association Test is based on the principle of automatic ac-tivation of attitudes (Greenwald, Banaji, Rudman, Farnham, Nosek, & Mellot, 2002; Greenwald, McGhee, & Schwartz, 1998). The overall procedure is more complex than we can describe here, but a number of results can be summa-rized. Nosek, Banaji, & Greenwald (2002) set up a Web site where "drop in" visitors could actually be subjects on-line. The authors were well aware of the problems associated with interpreting such data, but with appropriate safe-guards a number of clear results emerged from the over 600,000 volunteer subjects. These were most notable in comparisons of the IAT results with re-sults from explicit measures using standard attitude scale items. For example, preferences for whites over blacks declined steadily along a dimension of re-spondents from "strongly conservative" to "strongly liberal," but much less so for the implicit reaction time measures than for responses to standard atti-tude scales. Another result was that on an explicit measure, the preference for young over old declined steadily as a function of age of the respondents (from 8 to 71+ years). On the IAT, however, there was no drop at all—sug-gesting that older respondents really favored youth. The IAT does not neces-sarily uncover truth in our psyches, but such indirect approaches are provoca-tive new methods which should deepen our understanding of the nature of attitudes and stereotypes (Greenwald, et al., 2002).

When Do Attitudes Predict Behavior?

The ability of attitudes to predict behavior is one of the major topics in the field of attitude research and theory (Ajzen, 2001). Attitudes are not, and cannot be, the sole predictors of behavior. Let us remind ourselves that Be-havior = f (person, environment) and that multiple aspects of both the per-son and the environment determine behavior. Suppose we have a politician in favor of liberal legislation running for office in a conservative district. The politician may express attitudes that do not completely reflect her own views simply because she must get elected in order to have any effect on legislation at all. The expressed attitude might not be a very reliable predictor of subse-quent behavior. It is always a good idea to pay attention to what people do, not just what they say.

If attitudes are measured properly, they can predict behavior rather well, as shown by the success of political pollsters in recent years. Election outcomes can be accurately predicted within two or three percentage points, depending on the size of the sample. In a carefully conducted research study, Bowman and Fishbein (1978) found a very high correlation ($r = .80$) between attitudes and subsequent voting on a referendum for a nuclear power plant. Predictions are best if a number of different conditions prevail: (1) if the attitude measure is specific to an object or issue (e.g., attitude toward a nuclear power plant); (2) if the attitude measure is reliable; (3) if nonattitudinal considerations do not override accurate attitude statements; (4) if survey sampling is appropriate (e.g., random sampling from the relevant population); and (5) if the attitude does not change between the time the measure is collected and the time the to-be-predicted behavior occurs (e.g., voting). Intervening events may affect attitudes (e.g., a nuclear accident, war, change in economy, something about a candidate). Discussions of theories of the attitude-behavior relationship are discussed in Ajzen (2001).

Biology of Attitudes

Genetics.   Psychologists have historically treated attitudes as if they are entirely learned, but there is good evidence for biological inheritance as well. Tesser (1993, p. 129) observed that "the list of behavioral domains that appear to have sizable heritabilities is both long and surprising" and cites studies showing heritability coefficients in the range of 50 percent. These include studies of job satisfaction, attitudes toward God, attitudes toward drinking alcohol (but not drinking coffee or smoking cigarettes), the political attitude of authoritarianism, and radical political views. Attitudes with high heritability are stronger than attitudes with low heritability, they are responded to more quickly, and they are harder to change. The larger question then is, What are the mechanisms by which the genetic effects are demonstrated? Tesser suggests that sensory structures, body chemistry, intelligence, temperament and activity level, and conditionability all play a role. In a global way, genetic factors may affect such general dispositions as mood or extraversion (which has a genetic component), and these dispositions may affect the development of positive or negative attitudes. Genetic inheritance always interacts with environmental events.

Physiological measurement.   If attitudes are emotional responses, then we should expect some physiological responses to be correlated with attitude arousal. Cacioppo, Crites, and Gardner (1996) recorded **event-related brain potentials (ERPs)** from the scalp over the two hemispheres. Event-related potentials are specific electrical responses of the brain to stimuli. The ERPs were larger over the right hemisphere than the left when subjects were asked to categorize food items as positive or negative (evaluative judgments) than when asked to categorize them as vegetable versus nonvegetable (cognitive judgments). During the cognitive judgments, the right and left hemisphere ERPs were equal. This finding matches the pattern for emotional responsiveness by the brain discussed in Chapter Two. Specifically, there appears to be greater right-brain participation in emotional acts, including those related to attitudes.

SECTION SUMMARY

1. An **attitude** is a positive or negative affective response directed toward a specific person, object, or situation. The attitude object falls somewhere on a hedonic continuum. Attitudes influence our thoughts about an attitude object and our actions toward that object, but we can hold more than one attitude toward an object.
2. There are many ways of measuring attitudes. Two widely used self-report techniques are **Likert scales** and the **semantic differential.** The **Implicit Attitude Test** uses a less direct approach called the **automatic activation method,** which measures reaction times, and is less subject to social desirability effects.
3. Attitudes are not the only determinants of behavior, and measures of attitude do not always predict behavior well. A number of different factors determine how well attitude measures will predict behavior. For example, attitudes toward more specific objects or events predict future behavior better.
4. There is a genetic component to attitudes, although the mechanism by which this works is not clear. There is a greater right hemisphere involvement with attitudes, as with emotion in general.

PROCESSES UNDERLYING ATTITUDE DEVELOPMENT AND CHANGE

Dual Process Theories

Many different aspects of attitude development and change have in recent years been subsumed under dual process theories, notably the **elaboration likelihood model** (**ELM;** Petty & Cacioppo, 1986) and the **heuristic-systematic model** (**HSM;** Chaiken, Liberman & Eagly, 1989). These models assume that there are two different types of processes involved in attitude development and change. One process involves systematic, effortful thinking about a problem. The other is more mindless, using heuristics (shortcuts) to arrive at attitudes, without necessarily thinking at all (sometimes attitudes arise automatically in the presence of certain cues, or occur without our awareness of why they occur). In the ELM model, which we use to exemplify this theoretical approach, these are called two routes to attitude change, the **central route** and the **peripheral route** (Eagly & Chaiken, 1993; Myers, 2002; Petty & Cacioppo, 1986; Petty, Wegener, & Fabrigar, 1997).

The elaboration likelihood model.   The ELM proposes that the type of communication which will be most effective depends on the readiness and ability of an audience to elaborate on the message being sent. It is not a matter of one or the other route being "best" for changing attitudes, but under what conditions one or the other is more effective. Neither are the two routes mutually exclusive, they may reinforce each other.

The central route. This is the route of information and rational thought. When people are motivated and able to think systematically about an issue, this route is effective. For example, in the process of buying a car a person may compare prices, features, service histories of different models of car, and so on. Or, in reading job applications a manager may make careful comparisons of potential employees. The bigger, more important the problem is to a person, the more likely she will be ready and willing to scrutinize information carefully. The phrase elaboration likelihood refers to the extent to which a person is likely to engage in such effortful work. We might summarize central route processes by calling them more cognitive than peripheral route processes.

The peripheral route. If a person is unwilling, uninterested, or unable to engage in careful thought about attitude-related material, he or she may be more influenced by shortcut cues that trigger positive or negative attitudes without much thought. For example, if a person is tired, in a hurry, or preoccupied with something else, the peripheral route may be more effective in changing an attitude. Such cues may involve affect arousal by conditioned stimuli, by emotional priming stimuli, or by automatic activation of attitudes. For example, celebrities may be more influential in changing attitudes toward a product in a commercial. Many such shortcuts are motivational or emotional in nature and are hence of more interest in the context of this book.

Classical Conditioning

Classical conditioning plays an important role in attitude development and change (Staats, 1983; Staats & Staats, 1958). If the economy shows a sharp decline and people lose their jobs, they are likely to associate these events with the most visible person in the government, the president. We would diagram this association in classical conditioning terms as shown in Figure 13–4. The slander technique of guilt by association also seems a clear

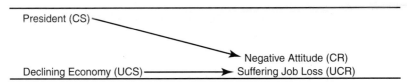

FIGURE 13–4. Classical conditioning of attitudes. If the president is associated with bad events, such as losing one's job, he is likely to be viewed negatively. Interestingly, in 1998 when President Clinton was in difficulty on account of his association with Monica Lewinsky, his popularity was reaching an all-time high. This trend was generally thought to be due in no small part to the fact that the economy had been doing exceptionally well for several years.

example of such conditioning. You associate someone's name with something bad, and by association that person becomes "guilty" and therefore also "bad." In the 1950s, the senator from Wisconsin, Joseph McCarthy, used this technique widely, associating the names of highly respectable citizens with communism, thereby causing them to lose jobs. This practice was particularly destructive in the Hollywood community of writers, directors, and actors. On the positive side, there is celebrity advertising, by which a product becomes "good" by being associated with a famous athlete or other personality. There are thought to be two types of conditioning, however, **signal conditioning** and **evaluative conditioning,** and attitudes are associated with the latter.

Signal conditioning.   In signal conditioning, an organism learns that one event will follow from another. The Pavlovian dog learns that food (unconditioned stimulus) will follow the sound of the can opener (conditioned stimulus). Subsequently, when the can opener sounds the animal makes a response (e.g., salivation) that it previously made only to the food. The process is conceived as being cognitive in nature, not that the dog will necessarily come to *like* the can opener itself.

Evaluative conditioning.   Evaluative conditioning refers to the transfer of emotional responses from one stimulus to another, and it is this evaluative transfer that characterizes attitude change through classical conditioning (Baeyens, Eelen, & Van den Bergh, 1990; De Houwer, Thomas, & Baeyens, 2001; Levey & Martin, 1987; Martin & Levey, 1978; Razran, 1954). The terminology and procedures for signal and evaluative conditioning are the same, but evaluative conditioning is said to differ from signal conditioning in several important ways: (1) evaluative conditioning can be unconscious and does not depend on the subject's awareness of the stimuli involved; (2) evaluative conditioning is thought to produce a long-lasting evaluative change that is highly resistant to extinction; and (3) evaluative conditioning does not necessarily involve such biologically significant UCSs as food or pain, although it may.

The most common paradigm to study evaluative conditioning has used a procedure like the following, introduced by Levey and Martin (1975). They had subjects sort a set of fifty unfamiliar paintings into three piles labeled "liked," "neutral," and "disliked." On the basis of these sorts, the pictures were paired and presented in these sequences: neutral-liked, neutral-disliked, neutral-neutral, liked-neutral, and disliked-neutral. The pictures were rated for subsequent liking after the paired presentations. The evaluation of the liked and disliked pictures was transferred to the neutral pictures, as judged by the change in ratings of the neutral pictures.

Other researchers have questioned whether evaluative conditioning is truly different from signal conditioning, or whether it is even conditioning at all (Davey, 1994; Öhman, 1983; Shanks & Dickinson, 1990). However, in a well-controlled experiment designed to take into account various criticisms, Olson and Fazio (2001) obtained results indicating that evaluative conditioning of attitudes occurs and can do so without the subjects' awareness. Under the guise of a study of vigilance, on a computer screen the researchers randomly paired several hundred words and images with either positive, neutral, or negative images. Consistently, however, they paired the image of one Pokemon character with positive images or words and a different character with negative ones. Then, in a surprise test, subjects were asked to rate their liking of the images. The Pokemon image paired with positive stimuli received significantly more positive ratings than the one paired with negative images, but subjects were found to be unaware of the pairings. The experiment thus appeared to demonstrate evaluative conditioning of attitude change.

The mere exposure effect. In Chapter Two we described the mere exposure effect, which is that "merely" experiencing some stimulus repeatedly may increase liking for that stimulus. But why should this occur? Robert Zajonc (2001), the person most identified with research and theory on this effect, suggests that the mere exposure effect may actually represent a form of classical conditioning. Instead of a bell as a conditioned stimulus and salivation as a conditioned response, we have a neutral repeated stimulus (such as a Chinese ideograph) as the conditioned stimulus and liking as the conditioned response. But what is the *unconditioned* stimulus? Zajonc proposes that the *absence* of any negative consequence of the stimulus is the unconditioned stimulus and that positive affect generated by the lack of an aversive outcome is the unconditioned response. We may recall the learned safety hypothesis from our earlier discussion of feeding behavior (Chapter Four). This hypothesis holds that if an animal finds that a new food is safe (doesn't make it sick) that the food becomes more attractive, much like Zajonc proposes. Most importantly, Zajonc and his colleagues (Monahan, Murphy & Zajonc, 2000) also demonstrated that (1) when people are exposed to repeated stimuli they develop a more positive mood than if exposed to nonrepeated stimuli, and (2) this positive mood produces a greater liking of various unrelated stimuli. In short, the procedure does appear to produce positive affect which transfers to other stimuli.

Affective priming. We have previously (Chapter Two) discussed research showing that neutral stimuli can be subconsciously primed by happy or angry faces (Murphy & Zajonc, 1993; Winkielman, Zajonc, & Schwarz, 1997). Specifically, when preceded by an angry or happy face presented too quickly to be recognized, Chinese ideographs were rated more negative or positive according to which face was presented. This suggests that fleeting stimuli, possibly random occurrences in everyday life, might influence our evaluative judgments of following events without our knowing this is happening.

Imitation and Reinforcement

Children tend to take on the attitudes of their parents. They hear parents say positive or negative things and imitate these statements or actions. In turn, they are reinforced by parents for the imitation. We talk about adolescent rebellion, but at the level of politics, there is a strong association between the way high school students vote in straw polls and the way elections actually come out. Since the students don't vote, they must be reflecting the political views of their voting elders. This possibility does not mean, of course, that high school students reflect their parents on all issues (e.g., music, sex, drinking, driving). Children may find more reinforcement (or punishment) from their peers than from their parents on many issues. What this says, however, is that there are multiple sources of imitation and reinforcement, not only parents.

SECTION SUMMARY

1. **Dual process models** of attitude development and change posit two different processes. One process (the **central route**) involves systematic, effortful thinking about an attitude-related object. The second process (the **peripheral route**) is more mindless, uses heuristics (shortcuts) to arrive at attitudes, and may not involve conscious thinking at all.

2. Classical (Pavlovian) conditioning plays an important role in attitude development and change. We have more positive or negative attitudes toward people who are associated with good or bad events. A conditioned stimulus itself may become emotionally good or bad (**evaluative conditioning**) in addition to being a **signal** that something good or bad is going to happen.

3. We are not necessarily **aware** of events that influence our attitudes. If we are simply exposed to neutral stimuli repeatedly, we tend to like them more even though we do not know why (the **mere exposure effect**). This may occur through a conditioning process. We can also be subconsciously primed by positive or negative stimuli to like or dislike the stimuli that follow.

4. Children tend to take on the attitudes of their parents, imitating their elders and being rewarded by their elders for attitude-related behaviors.

ATTITUDES AND COGNITIVE CONSISTENCY

Theories of cognitive consistency dominated the field of social psychology in the 1950s and 1960s, but in the last thirty years have fallen from favor as a major research topic. Greenwald et al. (2002, p. 3) suggest several reasons for this, not the least of which is that consistency theories became "so thoroughly woven into the fabric of social psychology as to have acquired the character of unquestioned wisdom, no longer requiring research investigation." Other factors were also involved, but represented a change of interest in the field rather than a lack of theoretical importance of consistency theories or demonstration of their ineffectiveness.

Meaning of Cognitive Consistency

Cognitive consistency refers to our perception that events are occurring as we expect them to. **Inconsistency,** or **incongruity,** exists when an event is perceived to be different from expectation. For example, a dog with wings would be incongruous only to a person who has already become familiar with dogs without wings and learned to expect them. In the *control theory* terminology of Chapter Twelve, the familiar (expected) dog is a *reference point,* and a mechanism called a *comparator* detects an *error* (the difference between the expected dog and the observed dog-with-wings). This detected error (the incongruity) triggers arousal in the observer, and the observer tries to reduce the arousal by reducing the incongruity. Incongruity has a *drivelike motivational property,* and the goal of the organism is to reduce such incongruity. It is this motivational property that interests us. We must deal with consistency as perceived by an individual, however, because consistency or inconsistency are often in the eye of the beholder. One person may detect in unfolding events a consistent pattern that completely eludes someone else.

Balance Theory

Suppose that I like you and you like me, but we are in strong disagreement about a political candidate. We are in what Heider (1958) called a state of **imbalance.** If we agreed on the merits of the candidate, we would be in a state of **balance.** Imbalance is considered aversive, and we would therefore do something to reduce the imbalance. When "equilibrium" is restored, we are "satisfied." Imbalance is therefore like drive: Imbalance initiates action, and its reduction reinforces that action. There are a variety of cognitive or behavioral things one might do to reduce imbalance. For example, you might change your mind about the candidate, or about me, or about both of us. Or you might avoid me until after the election. Heider's theory has been widely used in social psychology, often taken as a fundamental principle on which to build other concepts (e.g., Greenwald et al., 2002). It has also been used in consumer psychology (Woodside & Chebat, 2001).

A simple state of perceived **interpersonal imbalance** can occur with just two people. If Frank likes Jane, and Jane likes Frank, they both have a positive relation toward each other. If the **affective sign** of the relation is the same for both individuals (either positive or negative), the situation is balanced, and there is no **strain** (motivation) to change it. A particularly dramatic two-person example is unrequited love: One person has a strong positive sentiment for another, but the second person is uncaring toward the first. It is here that we may see rapidly changing love-hate relationships. The individual whose positive sentiment is not returned may quickly turn negative toward the second party, thus bringing the relationship back into balance. Since the problem is perceptual, there may be interesting distortions. For example, Frank may like Jane and perceive that she does not like him, when in fact she does. Frank's perception of the situation, not the "real" state of affairs, determines the imbalance in his mind. Hess (2000) used balance theory to predict a variety of strategies that people use to distance themselves from disliked partners. Davis and Rusbult (2001) also studied what they called "attitude alignment, the tendency of interacting partners to modify their attitudes in such a manner as to achieve attitudinal congruence" (p. 65). Their results also supported balance theory predictions, that people would tend to align their diverging attitudes if the attitudes were salient in the relationship.

The more general and more widely researched case, however, is like our initial illustration. It involves a person (A), another person (B), and an entity (X), which may be an object, a third person, an idea, or an event. Using the symbolism popularized by Theodore Newcomb, there are three possible pairs of relationships within an **ABX triad:** (1) AB, where A holds some affect toward B; (2) AX, where A holds some affect toward X; and (3) BX, where B holds some affect toward X. A is the person with whom, by definition, we are concerned at a particular time. It is A's perception of the relationships that we are examining. Each of these three relationships can be positive or negative, and the general rule is that a triad is **balanced** if the algebraic product of the three is positive and **imbalanced** if the product is negative. This rule gives four balanced and four imbalanced triads, summarized in Table 13–1. Figure 13–5 illustrates two balanced and two imbalanced triads involving you (A), me (B), and the president of the United States (X).

Let us put Relationship 3 (balanced) and Relationship 6 (imbalanced) from Figure 13–5 into verbal form. In 3, you are A and have negative affect toward both me (B) and the president (X); since I like the president, the triad is balanced from the point of view of the focal person (A, who is you). In Relationship 6, you have a negative attitude toward me, but we are both positive toward the president. By definition, this represents an imbalanced situation, and you are therefore expected to change your attitude toward one of us. In any real situation the *sign* (+ or −) and *intensity* of affect would be

TABLE 13–1. **Balanced and imbalanced relationships with all combinations of positive and negative *AB*, *AX*, and *BX* relationships.**

	BALANCED				IMBALANCED		
	AB	AX	BX		AB	AX	BX
1.	+	+	+	5.	−	−	−
2.	+	−	−	6.	−	+	+
3.	−	−	+	7.	+	+	−
4.	−	+	−	8.	+	−	+

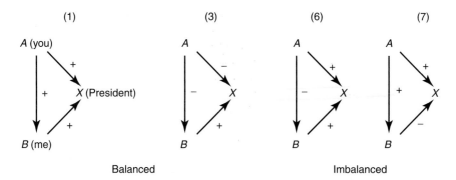

FIGURE 13–5. Balanced triads (1 and 3) and imbalanced triads (6 and 7). See text and Table 13–1 for details.

determined by many factors (you might like some of the president's policies, but not others), and the degree of imbalance would in turn depend on these intensities as well as on signs. A mild imbalance would not produce much effort toward reducing the imbalance. We also assume that X is of interest or relevance to both A and B before there could be any imbalance. If neither A nor B was concerned about X one way or another, there would be no triad.

Although imbalance is generally considered undesirable, we can readily see, from the point of view of activation theory, for example, that some imbalance (like some activation or some frustration) often may be sought. Up to a point, we may enjoy political arguments with our friends.

Newcomb (1968) proposed that balanced relations 1 and 2 in Table 13–1 are in fact different from 3 and 4. Considerable research cited by Newcomb indicates that although 1 and 2 are desirable, 3, 4, 5, and 6 are all mildly undesirable, and 7 and 8 are the most undesirable. Newcomb, therefore, prefers to consider 1 and 2 balanced (pleasant); 3, 4, 5, and 6 nonbalanced (relatively neutral); and 7 and 8 imbalanced (unpleasant). The reason for this view may be that negative relations are unpleasant, even though they may be balanced. Two people who do not like each other form a balanced situation, but neither may enjoy the situation. The evidence cited by Newcomb is not always consistent, but it does point up the fact that the logical relations (algebraic products) defining balance and imbalance do not necessarily coincide with the individual's perception of the situation or the affect that he or she experiences.

Are Consistency Effects Conscious?

Greenwald et al. (2002) found a number of predicted triadic relationships when they used the Implicit Association Test, but not with explicit self-report measures and the obvious question is Why? Until Nisbett and Wilson (1977) challenged the assumption that all the important psychological processes are available to consciousness, there was no reason to study unconscious consistency effects, and little methodology available for doing so. There is now reason to look more closely on cognitive consistency effects as unconscious processes, which, in the elaboration likelihood model, would put them into the peripheral route, as well as the central route.

ATTITUDES AND COGNITIVE DISSONANCE

When Prophecy Fails

For almost two millennia, there have been recurring predictions of the second coming of Christ, the impending end of the world, or other cataclysmic events. These have been accompanied by individuals claiming to have "divine warning," sometimes including very specific predicted dates for the catastrophic occurrences. In the early 1950s in Minnesota, a Mrs. Kreech began to receive messages, first from "Elder Brother" and then from a being named "Sananda," that such an event was going to occur. The messages were received via *automatic writing* (not under the volition of the writer) and warned that the Earth was going to split from the northern polar region down to Mexico, followed by great flooding. Mrs. Kreech told others of these spiritual messages, and a small group of believers formed. Over about three months, the messages continued, including word that a spaceship from the planet Ceron would come to take away the faithful. This event was to happen on December 21, which the group believed was the actual birth date of Christ. The group prepared for the event and held vigil, waiting for the spaceship. Needless to say the ship did not arrive, the Earth did not split, and there was no great flood. The members of the group, however, seemed undaunted and instead of losing faith some of them began to proselytize more strongly.

The preceding events were described at book length by Festinger, Riecken, & Schachter (1956), and the whole episode is often taken to be the prototypical example of **cognitive dissonance.** When faced with a firm belief (the cataclysm and the spaceship) and its disconfirmation, at least some of the believers held their belief even more strongly. Cognitive dissonance theory is an account of why people sometimes respond to contradictory events in such paradoxical ways.

Definition of Cognitive Dissonance

Cognitive dissonance is said to occur when two beliefs are incongruent or are logically contradictory. The cult members' belief that a spaceship was coming was incongruent with the fact that it did not come. Such inconsistencies are considered aversive. According to the theory, then, some of the members reduced this aversive state, not by surrendering their belief, but by rationalizing the failure of the spaceship to come. Perhaps the world was saved because they were strong believers. They then became even stronger believers.

There are many possible ways of reducing dissonance, but the ones most researched involve a change in cognitions. A chain-smoker thinking about possible lung cancer might add a new cognition ("the lung cancer research has produced ambiguous results") or might alter existing ones ("cancer really isn't all that likely"). Note that the cognitions (beliefs) are important, but not necessarily accurate. To deal with our dissonance, we might seek more information, such as reading further on the problem of lung cancer. Doing this could lead to the apocryphal outcome that "I read so much about lung cancer and smoking that I gave up reading." Facetious, perhaps, but not an entirely unreal possibility. On the other hand, a heavy smoker might change his behavior and give up cigarettes as a means of reducing dissonance.

Dissonance, however, would not be the only factor determining whether a person stops smoking. Dissonance theory is not all-encompassing and was never intended to be. Other desires and aversions might override dissonance, and we might even engage in dissonance-producing activities. Group pressure, for example, might push an adolescent into doing something that is at odds with her beliefs about herself.

Attitude Change and Forced Compliance

The most widely used approach to the study of cognitive dissonance employs a procedure involving **forced compliance** and **insufficient justification.** The experimental situation is structured so that the subjects find it difficult not to do what the experimenter asks (forced compliance), but at the same time they have little apparent reason for doing so (insufficient justification). Festinger and Carlsmith (1959) reported an experiment often used as the standard for explaining and describing dissonance. Their subjects were initially required to do the very tedious task of turning pegs in holes. When they were finished, the subjects were asked if they would help persuade other persons to be subjects. This persuasion would involve telling the potential subjects that the task was interesting. The only potential subject was in fact a confederate of the researchers.

Half the real subjects were told they would receive a $20 retainer for their services, and the rest that they would receive $1. All subjects agreed to serve (indicating the power of the forced-compliance aspect). The critical measure of dissonance reduction was how the subjects evaluated the task after trying to persuade the assistant. It was independently ascertained that the task really was boring and that making positive statements about the task would be discrepant with one's actual evaluation of the task. Incentive theory might say that the subjects receiving $20 would view the task as more attractive, since it is associated with a large incentive. Receiving $20 should produce little dissonance, however, because $20 is *adequate justification* for making the discrepant statements. Therefore, according to dissonance theory, the subjects receiving $1 should show the most positive evaluation of the task because they come to believe what they are saying because this reduces their dissonance. And that is how the experiment turned out. As Festinger commonly described the results, "You come to love what you suffer for." The experiment is diagrammed in Figure 13–6.

Another, more widely used procedure (Cohen, Brehm, & Fleming, 1958), asks college students to write essays supporting a view opposite to their own opinion on a matter of current interest, such as campus parking fees (students are uniformly against increased parking fees). Some students are given minimal reasons for arguing counter to their own position, but others are given such good reasons as that helping the experimenter will allow the experimenter to complete his dissertation so he can get his Ph.D. on time. Again, subjects with minimal justification change more favorably toward the view they had been forced to support than did subjects with greater justification.

Conditions Necessary to Produce Attitude Change

Research over the years has shown, however, that it takes more than just conflicting cognitions to produce attitude change in dissonance experiments. The following conditions are also necessary.

Belief in free choice. Research has consistently shown that subjects must perceive that they freely chose to engage in behavior that contradicts their attitudes. The subject must believe that he or she actually freely chose to engage in the counterattitudinal behavior. In fact, the "forced compliance" paradigm is one in which virtually all subjects choose to engage in the behavior, so there is little real choice, except in the subjects' minds. In practice, subjects are placed into high choice versus low choice conditions. In the Festinger and Carlsmith experiment, subjects in the $20 condition had low choice, whereas those in the $1 condition had high choice. So, a basic condi-

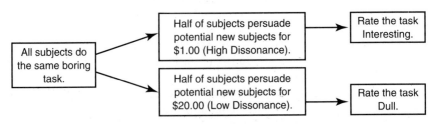

FIGURE 13–6. The experimental plan and results of the Festinger-Carlsmith cognitive dissonance experiment. The *High Dissonance* subjects seemed to convince themselves that the boring task was actually rather interesting.

tion for getting dissonance effects is that subjects be in a counterattitudinal, high choice condition. Proattitudinal essays, regardless of choice, are not expected to produce dissonance.

Intent to deceive.   The subject must believe that she or he is doing something (e.g., writing a counterattitudinal essay) that will be deceptive as far as real attitude is concerned. Deception is intended if a person (1) perceives she or he has a choice between making or not making a statement against her or his own attitude, (2) knows that someone will or will not be deceived, and (3) chooses to make the counterattitudinal statement. If a person does not foresee the consequences of her or his possible actions, then intent is not present or can be denied. In this case, attitude change does not occur (Cooper & Fazio, 1984).

Belief that the action affects someone.   Nel, Helmreich, and Aronson (1969) found that subjects giving counterattitudinal speeches to an audience changed their own attitude only if the audience was perceived as noncommittal with regard to the topic (legalization of marijuana). If the audience was perceived as either firmly for or against legalization and hence would not change, the speaker (the experimental subject) showed no attitude change. The subject must believe that he or she has had an effect on someone and must find this belief annoying. The subject finds it unpleasant to believe that he or she has deceived someone and does what he or she can (attitude change) to reduce the unpleasantness.

Major Questions about Dissonance Theory

Are dissonant cognitions necessary for dissonance effects?   The heart of dissonance theory is that aversive dissonance produces attitude change as a means of reducing the dissonance. Unfortunately, direct tests of this presupposition have not always supported the theory. Scher and Cooper (1989) had different groups of subjects write essays either in favor of (proattitudinal) or against (counterattitudinal) increasing student fees (another topic guaranteed to have all students on the same side). Half of each group believed that their essays would have the intended effect on the school's Board of Trustees, but the other half were led to believe that their essays would have the opposite effect (a boomerang effect). The conditions that were expected to have aversive consequences for the subjects, whether or not consistent with their real attitude, produced attitude change. The conclusion is that expected aversive consequences of writing the essay (probable increase in fees) produces attitude change, not inconsistency with one's own position. This outcome is not detected in the typical dissonance experiment.

Johnson, Kelly, and LeBlanc (1995) also tested the inconsistency hypothesis by having subjects telephone a confederate and make arguments that were either consistent or inconsistent with their own attitudes. The subjects were given controlled feedback indicating that the consequences would be aversive or not, regardless of the attitude position they took. Unlike the Scher and Cooper results, attitude toward the topic changed only when behaviors were both inconsistent and counterattitudinal, as predicted by dissonance theory. Harmon-Jones (2000) has also reported that dissonance increases negative affect and that negative affect is reduced following attitude change. We are thus left with the conclusion that aversion is necessary, but it is less sure that the aversion must be produced by negative consequences of one's actions.

Does dissonance produce physiological arousal? If dissonance has drive-like arousal properties, there should be evidence for such arousal independently of the measure of attitude change. Three lines of evidence are taken to support the existence of such arousal (Cooper & Fazio, 1984): (1) drive-like effects on simple versus complex tasks; (2) attribution effects, based on predictions from cognitive-arousal theory; and (3) physiological measures.

1. **Drivelike effects of dissonance on performance.** According to Hull's drive theory (Chapter Six, here), high levels of drive should facilitate performance on simple, dominant responses but interfere with performance on more complex, nondominant responses. Several early studies indicated that high dissonance did have performance effects similar to those produced by high anxiety (e.g., Cottrell & Wack, 1967; Waterman, 1969). Unfortunately, attitude changes were not demonstrated in the same experiments. Pallak and Pittman (1972) subsequently did report attitude change along with the drivelike effects, but the amount of evidence for both of these occurring together is not great.

2. **Attribution and dissonance.** Following the Schachter and Singer (1962) cognitive-arousal theory, it can be argued that dissonance-produced arousal should be subject to cognitive labeling the same as any other arousal. If the arousal is attributed to the dissonance, attitude change should occur. But if the attribution is directed to some other source, attitude change should not occur. In support of the attribution hypothesis, Zanna and Cooper (1974) found that subjects given a placebo pill with the supposed side effect of producing tension did not show as much attitude change as did subjects given the placebo without this supposed side effect. The arousal was presumably attributed to the pill rather than to dissonance, so the subjects did not engage in dissonance-reducing attitude change. Conversely, subjects under high dissonance conditions did not show attitude change if given phenobarbital, a central nervous system depressant (Cooper, Zanna, & Taves, 1978). Presumably, the drug reduced the dissonance-produced arousal, so that there was no need for further dissonance-reducing activity. Attitude change was also heightened by misattributing external arousal to dissonance. Subjects given a pill containing amphetamine (which increases physiological arousal) showed greater attitude change than control subjects.

3. **Physiological measures of dissonance arousal.** Dissonance theory was around for twenty-five years before anyone reported a direct measure of arousal in a dissonance experiment, when Croyle and Cooper (1983) attempted to measure arousal with the galvanic skin response (GSR). They used the standard proce-

dure of having subjects write essays in opposition to their own attitudes. Supporting dissonance theory, only high-dissonance subjects (high choice, counterattitudinal essay) showed elevated GSR levels immediately after writing their essays. Unfortunately, this experiment did not attempt to demonstrate a *reduction* of the GSR following attitude change, which the theory predicts should occur. In a later experiment, Elkin and Leippe (1986) found that high-dissonance subjects showed larger GSR increments than low-dissonance subjects, but the GSR did not go down within even five minutes after the subjects had expressed their changed attitude. This is in contradiction to the theory, which says that attitude change should be followed quickly by dissonance reduction. Thus in two experiments it appears that autonomic arousal (GSR) may be produced by dissonance, but there is no evidence that arousal reduction accounts for attitude change.

Although use of the GSR is a step in the right direction, we have also seen (Chapter Six) that arousal cannot necessarily be equated with any single physiological measure. Arousal can be separated into behavioral arousal, EEG arousal, and autonomic arousal, and there is no indication as to which of these would be relevant to dissonance. Elliot and Devine (1994) argued that GSR measures arousal but does not necessarily measure differences in affect (emotion). Therefore, they used a self-report measure of psychological discomfort collected at different times in their dissonance-producing experiment. They found that subjects had a higher level of discomfort after writing a counterattitudinal essay and that this discomfort decreased only after they reported their (changed) attitude toward the topic. This appears to be the best support available for the hypothesis that attitude change produces dissonance reduction.

In summary, the evidence seems fairly convincing that experimental procedures for producing dissonance may also produce arousal of the GSR. But there is little evidence that dissonance produces arousal and that attitude change is reinforced by dissonance reduction. The usual "dissonance" procedures may produce arousal, but for some reason other than dissonance per se. This distinction is illustrated in Figure 13–7.

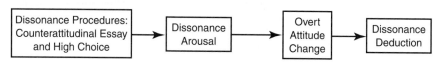

FIGURE 13–7A.   Illustration of Cognitive Dissonance Theory. (1) Freely writing an essay counter to one's own attitude produces (2) dissonance between one's attitude and one's behavior. This dissonance is a state of aversive arousal. (3) To get rid of this unpleasant arousal, a person expesses an attitude more in favor of the essay topic than previously expressed. (4) The attitude change reduces the dissonance, and arousal is therefore reduced.

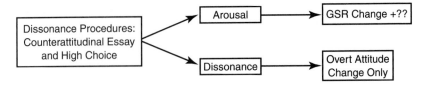

FIGURE 13–7B. Alternatives to the Dissonance Theory. Dissonance procedures may produce arousal for some reason other than cognitive dissonance. The dissonance may lead to attitude change following self-perception, or as a means of better self-presentation, or for some other reason. Arousal may not be a link in the chain of events leading from dissonance procedures to overt attitude change.

Alternative Explanations for Dissonance Effects

Aronson's expectancy interpretation. Aronson (1968) suggested that dissonance does not occur with just any contradiction but that it is specific to a violation of expectancies. Walking in the rain and not getting wet would create dissonance because walking in the rain arouses the expectancy of getting wet. If we did not have this expectancy, there would be no dissonance. According to Aronson, dissonance is especially likely to occur in relation to one's self-concept. He suggested that in the Festinger-Carlsmith experiment, for example, the dissonance was not just the result of telling someone that the task was interesting when in fact it was boring. Rather, the dissonance resulted from the subjects' violation of their self-concepts. The individual who lies for $1 is doing something out of line with her concept of how she normally behaves. Aronson concluded that the strongest dissonance effects have been obtained in experiments in which the self-concept was clearly involved.

Bem's self-perception theory. Bem (1967, 1970) proposed to account for all the cognitive dissonance research with an essentially nonmotivational, Skinnerian approach. Rather than argue that subjects perform as they do because inconsistent cognitions are aversive, Bem proposed that the individual views his or her own behavior and the situation just as he or she would view the behavior of another person in the same situation. In the Festinger-Carlsmith experiment, suppose we could invisibly observe a college student offered $20 to lie to someone and then see him do it. We also see another student tell the same lie for a mere $1. What might we conclude? One reasonable interpretation would be that "for $20 the subject doesn't have to believe in what he's doing, but if the other subject is doing it for a crummy dollar, maybe he does believe it." Bem's interpretation is that the subject may look at his own behavior and draw the same conclusion.

To test his hypothesis, Bem (1967) had subjects simply listen to tape-recorded descriptions of the Festinger-Carlsmith experiment (without hearing the actual results). Bem's subjects then rated the experimental task as they thought that the Festinger-Carlsmith subjects would. There were three

TABLE 13–2.   Comparison of Bem's (1967) results with the Festinger-Carlsmith (1959) results (see text for details).

| STUDY | CONTROL | EXPERIMENTAL CONDITION | |
		$1 COMPENSATION	$20 COMPENSATION
Festinger-Carlsmith	−0.45	+1.35	−0.05
Bem	−1.56	+0.52	−1.96

From Bem, 1967. Copyright © 1967 by the American Psychological Association. Used by permission.

different conditions: the $1 inducement, the $20 inducement, and a control group with no inducement. Bem's subjects rated the task on a scale from −5 (very dull) to +5 (very interesting). Table 13–2 compares Bem's ratings with those from the original experiment. The absolute numerical values in the two experiments are different, but the trend of results is the same: The $1 group is more positive than either of the other groups in the experiment.

Bem (1970) argued with many experimental and "real-life" illustrations that our behavior often determines our attitudes, rather than the other way around. For example, factory workers who become shop stewards suddenly shift their attitudes to a more prolabor position, whereas the attitudes of workers who are promoted to foreman suddenly become more promanagement. The proposition that we come to like (or believe) what we see ourselves do sounds intuitively backward, because we have all been brought up with the reverse notion, that our feelings determine our behavior. Note, however, that this "standard" belief is essentially the Cartesian dualistic interpretation of the mind-body relation discussed in Chapter One. That is, it is a statement that mind (attitudes, beliefs, etc.) causes behavior. Bem's position is that circumstances dictate behaviors and that we infer our mental state, at least in part, from these circumstances and behaviors. An especially pernicious consequence of this argument is that people who confess to a crime may come to believe that they are guilty, and the freer the confession, the firmer the guilt feeling (Bem, 1970).

Impression management.   We can imagine that a subject in a dissonance experiment might not want to give the impression that he could be cheaply bought to engage in self-contradictory behavior, such as writing a counterattitudinal essay. To give the experimenter a more favorable impression, the subject might report a changed attitude more in line with his inconsistent behavior. The subject fibs a little about his attitude so that the experimenter will believe that he has actually developed the attitude he is now expressing. By this interpretation, there is no great moral dilemma, no unpleasantly overpowering state of arousal, and no attempt to figure out the discrepant behavior. One prediction from the impression-management hypothesis would be that if subjects thought the experimenter did not know that they had changed their attitude or if they believed that the experimenter had a foolproof way to tell what their real attitude was, subjects should not show attitude change. Evidence for these hypotheses is ambiguous (Cooper & Fazio, 1984).

A potentially troublesome finding for the impression management interpretation is that subjects do appear to show increased arousal in the dissonance situation. If this arousal is actually related to their attitude change, then impression management theory would have to take this element into account. Schlenker (1982) has proposed that the activity of selling oneself cheaply produces arousal because the subject wants to protect her or his self-esteem. Attitude change is one way to do this. This interpretation runs into some of the same problems as the dissonance-reduction interpretation. That is, if the arousal (social anxiety? guilt?) does not decrease after the changed attitude is expressed, what does arousal do? It may be that arousal does nothing at all. Arousal and impression management may in fact be parallel events, neither one causing the other. This is like our previous proposal that arousal and dissonance might occur in parallel, but without causal significance for each other.

Change in the motivational basis of dissonance.   Greenwald and Ronis (1978) pointed out that there has been a drift in the nature of the motivational principle supposedly underlying cognitive dissonance. Initially, it was said that any two contradictory actions or beliefs were a source of dissonance. Then, inconsistency was said to be a major force only if the individual was committed to behaving in an inconsistent manner (Brehm & Cohen, 1962). Aronson (1968) then suggested that the self-concept was importantly involved. Wicklund and Brehm (1976) argued that dissonance reduction occurs only when the dissonant elements have been brought together through the personal responsibility of the individual who feels the dissonance. Impression management theorists argue that social anxiety is the motivating force. Greenwald and Ronis suggest that the more recent approaches are more akin to ego-defensive actions, as proposed by many personality theorists, than to dissonance and its reduction, as proposed by Festinger.

The increasing emphasis on the self-concept, suggest Greenwald and Ronis, is not bad. But it may not really be dissonance, either. It is possible that the shift in focus has been due to a greater emphasis on those aspects of dissonance procedures that happen to overlap with ego-defensive activities. If the ego-defensive behaviors are particularly powerful (and the procedures for manipulating threat to the ego or self-esteem are strong), then these behaviors would in the "natural course of things" lead to a greater concern with them. The net effect may then be that dissonance theory in its original formulation has not been fully tested, because the predictions made by subsequent revisions simply are not relevant to the original statement.

Cognitive dissonance theory has been a highly fruitful theory, generating much new research, controversy, and theory. The attitude change data generated by tests of the theory are often interpreted in other ways, and the theory is much less influential than it once was.

Conformity and Nonconformity

In a classic experiment, Solomon Asch (1951) had several subjects judge which of a set of lines matched the length of a standard line. All but one of the subjects were actually accomplices of the experimenter. The accomplices all made their judgments before the real subject made his, and on some occasions they made obviously incorrect judgments. Under these circumstances the real subjects frequently went along with what they thought were the judgments of the other subjects. In other words, they took what the other subjects said as a norm and conformed to that norm. In fact, the real subjects often did not privately believe that the false answer was actually correct, but they publicly went along with it. They were concerned about the effects of being different from the norm, and their "error correction" procedure was to "go along."

In general, research shows a strong tendency for individuals to conform to whatever standards are set by their group. A person is rewarded for conformity but sanctioned for nonconformity. A group, like an individual, has goals, such as to maintain production or win a game. The group pressure for cooperation helps attain these goals, and the group, or its leader, provides rewards and punishments for individuals who do or do not "go along." Schacter (1951) found that individuals who consistently differed from a group in their attitudes were rejected by other group members. This rejection can be severe punishment. The college freshman who dearly wants to become a member of a particular fraternity, for example, is not likely to deviate much from the norms of that group lest he not be invited. In terms of discrepancy, then, what we see are group mechanisms for keeping social behavior at an expected (reference) level. If individual behaviors depart from this, appropriate corrective actions are taken to bring the behavior back into line.

SECTION SUMMARY

1. **Cognitive inconsistency** occurs when an event is perceived to be different from expectation. Such inconsistencies may be arousing and may induce attitude change.
2. Heider's **balance theory** concerns the effects of consistency of perceived relations among different people. If A likes B, and B likes C, but A strongly dislikes C, there is an imbalance for A in relation to B. A then tries to restore balance, in part at least by changing his attitude toward B and/or C.
3. **Cognitive dissonance** is said to occur when the same individual holds **contradictory** beliefs, or acts contrary to his or her beliefs. Dissonance is aver-

sive, and dissonance reduction is reinforcing. Attitude change is one way to reduce dissonance.

4. In a typical dissonance experiment, subjects are subtly coerced to write essays against their own attitude regarding some topic (such as parking on campus). Subjects show attitude changes away from their original attitude if they believe that their inconsistent behavior has actually affected someone and if they believe that they have chosen freely to engage in the counterattitudinal behavior.

5. Evidence that dissonance is actually arousing is slight, and mostly inferred from behavior. Dissonance-arousing conditions produce an increase in the **galvanic skin response,** but the arousal may not be causally related to reported attitude change. Self-reported change in affect does seem to be related to attitude change.

6. There is some controversy over whether attitude change occurs because of **incongruence** between belief and behavior or whether one must anticipate an **aversive consequence** of the behavior, even though it might be consistent with one's beliefs.

7. There are several alternative explanations for the results of dissonance experiments. Bem's **self-perception theory** says that people infer their own attitudes the same way that they infer the attitudes of other people, by observing their own behavior. According to **impression management theory,** subjects wish to maintain their self-esteem; therefore, they report a changed attitude so that they will not appear to be easily swayed by the experimenter.

8. **Conformity** research shows the motivational importance of inconsistency in social situations. When individuals fail to conform to group norms, they may be ostracized and then conform to reduce the level of aversiveness of group reaction to their nonconformity.

CHAPTER FOURTEEN

Interpersonal Attraction

Why are people drawn to form relationships with others?

What makes some people more attractive than others?

Why are some people more desirable companions than others?

What defines physical attraction? Is it universal or culturally determined?

What costs are we willing to pay in return for good relationships with others?

How are liking and loving related?

Is there more than one kind of love?

AFFILIATION

Why Do People Affiliate?

In the most general of motivational terms, we affiliate with other people because they increase our pleasure or reduce our discomfort. Having said this, there are many specific questions to be answered. For example, is affiliating with others something we learn to do, and if so, how do we learn this? Or, how do others specifically increase our pleasure or reduce our distress?

Need to belong? Baumeister and Leary (1995) argue that the "need to belong" is a fundamental human motivation to form and maintain some minimum amount of relatively enduring and pleasant interpersonal relationships. In evolutionary terms, such a motive should have both survival and reproductive benefits. Groups share resources, protect members from outside harm, and make mates available. One prediction from this view is that if there is a basic biological need for belonging, then groups should form easily. Many studies confirm this with what is called the **minimal intergroup situation**. If a larger group of subjects is randomly divided into two smaller groups by some completely arbitrary and trivial criterion, the groups almost immediately show favoritism toward their group and some degree of antagonism toward the other. By the same token, people are reluctant to break established group bonds. If there is a biological need to belong, what biological processes underlie affiliation?

Biological Factors in Affiliation

Effects of early experience on later affiliation. Prolonged social isolation so frequently leads to loneliness and depression that these consequences appear to have some degree of genetic determination. John Bowlby (1969) suggested that such attachment behaviors as clinging to the mother or acting distressed when the mother departs are biologically determined. According to Cairns (1979), however, the degree of the child's attachment at one age is not a good predictor of degree of attachment for the same child just a few months later. This suggests that attachment behaviors have a strong learning component.

Experimental research with monkeys indicates that early experience with other members of one's species is an important determinant of later social behavior. Harlow (1958) reared infant rhesus monkeys in isolation, feeding them from surrogate mothers consisting of wire frames or terry cloth-covered models with bottles attached. The unexpected result was that, although well nurtured, when these animals reached adulthood they consistently failed to engage in normal social interactions, including sexual activity. Allowing the animals to interact with others for just a few minutes a day during infancy was sufficient for the development of normal social relations, however. Obviously, such experimental research is not done with humans, but there are periodic reports of children who have been reared in isolation by their parents. Since we don't know what these children might have been like if they had experienced normal human interactions, we have to interpret such reports with caution. Nevertheless, the behaviors described are often consistent with those reported for experimentally isolated animals.

In field research, Hunt (1984) found that infants in orphanages had high incidence of health problems that were not due to poor health care, but were attributable to lack of stimulation in a dull and unchanging environment. This had previously been described clinically under the name **miasmas**. Hunt concluded that stimulation from a changing and challenging environment is a necessary element for physical, intellectual, and emotional growth.

Considerable evidence therefore suggests that it is not inevitable that humans will seek affiliation. Environmental factors and experience interact with genetic factors to influence emotional responsiveness and behavior, and these may enhance or diminish affiliation with others. Clearly, however, affiliation with others is important to most humans and both positive and negative incentive motivational systems are involved.

Positive incentive systems.   If basic biological processes are important to affiliation, there should be some very basic biological markers. Dopamine release in the nervous system is such a marker. In one experiment, for example, experimental subjects were shown films with affiliation themes, a procedure intended to increase the need for affiliation. Subjects scoring high on a test of need for affiliation subsequently had higher levels of dopamine release than subjects who scored low on the test. There were no differences in levels of cortisol, epinephrine, or norepinephrine, which are measures of general arousal. Therefore, the dopamine effect appeared to be specific to affiliation (McClelland, Patel, Stier, & Brown, 1987).

The personality trait of extraversion is also associated with positive incentive motivation. Depue and Collins (1999), for example, say that one of two major characteristics of extraversion is "interpersonal engagement consisting of affiliation (enjoying and valuing close interpersonal bonds, being warm and affectionate) (p. 491)." Extraversion is also characterized by a high level of positive affect, which in turn is related to the ventral tegmental dopamine system and the nucleus accumbens endorphin system. Given the great variety of positive incentive situations in which the dopamine system/endorphin system is involved, it is but a short step to speculate that people are positive incentives for other people to approach.

We may affiliate with others because they are of some service to us. They produce positive emotional responses in us because they are rewarding to us or diminish our anxiety. For example:

- **Assistance.** We often need assistance from other people to achieve our goals, and we are reinforced for affiliating with them by the assistance they give us.

Such reinforcement, as in a work situation, may maintain our affiliative behavior over long periods of time.

- **Stimulation.** Stimulus variation is a source of pleasurable arousal. What is more variable, more full of surprises, or more stimulating than other people? Interesting people attract more friends than boring people but, as we have seen earlier, there also appears to be an optimal level of stimulation that varies from person to person. A given person may be too stimulating for some people, too dull for others, and just right for somebody else.
- **Information.** We have seen in an earlier chapter that behavior is reinforced by new information. Other people provide information or reduce uncertainty for us, so we associate with them. Information may be important (world news) or trivial (gossip), but it is reinforcing and sought.
- **Self-evaluation.** We all need to evaluate ourselves, our opinions, our abilities, or our work from time to time. Lacking objective standards, we often compare ourselves with other people. Festinger (1954) argued that we make **social comparisons** requiring affiliation when we are uncertain about ourselves. In order to judge ourselves, we seek information about social norms from someone who is similar to us (in age, background, interest, experience, etc.) rather than from someone who is very dissimilar.
- **Freedom from internal constraint.** Groups frequently restrain their members from engaging in "questionable" activities but sometimes do just the opposite and reinforce uninhibited behavior. If an individual at a particular time is seeking freedom from self-imposed or group-imposed constraints, she may choose to affiliate with others under conditions where the restraints can temporarily be discarded—at a party, for example. We may become relatively anonymous, free of responsibility, and "act crazy." Such **deindividuation** may temporarily be enjoyable, but after a while recognition from others again becomes desirable (Zimbardo, 1969).

Negative incentive systems: fear and anxiety.   When we feel afraid, we often want to be with someone to calm our fears. Even among laboratory rats, the presence of another animal reduces the fearful behaviors of an animal that has been shocked in an experimental apparatus. One such fearful response is "crouching in the corner," or freezing. A previously shocked animal is more active if another animal is present, and more active yet if the other animal has itself not been shocked (Davitz & Mason, 1955). Schachter (1959) studied fear and affiliation in humans by threatening subjects with either strong or weak electric shock, and then giving them the choice of waiting for their punishment alone or with someone else. The strong-shock subjects did prefer to be with someone else, and Wrightsman (1960) subsequently found that subjects in a threatening situation were less afraid when waiting with someone else.

SECTION SUMMARY

1. In the most general motivational terms, we **affiliate** with others because they increase our pleasure or reduce our discomfort.
2. Prolonged isolation in infancy may produce severe deficits in social behavior in later life. One explanation for this is that social stimulation is important for the normal development of social relations.

3. It has been suggested that there is a fundamental human **need to belong**, to form and maintain pleasant interpersonal relations. Arousal of the **dopamine/endorphin incentive approach system** is related to affiliation with others. Extraverts are gregarious individuals who appear to be particularly sensitive to the incentive motivational characteristic of other people.

4. People may affiliate with others because they provide **assistance, stimulation, information, self-evaluation**, and occasional **freedom from internal constraint**. All these are related to positive affect and reward.

5. The presence of others may be desirable and sought in unpleasant situations because they **reduce fearfulness**.

INTERPERSONAL ATTRACTION

Physical Attractiveness

Advantages of physical attractiveness. The physical attractiveness of another person makes affiliation more or less pleasant and most certainly plays an important role in love. Actual psychological research dates back only to the last half of the twentieth century, but a large body of data shows that the advantages of physical attractiveness are many. Physically attractive people draw preferential treatment from infancy through old age (Brehm, 1985; Langlois, Kalakanis, Rubenstein, Larson, Hallam, & Smoot, 2000; but also see Eagly, Ashmore, Makhijanai, & Longo, 1991). Attractive children are treated better in school; attractive adults receive more assistance and cooperation than their less-attractive counterparts, are reprimanded less severely for transgressions, and make more money. In just about any situation one can imagine, attractive people have the advantage. Why should this be? There are several possible explanations for such preferential treatment and more than one may apply in a particular instance.

- Many people seem to hold an **attractiveness stereotype**, an implicit assumption that attractive people have other virtues in addition to their appearance and preferential treatment is their due. (Baron & Byrne, 1997; Brehm, 1985). There also appear to be cultural differences in the stereotype, however. Wheeler and Kim (1997) predicted that Korean and American stereotypes would be somewhat different because different characteristics are valued in **individualist** (American) and **collectivist** (Korean) cultures. They found that Americans perceived attractive targets as higher in power, an individual characteristic, whereas Koreans perceived attractive targets as higher in integrity and concern for others, a collectivist characteristic. The conclusion is that an attractiveness stereotype exists in both cultures, but the stereotypes vary in detail.

- Attractive people are in fact more self-confident and have better mental health. These qualities may result from being treated better by others and having more opportunity to be reinforced for social skills. Thus, if you are more successful in dealing with others because you are attractive, you may become more confident in yourself, which further increases your successes (Langlois et al. 2000).

- Other people may wish to associate with attractive people because such an association enhances one's own self-image. Sigall and Landy (1973) found that a man was rated positively when associated with an attractive woman but was rated negatively when associated with an unattractive woman. Attractiveness seems to be relatively more important in dating than in marrying (Stroebe, Insko, Thompson, & Layton, 1971), but Mathes (1975) found that over a series of five dates, physical attractiveness was considered increasingly important.

- An attractive person produces a pleasant emotional response in others and thus elicits preferential treatment in hope of maintaining or increasing that emotion. In a classic study, a "computer dance" was arranged for University of Minnesota freshmen who signed up and were randomly paired. At the original sign-up, the experimenters rated the subjects' attractiveness to provide independent and relatively objective judgments. At the dance intermission, the subjects rated their partners on various characteristics, including attractiveness. A third of the most attractive women were later asked for dates by their partners but only 10 percent of the unattractive women were. The subjects' attractiveness ratings of their partners was the single best predictor of who would be asked out on a date, indicating both that attractiveness is important and that to some degree it was in the eye of the beholder (Walster, Aronson, Abrahams, & Rottman, 1966).

Standards of attractiveness.   Attractiveness has many dimensions, which may vary in importance to different people, for example, facial features, body characteristics, movement, and so on. Men are often thought to be taken more by attractiveness than women, but in fact women are just as concerned about male attractiveness (Wright, 1999) although men and women may express this in somewhat different ways. Men may just be more open about the issue. However, Coombs and Kenkel (1966) also found that males rated attractiveness more important before having a date with a particular woman, but women expressed more concern about the attractiveness of their date afterward.

The matching principle.   In spite of the importance of attractiveness, the physically most attractive member of the opposite sex is not necessarily the one who will be most sought after. In fact, extreme mismatches of attractiveness may draw attention because they are unusual. People tend to be attracted to others with similar physical characteristics, such as height and weight (Berscheid & Walster, 1969). This matching principle may work for reasons beyond attractiveness, however. A man might prefer an exceptionally attractive woman, but if he is of medium attractiveness himself, he might believe that she would not date him. He therefore seeks the most attractive woman who *would* date him. The optimal choice, then, might be to choose a woman of medium attractiveness so that there is a good probability of a successful relationship. This explanation is very similar to that of achievement theory, in which the tendency to choose a particular activity (in this case, asking for a date) depends on the probability of success (Ps) and the incentive value of success (Is). A very attractive date could have a high incentive value, but the probability of success in getting a date with her might be considered very low. Conversely, an unattractive date has a very low incentive value even though the perceived probability of success in getting a date is high. A man should then approach the most attractive woman that he could reasonably expect to date him. A highly attractive woman who does date an average man might express dissatisfaction with the experience, further leading the man to date more moderately attractive women.

In a study of the matching principle involving 120 couples with varying degrees of relationship (casual, serious, cohabiting, engaged/married), White (1980) found that couples more similar in attractiveness did stay together longer. There was a greater similarity of attractiveness (r = .63) between the engaged/married pairs than for the casually dating pairs (r = .18). In the casual and serious groups, the greater the dissimilarity, the more likely the couple were to break up during the time of the research (a school year). Part of the breakup was related to the desire of the more attractive pair member to have a relationship with someone else.

Other Determinants of Attractiveness

Proximity. As the song says, "How can I ignore/the boy next door?" We are more likely to become friends with people who are physically close to us. In dormitories, for example, people who are thrown together by the chance of alphabetical grouping are more likely to become friends with each other than with people who live farther away in the same dormitory (Newcomb, 1961; Priest & Sawyer, 1967; Segal, 1974). In the Segal study, there was a very high correlation (.90) between liking a person and how close in the alphabet that person's name was to the rater's name. In purely practical terms, it takes less effort to interact and become friendly with people close by.

Familiarity. The effects of proximity are partly explained by the fact that when individuals live or work close to each other, they can become more familiar with each other. As we have already seen with the mere exposure effect, we generally tend to like better the persons, objects, or even strange words in a foreign language the more that we have been exposed to them (Zajonc, 2001). The mere exposure effect may not always work but there are probably other factors involved in such situations. For example, Burgess and Sales (1971) obtained the mere exposure effect with subjects who felt good about the overall experimental context, but not with subjects who disliked the experimental situation. Similarly, the behavior of another person may enhance or diminish our liking for that person. If the behavior were agreeable, we would expect increased liking with increased exposure, but if the person were disagreeable or boring. we would expect disliking.

Similarity. According to the **need complementary hypothesis** (Winch, 1958), people with opposite interests or personal characteristics should be attracted to each other because they fulfill the deficiencies of each other. There is little support for this theory, however. For example, both dominant and submissive people prefer more dominant individuals as friends (Palmer

& Byrne, 1970), and introverts and extraverts both prefer extraverts (Hendrick & Brown, 1971).

People who are similar are more likely to get together—which would seem to be a variation on the matching principle. Research on attitudinal similarity indicates that the greater the percentage of topics on which two people have similar attitudes, the greater their liking for each other (Byrne & Nelson, 1965). Several general qualifications regarding similarity and liking that are worth noting, however (Sherrod, 1982): (1) physical attractiveness overrides attitudinal similarity, at least for a first date; (2) if the similar individual is unattractive in some way, such as being emotionally disturbed or obnoxious, liking is decreased; (3) a fear of rejection by similar individuals may direct a person to dissimilar individuals who might be more accepting; and (4) a too-similar person may be rejected because an individual wishes to appear unique.

Reciprocity.   We are more prone to like others if we think they reciprocate by liking us (Peplau, 1982). Salespeople use this principle in face-to-face contacts, immediately asking your first name and showing great interest in you. Large companies use it for mass advertising ("Fly the friendly skies of United"). In a group setting, subjects with low self-esteem are more prone to like the group if they believe that the group likes them, but subjects with high self-esteem are less likely to be swayed by how they thought the group felt (Dittes, 1959). An ingratiating person, however, can go too far in trying to attract reciprocity from others by expressing liking for them. Such ingratiation may work if it is perceived as sincere but have just the opposite effect, producing dislike, if perceived as a phony attempt to gain some advantage (Jones, 1964). What is perceived as "overdoing" praise or liking may depend on who is receiving the flattery, however. People starved for attention or praise may believe almost anything that will enhance their self-image, no matter how ingratiating or insincere.

Intellectual stimulation.   We use the phrase intellectual stimulation to refer broadly to what have been called the "pleasures of the mind" (Kubovy, 1999). These are the emotional experiences that come from such nonliving sources as music, art, and humor. People who are talented (music, art, dance, athletics) and/or funny are also attractive. How do these talents produce pleasure? For one answer to this question we turn to activation theory (Chapter Six), where we saw that humor and art are interesting partly because they produce an optimal level of arousal. The level of arousal produced by a particular stimulus depends on a number of other variables, such as the complexity and amount of prior experience with the stimulus. The same principles that apply to inanimate stimuli (music, art) can also apply to people. People who do or say unexpected things generate some level of arousal and pleasure. Seeking pleasures of the mind also has a characteristic of sensation-seeking, as measured by the experiencing seeking subscale. We also saw in Chapter Twelve that optimal level of arousal did not account for sensation seeking and was replaced by Zuckerman (1994) with a theory that says sensation seeking is rewarded by increased activity in the dopamine reward system.

Evolutionary Approaches to Attractiveness

Universality of interest in beauty.   Interest in beauty goes back at least to ancient Egypt. Etcoff (*Survival of the Prettiest,* 1999) notes that cosmetics dating back five thousands years have been found and that people all over the world and in all times have done a variety of things to make themselves prettier. They have had their bodies pierced and tattooed, their lips stretched, and their feet bound. Thanks to the miracles of modern science and surgery, people have had body parts tightened, loosened, enlarged and reduced. Aristotle referred to cosmetics as the false art of health, obviously believing that a healthy-looking body was more attractive.

Langlois et al. (2000) examined the concepts behind such statements as: "Beauty is in the eye of the beholder," "Never judge a book by its cover," and "Beauty is only skin deep" to determine whether these statements represent reality. They examined every research study from 1932 to 1999 (n = 1800 studies) and found that:

1. Within and across cultures, people agreed about who is and is not attractive.
2. Attractiveness is an advantage in a variety of important, real-life situations.
3. There were no gender differences (indicating attractiveness is equally important for males and females).
4. There were few age differences, indicating that attractiveness is equally important for young and old.

Since mating is essential for the normal transmission of human genes from generation to generation, it has been speculated that biologically determined aspects of beauty may facilitate this process. Therefore, it is of interest to know just what is beautiful. Several studies show that males or females with highly exaggerated physical features are not generally considered the most attractive (Beck, Ward-Hull, & McLear, 1976; Wiggins, Wiggins, & Conger, 1968). For example, Beck et al. (1976) presented female subjects with silhouette drawings of male and female figures in which chest/breast, buttocks, and leg size were varied. They found that moderate-size male and female silhouettes with small buttocks were preferred for either male or female figures.

Waist-to-hip ratio.   One evolutionary hypothesis links signals of female attractiveness to reproductive potential (fertility) (Singh, 1993). If men "wish" to pass on their genes to future generations, the most attractive females should be those with signs of good reproductive potential. Singh suggested that a waist-to-hip ratio of about 0.7 (e.g., 26″/36″ = .72) and a moderate overall body size are most attractive and most fecund (capable of child-birth). Tassinary and Hansen (1998) tested this hypothesis in an experiment where they independently varied weight, waist size, and hip size in schematic drawings. Figure 14–1 illustrates some of their stimuli. Male and female subjects ranked the stimuli for both attractiveness and fecundity. Light-weight and moderate-weight figures were judged more attractive, and moderate-weight and heavy-weight figures more fecund. There was almost no correlation between the two sets of judgments. The authors conclude that although the waist-to-hip ratio hypothesis may have some intuitive appeal, it has little predictive value.

Henss (2000), however, argued that line drawings are impoverished stimuli for research on beauty and turned to digitally manipulated photographs of attractive women to vary the waist-to-hip ratio. He found that the larger the waist-to-hip ratio, the less attractive the model, regardless of which stimulus figure it was. Henss concluded that his research provided compelling support for the waist-to-hip ratio as "an essential attribute of the at-

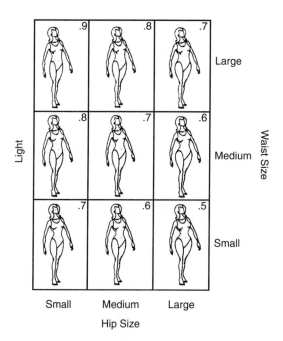

FIGURE 14–1. Schematic waist-to-hip ratios for light-weight women with different waist sizes. There are three different waist sizes (small, medium, large) and different hip sizes (small, medium, large) for each waist size. The number accompanying each figure is the ratio of waist-to-hip size. There were equivalent sets of nine drawings for moderate and heavy women used in the experiment. Overall, no specific waist-to-hip ratio was perceived as most attractive or fecund, contrary to evolutionary hypotheses that have been proposed. See text for details. (From Tassinary & Hansen, 1998, pp. 150–155, Figure 2. Used by permission.)

tractiveness of the female figure." We might observe that Henss's use of digitally manipulated photographs adds validity to his results, but that no one appears to have published research on the problem using videotaped images that involve movement and different perspectives of form.

Facial averageness. When we see a person with a spectacularly beautiful face, are we looking at an extremely average face? Sir Francis Galton in 1878 used photographic techniques to average different portraits and found that the composite faces were more attractive than their components, "a result that frustrated his attempts to create the prototypical criminal face" (Rhodes & Tremewan, 1996, p. 105). Langlois and Roggman (1990) used a computer technique to separately average thirty-two male faces and thirty-two female faces to form composite male and female faces. The averages literally were the statistical averages of numerical gray-scale values for photographs scanned into a computer and digitized. They were not the averages of subjective judgments about the faces. The composite faces were rated significantly more attractive than the average ratings of the sets of faces from which they had been generated.

The facial-average results provide a parsimonious explanation for two facts: Infants prefer attractive to unattractive faces, and cross-cultural judgments of attractiveness are more similar than different. Both these facts run contrary to the notion that what is attractive is learned within a specific cultural context. Instead, it is suggested that as a person views different faces, he or she develops a mental representation of the average of the faces, and this becomes the standard of attractiveness. This average face is more familiar even though it would be rare for any particular face to match it. Various criticisms have been leveled at the averaging procedure (Alley & Cunningham, 1991; Pittenger, 1991), but these seem to have been answered effectively (Langlois, Roggman, Musselman, & Acton, 1991). Rhodes and Tremewan (1996) also supported the averageness hypothesis, using a computerized caricature generator to vary averageness of line drawings of faces. They found that attractiveness was negatively correlated with distinctiveness. For reasons of their individual histories, we would expect that some persons will find particular deviations from the norm attractive, but that fact does not in itself negate the more general principle of attractiveness in the average. Furthermore, it has been found that composites of stimuli other than faces (dogs, birds, and wristwatches) are also judged to be more attractive (Halberstadt & Rhodes, 2000) This supports the idea that the development of mental representations is a general principle, of which facial averaging is only one example.

Health. It has also been hypothesized that visible signs of poor health should indicate a lower likelihood of offspring and therefore make a person a less attractive mate. Signs of health and attractiveness should therefore be correlated. Kalick, Zebrowitz, Langlois, and Robinson (1998) tested this hypothesis in a longitudinal study in which subjects rated facial photographs of adolescent males and females for attractiveness and health. They correlated these two ratings with each other, as well as with actual health records during adolescence, middle adulthood, and later adulthood. Subjects' ratings of attractiveness and *perceived* health correlated substantially (above .60), but attractiveness did not correlate with actual health at the time the photos were taken, nor did attractiveness predict future health (correlations approximately zero). The authors suggest that people may be "blinded by beauty" in their judgments of health. This finding seems to be another example of the beauty stereotype discussed earlier. Martin and Leary (1998) found that females who are thought to be exercising regularly, even though overweight, are considered more attractive than their nonexercising counterparts. This finding is at least congruent with the health hypothesis.

Tactics of mate attraction. Buss (1988) suggested that there are four components of competition for mates among humans that are more common than direct confrontations of competing individuals. These are (1) skill at locating mates, such as going to places where they "hang out"; (2) displaying mate-attracting behaviors (e.g., signaling interest or availability); (3) acquiring resources desired by members of the opposite sex; and (4) altering one's body shape or appearance to make it more attractive (exercising, dieting, surgery, cosmetics).

There was some support for these hypotheses. For example, men displayed and bragged about resources more than females did. Women, in turn, altered their appearance and wore jewelry more than men did. Many of the predicted sex differences in favor of females did not occur, including such behaviors as grooming, wearing sexy clothes, and flirting. Perhaps some of the differences that do occur (e.g., wearing jewelry) depend on what subculture is examined. Men's jewelry is increasingly popular, and men more frequently adorn their bodies with tattoos, although women are now doing this more. Furthermore, given the importance of male mating displays in other species, it seems rather paradoxical that displays of strength, athleticism, and showing off were not predicted to be differentiated by sex. However, males engaged in these behaviors more than females. This whole approach to human mate selection is so new that it is difficult to evaluate, partly because it is difficult to know what predictions to make. After the fact, any behaviors differing between the sexes could be rationalized to have evolutionary value.

SECTION SUMMARY

1. People who are physically attractive have many advantages throughout the life span. One reason for this is the presence of an **attractiveness stereotype** that says attractive people also have many other positive characteristics. Association

with attractive people may also enhance a person's own self-image, as well as producing pleasant feelings.

2. According to the **matching principle**, people tend to relate to others of similar attractiveness, which follows the general principles of achievement motivation. Such relationships seem to be more enduring.

3. We are more likely to be attracted to people who are geographically close to us (proximity), who are familiar to us, who are similar to us, and whom we believe to like us.

4. There appears to be a universal and timeless interest in beauty. People within the same culture and across different cultures show high agreement about who is or is not attractive.

5. An **evolutionary perspective** suggests that female attractiveness is linked to signals of **reproductive potential**, including body shape and general signs of health. Evidence for this hypothesis is not strong.

6. According to the **facial averageness hypothesis**, the most attractive face is a composite of all the faces a person has seen. The evidence for this hypothesis is strong, and accounts for the cross-cultural similarities in standards of beauty.

THEORIES OF LIKING AND LOVING

A Bit of Background

An historical shift in psychological research in interpersonal relationships took place when it was proposed that liking and loving are not the same thing, and that there may even be several kinds of love. A turning point was Rubin's (1970) theory of liking and loving. Liking was said to be based on *affection* and *respect*, whereas loving was said to be based on *attachment, caring,* and *intimacy*. Rubin's "liking scale" has items such as "I have great confidence in (name)'s good judgment," and his "love scale" has items such as "If I were lonely, my first thought would be to seek (name) out." Other scales have since been developed (e.g., Lee, 1977; Levinger, Rands, & Talober, 1977; Steffen, McLaney, & Hustedt, 1982; Swenson, 1972), but the most important aspect of them all is the attempt to measure what so often has been considered the unmeasurable. Theories are based on observation and observations involve measurement, so the better the measurement the better the ensuing theories.

Theories

Reinforcement Theory. If John experiences rewards at times when he is in the presence of Mary, she becomes a secondary reinforcer, and he comes to like her (Lott & Lott, 1974). Clore and Byrne (1974) suggested that a rewarding experience produces a positive emotional response that becomes attached to someone present at the time. Presumably this attachment would result from classical conditioning of the emotional response to a person present when the emotion was aroused. In one study, for example, children came to like their classmates more if they were systematically rewarded by their teacher for various activities not directly related to their classmates. Their classmates just happened to be there. The opposite also happens; the messenger who delivers the bad news is seldom popular. This theory was also related to research on attraction and attitudinal similarity (Byrne & Nelson, 1965). The more similar the attitudes of two people, the more they reinforce each other, hence the greater their attraction to each other. A wide range of things may be reinforcing, including intrinsic characteristics of the other person (such as attractiveness, sense of humor, or intelligence) and behaviors of the other person (such as giving attention or other favors).

Social exchange theory.   Using terminology from the marketplace, this approach deals with mutually rewarding behaviors between people (Rubin, 1973). Associating with another person involves **benefits** and **costs**. Positive attraction occurs when the anticipated benefits (rewards, positive affect) are greater than the costs (punishers, negative affect). Avoidance occurs when the costs exceed the benefits. A man and a woman may each have socially desirable qualities they can "trade off" to each other. A man gains more prestige by being seen with an attractive woman than with an unattractive one, and attractive women are more likely to date or marry men of higher social status than their own. A physically less-attractive man can bring money, prestige, and power to the interpersonal bargaining table, as well as intellect, wit, and charm. Political power seems to be a universal bargaining commodity, as is the prestige of rock stars and athletes that can be traded for sexual favors.

Equity theory.   The distinguishing characteristic of equity theory is that a person in a relationship compares his or her personal ratio of costs to benefits with those of some reference. The standard terminology of equity theory is in term of inputs and outputs, where input (I) = costs, and output (O) = benefits. There are then three general possibilities for ratios:

1. $Ip/Op = Ir/Or$. The ratio of I/O for the person (p) in question is the same as that for the reference (r). Person (p) perceives that there is equity between his or her inputs and outputs and those of the reference. The reference used may specifically be the other person in the relationship, or it may be some past relationship, or some abstract standard. An abstract standard might be some romantic ideal. When there is equity, there is satisfaction with the relationship.

2. $Ip/Op > Ir/Or$. If person (p) perceives that he or she puts relatively more into the relationship than the reference, there is a strain, and the person will try to restore equity. Equity is a matter of perception, as well as reality, so it is important to change perceived equity. For example, if a woman feels that a man does not spend enough time with her, he may try to persuade her that his time is being used (such as working) to their mutual long-term benefit, or he might try to restore equity with substitutes for time, such as flowers, candy, or other gifts.

3. $Ip/Op < Ir/Or$. What happens in a relationship if a person feels that she or he is getting more than is equitable out of a relationship? Equity may be restored by

putting more into the relationship or by getting the other person to put less into the relationship.

These are just a few of the many predictions of equity theory, and the theory has received rather good support in research (e.g., Walster, Walster, & Berscheid, 1978).

Inputs and outputs as affect.   Since interpersonal relationships at some level always involve affect, we may also think of equity in terms of affect. If we substitute "positive affect" (*PA*) for benefits and "negative affect" (*NA*) for costs, we could have the following equity situation for John and Mary:

$$PA_{John}/NA_{John} = PA_{Mary}/NA_{Mary}$$

This equity formula says that as long as both parties have equal ratios of positive and negative affect from the relationship, there is equity. Many factors combine to produce levels of positive affect and negative affect. In addition, this formula suggests that as absolute levels of negative affect increase, the parties involved may become more uncomfortable with the relationship regardless of the equity. This is because the ratio of positive to negative affect will get smaller. In general, negative affect is more salient than positive and people are more responsive to negative affect (Rozin & Royzman, 2001).

Investment theory.   Why does a person stay in a relationship or leave it? Rusbult (1983) proposed another economic theory of interpersonal relations that is aimed at answering this question. Her model combines features of several of the models previously discussed and adds the additional component of **investment** to account for why people become committed to relationships. Investment theory starts off by saying that:

Satisfaction with a relationship = (Rewards − Costs) − Comparison Level

A person will be satisfied with a relationship if there are many rewards and few costs and if the difference is greater than the person's expectations about what he or she should get out of a relationship (the comparison level). In addition, the net satisfaction from Relationship X should be greater than that of some alternative. If we can get the same rewards with fewer costs in a different relationship, then that alternative would be preferred. If one has invested a great deal of time, money, or emotional involvement in a relationship, it is more difficult to withdraw because one does not want to lose one's investment. It is rather like a poker game in which someone plays out a doubtful hand because the only possible way to recoup a large investment in the pot is to keep playing.

Commitment to a particular relationship depends on satisfaction with the relationship, investment in the relationship, and possible alternatives. Given that a person has a fixed comparison level for expectations about what relationships are generally like, then

$$\text{Commitment to Person X} = (\text{Rewards}_x - \text{Costs}_x) + \text{Investment}_x - \text{Alternatives}$$

Thus, if everything else were equal, there would be greater commitment to a relationship if there were a greater investment. The model says that satisfaction and commitment need not necessarily be highly correlated. Strong commitment to a relationship could result even with relatively few rewards if the costs were low, the investment high, and alternatives poor. Alternatively, a person might quit a relatively satisfactory relationship because there was little investment and a better alternative. Rusbult (1983) tested the model in a seven-month longitudinal study of dating college students. The data were gathered by periodic questionnaires. The results were that: (1) Increases in rewards led to greater satisfaction, but (2) variations in cost did not affect satisfaction. (3) Greater satisfaction and investment and poorer alternatives promoted a higher level of commitment. (4) For those individuals who stayed in relationships, rewards increased over time, costs rose slightly, satisfaction increased, investment increased, quality of alternatives declined, and commitment increased. For those who left relationships, the opposite changes occurred: rewards, satisfaction, and investment decreased, whereas costs and quality of alternatives increased. The data thus provide reasonable support for the model.

Cognitive-arousal theory.   In his *Ars Amatoria* (The Art of Love), a first-century how-to manual for romantic conquest, the Roman poet Ovid provided many helpful hints for would-be lovers. These involved grooming and behavior, as well as the suggestion that a good time to arouse passion in a woman was while watching gladiators fight in the arena. In modern times a football game, hockey match, or wrestling bout might suffice. A nineteenth-century German psychologist named Adolph Horwicz similarly proposed that any strong emotional arousal could facilitate love. The Ovid-Horwicz effect was originally just an empirical observation but cognitive-arousal theory has been used to account for the effect (Patterson, 1976; Rubin, 1973; Walster, 1971).

According to cognitive arousal theory, emotional arousal is diffuse until labeled as a particular emotion by the person experiencing the arousal (Schachter & Singer, 1962) (see Chapter Two here). This was illustrated in an experiment where an attractive person was rated as more attractive after two minutes of running in place than after fifteen seconds (White, Fishbein, and Rutstein, 1981). Such attractiveness might be interpreted as love. Similar results were obtained in an experiment with both pleasant arousal (produced by a Steve Martin comedy clip) and unpleasant arousal (a grisly murder/ mayhem clip). The authors conclude that type of arousal is irrelevant, again supporting cognitive arousal theory. In a rather dramatic setting, Dutton and Aron (1974) conducted a field study in which a female gathered information from males just after they had crossed a high, swinging bridge. She was more likely to be contacted later than when (for other subjects) she had been at the end of a low, stable bridge. The swinging bridge presumably produced greater arousal, which was attributed to the female experimenter. It is also possible that there was a subject selection factor for which males were on which bridge, so the authors also conducted a laboratory experiment with an attractive female as the experimenter. Male subjects were randomly assigned to high and low arousal conditions (threat of shock or no threat). Again, the experimenter was more likely to be contacted later by subjects in the high arousal condition, supporting the cognitive-arousal interpretation.

Applying the theory to passionate love, if a member of the opposite sex is present, arousal produced for any reason may be misinterpreted as love. Sexual arousal itself is readily interpreted as passionate because there are specific physiological and anatomical cues, but other sources of arousal (such as mild fear, frustration, excitement about an athletic contest, or exercise) may be labeled as love if a particular person happens along at the right time.

Recall from Chapter Two that there are problems with cognitive-arousal theory but that excitation transfer theory is better supported. This latter theory would say that if there is already some degree of sexual arousal, this may be intensified by additional arousal from an unrelated source. This effect explains a number of curious phenomena, for example, why a "hard-to-get" person may be more attractive. The apparently unobtainable person produces feelings of frustration, a form of arousal. This arousal may transfer to other feelings and be interpreted as heightened love. Even rejection or discovering that the object of one's romantic inclination has another partner may produce an emotional arousal that is interpreted as being even stronger love than existed before. Some people are also "turned on" by a certain amount of "danger" in lovemaking (for example, having sex in locations where they might be observed). All these situations make sense in terms of excitation-transfer theory.

Triangular theory of liking and loving.   Sternberg (1986, 1987) has proposed what he calls the triangular theory of love, based on the dimensions of **intimacy, passion**, and **decision/commitment**. Intimacy refers to feelings of closeness or connectedness between two people, including such factors as concern with the welfare of the loved one, mutual understanding, and sharing. Passion consists of the sources of arousal that we generally label as passion (emotional feelings and physical arousal). Sexual arousal is certainly a strong element, but such needs as for affiliation may also be involved. Decision/commitment refers to short-term and long-term elements. In the short term, one person makes the decision that he or she loves another person. In the long term, one makes a commitment to maintain that love and relationship. The two do not necessarily go together; one can decide that one is in love at the moment without making any long-term commitment. Likewise, one can make a long-term commitment (such as marriage) without necessarily deciding that one is in love at the moment.

The presence or absence of each of the preceding three components of love can result in eight possible combinations, which comprise eight different kinds of liking or loving, as summarized in Table 14–1. Sternberg's names for each are also given. Figure 14–2 also illustrates the theory.

Some brief descriptions of the eight types are as follows:

1. **Nonlove** means what the name implies, the absence of love (keep in mind that zero is a perfectly good mathematical quantity when describing something).
2. **Liking** is intimacy, without passion or commitment. Friendships can endure for decades without friends' seeing each other for years at a time; love often is not so durable in this manner.
3. **Infatuated love** (infatuation) is a kind of love at first sight phenomenon, passion without intimacy or commitment (students always refer to this as the "one-night stand").
4. **Empty love** seems as vacuous as nonlove but characterizes such social phenomena as arranged marriages, where there is commitment without intimacy or passion. It also characterizes a "burned-out marriage" or the end of some other long-term relation.

TABLE 14–1.   Sternberg's taxonomy of kinds of love based on his triangular theory of love.

| | COMPONENTS | | |
KIND OF LOVE	INTIMACY	PASSION	DECISION/COMMITMENT
1. Nonlove	0	0	0
2. Liking	+	0	0
3. Infatuated love	0	+	0
4. Empty love	0	0	+
5. Romantic love	+	+	0
6. Companionate love	+	0	+
7. Fatuous love	0	+	+
8. Consummate love	+	+	+

Note: + = component present; 0 = component absent. Most loving relationships fall somewhere between these "pure" types because the various components are present in various degrees, not in all-or-none fashion as indicated in the table.

From Sternberg, 1986, pp. 119–135, Table 2. Copyright © 1986 by the American Psychological Association. Used by permission.

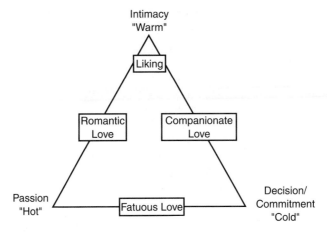

FIGURE 14–2. Sternberg's "triangular" theory of love. Different "types" of liking and loving relationships are defined by location with reference to the vertices of the triangle.

5. **Romantic love** has intimacy and passion, and is a kind of storybook love. There is stronger emotional bonding (intimacy) than with infatuated love, but not commitment.

6. **Companionate love** refers to a long-term, committed friendship. Such a friendship might characterize a marriage after the passion has died down.

7. **Fatuous love** is a combination of passion and decision/commitment, such as a whirlwind courtship and marriage. The commitment is based on passion rather than intimacy.

8. **Consummate love** represents a kind of ideal toward which we might strive, a kind of love to be found more in our dreams than in reality. And, if found, it may be very hard to maintain.

The range of theories and of types of love within a theory strongly indicates that love is not a single process that applies the same to all people in all situations. Love may mean different things to different people because there are different kinds of love masquerading under one name. As the different types or styles of love become more clearly distinguished by research, we should better be able to understand the development of love, the relationship of love to other behaviors, and perhaps how to increase the amount of love in people's lives.

SECTION SUMMARY

1. A major advance in the study of interpersonal relations was the recognition that liking and loving are not the same, and that there are different kinds of love.

2. According to **reinforcement theory**, if rewards are experienced while in the presence of someone, the positive emotion produced by the reward becomes associated with the person present.

3. **Social exchange theory, equity theory**, and **investment theory** are **economic** approaches to attraction. Each deals with the **costs** and **benefits** of being in a relationship. According to investment theory, the more resources that people have in a relationship, the stronger the commitment to that relationship if the rewards are greater than the costs.

4. **Cognitive-arousal theory** says that if diffuse arousal occurs while in the presence of another person, the first person may interpret the arousal as love. This phenomenon may also account for the attractiveness of the "hard to get" person, whereby frustration might be mislabeled as love.

5. Sternberg's **triangular theory** says that love is based on the three dimensions of **intimacy, passion**, and **decision/commitment**. The relative amounts of each of these define eight different types of love, ranging from "nonlove" to "consummate love."

CHAPTER FIFTEEN

Applications of Motivation Theory

How do our views about mankind affect the way we look at job motivation?

Is a large salary sufficient to get a worker to perform at his or her best?

Is there a fixed hierarchy of motives that applies to everyone?

How do expectations of success relate to work motivation?

What is the most effective way to set goals?

What is job satisfaction and why is it important?

Why do people play sports?

Why do people watch sports?

Does level of arousal affect all sports performances the same?

What causes aggression in sports?

Does playing at home really give a team an advantage?

What is the communication model of advertising and persuasion?

How is the elaboration likelihood model different from the communication model?

What specific factors influence advertising effectiveness?

Does subliminal advertising really work?

In this chapter we look at the application of general principles of motivation to three areas of psychology: job motivation and satisfaction, sports psychology, and advertising and persuasion. To say that we are looking at applications, however, does not mean that there is a difference between so-called "pure" and "applied" research as far as the rules for conducting research are concerned. The two kinds of research differ only in that pure research may be done because a problem is interesting in its own right or it contributes to theory and applied research is done with a more immediate practical goal in mind. For example, one psychologist might be interested in the general question of how people interact in groups, and another psychologist might be interested in specific interactions in sports teams. The same person might combine both interests in her research. Or one researcher might be interested in the reason why people are attracted to a particular kind of stimulus, whereas another researcher might be interested in attracting attention to an advertisement. In previous chapters we have often looked at specific applications through the lens of general theories. In this chapter we just do this in more detail for some selected problems.

JOB MOTIVATION AND SATISFACTION

Orientation to Job Motivation

A common question from managers is "How can I motivate people to work harder?" Job motivation theories in business and industry are not unlike the more general psychological theories of motivation discussed thus far. And the reason is simple: People are people whether at home or on the job. Quite separately from psychological research or theory, however, some managers might have philosophical views that affect how they treat their subordinates.

Philosophical views. Motivation "theory" in business used to be largely speculative, related to the perceived nature of humans. Such philosophical views as the following, accurate or not, have influenced managerial thinking about dealing with workers.

1. **Rational-economic person.** This view assumes that people are motivated solely by economic considerations and can make rational economic decisions. Workers are considered to be inherently lazy and will not work unless paid. Manipulation of wages and incentives should be sufficient to make them work. People are considered relatively interchangeable since they can be controlled by money.
2. **Social person.** In a famous set of studies conducted at the Hawthorne, Illinois, manufacturing plant of Western Electric Company, Roethlisberger and Dickson (1947) showed that such environmental conditions as lighting affected production far less than did such social factors as job satisfaction, social groupings, and conformity. The concept of the social person developed from these studies, sug-

gesting that workers are primarily motivated by social needs that are not met just by work. Workers may be more responsive to their peers than to their company.

3. **Self-actualizing person.** "According to the self-actualizing conception, man is seen as intrinsically motivated. He takes pride in his work because it is his work" (Wrightsman, 1972, p. 510). Pride and satisfaction are not always possible in large amounts in some jobs (as in menial labor), but where there is possibility for personal growth and accomplishment for the worker, a good leader will provide the opportunity.

4. **Complex person.** This view recognizes that motives, emotions, experiences, and abilities may differ greatly from person to person, and that they may also change over time. New motives and skills, as well as successes and failures, affect a worker's attitude about a job and how well the job can be handled. There is therefore no single strategy for dealing with all workers, and perhaps not even with the same worker at different times.

Theory X and theory Y.   Douglas McGregor (1960) distinguished two approaches to management and the worker that he simply identified as Theory X and Theory Y, summarized by DuBrin (1980, p. 39) as follows:

- Theory X assumes that people dislike work and must be coerced, controlled, and directed toward organizational goals. Furthermore, most people prefer to be treated this way so that they can avoid responsibility.
- Theory Y emphasizes people's intrinsic interest in their work, their desire to be self-directing and to seek responsibility, and their capacity to be creative in solving business problems.

A marketing manager who believes in Theory X might try to motivate sales representatives as follows, again quoting DuBrin (p. 39):

We have established sales quotas for each of you. Each year that your quota is reached, the company will pay for a five-day trip for you and your spouse. This will be in addition to your normal vacation. . . . Sales representatives who are unable to meet their quotas for three consecutive quarters will probably not be invited back for a fourth quarter.

On the other hand, a Theory Y believer might say the following:

You and your sales managers will get together on establishing sales quotas for each year. If you achieve your quotas, you will receive extra money. High performance in sales is one important factor in being considered for a management assignment. Another important part of your job besides selling is to keep our product-planning group informed about changes in consumer demand. Many of our new products in the past stemmed directly from the suggestions of sales representatives.

The newer views, departing from the economic person approach, have developed in part because research has shown that workers are indeed more complex than Theory X supposes. Unfortunately, it is still true that many employers believe that simply paying a person is sufficient to get the most there is to be gotten from a worker.

Theories of Job Motivation

The previous philosophical approaches indicate different orientations to the questions of worker motivation but are not articulated theories in any specific sense. We now look at more detailed theories.

Herzberg's two-factor theory. Frederick Herzberg (1966) suggested that some aspects of a job allow people to satisfy "higher level" needs, which he called satisfiers or motivators. He argued that people want more from their jobs than pay, such as recognition, responsibility, feelings of achievement, prestige, pleasure from social interactions, stimulation, and challenge. Some job elements are noticeable in their absence, however, and produce dissatisfaction. Such dissatisfiers tend to relate to annoying external conditions, such as company policy and its administration, supervision, working conditions, relations with others, status, and job security. Satisfaction of these needs is called hygiene. The heart of Herzberg's approach is that dissatisfaction may lower performance but that hygienic measures will not markedly improve performance.

Herzberg repeatedly claimed that external incentives are not motivators. The distinction that Herzberg seemed to be trying to convey was between external rewards and intrinsic motivation. This distinction is certainly not unimportant, but since Herzberg did not make it clear, his resulting ideas were sometimes unusual. To argue that supervision is not motivating (whether by threat of firing or control of rewards) and that achievement, recognition, and responsibility are motivating, simply flies in the face of any other major theoretical approach to motivation (e.g., see Locke, 1976). Achievement and recognition may be good motivators, but this observation is not equivalent to saying that supervisory practices or pay incentives have no role as motivators.

Maslow's need hierarchy. Maslow's need hierarchy theory (e.g., Maslow, 1970) stratifies needs from the most basic biological to the most ethereal psychological: (1) physiological (such as hunger-thirst), (2) safety and security, (3) love and belongingness, (4) self-esteem (achievement, recognition), and (5) self-actualization (reaching one's highest potential). The essence of the theory is that the needs lower in the hierarchy have to be at least partly fulfilled before the higher needs become active. As Maslow saw it, few individuals ever really reach the highest plateau, self-actualization, because of overconcern about lower-level needs, self-esteem, for example. A serious problem for the theory is posed by the prevalence of so-called suicide bombers who are willing, if not eager, to ignore the most basic principles in Maslow's scheme and sacrifice themselves for some principle. As was pointed out in Chapter One, people do have hierarchies of motives (some are more important than others), but they don't often match Maslow's theory.

Maslow's theory sometimes seems to make sense in the industrial situation. For example, lower-level workers seem to be more motivated by money (needed for food and shelter) and may not be much motivated to work creatively in their jobs. At higher levels, where income is sufficient to keep the wolf from the door, self-actualization seems more important. The theory is extremely difficult to test, however, because in lower-level jobs, there may be no opportunity for self-expression. Therefore, workers may seek more expressive satisfactions outside the job. Research indicates that two "levels" of motivation are sufficient to account for work motivation. One level combines physiological, safety and belonging needs and the other level combines esteem, achievement and actualization. This looks suspiciously like restatement of the external reward/intrinsic motivation distinction (e.g., see Landy & Trumbo, 1980; Steers & Porter, 1975).

Vroom's valence-instrumentality-expectancy (VIE) theory.   According to Vroom's (1964) theory, expectancy is the perceived probability that a particular amount of effort will be instrumental in achieving a valued goal. A worker might consider, "What are the chances I will get promoted if I work hard?" Based upon knowledge of the situation, the probability might be low, medium, or high. For example, a female in a male-dominated organization might consider the probability of advancement to be much lower than would a man in the same position. The second component of the expectancy is the valence (value) that some outcome (such as promotion) has for the worker. If a person does not value a promotion, we would not expect her or him to work hard for it. Putting this formulation into Vroom's terms produces Figure 15–1, which is the expectancy that work will lead to a certain level of performance and that this performance will be instrumental in achieving the long-term goal (promotion). If a person expects that hard work will not produce a high level of performance or that high performance will not achieve the goal, the perceived instrumentality will be low, and the person is not likely to work very hard.

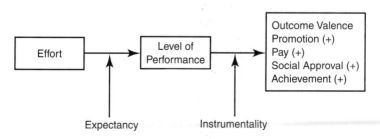

FIGURE 15–1. Vroom's VIE model of job motivation and performance.

Equity theory.   The author once listened to the complaint of a construction worker about having to do some welding one day when the regular welder was sick. His complaint was not that he disliked welding (he actually liked it) or that it was more difficult or harder work than his regular job (it was easier). Rather, he was dissatisfied because welders earn more than his own job paid, and he considered it unfair that he should be asked to weld but be paid at his own regular rate. This type of response is not readily explained by the previous theories but is exactly what equity theory was designed to explain.

Equity theory (Adams, 1975) is the idea that a person compares how hard he is working with what he is getting in return, and if he perceives a discrepancy, he is unhappy. The discrepancy may be between the person's internal standard for what is equitable return for a certain amount of effort, or it may be in comparison with some external reference. Our construction worker (let's call him Frank) used other welders as a reference rather than his own pay rate. Welders get paid so much an hour for their work, and Frank was getting paid less. Therefore, the ratio of his pay to his work was less than that of the regular welders. Thus

Frank's Pay for Welder's Work < Welder's Pay for Welder's Work

This discrepancy produced an aversive emotional state in Frank, a degree of frustration because Frank's goal was equity and he was not achieving it. How does Frank respond to this if he is forced to weld for the day? According to the theory, he would do something to make his ratio of pay to work more equal to the reference. He might reduce his own work until he perceives that his return is proportionally the same as that of a regular welder. Or he might try to get a raise. Or he might just complain and be rather unpleasant to be around (as he was).

Suppose that instead of Frank, there is Frieda, who is getting a perceived low return for effort compared with that of male workers. What might she do? She might accept one of the traditional excuses for paying women less, such as "a man has a family to support," while remaining unhappy. She might quit her job. She might ask for a raise. She might reduce her work output. She might file a complaint with the government under the Equal Pay Act or the Fair Employment Practices Act. In any event, neither Frank nor Frieda is going to be a happy camper until there is some resolution to their perceived inequities.

What would happen if a person received *more* than he or she perceives to be deserved? There is some evidence that people will actually work harder, for a while at least, apparently in order to restore equity. It does seem, however, that people adapt to the new level of return for their work so that it is no longer perceived as high, and work may drop back to where it had been previously.

Two particular problems for researchers working with equity theory in the industrial/organizational setting are that (1) pay is not the only work outcome and (2) the appropriateness of the reference person that an individual compares himself or herself with is not always clear (Gibson, Ivancevich, & Donnelly, 1979, p. 117). There certainly is enough evidence from a variety of sources, however, to indicate that such discrepancies may indeed produce tension and disharmony (Landy & Trumbo, 1980). Equitable treatment is important in most situations, not just business.

Behavior theory and goal setting. Any method of rewarding work or punishing nonwork (such as by threat of firing a recalcitrant worker) is an application of instrumental (operant) conditioning to job motivation. The problem is that usually the people who use these applications are often not well versed in the details of this approach. A more sophisticated operant conditioning approach proceeds in three parts:

1. Setting up environmental conditions to make particular behaviors more or less likely to occur. For example, working without interruption is easier if one's desk is not in a place that many people go by each day;
2. Setting goals so that the individual knows what performance is expected; and
3. Reinforcing individuals for achieving those goals. Many questions still arise, however. Who will set the goals? How will reinforcement (feedback about success) be given?

Emery air freight. One of the best-documented cases of companywide adoption of these principles is the experience at the Emery Air Freight Company (Feeney, 1972). The problem was simple: Employees were using the wrong size cardboard cartons for shipping. Because too-large cartons take up more space, there are fewer cartons per load and less profit. The "cure" for the problem was almost equally simple: Employees were told how to load cartons properly and were verbally reinforced for doing so. Improvement was immediate. Employees were also instructed to pay close attention to such details as the scheduling of pickups and deliveries, and goals were set for these. Again, performance improved markedly.

The "real" problem had been that the employees did not know either what they were doing or what they should have been doing. They estimated that they were about 90 percent efficient in their loading, whereas they were actually closer to 45 percent efficiency. Once it was determined where performance really was and careful records were being kept, it was possible to institute rapid change at little expense. An initial investment of $5,000 in the program brought about improved efficiency ultimately worth millions of dollars.

Locke's theory of goal setting. Edwin Locke (e.g., 1968; Latham, 2001; Locke & Latham, 1984) proposed two major principles of goal setting:

1. Hard goals produce higher performance than easy goals.
2. Specific goals produce higher performance than vague goals, such as "Do the best you can."

This proposal was illustrated in the Emery Air Freight case, but even better in a report by Latham and Baldes (1975). The problem was that logging trucks were not being loaded nearly to capacity, so that more runs than necessary were being made by each truck. The solution was to tell each driver specifically to load her or his truck to 94 percent of the truck's legal weight, as compared with the approximately 60 percent average that the drivers had been carrying. Figure 15–2 shows the result, a marked and sustained improvement. The drivers were given verbal praise for improving their load size, but they got no other reward, and there was no special training for either drivers or supervisors.

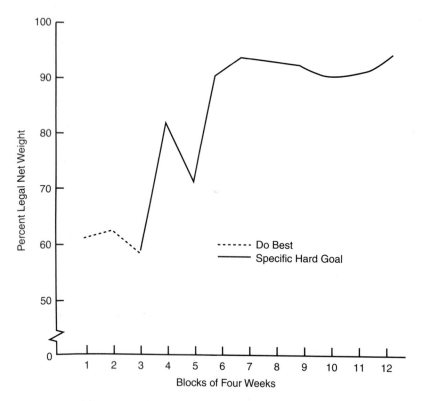

FIGURE 15–2.   When drivers were told to "do their best" loading trucks (dotted portion of curve), they loaded them only to about 60 percent of legal capacity. When given the specific instructions to load them to 94 percent, however, there was an immediate and sustained increase in load size. (From Latham & Baldes, 1975. Used with permission. Copyright © 1975 by the American Psychological Association.)

Two additional principles in the application of goal-setting techniques should be adhered to, however. First, goals should be attainable. Specific goals should be difficult, not impossible. Research on United Fund campaigns illustrates this principle. When a goal of 20 percent increase over the previous year was set, productivity went up 25 percent. But a goal of 80 percent increase resulted in only a 12 percent rise, and performance declined when the goal was doubled (Dessler, 1980). Second, goals should be relevant to the job at hand. A production supervisor should set goals for production, not sales. The goals should also be measured in objective and relevant terms, such as amount produced per unit time. There is also considerable value in employee participation in goal setting. What a supervisor sees as an attainable goal may differ sharply from what an employee sees. Therefore, if supervisor and employee jointly set a goal that is satisfactory to both, there is a greater chance of success because the goal is realistic and the employee is committed to trying to achieve the goal. Participation also increases job satisfaction.

Job Satisfaction

Between 1935 and 1976, there were over 3,000 published studies of job satisfaction, an average of one every five days (Locke, 1976). Between 1989 and 1998, PsycINFO (a computerized abstracting service for psychology-related journals and books, operated by the American Psychological Association) showed 3,191 entries with the phrase "job satisfaction" in the abstract. Interest in the topic seems not to have dimmed in the last ten years. Job satisfaction is considered so important because of the costs of dissatisfaction in employee turnover, absenteeism, and work performance. Turnover is one of the most expensive of personnel problems because of time and money that are lost in training workers. The relationship between job satisfaction and absenteeism is somewhat difficult to document, but Smith (1977) cleverly did so. During a snowstorm in Chicago, job satisfaction predicted rather well among a large number of managers who would or would not show up for work. Given a good excuse not to come to work, the less satisfied managers in a large corporation did not come to work, but better satisfied managers did. On the same day in New York City, where the weather was nice, job satisfaction did not predict absenteeism among comparable managers. It took the combination of environmental factors (storm) and personal factors (job satisfaction) to tease out the effect of job satisfaction on absenteeism.

Meaning and measurement of job satisfaction.   Job satisfaction may be defined as "the attitude one has toward his or her job" (McCormick & Ilgen, 1980, p. 303). An attitude, as we saw in Chapter Thirteen, is an emotional response toward something (in this case, a job), which can vary from positive to negative in any degree. Whatever might be said about attitudes in general applies to job satisfaction in particular. Thus, the measurement of job satisfaction, the relation of job satisfaction to behavior, and methods of improving job satisfaction are all special cases of the same problems raised about attitudes. Furthermore, just as a job has many characteristics, so job satisfaction is necessarily a summation of worker attitudes about all these characteristics. Good and bad features of a job are balanced so that job satisfaction "on the whole" is relatively high or low. Table 15–1 shows a dozen dimensions of work that are related to job satisfaction.

TABLE 15–1.   Job dimensions typically relevant to job satisfaction.

GENERAL CATEGORIES	SPECIFIC DIMENSION	DIMENSION DESCRIPTIONS
I. Events or Conditions		
1. Work	Work itself	Includes intrinsic interest, variety, opportunity for learning, difficulty, amount, chances for success, control over work flow, etc.
2. Rewards	Pay	Amount of fairness or equity of, basis for pay, etc.
	Promotions	Opportunities for, basis of, fairness of, etc.
	Recognition	Praise, criticism, credit for work done, etc.
3. Context of work	Working conditions	Hours, rest pauses, equipment, quality of the work space, temperature, ventilation, location of plant, etc.
	Benefits	Pensions, medical and life insurance plans, annual leave, vacations, etc.
II. Agents		
1. Self	Self	Values, skills and abilities, etc.
2. Others (in-company)	Supervision	Supervisory style and influence, technical adequacy, administrative skills, etc.
	Coworkers	Competence, friendliness, helpfulness, technical competence, etc.
3. Others (outside company)	Customers	Technical competence, friendliness, etc.
	Family members*	Supportiveness, knowledge of job, demands for time, etc.
	Others	Depending upon position, e.g., students, parents, voters

*Not included in Locke's discussion.
Adapted from Locke, 1976, 1302. Used by permission of Rand-McNally.

Job satisfaction and behavior.   It is only partly true that "happy workers are good workers." The relationship between job satisfaction and performance is considerably less than perfect, and where such a correlation does exist, the cause may not be the one implied. For example, good performance may lead to high job satisfaction rather than the other way around. Lawler and Porter (1967) proposed that performance that leads to rewards produces satisfaction with the work and also produces the expectation that future performance will also lead to rewards. This model is illustrated in Figure 15–3.

Several studies testing Lawler and Porter's model have indicated that there is greater job satisfaction when rewards are specifically related to job performance than when equal rewards are given but not specifically related to job performance. This finding suggests that job satisfaction comes with perceived control over events that produce success. Organizational attempts to "increase morale" by contrived programs may have some positive effects but do not necessarily lead to better performance, since the "morale building events" are not related to performance.

Theories of Job Satisfaction

Theories of job satisfaction involve motivational, emotional, and informational components. The following three theories are illustrative.

Instrumentality theory.   Job satisfaction is high to the extent that the job is instrumental in getting the worker what he or she values or wants from the job. This might be pleasure in the work, security, prestige, money, short hours, flex time, autonomy, convenient location, day care, or anything else the worker considers valuable.

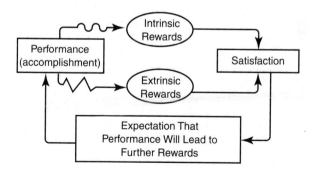

FIGURE 15–3. The Lawler-Porter model of job satisfaction, showing how performance leads to rewards and satisfaction and the expectation of future rewards. (From Lawler & Porter, 1967, Fig. 1. Figure slightly adapted by Dessler, 1980. Used with permission of Reston Publ. Co.)

Equity theory.   As discussed earlier, people generally want to get what they consider a fair (equitable) return for their behavior, suggesting that there is greater job satisfaction if the worker perceives that the return for her or his work is equitable.

The job characteristics model.   Hackman and Lawler (1971) defined six job attributes that might relate to job satisfaction: (1) variety of work on the job; (2) autonomy in doing work and making decisions; (3) task identity, doing a piece of work that can be clearly identified as the result of the worker's efforts; (4) receiving performance feedback about how well one is doing on the job; (5) dealing with other people; and (6) friendship opportunities on the job. Using a statistical procedure called path analysis, Hackman and Oldham (1976) found that the appropriate combinations of these factors did predict job satisfaction rather well.

Reith (1988) tested the generality of the Hackman-Oldham results by translating the model into academic terms. Her basic assumption was that going to school is a student's job and that all the elements that apply to satisfaction with other jobs would also apply to the classroom. Reith studied 180 students taking introductory psychology and found that measures of the combination of the various aspects of job satisfaction just described did correlate about +.60 with course satisfaction. Overall, Reith's results were very similar to those reported by Hackman and Oldham (1976), showing that job satisfaction can be fruitfully studied in academic settings. Although it would be unwise to study job satisfaction exclusively in academia, there is some value in being able to test theories in less formidable surroundings than unionized industries and in applying models that might suggest improvements in academia. Reith also found a significant relationship between degree of perceived equity in grading and course satisfaction.

SECTION SUMMARY

1. **Job motivation** refers to those motivational variables that influence worker productivity. **Job satisfaction** refers to worker attitudes (positive or negative) toward the job.

2. Many "theories" of worker behavior have been more philosophical than scientific. McGregor distinguished two broadly different approaches to worker motivation. **Theory X,** representing traditional views, assumes that workers dislike work and have to be coerced to do it. **Theory Y,** a more modern view, emphasizes that workers want self-satisfaction from work, which includes responsibility and autonomy.

3. Maslow's **need hierarchy theory** distinguishes physiological, safety, belongingness, self-esteem, and self-actualization needs. The latter become more dominant when the former have been satisfied. Research evidence supports only a two-level approach, however (combining the first three and the last two needs into two separate groupings).

4. **Expectancy theories,** much like achievement theory, emphasize workers' perceptions of the **probabilities** and **values** of successfully completing some job. **Vroom's instrumentality theory** emphasizes the importance of workers' perceptions that a given behavior will be **instrumental** in obtaining a desired goal.

5. **Equity theory** emphasizes workers' desires to get an equitable return for work done. What is considered equitable may be based on some internal standard or on some external reference, such as what another worker gets for doing similar work. Perceived inequity produces tension, which a worker may try to reduce by working less hard, trying to get more money, and so on.

6. **Goal-setting theory** emphasizes setting high (but reachable) and specific goals, and giving feedback about whether these goals are being achieved.

7. Job satisfaction is only partly related to job productivity. Performance that leads to rewards produces satisfaction, which leads to the expectation that future performance will also lead to rewards. Job satisfaction alone does not greatly increase productivity.

8. Theories accounting for job satisfaction include **instrumentality theory, equity theory,** and **job characteristics theory.**

MOTIVATION IN SPORTS

Orientation

Sports behavior is just as complex as any other form of behavior, involving many sets of skills, thoughts, motives, and environmental settings. We can take the formula

$$\text{Behavior} = f\,(\text{Person, Environment})$$

and just make it more specific.

$$\text{Sports Behavior} = f\,(\text{Person}_{\text{motives, skills, knowledge}}$$
$$\text{and Environment}_{\text{physical, social}})$$

this indicates some aspects of the person and the environment that might concern us. "Person" could refer to players, coaches, or fans. The environment could be physical surroundings, but could also include social aspects of other people participating in an event (e.g., trash talking), as well as people viewing an event (fans cheering, booing, or remaining eerily silent).

The problems to be addressed by sports psychologists are highly varied, depending on (1) what person(s) we are interested in, (2) what behavior we are interested in, and (3) the environment in which we are working, including rules (and their interpretations). These elements are illustrated in Table 15–2.

TABLE 15–2. Some topics that might be of interest to a sports psychologist.

	YOUTH SPORTS	YOUNG ADULT	ADULT
Players or Coaches	Recreational	Recreational	Recreational
	Competitive	Competitive	Competitive
	Elite	High school varsity	Elite amateur, e.g.,
		College varsity	Olympic
		Elite amateur	Professional
Behaviors	Skilled athletic performance (learning and maintenance)		
	Persistence in staying with sport (e.g., youth)		
	Violence or other rule-breaking (on field and in the stands)		
	Competitors only, no coaches or referees (e.g., pickup games)		
Environment	Parents and a few fans		
	Large audiences, many fans, television cameras		
	Home field versus away		

What Motivation Theories Apply to Sports?

Success or failure in sports depends on factors in addition to motivation, such as athletic ability, training, practice, and coaching. All these are relevant to skill levels. Motivational factors are relevant to many aspects of sports, however. These include the goals a person has for being involved in sport and willingness to overcome obstacles to participate (e.g., endure hardship of training, expense of participation, loss of time from other activities, and so on). Table 15–3, which refers to topics from previous chapters, shows theories of motivation that are obviously relevant to sports. We shall limit ourselves to a few selected issues here.

Why Do People Play Sports?

People engage in sports for many different reasons, just as they choose to participate in any other activity for different reasons. The following are some motivational factors.

Arousal.   The excitement produced by playing may make playful behavior rewarding for its own sake. In Chapter Six we discussed the fact that people and animals may engage in activities that serve to increase their arousal, bringing them more nearly to an optimum level. Sports may bring a degree of variety, or stimulus change, into one's life. Thus, a person who works at a routine job all day may enjoy the change of pace and challenge provided by recreational activities.

Achievement and competition.   The pride of achievement may be sought in sports, as well as in work. Similarly, competitiveness may also be experienced in sports.

TABLE 15–3. Some major theo. ...n relevant to sports.

Achievement Motivation (Hope of s... . of failure)
Task persistence, performance inten.. ..asks
Activation (Arousal) Theory
Optimal level of arousal and performanc..
Aggression Theory
Frustration-aggression, stimulus-aroused aggr..
Attribution Theory of Achievement (Weiner)
Effects of success/failure attributions (perceived ca... mental aggression
Drive Theory
Social facilitation effects and type of task
...bsequent performance
Expectancy-Value Theory
Effects of expected outcome and value of outcome on perfor..
Frustration Theory
Punishing effects of frustration, drive effects, frustration-aggressio..
Goal Setting Theory (Locke)
Types of goals (winning, mastery of task, social, money)
Determining what goal levels are most effective for performance
Reinforcement Theory
E.g., fans, other players, coaches selectively reinforcing certain behaviors
Schedules of reinforcement, choice of reinforcers
Self-Efficacy Theory ("Self-confidence")
How feelings of efficacy develop and what their effects are on performance

Self-expression. Sports can be a form of self-expression for some people in the same way that music, art, writing, or hobbies are vehicles for self-expression for other people (Weinberg, 1984). Self-expression could also be viewed in terms of intrinsic motivation.

Social rewards. Many people enjoy sports because sports satisfy an affiliation motive through opportunity for interaction with others. A friendly softball game can be a family affair as much as a sports competition. A game of tennis may be played at a level below the capabilities of the players just in order to keep the game friendly and to have a pleasant outing.

Changes in motivation with aging. As children get older, interest in organized sports depends on the rewards gained from sports as compared with the rewarding aspects of other activities. After about age twelve, there is a marked decline in the numbers of boys and girls engaging in organized sport. One reason is that children perceive that they are not mastering their particular sport and therefore do not find it rewarding (Roberts, 1984). At the same time, the other rewards (e.g., opportunities to socialize) are not strong enough to hold them if those rewards can be gained more easily elsewhere. From a strictly sports point of view, this tendency is unfortunate because slower-maturing children who are not the best of athletes in early adolescence may subsequently surpass the abilities of many of their

Applications of Motivation Theory) and could enjoy sports activities

earlier-maturing age mates (R ort as a social event persist longer in
later. Children who are attra to it because they believe they can get
the sport than those who a rs.
recognition by being goo t is rewarding for an individual depends
The extent to wh he sets. A mediocre athlete may play tennis
partly on the goals th some exercise, have a good time, and make a
regularly if the goal hievement theory (Chapter Twelve) suggests that
good shot now and es where there are about equal chances of winning
maximum enjoym how well a person plays. In team or individual sports,
or losing regard es into competitions where we can have some successes
we usually put Without that risk, the successes mean little.
but also risk f

Why eople Watch Sports?

Th 1982 World Cup soccer match final drew an estimated 1.4 billion
televisi viewers. Television advertising time during recent Superbowl
games has sold for about $1 million a minute. Several cable TV networks now
devote twenty-four hours a day to sports, and the major networks carry almost
every sporting event of national interest. What is so attractive to viewers about
sports

Basking in the reflected glory of the home team. Many viewers have a
favorite team with which they can identify. When the "home team" (which
might be the Atlanta Braves, which calls itself "America's Team") wins, its
fans feel proud and happy; when it loses, they are mightily unhappy. The
depth of this feeling is shown by the harassment of coaches who lose too
often, as if the fans themselves had been the losers. This possibility may be
true. The fans may have their self-esteem lowered if their team performs
badly because they feel that losing somehow reflects on them. At the very
least, their team losing does reflect on their ability to choose a winning team
to support. The "national pride" of "winning" the Olympics and the "shame"
of not winning highlights this whole phenomenon.

Watching sports for arousal. Many people go to sporting events because of the excitement of the crowd, the thrill of "being there." Sporting
events, like movies, are also a stimulus change, a variation in the everyday
routine of life and an opportunity for affiliation with one's friends.

Sport as art. Such events as gymnastics, diving, and figure skating are
judged by artistic standards as well as by athletic ones. In gymnastics there are
required moves, demonstrating strength and balance, for example, but
within these limits the ease and grace with which the moves are performed
also determine the winner. Ballet movements and choreography have indeed
become integral to gymnastics and figure skating. To a considerable extent,

particular athletes gain a following because of the artistic manner in which they perform. A balletic action slam dunk by a Michael Jordan or Kobe Bryant is a work of art by any standard.

Motivation and Sports Performance

Optimal levels of arousal.   It is a common observation that either an individual or a team can be "too psyched up" to perform well. According to the Yerkes-Dodson law, the more complex the behavior is, the lower the optimal level of motivation (Chapter Six). Different activities in different sports require different complexities of behavior and should therefore have different optimal levels of arousal. A football coach might try to work his team into a passionate frenzy for a big game ("Win this one for the Gipper!"), but a golf coach would hardly do so because golf requires delicately controlled movements and golfers have to remain calm (Silva & Stevens, 2002, Ch. 7).

Oxendine (1970) examined the question of optimal levels for different sports activities. He ranked different sports in terms of the amount of fine muscular control and judgment involved. Bowling, field goal kicking, skating, and tournament-level golfing require very delicate control, whereas weight lifting, sprinting, and football blocking and tackling do not require as much control. Weinberg and Genuchi (1980) reported that golfers performed better with low levels of anxiety, as expected. For basketball, however, it has been reported that medium anxiety levels are more effective (Sonstroem & Bernardo, 1982). Klavora (1978) assessed the pregame anxiety levels of ninety-five boys during a high school basketball season. Performance level was determined by having coaches rate the players in terms of their customary levels of ability. Performance was again found to be better with medium levels of anxiety.

Sonstroem (1984) and Neiss (1988) have both made the point, however, that there are several problems in applying the optimal level notion. First, it is difficult to quantify arousal levels. Psychologists usually look at motivation levels in terms of groups that have more or less motivation than do other groups. This procedure does not allow discovery of an optimal level because it takes a number of well-defined motivational values to determine any inverted function, much less to compare different ones. Consequently, we may not be able to define arousal levels precisely enough to test the inverted U hypothesis well. Second, even if we could define levels of arousal accurately, there are ethical sanctions against inducing extreme levels of arousal in experimental situations. Third, we must ask whether there is more than one kind of arousal.

In sports psychology, being "anxious" and being "psyched up" refer to two different kinds of arousal. These two kinds of arousal seem to be like Thayer's energetic-sleepy and tense-relaxed dimensions of arousal (see Chapter Two), and there is some physiological evidence for such a distinction.

Exercise-induced arousal produces an increase in epinephrine output, but not cortisol (an adrenal cortex stress hormone). Exercise plus fear produces an increase in both (Neiss, 1988). This being the case, we would then have to ask in any particular situation which arousal dimension we are referring to if we say that arousal is low, medium, or high. Furthermore, suppose that an athlete also gets angry. Is anger a third type of arousal? And for each of these types of arousal, is the optimal level of arousal the same?

A final consideration in evaluating the inverted U function hypothesis concerns the methods used to produce arousal. The operations for producing arousal may have both arousal effects and stimulus effects. Thus the crowd at an athletic event might be a "social facilitator," raising the level of irrelevant drive, but a screaming crowd might also be a distracting stimulus as well. If performance were worse with such a crowd, it would be diffficult to know whether the motivational element (irrelevant drive) or the stimulus element (distracting noise) were the important determinant of performance. Both might be important.

In the face of such difficulties, Neiss (1988) argues that the inverted U hypothesis is given only weak support in the motor performance literature. High arousal on one dimension (such as energetic-sleepy, or psyched up) might facilitate performance, but on another dimension (such as tensed-relaxed, or anxious) it might inhibit performance. We need to specify which kind of arousal is related to performance and an inverted U.

Ideally, we would try to help an athlete adjust his or her level of motivation to the optimal level for his or her sport at a given time. Part of the art of coaching is to recognize when individual performers are not aroused enough or are too highly aroused. At the beginning of an important game, for example, players may be too highly aroused (too tense) and make errors, and the coach may call time out to calm down the players. Or a team may be so confident of winning that the coach must work hard to get the team aroused to optimum performance. One of the most important motivational insights that we can have about motivation and athletics is that the highest possible level of arousal is seldom the best level of arousal for best performance.

Self-regulation of arousal.   Athletes themselves engage in various strategies to raise or lower their own arousal levels, just as people try to control their own anxiety or stress levels in other situations. Some athletes relax themselves with meditation before a contest, and others engage in relaxation exercises. Some pray. During the 1988 World Series, Dodgers pitcher Orel Hershiser sang hymns to himself in the dugout. Good athletes commonly engage in thought stopping, tuning out thoughts that would be disruptive or anxiety arousing in relation to performance. For example, a golfer who just shot a double-bogey cannot afford to dwell on that thought as she or he continues to play, nor can a player who makes an error in the World Series dwell on the error. Among world-class athletes of similar ability in any sport, the small edge gained by psychological training may be the difference between an Olympic medal and oblivion.

Aggression in Sports

Player aggression.   Violent behavior is inherent in such contact sports as hockey and football, but it is also frequent in such "noncontact" sports as basketball and soccer. It is important to distinguish between assertiveness and aggressiveness, however (Wann, 1997). In everyday conversation, people often label "trying hard" as being "aggressive," not using the term "aggressive" in the more precise sense of intending to harm someone. Two players diving to the floor for a loose basketball may be called aggressive when in fact they are being assertive. An injury resulting from the collision would be incidental to the assertiveness, an unintended harm. In contrast, intentional elbowing under the basket may be done to intimidate an opponent by hurting him or her. Such intimidation and other harmful activities become more acceptable if we blur the distinction between assertion and aggression. It is, of course, difficult for an observer to say when harmful behavior is in fact aggressive, so such behaviors are even more likely to pass unchallenged.

Why does truly aggressive behavior occur in sports? Some aggressive behavior may be stimulus-induced, following a painful encounter, for example. The frustration-aggression hypothesis makes much sense here. When a player or team is frustrated in attempts to win, aggression may ensue. The story is made more complicated, however, by instrumental aggression (Wann, 1997). In many sports, a certain degree of departure from the rules is allowed in order to maintain the flow of play. It is up to the referee(s) to keep play from getting out of hand. In important games, such as the NBA finals, referees are reluctant to "take the game out of the hands of the players" by too-frequent whistles. Under such conditions it is not uncommon for fights to erupt because players become frustrated but also because aggressive behavior may lead to greater success. Furthermore, fans, coaches, and fellow players often reward individual violent behavior. It is often said that hockey fans go more to see the fights than to see hockey. A hockey player on the bench may be expected to leap into a fight on the ice or be considered a coward or not a true team member if she or he fails to do so.

Fan aggression and mob behavior.   Chapter Ten presented two opposing views of the effects of observing violence: (1) Viewing is cathartic and reduces violence, and (2) observed violence is a model that leads to more violence. Considerable evidence suggests that the latter view is more nearly correct. For example, fans were interviewed before and after both the 1969 Army-Navy football game and the Army-Temple gymnastics meet held in the same month. There was a significant increase in reported hostility after the football game but not after the gymnastics meet, regardless of which team was supported (Goldstein & Arma, 1971). Similar results were found in a study of ice hockey and professional wrestling in contrast to swimming (Arma, Russell, & Sandelands, 1979). Such studies, along with casual observation, suggest that fan hostility increases with contact sports more than with noncontact sports. Player violence and fan violence may fuel each other. Soccer crowds have become so unruly on the European continent, especially when English teams are involved, that in 1985 several countries joined in a pact to reduce the violence. The critical incident was a riot between British and Italian fans in Belgium in which forty-one people were killed.

How can we account for such violent behavior? One reason offered for the Belgian riot was that the English fans came from an economically depressed area. They had time on their hands, their lives were dull, and they were livening things up for themselves. It is generally conceded that the English fans went to Belgium "looking for trouble." We may, then, partly account for the riot in terms of the frustration-aggression hypothesis. Frustrated in their everyday lives, the fans became aggressive elsewhere.

Fan violence is so often reported in soccer that it is sometimes considered the norm. In fact, however, fan violence in England and Europe is more a political problem than a sports problem. It is brought about by organized groups (e.g., the skinheads in England, and radical right-wing, neo-Nazi groups in Germany). The violence does not just erupt among fans of opposing sides, it is planned in advance, with battle plans drawn. In contrast, at the World Cup match between Mexico and Italy in Washington, D.C., in 1994, opposing fans took pictures with each other. They were just happy to be there.

There are other factors as well. The fans of one team may form a highly cohesive in-group that rejects outsiders, producing an "us versus them" feeling that is frequently related to aggressive behavior (Sherif, Harvey, White, Hood, & Sherif, 1961). Fans of one team reinforce each other for behavior that leads to trouble, such as shouting obscenities at opposing fans. It is also easier to be anonymous in a crowd, so that the chances of being identified and caught for illegal behavior is reduced.

Interestingly, there is little fan violence in the United States. We talk about the Cameron Crazies (the Duke University students at home basketball games in Cameron Indoor Stadium), but in fact they (and many other fans) only act that way. It is what they do, not who they are. They are not violent. There are several possible reasons why Americans may be somewhat "better socialized" (if we are):

- Our professional teams rarely cross national boundaries for regular competition (only to Canada for baseball and basketball), and there are no long-term national rivalries along political lines as there are in Europe.
- We diffuse our allegiances among many sports (football, basketball, baseball, hockey, and so on, whereas other countries around the world tend to be more limited, mostly to soccer).

- Many of our major allegiances are with college teams rather than professional teams, with a continually shifting audience and players.
- The density of professional teams is much greater in many other countries. For example, England, a country about the size of Oregon, has twenty-two professional soccer teams at the highest level. Imagine that we have twenty professional football teams in any U.S. state: Where would we put them? What rivalries would develop?

Environment and Performance

Social facilitation.   If you have ever stood in front of an audience and been afraid or excited, you have an idea of the effect of an audience on athletic performance. An audience may be just another competitor, or it may be a stadium full of people. Attempts to break track records invariably involve competition because runners run faster with competition, and a loud supportive audience is also an asset.

Audience effects depend on the type of activity, however. For well-learned or simple skills, an audience should improve performance. For complex or not-well-learned skills, an audience may make performance worse (see Chapter Six here; LeUnes & Nation, 2002). Most observers seem surprised when a very young competitor does well at a great sporting event, such as Wimbledon or the U.S. Open in tennis. We may equate the pressure with social facilitation. But these young players have been playing tournament tennis from very early ages, are used to audiences, and therefore were probably not as aroused as some other players their age might have been.

Home-field advantage.   It is widely held that there is a home-field advantage in sports, which might might be due to a supportive home crowd ("We've got to get the crowd into the game"), the disadvantages of traveling (especially in professional sports that have long road trips, such as baseball and basketball), or peculiarities of the field or court (e.g., a domed stadium). It was sometimes alleged that the Boston Celtics had a home-court advantage in the old Boston Garden because they knew the dead spots on the parquet floor! What do the data show about home-field advantage?

In general, the home-field advantage is relatively slight. Courneya and Carron (1991) examined 1,812 Double A baseball games and found that the home team won 55 percent of the games. However, this finding was unrelated to travel per se. The results were not predicted by such factors as length of home stand or visitor's road trip. Gayton and Coombs (1995) also concluded that the effects of travel on the home-court advantage was minimal in high school basketball games. Acker (1997) examined 1,568 professional football games between 1988 and 1994 and found that the home team outscored the opponent by 2.91 points. There was a slightly greater home-field advantage for teams with domed stadiums (3.22 points) as compared with open stadiums (3.01 points). There appears to be no single overwhelming factor determining home-field advantage.

Home-field disadvantage. Baumeister and Steinhilber (1984) suggested that a supportive home crowd might actually be disadvantageous to a team because the players might be more self-conscious and distracted from what they are doing. They found that in baseball World Series, home teams tend to win early games but to lose the final games, especially when these games were decisive for winning the series. Benjafield, Liddell, and Benjafield (1989), however, disputed the generality of a home-field disadvantage and said that it was true only for championship series involving the New York Yankees, the Boston Celtics (so much for the parquet floor), and the Montreal Canadiens. They suggest that the home crowds of persistent champions (as these teams were) communicate a pressure to win that interferes with these teams. This pressure might lead to heightened self-awareness or could be due to over arousal.

SECTION SUMMARY

1. The motivation for engaging in sports activities is much the same as for other activities: to provide arousal, achievement and competition, self-expression, and social rewards such as affiliation. After about age twelve, there is a sharp decline in participation in organized sports as children see that they are not mastering their sport.

2. An important problem for competitors is to achieve the **optimal level of motivation** for a sport. The optimal level of arousal varies with the kind of sport (e.g., golf has a lower optimal level than football), and many athletes learn effectively to increase or decrease their own arousal levels to make them more optimal.

3. **Player aggression** in sports may occur as the result of frustration or pain that occur during the course of play (stimulus aroused aggression), and because players and fans reinforce aggressive behavior, which is instrumental to winning.

4. Some of the reasons why people watch sports are that they feel good if the team they identify with is successful, they enjoy the excitement of the contest, and the contest provides opportunity for affiliation with others. **Fan aggression,** stimulated by athletic contests, is sometimes more severe than player aggression.

5. The **environment,** including arena and fans, may influence athletes. Arousal level may be increased because of social facilitation effects of an audience, sometimes thought to be an actual disadvantage of playing at home. There seems to be relatively little home-field advantage.

MOTIVATION AND ADVERTISING

Advertising is an attempt to persuade people to buy some product, commonly assuming that sales will be greater if attitudes toward the product are more positive. One of the most frequently used psychological frameworks for advertising has been the communication model of attitude change and persuasion (e.g., Faison, 1980; Petty & Cacioppo, 1984).

The Communication Model

The communication model says that the **source** of communication (sender) **encodes** an idea into a **message** that is transmitted to an **audience** (receiver) that **decodes** the message. Researchers have systematically studied characteristics of the source, message, and audience to determine what makes persuasive messages effective. We briefly outline some of the main findings of such research and then turn to the relevant motivational/emotional factors related to advertising.

1. The two most important source characteristics are **credibility** (a combination of trustworthiness and expertise) and **likability.**
2. Message characteristics are very complex, depending on the nature of the *medium* (e.g., visual, written, or oral), the type of *arguments* presented (one-sided versus two-sided), the order of presentation of arguments, and logical versus emotional appeals.
3. Audience characteristics include *interest* in and *knowledge* of the topic, and mood (which we may take to include motivational/emotional states in general).

The communication model is based on the idea that the transmission of information is the critical factor in persuasion. Motivational/emotional factors are something of a distracting issue. For example, should one communicate threat or fear in a message? If so, how much? Such issues were considered to be relevant only to the degree that the "real" message got communicated.

As we saw in Chapter Thirteen, however, such dual process attitude theories as the elaboration likelihood model take the point of view that attitude change and persuasion can follow a central route or a peripheral route, or both. The central route involves effortful thinking and scrutiny of attitude-related information. This route is used when a person is ready, willing, and able to engage in effortful processing of information. The peripheral route involves simpler thought processes, automatic arousal of positive or negative affect and the like. For example, a beer ad may evoke imagery of cool refreshment on a hot day or some kind of macho activity or some very vague information ("less calories") requiring little central processing. And, after all, who wants to spend a lot of time thinking carefully about different beers? Furthermore, the situations in which such ads appear (e.g., televised ball games, automobile races) hardly lend themselves to deep thought about products being advertised. Emotional appeals, such as having attractive people in advertisements, would also follow the peripheral route. It is to an advertiser's advantage to consider the conditions under which appeal to the central route or peripheral route might be more effective for their particular product advertised under certain conditions (e.g., time or place). In the discussion that follows, it is useful to consider which of these two routes is being used. Motivational and emotional appeals, the topic of this chapter, do lend themselves better to the peripheral route.

The Source

The primary purpose of appealing to motives in advertising is to attract attention to a product or to make a product more favorable (Petty & Cacioppo, 1984). Since the prospective audience is faced with literally hundreds of advertisements competing for attention, the advertiser's problem is to make its ad more attention-getting in some way. Other factors then determine whether a product will be purchased.

One method of increasing apparent source credibility is to have actors or actresses portray characters who symbolize credibility and honesty. The general assumption is that the association of the product with the credible or likable character will add credibility or likability to the product. This is classical conditioning at work. Thus, Robert Young, an actor well-known to TV audiences for his portrayal of a medical doctor, advertised Maxwell House coffee. Similarly, "Four out of five doctors prefer . . . (fill in the name of your favorite across-the-counter medical product)." Joe Namath, a football hero and all-around likable character, advertised popcorn poppers and panty hose (which he wore in TV commercials). General Mills puts famous athletes on the front of Wheaties packages. Perfumes (including men's), clothes, and other products have famous people associated with them; shoes are associated with athletes, and so on.

Such ads have been considered most effective in changing viewer attitudes, however, when the viewer is not greatly involved with the product, following the peripheral route to persuasion (Petty, Cacioppo, & Schumann, 1983; Chapter 13 here). Panty hose and popcorn poppers would seem to be in this category. Advertisements in recent years, however, have also used such celebrities to promote sales of automobiles, which are products that bear a hefty price tag and do have considerable consumer "involvement."

Research dating back to the 1950s (Hovland & Weiss, 1957) indicates that a source is more effective if he or she argues against his or her own self-interest and does not appear to be trying to influence us. If the source puts on a "hard sell" too strongly, the audience may react against the message. If people believe that they are being coerced or manipulated, they tend to react negatively. Obviously, a person in an ad is trying to sell the product, but this intention can be softened in various ways. For example, the ad may show apparently unsolicited testimonials for the product, the source of the message apparently not trying to sell. The viewer does not know how many people had to be filmed to get one unsolicited testimonial, and such "soft sells" may avoid reactance.

The Message

Approach arousal.   Sex in advertising is a time-honored way to attract attention to the ad, and pretty obviously follows the peripheral route. Semi-clad buxom females are associated with everything from shoes to motorcycles. The "Maidenform woman" and her brassieres have been around for years, but more recently ads for blue jeans and undershorts have drawn attention to other parts of the anatomy. Sex does not necessarily have a favorable result in advertising, however. In a study in which different versions of the same ad showed different amounts of clothing on a female model, it was found that explicit nudity lowered the perceived quality of either body oil or ratchet sets (Peterson & Kerin, 1977). A more modest but still sexy model enhanced body oil but not ratchet sets. Thus moderately sexy advertisements may enhance products for which an attractive body is relevant to the ad (such as body oil) but not if it is irrelevant (such as with tool kits). The Maidenform woman, of course, wears the relevant product, and rounded derrieres are covered by the denim product advertised. Too-explicit sexual advertising may arouse negative responses from viewers, regardless of the product. La Tour and Henthorne (1994) showed 199 adults in a shopping mall two different advertisements, one having a strong overt theme and the other a mild sexual theme. Regardless of their gender, respondents did not like the strongly sexual ads. What is considered too explicit by the viewing audience, however, does change with the times, and this factor has to be judged by continual research. Nudity is far more acceptable now than, say, twenty-five years ago.

Fear arousal.   Traders in persuasive messages have long debated the value of negative emotional appeals in advertising. It would appear, for example, that health products could be sold more effectively if a certain amount of fear were introduced into the product advertising. The difficulties in doing this, however, are made obvious by the relative ineffectiveness of the surgeon general's warnings on cigarette packages to cut down on cigarette consumption. Fear of lung cancer seems not to deter a great percentage of smokers. To the extent that fear arousal is effective, two fairly simple rules may be followed (Secord & Backman, 1974):

1. **"Action instructions" (what to do; following a more central route) are not very effective without any fear arousal at all, but a small amount of arousal is about as effective as a large amount.** Very strong fear arousal may, indeed, produce a defensive reaction such that the viewer puts the whole issue out of his or her mind. Faison (1980, p. 244) describes an audience reaction test to two different toothpaste commercials. One of them simply showed that a person using Brand X for a long time had few cavities. The other commercial showed acid dripping on a tooth, and the tooth disintegrating before the viewers' eyes. The product name associated with this fearsome scene was less well remembered than with the more mundane scene, apparently because the scene was so aversive that the viewers tuned out the name of the product.

2. **Fear arousal is more effective if the action proposed is something that will re-
    duce the fear.** An effective tire advertisement showed a woman on a lonely road
    gazing at a flat tire on her car. The caption said, "When there's no man around,
    Goodyear should be" (Kleppner, 1977). Two aspects of this ad are important.
    First, there is a small amount of fear arousal about the consequences of not hav-
    ing good tires. Second, there is something suggested that the viewer can do,
    that is, buy Goodyear tires. Fear arousal without instructions on how to reduce
    fear is just fear arousal.

The Audience

The motivational state of the consumer audience may determine the effectiveness of an advertisement. For example, an ad for a cold remedy is
much less likely to influence your purchase if you do not have a cold. But if
you have a sniffly cold in the middle of winter, a TV commercial with a well-
known actor extolling the virtues of a cold medicine may be very effective. In
politics the audience for a political speech is often "warmed up" by food and
drink to make it more receptive to the candidate's message.

Subliminal Advertising

Every few years the question arises whether persuasive techniques, including advertising, can be effective without people's being aware of them.
This is known as subliminal advertising, using stimuli below the threshold for
conscious awareness. Subliminal advertising would be the most extreme example of following a peripheral route to persuasion since, by definition,
there would be no effortful thought on the part of the advertising recipient.

Who believes in subliminal advertising? Two different studies have
looked at the extent to which people are familiar with subliminal advertising
and believe that it is effective and/or being used. In one telephone survey, it
was found that 81 percent of 209 respondents had knowledge of subliminal advertising and believed that it was being used and well-educated individuals were
more likely to have heard of it. Two-thirds of the respondents thought that it
was unethical (Zanot, Pincus, & Lamp, 1983). In the second study, it was found
that 74 percent of 400 people interviewed by telephone had heard of subliminal advertising, 61 percent believed that it is used by advertisers, and 45 percent
believed that it would affect whether they would buy the product (Rogers &
Smith, 1993). Again, respondents with more education believed more strongly
that subliminal advertising works. The numbers vary, but the percentages of
people who believe that subliminal advertising is effective are impressive in
both studies. What, then, do the data show about effectiveness?

How effective is subliminal advertising? The most notorious claims
came in 1957 when a marketer named James Vicary claimed he had flashed
slides saying BUY POPCORN on the screen during the showing of a film. Supposedly the slide presentations were so brief that the audience was not con-

sciously aware of them. He claimed a dramatic increase in popcorn sales as a result. The spectre of such powerful mind control caused something of a furor, and bills making subliminal advertising illegal were even introduced into Congress. A number of good experimental psychologists also went to their laboratories to research the subject, with the result that no one could substantiate the original claims. For example, subjects "subliminally" subjected to the word "beef" did not subsequently choose beef in preference to other meat sandwiches (Byrne, 1959). In a field study, local TV stations participated by sending out messages in the manner described for the "buy popcorn" report. Telephone surveys taken immediately afterwards showed no effect of these messages on any kind of viewer behavior. Research on this topic so repeatedly came up dry that Dixon (1971) was prompted to say that he knew of no evidence to support the "buy popcorn" effect. There has been no evidence for the effect since then, either. Three different analyses of available research results concluded that any such effects are minimal, if present at all (Moore, 1982; Theus, 1994; Trappey, 1996). The dates of these reviews indicate that the yield has not improved with time.

In one experiment, however, there was an interesting nonspecific effect of subliminal stimulation (Channouf, Canac, & Gosset, 1999). French university students who were exposed to a subliminal image of Coca-Cola did not subsequently choose Coca-Cola more frequently than Orangina (a popular European soft drink), and those exposed to Orangina did not choose Orangina more often than Coca-Cola. However, subjects exposed to either of these products chose one of them more often than subjects exposed to a neutral stimulus (a table). This suggests that the subliminal stimulation might have a general motivational priming effect for drinking in general, but not for a specific drink.

Self-Help Tapes

For a few dollars, you can buy audiotapes to play throughout the day and that supposedly carry subliminal messages to your brain. These messages range from telling you how to gain self-confidence, to being less anxious, to how to play better golf. Sometimes these messages are disguised by music that you can enjoy. Sometimes it is claimed that there are only subliminal messages and that these will help you. Do they work? In an extensive field experiment, the effectiveness of several such tapes was studied (Greenwald, Spangenberg, Pratkanis, & Eskenazi, 1991). Greenwald et al. used commercially available tapes sold with the claims of improving either memory or self-esteem. The experiment was done under realistic conditions, following manufacturers' instructions. The subjects used the tapes for a month and then were tested for both their real effects on the subjects and for the effects that the subjects perceived to have happened. What the subjects did not know was that the tapes were labeled in different ways and that the subjects had been randomly assigned to the different labeling conditions with a double-blind procedure. That is, neither the person giving out the tapes to the subjects nor the subjects knew what the real content of the tapes was. For some subjects, self-esteem tapes were labeled "self-esteem," but for others they were labeled "memory." Similarly, memory tapes were labeled either "memory" or "self-esteem." Following the month's use of a tape, each subject completed several tests of self-esteem and of memory.

The results were that the subjects showed significant effects of listening to the tapes but that these effects resulted from the labels on the tapes, not the contents of the tapes. They showed better memory if the tapes were labeled memory than if they were labeled self-esteem, but actual tape content made no difference. Presumably the same effects could have been obtained with any tape content as long as the buyer knew the tape label. Had the subjects actually purchased and used these tapes, they probably would have been pleased with what they thought were the results—even though those results did not actually occur.

Actually, psychologists had been researching the topics of perception and persuasion for many years prior to the popcorn claim, and there was no reason to believe that so-called subliminal (below-threshold) messages should have been effective. First, whether or not consciously perceived, a message would have to get through the eyes and into the nervous system in order to affect behavior. It is doubtful that such messages could be received with brief flashes of a slide mixed in with thousands of other unrelated movie frames. Second, even if the signal did reach the nervous system, there is no reason to expect that a viewer should perform like a robot to go out and buy anything. Although we may perceive some messages via stimuli of near-threshold intensity or duration, such effects are difficult-to-achieve laboratory phenomena obtained under very restricted conditions. The most recent claims of any behavioral effects of such messages (e.g., Silverman, 1982) have been severely challenged on grounds of weak methodology and the failure of other researchers to reproduce the phenomena (Balay & Shevrin, 1988). The general conclusion to be reached about subliminal advertising is that it is truly a subliminal phenomenon. This is not to say that subliminal stimuli have no effects on us. We have already seen that they do. The data do suggest, however, that such effects are relatively narrow. They do not seem to be strong enough to support the claims that subliminal advertisers have made. Given the apparent widespread belief in subliminal advertising, however, the topic calls for continued research.

SECTION SUMMARY

1. A framework for encompassing many aspects of advertising is the **communication model,** which looks upon **persuasive communications** from the points of view of the **source** of a message, the **message** itself, and characteristics of the **audience.**

2. According to the **elaboration likelihood model** of persuasion, there are two "routes" to persuasion, central and peripheral. The central route requires a more thoughtful analysis of information, whereas the peripheral route involves cues that influence a person more directly. The arousal of motives and emotions would involve the peripheral route more.

3. The two most important source characteristics are **credibility** and **likability.** A source is considered to be more effective if she or he does not appear to be trying to influence the audience too heavily.

4. A major **emotional content** of advertising messages is sexual, but research suggests that moderate sexuality that is relevant to the product advertised is most effective. Too-explicit nudity or sexual connotations for irrelevant products may backfire and engender negative attitudes toward an ad.

5. Some **fear arousal** in advertising may be effective if accompanied by instructions about what to do to reduce the threat that produces the fear. Overly strong fear arousal may simply cause the audience to tune out the message.

6. The motivational state or mood of an audience modifies the effect of an advertising message. A person with a cold is more likely to pay attention to cold remedy ads.

7. Claims have been made that **subliminal advertising** is a powerful tool for **influencing** consumers. There is virtually no evidence, however, that advertising messages below the level of conscious awareness have any unique or strong influence on consumer behavior.

References

Abramson, L. Y., Seligman, M. E. P., & Teasdale, J. (1978). Learned helplessness in humans: Critique and reformulation. *Journal of Abnormal Psychology, 87,* 49–74.

Acker, J. C. (1997). Location variations in professional football. *Journal of Sport Behavior, 20,* 247–259.

Adametz, J. H. (1959). Rate of recovery of functioning in cats with rostral reticular lesions. *Journal of Neurosurgery, 16,* 85–98.

Adams, J. S. (1975). Inequity in social exchange. In R. M. Steers & L. W. Porter (Eds.), *Motivation and work behavior.* New York: McGraw-Hill.

Adorno, T. W., Frenkel-Brunswik, E., Levinson, D. J., & Sanford, R. N. (1950). *The authoritarian personality.* New York: Harper & Brothers.

Aggleton, J. P., & Young, A.W. (2000). The enigma of the amygdala: On its contribution to human emotion. In R. D. Lane & L. Nadel (Eds.), *Cognitive neuroscience of emotion.* New York: Oxford University Press.

Ajzen, I. (2001). Nature and operation of attitudes. *Annual Review of Psychology, 52,* 27–58.

Alcott, J. (1979). *Animal behavior: An evolutionary approach* (2d ed.). Sunderland, M.: Sinauer Associates, Inc.

Alley, T. R., & Cunningham, M. R. (1991). Averaged faces are attractive, but attractive faces are not average. *Psychological Science, 2,* 123–125.

Allport, G. (1937). *Personality: A psychological interpretation.* New York: Holt.

Amorose, A. J., & Horn, T. S. (2000). Intrinsic motivation: Relationships with collegiate athletes' gender, scholarship status, and perceptions of their coach's behavior. *Journal of Sport & Exercise Psychology, 22,* 63–84.

Amsel, A. (1992). *Frustration theory.* New York: Cambridge University Press.

Amsel, A., & Roussel, J. (1952). Motivational properties of frustration: I. Effect on running response of the addition of frustration to the motivational complex. *Journal of Experimental Psychology, 43,* 363–368.

Anderson, C. A., & Bushman, B. J. (2002). Human aggression. *Annual Review of Psychology, 53,* 27–51.

Anderson, G., & Anderson, D. (1984). Ambient temperature and violent crimes: Tests of the linear and curvilinear hypotheses. *Journal of Personality and Social Psychology, 46,* 91–97.

Anderson, K. J. (1994). Impulsivity, caffeine, and task difficulty: A within-subjects test of the Yerkes-Dodson Law. *Personality and Individual Differences, 16,* 813–829.

Anderson, R., Manoogian, S., & Reznick, S. (1976). The undermining and enhancing of intrinsic motivation in preschool children. *Journal of Personality and Social Psychology, 34,* 915–922.

Andersson, B. (1952). Polydipsia caused by intrahypothalamic injections of hypertonic NaCl solutions. *Experientia, 8,* 157–158.

Anger, D. (1963). The role of temporal discrimination in the reinforcement of Sidman avoidance behavior. *Journal of the Experimental Analysis of Behavior, 6,* 477–506.

Ardrey, R. *The territorial imperative.* New York: Dell, 1966.

Arma, R., Russell, G., & Sandelands, M. (1979). Effects of the hostility of spectators on viewing aggressive sports. *Social Psychology Quarterly, 42,* 274–279.

Aronson, E. (1968). Dissonance theory: Progress and problems. In R. P. Abelson, E. Aronson, W. J. McGuire, T. M. Newcomb, M. J. Rosenberg, & P. H. Tannenbaum (Eds.), *Theories of cognitive consistency: A source book.* Chicago: Rand McNally.

Arthur, A. Z. (1986). Stress of predictable and unpredictable shock. *Psychological Bulletin, 100,* 379–383.

Asch, S. (1951). Effects of group pressure upon the modification and distortion of judgment. In Z. H. Guetzkokw (Ed.), *Groups, leadership, and men.* Pittsburgh: Carnegie.

Asch, S. E. (1946). Forming impressions of personality. *Journal of Abnormal and Social Psychology, 41,* 258–290.

Atkinson, J. W. (1958). *Motives in fantasy, action, and society.* New York: D. Van Nostrand.

Atkinson, J. W. (1964). *An introduction to motivation.* New York: D. Van Nostrand.

Atkinson, J. W., & Litwin, G. H. (1960). Achievement motive and test anxiety conceived as motive to approach success and motive to avoid failure. *Journal of Abnormal and Social Psychology, 60,* 52–63.

Atkinson, J. W., & Birch, D. (1978). *Introduction to motivation* (2d ed.). New York: D. Van Nostrand.

Averill, J. (1983). Studies on anger and aggression: Implications for theories of emotion. *American Psychologist, 38,* 1145–1160.

Azrin, N. H., & Holz, W. C. (1966). Punishment. In W. K. Honig (Ed.), *Operant behavior: Areas of research and application.* New York: Appleton-Century-Crofts.

Baeyens, F., Eelen, P., & Van den Bergh, O. (1990). Contingency awareness in evaluative conditioning: A case for unaware effective-evaluative learning. *Cognition and Emotion, 4,* 3–18.

Bailey, C. J. (1955). The effectiveness of drives as cues. *Journal of Comparative and Physiological Psychology, 48,* 183–187.

Balay, J., & Shevrin, H. (1988). The subliminal psychodynamic activation method: A critical review. *American Psychologist, 43,* 161–174.

Balleine, B. W. (2001). Incentive processes in instrumental conditioning. In R. R. Mowrer & S. B. Klein (Eds.), *Contemporary learning theories.* Mahwah, NJ: Lawrence Erlbaum Associates.

Bandura, A. (1973). *Aggression: A social learning analysis.* Englewood Cliffs, NJ: Prentice-Hall, Inc.

Bandura, A. (1977). Self-efficacy: Toward a unifying theory of behavioral change. *Psychological Review, 84,* 191–215.

Bandura, A. (1982). Self-efficacy mechanism in human agency. *American Psychologist, 37,* 122–147.

Bandura, A., Ross, D., & Ross, S. A. (1963). Imitation of film-mediated aggressive models. *Journal of Abnormal and Social Psychology, 66,* 3–11.

Barlow, D. H. (1988). *Anxiety and its disorders.* New York: Guilford Press.

Barlow, D. H. (2000). Unraveling the mysteries of anxiety and its disorders from the perspective of emotion theory. *American Psychologist, 55,* 1245–1263.

Baron, R. A., & Byrne, D. (1977). *Social psychology: Understanding human interaction.* Boston: Allyn and Bacon.

Baron, R. A., & Byrne, D. (1997). *Social Psychology,* 8th ed. Boston: Allyn and Bacon.

Baumeister, R. F., & Leary, M. R. (1995). The need to belong: Desire for interpersonal attachments as a fundamental human motivation. *Psychological Bulletin, 117,* 497–529.

Baumeister, R. F., & Steinhilber, A. (1984). Paradoxical effects of supportive audiences on performance under pressure: The home field disadvantage in sports championships. *Journal of Personality and Social Psychology, 47,* 85–93.

Beach, F. A. (1942). Analysis of factors involved in the arousal, maintenance, and manifestation of sexual excitement in male animals. *Psychosomatic Medicine, 4,* 173–179.

Beach, F. A. (1955). The descent of instinct. *Psychological Review, 62,* 401–410.

Beach, F. A. (1969). Locks and beagles. *American Psychologist, 24,* 971–989.

Beamer, W., Bermont, G., & Clegg, M. (1969). Copulatory behavior of the ram, Ovis aries. II. Factors affecting copulatory satiety. *Animal Behavior, 17,* 706–711.

Beck, A. T. (1967). *Depression: Clinical, experimental and theoretical aspects.* New York: Harper and Row.

Beck, A. T., & Rush, A. J. (1980). A cognitive model of anxiety formation and anxiety reduction. In C. D. Spielberger & I. W. Sarason (Eds.), *Stress and anxiety* (Vol. 10, pp. 349–365) Oxford, Eng.: Hemisphere.

Beck, R. C. (1983). *Motivation: Theories and principles,* 2d ed. Englewood Cliffs, NJ: Prentice-Hall.

Beck, R. C. (1990). *Motivation: Theories and principles,* 3d ed. Englewood Cliffs, NJ: Prentice- Hall.

Beck, R. C., & Bidwell, L. D. (1974). Incentive properties of sucrose and saccharin under different deprivation conditions. *Learning and Motivation, 5,* 328–335.

Beck, R. C., Gibson, C., Elliot, W., Simmons, C., Matteson, N., & McDaniel, L. (1988). False physiological feedback and emotion. *Motivation and Emotion, 12,* 217–256.

Beck, R. C., & McBee, W. (1995). Mood-dependent memory for generated and repeated words: Replication and extinction. *Cognition and Emotion, 9,* 289–307.

Beck, R. C., Nash, R., Viernstein, L., & Gordon, L. (1972). Sucrose preferences of hungry and thirsty rats as a function of duration of presentation of test solutions. *Journals of Comparative and Physiological Psychology, 78,* 40–50.

Beck, S. B., Ward-Hull, C., & McLear, P. M. (1976). Variables related to women's somatic preferences of the male and female body. *Journal of Personality and Social Psychology, 34,* 1200–1210.

Bell, P. A., Fisher, J. D., & Loomis, R. J. (1978). *Environmental psychology.* Philadelphia: W. B. Saunders.

Bell, R. W., Noah, J. C., & Davis, J. R., Jr. (1965). Interactive effects of shock intensity and delay of reinforcement on escape conditioning. *Psychonomic Science, 3,* 505–506.

Bellows, R. T. (1939). Time factors in water drinking in dogs. *American Journal of Physiology, 125,* 87–97.

Bem, D. J. (1967). Self-perception: An alternative interpretation of cognitive dissonance phenomena. *Psychological Review, 74,* 183–200.

Bem, D. J. (1970). *Beliefs, attitudes, and human affairs.* Monterey, CA: Brooks/Cole.

Benjafield, J., Liddell, W. W., & Benjafield, I. (1989). Is there a home field disadvantage in professional sports championships? *Social Behavior and Personality, 17,* 45–50.

Bentley, D. R. (1977) Control of cricket song patterns by descending interneurons. *Journal of Comparative Physiology,* 19–38.

Bentley, D. R., & Hoy, R. R. (1972). Genetic control of the neuronal network generating cricket song patterns. *Animal Behavior, 20,* 478–492.

Berkeley, G. (1939). Principles of human knowledge. In E. A. Burtt (Ed.), *The English philosophers from Bacon to Mill.* New York: Modern Library. (Original work published 1710.)

Berkowitz, L. (1974). Some determinants of impulsive aggression: Role of mediated associations with reinforcements for aggression. *Psychological Review, 81,* 165–176.

Berkowitz, L. (1983). Aversively stimulated aggression: Some parallels and differences in research with animals and humans. *American Psychologist, 38,* 1135–1144.

Berkowitz, L. (1984). Some effects of thoughts on anti- and prosocial influences of media events: A cognitive-neoassociation analysis. *Psychological Bulletin, 95,* 410–427.

Berkowitz, L. (1988). Frustrations, appraisals, and aversively stimulated aggression. *Aggressive Behavior, 14* (1), 3–11.

Berkowitz, L., & Le Page, A. (1967). Weapons as aggression-eliciting stimuli. *Journal of Personality and Social Psychology, 7,* 202–207.

Berlyne, D. E. (1960). *Conflict, arousal, and curiosity.* New York: McGraw-Hill.

Berlyne, D. E. (1970). Novelty, complexity and hedonic value. *Perception and Psychophysics, 8,* 279–286.

Berlyne, D. E. (1971). *Aesthetics and psychobiology.* New York: Appleton-Century-Crofts.

Berman, M. E., & Coccaro, E. F. (1998). Neurobiological correlates of violence: Relevance to criminal responsibility. *Behavioral Sciences & the Law, 16,* 303–318.

Bermond, B., Nieuwenhuyse, B., Fasotti, L., & Schuerman, J. (1991). Spinal cord lesions, peripheral feedback, and intensities of emotional feelings. *Cognition and Emotion, 5,* 201–220.

Bernard, C. (1957). *An introduction to the study of experimental medicine* (H. C. Greene, trans.). New York: Dover. (Original work published 1865.)

Bernardis, L. L., & Bellinger, L. L. (1996). The lateral hypothalamic area revisited: Ingestive behavior. *Neuroscience and Biobehavioral Reviews, 20,* 189–287.

Berridge, K. (1999). Pleasure, pain, desire, and dread: Hidden core processes of emotion. In Kahneman, D., Diener, E. & Schwarz, N. (Eds.), *Well-being: The foundations of hedonic psychology.* New York: Russell Sage Foundation.

Berridge, K. (2001). Reward learning: Reinforcement, incentives and expectations. In D. L. Medin (Ed.), *Psychology of Learning and Motivation.* New York: Academic Press, Vol. 40, 223–278.

Berridge, K. C. (1991). Modulation of taste affect by hunger, caloric satiety, and sensory-specific satiety in the rat. *Appetite, 16,* 103–120.

Berridge, K. C. (1996). Food reward: Brain substrates of wanting and liking. *Neuroscience & Biobehavioral Reviews, 20,* 1–25.

Berridge, K. C. (2000). Measuring hedonic impact in animals and infants: Microstructure of affective taste reactivity patterns. *Neuroscience and Biobehavioral Reviews, 24,* 173–198.

Berridge, K. C. & Robinson, T. E. (1995). The mind of an addicted brain: Neural sensitization of wanting versus liking. *Current Directions in Psychological Science, 4,* 71–76.

Berscheid, E., & Walster, E. H. (1969). *Interpersonal attraction.* Reading, MA: Addison-Wesley.

Bettleheim, B. (1960). *The informed heart.* New York: Free Press.

Bexton, W. H., Heron, W., & Scott, T. H. (1954). Effects of decreased variation in the sensory environment. *Canadian Journal of Psychology, 8,* 70–76.

Bindra, D. (1969). The interrelated mechanisms of reinforcement and motivation, and the nature of their influence on response. In W. J. Arnold & D. Levine (Eds.), *Nebraska symposium on motivation*. Lincoln: University of Nebraska Press.

Bindra, D. (1974). A motivational view of learning, performance, and behavior modification. *Psychological Review, 81*, 199–213.

Bindra, D. (1978). How adaptive behavior is produced: A perceptual-motivational alternative to response-reinforcement. *Behavioral and Brain Sciences, 1*, 41–91.

Bindra, D., & Palfai, T. (1967). Nature of positive and negative incentive-motivational effects on general activity. *Journal of Comparative and Physiological Psychology, 52*, 165–166.

Birch, L. L., & Fisher, J. A. (1996). The role of experience in the development of children's eating behavior. In E. D. Capaldi (Ed.), *Why we eat what we eat: The psychology of eating*. Washington, DC: American Psychological Association.

Black, A. H., Carlson, N. J., & Solomon, R. L. (1962). Exploratory studies of the conditioning of autonomic responses on curarized dogs. *Psychological Monographs, 76* (Whole No. 548).

Black, R. W. (1969). Incentive motivation and the parameters of reward in instrumental conditioning. In W. J. Arnold & D. Levine (Eds.), *Nebraska symposium on motivation*. Lincoln: University of Nebraska Press.

Blaney, P. H. (1986). Affect and memory: A review. *Psychological Bulletin, 99*, 229–246.

Bolles, R. C. (1967). *Theory of motivation*. New York: Harper & Row.

Bolles, R. C. (1972). Reinforcement, expectancy, and learning. *Psychological Review, 79*, 394–409.

Bolles, R. C. (1975). *Theory of motivation*, 2d ed. New York: Harper & Row.

Bolles, R. C., & Moot, S. A. (1972). Derived motives. *Annual Review of Psychology, 23*, 51–72.

Boulze, D., Montratruc, P., & Cabanac, M. (1983). Water intake, pleasure and water intake in humans. *Physiology and Behavior, 30*, 97–102.

Bower, G. H. (1981). Mood and memory. *American Psychologist, 36*, 129–148.

Bower, G. H., Fowler, H., & Trapold, M. A. (1959). Escape learning as a function of amount of shock reduction. *Journal of Experimental Psychology, 58*, 482–484.

Bower, G. H., McLean, J., & Meacham, J. (1966). Value of knowing when reinforcement is due. *Journal of Comparative and Physiological Psychology, 62*, 183–192.

Bowlby, J. (1969). *Attachment and loss* (Vol. 1. Attachment). London: Hogarth.

Bowman, C. H. & Fishbein, M. (1978). Understanding public reaction to energy proposals: An application of the Fishbein model. *Journal of Applied Social Psychology, 8*, 319–340.

Brehm, J. W., & Cohen, A. R. (1962). *Explorations in cognitive dissonance*. New York: Wiley.

Brehm, S. S. (1985). *Intimate relationships*. New York: Random House.

Breland, K., & Breland, M. (1961). The misbehavior of organisms. *American Psychologist, 16*, 681–684.

Bridgman, P. W. (1927). *The logic of modern physics*. New York: Macmillan.

Broadhurst, P. L. (1957). Emotionality and the Yerkes-Dodson law. *Journal of Experimental Psychology, 54*, 345–352.

Brogden, W. J., Lipman, E. A., & Culler, E. (1938). The role of incentive in conditioning and learning. *American Journal of Psychology, 51*, 109–117.

Brown, J. S. (1948). Gradients of approach and avoidance responses and their relation to level of motivation. *Journal of Comparative and Physiological Psychology, 41*, 451–465.

Brown, J. S. (1961). *The motivation of behavior*. New York: McGraw-Hill.

Brown, J. S., & Farber, I. E. (1951). Emotions conceptualized as intervening variables—With suggestions toward a theory of frustration. *Psychological Bulletin, 48*, 465–495.

Brown, J. S., Kalish, H. I., & Farber, I. E. (1951). Conditioned fear as revealed by magnitude of startle response to an auditory stimulus. *Journal of Experimental Psychology, 41*, 317–328.

Bryan, J. H., & Test, M. A. (1967). Models and helping: Naturalistic studies in aiding behavior. *Journal of Personality and Social Psychology, 6*, 400–407.

Burger, J. (1989). Negative reactions to increases in perceived personal control. *Journal of Personality and Social Psychology, 56*, 246–256.

Burger, J. M., & Cooper, H. M. (1979). The desirability of control. *Motivation and Emotion, 3*, 381–393.

Burgess, T. D. G., & Sales, S. M. (1971). Attitudinal effects of "mere exposure": A reevaluation. *Journal of Experimental Social Psychology, 7*, 461–472.

Burnstein, E., & Worchel, P. (1962). Arbitrariness of frustration and its consequences for aggression in a social situation. *Journal of Personality, 30*, 528–541.

Bushman, B. J., Baumeister, R. F. & Phillips, C. M. (2001). Do people aggress to improve their mood? Cartharsis beliefs, affect regulation opportunity, and aggressive responding. *Journal of Personality and Social Psychology, 81,* 17–32.

Buss, A. H., Booker, A., & Buss, E. (1972). Firing a weapon and aggression. *Journal of Personality and Social Psychology, 22,* 296–302.

Buss, D. M. (1988). The evolution of human intrasexual competition: Tactics of mate attraction. *Journal of Personality and Social Psychology, 54,* 616–628.

Buss, D. M., Haselton, M. G., Shackelford, T. K., Bleske, A. L., & Wakefield, J. C. (1998). Adaptations, exaptations, and spandrels. *American Psychologist, 53,* 533–548.

Bykov, K. M. (1957). *The cerebral cortex and the internal organs* (W. H. Gantt, Trans. and Ed.). New York: Chemical Publishing.

Byrne, D. (1959). The effects of a subliminal food stimulus on verbal responses. *Journal of Applied Psychology, 43,* 249–252.

Byrne, D. (1974). *An introduction to psychology,* 2d ed. Englewood Cliffs, NJ: Prentice-Hall.

Byrne, D., & Nelson, D. (1965). Attraction as a linear function of proportion of positive reinforcements. *Journal of Personality and Social Psychology, 1,* 659–663.

Cabanac, M. (1979). Sensory pleasure. *Quarterly Review of Biology, 54,* 1–29.

Cabanac, M. (1990). Taste: The maximization of multidimensional pleasure. In E. Capaldi & T. Powley (Eds.). *Taste, experience, and feeding.* Washington, DC: American Psychological Association.

Cacioppo, J. T., & Berntson, G. G. (1994). Relationship between attitudes and evaluative space: A critical review, with emphasis on the separability of positive and negative substrates. *Psychological Bulletin, 115,* 401–423.

Cacioppo, J. T., Crites, S. L., Gardner, W. L. (1996). Attitudes to the right: Evaluative processing is associated with lateralized late positive event-related brain potentials. *Personality and Social Psychology Bulletin, 22,* 1205–1219.

Cacioppo, J. T., & Gardner, W. L. (1999). Emotion. *Annual Review of Psychology, 50,* 191–214.

Cacioppo, J. T., Gardner, W. L., & Berntson, G. G. (1997). Beyond bipolar conceptualizations and measures: The case of attitudes and evaluative space. *Personality and Social Psychology Review, 1,* 3–25.

Cacioppo, J. T., & Petty, R. E. (1982). The need for cognition. *Journal of Personality and Social Psychology, 42,* 116–131.

Cacioppo, J., Petty, R., Losch, M., & Kim, H. (1986). Electromyographic activity over facial muscle regions can differentiate the valence and intensity of affective reactions. *Journal of Personality and Social Psychology, 50(2),* 260–268.

Cairns, R. B. (1979). *Social development.* San Francisco: Freeman.

Calhoun, J. B. (1962). Population density and social pathology. *Scientific American, 206,* 139–148.

Cameron, J., & Pierce, W. D. (1994). Reinforcement, reward and intrinsic motivation: A meta-analysis. *Review of Educational Research, 64,* 363.

Camp, D. S., Raymond, G. A., & Church, R. M. (1967). Temporal relationship between response and punishment. *Journal of Experimental Psychology, 74,* 114–123.

Campbell, B. A. (1964). Theory and research on the effects of water deprivation on random activity in the rat. In M. J. Wayner (Ed.), *Thirst.* Oxford: Pergamon.

Campbell, B. A., & Church, R. M. (1969). *Punishment and aversive behavior.* New York: Appleton-Century-Crofts.

Campbell, B. A., & Kraeling, D. (1953). Response strengths as a function of drive level and amount of drive reduction. *Journal of Experimental Psychology, 45,* 97–101.

Campbell, B. A., & Masterson, F. A. (1969). Psychophysics of punishment. In B. A. Campbell & R. M. Church (Eds.), *Punishment and aversive behavior.* New York: Appleton-Century-Crofts.

Campbell, B. A., Smith, N. F., Misanin, J. R., & Jaynes, J. (1966). Species differences in activity during hunger and thirst. *Journal of Comparative and Physiological Psychology, 61,* 123–127.

Cannon, W. B. (1927). The James-Lange theory of emotions: A critical examination and an alternative theory. *American Journal of Psychology, 39,* 106–124.

Cannon, W. B. (1934). Hunger and thirst. In C. Murchison (Ed.), *Handbook of general experimental psychology.* Worcester, MA: Clark University Press.

Cannon, W. B. (1939a). *Bodily changes in pain, hunger, fear and rage: An account of recent researches into the function of emotional excitement,* 2d ed. New York: Appleton-Century-Crofts.

Cannon, W. B. (1939b). *The wisdom of the body.* New York: Norton.

Gallistel, C. R., & Gibbon, J. (2001). Computational versus associative models of simple conditioning. *Current Directions in Psychological Science, 10,* 146–150.

Garcia, J., & Ervin, R. R. (1968). Gustatory visceral and telereceptor cutaneous conditioning—Adaptation in external and internal milieus. *Communications in Behavioral Biology, 1* (Part A), 389–415.

Garcia, J., & Koelling, R. A. (1966) Relation of cue to consequence in avoidance learning. *Psychonomic Science, 4,* 123–124.

Garfinkel, P., Molodofsky, H., & Garner, D. (1979). The stability of perceptual disturbances in anorexia nervosa. *Psychological Medicine, 9,* 703–708.

Garfinkel, P. E. (1995). Classification and diagnosis of eating disorders. In K. D. Brownell & C. G. Fairburn (Eds.), *Eating disorders and obesity.* New York: Guilford Press.

Gayton, W. F., & Coombs, R. (1995). The home advantage in high school basketball. *Perceptual and Motor Skills, 81,* 1244–1246.

Gazzaniga, M. S. (1967). The split brain in man. *Scientific American, 217,* 24–29.

Geen, R. G., & Berkowitz, L. (1967). Some conditions facilitating the occurrence of aggression after the observation of violence. *Journal of Personality, 35,* 666–667.

Geen, R. G., & O'Neal, E. C. (1969). Activation of cue-elicited aggression by general arousal. *Journal of Personality and Social Psychology, 11,* 289–292.

Gibson, J. L., Ivancevich, J. M., & Donnelly, J. H. (1979). *Organization: Behavior, structure, processes.* Dallas: Irwin-Dorsey.

Gilbert, D. T., & Wilson, T. D. (2000). Miswanting: Some problems in the forecasting of future affective states. In J. P. Forgas (Ed.), *Feeling and thinking: The role of affect in social cognition.* Cambridge, England: Cambridge University Press.

Gilman, A. (1937). The relation between blood osmotic pressure, fluid distribution, and voluntary water intake. *American Journal of Physiology, 120,* 323–328.

Gladue, B. A., Green, R., & Hellman, R. E. (1984). Neuroendocrine response to estrogen and sexual orientation. *Science, 225,* 1496–1499.

Glickman, S. E., & Schiff, B. B. (1967). A biological theory of reinforcement. *Psychological Review, 74,* 81–109.

Goldsmith, H. H. (1993). Temperament: Variability in developing emotion systems. In M. Lewis & J. M. Haviland (Eds.), *Handbook of emotions.* New York: Guilford Press.

Goldstein, J., & Arma, R. (1971). Effect of observing athletic contests on hostility. *Sociometry, 54,* 83–91.

Goodson, P., McCormick, D., & Evans, A. (2000). Sex on the internet: College students' emotional arousal when viewing sexually explicit materials. *Journal of Sex Education and Therapy, 25,* 252–260.

Goranson, R., & Berkowitz, L. (1966). Reciprocity and responsibility reactions to prior help. *Journal of Personality and Social Psychology, 3,* 227–232.

Gordon, W. C. (1989). *Learning.* Belmont, CA: Wadsworth.

Gould, S. J. (1991). Exaptation: A crucial tool for evolutionary psychology. *Journal of Social Issues, 47,* 43–65.

Gray, J. (1971). *The psychology of fear and stress.* New York: McGraw-Hill.

Gray, J. A. (1982a). *The neuropsychology of anxiety: An enquiry into the the functions of the septohippocampal system.* Oxford: Oxford University Press.

Gray, J. A. (1982b). Precis of "The neuropsychology of anxiety: An enquiry into the functions of the septo-hippocampal system." *Behavioral and Brain Sciences, 5,* 469–534.

Green, D. P., Goldman, S. L., & Salovey, P. (1993). Measurement error masks bipolarity in affect ratings. *Journal of Personality and Social Psychology, 64,* 1029–1041.

Greenwald, A. G., Banaji, M. R., Rudman, L. A., Farnham, S. D., Nosek, B. A., & Mellot, D. S. (2002). A unified theory of implicit attitudes, stereotypes, self-esteem, and self-concept. *Psychological Review, 109,* 3–25.

Greenwald, A. G., McGhee, D. E., & Schwartz, J. L. K (1998). Measuring individual differences in implicit cognition: The implicit association test. *Journal of Personality and Social Psychology, 74,* 1464–1480.

Greenwald, A. G., & Ronis, D. L. (1978). Twenty years of cognitive dissonance: Case study of the evolution of a theory. *Psychological Review, 85,* 53–57.

Greenwald, A. G., Spangenberg, E. R., Pratkanis, A. R., & Eskenazi, J. (1991). Double-blind tests of subliminal self-help audiotapes. *Psychological Science, 2,* 119–122.

Gregory, E., Engle, K., & Pfaff, D. (1975). Male hamster preference for odors of female hamster vaginal discharges: Studies of experiential and hormonal determinants. *Journal of Comparative and Physiological Psychology, 89,* 442–446.

Grill, H. J., & Kaplan, J. M. (1990). Caudal brainstem participates in the distributed neural control of feeding. In E. M. Stricker (Ed.), *Handbook of behavioral neurobiology* (Vol. 10: *Neurobiology of food and fluid intake*). New York: Plenum.

Gross, J. J. (2001). Emotion regulation in adulthood: Timing is everything. *Current Directions in Psychological Science, 10,* 214–218.

Guerin, B., & Innes, J. M. (1984). Explanations of social facilitation: A review. *Current Psychological Research and Reviews, 3,* 32–52.

Guttman, N. (1953). Operant conditioning, extinction, and periodic reinforcement in relation to concentration of sucrose used as reinforcing agent. *Journal of Experimental Psychology, 46,* 213–224.

Guttman, N. (1954). Equal-reinforcement values for sucrose and glucose solutions compared with equal-sweetness values. *Journal of Comparative and Physiological Psychology, 47,* 358–361.

Hackman, J. R., & Lawler, E. E. (1971). Employee reactions to job characteristics. *Journal of Applied Psychology, 55,* 259–286.

Hackman, J. R., & Oldham, G. R. (1976). Motivation through the design of work: Test of a theory. *Organizational Behavior and Human Performance, 16,* 250–279.

Halberstadt, J., & Rhodes, G. (2000). The attractiveness of nonface averages: Implications for an evolutionary explanation of the attractiveness of average faces. *Psychological Science, 11,* 285–289.

Hall, J. F. (1958). The influence of learning in activity wheel behavior. *Journal of Genetic Psychology, 92,* 121–125.

Hall, W. G., Arnold, H. M., & Myers, K. P. (2000). The acquisition of an appetite. *Psychological Science, 11,* 101–105.

Hamann, S. B., Ely, T. D., Hoffman, J. M., & Kilts, C. D. (2002). Ecstasy and agony: Activation of the human amygdala in positive and negative emotion. *Psychological Science, 13,* 2, 135–141.

Hamer, D. (1997). The search for personality genes: Adventures of a molecular biologist. *Psychological Science, 6,* 111–114.

Hamilton, W. D. (1964). The genetical theory of social behavior: I. and II. *Journal of Theoretical Biology, 7,* 1–52.

Hammen, C. L. (1985). Predicting depression: A cognitive-behavior perspective. In P. C. Kendall (Ed.), *Advances in cognitive-behavioral research and therapy* (Vol. 4, pp. 30–71). New York: Academic Press.

Harlow, H. F. (1953). Mice, monkeys, men, and motives. *Psychological Review, 60,* 23–32.

Harlow, H. F. (1958). The nature of love. *American Psychologist, 13,* 673–685.

Harmon-Jones, E. (2000). Cognitive dissonance and experienced negative affect: Evidence that dissonance increases experienced affect even in the absence of aversive consequences. *Personality and Social Psychology Bulletin, 26,* 1490–1501.

Harmon-Jones, E., & Allen, J. B. (1998). Anger and frontal brain activity: EEG asymmetry consistent with approach motivation despite negative affective valence. *Journal of Personality and Social Psychology, 74,* 1210–1216.

Harmon-Jones, E., & Allen, J. J. B (2001). The role of affect in the mere exposure effect: Evidence from psychophysiological and individual difference approaches. *Personality and Social Psychology Bulletin, 27,* 889–898.

Harris, L. J., Clay, J., Hargreaves, F. J., & Ward, A. (1933). Appetite and choice of diet: The ability of the vitamin B deficient rat to discriminate between diets containing and lacking the vitamin. *Proceedings of the Royal Society, London, 113* (Serial B), 161–190.

Hebb, D. O. (1946). On the nature of fear. *Psychological Review, 53,* 259–276.

Hebb, D. O. (1955). Drives and the CNS (conceptual nervous system). *Psychological Review, 62,* 243–254.

Hecker, M. H., Chesney, M. A., Black, G. W., & Frautschi, N. (1988). Coronary-prone behaviors in the Western Collaborative Group Study. *Psychosomatic Medicine, 50,* 153–164.

Heckhausen, H. (1975). Effort expenditure, aspiration level and self-evaluation before and after unexpected performance shifts. Cited in McClelland (1985).

Heider, F. (1958). *The psychology of interpersonal relations.* New York: Wiley.

Hendrick, C., & Brown, S. R. (1971). Introversion, extroversion, and interpersonal attraction. *Journal of Personality and Social Psychology, 20,* 31–36.

Hendry, D. P. (Ed.). (1969). *Conditioned reinforcement.* Homewood, IL: Dorsey.

Henss, R. (2000). Waist-to-hip ratio and female attractiveness. Evidence for photographic stimuli and methodological considerations. *Personality and Individual Differences, 28,* 501–513.

Hergenhahn, B. R. (1997). *An introduction to the history of psychology,* 3d ed. Belmont, CA: Brooks/Cole Publishing Co.

Herman, C. P. (1996). Human eating: Diagnosis and prognosis. *Neuroscience and Biobehavioral Reviews, 20,* 107–111.

Herrnstein, R. J. (1969). Method and theory in the study of avoidance. *Psychological Review, 76,* 49–69.

Herzberg, F. (1966). *Work and the nature of man.* New York: New American Library.

Hess, E. H. (1962). Ethology: An approach toward the complete analysis of behavior. In R. Brown, E. Galanter, E. H. Hess, & G. Mandler (Eds.), *New directions in psychology.* New York: Holt, Rinehart and Winston.

Hess, J. A. (2000). Maintaining nonvoluntary relationships with disliked partners: An investigation into the use of distancing behaviors. *Human Communication Research, 26,* 458–488.

Hetherington, M. M., & Rolls, B. J. (1996). Sensory-specific satiety: Theoretical frameworks and central characteristics. In E. D. Capaldi (Ed.), *Why we eat what we eat: The psychology of eating* (pp. 267–290). Washington, DC: American Psychological Association.

Hinde, R. (1997). Is war a consequence of human aggression? In S. Feshbach and J. Zagrodzka (Eds.), *Aggression: Biological, developmental, and social perspectives.* New York: Plenum.

Hinde, R. A., Thorpe, W. H., & Vince, M. A. (1956). The following response in young coots and moorhens. *Behaviour, 9,* 214–242.

Hiroto, D. S. (1974). Locus of control and learned helplessness. *Journal of Experimental Psychology, 102(2),* 187–193.

Hiroto, D. S., & Seligman, M. E. P. (1975). Generality of learned helplessness in man. *Journal of Comparative and Physiological Psychology, 31,* 211–217.

Hobbes, T. (1962). *Leviathan.* New York: MacMillan. (Original work published in 1651.)

Hoebel, B. G. (1969). Feeding and self-stimulation. Neural regulation of food and water intake. *Annals of the New York Academy of Science, 157,* 758–778.

Hoffman, H. S., & Fleshler, M. (1962). The course of emotionality in the development of avoidance. *Journal of Experimental Psychology, 64,* 288–294.

Hohmann, G. W. (1966). Some effects on spinal cord lesions on experienced emotional feelings. *Psychophysiology, 3,* 143–156.

Hokanson, J. E. (1970). Psychophysiological evaluation of the catharsis hypothesis. In E. I. Megargee & J. E. Hokanson (Eds.), *The dynamics of aggression.* New York: Harper & Row.

Holmes, D. S. (1984). Meditation and somatic arousal reduction: A review of the experimental evidence. *American Psychologist, 39,* 1–10.

Holmes, T. H., & Rahe, R. H. (1967). The social readjustment rating scale. *Journal of Psychosomatic Research, 11,* 213–218.

Hovland, C., & Weiss, W. (1957). The influence of source credibility on communication effectiveness. *Public Opinion Quarterly, 15,* 635–650.

Hoy, R. R., & Casaday, G. B. (1979). Acoustic communication in crickets: Physiological analysis of auditory pathways. In G. Burghardt and M. Bekoff (Eds.), *The development of behavior: Comparative and evolutionary aspects.* New York: Garland.

Huesmann, L. R., & Eron, L. D. (1984). Cognitive processes and the persistence of aggressive behavior. *Aggressive Behavior, 10,* 243–251.

Hull, C. L. (1931) Goal attraction and directing ideas conceived as habit phenomena. *Psychological Review, 38,* 487–506.

Hull, C. L. (1943). *Principles of behavior.* New York: Appleton-Century-Crofts.

Hull, C. L. (1952). *A behavior system.* New Haven, CT: Yale University Press.

Hume, D. (1939). An enquiry concerning human understanding. In E. A. Burtt (Ed.), *The English philosophers from Bacon to Mill.* New York: Random House (Modern Library). (Original work published 1748).

Hunt, H. F., & Brady, J. V. (1955). Some effects of punishment and intercurrent "anxiety" on a simple operant. *Journal of Comparative and Physiological Psychology, 48,* 305–310.

Hunt, J. McV. (1965). Intrinsic motivation and its role in psychological development. In D. Levine (Ed.), *Nebraska symposium on motivation*. Lincoln: University of Nebraska Press.

Hunt, J. McV. (1984). The role of early experience in the development of intelligence and personality. In N. Endler & J. M. Hunt (Eds.), *Personality and the behavior disorders*, 2d ed. New York: John Wiley and Sons.

Hutchinson, B. R. (1972). The environmental causes of aggression. In J. K. Cole & D. D. Jensen (Eds.), *Nebraska symposium on motivation*. Lincoln: University of Nebraska Press.

Hyland, M. (1988). Motivational control theory: An integrated framework. *Journal of Personality and Social Psychology, 55*, 542–551.

Irwin, F. W. (1971). *Intentional behavior and motivation: A cognitive theory*. Philadelphia: Lippincott.

Izard, C. E. (1977). *Human emotion*. New York: Plenum Press.

Jacobs, G. D., & Snyder, D. (1996). Frontal brain asymmetry predicts affective style in men. *Behavioral Neuroscience, 110*, 3–6.

James, W. (1884). What is an emotion? *Mind, 9*, 188–205.

James, W. (1890). *Principles of psychology*. New York: Holt.

Jemmott, J. B. (1987). Social motives and susceptibility to disease: Stalking individual differences in health risks. *Journal of Personality, 55*, 267–298.

Johnson, R. W., Kelly, R. J., & Leblanc, B. A. (1995). Motivational basis of dissonance: Aversive consequences or inconsistency. *Personality and Social Psychology Bulletin, 8*, 850–855.

Jones, H. E., & Jones, M. C. (1928). A study of fear. *Childhood Education, 5*, 136–143.

Jones, M. C. (1924). The elimination of children's fears. *Journal of Experimental Psychology, 7*, 382–390.

Jones, E. E. (1964). *Ingratiation*. New York: Appleton-Century-Crofts.

Kagan, J., Reznick, J. S., & Snidman, N. (1988). Biological bases of childhood shyness. *Science, 240*, 167–171.

Kahneman, D., Diener, E., & Schwarz, N. (Eds) (1999). *Well-being: The foundations of hedonic psychology*. New York: Russell Sage Foundation.

Kalat, J. (1988). *Biological psychology*, 3d ed. Belmont, CA: Wadsworth Publishing Company.

Kalat, J. W. (1995). *Biological psychology*, 5th ed. Pacific Grove, CA: Brooks/Cole.

Kalick, S. M., Zebrowitz, L. A., Langlois, J. H., & Rohnson, R. M. (1998). Does human facial attractiveness honestly advertise health? Longitudinal data on an evolutionary question. *Psychological Science, 9*, 8–13.

Kalish, H. J. (1954). Strength of fear as a function of number of acquisition and extinction trials. *Journal of Experimental Psychology, 47*, 1–9.

Kallman, F. J. (1946). The genetic theory of schizophrenia. *American Journal of Psychiatry, 103*, 309–322.

Kamin, L. J. (1956). The effects of termination of the CS and avoidance of the US on avoidance learning. *Journal of Comparative and Physiological Psychology, 49*, 420–424.

Kamin, L. J., Brimer, C. J., & Black, A. H. (1963). Conditioned suppression as a monitor of fear of the CS in the course of avoidance learning. *Journal of Comparative and Physiological Psychology, 56*, 497–501.

Kane, T. R., Doerge, P., & Tedeschi, J. T. (1973). When is intentional harm-doing perceived as aggressive? A naive reappraisal of the Berkowitz aggression paradigm. *Proceedings of the 81st Annual Convention of the American Psychological Association, Montreal, Canada, 8*, 113–114. Washington, DC: American Psychological Association.

Karniol, R., & Ross, M. (1996). The motivational impact of temporal focus: Thinking about the future and the past. *Annual Review of Psychology, 47*, 593–620.

Kaufman, E. L., & Miller, N. E. (1949). Effect of number of reinforcements on strength of approach in an approach-avoidance conflict. *Journal of Comparative and Physiological Psychology, 42*, 65–74.

Keesey, R. E., & Powley, T. L. (1986). The regulation of body weight. *Annual Review of Psychology, 37*, 109–133.

Kelley, H. H. (1967). Attribution theory in social psychology. In D. Levine (Ed.), *Nebraska symposium on motivation*. Lincoln: University of Nebraska Press.

Keltner, D., & Anderson, C. (2000). Saving face for Darwin: The functions and uses of embarrassment. *Current Directions in Psychological Science*, 187–192.

Keltner, D., & Gross, J. J. (1999). Functional analyses of emotion. *Cognition and Emotion, 13*, 476–480.

Kimble, G. A. (1994a). A frame of reference for psychology. *American Psychologist, 49,* 510–519.

Kimble, G. A. (1994b). A new formula for behaviorism. *Psychological Review, 101,* 254–258.

Kirsch, I., & Henry, D. (1979). Self-desensitization and meditation in the reduction of public speaking anxiety. *Journal of Consulting and Clinical Psychology, 47,* 536–541.

Kitayama, S., & Markus, H. R. (1994). *Emotion and culture.* Washington, DC: American Psychological Association.

Klavora, P. (1978). An attempt to derive inverted-U curves based on the relationship between anxiety and athletic performance. In D. M. Landers & R. W. Christina (Eds.), *Psychology of motor behavior and sport—1977.* Champaign, IL: Human Kinetics.

Kleppner, O. (1977). *Advertising procedure,* 6th ed. Englewood Cliffs, NJ: Prentice-Hall.

Klinger, E. (1975). Consequences of commitment to and disengagement from incentives. *Psychological Review, 82,* 1–25.

Klinger, E. (1977). *Meaning and void: Inner experience and the incentives in people's lives.* Minneapolis: University of Minnesota Press.

Kluger, M. J., & Rottenberg, B. A. (1979). Fever and reduced iron: Their interaction as a host defense response to bacterial infection. *Science, 203,* 374–376.

Kobasa, S. C. (1979). Stressful life events, personality and health: An inquiry into hardiness. *Journal of Personality and Social Psychology, 37,* 1–11.

Kohlberg, L. (1964). Development of moral character and moral ideology. In M. L. Hoffman & L. W. Hoffman (Eds.), *Review of child development research* (Vol. 1). New York: Russell Sage Foundation.

Kohn, A. (1993a). *Punished by rewards.* Boston: Houghton Mifflin.

Kohn, A. (1993b, September–October). Why incentive plans cannot work. *Harvard Business Review, 71,* 54–63.

Kraley, F. S., Simansky, K. J., Coogan, L. A., & Trattner, M. S. (1985). Histamine and serotonin independently elicit drinking in the rat. *Physiology and Behavior, 34,* 963–967.

Kraly, S. F. (1984). Physiology of drinking elicited by eating. *Psychological Review, 91(4),* 478–490.

Kraut, R. E., & Johnston, R. E. (1979). Social and emotional messages of smiling: An ethological approach. *Journal of Personality and Social Psychology, 37,* 1539–1553.

Krieckhaus, E. E., & Wolf, G. (1968). Acquisition of sodium by rats: Interaction of innate mechanisms and latent learning. *Journal of Comparative and Physiological Psychology, 65,* 197–201.

Kruglanski, A. (1978). Endogeneous attribution and intrinsic motivation. In M. R. Leppen & D. Greene (Eds.), *The hidden costs of reward.* Hillsdale, NJ: Erlbaum.

Kruglanski, A. W., & Webster, D. M. (1996). Motivated closing of the mind: "Seizing" and "freezing." *Psychological Review, 103,* 263–283.

Kubovy, M. (1999). On the pleasures of the mind. In D. Kahneman, E. Diener, & N. Schwarz, (Eds). *Well-being: The foundations of hedonic psychology.* New York: Russell Sage Foundation.

Kuo, Z. Y. (1922). How are instincts acquired: *Psychological Review, 29,* 244–265.

Kuo, Z. Y. (1930). The genesis of the cat's response to the rat. *Journal of Comparative Psychology, 11,* 1–30.

Kuo, Z. Y. (1932). Ontogeny of embryonic behavior in aves. *Journal of Experimental Biology, 61,* 395–430, 453–489.

Laird, J. D. (1974). Self-attribution of emotion: The effects of expressive behavior on the quality of emotional experience. *Journal of Personality and Social Psychology, 29,* 475–486.

Landy, F. J., & Trumbo, D. H. (1980). *Psychology of work behavior.* Homewood, IL: Dorsey Press.

Lang, P. J., Bradley, M. M., & Cuthbert, B. N. (1989). Emotion, attention, and the startle reflex. *Psychological Review, 97,* 377–395.

Lange, G. C. (1885). *Om sinds bivogelser.* Copenhagen.

Langlois, J. H. Kalakanis, L., Rubenstein, A. J., Larson, A., Hallam, M., & Smoot, M. (2000). Maxims or myths of beauty? A meta-analytic and theoretical review. *Psychological Bulletin, 126,* 390–423.

Langlois, J. H., & Roggman, L. A. (1990). Attractive faces are only average. *Psychological Science, 1,* 115–121.

Langlois, J. H., Roggman, L. A., Musselman, L., & Acton, S. (1991). A picture is worth a thousand words: Reply to "On the difficulty of averaging faces." *Psychological Science, 5,* 354–357.

Larsen, J. T., McGraw, A. P., & Cacioppo, J. T. (2001). Can people feel happy and sad at the same time? *Journal of Personality and Social Psychology, 81,* 684–696.

Lashley, K. (1950). In search of the engram. *Symposium of the Society of Experimental Biology, 4,* 454–582.

Lashley, K. S. (1938). Experimental analysis of instinctive behavior. *Psychological Review, 45,* 445–471.

Latane, B. (1981). The psychology of social impact. *American Psychologist, 36,* 343–356.

Latane, B., & Darley, J. M. (1970). *The unresponsive bystander: Why doesn't he help?* New York: Appleton-Century-Crofts.

Latham, G. (2001). The reciprocal effects of science on practice: Insights from the practice and science of goal setting. *Canadian Psychology, 42,* 1–11.

Latham, G. P., & Baldes, J. J. (1975). The "practical significance" in Locke's theory of goal setting. *Journal of Applied Psychology, 60,* 122–124.

LaTour, M. S., & Henthorne, T. L. (1994). Female nudity in advertisements, arousal and response: A parsimonious extension. *Psychological Reports, 75,* 1683–1690.

Lawler, E. E., & Porter, L. W. (1967). The effects of performance on job satisfaction. *Industrial Relations, 20,* 20–28.

Lawson, R. (1965). *Frustration: The development of a scientific concept.* New York: Macmillan.

Lazarus, R. S. (1968). Emotion and adaption: Conceptual and empirial relations. In E. J. Arnold (Ed.), *Nebraska symposium on motivation.* Lincoln: University of Nebraska Press.

Lazarus, R. S. (1981). Little hassles can be dangerous to your health. *Psychology Today, 15,* 58–61.

Lazarus, R. S. (1984). On the primacy of cognition. *American Psychologist, 39* (2), 124–129.

Lazarus, R. S., & Folkman, S. (1984). *Stress, appraisal, and coping.* New York: McGraw-Hill.

Lea, S. E. G. (1978). The psychology of economics of demand. *Psychological Bulletin, 85,* 441–466.

Leaf, R. C. (1964). Avoidance response evocation as a function of prior discriminative fear conditioning under curare. *Journal of Comparative and Physiological Psychology, 58,* 446–449.

LeDoux, J. E. (1993). Emotional networks in the brain. In M. Lewis & J. M. Haviland (Eds.), *Handbook of emotions.* New York: Guilford Press.

LeDoux, J. E. (1994). Cognitive-emotional interactions in the brain. In P. Ekman & R. Davidson (Eds.), *The nature of emotion: Fundamental questions.* New York: Oxford.

LeDoux, J. E. (2000). Emotion circuits in the brain. *Annual Review of Neuroscience, 23,* 155–184.

Lee, J. A. (1977). A typology of styles of loving. *Personality and Social Psychology Bulletin, 3,* 173–182.

Lepper, M., & Greene, D. (1978). *The hidden cost of reward.* New York: Lawrence Erlbaum Associates, Inc.

Leeper, R. (1935). The role of motivation in learning: A study of the phenomenon of differential motivational control of the utilization of habits. *Journal of Genetic Psychology, 46,* 3–40.

Lerner, J. S., & Keltner, D. (2000). Beyond valence: Toward a model of emotion-specific influences on judgment and choice. *Cognition and Emotion, 14,* 473–493.

LeUnes, A., & Nation, J. R. (2002). *Sport psychology,* 3d ed. Pacific Grove, CA: Wadsworth.

Leventhal, H., & Tomarken, A. (1986). Emotion: Today's problems. *Annual Review of Psychology, 37,* 565–610.

Levey, A. B., & Martin, I. (1987). Evaluative conditioning: A case for hedonic transfer. In H. J. Eysenck & I. Martin (Eds.). *Theoretical foundations of behaviour therapy* (pp. 113–132). London: Plenum.

Levey, A. B., & Martin, I. (1975). Classical conditioning of human "evaluative" responses. *Behaviour Research and Therapy, 13,* 116–221.

Levine, S. (1960). Stimulation in infancy. *Scientific American, 202,* 80–86.

Levinger, G., Rands, M., & Talober, R. (1977). *The assessment of involvement and rewardingness in close and casual pair relationships* (National Science Foundation Tech. Dept. DIC). Amherst: University of Massachusetts.

Levis, D. J., & Brewer, K. E. (2001). The neurotic paradox: Attempts by two-factor fear theory and alternative avoidance models to resolve the issues associated with sustained avoidance responding in extinction. In R. R. Mowrer & S. B. Klein (Eds.), *Handbook of contemporary learning theories,* pp. 561–597. Mahwah, NJ: Lawrence Erlbaum Associates.

Lewin, K. (1935). *A dynamic theory of personality.* New York: McGraw-Hill.

Lewin, K., Dembo, T., Festinger, L., & Sears, P. S. (1944). Level of aspiration. In J. McV. Hunt (Ed.), *Personality and the behavior disorders.* New York: Ronald Press.

Lewis, M., & Haviland-Jones, J. (Eds.). (2000). *Handbook of emotions,* 2d ed. New York: Oxford University Press.

Lindsley, D. B. (1951). Emotion. In S. S. Stevens (Ed.), *Handbook of experimental psychology.* New York: Wiley.

Lindsley, D. B., Schreiner, L. H., Knowles, W. B., & Magoun, H. W. (1950). Behavioral and EEG changes following chronic brain stem lesions in the cat. *Electroencephalography and Clinical Neurophysiology, 2,* 483–498.

Lippsitt, L., Reilly, B. M., Butcher, M. J., & Greenwood, M. M. (1976). The stability and interrelationships of newborn sucking and heart rate. *Developmental Psychobiology, 9,* 305–310.

Little, B. R. (1983). Personal projects: a rationale and method for investigation. *Environment and Behavior, 15,* 273–309.

Locke, E. A. (1968). Toward a theory of task motivation and incentives. *Organizational Behavior and Human Performance, 3,* 157–189.

Locke, E. A. (1976). Nature and causes of job satisfaction. In M. Dunnette (Ed.), *Handbook of industrial and organizational psychology.* New York: Rand-McNally.

Locke, E. A., & Latham, G. P. (1984). *Goal setting: A motivational technique that works!* Englewood Cliffs, NJ: Prentice-Hall, Inc.

Loewenstein, G. (1994). The psychology of curiosity: A review and reinterpretation. *Psychological Bulletin, 116,* 75–98.

Loewenstein, G., Adler, D., Behrens, D., & Gillis, J. (1992). Why Pandora opened the box: Curiosity as a desire for missing information. Working paper, Department of Social and Decision Sciences, Carnegie Mellon University, Pittsburgh, PA.

Logan, F. A. (1960). *Incentive.* New Haven, CT: Yale University Press.

Logan, F. A. (1968). Incentive theory and changes in reward. In G. H. Bower (Ed.), *The psychology of learning and motivation* (Vol. 2). New York: Academic.

Lorenz, K. (1965a). *Evolution and modification of behavior.* Chicago: University of Chicago Press.

Lorenz, K. (1965b). *On aggression.* New York: Harcourt Brace Jovanovich.

Lott, A. J., & Lott, B. E. (1974). The role of reward in the foundation of positive interpersonal attitudes. In T. C. Huston (Ed.), *Foundations of interpersonal attraction.* New York: Academic Press.

Maier, S. F., Seligman, M. E. P., & Solomon, R. L. (1969). Pavlovian fear conditioning and learned helplessness: Effects on escape and avoidance behavior of (a) the CS-UCS contingency and (b) the independence of UCS and voluntary responding. In B. A. Campbell & R. M. Church (Eds.), *Punishment and aversive behavior.* New York: Appleton-Century-Crofts.

Maier, S. F., & Watkins, L. R. (1998). Stressor controllability, anxiety, and serotonin. *Cognitive Therapy and Research, 22,* 595–613.

Maisto, S. A., Galizio, M., & Connors, G. J. (1991). *Drug use and misuse.* Philadelphia: Holt, Rinehart & Winston.

Malmo, R. B. (1959). Activation: A neuropsychological dimension. *Psychological Review, 66,* 367–386.

Malmo, R. B. (1975). *Our emotions, needs, and our archaic brain.* New York: Holt, Rinehart and Winston.

Mandler, G. (1962). Emotions. In T. M. Newcomb (Ed.), *New directions in psychology.* New York: Holt, Rinehart and Winston.

Marler, P. (1976). On animal aggression: The roles of strangeness and familiarity. *American Psychologist, 31,* 239–246.

Marshall, G. D., & Zimbardo, P. G. (1979). Affective consequences of inadequately explained physiological arousal. *Journal of Personality and Social Psychology, 37,* 970–988.

Martin, I., & Levey, A. B. (1978). Evaluative conditioning. *Advances in Behavioural Therapy, 1,* 57–102.

Martin, K. A., & Leary, M. R. (1998). Single, female, physically active: Effects of exercise status and body weight on stereotyped perceptions of young women. Unpublished manuscript, Wake Forest University.

Maslach, C. (1979). Negative emotional biasing of unexplained arousal. *Journal of Personality and Social Psychology, 37,* 953–969.

Maslow, A. H. (1970). *Motivation and personality,* 2d ed. New York: Harper & Row.

Masserman, J. H. (1943). *Behavior and neurosis.* Chicago: University of Chicago Press.

Masters, W. H., & Johnson, V. (1966). *Human sexual response.* Boston: Little, Brown.

Mathes, E. W. (1975). The effects of physical attractiveness and anxiety on heterosexual attraction over a series of five encounters. *Journal of Marriage and the Family, 37,* 769–774.

Matsumoto, D. (1987). The role of facial response in the experience of emotion: More method-ological problems and a meta-analysis. *Journal of Personality and Social Psychology, 52* (4), 769–774.

McAdams, D. P. (1997). A conceptual history of personality psychology. In R. Hogan, J. Johnson, & S. Briggs (Eds.), *Handbook of personality psychology*. New York: Academic Press.

McAdams, D. P., & McClelland, D. C. (1983). Social motives and memory. Unpublished manu-script, Harvard University, Department of Psychology and Social Relations. Cited in Mc-Clelland (1985, p. 279).

McAllister, W. R., McAllister, D. E., Scoles, M. T., & Hampton, S. R. (1986). Persistence of fear-reducing behavior: Relevance for the conditioning theory of neurosis. *Journal of Abnormal Psychology, 95,* 365–372.

McClelland, D. C. (1958). Risk-taking in children with high and low need for achievement. In J. W. Atkinson (Ed.), *Motives in fantasy, action, and society*. Princeton: Van Nostrand.

McClelland, D. C. (1961). *The achieving society*. Princeton: Van Nostrand.

McClelland, D. C. (1965). N achievement and entrepreneurship: A longitudinal study. *Journal of Personality and Social Psychology, 1,* 389–392.

McClelland, D. C. (1985). *Human motivation*. New York: Scott-Freeman.

McClelland, D. C., Atkinson, J. W., Clark, R. A., & Lowell, E. L. (1953). *The achievement motive*. New York: Appleton-Century-Crofts.

McClelland, D. C., Davidson, R., Saron, C., & Floor, E. (1980). The need for power, brain norep-inephrine turnover, and learning. *Biological Psychology, 10,* 93–102.

McClelland, D. C., Davis, W. W., Kalin, R., & Wanner, E. (1972). *The drinking man: Alcohol and human motivation*. New York: Free Press.

McClelland, D. C., Patel, V., Stier, D., & Brown, D. (1987). The relationship of affiliative arousal to dopamine release. *Motivation and emotion, 2,* 51–66.

McClelland, D. C., Rindlisbacher, A., & DeCharms, R. C. (1955). Religious and other sources of parental attitudes toward independence training. In D. C. McClelland (Ed.), *Studies in mo-tivation*. New York: Appleton-Century-Crofts.

McCormick, E. J., & Ilgen, D. R. (1980). *Industrial psychology*, 7th ed. Englewood Cliffs, NJ: Prentice-Hall.

McCrae, R. R., & Costa, P. T. (1987) Validation of the five-factor model of personality across in-struments and observers. *Journal of Personality and Social Psychology, 52,* 81–90.

McCrae, R. R. & John, O. P. (1992). An introduction to the five factor model and its applica-tions. *Journal of Personality, 60,* 175–215.

McDougall, W. (1923). *Outline of psychology*. New York: Charles Scribner's Sons.

McGrath, J. E. (1970). *Social and psychological factors in stress*. New York: Holt, Rinehart and Win-ston.

McGregor, D. (1960). *The human side of enterprise*. New York: McGraw-Hill.

McNally, R. J. (1987). Preparedness and phobias: A review. *Psychological Bulletin, 101,* 283–303.

Mehrabian, A. (1976). *Public spaces and private places*. New York: Basic Books.

Mellgren, R. (1972). Positive and negative contrast effects using delayed reinforcement. *Learning and Motivation, 3,* 185–193.

Mendelson, J., & Chillag, D. (1970). Tongue cooling: A new reward for thirsty rodents. *Science, 170,* 1418–1421.

Mesquita, B., & Frijda, N. (1992). Cultural variations in emotion: A review. *Psychological Bulletin, 112,* 179–204.

Milgram, S. (1974). *Obedience to authority: An experimental view*. New York: Harper & Row.

Miller, N. E. (1948). Studies of fear as an acquirable drive: I. Fear as motivation and fear-reduction as reinforcement in the learning of new responses. *Journal of Experimental Psy-chology, 38,* 89–101.

Miller, N. E. (1951a). Comments on multi-process conceptions of learning. *Psychological Review, 58,* 375–381.

Miller, N. E. (1951b). Learnable drives and rewards. In S. S. Stevens (Ed.), *Handbook of experimen-tal psychology*. New York: Wiley.

Miller, N. E. (1959). Liberalization of basic S-R concepts: Extensions to conflict behavior, motiva-tion and social learning. In S. Koch (Ed.), *Psychology: A study of a science* (Vol. 2). New York: McGraw-Hill.

Miller, N. E. (1960). Learning resistance to pain and fear: Effects of overlearning, exposure, and rewarded exposure in context. *Journal of Experimental Psychology, 60,* 137–145.

Miller, N. E., & Kessen, M. L. (1952). Reward effects of food via stomach fistula compared with those of food via mouth. *Journal of Comparative and Physiological Psychology, 45,* 555–564.

Miller, R. R., Greco, C., Vigorito, M., & Marlin, N. A. (1983). Signaled tailshock is perceived as similar to a stronger unsignaled tailshock: Implications for a functional analysis of classical conditioning. *Journal of Experimental Psychology: Animal Behavior Processes, 9,* 105–131.

Mineka, S. (1979). The role of fear in theories of avoidance learning, flooding, and extinction. *Psychological Bulletin, 5,* 985–1010.

Mineka, S., & Cook, M. (1993). Mechanisms involved in the observational conditioning of fear. *Journal of Experimental Psychology: General, 122,* 23–38.

Mineka, S., & Henderson, R. W. (1985). Controllability and predictability in acquired motivation. *Annual Review of Psychology, 36,* 495–529.

Mischel, W. (1973). Toward a cognitive social learning reconceptualization of personality. *Psychological Review, 80,* 252–283.

Mitchell, J. E. (1986). Bulimia: Medical and physiological aspects. In K. D. Brownell & J. P. Foreyt (Eds.), *Handbook of eating disorders.* New York: Basic Books.

Moltz, H. (1960). Imprinting: Empirical basis and theoretical significance. *Psychological Bulletin, 57,* 291–314.

Monahan, J. L., Murphy, S. T., & Zajonc, R. B. (2000). Subliminal mere exposure: Specific, general, and diffuse effects. *Psychological Science, 11,* 462–466.

Monat, A., & Lazarus, R. S. (1985). Stress and coping—some current issues and controversies. In A. Monat & R. Lazarus (Eds.), *Stress and coping,* 2d ed. New York: Columbia University Press.

Money, J. (1987). Sin, sickness, or status: Homosexual gender identity and psychoneuroendocrinology. *American Psychologist, 42,* 284–299.

Money, J., & Ehrhardt, A. (1972). *Man & woman, boy & girl.* Baltimore, MD: Johns Hopkins University Press.

Montgomery, K. C. (1953). The effect of hunger and thirst drives upon exploratory behavior. *Journal of Comparative and Physiological Psychology, 46,* 315–319.

Moore, T. E. (1982). Subliminal advertising: What you see is what you get. *Journal of Marketing, 46,* 38–47.

Morgan, C. T. (1943). *Physiological psychology.* New York: McGraw-Hill.

Morgan, C. T. (1959). Physiological theory of drive. In S. Koch (Ed.), *Psychology: A study of science* (Vol. 1). New York: McGraw-Hill.

Morris, C. W. (1938). Foundations of the theory of signs. In O. Neurath, R. Carnap, & C. Morris (Eds.), *International encyclopedia of unified science* (Vol. 1). Chicago: University of Chicago Press.

Morris, D. (1967). *The naked ape.* New York: Dell.

Morris, W. N. (1989). *Mood: The frame of mind.* New York: Springer-Verlag.

Morrison, A. R. (1983). A window on the sleeping brain. *Scientific American, 248(4),* 94–102.

Moruzzi, G., & Magoun, H. W. (1949). Brain stem and reticular formation and activation of the EEG. *Electroencephalography and Clinical Neurophysiology, 1,* 455–473.

Mosher, D. L., & O'Grady, K. E. (1979). Sex guilt, trait anxiety, and females' subjective sexual arousal to erotica. *Motivation and Emotion, 3,* 235–249.

Moss, M. K., & Page, R. A. (1972). Reinforcement and helping behavior. *Journal of Applied Social Psychology, 2,* 360–371.

Moulton, R. W. (1965). Effects of success and failure on level of aspiration as related to achievement motives. *Journal of Personality and Social Psychology, 1,* 399–406.

Mower, G. D. (1976). Perceived intensity of peripheral thermal stimuli is independent of internal body temperature. *Journal of Comparative and Physiological Psychology, 90,* 1152–1155.

Mowrer, O. H. (1939). A stimulus-response analysis of anxiety and its role as a reinforcing agent. *Psychological Review, 46,* 553–564.

Mowrer, O. H. (1948). Learning theory and the neurotic paradox. *American Journal of Orthopsychiatry, 18,* 571–610.

Mowrer, O. H. (1960). *Learning theory and behavior.* New York: Wiley.

Mowrer, O. H., & Lamoreaux, R. R. (1946). Fear as an intervening variable in avoidance conditioning. *Journal of Comparative Psychology, 39,* 29–50.

Mowrer, O. H., & Viek, P. (1948). An experimental analogue of fear from a sense of helplessness. *Journal of Abnormal and Social Psychology, 83,* 193–200.

Moyer, K. E. (1971). The physiology of aggression and the implications of aggression control. In J. L. Singer (Ed.), *The control of aggression and violence: cognitive and physiological factors.* New York: Academic.

Munton, A. G. (1985–1986). Learned helplessness, attribution theory, and the nature of cognitions: A critical evaluation. *Current Psychological Research and Reviews,* Winter, 331–348.

Murphy, S., & Zajonc, R. B. (1993). Affect, cognition, and awareness: Affective priming with optimal and suboptimal stimulus exposures. *Journal of Personality and Social Psychology, 64,* 723–739.

Murray, H. A. (1938). *Explorations in personality.* New York: Oxford University Press.

Myers, D. G. (2002). *Social psychology,* 7th ed. New York: McGraw-Hill.

Neiss, R. (1988). Reconceptualizing arousal: Psychobiological states in motor performance. *Psychological Bulletin, 103,* 345–366.

Nel, E., Helmreich, R., & Aronson, E. (1969). Opinion change in the advocate as a function of the persuasibility of the audience: A clarification of the meaning of dissonance. *Journal of Personality and Social Psychology, 12,* 117–124.

Newcomb, T. (1968). Interpersonal balance. In R. P. Abelson, E. Aronson, W. J. McGuire, T. M. Newcomb, M. J. Rosenberg, & P. H. Tannenbaum (Eds.), *Theories of cognitive consistency: A sourcebook.* Chicago: Rand McNally.

Newcomb, T. M. (1961). *The acquaintance process.* New York: Holt, Rinehart and Winston.

Nicholaidis, S. (1968). Réponses des unites osmosensibles hypothalamiques aux stimulations saliens at aqueuses de la langue. *Competes rendus hebdomadaires des séances de l'académie des sciences, Series C, 267,* 2352–2355.

Nisbett, R. E., & Wilson, T. D. (1977). Telling more than we can know: Verbal reports on mental processes. *Psychological Review, 84,* 231–259.

Nosek, B. A., Banaji, M. R., & Greenwald, A. G. (2002). Harvesting implicit group attitudes and beliefs from a demonstration web site. *Group Dynamics, 6,* 101–115.

Notz, W. W. (1975). Work motivation and the negative effects of extrinsic rewards: A review with implications for theory and practice. *American Psychologist, 9,* 844–891.

Novin, D. (1962). The relation between electrical conductivity of brain tissue and thirst in the rat. *Journal of Comparative and Physiological Psychology, 55,* 145–154.

Oatley, K., & Jenkins, J. M. (1996). *Understanding emotions.* Cambridge, MA: Blackwell Publishers.

Öhman, A. (1983). Evaluating evaluative conditioning. Some comments on "Cognitions, Evaluations, and Conditioning: Rules of Sequence and Rules of Consequence" by Levey and Martin. *Advances in Behavior Research & Therapy, 4,* 213–218.

Öhman, A. (1986). Face the beast and fear the face: Animal and social fears as prototypes for evolutionary analyses of emotion. *Psychophysiology, 23(2),* 123–145.

Öhman, A., & Mineka, S. (2001). Fears, phobias and preparedness: Toward an evolved module of fear and fear learning. *Psychological Review, 108,* 483–522.

O'Kelly, L. I., & Beck, R. C. (1960). Water regulation in the rat: III. The artificial control of thirst with stomach loads of water and sodium chloride. *Psychological Monographs, 74*(13, Whole No. 500).

Olds, J. (1958). Satiation effects in self-stimulation of the brain. *Journal of Comparative and Physiological Psychology, 51,* 675–678.

Olds, J., & Milner, P. (1954). Positive reinforcement produced by electrical stimulation of the septal area and other regions of the rat brain. *Journal of Comparative and Physiological Psychology, 47,* 419–427.

O'Leary, C. J., Willis, F. N., & Tomich, E. (1969). Conformity under deceptive and nondeceptive techniques. *Sociological Quarterly,* Winter, 87–93.

Olson, M. A. & Fazio, R. H. (2001). Implicit attitude formation through classical conditioning. *Psychological Science, 10,* 413–417.

Ornstein, R. (1986). *The psychology of consciousness.* New York: Penguin.

Osgood, C. E. (1950). Can Tolman's theory of learning handle avoidance training? *Psychological Review, 57,* 133–137.

Osgood, C. E., Suci, G. J., & Tannenbaum, P. H. (1957). *The measurement of meaning.* Urbana: University of Illinois Press.

Overmier, J. B., & Seligman, M. E. P. (1967). Effects of inescapable shock upon subsequent escape and avoidance responding. *Journal of Comparative and Physiological Psychology, 63,* 28–33.

Oxendine, J. B. (1970). Emotional arousal and motor performance. *Quest, 13,* 23–32.

Page, H. A. (1955). The facilitation of experimental extinction by response prevention as a function of the acquisition of a new response. *Journal of Comparative and Physiological Psychology, 48,* 14–16.

Page, M. M., & Scheidt, R. J. (1971). The elusive weapons effect: Demand awareness, evaluation apprehension, and slightly sophisticated subjects. *Journal of Personality and Social Psychology, 20,* 304–318.

Pallak, M. S., & Pittman, T. S. (1972). General motivational effects of dissonance arousal. *Journal of Personality and Social Psychology, 21,* 349–358.

Palmer, J., & Byrne, D. (1970). Attraction toward dominant and submissive strangers: Similarity versus complementarity. *Journal of Experimental Research in Psychology, 4,* 108–115.

Papez, J. W. (1937). A proposed mechanism of emotion. *Archives of Neurology and Psychiatry, 38,* 725–743.

Papini, M. R. (2002). Pattern and process in the evolution of learning. *Psychological Review, 109,* 186–201.

Papini, M. R., & Dudley, R. T. (1997). Consequences of surprising reward omission. *Review of General Psychology, 1,* 175–197.

Pashler, H., & Gallistel, R. (Eds.), *Stevens' handbook of experimental psychology,* 3d ed. (Vol. 3). New York: John Wiley & Sons.

Pastore, N. (1952). The role of arbitrariness in the frustration-aggression hypothesis. *Journal of Abnormal and Social Psychology, 57,* 728–731.

Patterson, M. L. (1976). An arousal model for interpersonal intimacy. *Psychological Review, 83,* 235–245.

Pavlov, I. P. (1927). *Conditioned reflexes.* London: Oxford University Press.

Pelletier, L. G., Fortier, M.S., Vallerand, R. J., Tuson, K. M., Briere, N. M., & Blais, M. R. (1995). Toward a new measure of intrinsic motivation, extrinsic motivation, and amotivation in sports: The Sport Motivation Scale (SMS). *Journal of Sport & Exercise Psychology, 17,* 35–53.

Peplau, L. A. (1982). Interpersonal attraction. In D. Sherrod (Ed.), *Social psychology.* New York: Random House.

Pepper, S. (1959). A neural-identity theory of mind. In S. Hook (Ed.), *Dimensions of mind.* New York: Collier.

Perin, C. T. (1942). Behavioral potentiality as a joint function of the amount of training and the degree of hunger at the time of extinction. *Journal of Experimental Psychology, 30,* 93–113.

Peterson, R. A., & Kerin, R. A. (1977). The female role in advertising: Some experimental evidence. *Journal of Marketing, 41,* 59–63.

Petty, R. E., & Cacioppo, J. T. (1984). Motivational factors in consumer response to advertisements. In R. G. Geen, W. W. Beatty, & R. M. Arkin (Eds.), *Human motivation.* New York: Allyn and Bacon.

Petty, R. E. & Cacioppo, J. T. (1986). The Elaboration Likelihood Model of Persuasion. *Advances in Experimental Social Psychology, 19,* 123–205.

Petty, R. E., Cacioppo, J. T., & Schumann, D. (1983). Central and peripheral routes to advertising effectiveness: The moderating role of involvement. *Journal of Consumer Research, 10,* 135–146.

Petty, R. E., Wegener, G. T., Fabrigar, L. R. (1997). Attitudes and attitude change. *Annual Review of Psychology, 48,* 609–647.

Pfaff, D. W., & Ågmo, A. (2002). Reproductive motivation. In H. Pashler & R. Gallistel (Eds.), *Stevens' handbook of experimental psychology,* 3d ed. (Vol. 3). New York: John Wiley & Sons.

Pfaffmann, C., & Bare, J. K. (1950). Gustatory nerve discharges in normal and adrenalectomized rats. *Journal of Comparative and Physiological Psychology, 43,* 320–324.

Pilliavin, I., Rodin, J., & Piliavin, J. (1969). Good Samaritanism: An underground phenomenon? *Journal of Personality and Social Psychology, 13,* 289–299.

Pittenger, J. B. (1991). On the difficulty of averaging faces: Comments on Langlois and Roggman. *Psychological Science, 5,* 351–353.

Platt, J. R. (1961). Beauty: Pattern and change. In D. W. Fiske & S. R. Maddi (Eds.), *Functions of varied experience.* Homewood, IL: Dorsey Press.

Plomin, R., Fulker, D. W., Corley, R., & DeFries, J. C. (1997). Nature, nurture, and cognitive development from 1 to 16 years: A parent-offspring adoption study. *Psychological Science, 6,* 442–447.

Plutchik, R. (1980). *Emotion: A psychoevolutionary synthesis.* New York: Harper & Row.

Popper, K. R. (1959). *The logic of scientific discovery.* New York: Harper & Row.

Postman, L., & Phillips, L. W. (1965). Short term temporal changes in free recall. *Quarterly Journal of Experimental Psychology, 17,* 132–138.

Premack, D. (1959). Toward empirical behavioral laws: I. Positive reinforcement. *Psychological Review, 66,* 219–233.

Premack, D. (1971). Catching up with common sense or two sides of a generalization: Reinforcement and punishment. In R. Glaser (Ed.), *The nature of reinforcement.* New York: Academic.

Preston, S. D., & de Waal, F. B. M. (2002). Empathy: Its ultimate and proximate bases. *Behavioral and Brain Sciences, 25,* 1–20.

Priest, R. F., & Sawyer, J. (1967). Proximity and peership: Bases of balance in interpersonal attraction. *American Journal of Sociology, 7,* 21–27.

Pritchard, R. M. (1961). Stabilized images on the retina. *Scientific American, 204,* 72–78.

Ramirez, I., & Fuller, J. L. (1976). Genetic influence on water and sweetened water consumption in mice. *Physiology and Behavior, 16,* 163–168.

Ramsay, D. S., Seeley, R. J., Bolles, R. C., & Woods, S. C. (1996). Ingestive homeostasis: The primacy of learning. In E. D. Capaldi (Ed.), *Why we eat what we eat: The psychology of eating.* Washington, DC: American Psychological Association.

Ranson, S. W., Fischer, C., & Ingram, W. R. (1938). The hypothalamicohypophyseal mechanism in diabetes insipidus. Paper read before Association for Research in Nervous and Mental Diseases, December 1936. In *The pituitary gland.* Baltimore, MD: Williams and Wilkins.

Ray, O. (1963). The effects of tranquilizers on positively and negatively motivated behavior in rats. *Psychopharmacologia, 4,* 326–342.

Raynor, H. A. (2001). Dietary variety, energy regulation, and obesity. *Psychological Bulletin, 127,* 325–341.

Razran, G. (1954). The conditioned evocation of attitudes (cognitive conditioning?). *Journal of Experimental Psychology, 48,* 278–282.

Razran, G. (1961). The observable unconscious and the inferable conscious in current Soviet psychophysiology: Interoceptive conditioning, semantic conditioning, and the orienting reflex. *Psychological Review, 68,* 81–147.

Reisenzein, R. (1983). The Schachter theory of emotion: Two decades later. *Psychological Bulletin, 94,* 239–264.

Reith, J. (1988). Job satisfaction parallels in higher education. Unpublished master's thesis, Wake Forest University, Winston-Salem, NC.

Rescorla, R. A. (1969). Establishment of a positive reinforcer through contrast with shock. *Journal of Comparative and Physiological Psychology, 67,* 260–263.

Rescorla, R. A. (1987). A Pavlovian analysis of goal-directed behavior. *American Psychologist, 42,* 119–129.

Rescorla, R. A., & Lolordo, V. M. (1965). Inhibition of avoidance behavior. *Journal of Comparative and Physiological Psychology, 59,* 406–412.

Rescorla, R. A., & Solomon, R. L. (1967). Two-process learning theory: Relationships between Pavlovian conditioning and instrumental learning. *Psychological Review, 74,* 151–182.

Revusky, S. H. (1967). Hunger level during food consumption: Effects on subsequent preferences. *Psychonomic Science, 7,* 109–110.

Revusky, S. H. (1968). Effects of thirst level during consumption of flavored water on subsequent preference. *Journal of Comparative and Physiological Psychology, 66,* 777–779.

Revusky, S. H., & Garcia, J. (1970). Learned associations over long delays. In C. H. Bower & J. T. Spence (Eds.), *The psychology of learning and motivation: Advances in research and theory* (Vol. 4). New York: Academic.

Rhodes, G., & Tremewan, T. (1996). Averageness, exaggeration, and facial attractiveness. *Psychological Science, 2,* 105–110.

Richter, C. P. (1936). Increased salt appetite in adrenalectomized rats. *American Journal of Physiology, 115,* 155–161.

Rilling, M., Askew, H. R., Ahlskog, J. E., & Kramer, T. J. (1969). Aversive properties of the negative stimulus in a successive discrimination. *Journal of the Experimental Analysis of Behavior, 12,* 917–932.

Rimm, D. C., & Masters, J. C. (1979). *Behavior therapy: Techniques and empirical findings,* 2d ed. New York: Academic Press.

Rinn, W. (1984). The neuropsychology of facial expression: A review of the neurological and psychological mechanisms for producing facial expressions. *Psychological Bulletin, 95(1),* 52–77.

Robbins, D. (1969). Effect of duration of water reinforcement on running behavior and consummatory activity. *Journal of Comparative and Physiological Psychology, 69,* 311–316.

Roberts, G. C. (1984). Toward a new theory of motivation in sport: The role of perceived ability. In R. M. Silva & R. S. Weinberg (Eds.), *Psychological foundations of sport.* Champaign, IL: Human Kinetics Publishers.

Robins, C. J. (1988). Attributions and depression: Why is the literature so inconsistent? *Journal of Personality and Social Psychology,* 54(5), 880–889.

Rodin, J., Bartoshuk, L., Peterson, C., & Schank, D. (1990). Bulimia and taste: Possible interactions. *Journal of Abnormal Psychology, 99,* 32–39.

Rodin, J., & Langer, E. J. (1977). Long-term effects of control-relevant intervention with the institutionalized aged. *Journal of Personality and Social Psychology, 35,* 897–902.

Roethlisberger, F. J., & Dickson, W. J. (1947). *Management and the worker.* Cambridge, MA: Harvard University Press.

Rogers, M., & Smith, K. H. (1993). Public perceptions of subliminal advertising: Why practitioners shouldn't ignore this issue. *Journal-of-Advertising Research, 33,* 10–18.

Rolls, E. T. (1999). *The brain and emotion.* New York: Oxford University Press.

Rothbaum, F., Weisz, J. R., & Snyder, S. S. (1982). Changing the world and changing the self: A two process model of perceived control. *Journal of Personality and Social Psychology, 42,* 5–37.

Rotter, J. B. (1966). Generalized expectancies for internal versus external control of reinforcement. *Psychological Monographs, 80* (Whole No. 609).

Rowland, N. E. (2002). Thirst and water-salt appetite. In H. Pashler & R. Gallistel (Eds.), *Stevens' handbook of experimental psychology,* 3d ed. (Vol. 3). New York: John Wiley & Sons.

Rozin, P. (1996). Sociocultural influences on human food selection. In E. D. Capaldi (Ed.), *Why we eat what we eat: The psychology of eating.* Washington, DC: American Psychological Association.

Rozin, P., & Kalat, J. W. (1971). Specific hungers and poison avoidance as adaptive specializations of learning. *Psychological Review, 78,* 459–486.

Rozin, P., & Royzman, E. B. (2001). Negativity bias, negativity dominance, and contagion. *Personality and Social Psychology Review, 5,* 296–320.

Rubin, Z. (1970). Measurement of romantic love. *Journal of Personality and Social Psychology, 16,* 265–273.

Rubin, Z. (1973). *Liking and loving.* New York: Holt, Rinehart and Winston.

Rusbult, C. (1983). A longitudinal test of the investment model: The development (and deterioration) of satisfaction and commitment in heterosexual involvements. *Journal of Personality and Social Psychology, 45,* 101–117.

Russell, J. A. (1980). A circumplex model of affect. *Journal of Personality and Social Psychology, 39,* 1161–1178.

Russell, J. A., & Mehrabian, A. (1977). Evidence for a three-factor theory of emotions. *Journal of Research in Psychology, 11,* 273–294.

Ryle, G. (1949). *The concept of mind.* New York: Barnes & Noble.

Salovey, P., Mayer, J. D., & Rosenhan, D. L. (1991). Mood and helping: Mood as a motivator of helping and helping as a regulator of mood. In M. S. Clark (Ed.), *Review of Personality and Social Psychology* (Vol. 12: *Prosocial behavior,* pp. 295–237). Newbury Park, CA: Sage.

Sansone, C., & Harackiewicz, J. M., Eds (2000). *Intrinsic and extrinsic motivation.* New York: Academic Press.

Satinoff, E. (1983). A reevaluation of the concept of the homeostatic organization of temperature regulation. In E. Satinoff & P. Teitelbaum (Eds.), *Handbook of behavioral neurobiology* (Vol. 6). New York: Plenum.

Schachter, S. (1951). Deviation, rejection, and communication. *Journal of Abnormal and Social Psychology, 46,* 190–207.

Schachter, S. (1959). *The psychology of affiliation.* Palo Alto, CA: Stanford University Press.

Schachter, S., & Singer, J. E. (1962). Cognitive, social, and physiological determinants of emotional state. *Psychological Review, 69,* 379–399.

Schafe, G. E., & Bernstein, I. L. (1996) Taste version learning. In E. D. Capaldi (Ed.), *Why we eat what we eat: The psychology of eating.* Washington, DC: American Psychological Association.

Scher, S. J., & Cooper, J. (1989). Motivation basis of dissonance: The singular role of behavioral consequences. *Journal of Personality and Social Psychology, 56,* 899–906.

Schlenker, B. (1982). Translating actions into attitudes: An identity analytic approach to the explanation of social conduct. In L. Berkowitz (Ed.), *Advances in experimental social psychology* (Vol. 15). New York: Academic Press.

Schmidt, D. E., & Keating, J. P. (1979). Human crowding and personal control: An integration of the research. *Psychological Bulletin, 86*, 680–700.

Schwartz, S. (1968). Words, deeds, and the perception of consequences and responsibility in action situations. *Journal of Personality and Social Psychology, 10*, 232–242.

Schwartz, S., & Clausen, G. T. (1970). Responsibility, norms, and helping in an emergency. *Journal of Personality and Social Psychology, 16*, 299–310.

Sclafani, A. (1991). The hedonics of sugar and starch. In R. Bolles (Ed.), *The hedonics of taste.* Hillsdale, NJ: Lawrence Erlbaum Associates.

Sclafani, A., & Nissenbaum, J. W. (1987). Taste preference thresholds for polycose, maltose, and sucrose in rats. *Neuroscience and Biobehavioral Reviews, 11*, 181–185.

Scott, J. P. (1958). *Aggression.* Chicago: University of Chicago Press.

Scott, J. P. (1962). Critical periods in behavioral development. *Science, 138*, 949–958.

Scott, J. P. (1971). Theoretical issues concerning the origin and causes of fighting. In B. E. Eleftheriou & J. P. Scott (Eds.), *The physiology of aggression and defeat.* New York: Plenum.

Scott, T. R. (1990). Gustatory control of food selection. In E. M. Stricker (Ed.), *Handbook of behavioral neurobiology* (Vol. 10: *Neurobiology of food and fluid intake*). New York: Plenum.

Scott, T. R. (2001). The role of taste in feeding. *Appetite, 37*, 111–113.

Searle, J. R. (2000). Consciousness. *Annual Review of Neuroscience, 23*, 557–578.

Secord, P. F., & Backman, C. W. (1974). *Social psychology.* New York: McGraw-Hill.

Segal, M. W. (1974). Alphabet and attraction: An unobtrusive measure of the effect of propinquity in a field setting. *Journal of Personality and Social Psychology, 30*, 654–657.

Segall, M. H., Ember, C. R., & Ember, M. (1997). Aggression, crime, and warfare. In J. W. Berry, M. H. Segall, & C. Kagitcibasi (Eds.), *Handbook of cross-cultural psychology* (Vol 3. *Social and behavioral applications*). Boston: Allyn and Bacon.

Seligman, M. E. P. (1970). On the generality of the laws of learning. *Psychological Review, 77*, 406–418.

Seligman, M. E. P. (1971). Phobias and preparedness. *Behavior Therapy, 2*, 307–320.

Seligman, M. E. P. (1975). *Helplessness: On depression, development and death.* San Francisco: W. H. Freeman.

Seligman, M. E. P., Abramson, L. Y., Semmel, A., & von Bayer, C. (1979). Depressive attributional style. *Journal of Abnormal Psychology, 88*, 242–247.

Seligman, M. E. P., & Johnston, J. C. (1973). A cognitive theory of avoidance learning. In F. J. McGurgan & D. B. Lumsden (Eds.), *Contemporary approaches to conditioning and learning.* Washington, DC: Winston.

Seligman, M. E. P., & Maier, S. F. (1967). Failure to escape traumatic shock. *Journal of Experimental Psychology, 74*, 1–9.

Selye, H. (1956). *The stress of life.* New York: McGraw-Hill.

Shanks, D. R., & Dickinson, A. (1990). Contingency awareness in evaluative conditioning: A comment on Baeyens, Eelen, and Van den Bergh. *Cognition and Emotion, 4*, 19–30.

Sheffield, F. D. (1948). Avoidance training and the contiguity principle. *Journal of Comparative and Physiological Psychology, 41*, 165–177.

Sheffield, F. D. (1966). New evidence on the drive-induction theory of reinforcement. In R. N. Haber (Ed.), *Current research in motivation.* New York: Holt, Rinehart and Winston.

Sheffield, F. D., & Roby, T. B. (1950). Reward value of a non-nutritive sweet taste. *Journal of Comparative and Physiological Psychology, 43*, 471–481.

Sheffield, F. D., Wulff, J. J., & Backer, R. (1951). Reward value of copulation without sex drive reduction. *Journal of Comparative and Physiological Psychology, 44*, 3–8.

Sheridan, C. L., & King, R. G. (1972). Obedience to authority with an authentic victim. *Proceedings, eightieth annual convention, American Psychological Association, Honolulu,* 165–166. Washington, DC: American Psychological Association.

Sherif, M., Harvey, O. J., White, B., Hood, W., & Sherif, C. (1961). *Intergroup conflict and cooperation: The robber's cave experiment.* Norman: Institute of Group Relations, University of Oklahoma.

Sherrod, D. (1982). *Social psychology.* New York: Random House.

Sidman, M. (1966). Avoidance behavior. In W. K. Honig (Ed.), *Operant behavior: Areas of research and application.* New York: Appleton-Century-Crofts.

Sigall, H., & Landy, D. (1973). Radiating beauty: Effects of having a physically attractive partner on person perception. *Journal of Personality and Social Psychology, 28*, 218–224.

Silva, J. M., III, & Stevens, D. E. (2002). *Psychological foundations of sport.* Boston, MA: Allyn & Bacon.

Silverman, L. (1982, May). Mommy and I are one. *Psychology Today*, 24–36.

Singh, D. (1993). Adaptive significance of female physical attractiveness: Role of waist-to-hip ratio. *Journal of Personality and Social Psychology, 65*, 293–307.

Skinner, B. F. (1938). *The behavior of organisms*. New York: Appleton-Century-Crofts.

Skinner, B. F. (1948). *Walden II*. New York: Macmillan.

Skinner, B. F. (1953). *Science and human behavior*, New York: Macmillan.

Smith, F. J. (1977). Work attitudes as predictors of attendance on a specific day. *Journal of Applied Psychology, 62*, 16–19.

Smith, G. F., & Dorfman, D. D. (1975). The effect of stimulus uncertainty on the relationship between frequency of exposure and liking. *Journal of Personality and Social Psychology, 31*, 150–155.

Smith, G. P., & Gibbs, J. (1995). Peripheral physiological determinants of eating and body weight. In K. D. Brownell & C. G. Fairburn (Eds.), *Eating disorders and obesity: A comprehensive handbook*. New York: Guilford Press.

Sokolov, E. N. (1960). Neuronal models of the orienting reflex. In M. A. B. Brazier (Ed.), *The central nervous system and behavior: Transaction of the third conference*. New York: Josiah Macy, Jr., Foundation.

Solomon, R. L. (1980). The opponent-process theory of acquired motivation: The costs of pleasure and the benefits of pain. *American Psychologist, 35*, 691–712.

Solomon, R. L., & Corbit, J. D. (1974). An opponent-process theory of motivation: I. Temporal dynamics of affect. *Psychological Review, 81*, 119–145.

Solomon, R. L., & Turner, L. H. (1962). Discriminative classical conditioning in dogs paralyzed by curare can later control discriminative avoidance responses in the normal state. *Psychological Review, 69*, 202–219.

Solomon, R. L., & Wynne, L. C. (1950). Avoidance conditioning in normal dogs and in dogs deprived of normal autonomic functioning. *American Psychologist, 5*, 264.

Solomon, R. L., & Wynne, L. C. (1954). Traumatic avoidance learning: The principles of anxiety conservation and partial irreversibility. *Psychological Review, 61*, 353–385.

Sonstroem, R. J. (1984). An overview of anxiety in sport. In J. M. Silva & R. S. Weinberg (Eds.), *Psychological foundations of sport*. Champaign, IL: Human Kinetics.

Sonstroem, R. J., & Bernado, P. B. (1982). Intraindividual pregame state anxiety and basketball performance: A re-examination of the inverted-U curve. *Journal of Sport Psychology, 4*, 235–245.

Spence, J., & Helmreich, R. (1983). Types of achievement and achievement-related motives and rewards. In J. Spence (Ed.), *Achievement and achievement motives*. San Francisco, CA: W. H. Freeman.

Spence, K. W. (1944). The nature of theory construction in contemporary psychology. *Psychological Review, 51*, 47–68.

Spence, K. W. (1956). *Behavior theory and conditioning*. New Haven, CT: Yale University Press.

Spence, S., Shapiro, D., & Zaidel, E. (1996). The role of the right hemisphere in the physiological and cognitive components of emotional processing. *Psychophysiology, 33*, 112–122.

Spielberger, C. D. (1966). Theory and research on anxiety. In C. D. Spielberger (Ed.), *Anxiety and behavior*. New York: Academic.

Spielberger, C. D. (1976). The nature and measurement of anxiety. In C. D. Spielberger & R. Diaz-Guerrero (Eds.), *Cross-cultural anxiety*. Washington, DC: Hemisphere.

Spielberger, C. D., Gorsuch, R. L., & Lushene, R. F. (1970). *Manual for the State-Trait Anxiety Inventory*. Palo Alto, CA: Consulting Psychologists Press.

Sprague, J. M., Chambers, W. W., & Stellar, E. (1961). Attentive, affective, and adaptive behavior in the cat. *Science, 133*, 165–173.

Staats, A. W. (1983). Paradigmatic behaviorism: Unified theory for social psychology. In L. Berkowitz (Ed.), *Advances in experimental social psychology*, (Vol. 16). Orlando, FL: Academic Press.

Staats, A. W., & Staats, C. (1958). Attitudes established by classical conditioning. *Journal of Abnormal and Social Psychology, 57*, 35–40.

Starr, M. D., & Mineka, S. (1977). Determinants of fear over the course of avoidance learning. *Learning and Motivation, 8*, 332–350.

Stavely, H. E., Jr. (1966). Effect of escape duration and shock intensity on the acquisition and extinction of an escape response. *Journal of Experimental Psychology, 72*, 698–703.

Steele, R. S. (1977). Power motivation, activation, and inspirational speeches. *Journal of Personality, 45*, 53–64.

Steers, R. M., & Porter, L. W. (1975). *Motivation and work behavior.* New York: McGraw-Hill.

Steffen, J. J., McLaney, M. A., & Hustedt, T. K. (1982). The development of a scale of limerence. Paper presented at the annual convention of the American Psychological Association, Washington, DC.

Steggerda, F. R. (1941). Observations on the water intake in an adult man with dysfunctioning salivary glands. *American Journal of Psychology, 132,* 517–521.

Stellar, E. (1954). The physiology of motivation. *Psychological Review, 61,* 5–22.

Stellar, J. R., & Stellar, E. (1985). *The neurobiology of motivation and reward.* New York: Springer-Verlag.

Sternberg, R. J. (1986). A triangular theory of love. *Psychological Review, 93,* 119–135.

Sternberg, R. J. (1987). Liking versus loving: A comparative evaluation of theories. *Psychological Bulletin, 102,* 331–345.

Storms, M. D. (1983a). *Development of sexual orientation.* Washington, DC: Office of Social and Ethical Responsibility, American Psychological Association.

Storms, M. D. (1983b). A theory of erotic orientation development. *Psychological Review, 88,* 340–353.

Stroebe, W. C., Insko, A., Thompson, V. D., & Layton, B. D. (1971). Effects of physical attractiveness, attitude similarity, and sex on various aspects of interpersonal attraction. *Journal of Personality and Social Psychology, 18,* 79–91.

Sue, D. (1979). Erotic fantasies of college students during coitus. *Journal of Sex Research, 15,* 299–305.

Suedfield, P. (1998). Homo invictus: The indomitable species. *Canadian Psychology, 38,* 164–173.

Sullivan, M., & Bender, W. (1986). Facial electromyography: A measure of affective processes during sexual arousal. *Psychophysiology, 23(2),* 182–188.

Sweeney, P. D., Anderson, K., & Bailey, S. (1986). Attributional style in depression: A meta-analytic review. *Journal of Personality and Social Psychology, 50,* 947–991.

Swenson, C. H. (1972). The behavior of love. In H. A. Otto (Ed.), *Love today.* New York: Associations Press.

Tannenbaum, P. H., & Zillmann, D. (1975). Emotional arousal in the facilitation of aggression through communication. In L. Berkowitz (Ed.), *Advances in experimental social psychology* (Vol. 8). New York: Academic.

Tassinary, L. G., & Hansen, K. A. (1998). A critical test of the waist-to-hip-ratio hypothesis of female physical attractiveness. *Psychological Science, 9,* 150–155.

Tavris, C. (1983). Anger: *The misunderstood emotion.* New York: Simon & Schuster.

Taylor, S. E. (1989). *Positive illusions: Creative self-deception and the healthy mind.* New York: Basic Books.

Tedeschi, J. T., & Felson, R. B. (1994). *Violence, aggression, & coercive actions.* Washington, DC: American Psychological Association.

Tedeschi, J. T., Smith, R. B., III., & Brown, R. C., Jr. (1974). A reinterpretation of research on aggression. *Psychological Bulletin, 81,* 540–562.

Teitelbaum, P., & Epstein, A. N. (1962). The lateral hypothalamic syndrome: Recovery of feeding and drinking after lateral hypothalamic lesions. *Psychological Review, 69,* 74–90.

Tesser, A. (1993). The importance of heritability in psychological research: The case of attitudes. *Psychological Review, 100,* 129–142.

Thayer, R. E. (1978). Toward a psychological theory of multidimensional activation (arousal). *Motivation and Emotion, 2,* 1–34.

Theus, K. T. (1994). Subliminal advertising and the psychology of processing unconscious stimuli: A review of research. *Psychology and Marketing, 11,* 271–290.

Thistlewaite, D. (1951). A critical review of latent learning and related experiments. *Psychological Bulletin, 48,* 97–129.

Thompson, S. C. (1981). Will it hurt less if I control it?: A complex answer to a simple question. *Psychological Bulletin, 90,* 89–101.

Thorndike, E. L. (1913). *The psychology of learning.* New York: Teachers College.

Thurstone, L. L., & Chave, E. J. (1929). *The measurement of attitude: A psychophysical method and some experiments with a scale for measuring attitude toward the church.* Chicago: University of Chicago Press.

Tinbergen, N. (1951). *The study of instinct.* Oxford: Clarendon.

Tinklepaugh, O. L. (1928). An experimental study of representative factors in monkeys. *Journal of Comparative Psychology, 8,* 197–236.

Toates, F. M. (1979). Homeostasis and drinking. *The Behavioral and Brain Sciences, 2,* 95–139.

Toates, F. M. (2001). *Biological psychology: An integrated approach.*. New York: Prentice-Hall.

Toch, H. (1970). The social psychology of violence. Division 8 invited address, American Psychological Association Meeting, New York, September, 1966. Reprinted in E. I. Megargee & J. E. Hokanson (Eds.), *The dynamics of aggression: Individual, group and international analyses.* New York: Harper & Row.

Tolman, E. C. (1932). *Purposive behavior in animals and men.* New York: Appleton-Century-Crofts.

Tolman, E. C. (1938). The determiners of behavior at a choice point. *Psychological Review, 45,* 1–41.

Tolman, E. C. (1948). Cognitive maps in rats and men. *Psychological Review, 55,* 189–208.

Tolman, E. C. (1959). Principles of purposive behavior. In S. Koch (Ed.), *Psychology: A study of a science* (Vol. 2). New York: McGraw-Hill.

Tolman, E. C., & Honzik, C. H. (1930). Degrees of hunger; reward and nonreward; and maze learning in rats. *University of California Publications in Psychology, 4,* 241–256.

Tomarken, A. J., Davidson, R. J., Wheeler, R. E., & Doss, R. C. (1992). Individual differences in anterior brain asymmetry and fundamental dimensions of emotion. *Journal of Personality and Social Psychology, 62,* 676–687.

Tomkins, S. (1962). *Affect, imagery, and consciousness: The positive affects* (Vol. 1). New York: Springer.

Tomkins, S. (1981). The quest for primary motives: Biography and autobiography of an idea. *Journal of Personality and Social Psychology, 41,* 306–329.

Toulmin, S. (1953). *The philosophy of science—An introduction.* London: Hutchinson.

Towbin, E. J. (1949). Gastric distention as a factor in the satiation of thirst in esophagustomized dogs. *American Journal of Physiology, 159,* 533–541.

Trappey, C. (1996). A meta-analysis of consumer choice and subliminal advertising. *Psychology and Marketing, 13,* 517–530.

Triandis, H. C. (1994). *Culture and social behavior.* New York: McGraw-Hill.

Tripplet, N. (1897). The dynamogenic factors in pacemaking and competition. *American Journal of Psychology, 9,* 507–533.

Tryon, R. C. (1940). Genetic differences in maze learning in rats. In *National Society for the Study of Education, the Thirty-ninth Yearbook.* Bloomington, IL: Public School Publishing.

Tucker, D. M. (1981). Lateral brain function, emotion, and conceptualization *Psycholgical Bulletin, 89,* 19–46.

Valenstein, E. S. (1973). *Brain control: A critical examination of brain stimulation and psychosurgery.* New York: Wiley.

Valentine, C. W. (1930). The innate bases of fear. *Journal of Genetic Psychology, 37,* 394–419.

Valins, S. (1966). Cognitive effects of false heart-rate feedback. *Journal of Personality and Social Psychology, 4,* 400–408.

Valins, S. (1970). The perception and labeling of bodily changes as determinants of emotional behavior. In P. Black (Ed.), *Physiological correlates of emotion.* New York: Academic.

Van Itallie, T. B., & Kissileff, H. R. (1990). Human obesity: A problem in body energy economics. In E. M. Stricker (Ed.), *Handbook of Behavioral Neurobiology,* Vol. 10: *Neurobiology of food and fluid intake,* 207–240.

Vernon, W. (1969) Animal aggression: Review of research. *Genetic Psychology Monographs, 80,* 3–28.

Vernon, W., & Ulrich, R. E. (1966). Classical conditioning of pain-elicited aggression. *Science, 152,* 668–669.

Vitz, P. (1966). Affect as a function of stimulus variation. *Journal of Experimental Psychology, 71,* 7479.

Von Holst, E., & Von St. Paul, U. (1962). Electrically controlled behavior. *Scientific American, 206,* 50–59.

Vroom, V. H. (1964). *Work and motivation.* New York: Wiley.

Wagner, A. R. (1963). Conditioned frustration as a learned drive. *Journal of Experimental Psychology, 66,* 142–148.

Wallace, D. H., & Wehmer, G. (1972). Evaluation of visual erotica by sexual liberals and conservatives. *Journal of Sex Research, 8,* 147–153.

Walster, E. (1971). Passionate love. In B. Murstein (Ed.), *Theories of attraction and love.* New York: Springer.

Walster, E., Aronson, E., Abrahams, D., & Rottman, L. (1966). Importance of physical attractiveness in dating behavior. *Journal of Personality and Social Psychology, 4,* 508–516.

Walster, E., Walster, G. W., & Berscheid, E. (1978). *Equity: Theory and research.* Boston: Allyn & Bacon.

Wann, D. L. (1997) *Sport psychology.* Upper Saddle River, NJ: Prentice-Hall.

Warden, C. J. (1931). *Animal motivation: Experimental studies on the albino rat.* New York: Columbia University Press.

Warren, R. M., & Pfaffmann, C. (1958). Early experience and taste aversion. *Journal of Comparative and Physiological Psychology, 52,* 263–266.

Waterman, C. K. (1969). The facilitating and interfering effects of cognitive dissonance on simple and complex paired associates learning tasks. *Journal of Experimental Social Psychology, 5,* 31–42.

Watson, D., & Clark, L. A. (1994). *The PANAS-X: Manual for the positive and negative affect schedule-expanded form.* Unpublished manuscript, University of Iowa.

Watson, D., Wiese, D., Vaidya, J. & Tellegen, A. (1999). The two general activation systems of affect: Structural findings, evolutionary considerations, and psychobiological evidence. *Journal of Personality and Social Psychology, 76,* 820–838.

Watson, J. B. (1924). *Psychology from the standpoint of a behaviorist.* Philadelphia: Lippincott.

Watson, J. B., & Rayner, R. (1920). Conditioned emotional reactions, *Journal of Experimental Psychology, 3,* 1–14.

Weber, M. (1930). *The protestant ethic and the spirit of capitalism* (T. Parsons, Trans.). New York: Scribner. (Original work published 1904.)

Webster, D. M., & Kruglanski, A. W. (1994). Individual differences in need for cognitive closure. *Journal of Personality and Social Psychology, 67,* 1049–1062. (Contains the detailed development of the scale items, including five dimensions.)

Weinberg, R. S. (1984). The relationship between extrinsic rewards and intrinsic motivation in sports. In R. M. Silva & R. S. Weinberg (Eds.), *Psychological foundations of sport.* Champaign, IL: Human Kinetics Publishers.

Weinberg, R. S., & Genuchi, M. (1980). Relationship between competitive trait anxiety, state anxiety, and golf performance: A field study. *Journal of Sport Psychology, 2,* 148–154.

Weiner, B. (1985). An attributional theory of achievement motivation and emotion. *Psychological Review, 92,* 548–573.

Weiss, J. M. (1972). Psychological factors in stress and disease. *Scientific American, 226,* 104–113.

Weiss, J. M. (1977). Psychological and behavioral influences on gastrointestinal lesions in animal models. In J. Maser & M. E. P. Seligman (Eds.), *Psychopathology: Experimental models* (pp. 232–269). San Francisco: Freeman.

Weiss, R. F., & Miller, F. G. (1971). The drive theory of social facilitation. *Psychological Review, 78,* 44–57.

Werboff, J., Duane, D., & Cohen, B. D. (1964). Extinction of conditioned avoidance and heart rate responses in rats. *Journal of Psychosomatic Research, 8,* 29–33.

West, M. J., King, A. P., & Eastzer, D. H. (1981). The cowbird: Reflections on development from an unlikely source. *American Scientist, 69,* 57–66.

Whalen, R. E. (1966). Sexual motivation. *Psychological Review, 73,* 151–163.

Wheeler, L. & Kim, Y. (1997). What is beautiful is culturally good: The physical attractiveness stereotype has different content in collectivistic cultures. *Personality and Social Psychology Bulletin, 23,* 795–800.

White, G. L. (1980). Physical attractiveness and courtship progress. *Journal of Personality and Social Psychology, 39,* 660–668.

White, G. L., Fishbein, E., & Rutstein, J. (1981). Passionate love: The misattribution of arousal. *Journal of Personality and Social Psychology, 41,* 56–62.

White, R. W. (1959). Motivation reconsidered: The concept of competence. *Psychological Review, 66,* 297–333.

Wicklund, R. A., & Brehm, J. W. (1976). *Perspectives on cognitive dissonance.* Hillsdale, NJ: Erlbaum.

Wiggins, J. S., Wiggins, N., & Conger, J. C. (1968) Correlates of heterosexual somatic preference. *Journal of Personality and Social Psychology, 10,* 82–90.

Wike, E. L. (1966). *Secondary reinforcement: Selected experiments.* New York: Harper & Row.

Wilcoxin, H. C., Dragoin, W. B., & Kral, P. A. (1971). Illness-induced aversions in rat and quail: Relative salience of visual and gustatory cues. *Science, 171,* 826–828.

Williams, D. R., & Teitelbaum, P. (1956). Control of drinking by means of an operant conditioning technique. *Science, 124,* 1294–1296.

Williams, J. J. G., Watts, F. N., MacLeod, C., & Mathews, A. (1997). *Cognitive psychology and emotional disorders*, 2d ed. Chichester: Wiley.

Williams, R. B. (1994). *Anger kills: Seventeen strategies for controlling the hostility that can harm your health.* New York: HarperCollins.

Wilson, E. O. (1975). *Sociobiology, the new synthesis.* Cambridge, MA: Harvard University Press.

Wilson, T. D., Lindsey, S., & Schooler, T. Y. (2000). A model of dual attitudes. *Psychological Review, 107,* 101–126.

Winch, R. F. (1958). *Mate selection: A study of complementary needs.* New York: Harper & Row.

Winkielman, P., Zajonc, R. B., & Schwarz, N. (1997). Subliminal affective priming resists attributional interventions. *Cognition and Emotion, 11,* 433–465.

Winter, D. G. (1973). *The power motive.* New York: Free Press.

Wise, R. A. (1989). Opiate reward: Sites and substrates. *Neuroscience & Biobehavioral Reviews, 13,* 129–133.

Wolf, A. V. (1958). *Thirst: Physiology of the urge to drink and problems of water lack.* Springfield, IL: Thomas.

Wolfe, J. (1933). Effectiveness of token rewards for chimpanzees. *Comparative Psychology Monographs, 12,* (60), 1–72.

Wolfgang, M. E. (1957). Victim-precipitated criminal homicide. *Journal of Criminal Law, Criminology, and Police Science, 48,* 1–11.

Wolpe, J., & Rachman, S. (1960). Psychoanalytic "evidence": A critique based on Freud's case of Little Hans. *Journal of Nervous and Mental Disease, 131,* 135–148.

Wood, W., Wong, F. Y., & Chachere, G. (1991). Effects of media violence on viewers' aggression in unconstrained social interaction. *Psychological Bulletin, 109,* 371–383.

Woods, P. J. (1967). Performance changes in escape conditioning following shifts in the magnitude of reinforcement. *Journal of Experimental Psychology, 75,* 487–491.

Woods, P. J., Davidson, E. H., & Peters, R. J., Jr. (1964). Instrumental escape conditioning in water tank: Effects of variations in drive stimulus intensity and reinforcement magnitude. *Journal of Comparative and Physiological Psychology, 57,* 466–470.

Woods, S. C. (1991). The eating paradox: How we tolerate food. *Psychological Review, 98,* 488–505.

Woodside, A. G., & Chebat, J. C. (2001). Updating Heider's blance theory in consumer behavior: A Jewish couple buys a German car and additional buying-consuming transformation stories. *Psychology and Marketing, 18,* 475–495.

Woodworth, R. S. (1918). *Dynamic psychology.* New York: Columbia University Press.

Woodworth, R. S., & Schlosberg, H. (1954). *Experimental psychology* (rev. ed.). New York: Holt, Rinehart and Winston.

Wright, D. E. (1999). *Personal relationships.* Mountain View, CA: Mayfield Publishing.

Wrightsman, L. S. (1972). *Social psychology in the 70's.* Monterey, CA: Brooks/Cole.

Wrightsman, L. S., Jr. (1960). Effects of waiting with others on changes in level of felt anxiety. *Journal of Abnormal and Social Psychology, 61,* 216–222.

Wyer, R., & Hartwick, J. (1980). The role of information retrieval and conditional inference processes in belief formation and change. In L. Berkowitz (Ed.), *Advances in experimental social psychology* (Vol. 13, pp. 243–284). New York: Academic Press.

Yates, A. J. (1962). *Frustration and conflict.* New York: Wiley.

Yerkes, R. M., & Dodson, J. D. (1908). The relation of strength of stimulus to rapidity of habit-formation. *Journal of Comparative and Neurological Psychology, 18,* 459–482.

Young, P. T. (1959). The role of affective processes in learning and motivation. *Psychological Review, 66,* 104–125.

Young, P. T. (1966). Hedonic organization and regulation of behavior. *Psychological Review, 73,* 59–86.

Young, P. T. (1968). Evaluation and preferences in behavioral development. *Psychological Review, 75,* 222–241.

Young, P. T., & Chaplin, J. P. (1945). Studies of food preference, appetite and dietary habit: III. Palatability and appetite in relation to bodily need. *Comparative Psychology Monographs, 1945, 18,* No. 3, 1–45.

Zajonc, R. B. (1965). Social facilitation. *Science, 149,* 269–274.

Zajonc, R. B. (1968). Attitudinal effects of mere exposure. *Journal of Personality and Social Psychology Monograph Supplements, 9* (2, Pt. 2), 1–27.

Zajonc, R. B. (1984). On the primacy of affect. *American Psychologist, 39(2),* 117–123.

Zajonc, R. B. (in press). The zoomorphism of human collective violence. In L. Newman & R. Erber (Eds.), *What social psychology can tell us about the Holocaust: Understanding the perpetrators of genocide.* Oxford: Oxford University Press.

Zajonc, R. B. (2000). Feeling and thinking: Closing the debate over the independence of affect. In J. P. Forgas (Ed.), *Feeling and thinking: The role of affect in social cognition.* Cambridge, England: Cambridge University Press.

Zajonc, R. B, (2001). Mere exposure: A gateway to the subliminal. *Current Directions in Psychological Science, 10,* 224–228.

Zajonc, R. B., & Sales, S. M. (1966). Social facilitation of dominant and subordinate responses. *Journal of Experimental and Social Psychology, 2,* 160–168.

Zanna, M. P., & Cooper, J. (1974). Dissonance and the pill: An attribution approach to studying the arousal properties of dissonance. *Journal of Personality and Social Psychology, 29,* 703–709.

Zanot, E. J., Pincus, J. D., & Lamp, E. J. (1983). Public perceptions of subliminal advertising. *Journal of Advertising, 12,* 39–45.

Zeigler, H. P. (1964). Displacement activity and motivational theory: A case study in the history of ethology. *Psychological Bulletin, 61,* 362–376.

Zillman, D. (1978). Attribution and misattribution of excitatory reactions. In J. H. Harvey, W. J. Ickes, & R. F. Kidd, (Eds.), *New directions in attribution research* (Vol. 2, pp. 355–368). Hillsdale, NJ: Erlbaum.

Zimbardo, P. G. (1969). The human choice: Individualization, reason, and order versus deindividuation, impulse, and chaos. In W. Arnold & M. Levine (Eds.), *Nebraska symposium on motivation.* Lincoln: University of Nebraska Press.

Zimmerman, D. W. (1957). Durable secondary reinforcement: Method and theory. *Psychological Review, 64,* 373–383.

Zimmerman, D. W. (1959). Sustained performance in rats based on secondary reinforcement. *Journal of Comparative and Physiological Psychology, 52,* 353–358.

Zuckerman, M. (1979). *Sensation seeking: Beyond the optimal level of arousal.* Hillsdale, NJ: Lawrence Erlbaum Associates.

Zuckerman, M. (1994). *Behavioral expressions and biosocial bases of sensation seeking.* Cambridge: Cambridge University Press.

Author Index

Subject Index